Foreign Exchange in Practice

CW01618851

HEAD OFFICE: 50 Waterloo Road NORTH RYDE NSW 2113
Tel: (02) 9936 6444 Fax: (02) 9888 2287

For all sales inquiries please ring 1800 650 522

NEW ZEALAND

Brooker's

Wellington, Auckand

SINGAPORE AND MALAYSIA

Thompson Information

(SE Asia)

CANADA

Carswell

Ontario

UNITED KINGDOM

Sweet & Maxwell Ltd

London

HONG KONG

Bloomsbury Books Ltd

USA

Wm W Gaunt & Sons Inc

Holmes Beach, Florida

Foreign Exchange in Practice

by

STEVE ANTHONY

B Ec (Hons) (Syd)
PGCE (Cantab)

Second Edition

LBC INFORMATION SERVICES 1997

Published in Sydney by

LBC Information Services
50 Waterloo Road, North Ryde, NSW 2113

1st Edition 1989
2nd Edition 1997

National Library of Australia
Cataloguing-in-Publication entry

Anthony, Steve.
Foreign exchange in practice.

2nd ed.
Includes index.
ISBN 0 455 21509 X.

1. Foreign exchange. 2. Money market — Australia. I. Title

332.45

©Steve Anthony 1997

This publication is copyright. Other than for the purposes of and subject to the conditions prescribed under the Copyright Act, no part of it may in any form or by any means (electronic, mechanical, microcoping, photocopying, recording or otherwise) be reproduced, stored in a retrieval system or transmitted without prior written permission. Inquiries should be addressed to the publishers.

Designed and edited by Kathryn Fairfax

Typeset by LBC Information Services, North Ryde NSW
Printed by Star Printery Pty Ltd, Erskineville, NSW

To Nicola, Patrick and James

All royalties from this book will be donated to Giant Steps Sydney which is a school for children with autism.

Preface

This book was written for participants in the foreign exchange market. It attempts to explain the concepts involved in foreign exchange and the application of these concepts to a large number of day-to-day situations. Numerous worked examples appear in the text and practice problems are set out at the end of each chapter to enable the student to test his or her understanding. The solutions to the practice problems appear at the end of the book.

The book was written as a textbook for the Citibank Bourse Course. The Bourse Course is an intensive one week course available to the customers and staff of Citibank. It has been taught in over 50 countries since 1975. The course has evolved with the changing financial environment and is tailored in each country to suit the local marketplace.

The Bourse Course includes a simulated trading game. Participants trade in fictitious currencies called pesos, rials, crowns and francs. Several of the examples and practice problems refer to these fictitious currencies. In these currencies it is assumed that interest rates are quoted on a 21 days per year basis. This is to emphasise the importance of interest in the simulation which runs for only a few days.

A recurring theme throughout the book involves the interrelationship between interest rates and exchange rates. These two markets are inextricably linked. Changes in interest rates cause changes in exchange rates and vice versa. The pricing of forward exchange rates and currency options depends on the interest rates of the two currencies. Accordingly, considerable attention is given to interest rates, particularly in Chapter 2 and Chapter 4.

Two other themes which recur throughout the book are that arbitrage forces equilibrium pricing and that break-even rates occur where the two alternatives have equal value.

The first edition of this book was published in 1989. Examples in the first edition used rates which prevailed at that time. They were predominantly Australian applications. In the second edition, the rates used in the examples are current at the time of writing and most of the applications relate to currencies other than Australian dollars.

The chapter on Eurocurrency Markets has been dropped because exchange controls have been removed in most countries. The second edition expands the coverage of option pricing in Chapter 10 and introduces option derivatives such as barrier and digital options and correlation hedges in Chapter 12. The concept of NPV accounting and its application is also introduced in Chapter 3.

Chapter 14 covers the risks associated with foreign exchange transactions — price risk, credit risk and liquidity risk — and how they are measured and controlled.

The reference to use of an HP-12C calculator has been removed because of the increased use of spreadsheet models such as Excel and Lotus.

Supplementary questions are provided following the practice problems at the end of each chapter. Academics can obtain solutions to the supplementary questions by contacting the publisher.

The author wishes to acknowledge the assistance provided by Matthew Dyer, Rachel Knox, Peter Beaumont and Steven Koulas for proofreading chapters. Needless to say, any errors are those of the author.

STEVE ANTHONY

Sydney

August 1997

Glossary of Terms

American option—an option which can be exercised for spot value on any date between the contract date and the expiry date

arbitrage—the practice of taking advantage of inconsistent pricing to lock in profit free of price risk

arbitrageur—a person who performs an arbitrage transaction

Asian option—an average rate option

at-the-money (ATM)—an option with a strike price equal to the current market price

average rate option—an option where the pay-out equals the difference between the average rate and the strike price or zero whichever is higher

average strike option—an option for which the strike price is the average rate of the market price during the life of the option

backwardation—the forward discount of a commodity

barrier option—options which can be knocked-out or which only kick-in if the market price reaches a specified level

basis point — one unit in the second decimal place of an interest rate quotation

basket option—an option for which the underlying is a basket (of currencies)

bid-offer spread—the difference between the bid rate and the offer rate

bid rate (foreign exchange)—the rate at which the quoting bank is willing to buy the commodity currency

bid rate (money market)—the rate at which the quoting bank is willing to borrow.

binary option—a digital option

binomial model—a mathematical model which can be used for pricing options

Black-Scholes model—a mathematical model for pricing European options

blotter—a rough copy of a net exchange position sheet

break-even rate—the rate at which the outcome will be the same under two or more different scenarios

brokerage—a fee which brokers charge for their services

call—the right without the obligation to buy (a currency)

calling bank—the bank that calls to ask the quoting bank for a price

central bank swaps—the practice of central banks using currency swaps to inject or withdraw liquidity from the local money market without creating a net exchange positon

chain rule—a procedure for calculating cross rates

chooser option—an option with a defined strike price for which on a specified date the buyer can choose whether it is a call or a put

commodity currency — the currency being priced in an exchange rate quotation

compound interest — interest earned when the amount of principal plus interest is reinvested for subsequent periods

compound option—an option to enter into an option

contango—the forward premium of a commodity

contingent option—an option which kicks-in if a specified, possibly unrelated, event occurs

contingent premium option—an option for which the premium is only paid if it expires in-the-money

contract date—the date on which a transaction is contracted

coupons—interim interest payments on a bond

covered interest arbitrage—the practice of transacting a currency swap and two money market transactions to make a rate risk-free profit by taking advantage of a set of inconsistent market rates

credit collar—a collar where the net premium is positive

cross rate—an exchange rate derived from two other exchange rates

currency option—the right without the obligation to buy or sell one currency against another currency at a specified price at a specified time

currency swap—the simultaneous purchase and sale of equivalent amounts of one currency against another currency for different maturities

current account balance—the net outcome of receipts and payments for exports and imports of goods and services

current account deficit—a negative balance reflecting an excess of import payments over export receipts

current account surplus—a positive balance reflecting an excess of export receipts over import payments

collar—the strategy of buying an option and writing the opposite type of option (call/put) for the same face value and same expiry date but at a different strike price

correlation—the extent to which two variables are related

debit collar—collar where the net premium is negative

delivery risk—the risk that a counterparty will be unable or unwilling to deliver a currency at the maturity of a contract

delta hedging—the practice of hedging a variable portion of an option position

digital option—an option which has a fixed pay-out regardless of how far it is in-the-money

down and in—an option which kicks-in if the price falls to the barrier level

down and out—an option which knocks-out if the price falls to the barrier level

early take-up—a swap which shortens the maturity of a forward exchange transaction without cash flows at the original maturity date

effective interest rate—an equivalent interest rate which is expressed under a different convention

engineered swap—a swap in which the spot and forward transactions are done with different counterparties

Eurocurrency deposits—deposits of a currency held outside the jurisdiction of that currency's government and central bank

Eurodollar—dollar deposits held outside the United States (initially in Europe)

European option—an option which, theoretically, can only be exercised for spot value on the expiry date

exchange rate—the price of one currency expressed in terms of another currency

exchange-traded options—a contract traded through certain stock, futures or commodity exchanges

expected volatility—the extent to which the exchange rate is expected to change during the life of the option

expiration date or expiry date—the date on which the buyer's right to exercise an option ends

flat yield curve—a horizontal yield curve reflecting the fact that interest rates are the same for different tenors

forward bid rate—the rate at which the quoting bank is willing to buy forward the commodity currency

forward discount—the excess of the spot rate over the forward rate

forward exchange agreement (FXA)—a non-deliverable currency swap

forward exchange rate—the rate agreed upon today at which one currency is sold against another for delivery on a specified future date

forward interest rate—an interest rate which can be determined today for a period from one future date till another future date

forward offer rate—the rate at which the quoting bank would sell forward the commodity currency

forward premium—the excess of the forward rate over the spot rate

forward value date—a value date which is farther into the future than spot value

FOTPI—the future obligation to pay interest

FOTRI—the future obligation to receive interest

FRA—forward rate agreement - a contract to fix a forward interest rate

future value — the value of an investment (principal plus interest) at a designated time into the life of the investment

futures contract—forward contracts traded through a futures exchange

gapping—the deliberate mismatch of maturity dates of assets and liabilities

hedging—eliminating a risk

historical rate rollover—a swap based on a spot rate which is set equal to the historic rate to avoid cash flows at the spot date

hybrids—derivatives which establish a price based on the relationship between two variables which might not normally be associated with each other

instalment option—an option whose premium is paid in periodic instalments. The owner has the right to discontinue paying the instalments but then loses the option

interest—the price paid for the use of money

interest rate—the ratio of the amount of interest to the amount of principal

interest rate parity theory—a theory which purports that in the long run, exchange rates adjust to reflect the relative interest rates of the two currencies

in-the-money (ITM)—an option with a strike price which is better than the market price

intrinsic value—the extent to which an option is in-the-money

inverse yield curve—a yield curve which is downward sloping to the right, reflecting the fact that the market generally expects interest rates to fall

jobbing—the practice of a price-maker moving prices to be hit on the side which will square off a position

knock-out option—an option which has zero pay-out if the barrier level is reached even if the market price at expiry is better than the strike price

ladder option—a reset option with multiple triggers

LIBID—London Interbank Bid Rate

LIBOR—London Interbank Offer Rate

liquidity—the ability to obtain cash

liquidity position—a situation in which there is a risk that insufficient funds will be available to meet a negative cash flow commitment

lognormal distribution—an asymmetrical distribution with known properties which include no negative values

long—a positive net exchange position

LTFX—long term foreign exchange (usually taken as beyond one year)

market making—the strategy which some banks follow of dealing at narrow bid-offer spreads in the expectation of doing large volumes on both sides of their prices

negative carry—the cost of borrowing at a high rate and lending at a low rate

negative cash flow—a payment of cash to another party

negative gapping—the strategy of borrowing short term and lending long term

net cash flow position—the difference between positive and negative cash flows on a particular value date

net exchange position — the difference between the amount of a foreign currency purchased and sold at a particular point of time (or the net present value of that amount)

net exchange position sheet—a running tally of the net exchange position in a particular foreign currency as a result of a series of foreign exchange transactions

nominal interest rate—a number which measures an interest rate quotation under a particular convention

normal distribution—a symmetrical distribution with known properties which are determined by specifying its mean and standard deviation

normal yield curve—a yield curve which is slightly upward sloping to the right, reflecting the fact that interest rates for longer tenors are "normally" higher than for shorter tenors

NPV—net present value

offer rate (foreign exchange) the rate at which the quoting bank is willing to sell the commodity currency

offer rate (money market)—the rate at which the quoting bank is willing to lend

option premium—the price of an option

out-of-the-money (OTM)—an option with a strike price which is worse than the current market price

outright exchange rate—a forward exchange rate (to be distinguished from a swap rate)

over-the-counter (OTC) option — an option written by banks and other institutions but not traded through public exchanges

parallel shift of the swaps curve—a movement of a swaps curve which reflects an equal increase or decrease in the swap rate for a range of tenors

parallel shift of the yield curve—a movement of a yield curve which reflects an equal increase or decrease in interest rates for a range of tenors

participating collar—the strategy of buying and writing opposite types of options (call/put) with different strike prices and different face values

participating option—the strategy of buying and writing opposite types of options (call/put) with the same strike price but for different face values

path dependent option—an option whose pay-out depends on the path which the market price follows during the life of the option

point (or pip)—one unit in the last decimal place to which a particular exchange rate is usually quoted

position—a situation in which a change in a price will result in a profit or loss

positive carry—the benefit of borrowing at a low rate and lending at a high rate

positive cash flow—a receipt of cash from another party

positive gapping—the strategy of borrowing long term and lending short term

positive yield curve—a yield curve which is more steeply upward sloping to the right than a normal yield curve, reflecting the fact that the market generally expects interest rates to rise

present value — the amount of money which, if invested today, would accumulate into a future value at a designated time in the future

price quotation—an exchange rate which is quoted with the foreign currency as the commodity currency and the local currency as the terms currency

principal—the amount of money borrowed or invested in a money market transaction

purchasing power parity theory—a theory which purports that in the long run, exchange rates adjust to reflect the relative inflation rates of the two currencies

pure swap—a swap in which both the spot and forward transactions are done simultaneously with the same counterparties

put—the right without the obligation to sell (a currency)

quanto—an option for which the quantity of the face value varies with some other variable

quoting bank—the bank that quotes the price

real exchange rate—the exchange rate adjusted for changes in the relative rates of inflation

real interest rate—the nominal interest rate adjusted for the effect of inflation

realised profit or loss—an exchange profit or loss where both the buy side and the sell side of the transaction are completed

reserve requirements — requirements that central banks impose on commercial banks to hold a minimum specified percentage of their commercial deposits in accounts with the central bank, generally at rates below market interest rates

reset option—an option for which the strike price may change during the life of the option

riding the swaps curve—opening a gap to take advantage of the non-linear shape of the swaps curve

riding the yield curve—gapping in the money market to take advantage of the shape of the yield curve

risk-free interest rate — the interest rate used to determine the up-front premium of an option

rolling a position—extending the maturity date

rotation of the swaps curve—a movement of the swaps curve which reflects a proportional increase or decrease in swap rates resulting in a change in the slope of the swaps curve

rotation of the yield curve—a proportional increase or decrease in interest rates resulting in a change in the slope of the yield curve

SIBID—Singapore Interbank Bid Rate

SIBOR—Singapore Interbank Offer Rate

short—a negative net exchange position

short dates—value dates which occur sooner than spot value

shout option—an option which gives the owner the right to lock-in a minimum pay-out equal to the then intrinsic value by declaring his intention

simple interest—the amount of interest paid at maturity on a money market transaction

simulated investment — investing in a currency indirectly by investing in another currency and entering into a currency swap

simulated loan—generating liquidity by borrowing one currency and entering into a currency swap

spot value—a payment which will be made two business days from the contract date

square position—a situation in which a change in a rate will not cause a profit or loss

standard deviation—a measure of dispersion of a distribution

swap bid rate—the differential at which the quoting bank is willing to buy forward the commodity currency in the swap

swap offer rate—the differential at which the quoting bank is willing to sell forward the commodity currency in the swap

swap rate—the differential between a forward exchange rate and the spot rate

swaps curve—the curve obtained when swap rates are plotted against tenors

T-accounts—a simple notation for specifying the cash flows associated with financial transactions

terms currency—the currency in terms of which an exchange rate is quoted

time decay—the decline in time value as an option approaches expiry

time value—the value that an option has because it has not expired

trending rates—the practice of moving quotations up or down to pre-empt an expected movement in the market

unrealised profit or loss—an (exchange) profit or loss where only one side of the transaction has been completed

up and in—an option which kicks-in if the price rises to the barrier level

up and out—an option which knocks-out if the price rises to the barrier level

value date—the date on which a cash flow occurs

value today—a cash flow which occurs today

value tomorrow—a cash flow which will occur on the next business day

volatility—a measure of the extent to which the (exchange) rate changes over a given period

volume quotation—an exchange rate which is quoted with the local currency as the commoditv currency and the foreign currency as the terms currency

yield curve—the curve obtained when yield (interest rate) is plotted on the vertical axis and tenor on the horizontal axis

zero coupon bond—a bond with all coupons equal to zero

zero premium collar—collar where the net premium is zero

Contents

1
Exchange Rates

This chapter introduces the basic conventions used to describe exchange rates and the profits or losses which result from changes in exchange rates. In pricing physical commodities, it is apparent that a particular commodity is being priced in terms of a particular currency. In exchange rate quotations, confusion sometimes arises because both the commodity being priced and the terms in which the commodity is being priced are currencies. To avoid this potential confusion, distinction is drawn between the commodity currency and the terms currency.

Definition

An ***exchange rate*** is the price of one currency expressed in terms of another currency.

Exchange rates

£1 = $1.5500

$1 = DM1.4450

Commodity Currency and Terms Currency

In every exchange rate quotation, there are two currencies. The currency being priced is known as the ***commodity currency***. The exchange rate is quoted such that a fixed number of units (usually one) of the commodity currency is expressed in terms of a variable number of units of the other currency. The other currency is known as the ***terms currency***.

In the exchange rate quotation £1 = $1.5500, the commodity being priced is the pound sterling. One pound is expressed as 1.5500 units of dollars. The unit of account is the dollar. The pound is the commodity currency; the dollar the terms currency.

In the exchange rate quotation $1 = DM1.4450, the dollar is the commodity currency and the deutschemark is the terms currency. The dollar is priced in deutschemark terms.

Notice that in one case, the dollar is the terms currency and in another, it is the commodity currency. There is no convention which dictates which currency should be the commodity currency.

In the days when the pound sterling was the principal world currency, it was customary for the Commonwealth currency to be quoted as the commodity currency. With the rise to prominence of the United States economy, most exchange rates are now quoted with the US dollar as the commodity currency. However, the old convention still applies for several of the former Commonwealth currencies.

Exhibit 1.1
Exchange rate quotations

Commonwealth Currencies

Commodity currency		*Terms currency*
£1	=	US$1.5500
A$1	=	US$0.7420
NZ$1	=	US$0.6375
US$1	=	C$1.3740
US$1	=	HK$7.8020

Other Currencies

Commodity currency		*Terms currency*
US$1	=	DM1.4450
US$1	=	¥102.50
US$1	=	FF4.9980
US$1	=	S$1.4370
US$1	=	BHT25.25

A good rule of thumb is that the commodity currency is the currency of which there is *one* in the exchange rate quotation.

Reciprocal Rates

If the price of an apple is 20 cents, it is possible to express the price as five apples for $1.

Exhibit 1.2
Reciprocal rates—physical example

Price of apples

Commodity		*Terms*
$1	=	5 apples
1 apple	=	20 cents

To convert the commodity to the terms, take reciprocals.

Similarly, it is possible to change the terms in which an exchange rate is expressed by taking reciprocals.

Example 1.1

Express the exchange rate quotation $ 1 = DM1.4450 with the deutschemark as the commodity currency and the dollar as the terms currency.

	Commodity currency		Terms currency
Original quotation	$1	=	DM1.4450
Reciprocal rate	DM1	=	$ $\frac{1}{1.4450}$
ie	DM1	=	$0.6920

Price Changes

If the price of the commodity rises, it will be worth more units of the terms currency. If the price of the commodity falls, it will be worth less units of the terms currency.

Exhibit 1.3
Commodity price changes—physical example

Original price	Commodity price rise	Commodity price fall
1 apple = 20 cents	1 apple = 25 cents An apple is more valuable in terms of dollars	1 apple = 15 cents An apple is less valuable in terms of dollars

A rise in the value of the commodity is equivalent to a fall in the value of the terms currency and a fall in the value of the commodity is equivalent to a rise in the value of the terms currency.

Price and Volume Quotations

If an exchange rate is expressed such that the foreign currency is the commodity currency and the local currency is the terms currency, this is described as a ***price quotation***. In a price quotation, the foreign currency is priced in terms of the local currency.

Exhibit 1.4
Price quotations

	Commodity currency		Terms currency
In Germany	$1	=	DM1.4450
In Japan	$1	=	¥102.50

If an exchange rate is expressed such that the foreign currency is the terms currency and the local currency is the commodity currency, this is described as a ***volume quotation***. Under the volume quotation system, the local currency is priced in terms of the foreign currency.

Exhibit 1.5
Volume quotations

	Commodity currency		Terms currency
In Australia	A$1	=	US$0.7420
In the United States	US$1	=	DM1.4450

Notice that the quotation US$1 = DM1.4450 constitutes a price quotation in Germany but a volume quotation in the United States.

Exhibit 1.6
Price changes in currency terms—physical example

Original price	Terms currency price rise	Terms currency price fall
$1 = 5 apples	$1 = 4 apples $1 is less valuable in terms of apples	$1 = 6 apples $1 is more valuable in terms of apples

A rise in the price of the terms currency corresponds to a fall in the number of units in which the price is expressed. Conversely, a fall in the price of the terms currency corresponds to a rise in the number of units in which the price is expressed.

Exhibit 1.7
Reciprocal Rate Relationships

Original exchange rate	Commodity currency price rises	Commodity currency price falls
US$1 = DM1.4450	US$1 = DM1.4460	US$1 = DM1.4440
Reciprocal rate	Terms currency price falls	Terms currency price rises
DM1 = US$0.6920	DM1 = US$0.6916	DM1 = US$0.6925

A rise in the exchange rate reflects an increase in the value of the commodity currency. Conversely, a fall in the exchange rate reflects a drop in the value of the commodity currency.

A *direct* relationship exists between a rise or fall in the exchange rate and a rise or fall in the value of the commodity currency. An *inverse* relationship exists between a rise or fall in the exchange rate and a rise or fall in the value of the terms currency. The terms currency proceeds from the sale of a fixed amount of the commodity currency and the terms currency cost of purchasing a fixed amount of the commodity currency will vary directly with the exchange rate. However, if the proceeds of the sale of a fixed amount of the terms currency is measured in terms of the commodity currency, a reciprocal relationship will exist.

In general, the concepts developed in the following chapters consider a constant amount of the commodity currency measured in terms of varying amounts of the terms currency. This preserves the direct relationship. In some cases, the context requires the terms currency amount to be measured in units of the commodity currency. In these cases, the reciprocal relationship applies.

Cross Rates

Provided there is a common currency, it is possible to derive an exchange rate between two currencies from the exchange rates at which the two currencies are quoted against the common currency.

An exchange rate which is derived from two other exchange rates is known as a *cross rate*.

Example 1.2

$$\begin{aligned} \$1 &= ¥100 \\ \$1 &= FF5 \end{aligned}$$

What is the exchange rate for French francs in yen terms?

Algebraically, $\$1 = ¥100 = FF5$

$$\therefore \quad FF1 = \frac{¥100}{5} = ¥20$$

Example 1.3

$$\begin{aligned} \$1 &= ¥100 \\ £1 &= \$1.5000 \end{aligned}$$

What is the exchange rate for pounds in yen terms?

Algebraically, $£1 = ¥100 \times 1.5000 = ¥150$

Chain Rule

The cross rate in Example 1.3 was calculated by multiplying the two exchange rates (100 × 1.5 = 150). The cross rate in Example 1.2 was calculated by dividing one of the exchange rates by the other (100/5 = 20).

The chain rule provides a foolproof procedure for determining whether the exchange rates should be multiplied or divided.

Chain rule

1. Start with the question to be answered: how many units of the terms currency equal one unit of the commodity currency?
2. Start the next question with the currency with which the previous question finished.
3. Again, start the next question with the currency with which the previous question finished.

   If the first three steps have been correctly followed, the third question will finish with the terms currency.
4. Multiply the numbers on the right hand side and divide by the product of the numbers on the left hand side.

Example 1.4

Using the chain rule

$$\begin{aligned} ¥? &= FF1 \\ FF5 &= US\$1 \\ US\$1 &= ¥100 \\ \therefore \quad FF1 &= \frac{¥1 \times 1 \times 100}{5 \times 1} = ¥\,20 \end{aligned}$$

Example 1.5

Using the chain rule

$$\begin{aligned} ¥? &= £1 \\ £1 &= US\$1.5 \\ US\$1 &= ¥100 \\ \therefore \quad £1 &= \frac{¥1 \times 1.5 \times 100}{1 \times 1} = ¥150 \end{aligned}$$

Example 1.6

$$\begin{aligned} A\$1 &= US\$0.7420 \\ US\$1 &= SF1.2320 \end{aligned}$$

What is the cross rate for Australian dollars in terms of Swiss francs?

Using the chain rule

$$\begin{aligned} SF? &= A\$1 \\ A\$1 &= US\$0.7420 \\ US\$1 &= SF1.2320 \\ \therefore \quad A\$1 &= \frac{SF\,1 \times 0.7420 \times 1.2320}{1 \times 1} \\ \text{ie} \quad A\$1 &= SF0.9141 \end{aligned}$$

Example 1. 7

$$\begin{aligned} \text{NZ\$1} &= \text{US\$0.6370} \\ \text{£1} &= \text{US\$1.5500} \end{aligned}$$

What is the cross rate for New Zealand dollars in terms of pounds?

Using the chain rule

$$\begin{aligned} \text{£?} &= \text{NZ\$1} \\ \text{NZ\$1} &= \text{US\$0.6370} \\ \text{US\$1.5500} &= \text{£1} \\ \therefore \quad \text{NZ\$1} &= \frac{\text{£1} \times 0.6370 \times 1}{1 \times 1.5500} \\ \text{ie} \quad \text{NZ\$1} &= \text{£0.4110} \end{aligned}$$

Points

It is arbitrary how many significant figures are used in an exchange rate quotation:

$$\begin{aligned} \text{US\$1} &= \text{DM1.4450} \\ \text{US\$1} &= \text{¥102.50} \\ \text{US\$1} &= \lambda\ 1528.00 \\ \text{A\$1} &= \text{US\$0.7420} \end{aligned}$$

The last decimal place to which a particular exchange rate is usually quoted is referred to as a ***point*** or ***pip***.

In the quotation US\$1 = DM1.4450, one point means DM0.0001.

In the quotation US\$1 = ¥102.50, one point means ¥0.01.

It is worth noting that all points are not of equal value. In the above example, DM1.4450 = λ 1528.00.

It follows that $$\text{DM 1} = \lambda\ \frac{1528.00}{1.4450} = \lambda\ 1057.44$$

so $$\text{DM0.0001} = \lambda\ \frac{1057.44}{10{,}000} = \lambda\ 0.1057$$

That is, one deutschemark point is worth more than ten times as much as one lira point.

If the exchange rate for the Australian dollar rises from A\$1 = US\$0.7420 to A\$1 = US\$0.7820, the value of each point remains constant at US\$0.0001. However, A\$1 is now worth more US dollars so the Australian dollar equivalent of one point is less at the higher exchange rate.

Calculating Exchange Profits and Losses

Exchange profits and losses are generated by buying and selling currencies at different exchange rates. The profit or loss is calculated by keeping the units of one of the currencies constant and determining the difference in the number of units of the other currency. Consequently, the method of calculating exchange profits and losses varies depending on whether the commodity currency or the terms currency is kept constant. The profit or loss will be expressed in units of the currency which is not kept constant.

Example 1.8

Calculate the profit when $1,000,000 are purchased at a rate of $1 = DM1.4450 and sold at a rate of $1 = DM1.4451.

DM profit	= proceeds of sale of $1,000,000	– cost of purchase of $1,000,000
	= 1,000,000 × 1.4451	– 1,000,000 × 1.4450
	= 1,000,000 (1.4451	– 1.4450)
	= 1,000,000 × 0.0001	
	= DM100	

There is a profit of one point on $1,000,000 which is equal to DM100.

Example 1.9

Calculate the profit or loss when DM1,000,000 are purchased at a rate of $1 = DM1.4451 and sold at a rate of $1 = DM1.4450.

$ Profit	= proceeds of sale of DM1,000,000	– cost of purchase of DM1,000,000
	$= \frac{1,000,000}{1.4450}$	$- \frac{1,000,000}{1.4451}$
	= 692,041.52	– 691,993.63
	= $47.89	

There is a profit of one point on DM1,000,000 which is equal to $47.89.

Realised and Unrealised Profits and Losses

Exchange profits and losses can be either realised or unrealised. They are said to be ***realised*** if *both* the buy side and sell side of the transaction are completed and ***unrealised*** if only *one* side of the transaction has been completed.

Example 1.10

Calculate the unrealised profit or loss if \$1,000,000 were purchased at a rate of \$1 = DM1.4450 and could be sold at a rate of \$1 = DM1.4435.

$$\text{Unrealised profit} = \text{proceeds of potential sale of dollars} - \text{cost of purchase of dollars}$$
$$= 1{,}000{,}000 - 1.4435 - 1{,}000{,}000 \times 1.4450$$
$$= 1{,}000{,}000\,(1.4435 - 1.4450) = 1{,}000{,}000\,(-\,0.0015)$$
$$= -\,\text{DM}1{,}500$$

A negative profit is a ***loss.***

There is an unrealised loss of 15 points or DM1,500. Until the second leg of the buy/sell transaction is complete, the profit or loss will remain unrealised. The size of the unrealised profit or loss will vary with the exchange rate.

Example 1.11

Calculate the realised profit or loss if the exchange rate rises from \$1 = DM1.4450 to \$1 = DM1.4460 and the \$1,000,000 are then sold.

$$\text{Realised profit} = \text{proceeds of sale of dollars} - \text{cost of purchase of dollars}$$
$$= 1{,}000{,}000 \times 1.4460 - 1{,}000{,}000 \times 1.4450$$
$$= 1{,}000{,}000\,(1.4460 - 1.4450)$$
$$= 1{,}000{,}000 \times 0.0010$$
$$= \text{DM}1{,}000$$

Once the profit or loss is realised, the size of the profit or loss ceases to vary with the exchange rate.

Practice Problems

1.1 Reciprocal rates

Given the following exchange rates,

US\$1 = FF4.5420

£1 = A\$2.0465

NZ\$1 = US\$0.6250

(a) Calculate the reciprocal rate for French francs in US dollar terms.

(b) Calculate the reciprocal rate for Australian dollars in pound terms.

(c) Calculate the reciprocal rate for US dollars in New Zealand dollar terms.

1.2 Cross rates

Given

US$1	= ¥103.25
US$1	= DM1.4525
£1	= US$1.5560
A$1	= US$0.7420

(a) Calculate the cross rate for pounds in deutschemark terms.

(b) Calculate the cross rate for deutschemarks in yen terms.

(c) Calculate the cross rate for deutschemarks in Australian dollar terms.

(d) Calculate the cross rate for yen in Australian dollar terms.

1.3 Calculating profits and losses

(a) Calculate the profit or loss as an amount in pesos when Crowns 8,540,000 are purchased at a rate of C1 = P1.4870 and sold at a rate of C1 = P1.4675.

(b) Calculate the unrealised profit or loss as an amount in pesos on P17,283,945 which were purchased at a rate of Rial 1 = P0.4980 and could now be sold at a rate of R1 = P0.5072.

Supplementary Questions

1.4 Reciprocal rates

Given the following exchange rates calculate the reciprocal rates:

	Original Exchange rate	Reciprocal rate
(a)	US$1 = FF5.6830	FF1 = US$?
(b)	US$1 = DM1.6670	DM1 = US$?
(c)	NZ$1 = US$0.5920	US$1 = NZ$?

1.5 Realised profit

Calculate the profit or loss when C9,360,000 are purchased at a rate of C1 = P1.4510 and sold at a rate of C1 = P1.4620.

1.6 Unrealised profit

Calculate the unrealised profit or loss on P17,283,945 which were purchased at a rate of R1 = P0.4720 and could now be sold at a rate of R1 = P0.4860.

2
Interest Rates

This chapter introduces the basic conventions used to describe interest rates. In practice, interest rates are quoted under a variety of different conventions. Measuring interest rates using different conventions makes the comparison of interest rates potentially confusing. The concept of effective interest rates is introduced as a means of comparing interest rates described under different conventions.

Definition

Interest is the price paid for the use of money. An ***interest rate*** is the ratio of the amount of interest to the amount of money. Interest rates are generally expressed in terms of per cent per annum.

Nominal and Effective Interest Rates

There are various conventions used in interest rate quotations. To compare two interest rates which are expressed using different conventions, it is necessary to express both interest rates in equivalent terms using a common convention. The number that measures an interest rate under a particular convention is called the ***nominal interest rate.*** When an interest rate quotation is converted so as to be expressed under a different convention, it is known as an ***effective interest rate.***

Basis points

Interest rates are often expressed as proper fractions or decimals, for example 8¾% or 8.75%. When interest rates per cent are expressed to two decimal places, one unit in the second decimal place is known as a ***basis point.*** The same interest rate could be expressed in decimal notation as 0.0875. In this case, a basis point refers to one unit in the fourth decimal place. Exchange points and basis points do not generally have equal value.

Days per year

There are 365 days to a year and 366 in leap years. Some interest rates are quoted as if there were 360 days per year; others on the basis of 365 days per year. To convert an interest rate based on 360 days per year to one based on 365 days per year, it is necessary to multiply by the factor 365/360.

For example if a three month Eurodollar rate which, by convention, is quoted on a 360 day year basis is 8.25% pa, the effective interest rate on a 365 days per year basis would be:

$$8.25 \times 365/360 \quad = \quad 0.0836 \quad = \quad 8.36\%$$

Similarly, an interest rate based on a 365 day year can be converted into a 360 days per year basis by multiplying by a factor of 360/365.

Simple Interest

The amount of interest earned on an investment is a function of the amount invested (known as the ***principal***), the interest rate and the period for which the investment is made.

$$\boxed{I = Prt} \qquad \textbf{Equation 2.1}$$

where

$$\begin{aligned} I &= \text{interest amount} \\ P &= \text{principal sum invested} \\ r &= \text{interest rate per annum} \\ t &= \text{time period in years} \end{aligned}$$

Example 2.1

$100 is invested at a simple interest rate of 8% pa (365 dpy) for a period of 30 days.

$$\begin{aligned} P &= \$100 \\ r &= 8\% = 0.08 \\ t &= 30/365 \\ \therefore \quad I &= Prt \\ &= \$100 \times 0.08 \times 30/365 \\ &= \$0.66 \end{aligned}$$

The investor receives the interest at **maturity** (ie at the end of the investment period) together with the principal sum invested.

$$\boxed{F = P + I} \qquad \textbf{Equation 2.2}$$

where F = final amount received at maturity or future value of the investment. From Example 2.1, P = $100 and I = $0.66 so that at the end of the 30 day period, the investor would have a final amount.

$$\begin{aligned} F &= P + I \\ &= \$100 + 0.66 \\ &= \$100.66 \end{aligned}$$

Figure 2.1

Simple interest

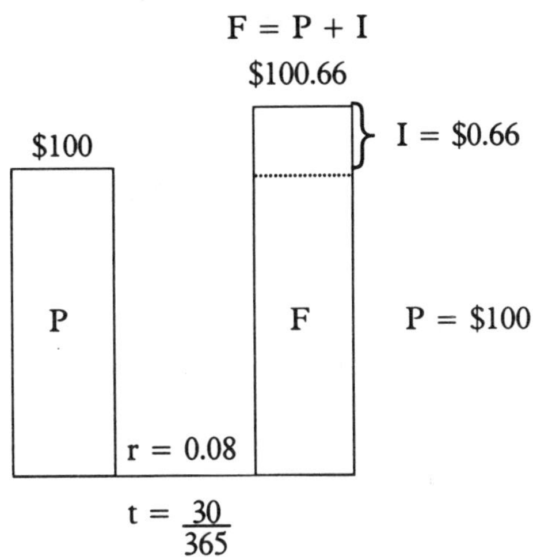

By substitution,

$$F = P + I$$
$$= P + Prt$$

$$\therefore \quad \boxed{F = P(1 + rt)} \qquad \textbf{Equation 2.3}$$

Continuing Example 2.1:

$$F = P(1 + rt)$$
$$= \$100(1 + 0.08 \times 30/365)$$
$$= \$100.66$$

Compound Interest

Compound interest assumes that the investor reinvests the amount of principal plus interest for subsequent periods. Under compound interest, the investor earns interest on the interest.

Example 2.2

A principal sum of $ 100 is invested for three years at an annually compounding rate of 10% pa.

Figure 2.2

Compound interest

$$F = P(1 + rt)^n$$

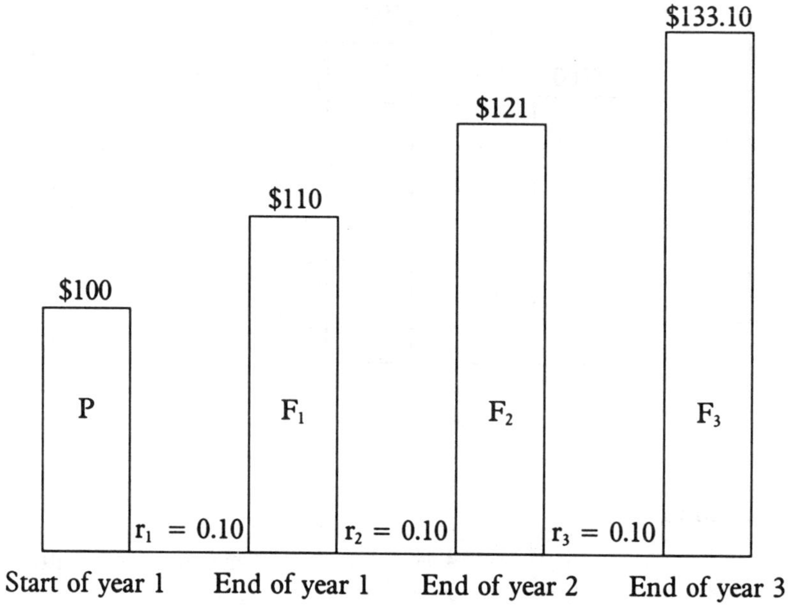

$$\begin{aligned} F_1 &= P(1 + r_1t_1) \\ &= \$100\,(1 + 0.10) \\ &= \$110 \end{aligned}$$

At the end of year 2, the value of the investment

$$\begin{aligned} F_2 &= F_1(1 + r_2t_2) \\ &= \$110\,(1 + 0.10) \\ &= \$121 \end{aligned}$$

At the end of year 3, the final value of the investment

$$\begin{aligned} F_3 &= F_2(1 + r_3t_3) \\ &= \$121\,(1 + 0.10) \\ &= \$133.10 \end{aligned}$$

Assuming the investment is rolled over each year at the fixed rate of 10% pa,

$$r_1 = r_2 = r_3 = 0.10 = r$$

then

$$\begin{aligned} F_3 &= F_2(1 + rt) \\ &= F_1(1 + rt)(1 + rt) \\ &= P(1 + rt)(1 + rt)(1 + rt) \\ &= P(1 + rt)^3 \end{aligned}$$

In general,

$$\boxed{FV = P\,(1+rt)^n} \qquad \textbf{Equation 2.4}$$

where

$$\begin{aligned} FV &= \text{future value of the investment} \\ P &= \text{principal amount} \\ rt &= \text{compound interest rate per period} \\ n &= \text{number of periods} \end{aligned}$$

If i = rt, Equation 2.4 becomes:

$$\boxed{FV = P(1 + i)^n} \qquad \textbf{Equation 2.5}$$

Semi-annual Interest

The more frequently interest is paid, the faster the compounding effect will tend to occur. Interest is commonly accrued semi-annually, quarterly or monthly.

Example 2.3

A principal sum of $100 is invested for four years at a semi-annually compounding rate of 9% pa. Calculate the value of the investment after two years.

At the end of the first half-yearly period,

$$\begin{aligned} FV_1 &= P\,(1 + r_1 t_1) \\ &= \$100\,(1 + 0.09/2) \\ &= \$100\,(1 + 0.045) \\ &= \$104.50 \end{aligned}$$

At the end of the second half-yearly period,

$$\begin{aligned} FV_2 &= FV_1(1 + r_2 t_2) &&= P\,(1 + rt)\,(1 + rt) \\ &= \$104.50\,(1 + 0.09/2) &&= P\,(1 + rt)^2 \\ &= \$104.50\,(1.045) &&= 100\,(1.045)^2 \\ &= \$109.20 \end{aligned}$$

And so on,

$$\begin{aligned} FV_3 &= FV_2\,(1 + r_3 t_3) &&= P\,(1 + rt)\,(1 + rt)\,(1 + rt) \\ &= \$109.20\,(1.045) &&= P\,(1 + rt)^3 \\ &= \$114.12 &&= 100\,(1.045)^4 \\ FV_4 &= FV_3\,(1 + r_4\,t_4) &&= P\,(1 + rt)(1 + rt)(1 + rt)(1 + rt) \\ &= \$114.12\,(1.045) &&= P\,(1 + rt)^4 \\ &= \$119.25 &&= 100\,(1.045)^4 \end{aligned}$$

Figure 2.3

Semi-annually compounding interest

$$FV = P\,(1 + i)^n$$

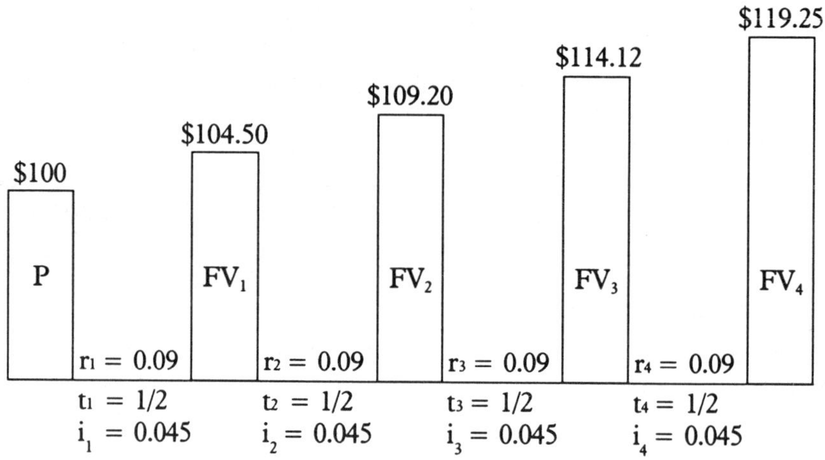

The formula for semi-annually compounding interest is identical to Equation 2.4. In applying the formula for semi-annual rests, it must be appreciated that the interest rate per period will be half the annual rate and there will be twice as many periods as years. Similarly, Equation 2.4 applies when interest accrues at quarterly, monthly or daily rests.

Applying the general formula to Example 2.3:

$$\begin{aligned} P &= \$100 \\ i &= rt = 0.09 \text{ x } 1/2 = 0.045 \\ n &= 2 \times 2 = 4 \\ FV &= P\,(1 + i)^n \\ &= \$100\,(1.045)^4 \\ &= \$119.25 \end{aligned}$$

Compounding interest on quarterly, monthly or other rests simply implies different values of t, that is, a different frequency.

$$\begin{aligned} t &= 1 && \text{annual rests} \\ t &= 1/2 && \text{semi-annual rests} \\ t &= 1/4 && \text{quarterly rests} \\ t &= 1/12 && \text{monthly rests} \\ n &= \text{number of periods} = \text{number of years} \times 1/t \end{aligned}$$

It is possible to convert a nominal interest rate based on, say, quarterly rests to an effective interest rate based on, say, semi-annual rests.

$$\left(1 + \frac{r_2}{2}\right)^2 = \left(1 + \frac{r_4}{4}\right)^4$$

$$\therefore \quad 1 + \frac{r_2}{2} = \left(1 + \frac{r_4}{4}\right)^2$$

$$\therefore \quad r_2 = 2\left[\left(1 + \frac{r_4}{4}\right)^2 - 1\right]$$

For example, a quarterly compounding interest rate of 10% pa is equivalent to 10.125% pa on a semi-annual basis.

If

$$r_4 = 0.10$$
$$r_2 = 2\,[(1 + 0.10/4)^2 - 1]$$
$$= 0.10125$$

It is similarly possible to convert any compounding interest rate to the equivalent compounding rate based on a different frequency.

Forward Interest Rates

A ***forward interest rate*** is an interest rate that can be determined today for a period from one future date until another future date.

Example 2.4

If the one month interest rate is 10% pa and the six month interest rate is 11% pa, calculate the forward interest rate for the period extending from one month from now to six months from now.

To describe forward interest rates, it is necessary to specify the starting date and the ending date of the period. The notation $r_{1/6}$ is used to denote the forward interest rate from one month till six months. The one month (from today) interest rate could be denoted $r_{0/1}$, and the six month interest rate, $r_{0/6}$.

Figure 2.4

Forward interest rate

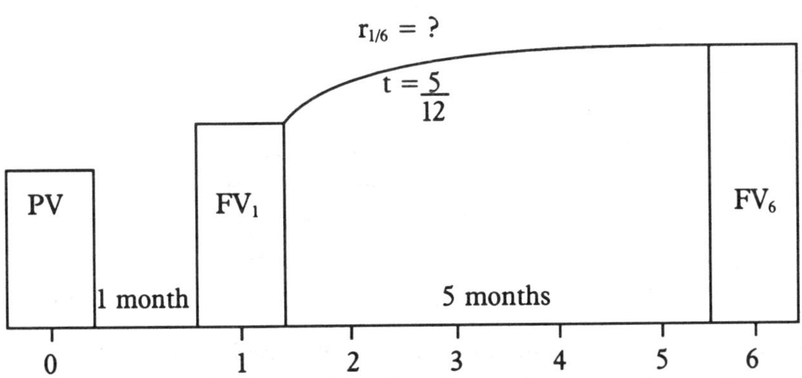

The future value of a one month investment of $1,000,000 would be

$$\begin{aligned} FV_1 &= PV\,(1 + r_{0/1} \times 1/12) \\ &= 1{,}000{,}000 \times (1 + 0.10 \times 1/12) \\ &= 1{,}008{,}333.33 \end{aligned}$$

The future value of a six month investment of $1,000,000 would be

$$\begin{aligned} FV_6 &= PV\,(1 + r_{0/6} \times 6/12) \\ &= 1{,}000{,}000 \times (1 + 0.11 \times 6/12) \\ &= 1{,}055{,}000.00 \end{aligned}$$

The forward interest rate is that rate which would make $1,008,333.33 accumulate to $1,055,000.00 after 5 months.

$$\begin{aligned} \text{ie} \quad 1{,}008{,}333.33 \times (1 + r_{1/6} \times 5/12) &= 1{,}055{,}000.00 \\ \therefore \quad r_{1/6} &= \left(\frac{1{,}055{,}000.00}{1{,}008{,}333.33} - 1\right) \times \frac{12}{5} \\ &= 0.11107 = 11.1\%\text{ pa} \end{aligned}$$

The forward interest rate is higher than the six month interest rate because the six month interest rate is higher than the one month rate. If the six month rate had been less than the one month rate, then the forward interest rate would have been less than the six month rate. It might be expected that if the one month and six month interest rates were equal, the forward interest rate would have the same value. In fact, in this case, the forward interest rate would be slightly less than the equal nominal rates because the interest earned in the first month will be part of the amount invested for the forward period.

In general, the forward interest rate from time t_1 to t_2 will be

$$r_{t_1/t_2} = \frac{FV_{t_2} - FV_{t_1}}{FV_{t_1}} \times \frac{12}{t_2 - t_1}$$

which can be expressed as

$$r_{t_1/t_2} = \left(\frac{FV_{t_2}}{FV_{t_1}} - 1\right) \times \frac{12}{t_2 - t_1} \qquad \textbf{Equation 2.6}$$

Present Value

To compare cash flows which apply at different points of time, it is necessary to ascertain their equivalent values at a common point of time, say, at present. The ***present value*** of a future cash flow can be calculated using Equation 2.7 which is derived by rearranging Equation 2.5.

From Equation 2.5:

$$PV = \frac{FV}{(1 + i)^n} \qquad \textbf{Equation 2.7}$$

where PV = present value
FV = future value
i = interest rate per period
n = number of periods

Example 2.5

Calculate the present value of a cash flow of \$800 due in two years time using a semi-annual interest rate of 6.5% pa.

$$FV = \$800$$
$$i = 0.065 \times 1/2 = 0.0325$$
$$n = 2 \times 2 = 4$$
$$\therefore \quad PV = \frac{\$800}{(1.0325)^4}$$
$$= \$703.93$$

Bonds

A ***bond*** is a long term note. The issuer promises to pay the investor the face value of the bond at a specified future date. The issuer may also agree to pay the investor an amount of interest at regular intervals throughout the life of the bond. These interim interest payments are known as ***coupons***.

Figure 2.5

Cash flows of an investor who has purchased a bond

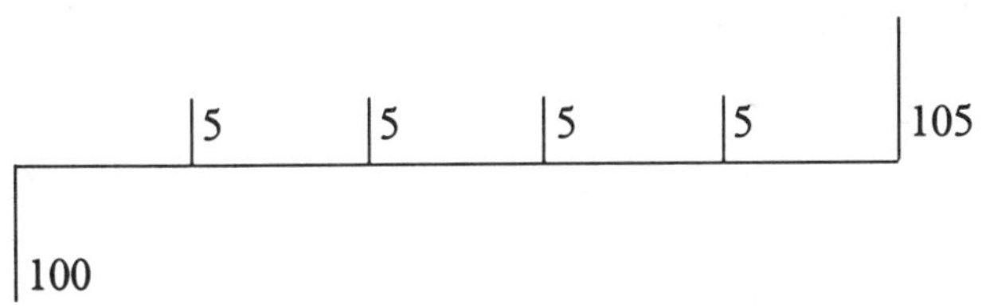

A coupon at end of each period and repayment of principal at maturity

Zero Coupon Bonds

A ***zero coupon bond*** is a bond with all coupons equal to zero.

Figure 2.6

Cash flows of a zero coupon bond

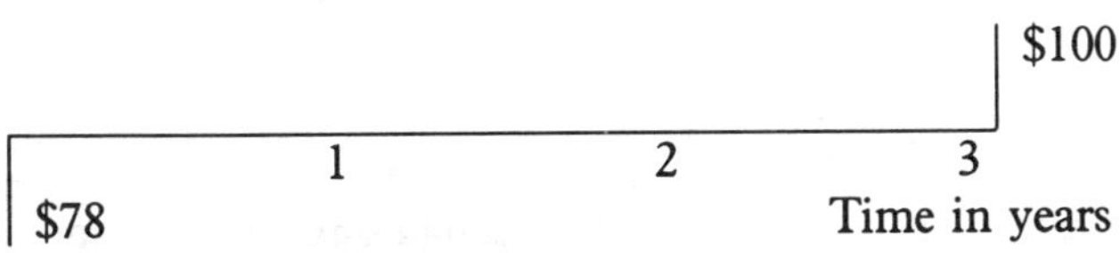

Example 2.6

An investor purchases a zero coupon bond with the face value of $100 maturing in three years for $78. What is the effective yield quoted in annual interest terms?

From Equation 2.5:

$$FV = P(1 + i)^n$$
$$FV = 100$$
$$P = 78$$
$$n = 3$$
$$i = ?$$

Rearranging Equation 2.5:

$$(1 + i)^n = FV/P$$
$$\therefore \quad 1 + i = (FV/P)^{1/n}$$
$$\therefore \quad \boxed{i = (FV/P)^{1/n} - 1} \qquad \textbf{Equation 2.8}$$
$$\therefore \quad i = (100/78)^{1/3} - 1$$
$$= 1.0863 - 1$$
$$= 0.0863$$
$$= 8.63\%$$

Practice Problems

2.1 Simple interest

(a) Calculate the interest earned on an investment of $2,000 for a period of three months at a simple interest rate of 6.75% pa.

(b) Calculate the interest earned on an investment of P4,750,000 for a period of 12 days at a simple interest rate of 8.25% pa (21 dpy).

2.2 Future value with simple interest

Calculate the future value of the investment in 2.1 (a).

2.3 Compound interest

An amount of $100,000 is invested for five years at a compounding interest rate of 8.25% pa at semi-annual rests. Calculate the accumulated value at maturity.

2.4 Varying rests

An interest rate is quoted as 9.8% pa compounding semi-annually. Calculate the effective interest rate allowing for compounding at monthly rests.

2.5 Forward interest rate

Calculate the forward interest rate for the period from six months from now to nine months from now if the six month rate is 7.5% pa and the nine month rate is 7.0% pa.

2.6 Present value

Calculate the present value of a cash flow of $10,000,000 due in three years time assuming a quarterly compounding interest rate of 7.25% pa.

2.7 Effective yield on zero coupon bond

An investor purchases a zero coupon bond with a face value of $1,000,000 maturing in five years for $500,000. What is the effective yield quoted in annual interest terms?

Supplementary Questions

2.8 Simple interest

Calculate the interest earned on an investment of $3,000 for a period of 78 days at a simple interest rate of 8.75 % per annum (365 days basis).

2.9 Future value

Calculate the future value of the $3,000 investment in 2.8.

2.10 Compound interest

An amount of $100,000 is invested for two years at a compounding interest rate of 12.25% pa at semi-annual rests. Calculate the accumulated value at maturity.

2.11 Compound interest

An amount of $100,000 is invested for three years at a compounding interest rate of 8.25% pa at semi-annual rests. Calculate the accumulated value at maturity.

2.12 Forward interest rate

Calculate the forward interest rate for a period from four months from now till nine months from now if the four month rate is 7.5% pa and the nine month rate is 7.0% pa.

3 Cash Flows and Value Dates

In this chapter, the concepts of cash flows and value dates are introduced. The T-account is presented as a simple notation for defining cash flows. The conventions used to describe value dates and the concepts of net cash flow and net exchange positions are also introduced.

Specifications of Cash Flows

Money market and foreign exchange transactions involve cash flows. To fully define the cash flows associated with a financial transaction, it is necessary to specify:

- the direction of the cash flows;
- the currencies of the cash flows;
- the amounts of the cash flows;
- the timing of the cash flows.

Positive and Negative Cash Flows

The receipt of cash from another party is described as an ***inflow of cash*** and designated a ***positive cash flow***. The payment of cash to another party is described as an ***outflow of cash*** and designated a ***negative cash flow***.

Exhibit 3.1

Examples of positive and negative cash flows of a commercial bank

Inflows (+)	Outflows (-)
Receipt of a deposit from a customer	Withdrawal of a deposit by a customer
Receipt of a loan repayment from a customer	Granting a loan to a customer
Termination of a deposit with another branch	Deposit of excess funds with another branch
Purchase of a currency	Sale of a currency
Sale of a bond	Purchase of a bond

T-accounts

T-accounts provide a simple notation for specifying the cash flows associated with a financial transaction.

> Money market transactions involve a positive and a negative cash flow in **one** currency at ***different*** times

Exhibit 3.2

Cash flow representation money market transactions

Taking a deposit of £1,000,000 for 3 months at 8% pa

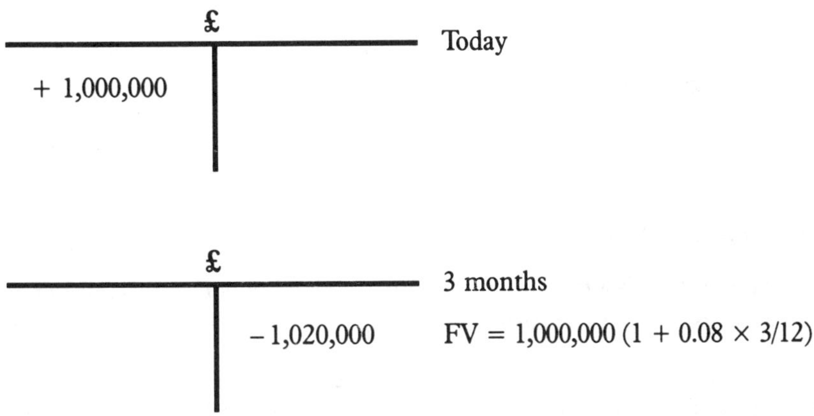

Making a loan of $1,500,000 for 1 month at 6% pa

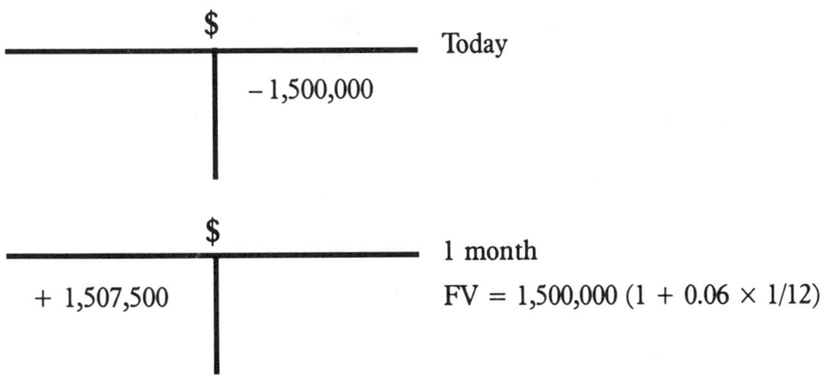

The cash flows in the future dates represent amounts of principal plus interest.

A foreign exchange transaction involves a positive and a negative cash flow in ***different*** currencies at the ***same*** time.

Exhibit 3.3
Cash flow representation foreign exchange transaction

Buying $1,000,000 against DM at 1.4450

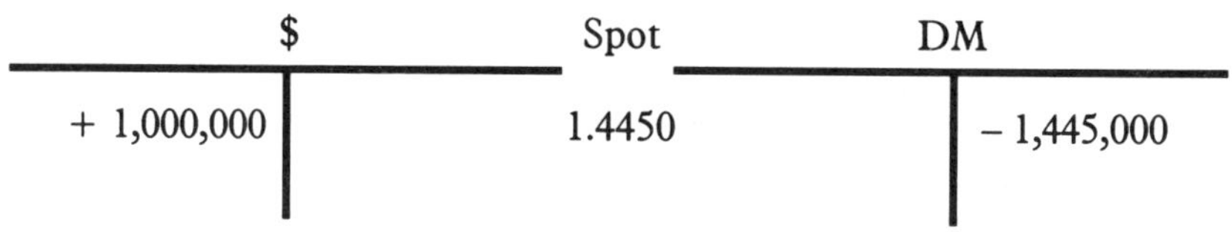

Spot Value Dates

The date on which a transaction is contracted is known as the ***contract date.*** The dates on which the cash flows occur are known as ***value dates.***

In international transactions, two business days are usually allowed between the contract date and the value date. This allows time for payments to be made to accounts in banks in other countries which are possibly in different time zones. ***Spot value*** refers to a payment which will be made two business days from the contract date. If there is a holiday in either or both countries in which the cash flows are to occur, the spot date moves forward to the next eligible date.

Exhibit 3.4

Spot value dates

JANUARY						
SUN	MON	TUE	WED	THU	FRI	SAT
	JA1	J2	3	4	5	6
7	8	9	10	11	12	13
14	H15	16	17	18	19	20
21	22	23	24	25	A26	27
28	29	30	31			

J Holiday in Japan
H Holiday in Hong Kong
A Holiday in Australia

Spot transactions	Contract date	Spot value date
Buys US$ against DM	Mon 8 Jan	Wed 10 Jan
Sells US$ against £	Thurs 4 Jan	Mon 8 Jan
Buys US$ against HK$	Thurs 11 Jan	Tues 16 Jan
Buys A$ against ¥	Wed 24 Jan	Mon 29 Jan
Sells £ against DM	Wed 17 Jan	Fri 19 Jan

During holiday periods, it is possible for spot value to extend for four, five or six days. For example, if Christmas Day falls on a Monday and Boxing Day is also a holiday on the Tuesday, a transaction dealt on Friday 22 December will have spot value the following Thursday 28 December — a six day run.

Forward Value Dates

If the cash flows associated with a transaction are to occur on a date or dates which are further into the future than spot, these are said to have ***forward value***. It is common for transactions to mature a round number of months after spot. For example, if £1,000,000 is borrowed for three months from spot, there would be a receipt of pounds on the spot date and a repayment of principal plus interest three months later. If that date is a weekend or public holiday, the repayment will occur on the next available business date, unless it requires going beyond month end, in which case the forward value date would be the first available business day prior to month end.

Exhibit 3.5

Forward value dates

JANUARY						
SUN	MON	TUE	WED	THU	FRI	SAT
	JA1	J2	3	4	5	6
7	8	9	10	11	12	13
14	H15	16	17	18	19	20
21	22	23	24	25	A26	27
28	29	30	31			

FEBRUARY						
SUN	MON	TUE	WED	THU	FRI	SAT
				1	2	3
4	5	6	7	8	9	10
11	12	13	14	15	16	17
18	19	20	UK21	UK22	23	24
25	26	27	28			

1 Month Forward Value Transactions

Contract date	Spot value date	1 month forward value date
3 Jan	5 Jan	5 Feb
5 Jan	9 Jan	9 Feb
8 Jan	10 Jan	12 Feb
18 Jan	22 Jan	23 Feb
25 Jan	29 Jan	28 Feb
29 Jan	31 Jan	28 Feb

Short Dates

On occasions, it is necessary for transactions to mature and the cash flows to occur prior to spot value. By definition, there are only two eligible business days before spot value: today *(tod)* and tomorrow *(tom)*. These are known as ***short dates.*** Transactions with cash flows that occur on the same day as the contract date are known as ***value today*** transactions. Similarly, transactions with cash flows that occur on the business day following the contract date are described as ***value tomorrow.***

Net Cash Flow Position

There is said to be a ***position*** if circumstances are such that a change in a rate will create a profit or loss. If cash inflows and cash outflows are unequal or have mismatched value dates, there is a ***net cash flow position.*** Separate net cash flow positions apply for each value date.

Net cash flow position = cash inflow – cash outflow **Equation 3.1**

A ***positive net cash flow position*** reflects an excess of cash inflow over cash outflow on the relevant value date. The surplus cash will be available for investment. If interest rates rise, the return will be higher. If interest rates fall, the return will be lower.

A ***negative net cash flow position*** reflects an excess of cash outflow over cash inflow on the relevant value date. Assuming there is no idle balance, the account will become overdrawn. The shortfall of cash will require funding. If interest rates rise, it will become more expensive to fund the account. If interest rates fall, it will become less expensive to fund the account.

A negative net cash flow position also implies a ***liquidity position***. There is a risk that there will be insufficient funds available for borrowing, in which case the account must remain overdrawn. Being overdrawn may involve financial and non-financial penalties.

Exhibit 3.6

Net cash flow positions

cash inflow	cash outflow	net cash flow position	
+ 300	- 200	+ 100	**Positive cash flow position** Potential gain if interest rates rise Potential loss if interest rates fall
+200	- 350	- 150	**Negative cash flow position** Potential gain if interest rates fall Potential loss if interest rates rise
+ 100	- 100	0	**Square cash flow position** No gain or loss from interest rate changes

If cash inflow equals cash outflow on a particular value date, then the net cash flow position is zero. This is referred to as a ***square cash flow position***. Changes in interest rates will have no net impact on profits or losses.

Net Exchange Position

Buying and selling foreign currencies create exposures to changes in exchange rates. Buying a foreign currency creates an asset. The position is said to be ***long*** the foreign currency. If the foreign currency appreciates, there will be an exchange gain. If the currency depreciates, there will be an exchange loss.

Selling a foreign currency creates a liability. The position is said to be ***short*** the foreign currency. If the foreign currency depreciates, there will be an exchange gain. If the foreign currency appreciates, there will be an exchange loss.

The excess amount of a foreign currency which has been purchased over the amount of the same foreign currency which has been sold is described as the ***net exchange position***. There is a separate net exchange position for each foreign currency.

net exchange position = foreign currency purchased – foreign currency sold	**Equation 3.2**

Being long a currency implies having a positive net exchange position. Provided the exchange rate is quoted with the currency as the commodity currency, a rise in the exchange rate will yield an exchange gain and a fall in the exchange rate will result in an exchange loss.

Being short a currency implies having a negative net exchange position. Provided the foreign currency is the commodity currency, a rise in the exchange rate will involve an exchange loss and a fall in the exchange rate will involve an exchange gain.

If the amount of currency purchased equals the amount of that currency which has been sold, then the net exchange position will be zero. This is referred to as a ***square exchange position***. Changes in exchange rates will have no impact on profit or loss.

A net exchange position is created or removed at the time at which the purchase or sale of foreign currency is contracted, not at the time at which the related cash flows occur. For example, if a spot contract is entered into today to purchase US$1,000,000 against deutschemarks at a rate of US$1 = DM 1.4450, the buyer immediately becomes long dollars and short deutschemarks regardless of the fact that he or she will not receive the dollars nor pay away the deutschemarks until two business days later. Similarly, forward purchases or sales of foreign currency immediately create or remove a net exchange position.

Exhibit 3. 7

Net exchange position

Foreign currency purchased	Foreign currency sold	Net exchange position	
+40	-30	+10	**Long foreign currency** Potential gain if exchange rate rises Potential loss if exchange rate falls
+ 20	– 40	– 20	**Short foreign currency** Potential gain if exchange rate falls Potential loss if exchange rate rises
+ 10	– 10	0	**Square exchange position** No gain or loss from exchange rate changes

Distinction between Net Exchange Position and Net Cash Flow Position

It is important to appreciate the distinction between a net exchange position and a net cash flow position. Money market transactions create net cash flow positions but do not create net exchange positions. Merely borrowing or lending a foreign currency does not create a net exchange position. Only buying or selling a currency can create a net exchange position. Borrowing Swiss francs for three months will cause a positive cash flow of Swiss francs now and a negative cash flow of Swiss francs in three months time but no exposure to the exchange rate. Unless the Swiss francs are sold (which would create a net exchange position), they will be available to repay the loan on maturity and so exchange rate changes will bear no relevance to profit or loss.[1]

Foreign exchange transactions create both net cash flow positions and net exchange positions. Mismatched cash flows may be offset by either money market transactions or foreign exchange transactions. However, net exchange positions can only be offset by foreign exchange transactions.

Example 3.1

Consider the net cash flow and net exchange implications of a corporation whose local currency is the dollar entering into a number of different transactions on 1 February.

Transaction 1: Buys foreign currency spot

Exhibit 3.8

Buys DM2,890,000 against dollars at $1 = DM1.4450 value Feb 3

Cash flows			Net exchange position
$	Feb 3	DM	from Feb 1
– 2,000,000	1.4450	+ 2,890,000	long DM 2,890,000

1. A net exchange position is created to the extent that the future obligation to pay interest (FOTPI) and future obligation to receive interest (FOTRI) will require a future purchase or sale of foreign currency. An alternative treatment is to define the net exchange position as the net present value of foreign currency cash flows. See p 33-34 for an example using the NPV method.

Transaction 2: Sells foreign currency spot

Exhibit 3.9

Buys $1,000,000 against DM1,445,000 at $1= DM1.4450 value Feb 3

$	Cash flows	DM	Net exchange position
	Feb 3		from Feb 1
+ 1,000,000	1.4450	– 1,445,000	short DM 1,445,000

Transaction 3: Borrows local currency

Exhibit 3.10

Borrows $1,000,000 at 10% pa from Feb 1 until Mar 1 (28 days)

$	Cash flows	DM	Net exchange position
	Feb 1		from Feb 1
+1,000,000			none
$	Mar 1	DM	
– 1,000,000	(P)		
– 7,778	(I)		
– 1,007,778	(P+I)		

Transaction 4: Lends local currency

Exhibit 3.11

Lends $2,000,000 at 7% pa from Feb 1 until April 1 (59 days)

$	Cash flows	DM	Net exchange position
	Feb 1		from Feb 1
– 2,000,000			none
$	Apr 1	DM	
+ 2,000,000	(P)		
+ 22,944	(I)		
+ 2,022,944	(P+I)		

Transaction 5: Borrows foreign currency

Exhibit 3.12

Borrows DM2,500,000 from Feb 3 until Feb 17 (14 days) at 6% pa

$	Cash flows	DM	Net exchange position
	Feb 3		from Feb 1
	+ 2,500,000		
	Feb 17		
	(P)	– 2,500,000	
	(I)	– 5,833	short DM 5,833
	(P+I)	– 2,505,833	(FOTPI)

Transaction 6: Lends foreign currency

Exhibit 3.13

Lends DM1,500,000 from Feb 3 until Feb 10 (7 days) at 5.1% pa

$	Cash flows	DM	Net exchange position
	Feb 3		from Feb 1
		– 1,500,000	
	Feb 17		
	1,500,000		
	+ 1,604		long DM 1,604
	1,501,604		(FOTRI)[3]

Transaction 7: Cross rate

Exhibit 3.14

Buys DM 1,000,000 against yen at DM 1 = ¥ 70.00 value Feb 3

$	Cash flows	DM		¥	Net exchange position
	Feb 3		Feb 3		from Feb 1
	+ 1,000,000		70.00	–70,000,00	long DM 1,000,00
					short ¥70,000,000

2. FOTPI stands for future obligation to pay interest

3. FOTRI stands for future obligation to receive interest

Net Exchange Position Sheet

A running tally of the net exchange position in each foreign currency can be kept for successive transactions. The net exchange position can be tracked throughout the day in the following manner. It is assumed that there was a square position before the first transaction.

Exhibit 3.15

Net exchange position sheet for Feb 1

	DM		¥	
		NEP		NEP
Opening position		0		0
Transaction 1	+ 2,890,000	+ 2,890,000		
Transaction 2	– 1,445,000	+ 1,445,000		
Transaction 5	– 5,833	+ 1,439,167		
Transaction 6	+ 1,604	+ 1,440,771		
Transaction 7	+ 1,000,000	+ 2,440,771	– 70,000,000	– 70,000,000

After the seven transactions, the net exchange position is long DM 2,440,771 and short ¥ 70,000,000.

Transactions 3 and 4 are excluded because they do not impact the net exchange position.

Blotter

Foreign exchange dealers who do many transactions a day keep a rough copy of a net exchange sheet known as a ***blotter***. It is vitally important that a dealer always knows his or her net exchange position, at least approximately. Amounts are usually rounded to the nearest 100,000 units.

Exhibit 3.16

Blotter

	DM		¥	
		NEP		NEP
Opening position		0		0
Transaction 1	+ 2.9	+ 2.9		
Transaction 2	– 1.5	+ 1.4		
Transaction 7	+ 1.0	+ 2.4	– 70	– 70

Transactions 5 and 6, which are FOTPI and FOTRI entries, are excluded from the blotter as trivial.

At the end of each day, the blotter should be reconciled with the complete net exchange position sheet. These days, most banks have real time systems which display accurate cash flow and net exchange positions. It is important for dealers to input deals as soon as possible once a transaction is done.

> A cardinal rule of trading is for the dealer to know her or his position at all times

NPV Method

A superior definition of the ***net exchange position*** is the net present value of foreign currency cash flows.

Example 3.2

Prepare a net exchange position sheet for a dealer who does the following three transactions using the NPV method assuming the following interest rates and a square starting position:

(a) bought ¥1,000,000,000 against dollars value spot at $1 = ¥105.75

(b) sold ¥500,000,000 against dollars value three months at $1 = ¥104.90

(c) sold $4,000,000 against yen value six months at $1 = ¥104.70

Prevailing interest rates:

	3 months	6 months
Dollar	5.25% pa	5.50% pa
Yen	0.75% pa	1.00% pa

Cash flows:

Trans-action	$	¥	Rate	Term	Working
(a)	– 9,456,264.78	+ 1,000,000,000	105.75	spot	$\frac{1,000,000,000}{105.75} = 9,456,264.78$
(b)	+ 4,766,444.27	– 500,000,000	104.90	3 months	$\frac{500,000,000}{104.90} = 4,766,444.27$
(c)	– 4,000,000.00	+ 418,800,000	104.70	6 months	4,000,000 × 104.70 = 418,800,000

Present values:

Term	Cash flow	Rate	PV	Working
spot	– $9,456,264.78	—	– $9,456,264.78	
spot	+ ¥1,000,000,000	—	+ ¥1,000,000,000	
3 months	+ $4,766,444.27	5.25%	+ $4,704,695.15	$\frac{4,766,444.27}{1 + 0.0525 \times 3/12} = 4,704,695.15$
3 months	– ¥500,000,000	0.75%	– ¥499,064,255	$\frac{500,000,000}{1 + 0.0075 \times 3/12} = 499,064,255$
6 months	– $4,000,000	5,50%	– $3,892,944.04	$\frac{4,000,000}{1 + 0.055 \times 6/12} = 3,892,944.04$
6 months	+ ¥418,800,000	1.00%	+ ¥420,894,000	$\frac{418,800,000}{1 + 0.01 \times 6/12} = 420,894,000$

Trans-action	$PV	NEP	¥PV	NEP
(a)	− 9,456,264.78	− 9,456,264.78	+ 1,000,000,000	+ 1,000,000,000
(b)	+ 4,704,695.15	− 4,751,569.63	− 499,064,255	+ 500,935,745
(c)	− 3,892,944.04	−8,644,513.67	+ 420,894,000	+ 921,829,745

Net Exchange Position is long ¥921,829,745 at an average spot equivalent rate of $\frac{921,829,745}{8,644,513.67}$ = ¥106.64 per $1.

The present value of a future cash flow is sometimes referred to as its ***delta***. This represents the amount which needs to pur`hased or sold value spot to accumulate to the face value of the foreign currency amount by the future date. If the time period is sufficiently long or interest rates sufficiently high, the delta can be significantly less than the future value.

The benefits of the NPV method will be better appreciated when forward exchange transactions have been explained in Chapter 6.

Applying the NPV method requires a reasonably sophisticated system, which can continually discount future cash flows into present values.

Practice Problems

3.1 Cash flow representation: forward interest rate transaction

Show the cash flows when $2,000,000 is borrowed from one month till six months at a forward interest rate $r_{1/6}$ of 9% pa.

3.2 Cash flow representation: forward exchange rate transaction

Show the cash flows when $2,000,000 is purchased three months forward against deutschemarks at a forward rate of $1 = DM1.4420.

3.3 Net exchange position sheet

Prepare a net exchange position sheet for a dealer whose local currency is the dollar who does the following five transactions. Assuming he or she is square before the first transaction, the dealer:

(a) borrows DG7,000,000 for four months at 4% pa;
(b) sells DG7,000,000 spot at $1 = DG1.6500;
(c) buys ¥500,000,000 spot at $1 = ¥103.00;
(d) sells ¥200,000,000 spot against DG at DG1 = ¥62.50;
(e) buys DG4,000,000 one month forward at $1 = DG62.70.

Supplementary Questions

3.4 Cash flow representation: forward investment

Show the cash flows when $1,000,000 is invested from three months for six months at a forward rate $r_{3/9}$ of 7.5% pa.

3.5 Cash flow representation: forward exchange transaction

Show the cash flows when ¥4,000,000,000 is sold against DM for value 3 November at an outright rate of DM1 = ¥73.60.

4

Yield Curves and Gapping in the Money Market

In this chapter, the concept of the yield curve is introduced and the factors that give rise to changes in the shape and position of the yield curve are examined. The practice of gapping in the money market enables profit to be made from expected changes in interest rates.

The Yield Curve

At any point of time, different interest rates are likely to apply for different tenors. For example, the one month interest rate might be 7.0% pa, the two month interest rate 7.2% pa, the three month interest rate 7.4% pa, the four month interest rate 7.6% pa, and so on.

Tenor in months	Interest rate yield % pa
1	7.0%
2	7.2%
3	7.4%
4	7.6%
5	7.8%
6	8.0%

It is possible to plot yield against tenor for these and other tenors. The curve obtained when yield is plotted on the vertical axis and tenor on the horizontal axis is known as the ***yield curve.***

Figure 4.1

Yield curve

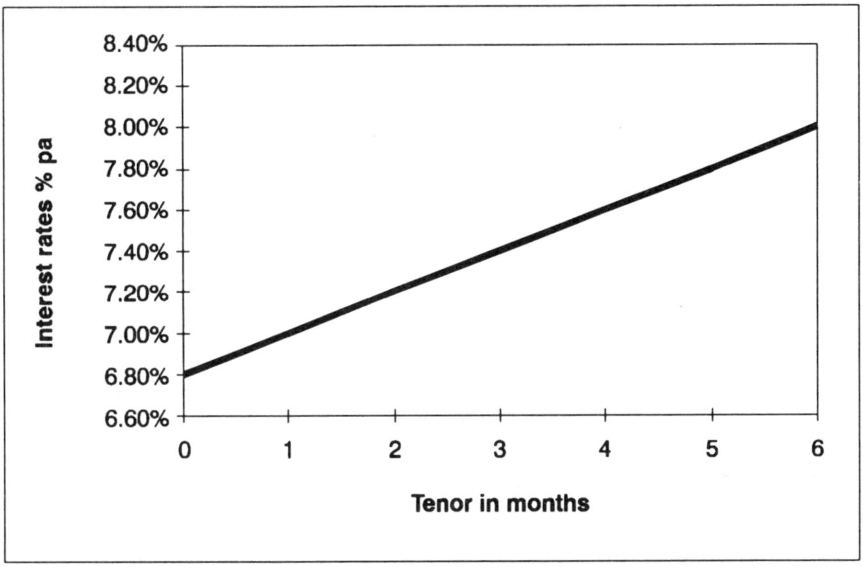

The shape and position of the yield curve will change over time. Figure 4.2 shows how the US dollar yield curve moved between 1 February 1994 and 31 December 1994.

Figure 4.2

Shift in US dollar yield curve

1 Feb 1994 to 31 Dec 1994

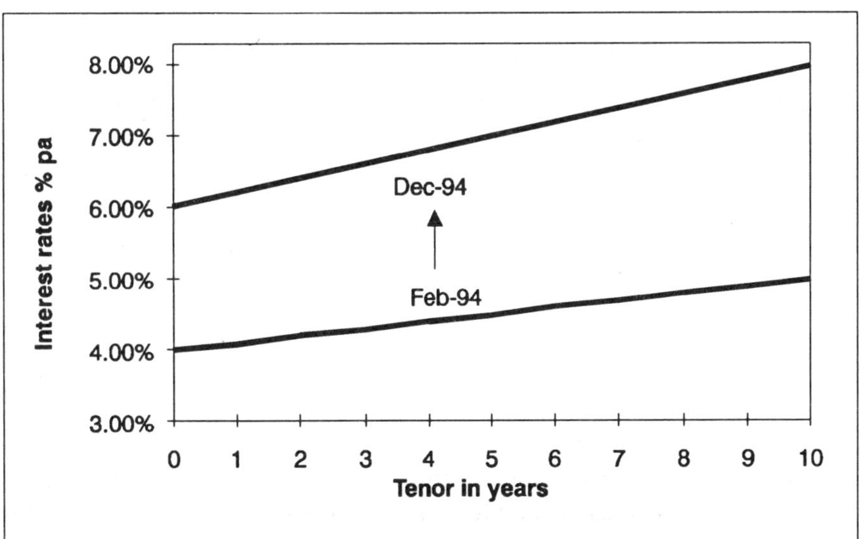

Normal Yield Curve

It is normal that interest rates for longer tenors are higher than for shorter tenors. A ***normal yield curve*** is therefore slighly upward sloping to the right.

Figure 4.3

Normal yield curve

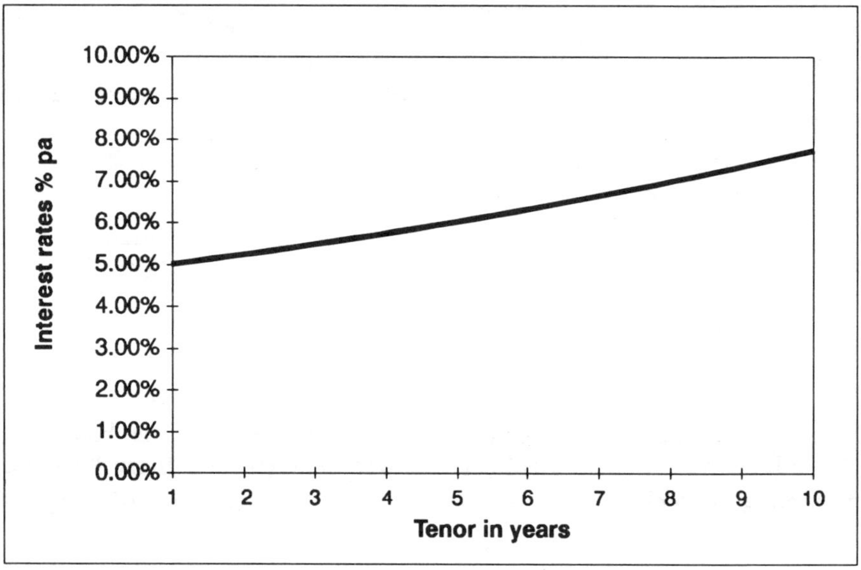

Reasons for the Normal Yield Curve

1. Liquidity preference

If yields were the same for all tenors, the yield curve would be horizontal. Such a yield curve would be described as a ***flat yield curve***. In this situation, investors would prefer to be repaid sooner rather than later. By lending money, an investor foregoes the opportunity to spend it, and so the longer the tenor, the more liquidity is sacrificed by the investor. As a result, the investor usually commands a higher return for an investment for a longer tenor.

2. Time value of money

Interest is usually paid at the maturity of the investment. By investing for shorter periods, an investor receives interest sooner. The investor is then free to reinvest or rollover the principal plus interest for another period, to enjoy the compounding of interest. The investor, therefore, normally requires a higher yield as an enticement to invest for longer tenors.

3. Credit risk

When an investor lends money to a borrower, he or she takes a risk that the borrower may be unwilling or unable to repay the principal plus interest at maturity. This risk is greater the longer the period of the loan. The investor normally commands a higher yield as an enticement to extend credit for a longer term.

4. Rate risk

Interest rates change over time. When lending money to a borrower, the investor takes a risk that interest rates may rise, in which case he or she will have invested at a lower return than subsequently becomes available. To compensate for taking this risk, the investor commands a higher yield for longer tenors.

Impact of Interest Rate Expectations

It can be seen from Figure 4.8 that yield curves are not always gradually upward sloping to the right. For example, on 1 May 1996 the ten year NZ$ yield was less than the five year yield and the five year yield was less than the one year yield and so on.

In addition to the factors that give normality to the yield curve, the shape of the yield curve is also influenced by how the market expects interest rates to change.

If market participants generally expect interest rates to rise, borrowers will be inclined to borrow for long tenors to lock into relatively low interest rates before they rise. Consequently, long term interest rates will tend to rise. At the same time, investors will be inclined to lend for short tenors in the expectation that they will be able to rollover their investments at higher interest rates in the future. Consequently, short term interest rates will tend to fall. The combined effect of long term rates rising and short term rates falling will cause the yield curve to become steeper.

Figure 4.4

Market expects interest rates to rise causing more positive yield curve

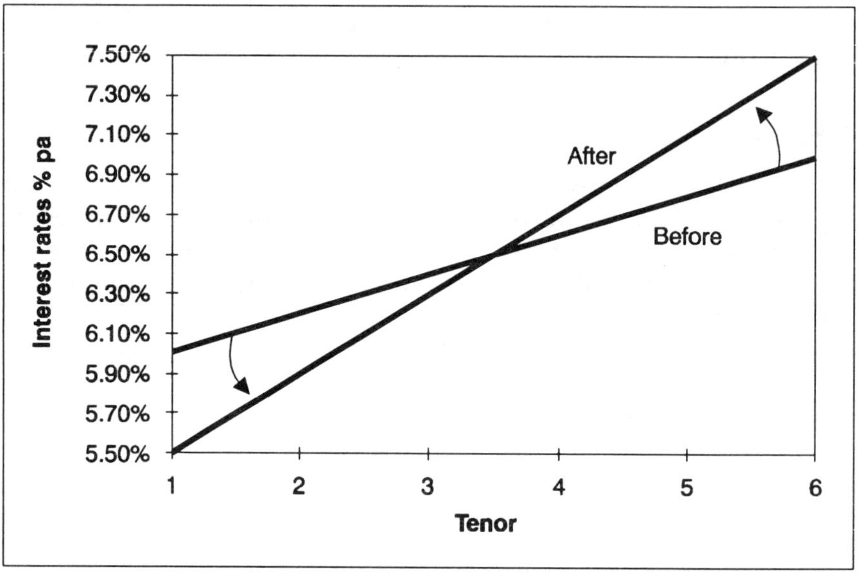

Conversely, if market participants generally expect interest rates to fall, borrowers will be inclined to borrow for short periods in the expectation that they will be able to rollover their borrowings at lower interest rates in the future. Consequently, short term interest rates will tend to rise. At the same time, investors will be inclined to lend for long periods to lock in relatively high yields before they fall. Consequently, long term interest rates tend to fall. The combined effect of short term rates rising and long term rates falling will cause the yield curve to become flatter. If interest rates are expected to fall more than sufficiently to outweigh the factors giving rise to normality, then the yield curve will be downward sloping to the right. Such a yield curve is described as an ***inverse yield curve***.

Figure 4.5

Market expects interest rates to fall causing inverse yield curve

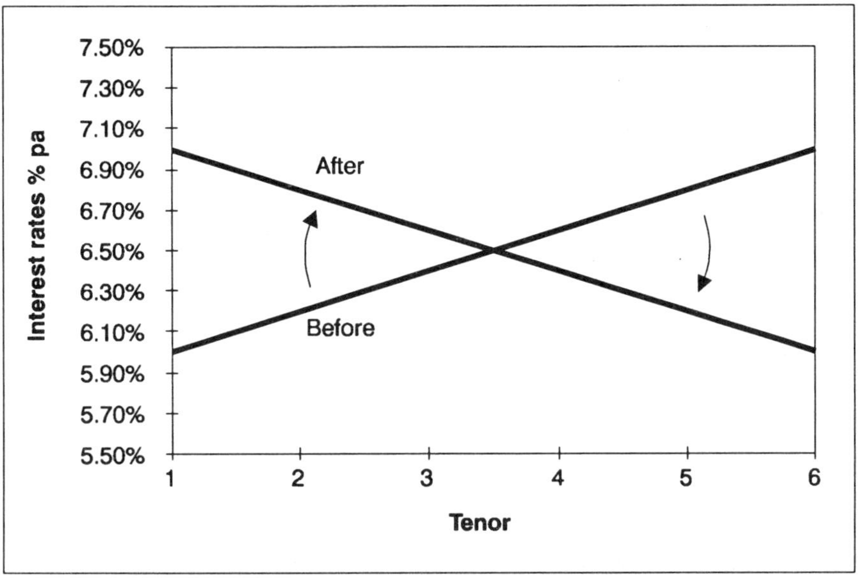

The shape of the yield curve shows what the market expects to happen to interest rates.

If the yield curve is more positive than the normal market, participants must generally expect interest rates to rise. If the yield curve is inverse, the market must generally expect interest rates to fall. Indeed, when the yield curve is flat, the market must generally expect interest rates to fall slightly, because in the absence of interest rate expectations, the yield curve would be normal.

Figure 4.6

Normal yield curve

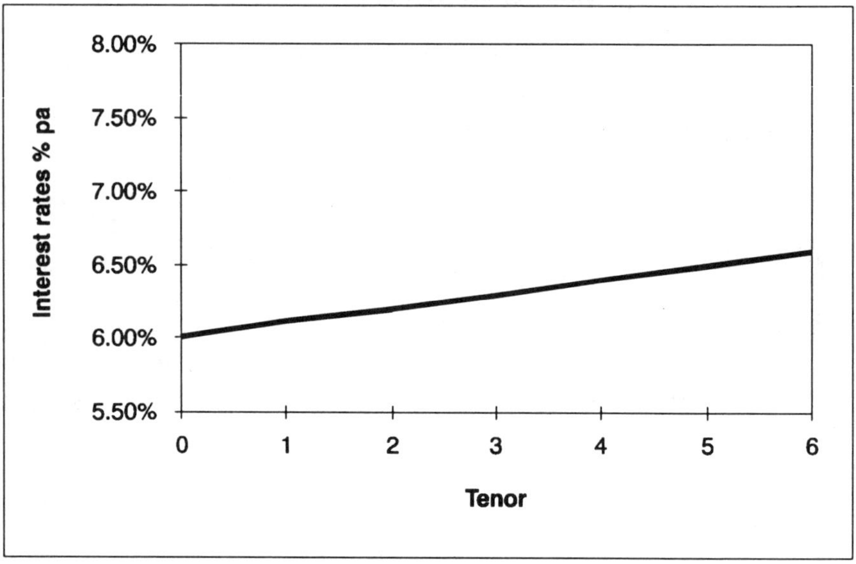

Market expects interest rates to remain at current levels.

Figure 4.7

Positive yield curve

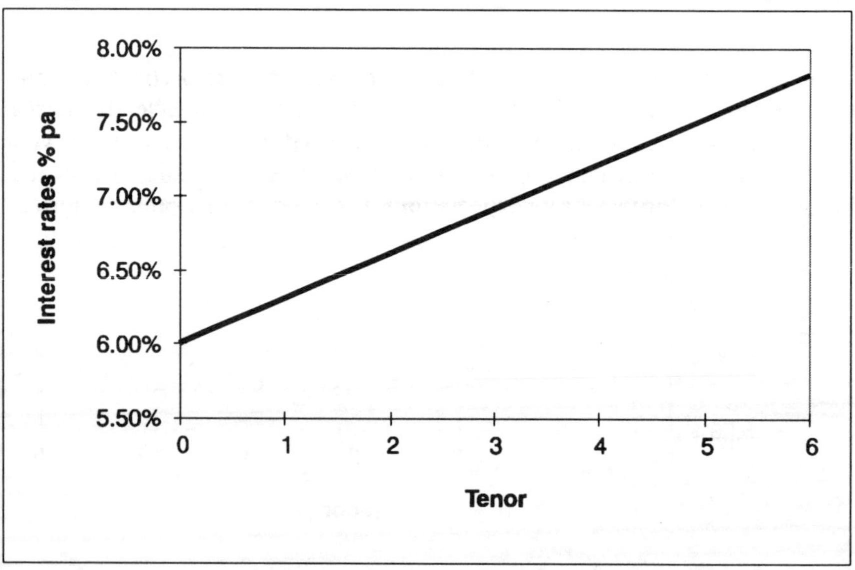

Market expects interest rates to rise.

Figure 4.8
Inverse yield curve

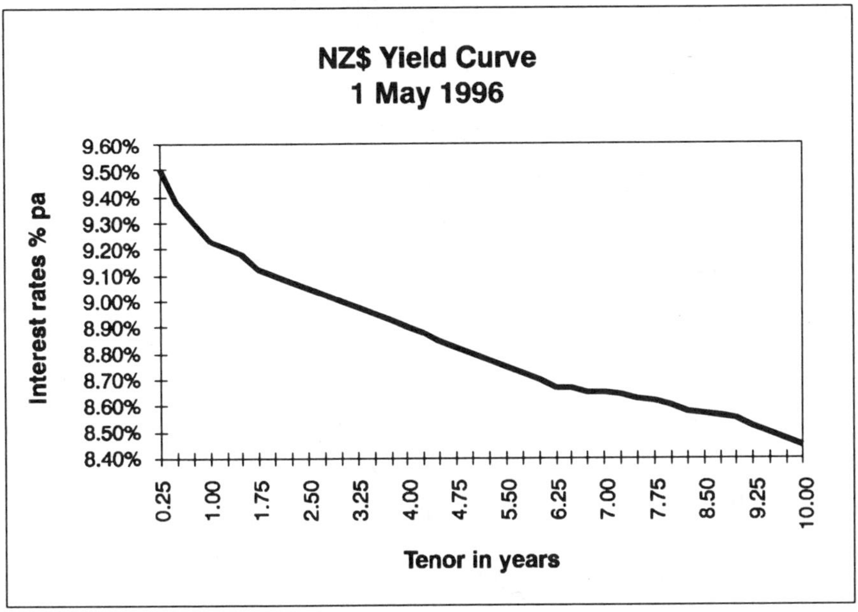

Market expects interest rates to fall sharply.

Figure 4.9
Flat yield curve

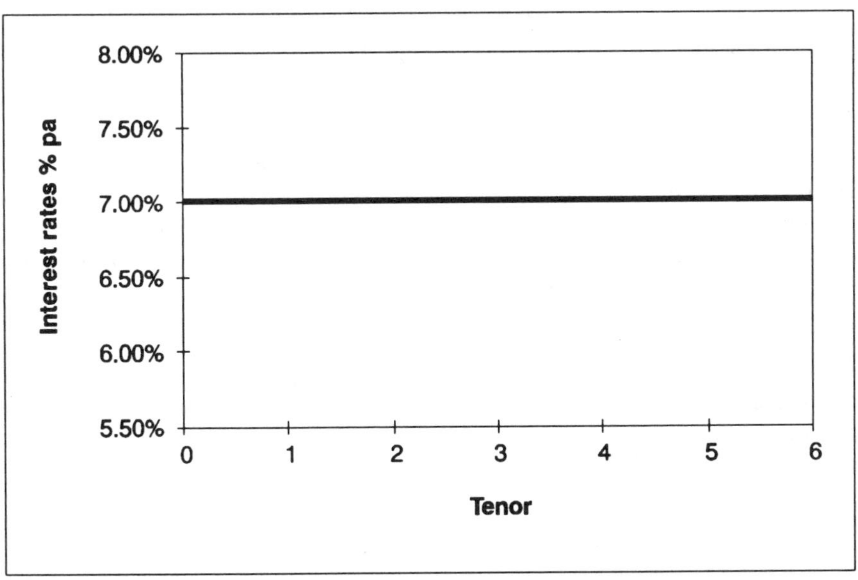

Market expects interest rates to fall slightly.

In practice, the slope of the yield curve is not always uniform. Market expectations for future interest rates represent a complex combination of the views of many borrowers and investors whose expectations will vary for different tenors. Even so, the shape of thc yield curve reveals a mass of market intelligence about interest rate expectations.

Figure 4.10

Italian lira yield curve 12 March 1996

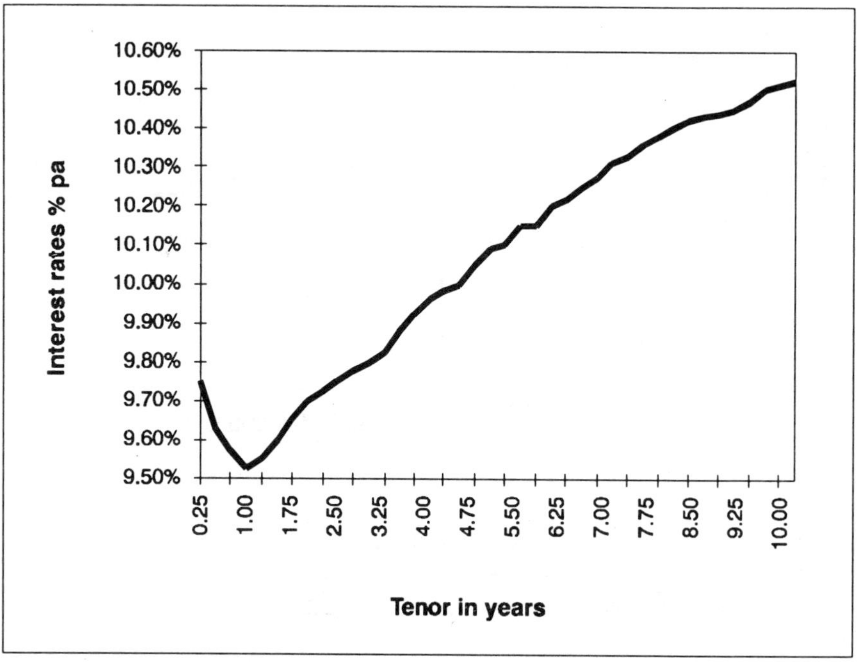

Figure 4.10 shows the actual Italian lira yield curve as at 12 March 1996. Unlike any of the theoretical yield curves shown in Figures 4.6 to 4.9, this yield curve is not regular. Even so, the shape of the yield curve reflects market expectation for interest rates. Interest rates were expected to fall in the coming five quarters and then increase.

Interest rates do not always move in accordance with market expectations. However, the shape of the yield curve is a good barometer of what is likely to happen to interest rates. Unlike the forecasts of business commentators and economists, the yield curve reflects the views of borrowers and investors speaking through their pockets.

Parallel Shift of the Yield Curve

It is convenient to distinguish between parallel shifts and rotations of the yield curve. A parallel shift of the yield curve would reflect an equal increase or decrease in interest rates over a range of tenors. The slope of the yield curve is unchanged; it merely moves up or down.

Tenor in months	Interest rate before shift % pa	Interest rate after shift % pa	Increase in interest rate % pa
1	6.0	6.5	+0.5
2	6.1	6.6	+0.5
3	6.2	6.7	+0.5
4	6.3	6.8	+0.5
5	6.4	6.9	+0.5
6	6.5	7.0	+0.5

Figure 4.11

Parallel shift of the yield curve

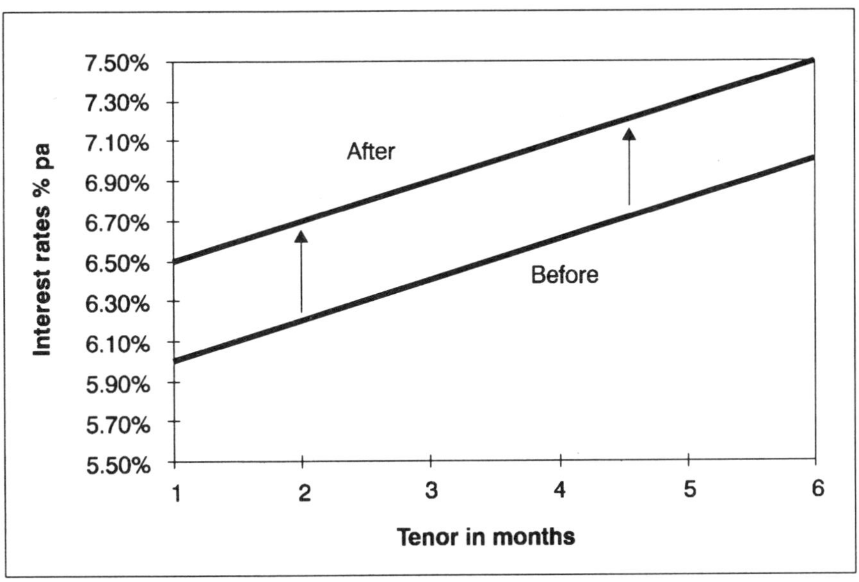

Rotation of the Yield Curve

A rotation of the yield curve would reflect a proportional increase or decrease in interest rates resulting in a change in the slope of the yield curve. The yield curve would become steeper or flatter.

Tenor in months	Interest rate before rotation % pa	Interest rate after rotation % pa	Increase in interest rate % pa
1	6.0	5.8	–0.2
2	6.1	6.0	–0.1
3	6.2	6.2	0
4	6.3	6.4	+0.1
5	6.4	6.6	+0.2
6	6.5	6.8	+0.3

Figure 4.12

Rotation of the yield curve

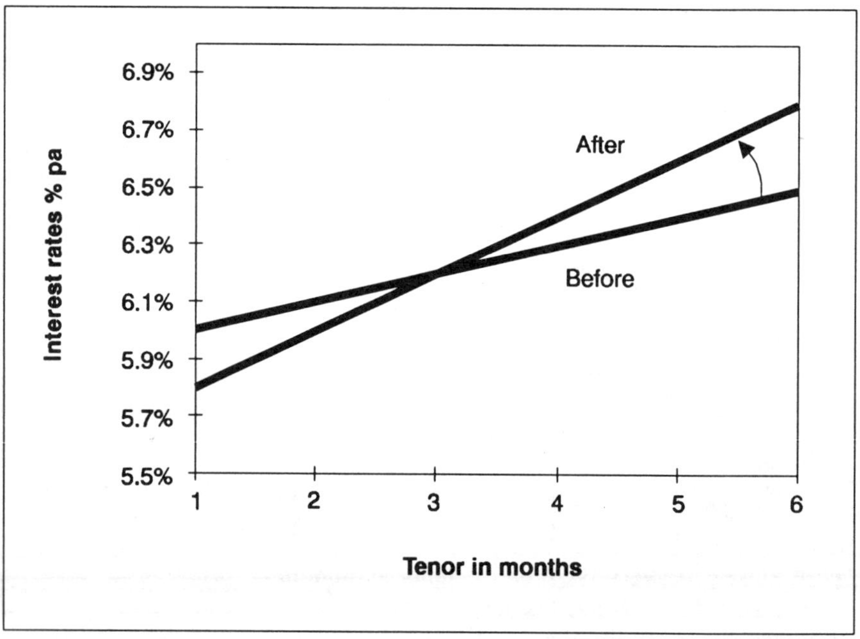

The yield curve rotated about a pivotal point at three months.

In practice, movements of the yield curve will involve various combinations of shifts and rotations.

The Australian dollar yield curve as shown in Figure 4.13 moved from being steeply inverse in January 1990 to being positive in February 1994. This move constitutes both a translation and rotation of the curve.

Figure 4.13

A$ yield curve

January 1990 and February 1994

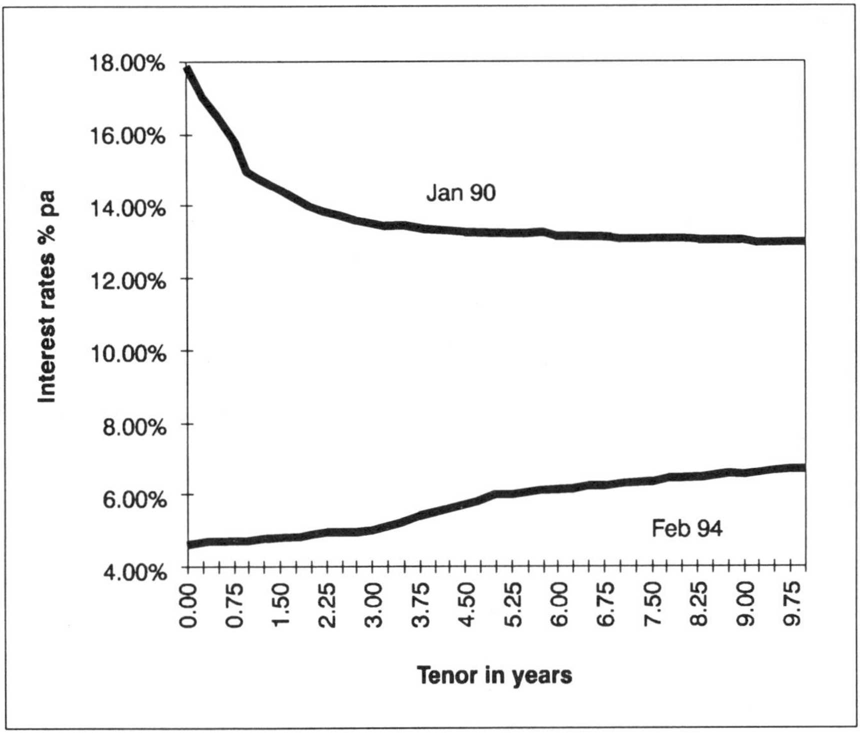

Traditional Banking Strategy: Riding the Yield Curve

Traditionally, banks borrowed by taking short term deposits and lent by making long term housing loans.

While the yield curve remained fixed, the banks had a profitable business. They borrowed at 3% pa and lent at 7% pa, making a healthy spread of 4%. Taking advantage of the shape of the normal yield curve is known as "riding the yield curve".

During the mid 1970s, interest rates jumped dramatically in response to the inflationary shock of the oil price hike. Suddenly banks found they had to pay, say, 10% pa to attract short term deposits, while they were locked into fixed mortgages yielding only 7% pa with perhaps several years to maturity. Mortgage loans, which had traditionally provided healthy profits when the yield curve had been relatively steady, were suddenly suffering losses following the jump in deposit rates.

Banks soon realised that to remain profitable in their money market activities they could no longer rely on merely riding the yield curve. In an environment where interest rates can rise or fall significantly, active interest rate management is required to ensure profitability.

Gapping in the Money Market: How to Profit from Expected Changes in Interest Rates

The deliberate mismatch of maturity dates of assets and liabilities is called ***gapping***. The traditional banking strategy, referred to as riding the yield curve, was profitable while interest rates remained steady. Indeed, this strategy would have proved even more profitable had short term deposit rates fallen. However, following this strategy involved the risk that interest rates might rise. Banks which had taken an interest rate position by borrowing short term and lending long term stood to lose when interest rates rose.

The strategy of borrowing short term and lending long term is known as opening a ***negative gap***. At the maturity of the short term deposit, the bank will find itself out of funds. It will need to borrow again by taking further deposits. If interest rates have fallen, it can borrow more cheaply and so it will make an even greater profit, but if deposit rates have risen above the rate at which it made the long term loan, it will begin to lose.

Exhibit 4.1

Negative gapping

Borrow short	++
Lend long	– – – – – – – – –

Strategy to take advantage of an expected fall in interest rates

The opposite strategy, which involves borrowing long term and lending short term, is known as opening a ***positive gap***. At the maturity of the short term loan, the bank will find itself with surplus funds to reinvest. If yields have risen, it will enjoy an increase in profit but if yields have fallen, it will suffer a decrease in profit. If yields have fallen below the rate at which the bank borrowed long term, the bank will start to incur a loss.

Exhibit 4.2

Positive gapping

Lend short	– –
Borrow long	+ + + + +

Strategy to take advantage of an expected rise in interest rates

Opening a Negative Gap

Example 4. 1

For simplicity, assume the yield curve for dollar interest rates is flat at 6% pa for tenors from one month through to six months.

Tenor in months	Interest rate % pa
1	6.0 %
2	6.0 %
3	6.0 %
4	6.0 %
5	6.0 %
6	6.0 %

A bank expects interest rates to fall. It opens a negative gap by borrowing $1,000,000 for one month and lending $1,000,000 for six months.

For the first month, the bank will break-even. It pays 6% pa ($5,000) for its deposit and receives 6% pa ($5,000) on its loan.

While the gap is open, the bank has an interest rate position. If interest rates rise, it will lose because it will have to borrow for the remaining five months at a higher rate. If interest rates fall, it will gain because it will be able to borrow for the remaining five months at a lower rate.

Exhibit 4.3

Opening a negative gap

$		Spot
+ 1,000,000		
	− 1,000,000	
1,000,000	1,000,000	

$		1 month
	− 1,005,000	FV = 1,000,000 (1 + 0.06 × 1/12)

$		6 months
+ 1,030,000		FV = 1,000,000 (1 + 0.06 × 6/12)

Opening the negative gap by borrowing $1,000,000 for one month and lending $1,000,000 for six months is equivalent to forward lending $1,005,000 from one month till six months at the forward interest rate $r_{1/6}$.

$$\text{Note:} \quad (1 + r_{1/6} \times 5/12) = \frac{(1 + 0.06 \times 6/12)}{(1 + 0.06 \times 1/12)}$$

$$= 1.024876$$

$$\therefore \quad r_{1/6} = 0.059701$$

$$= 5.97\% \text{ pa}$$

Effective forward interest rate from the cash flows in Exhibit 4.3

$$= \frac{1{,}030{,}000 - 1{,}005{,}000}{1{,}005{,}000} \times \frac{1200}{5}$$

$$= 5.97\% \text{ pa}$$

Closing a Negative Gap

Suppose the bank's expectation is fulfilled and after one month there has been a 1% pa downward shift in the yield curve so that all interest rates fall from 6% pa to 5% pa. The bank could then close the gap by borrowing $1,005,000 for the remaining five months.

Exhibit 4.4

Closing the negative gap after a parallel shift in a flat yield curve

One month later ...

$ (debit)	$ (credit)	Spot
+ 1,005,000	– 1,005,000	
1,005,000	1,005,000	

$ (debit)	$ (credit)	5 months
+ 1,030,000		
	– 1,025,937.50	FV = 1,005,000 (1 + 0.05 × 5/12)
	4,062.50	Profit
1,030,000	1,030,000.00	

By closing the gap, the bank realises a profit of $4,062.50 and eliminates its interest rate position. Further rises or falls in interest rates will have no impact on the bank's profit or loss.

Gapping with a Normal Yield Curve

When the yield curve is not flat at the time a gap is opened, there will be a benefit or cost involved in running the gap. If the yield curve is normal or positive, there will be a benefit in running a negative gap and a cost in carrying a positive gap. Conversely, if the yield curve is inverse, there will be a benefit in running a positive gap or a cost in carrying a negative gap.

> The yield curve either works in favour of the gap or against it.

Example 4.2

Consider a case where a negative gap is opened with a normal yield curve. Suppose the bank follows a strategy identical to that in Example 4.1, assuming the normal yield curves as in Exhibit 4.5.

Exhibit 4.5

Negative gap with a normal yield curve

Tenor in months	Interest rates when gap is opened % pa	Interest rates when gap is closed % pa (1 month later)
1	6.0	5.0
2	6.1	5.1
3	6.2	5.2
4	6.3	5.3
5	6.4	5.4
6	6.5	5.5

Following the same strategy as in Example 4.1, the bank opens a negative gap by borrowing $1,000,000 for one month at 6.0% pa and lending $1,000,000 for six months at 6.5% pa.

Opening the negative gap is equivalent to forward lending $1,005,000 from one month to six months at the forward interest rate of 6.57% pa.

$$(1 + r_{1/6} \times 5/12) = \frac{(1 + 0.065 \times 6/12)}{(1 + 0.06 \times 1/12)}$$

$$\therefore \quad r_{1/6} = 0.065672$$

$$= 6.57\% \text{ pa}$$

While the gap is open, the bank earns the 50 basis points difference between the borrowing rate and the lending rate. This reflects the benefit of running the negative gap with a positive yield curve. Until the gap is closed, the bank has an interest rate position. If interest rates rise, it may have to borrow for the remaining five months at a higher rate. The benefit of running the gap, which is known as ***positive carry***, is that it will reduce the unfavourable impact of a rise in rates or add to the favourable impact of a fall in rates.

Exhibit 4.6

Opening a negative gap with a normal yield curve

$		
+ 1,000,000		Spot
	− 1,000,000	
1,000,000	1,000,000	

$		
	− 1,005,000	1 month
		FV = 1,000,000 (1 + 0.06 × 1/12)

$		
+ 1,032,500		6 months
		FV = 1,000,000 (1 + 0.065 × 6/12)

Assuming that after one month there has been a 1% pa downward shift in interest rates, as portrayed in Exhibit 4.5, the bank can close the gap by borrowing $1,005,000 for five months at 5.4 % pa.

Exhibit 4.7

Closing the negative gap after a parallel shift in a normal yield curve

One month later ...

$		
		Spot
+ 1,005,000		
	– 1,005,000	
1,005,000	1,005,000	

$		
		5 months
+ 1,032,500		
	– 1,027,612.50	FV = 1,005,000.00 (1 + 0.054 × 5/12)
	4,887.50	Profit
1,032,500	1,032,500.00	

By closing the gap, the bank realises a profit of $4,887.50 and eliminates its interest rate position. Further rises or falls will have no impact on the bank's profit or loss.

Opening a Positive Gap

A bank expecting interest rates to rise would be inclined to open a positive gap. For example, the bank might borrow $1,000,000 for six months at 6.5% pa and lend $1,000,000 for one month at 6.0% pa. For a positive gap to prove profitable when the yield curve is normal, it is necessary for interest rates to rise faster than the slope of the yield curve.

Exhibit 4.8

Opening a positive gap with a normal yield curve

$		
		Spot
+ 1,000,000		
	− 1,000,000	
1,000,000	1,000,000	

$		
		1 month
+1,005,000		FV = 1,000,000 (1 + 0.06 × 1/12)

$		
		6 months
	− 1,032,500	FV = 1,000,000 (1 + 0.065 × 6/12)

Opening the positive gap by borrowing $1,000,000 for six months and lending $1,000,000 for one month is equivalent to forward borrowing $1,005,000 from one month till six months at the forward interest rate 6.57% pa.

$$(1 + r_{1/6} \times 5/12) = \frac{(1 + 0.065 \times 6/12)}{(1 + 0.06 \times 1/12)}$$

$$\therefore \quad r_{1/6} = 0.065672$$

$$= 6.57\%\ \text{pa}$$

While the gap is open, the bank pays the 0.5% pa difference between the borrowing rate and the lending rate. This represents the cost of carrying the positive gap with a positive yield curve. The cost of carrying the gap, which is known as ***negative carry,*** will reduce the favourable impact of a rise in interest rates and add to the unfavourable impact of a fall in interest rates.

Closing a Positive Gap

Assuming that after one month there has been a 1% pa upward shift in interest rates, as portrayed in Exhibit 4.9, the bank could close the gap by lending $1,005,000 for five months at 7.4% pa.

By closing the gap, the bank eliminates its interest rate position and realises a profit of $3,487.50. Notice that this is less than the $4,887.50 profit that would have been realised from an equivalent fall in interest rates under a negative gapping strategy. This $1,400 difference reflects the impact of the normal yield curve working in favour of the negative gap and against the positive gap.

Exhibit 4.9

Closing a positive gap after a parallel shift in a normal yield curve

Tenor in months	Interest rates when gap is opened % pa	Interest rates when gap is closed % pa (1 month later)
1	6.0 %	7.0 %
2	6.1 %	7.1 %
3	6.2 %	7.2 %
4	6.3 %	7.3 %
5	6.4 %	7.4 %
6	6.5 %	7.5 %

One month later ...

$		Spot
1,005,000.00		
	– 1,005,000.00	
1,005,000.00	– 1,005,000.00	

$		5 months
	1,032,500.00	
+1,035,987.50		FV = 1,005,000.00 (1 + 0.074 × 5/12)
	3,487.50	Profit
1,035,987.50	1,035,987.50	

Break-even Rates

It is possible at the time of opening the gap to calculate the ***break-even interest rate***, at which the gap will result in zero profit or loss. Assuming the normal yield curve as in Example 4.2, the break-even five month interest rate one month after opening the gap would be:

1. Under the negative gap scenario, such that:

$$\text{interest earned for six month period} = \text{interest paid for six month period}$$

$$(1{,}000{,}000 \times 0.06 \times 1/12) + (1{,}005{,}000 \times b \times 5/12) = 1{,}000{,}000 + 0.065 \times 6/12$$

$$5{,}000 + 418{,}750 \times b = 32{,}500$$

$$\therefore \quad b = \frac{27{,}500}{418{,}750}$$

$$= 0.065672$$

$$= 6.57\% \text{ pa}$$

That is, the five month interest rate could rise to 6.57% pa before the gap would start to lose money.

> The break-even rate equals the forward interest rate at the time of opening the gap.

2. Under the positive gap scenario, such that:

$$\text{interest earned for six month period} = \text{interest paid for six month period}$$

$$1{,}000{,}000 \times 0.065 \times 1/12 = (1{,}000{,}000 \times 0.06 \times 1/12) + (1{,}005{,}000 \times b \times 5/12)$$

$$\therefore \quad b = 6.57\% \text{ pa}$$

That is, the five month interest rate would have to rise to 6.57% pa before the gap would start to make money. Again, the break-even rate equals the original forward interest rate.

Notice the calculation of the break-even rate is identical for both the negative and positive gaps. The break-even rate is a function of the *shape* of the yield curve. It does not depend on whether the gap is positive or negative.

Early Closure of a Gap

It is possible to close out a gap at a date other than the maturity of the near leg. This can be done by doing the reverse money market transactions. For example, to close out the gap opened in Example 4.1 one week after it was opened, it would be necessary to lend for three weeks and borrow for five and three quarter months. For the profit or loss from the gap to occur at the far date (ie six months from the date of opening the gap), the amount to be lent for three weeks should be such that the future value at the three week maturity will exactly offset the future value of the original one month borrowing, ie

$1,005,000. The amount to be borrowed for five and three quarter months should exactly offset the amount being lent for three weeks.

Suppose that one week after opening the gap, the three week interest rate is 5.5% pa and the five and three quarter month interest rate is 5.7% pa, ie the yield curve has dropped, but farther at the short end than at the long end. The cash flows in Exhibit 4.10 show that closing the gap would generate a profit of $1,087.82 at the far date.

An alternative and equivalent means of closing the gap would be to borrow $1,005,000 at the forward interest rate of 5.71% pa from three weeks till five and three quarter months.

$$(1 + r_{0.75/5.75} \times 5/12) = \frac{(1 + 0.057 \times 5.75/12)}{(1 + 0.055 \times 0.75/12)}$$

$$r_{0.75/5.75} = 0.057104$$

$$= 5.71\ \%\ \text{pa}$$

Exhibit 4.10

Early closure of a negative gap

One week after opening ...

$ (in)	$ (out)	Spot
	– 1,001,557.15	$PV = \frac{1,005,000}{(1 + 0.055 \times 0.75/12)}$
+ 1 001,557.15		
1,001,557.15	1,001,557.15	

$ (in)	$ (out)	3 weeks
	1,005,000	
1,005,000		
1,005,000	1,005,000	

$ (in)	$ (out)	5.75 months
1,030,000		
	– 1,028,912.18	FV = 1,001,557.15 (1 + 0.057 × 5.75/12)
	1,087.82	Profit
1,030,000	1,030,000.00	

Extending a Gap

To extend a gap beyond the maturity date of the near leg merely requires rolling the near leg through the money market. For example, to extend the negative gap opened in Example 4.1 for a further month simply requires rolling the original one month borrowing plus interest for an additional month. This strategy would be appropriate if interest rates were expected to fall during the coming month. Assuming it is intended that profits be realised at the far date of the gap, it would be necessary to roll the original borrowing so as to capitalise the interest from the first month.

Assuming that one month after the gap was opened the five month interest rate was 5.7% pa, extending the life of the gap would merely require the bank to borrow $1,005,000 for an additional month at 5.7% pa.

Exhibit 4.11

Extending the gap

One month after opening the gap ...

$		
		Spot
	– 1,005,000	
+ 1,005,000		
1,005,000	1,005,000	

$		
		1 month
	– 1,009,773.75	FV = 1,005,000 × (1 + 0.057 × 1/12)

Practice Problems

4.1 Gapping: normal yield curve – expect upward shift of yield curve

The dollar yield curve is currently:

1 month	5.00%
2 months	5.25%
3 months	5.50%

Interest rates are expected to rise.

(a) What two money market transactions would be performed to open a positive gap three months against one month?

Assume this gap was opened on a principal amount of $1,000,000 and after one month rates have risen such that the yield curve is now:

1 month	6.00%
2 months	6.25%
3 months	6.50%

(b) What money market transaction should be performed to close the gap?

(c) How much profit or loss would be made from opening and closing the gap?

4.2 Gapping: inverse yield curve – expect downward shift of yield curve

The dollar yield curve is currently inverse and expectations are that one month from now the yield curve will be 50 basis points below current levels as reflected in the following table.

Tenor in months	Current interest rates % pa	Expected interest rates % pa
1	8.0	7.5
2	7.5	7.0
3	7.0	6.5

A corporation borrows $10,000,000 for one month and lends $10,000,000 for three months to open a negative gap position.

(a) Calculate the break-even interest rate at which it will need to be able to borrow $10,000,000 for two months in one month's time.

(b) Assuming the yield curve moves according to expectation, calculate the profit or loss that will be realised on closing the gap.

4.3 Gapping: normal yield curve – expect rotation of yield curve

The crown yield curve is currently normal and expectations are that it will become steeper with the pivotal point at six months as reflected below:

Months	Current rates	Expected rates 3 months from now
3	5.0 %	4.5 %
6	5.5 %	5.5 %
9	6.0 %	6.5 %
12	6.5 %	7.5 %

Two gapping strategies are contemplated:

(a) borrowing C 1,000,000 for 3 months and lending C 1,000,000 for 6 months;

(b) borrowing C 1,000,000 for 3 months and lending C 1,000,000 for 12 months.

Assuming that interest rates move according to expectations and that the gap is closed after three months, which strategy will prove more profitable?

4.4 Gapping: calculation for exact number of days

On 1 July a company borrows $10,000,000 at a three month floating rate of 6.75% pa (360 days per year basis). This debt will be rolled on 1 October (92 days). The company also placed $10,000,000 on deposit maturing on 3 January (186 days) also at a rate of 6.75% pa.

(a) Is the gap which the company has opened positive or negative?

(b) Would the company like the three month rate on 1 October to be higher or lower than at present?

(c) Calculate the profit or loss if the company rolls the floating rate borrowing for 94 days from 1 October at exactly 6.75% pa.

Supplementary Question

4.5 Gapping: normal yield curve – expect rates to fall

The dollar yield curve is currently:

1 month	5.00%
2 months	5.25%
3 months	5.50%

Interest rates are expected to fall.

(a) Which two money market transactions should be performed to open a gap three months against one month?

(b) Assuming the gap was opened on a principal amount of $1,000,000 and after 1 month interest rates have fallen such that the yield curve is then:

1 month	4.75%
2 months	5.00%
3 months	5.25%

What money market transaction should be performed to close the gap?

(c) How much profit or loss would have been made from opening and closing the gap?

5

Bid and Offer Rates

In this chapter, the concept of bid and offer rates is introduced. Potential confusion arises because with bid and offer quotations there are two parties, two prices and, in the case of foreign exchange rates, two currencies. Dealers use bid and offer rates to make money by making markets and at times by exploiting arbitrage when the opportunity arises.

Quoting Bank and Calling Bank

It is customary in interbank markets for banks to quote two-way prices. There are two parties to the quotation, the quoting bank and the calling bank. The ***quoting bank*** is the bank that quotes the price. The ***calling bank*** is the bank that calls to ask the quoting bank for a price. Having been quoted the price, the calling bank either accepts it, in which case a deal is done, or rejects it, in which case no transaction occurs.

Whenever two-way prices are quoted, the first rate quoted is known as the ***bid rate*** and the second rate quoted is known as the ***offer rate***.

Bid and Offer Rates in the Money Market

In the money market, the ***bid rate*** is the rate at which the quoting bank is willing to borrow. The ***offer rate*** is the rate at which the quoting bank is willing to lend.

A bank quotes three month dollars at 7.00%/7.25%. The bid rate is 7.00% pa and the offer rate 7.25% pa. In full, the quoting bank is saying that it is willing to borrow dollars for three months at a rate of 7.00% pa and to lend dollars for three months at a rate of 7.25% pa.

The calling bank performs the opposite side of the transaction to the quoting bank. If the quoting bank borrows, then the calling bank lends and if the quoting bank lends, then the calling bank borrows.

If the calling bank wishes to borrow dollars from the quoting bank, it must borrow at the offer rate (that is the quoting bank's lending rate) of 7.25% pa.

If the calling bank wishes to lend dollars to the quoting bank, it must lend them at the bid rate (that is the quoting bank's borrowing rate) of 7.00% pa. An alternative definition of the bid rate would be the rate at which the calling bank can lend. Similarly, an alternative definition of the offer rate would be the rate at which the calling bank can borrow.

Exhibit 5. 1

Bid and offer rates in the money market

	3 month dollars	
	Bid rate	Offer rate
Quote	7.00% pa	7.25% pa
Quoting bank	Borrows	Lends
Calling bank	Lends	Borrows

Bid and Offer Rates in the Foreign Exchange Market

In the foreign exchange market, the ***bid rate*** is the rate at which the quoting bank is willing to buy the commodity currency.

The ***offer rate*** is the rate at which the quoting bank is willing to sell the commodity currency.

A bank quotes spot $1 = DM1.4410/ 1.4415. The bid rate is 1.4410 and the offer rate is 1.4415. In full, the quoting bank is saying that it is willing to buy dollars at a rate of $1 = DM1.4410 and to sell dollars at a rate of $1 = DM1.4415.

The calling bank performs the opposite side of the transaction to the quoting bank. If the quoting bank buys dollars, then the calling bank sells dollars and if the quoting bank sells dollars, then the calling bank buys dollars.

If the calling bank wishes to buy dollars from the quoting bank, it must buy dollars at the quoting bank's offer rate (that is its selling rate) of 1.4415. If the calling bank wishes to sell dollars to the quoting bank, it must sell dollars at the quoting bank's bid rate (that is its buying rate) of 1.4410. An alternative definition of the bid rate would be the rate at which the calling bank can sell the commodity currency. Similarly, an alternative definition of the offer rate would be the rate at which the calling bank can buy the commodity currency.

Exhibit 5.2

Bid and offer rates in the foreign exchange market
Commodity Currency

	Spot $/DM	
	Bid rate	Offer rate
Quote $1 = DM	1.4410	1.4415
Quoting Bank	Buys dollars	Sells dollars
Calling Bank	Sells dollars	Buys dollars

In the quotation $1 = DM1.4410/1.4415, the dollar is the commodity currency and the deutschemark is the terms currency. When a bank buys the commodity currency, it sells the terms currency and when it sells the commodity currency it buys the terms currency. The bid rate could also be defined as the rate at which the quoting bank is willing to sell the terms currency or the rate at which the calling bank is able to buy the terms currency. The offer rate could also be defined as the rate at which the quoting bank is willing to buy the terms currency or the rate at which the calling bank is able to sell the terms currency.

Exhibit 5.3

Bid and offer rates in the foreign market exchange
Terms Currency

	Spot $/DM	
	Bid rate	Offer rate
Quote $1 = DM	1.4410	1.4415
Quoting bank	Sells DM	Buys DM
Calling bank	Buys DM	Sells DM

To avoid confusion, observe the convention of concentrating on the commodity currency. When asked a question about the terms currency, convert it into a question about the commodity currency. This is referred to as the "mental switch". For example, if asked "at what rate will the quoting bank buy deutschemarks?", convert the question to "at what rate will the quoting bank sell dollars?".

The answer is at the offer rate, DM 1.4415.

Example 5. 1

A bank quotes $1 = ¥105.50 – 105.60.

At what rate:

1. Will the quoting bank buy dollars?	Its bid rate,	105.50.
2. Will the quoting bank sell dollars?	Its offer rate,	105.60.
3. Can the calling bank buy dollars?	Their offer rate,	105.60.
4. Can the calling bank sell dollars?	Their bid rate,	105.50.
5. Will the quoting bank buy yen? *Mental switch*: at what rate will the quoting bank sell dollars?	Its offer rate,	105.60.
6. Will the quoting bank sell yen? *Mental switch*: at what rate will the quoting bank buy dollars?	Its bid rate,	105.50.
7. Can the calling bank buy yen? *Mental switch:* at what rate can the calling bank sell dollars?	Their bid rate,	105.50.
8. Can the calling bank sell yen? *Mental switch:* at what rate can the calling bank buy dollars?	Their offer rate,	105.60.

Bid-offer Spreads

The difference between the bid rate and the offer rate is called the ***bid-offer spread.***

As the quoting bank is seeking to make profit by borrowing at lower rates than it lends or buying the commodity currency more cheaply than it sells it, the bid rate will be a smaller number than the corresponding offer rate.

Example 5.2

	Bid rate	Offer rate
Money market 3 month	7.00% pa	7.25% pa
Foreign exchange market	$1 = DM1.4410	1.4415

If the quoting bank is simultaneously able to deal equal amounts at its bid rate and its offer rate, it would lock in a profit without acquiring a net cash flow position or a net exchange position.[1]

1 This is not exactly true because the profit generated would create a net cash flow position. If the profit is in units of foreign currency it would create a net exchange position.

If the quoting bank borrows $1,000,000 for three months at 7.00% pa and lends $1,000,000 for three months at 7.25% pa, how much profit would it make?

It would have the following cash flows:

Exhibit 5.4

Money market cash flows

$		**Spot**
+ 1,000,000		7.00 %
	− 1,000,000	7.25 %
1,000,000	1,000,000	

$		**3 months**
	− 1,017,500	FV = 1,000,000 (1 + 0.07 × 3/12)
+ 1,018,125		FV = 1,000,000 (1 + 0.0725 × 3/12)
	625	**Profit**
1,018,125	1,018,125	
Profit =	$625	

Example 5.3

If the quoting bank buys $1,000,000 at DM1.4410 and sells $1,000,000 at DM1.4415, how much profit would it make?

It would have the following cash flows and net exchange position:

Exhibit 5.5

Foreign exchange market cash flows

$		**Spot**	**DM**		**Net Exchange Position**
+ 1,000,000		1.4410		− 1,441,000	
	− 1,000,000	1.4415	+ 1,441,500		**Square**
		Profit		500	
1,000,000	1,000,000		1,441,500	1,441,500	

Profit = DM 500

If the quoting bank widens its spread, it will make a larger profit each time it is able to deal on both sides of its quote. For example, if it quoted 7.00/7.50, it would make a profit of $1,250 per $1,000,000 and if it quoted $1 = DM 14410/ 1.4420, it would make a profit of DM1,000 per $1,000,000.

However, the wider the bid-offer spread, the less attractive the prices are to calling banks. Banks which quote narrow spreads will tend to have higher turnovers than banks which quote wide spreads.

Exhibit 5.6

Bid-offer spreads

		$1 = DM		
		Bid	Offer	
Bank A	Aggressive quote	1.4411	1.4414	Narrow spread high turnover
Bank B	Non-competitive quote	1.4405	1.4420	Wide spread low turnover

Calling banks will be inclined to deal with Bank A in preference to Bank B. Banks wishing to buy dollars will be inclined to buy at the lower offer rate. As Bank A's offer of DM1.4414 is lower than Bank B's offer of DM1.4420, banks wanting to buy dollars will deal with Bank A.

Similarly, banks wishing to sell dollars will be inclined to sell at the higher bid rate. As Bank A's offer of DM1.4411 is higher than Bank B's bid of DM1.4405, banks wanting to sell dollars will deal with Bank A. When quoting banks become more keen to deal, they narrow their bid-offer spread. When they become less keen to deal, they widen their bid-offer spread.

Narrowness of bid-offer spread is not the only factor that influences the decision to deal with the quoting bank. Credit lines need to be available for the transaction to proceed. A calling bank may deal with Bank B, even though Bank A has a more competitive price, because it has no credit lines for Bank A. Speed of quotation is also an important determinant of which bank does the deal. Waiting for a slow quote involves the risk that rates may move against the calling bank.

Brokers

Brokers facilitate the coming together of buyers and sellers by collecting prices from a variety of banks. The broker selects the highest bid rate and the lowest offer rate and combines them to establish the best two-way price available to calling banks. For example, if banks quote different prices as reflected in Exhibit 5.7, the broker price would be $1 = DM1.4411/1.4414. Calling banks find it easier and quicker to call the broker than to call all of the banks separately. Brokers charge a fee for their service which is known as ***brokerage***.

Exhibit 5.7

Broking exchange rates

$1 = DM

	Bid	Offer
Bank A	1.4409	**1.4414**
Bank B	1.4410	1.4415
Bank C	**1.4411**	1.4416
Broker price	1.4411	1.4414

Trending Rates

Money markets and foreign exchange markets are dynamic. Prices change to reflect changes in supply and demand. Quoting banks move their prices to reflect changes in their willingness to borrow and lend or buy and sell.

Exhibit 5.8

Rising interest rates

Previous rates % pa	7.00	7.25
New rates % pa	7.10	7.35

Trending upwards or trending to the right

By increasing its quote from 7.00/7.25 to 7.10/7.35, the quoting bank makes its bid rate more attractive to potential lenders and its offer rate less attractive to potential borrowers.

Exhibit 5.9

Falling interest rates

Previous rates % pa	7.00	7.25
New rates % pa	6.90	7.15

Trending downwards or trending to the left

By dropping its quote from 7.00/7.25 to 6.90/7.15, the quoting bank makes its bid rate less attractive to potential lenders and its offer rate more attractive to potential borrowers.

Exhibit 5.10

Rising exchange rates

Previous rates	$1 = DM	1.4410	1.4415
New rates	$1 = DM	1.4412	1.4417

Trending upwards or trending to the right

By increasing its quote from 1.4410/ 1.4415 to 1.4412/ 1.4417, the quoting bank makes its bid rate more attractive to potential sellers of dollars and its offer rate less attractive to potential buyers of dollars.

Exhibit 5.11

Falling exchange rates

Previous rates	$1 = DM	1.4410	1.4415
New rates	$1 = DM	1.4407	1.4412

Trending downwards or trending to the left

By lowering its quote from 1.4410/1.4415 to 1.4407/1.4412, the quoting bank makes its bid rate less attractive to potential sellers of dollars and its offer rate more attractive to potential buyers of dollars.

Covering a Spot Exchange Position at Market Rates

Example 5.3

If a bank quotes $1 = DM1.4410/ 1.4415 and a customer calls and sells the bank $1,000,000 at 1.4410, it becomes long $1,000,000 (short DM1,441,000). If the bank goes to another bank to sell dollars to square its position, it will find it needs to sell dollars at the other bank's bid rate.

Assuming that bank's bid rate is also 1.4410, the original bank would be square without making a profit or a loss.

If a quoting bank buys $1,000,000 from the customer at 1.4409 (its bid rate) and sells $1,000,000 to another bank at 1.4410 (their bid rate), it would lock in a profit of one point or DM100.[2]

---

2 Profit = 1,000,000 (1.4410 – 1.4409) = DM 100.

To make a profit from a transaction with a customer who deals at its rates, a quoting bank should lower its bid rate or increase its offer rate.

If a different customer calls wanting to buy $1,000,000 and the bank intends to square its position by dealing with the market, it should increase its offer rate. If the market rate is 1.4410/1.4415, it might quote the customer an offer rate of 1.4416. If it sells $1,000,000 to the customer at 1.4416 (its rate) and buys $1,000,000 from another bank at 1.4415 (their rate), it would lock in a profit of one point or DM 100.[3]

Covering a Spot Exchange Position at Own Rates: Jobbing

Banks generally prefer to deal at their own prices than to deal at the bid or offer rate of another bank. In practice, it is extremely rare for a quoting bank to be able to deal simultaneously on both sides of its quote for the same amount. Once a bank has been hit on one side of its quote, it has a net cash flow position and possibly a net exchange position. If market rates move in a particular direction, it may find it is unable to deal on the other side at a profit.

Example 5.4

A bank quoting $1 = DM1.4410/ 1.4415 is hit for $2,000,000 on its bid rate, that is it buys $2,000,000 at a rate of DM1.4410. It has a net exchange position long $2,000,000 (short DM3,282,000). To square its net exchange position, it will need to sell $2,000,000. If market rates rise, it will gain but if market rates fall, it may lose. For example, if banks generally begin to quote 1.4400/ 1.4405, the highest rate at which the bank can hope to sell is 1.4405. It could only achieve this if it lowered its offer rate to 1.4405 and it was lucky enough to be hit there by a buyer of dollars. In this best case, it would lock in a loss of five points or DM 1,000.[4] If it were forced to sell the dollars by hitting another bank's bid rate of 1.4400, it would incur an even larger loss of ten points or DM2,000.[5]

Having purchased $2,000,000 at 1.4410, the bank might drop its quote to say, 1.4407/ 1.4412. If the market generally is still quoting 1.4410/ 1.4415, it will now have an attractive offer and an unattractive bid. It is quite likely that its next transaction will be a sale of dollars at 1.4412 and fairly unlikely that it will be a further purchase of dollars at 1.4407. If the bank sells $2,000,000 at 1.4412, it will make a profit of two points or DM 400 and it will be square.[6]

The practice of trending prices to be hit on the side which will square off a net exchange position is known as ***jobbing***.

---

3 Profit = 1,000,000 (1.4416 – 1.4415) = DM 100.
4 Loss = 2,000,000 (1.4410 – 1.4405) = DM 2,000.
5 Loss = 2,000,000 (1.4410 – 1.4400) = DM 2,000.
6 Profit = 2,000,000 (1.4412 – 1.4410) = DM 400.

Exhibit 5.12

Jobbing exchange rates

Original quote	$1 = DM	**1.4410**	1.4415
Next quote	$1 = DM	1.4407	**1.4412**

Trending downwards to encourage potential buyers to buy dollars at 1.4412

Market Making

Some banks adopt the strategy of dealing at narrow bid-offer spreads in the expectation that they will deal large volumes on both sides, thereby capturing substantial profits. This strategy is known as ***market making***.

An additional benefit of market making is that the bank obtains more market intelligence. Being aware of the transactions taking place in the market is important if the bank follows a strategy of position taking.

It is not always desirable for banks to deal at their own prices. If rates are moving quickly in one direction because there is a bias in the market, banks will be better off if they square their positions by dealing at market rates.

For example, if a bank is long $2,000,000 at 1.4410 and a news release comes out revealing a very large trade deficit, all market participants may expect the exchange rate to fall. Banks will tend to lower their quotes and possibly to widen them as uncertainty grows. In this type of market, there is no sense in a bank waiting and hoping to be hit on its offer rate. As there will be many keen sellers and possibly no keen buyers, it would be folly for a bank to wait in the vain hope of being able to sell at its offer rate. The prudent action to take would be to square off its position by dealing at another bank's bid rate and to trend its rates down accordingly. This will probably result in the bank taking a loss but it is better to take a small loss now than to be caught and end up with a much larger loss later.

Arbitrage

Arbitrage refers to the practice of taking advantage of inconsistent pricing to lock in risk-free profits. If two banks are quoting bid and offer rates such that one bank's bid rate is higher than the other bank's offer rate, then an arbitrage opportunity exists.

Example 5.5

				Bid	Offer
Bank A quotes	$1	=	DM	1.4410	**1.4415**
Bank B quotes	$1	=	DM	**1.4417**	1.4422

As Bank B's bid rate of 1.4417 is higher than Bank A's offer rate of 1.4415, it is possible to buy dollars from Bank A at 1.4415 and to sell them to Bank B at 1.4417 for a profit of two points without creating a net exchange position.

Once they realise that this situation has arisen, one or both banks will quickly trend their rates so that the arbitrage opportunity soon disappears.

Cross Rates

Cross rate calculations with bid and offer rates involve two steps:

- establish which rates to cross
- apply the chain rule.

Example 5. 6

$1	=	¥	105.50	105.60
$1	=	DM	1.4410	1.4415

(a) A Japanese importer needs to buy deutschemarks against yen. What is the cross rate in yen terms? Assume the bank quotes to make one point profit.

Step 1. The Japanese importer needs to *buy* deutschemarks and *sell* yen. The cash flows are as portrayed in Figure 5.1. When it deals with the importer, the bank will be selling DM and buying yen. To cover its net exchange positions with the market, the bank will need to sell dollars / buy DM at 1.4410 and buy dollars / sell yen at 105.60.

Step 2. Applying the chain rule:

$$\begin{aligned} ¥\,? &= \text{DM}1 \\ \text{DM}1.4410 &= \$1 \\ \$1 &= ¥105.60 \\ \text{DM}1 &= \frac{¥1 \times 1 \times 105.60}{1.4410 \times 1} = ¥73.28 \end{aligned}$$

This would be the break-even offer rate for deutschemarks in yen terms. To make one point profit, the bank should quote the customer ¥73.29, ie an offer rate which is one point higher than the break-even offer rate.

Figure 5.1

Flow Chart Representation of Cross Rate Transaction Offer Rate

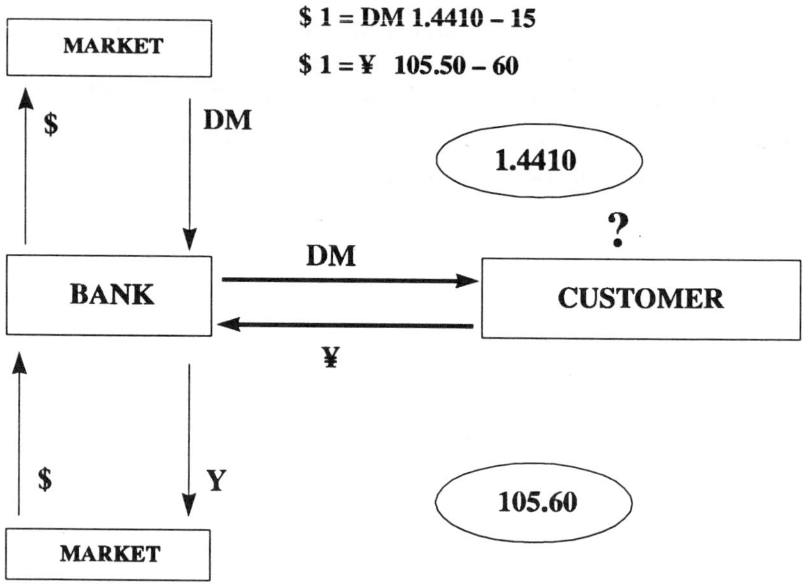

(b) A Japanese exporter needs to sell deutschemarks against yen. What cross rate should the bank quote to make two points profit? Express the cross rate in yen terms.

Step 1. The Japanese exporter needs to *sell* deutschemarks and *buy* yen. The cash flows are portrayed in Figure 5.2. To cover itself, the bank would need to buy dollars / sell DM at 1.4415 and to sell dollars / buy yen at 105.50.

Step 2. Applying the chain rule:

$$\begin{aligned} ¥\,? &= \text{DM}1 \\ \text{DM}1.4415 &= \$1 \\ \$1 &= ¥105.50 \\ \therefore \quad \text{DM}1 &= \frac{1 \times 1 \times 105.50}{1.4415 \times 1} \\ &= ¥73.19 \end{aligned}$$

Figure 5.2

Flow chart representation of cross rate transaction
Bid rate

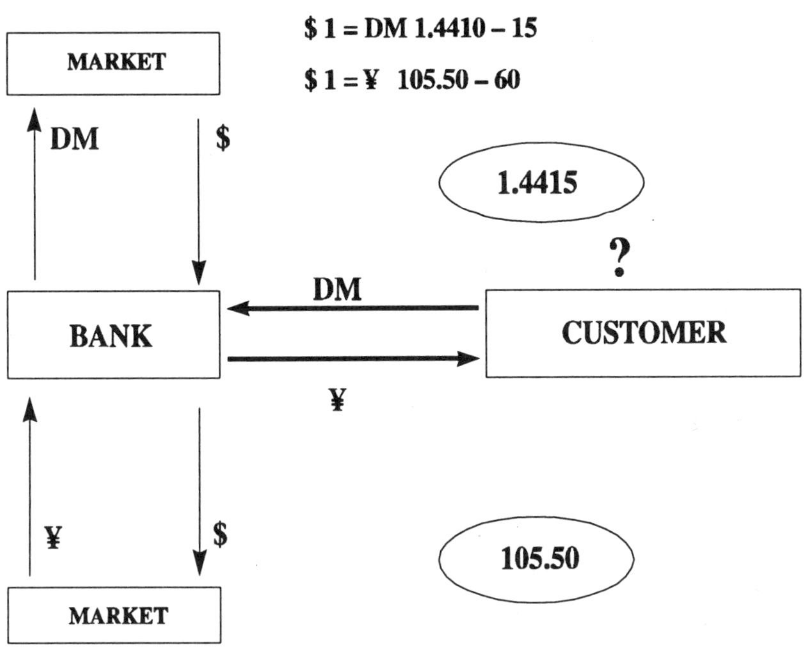

This would be the break-even bid rate for deutschemarks in yen terms. To make two points profit, the bank should quote the customer ¥73.17, that is a bid rate which is two points lower than the break-even bid rate.

Arbitraging Cross Rates

Example 5.7

A Reuters machine displays the following market rates:

In London: £1	=	$	1.5490	1.5500
In New York: R1	=	$	0.0250	0.0255
In Bombay: £1	=	R	62.08	62.88

(a) Calculate the bid and offer cross rates for pounds in rupee terms when working the London and New York markets.

Bid			Offer		
R?	=	£1	R?	=	£1
£1	=	$1.5490	£1	=	$1.5500
$0.0255	=	R1	$ 0.0250	=	R1
∴ £1	=	R $\frac{1.5490}{0.0255}$	∴ £1	=	R $\frac{1.5500}{0.0250}$
ie £1	=	R60.75	£1	=	R62.00

(b) What arbitrage opportunity is available when these rates are compared with those available in Bombay?

London/New York	£1	=	R60.75	**62.00**
Bombay	£1	=	**R62.08**	62.88

An arbitrage opportunity exists because the offer rate available through London and New York is lower than the bid rate available in Bombay. To arbitrage:

Buy £ sell R through London/New York at	£1	=	R62.00
Sell £ buy R in Bombay at	£1	=	R62.08
Profit			R 0.08 per £

There is a potential profit of R0.08 per £1. On a principal amount of £1,000,000, the arbitrageur would make a profit of R80,000.

Exhibit 5.13

Cash Flows in Cross Rate Arbitrage

	Rate	£	$	R
London	1.5500	+ 1,000,000	– 1,550,000	
New York	0.0250		+1,550,000	– 62,000,000
Bombay	62.08	– 1,000,000		+ 62,080,000
Profit		0	0	+ 80,000

Practice Problems

5.1 Bid-offer rates

A bank quotes £1 = $1.6020 / 1.6025.

(a) At what rate will the bank buy dollars?

(b) At what rate can a customer sell pounds?

(c) At what rate can a customer sell dollars?

5.2 Bid-offer rates

Bank A calls and asks bank B for a price for dollar/ deutschemarks. Bank B quotes

$1 = DM1.5640 / 1.5650. At what rate can Bank A sell DM?

5.3 Bid-offer rates and spreads

A customer in Crownland asks a bank for a crown/peso quote. The bank quotes

C1 = P1.4935 / 1.4945.

(a) How many pesos will it cost the customer to buy C1,000,000 ?

(b) How many pesos will the customer receive if he or she sells C1,000,000?

(c) What is the pesos value of the 10 point bid-offer spread?

(d) How many crowns will it cost the customer to buy P1,000,000 ?

(e) How many crowns will the customer receive if he or she sells P1,000,000?

(f) What is the crown value of the 10 point bid-offer spread?

5.4 Bid-offer rates

A bank quotes overnight at 8.25 / 8.50% pa.

(a) At what rate can a customer borrow dollars?

(b) At what rate can a customer invest dollars?

5.5 Bid-offer rates and spreads

A bourse bank quotes seven day francs at 4.50 / 4.75 % pa. There are 21 bourse days per year.

(a) Calculate the interest due if a customer borrows Fl,000,000 for seven days.

(b) Calculate the interest due if a customer invests Fl,000,000 for seven days.

(c) Calculate the franc value of the 25 basis point bid-offer spread.

5.6 Brokers

A broker has dollar/yen prices from three banks

Bank A	$1	=	¥105.60	105.65
Bank B	$1	=	¥105.62	105.67
Bank C	$1	=	¥105.63	105.68

What is the broker price?

5.7 Jobbing

A bank quotes Fl = Pl.2130 / 1.2140. A customer calls and sells the bank F10,000,000 at its bid rate 1.2130. The bank would like to square its position (if possible at a profit). If another customer calls a minute later, which of the following rates should the bank quote?

Rate A	Fl	=	Pl.2125	1.2135
Rate B	Fl	=	Pl.2130	1.2140
Rate C	Fl	=	Pl.2135	1.2145

5.8 Arbitrage

Bank A quotes	NZ$1	=	US$ 0.6820	0.6825
Bank B quotes	NZ$1	=	US$ 0.6826	0.6831

What arbitrage opportunity exists? How much profit could be made by performing this arbitrage on a principal amount of NZ$10,000,000?

5.9 Cross rates

US$1	=	S$ 1.4050	1.4060
FF1	=	US$ 0.2490	0.2500

A Singaporean exporter wants to sell French francs and buy Singapore dollars. What is the break-even rate for French francs in Singapore dollar terms?

5.10 Cross rates

US$1	=	M$ 2.5810	2.5830
£1	=	US$ 1.5470	1.5490

What bid and offer rates should a bank quote for pounds against ringitt in Malaysian terms to make a ten point spread on either side of the break-even rates?

Supplementary Questions

5.11 Brokers

A bank calls four brokers for dollar/Swiss franc rates.

Broker A	$1	=	SF1.2430	1.2433
Broker B	$1	=	SF1.2430	1.2432
Broker C	$1	=	SF1.2431	1.2433
Broker D	$1	=	SF1.2430	1.2433

The bank wishes to sell Swiss francs through the broker. With which broker and at what rate should it deal?

5.12 Cross rates

US$1	=	¥104.50	104.60
US$1	=	DM1.5460	1.5470

A Japanese importer wants to buy deutschemarks and sell yen. What is the break-even rate for deutschemarks in yen terms?

5.13 Cross rates

A customer calls and wants to buy Hong Kong dollars against Australian dollars. What rate should a bank quote for Hong Kong dollars in terms of Australian dollars to ensure a one point profit?

US$1	=	HK$7.7360	7.7370
A$1	=	US$0.7740	0.7745

6

Forward Exchange Rates

In this chapter, the concept of forward exchange rates is developed. The forward exchange rate can be calculated from the spot rate and the interest rates of two currencies. The concept is extended to cover short dates and long term foreign exchange.

If the one year dollar interest rate is 5% pa, $100 has a future value of $105 one year from now. It follows that if the spot price of gold is $400, the one year forward price of gold is $420. Gold could be said to command a forward premium of $20 (or 5%) as the forward price is $20 (or 5%) higher than the spot price.

Forward exchange rates are determined in the same way as the forward gold price, except that as exchange rates involve two currencies, there are two interest rates.[1]

Definition

A ***forward exchange rate*** is a rate agreed today at which one currency is sold against another for delivery on a specified future date.

For example on 2 September, $1,000,000 is sold against ¥98,050,000 for value 4 March at a forward rate of $1 = ¥98.05. The rate is agreed on 2 September. The currencies are exchanged six months later on 4 March.

Calculation of Forward Exchange Rates

Forward rates differ from spot rates to reflect the differing interest rates prevailing in the two currencies.

Example 6. 1

If the spot rate is $1 = ¥100 and six months dollar and yen interest rates are 6% and 2% respectively, calculate the six month forward exchange rate.

1. In reality gold interest rates are not equal to zero so the forward gold price is a function of the gold interest rate as well as spot gold and the dollar interest rate.

By the end of the six month period:

\$1,000,000 would be worth	$1{,}000{,}000 \times (1 + 0.06 \times 6/12)$	= \$1,030,000
¥100,000,000 would be worth	$100{,}000{,}000 \times (1 + 0.02 \times 6/12)$	= ¥101,000,000

The six month forward exchange rate would be such that:

\$1,030,000 = ¥101,000,000

$$\text{ie } \$1 = \frac{¥101{,}000{,}000}{1{,}030{,}000} = ¥98.06$$

Example 6.2

In practice, it is necessary to base the forward rate calculation on the exact number of days rather than a round number of months. Working in exact number of days the six month period from 4 September (spot value) until 4 March (six months forward value) is 181 days:

On 2 September market rates are:

Spot	\$1 =	¥100.00
\$ interest rate		6.0% pa (360 dpy)
¥ interest rate		3.0% pa (360 dpy)

At the spot rate \$1,000,000 = ¥100,000,000.

If the principal sum of \$1,000,000 is invested for 181 days at an interest rate of 6.0% pa, it would accumulate to a forward value of \$1,030,166.66.

Forward value	=	Principal	+	Interest
	=	\$ 1,000,000	+	$1{,}000{,}000 \times 0.06 \times 181/360$
	=	\$ 1,000,000	+	30,166.66
	=	\$ 1,030,166.66		

Similarly, if a principal sum of ¥100,000,000 is invested for 181 days at an interest rate of 2.0 % pa, it would accumulate to a forward value of ¥101,005,555.

Forward value	=	Principal	+	Interest
	=	¥ 100,000,000	+	$100{,}000{,}000 \times 0.02 \times 181/360$
	=	¥ 100,000,000	+	1,005,555
	=	¥ 101,005,555		

The market forward exchange rate is the rate at which traders would agree today to exchange dollars and yen for value 4 March. As they are willing to exchange \$1,000,000 for ¥100,000,000 value spot, it follows that they will be willing to exchange the corresponding forward values of the two currencies.

ie, value 4 March	$1,030,166.66	=	¥101,005,555
	$1	=	$\frac{¥101,005,555}{1,030,166.66}$
ie	$1	=	¥98.05

In general,

$$\text{Forward rate} = \frac{\text{forward value of terms currency}}{\text{forward value of commodity currency}} \quad \textbf{Equation 6.1}$$

Calculation of Forward Margins

The difference between the spot rate and the forward rate is known as the ***forward margin.***

$$\text{Forward margin} = \text{forward rate} - \text{spot rate} \quad \textbf{Equation 6.2}$$

In Example 6.1

Forward margin	=	98.06 – 100.00
	=	– 1.94

In Example 6.2

Forward margin	=	99.05 – 100.00
	=	– 0.95

If the forward margin is positive, the commodity currency is said to be at a ***forward premium,*** ie, the forward price is higher than the spot price. In the gold analogy, gold was at a forward premium. If the forward margin is negative, the commodity currency is said to be at a ***forward discount.***

Forward Discounts

In Examples 6.1 and 6.2, the forward margin is a negative number, indicating that the commodity currency (dollar) is at a forward discount against the terms currency (yen). That is, the forward price of the dollar is less than its spot price when priced in terms of yen. This reflects the fact that the dollar interest rate is higher than the yen interest rate.

> The higher interest rate currency is at a forward discount against the lower interest rate currency.

Example 6.3

Spot	$1	=	λ1550
6 month dollar interest rate			6.0% pa (360 dpy)
6 month lira interest rate			9.5% pa (360 dpy)

At the spot rate, $1,000,000 = λ1,550,000,000.

After 6 months (184 days), $1,000,000 would accumulate to a forward value of $1,030,666.66.

Forward value	=	Principal	+	Interest
	=	$1,000,000	+	1,000,000 × 0.06 × 184/360
	=	$1,000,000	+	30,666.66
	=	$1,030,666.66		

Similarly, λ1,550,000,000 would accumulate to a forward value of λ1,625,261,112.

Forward value	=	Principal	+	Interest
	=	1,550,000,000	+	1,550,000,000 × 0.095 × 184/360
	=	1,550,000,000	+	75,261,112
	=	λ1,625,261,112		

$$\text{Thus, forward rate} = \frac{\text{forward value of terms currency}}{\text{forward value of commodity currency}}$$

$$= \frac{\lambda\ 1{,}625{,}261{,}112}{\$\ 1{,}030{,}666.66}$$

ie $1 = λ1,577

Forward margin	=	Forward rate	–	Spot rate
	=	1,577	–	1,550
	=	+ 27		

Forward Premiums

In Example 6.3, the forward margin is a positive number indicating that the commodity currency (dollar) is at a forward premium against the terms currency (lira). That is, the forward price of a dollar is higher than the spot price in terms of lira. This reflects the fact that the dollar interest rate is lower than the lira interest rate.

> The lower interest rate currency is at a forward premium against the higher interest rate currency.

If one currency is at a forward premium, the other currency is at a forward discount. The dollar is at a forward premium against the lira, so it follows that the lira is at a forward discount against the dollar. It could also be said that if gold is at a forward premium against the dollar, then the dollar is at a forward discount against gold.

Compensation Argument

Between the spot date and the value date of a forward exchange agreement, one party holds the higher yielding currency. The other party holds the lower yielding currency. In effect, the forward rate differs from the spot rate to the extent to which the holder of the higher interest currency is willing to and expected to compensate the holder of the lower interest currency.

Forward Rate Formula

The general formula can be expanded to:

$$f = \frac{s\,(1 + r_T t)}{(1 + r_C t)} \qquad \textbf{Equation 6.3}$$

where

f	=	forward exchange rate
s	=	spot exchange rate
r_T	=	interest rate of terms currency
r_C	=	interest rate of commodity currency
t	=	time period

Derivation of Forward Rate Formula (Equation 6.3)

By definition, the forward rate is the ratio of the forward value of the terms currency to the forward value of the commodity currency.

$$f = \frac{FV_T}{FV_C}$$

Similarly, by definition the spot rate is the ratio of the present value of the terms currency to the present value of the commodity currency.

$$s = \frac{PV_T}{PV_C}$$

Using FV = PV(1 + rt),

$$f = \frac{FV_T}{FV_C} = \frac{PV_T(1 + r_T t)}{PV_C(1 + r_C t)} = \frac{s(1 + r_T t)}{(1 + r_C t)}$$

If the time period is expressed in days, $t = d/dpy$

where

d = number of days

dpy = days per year

Therefore,

$$f = \frac{s\,(1 + r_T.d/dpy_T)}{(1 + r_C.d/dpy_C)}$$

Equation 6.4

Generalising, $t = p/ppy$

where

p = period

ppy = periods per year

For example, when considering quarterly periods ppy = 4; monthly periods ppy = 12; weekly periods ppy = 52; and so on.

Role of Price Expectations

Many people think that the forward rate is merely what the market expects the spot rate to be at the future date. In general this is not true. The forward rate differs from the spot rate only because of the interest differential. If the forward rate was not as determined by Equation 6.1, then arbitrageurs would be able to take advantage of the price inconsistency. So, provided it is possible to borrow and lend the two currencies, the forward price is merely a mechanical function of the spot rate and the two interest rates.

In Example 6.2 the equilibrium forward rate was \$1 = ¥98.05. If someone who expected that the spot rate would fall below \$1 = ¥98.00 by 4 March was prepared to sell dollars against yen at a forward rate of $1 = ¥98.00 (ie 5 points below the equilibrium rate), arbitrageurs would be willing to buy them. The arbitrageur would buy dollars value 4 March directly and sell dollars value 4 March synthetically by selling dollars spot (value 4 September) at $1 = ¥100.00 and borrowing dollars at 6% and lending yen at 2%.

Proceeds of synthetic sale of dollars	$1	=	¥98.05	
Cost of direct purchase of dollars	$1	=	¥98.00	
Profit from arbitrage		=	¥0.05	per $1

Unless artificial constraints such as exchange controls prevent one or more legs of this from happening, arbitrageurs will continue to do the above transactions until the forward rate moves into line with the equilibrium rate.

In contrast, in the market for most commodities the futures price is primarily a function of price expectations. No liquid market exists in which people can borrow and lend the commodities, so the above arbitrage process cannot happen. For example, in mid-1995 the one-year copper futures price was around US$2,200 per tonne when the cash (ie spot) price was around US$3,200 per tonne. Producers knew that many new mines would be coming into production within the year and so the world supply of copper would increase significantly but not in the short term. Consequently, the one-year forward copper price was at a deep discount to the cash price[2].

Some commodities such as gold do have very liquid interest rate markets. For these commodities, like most exchange rates, the arbitrage process ensures that the forward price is merely a reflection of the spot rate and the two interest rates and not a matter of price expectations.

Net Accessible Rates

The rates used to calculate forward exchange rates are those which are net and accessible to the parties involved. For example, if a resident borrows from or lends to a non-resident, the transaction may be subject to interest withholding tax. The interest rates used to calculate forward exchange rates should be inclusive of withholding tax.

Bid and Offer Rates

In practice, in the foreign exchange and money markets, prices are quoted with bid and offer rates. This adds a further consideration in calculating forward exchange rates. Example 6.2 can be expanded to include bid and offer pricing as follows.

---

[2] In commodity markets, forward premiums are known as ***contango*** and forward discounts are known as ***backwardation***.

Example 6.4

Spot	\$1	=	¥ 100.00	100.05
6 month \$ interest rate			5.9	6.0 % pa (360 dpy)
6 month ¥ interest rate			2.0	2.1 % pa (360 dpy)

Calculate the forward bid and offer rates given that there are 181 days in the 6 month period.

Forward Bid Rates

The ***forward bid rate*** is the rate at which the quoting bank is willing to buy forward the commodity currency. A forward purchase of dollars could be represented on a cash flow diagram as in Exhibit 6.1.

Exhibit 6. 1

Cash flow diagram: forward purchase of dollars

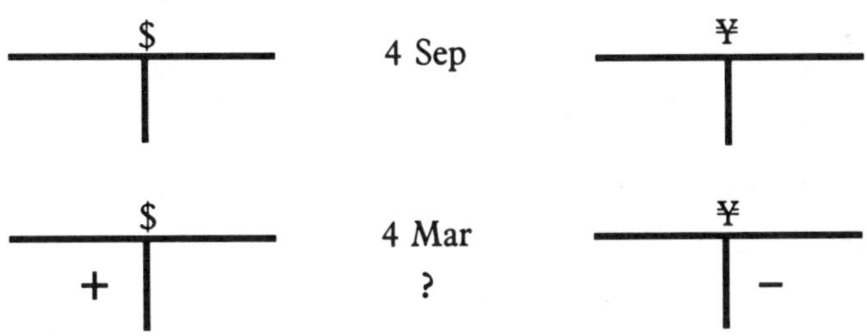

If the bank purchases dollars forward, it will create a net exchange position. It will become long dollars. It could square its net exchange position by selling dollars spot at the market bid rate of \$1 = ¥ 100.00.

Exhibit 6.2

Cash flow diagram:

Forward purchase of dollars covered by spot sale of dollars

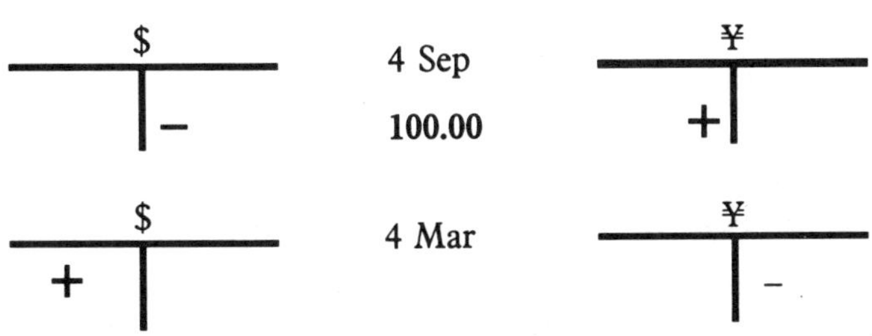

Using the spot market to square the net exchange position would leave the bank with a mismatched cash flow position as in Exhibit 6.2. The cash flows could be matched by two money market transactions:

1. Borrow dollars for 6 months at the market offer rate of 6.0%.
2. Lend yen for 6 months at the market bid rate of 2.0%.

Exhibit 6.3

Cash flow diagram:

Mismatched cash flows covered through money market

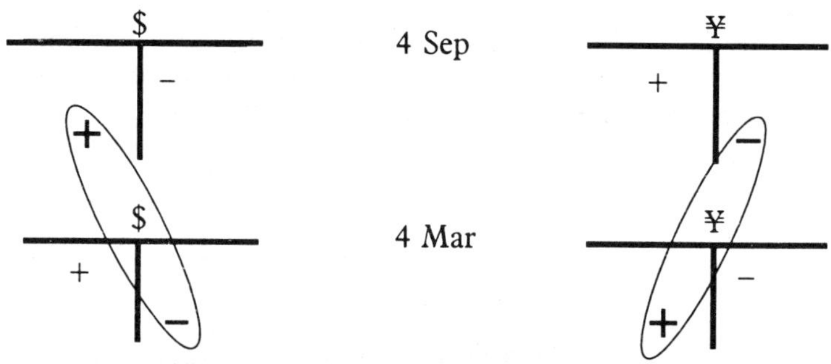

$$s = 100.00$$

$$r_T = 2.0\ \%\ (360\ \text{dpy})$$

$$r_C = 6.0\ \%\ (360\ \text{dpy})$$

$$t = 181\ \text{days}$$

$$f = \frac{s\,(1 + r_T t)}{(1 + r_C t)}$$

$$\therefore\ f = 100.00\ \frac{(1 + 0.02 \times 181/360)}{(1 + 0.06 \times 181/365)}$$

$$= 98.05$$

Forward Offer Rates

The ***forward offer rate*** is the rate at which the quoting bank would sell forward the commodity currency. A forward sale of dollars could be represented on a cash flow diagram as in Exhibit 6.4.

Exhibit 6.4

Cash flow diagram: forward sale of dollars

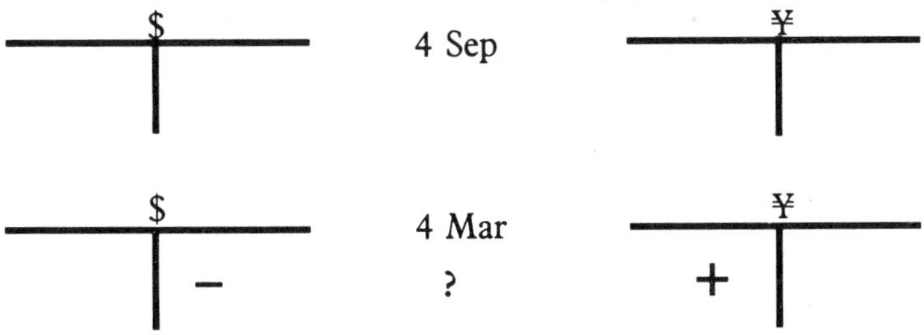

If the bank sells dollars forward, it will create a net exchange position. It will become short dollars. It could square its net exchange postion by buying dollars spot at the market offer rate of $1 = ¥100.05.

Exhibit 6.5

Cash flow diagram:

Forward sale of dollars covered by spot purchase of dollars

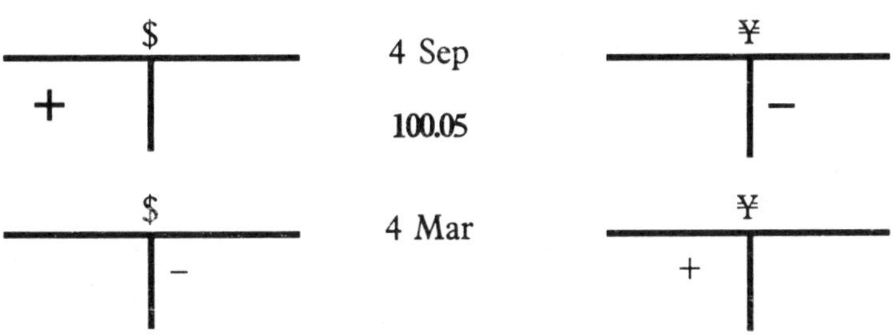

Using the spot market to square the net exchange position would leave the bank with a mismatched cash flow postion as shown in Exhibit 6.5. The cash flows could be matched by two money market transactions:

1. Borrow yen for 6 months at the market offer rate of 3.1% pa.
2. Lend dollars for 6 months the market bid rate of 5.9% pa.

Exhibit 6.6

Cash flow diagram:

Mismatched cash flows covered through money market

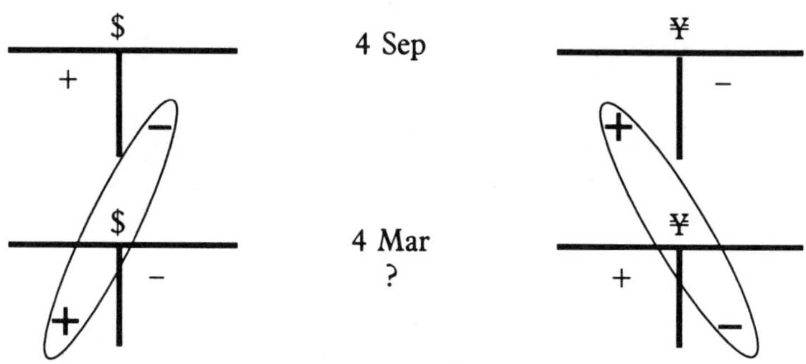

$s = 100.05$

$r_T = 2.1\ \%\ (360\ \text{dpy})$

$r_C = 5.9\ \%\ (360\ \text{dpy})$

$t = 181\ \text{days}$

$$\therefore f = 100.05 \frac{(1 + 0.021 \times 181/360)}{(1 + 0.059 \times 181/360)}$$

$$= 98.19$$

The market forward rate quoted in bid and offer terms is:

$1 = ¥98.05 98.19

If a bank wishes to quote a customer bid-offer forward rates so as to be sure of making one point profit if the customer deals, it would widen the spread by lowering the bid rate by one point and raising the offer rate by one point.

	Bid	Offer
Break-even forward rate	98.05	98.19
Profit margin	-0.01	+0.01
Customer rate	98.04	98.20

Forward Cross Rates

It is possible to cross two forward exchange rates to determine a forward cross rate.

Example 6.5

Spot	\$1	=	¥100.00	and	\$1	=	DM1.5000
3 month forward margin			– 1.00				– 0.0100
3 month forward rate	\$1	=	¥99.00		\$1	=	DM1.4900

Using the chain rule:

Spot cross rate DM1 = $\frac{¥100.00}{1.5000}$ = ¥66.66

Forward cross rate DM1 = $\frac{¥99.00}{1.4900}$ = ¥66.44

It follows that the forward margin for DM against ¥:

= f – s

= 66.44 – 66.66

= – 0.22

The deutschemark is at a forward *discount* of 22 points against the yen.

The forward margin of the cross rate cannot be determined directly from the forward margins of the currencies being crossed. This is because forward margins are not exchange rates; they are merely differentials.

Currency Futures

Currency futures are forward foreign exchange contracts which are traded through a futures exchange. The same concept applies and the pricing calculation is identical except that to facilitate uniformity through the exchange, currency futures are based on standard amounts, have specified maturity dates (usually one each quarter) and are net settled against the rate prevailing on the quarterly settlement date.

Currency futures contracts typically have their face value in the non-US dollar currency (eg each deutschemark contract is for face value DM125,000). The price is typically expressed in the non-US dollar currency. For example the DM June futures contract is quoted as 0.6660 meaning DM1 = US\$0.6660, which in the over-the-counter market would normally be quoted as 1.5011 meaning US\$1 = DM1.5011. On the Chicago Mercantile Exchange, which is the largest centre for currency futures, contracts are traded for settlement on the third Wednesday of March, June, September and December.

Credit risk is addressed by requiring traders to place a margin deposit with the exchange and to top up if the contract moves out-of-the-money.

Long Term Foreign Exchange (LTFX)

When interest periods extend beyond one year, calculating interest will normally require the use of a compound interest formula. Consequently, the formula for calculating forward exchange rates for long tenors needs to provide for compounding interest.

$$f = \frac{s\,(1 + i_T)^n}{(1 + i_C)^n}$$

Equation 6.5

Example 6.6

Spot	£1	=	A$2.0000
3 year A$ interest rate			9.5% pa (semi-annual zero coupon)
3 year £ interest rate			7.0% pa (semi-annual zero coupon)

$$f = 2.0000\,\frac{(1 + 0.0475)^{2 \times 3}}{(1 + 0.035)^{2 \times 3}}$$

$$= 2.1494$$

Derivation of long term foreign exchange formula (Equation 6.3)

$$f = \frac{FV_T}{FV_C}$$

$$FV_T = PV_T\,(1 + i_T)^n$$

$$FV_C = PV_C\,(1 + i_C)^n$$

$$\therefore\ f = \frac{PV_T\,(1 + i_T)^n}{PV_C(1 + i_C)^n}$$

$$= \frac{s\,(1 + i_T)^n}{(1 + i_C)^n}$$

Extending Example 6.6 to include bid and offer rates,

Spot	£1	=	A$2.0000	2.0005
3 year A$ interest rate			9.5	10.0% pa (semi-annual)
3 year £ interest rate			6.6	7.0% pa (semi-anuual)

$$\text{Bid rate} = 2.0000\,\frac{(1 + 0\ 0475)^6}{(1 + 0.035)^6} = 2.1494 \qquad \text{Offer rate} = 2.0005\,\frac{(1 + 0.05)^6}{(1 + 0.0325)^6} = 2.2128$$

Notice the bid-offer spread is very large for long term foreign exchange rates (e.g., 624 points in Example 6.6). This does not constitute windfall profits for the quoting bank, but merely reflects the bid-offer spread of the two interest rates applied over a long period.

NPV Accounting

It was pointed out in Chapter 3 that a superior definition of Net Exchange Position is the *net present value* of foreign currency cash flows. For long term transactions, the difference between the face value (that is future value) and the present value can be significant and so the benefits of using NPV accounting are greater.

Example 6.7

A trader who starts with a square position does the following transactions:

Currency bought	Currency Sold	Rate	Value date
$1,000,000	¥ 96,230,000	96.23	1 year
$4,000,000	¥ 370,440,000	92.61	2 years
¥267,450,000	$3,000,000	89.15	3 years
¥85,830,000	$1,000,000	85.83	4 years

Calculate the net exchange position using the NPV method.

Transaction	$ Cash flows	Years	$ rate	$ NPV
A	+ 1,000,000	1	6.00 %	+ 943,396
B	+ 4,000,000	2	6.25 %	+ 3,543,253
C	– 3,000,000	3	6.50 %	– 2,483,547
D	– 1,000,000	4	6.75 %	– 770,067
Total	+ 1,000,000			**+ 1,233,035**

Transaction	¥ Cash flows	Years	¥ rate	¥ NPV
A	– 96,230,000	1	2.00 %	– 94,339,630
B	– 370,440,000	2	2.25 %	– 354,325,290
C	+ 267,450,000	3	2.50 %	+248,354,728
D	+ 85,830,000	4	2.75 %	+77,006,692
Total	– 113,390,000			**– 123,303,500**

In NPV terms, the dealer is long $1,233,035 and short ¥123,303,500. To square his or her position in the spot market, the dealer could sell $1,233,035 against yen at the prevailing rate $1 = ¥100.00. As each of the four deals has been done at market rates, there is zero revaluation gain or loss.

	NPV Position	Revaluation	Profit/(Loss)
Dollars	+ 1,233,035	– 1,233,035	**0**
Yen	– 123,303,500	+ 123,303,500	**0**
Effective rate	100.00	100.00	

Suppose the same four transactions had been done except that in Transaction C $3,000,000 was sold at a rate of $1 = ¥89.20, implying a five point profit. The cash flows and NPVs would be as above except for the profit made on Transaction C.

Transaction	$ Cash flows	Years	$ rate	$ NPV
A	+ 1,000,000	1	6.00 %	+ 943,396
B	+ 4,000,000	2	6.25 %	+ 3,543,253
C	– 3,000,000	3	6.50 %	– 2,483,547
D	– 1,000,000	4	6.75 %	– 770,067
Total	+ 1,000,000			**+ 1,233,035**

Transaction	¥ Cash flows	Years	¥ rate	¥ NPV
A	– 96,230,000	1	2.00 %	– 94,339,630
B	– 370,440,000	2	2.25 %	– 354,325,290
C	+ **267,600,000**	3	2.50 %	+ **248,493,202**
D	+ 85,830,000	4	2.75 %	+ 77,006,692
Total	– 113,390,000			**– 123,165,026**

	NPV Position	Revaulation	Profit/(Loss)
Dollars	+ 1,233,035	– 1,233,035	0
Yen	– 123,165,026	+ 123,303,500	**¥ 138,474**
Effective rate	99.89	100.00	

Note: The effective rate = $\frac{\text{¥NPV position}}{\text{\$NPV position}}$

In NPV terms, the dealer has made 11 points profit on the net $1,233,035 long position which is equivalent to making five points on $3,000,000 for value three years from now.

Par Forwards

The NPV methodology can be used to price par forwards. A ***par forward*** is a series of forward foreign exchange rates for various maturities all at the same (average) rate.

Example 6.8

An exporter with receipts of ¥100,000,000 each year for five years could hedge the yen currency risk by doing five separate forward deals in which ¥100,000,000 would be sold against dollars at the different forward rates for each of the five maturities.

Year	¥ amount sold	$ proceeds	Forward rate
1	100,000,000	1,039,177	96.23
2	100,000,000	1,079,797	92.61
3	100,000,000	1,121,705	89.15
4	100,000,000	1,165,094	85.83
5	100,000,000	1,209,921	82.65
Total	500,000,000	5,615,694	89.04

The dollar proceeds rise each year because the forward rate is lower the further forward the maturity date.

Alternatively, the exporter could hedge by selling ¥100,000,000 each year for five years at the same (par forward) rate. The market par forward rate is that rate for which the net present value of the dollar cash flows is the same as the net present value of the dollar cash flows for the five separate forward deals.

It turns out that a par forward rate of $1 = ¥89.51 has the same NPV as the five separate forward deals. ¥100,000,000 at 89.51 would produce dollar proceeds of $1,117,194 for each of the five years.

Year	Rate	$ proceeds	NPV	Par rate	$ proceeds	NPV
1	96.23	1,039,177	980,392	89.51	1,117,194	1,053,956
2	92.61	1,079,797	956,474	89.51	1,117,194	989,625
3	89.15	1,121,705	928,599	89.51	1,117,194	924,868
4	85.83	1,165,094	897,166	89.51	1,117,194	860,314
5	82.65	1,209,921	862,609	89.51	1,117,194	796,544
Total		5,615,694	**4,625,241**		5,585,968	**4,625,306**

The small difference ($66) between the NPV amounts is merely rounding.

The exporter receives the dollar proceeds earlier under the par forward than with five separate outright forward transactions. For example, at the end of Year 1, the exporter would receive $1,117,194 from the par forward versus $1,039,177 from an outright forward at $1 = ¥96.23. Effectively, the bank is lending the exporter the difference. The bank is compensated for this extension of credit because the par forward rate ¥89.51 is higher (and, therefore, less attractive to the exporter) than the average rate of $1 = ¥89.04.

Figure 6.1

Par Forward

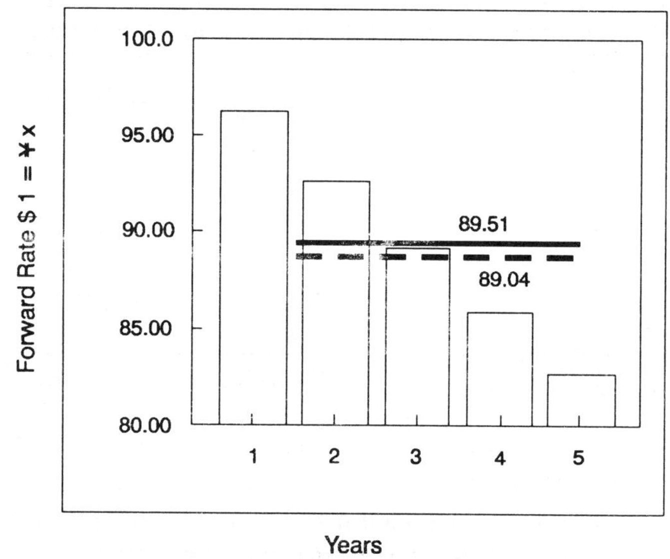

Short Dates

On occasions, it is necessary to do foreign exchange transactions for maturities before spot value. It is possible to calculate exchange rates for value today or value tomorrow. The procedure used to engineer exchange rates for short date maturities is identical to that for forward exchange rates. However, because the maturities are prior to spot, the formula used to calculate short dates is different to Equation 6.3.

$$t = \frac{s\,(1 + r_C d/dpy_C)}{(1 + r_T d/dpy_T)}$$

Equation 6.6

where t = today (tod) or tomorrow (tom) rate.

Example 6.9

Spot rate (value 3 August)	$1 = ¥ 104.50	104.55	
Overnight $ interest rate	6.00	6.25% pa (360 dpy)	
Overnight ¥ interest rates	2.50	2.25% pa (360 dpy)	

Calculate the value tom bid rate, ie the rate at which the quoting bank would be willing to buy dollars value tom (2 August).

Exhibit 6.7
Cash flow diagram:
Tom purchase of dollars against yen

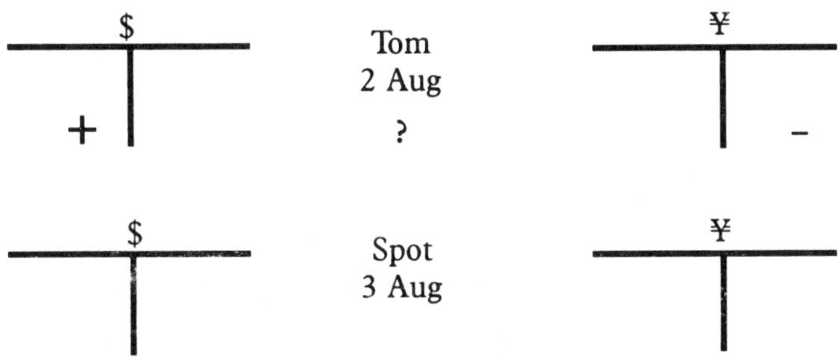

If the bank purchases dollars value tom, it will create a net exchange position. It will become long dollars. It could square this position by selling dollars spot at the market bid rate $1 = ¥104.50.

Exhibit 6.8
Cash flow diagram:
Tom purchase of dollars covered by spot sale of dollars

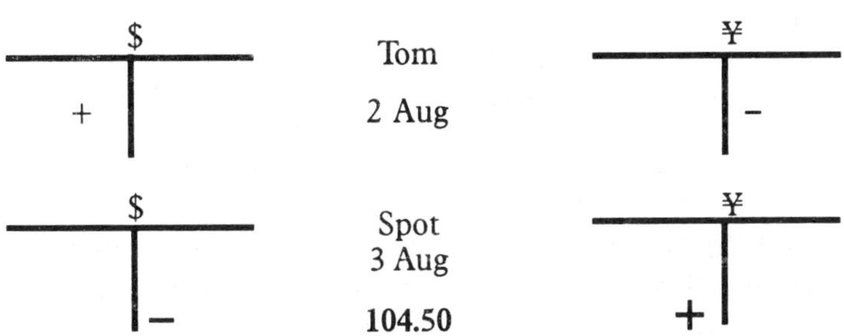

Using the spot market to cover the net exchange position would leave the bank with a mismatched cash flow position as in Exhibit 6.8. The cash flows could be matched by two money market transactions:

1. Lend dollars overnight at the market bid rate of 6.00 % pa.
2. Borrow yen overnight at the market offer rate of 3.00 % pa.

Exhibit 6.9
Cash flow diagram:
Mismatched cash flows covered through money market

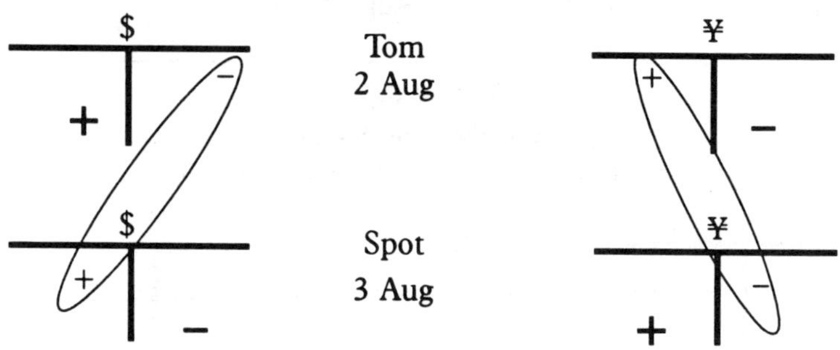

s	=	104.50
r_T	=	3.00% (360 dpy)
r_C	=	6.00% (360 dpy)
d	=	1 day

From Equation 6.6,

$$t = s\frac{(1 + r_C d/dpy_C)}{(1 + r_T d/dpy_T)}$$

$$= 104.50\frac{(1 + 0.06 \times 1/360)}{(1 + 0.03 \times 1/360)}$$

$$= 104.509$$

Note: Because of the size of the numbers, it is common to quote short date rates to an extra decimal place.

Short date margins

The tom rate is higher than the spot rate, reflecting the fact that the dollar is at a forward discount and therefore a short date premium against the yen.

tom margin	=	tom rate	−	spot rate
	=	104.509	−	104.50
	=	+ 0.009		

The tom/next margin is 0.9 of a point.

Exhibit 6.10
Short Date Margins

	1 Aug Tod	2 Aug Tom	3 Aug Spot	10 Aug Forward rates	17 Aug
	104.517	104.509	104.50	104.44	104.38
Margin	+ 0.017	+ 0.009		– 0.06	– 0.12

Because dollar interest rates are higher than yen interest rates, the short date exchange rates are higher than spot (ie at a premium) and the forward exchange rates are lower than spot (ie at a discount). If the commodity currency is the low interest rate currency, the short date exchange rates will be lower than spot (ie at a discount) and the forward exchange rates will be higher than spot (ie at a premium).

Derivation of short date formula (Equation 6.4)

$$t = \frac{PV_T}{PV_C}$$

$$s = \frac{FV_T}{FV_C}$$

$$= \frac{PV_T\,(1 + r_T d/dpy_T)}{PV_C\,(1 + r_C d/dpy_C)}$$

$$\therefore \quad s = \frac{t\,(1 + r_T d/dpy_T)}{(1 + r_C d/dpy_C)}$$

$$\therefore \quad t = \frac{s(1 + r_C d/dpy_C)}{(1 + r_T d/dpy_T)}$$

Note: In the short date formula, the factor is the reciprocal of the forward rate formula because for short date deals, the future value is on the spot date and the present value is at the tod or tom value date.

Practice Problems

6.1 Forward exchange rate and forward margin

Spot rate	$1 =	DM1.5000
3 month $ interest rate		6% pa
3 month DM interest rate		3% pa

(a) Calculate the three month forward rate for dollars in deutschemark terms.

(b) Calculate the three month forward margin.

6.2 Forward exchange rate and forward margin

Spot rate	DM1	=	¥70.00
7 month DM			6.5% pa
7 month ¥			3.5% pa

Calculate the seven month forward rate and forward margin.

6.3 Forward bid rate

Spot rate	F 1	=	$1.8090	1.8100
5 month F			6.00	7.00% pa
5 month $			11.00	12.00% pa

A customer wishes to buy dollars five months forward. What rate should a bank quote to break-even?

6.4 Forward offer rate

Assuming the same market rate scenario as in Practice Problem 6.3, what rate should a bank quote a customer who wishes to buy dollars five months forward if the bank is to make two points profit?

6.5 Long term foreign exchange

Spot rate	A$1	=	US$0.7500	
2 year A$ interest rate			8.0%	8.25% pa (semi-annually)
2 year US$ interest rate			6.5%	6.75% pa (semi-annually)

Calculate the break-even two year forward bid and offer rates.

6.6 Short dates

Spot rate	$1	=	DM1.4780	1.4785
Overnight $ interest rate			5.25%	5.375% pa (360 dpy)
Overnight DM interest rate			3.25%	3.375% pa (360 dpy)

Calculate the break-even bid and offer rates for value tomorrow.

Supplementary Questions

6.7 Forward exchange rate and forward margin

Spot rate	C1	=	P1.4560
1 week C			8% pa (21 dpy)
1 week P			10% pa (21 dpy)

Calculate the one week forward rate and the forward margin.

6.8 Short dates

Spot	NZ$1	=	US$0.6940 / 0.6950
Overnight NZ$			9.0% / 9.5% (365 dpy)
Overnight US$			5.0% / 5.5% (360 dpy)

Quote the break-even bid and offer rates outright value tomorrow (1 day).

6.9 Long term foreign exchange

Spot	$1	=	¥107.00
2 year dollars			6.00% / 6.25%
2 year yen			1.75% / 2.00%

Interest paid semi-annually in arrears.

Calculate the break-even two year bid and offer rates.

7

Applications of Forward Exchange

Forward exchange rates provide a means of hedging foreign currency exposures. This chapter covers applications of forward exchange rates for importers, exporters, borrowers and investors.

Hedging import payables

Importers are generally required to pay their foreign suppliers in foreign currency. For example, if an importer buys cars from Japan, it will probably be necessary to pay the Japanese supplier in yen. The importer has an exchange rate exposure upon committing to pay the supplier a fixed amount of foriegn currency. The lower the exchange rate of the dollar against the yen at the time the importer purchases the fixed amount of yen, the greater will be the dollar cost.

Example 7.1

An importer has an obligation to pay ¥1,000,000,000 to a Japanese supplier three months from now. This obligation to pay constitutes a net exchange position. The importer is short ¥1,000,000,000 against the dollar.

If the importer does not hedge the exposure, ie the importer waits for three months and purchases ¥1,000,000,000 at the then prevailing spot rate, the dollar cost of buying the yen will increase if the dollar falls against the yen.

If the importer expects the dollar to depreciate against the yen, he or she can ***hedge*** (ie eliminate) the exposure by using the forward exchange market to purchase the yen before the exchange rate falls.

Market rates are:

Spot rate	$1 = ¥100.00	100.05
3 month forward margin	− 2.00	− 1.90
3 month forward rate	$1 = ¥ 98.00	98.15

Figure 7.1
Unhedged imports

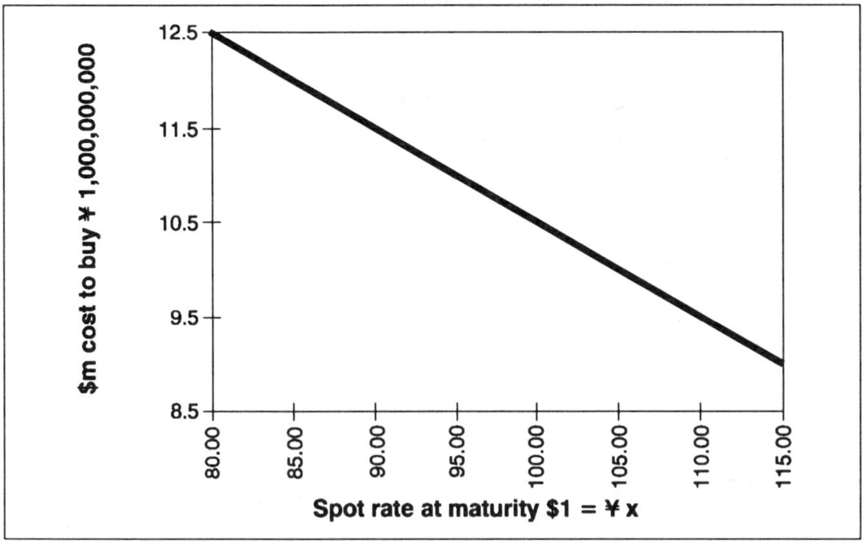

The importer could hedge by buying forward ¥1,000,000,000 at the forward bid rate $1 = ¥98.00

$$\text{The dollar cost if hedged} = \frac{1{,}000{,}000{,}000}{98.00} = \$10{,}204{,}081.63$$

Figure 7.2
Hedged imports

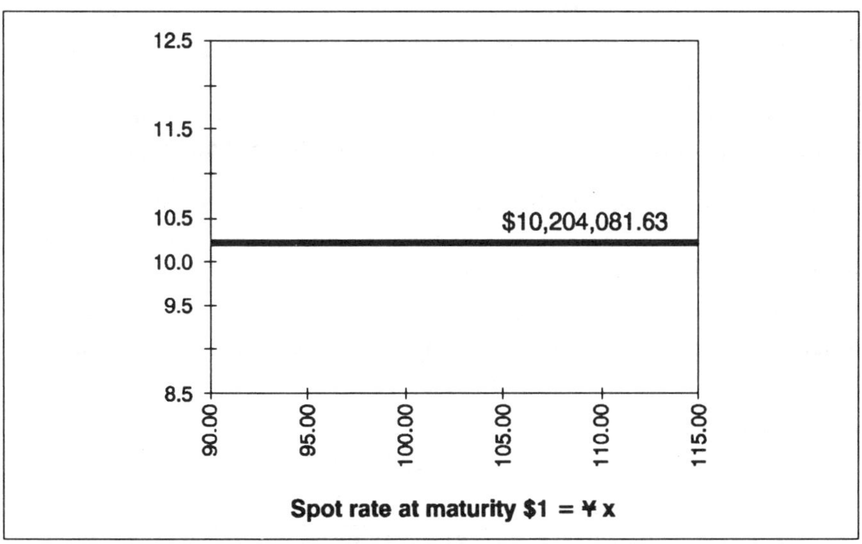

Once hedged, the importer knows with certainty that it will cost $10,204,081.63 to pay for the imports regardless of the spot rate in three months time. By hedging, the importer has eliminated the exposure to exchange rate movements.

Figure 7.3

Hedged and unhedged imports

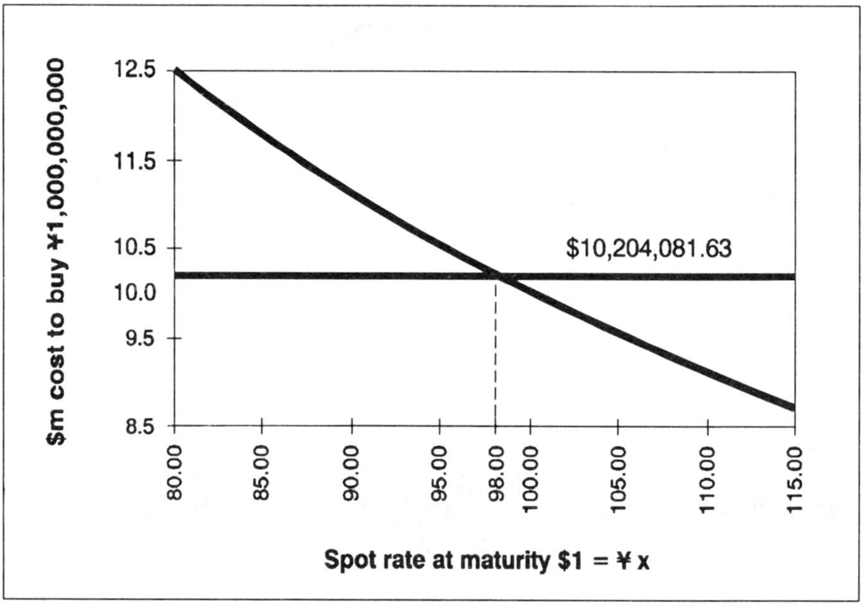

The forward rate $1 = ¥98.00 represents the break-even rate between being hedged and unhedged.[1] If at maturity the spot rate is less than 98.00, the importer would be better off hedged than unhedged. For example, if the spot rate at maturity is 80.00, the cost to the importer would be $10,204,081 if hedged and $12,500,000 if unhedged. On the other hand, if at maturity the spot rate is greater than 98.00, the importer would be better off unhedged than hedged. For example, if the spot rate at maturity is 100.00, the cost to the importer would be $10,000,000 if unhedged and $10,204,081 if hedged.

Partial hedging

The importer may elect to hedge part or all of the exposure. For example, the importer may choose to hedge 50% (ie ¥500,000,000) and leave the other 50%

1. At the break-even rate, cost if hedged = cost if unhedged

$$\text{ie} \quad \frac{1{,}000{,}000{,}000}{f} = \frac{1{,}000{,}000{,}000}{b}$$

$$\therefore \quad b = f = 98.00$$

unhedged. This would reduce rather than eliminate the foreign currency exposure. If the dollar falls, the loss will be only half what it would have been if the importer had been totally unhedged. It is possible to hedge any selected proportion of the exposure. Unhedged means 0% hedged. Hedged or "fully" hedged means 100% hedged.

Figure 7.4

Partially (50%) hedged imports

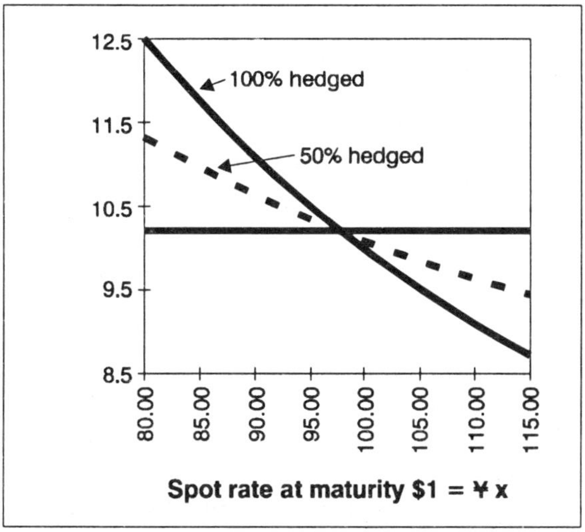

Hedging export receivables

If the proceeds of an export sale are denominated in a foreign currency, then the exporter has a net exchange position. It would be possible to hedge this net exchange position by selling forward the future foreign currency receipts.

Example 7.2

A French winegrower exports wine to the United Kingdom and, two months from now, will be paid £2,000,000. The French exporter is long £2,000,000 against French francs.

If the pound appreciates against the French franc, the unhedged exporter will receive more French francs for the sale of the wine. However, if the pound depreciates against the French franc, the unhedged exporter will receive fewer French francs. If he or she expects the pound to depreciate, the exporter can hedge the net exchange position by selling £2,000,000 forward in the foreign exchange market before the exchange rate falls.

Figure 7.5

Unhedged exports

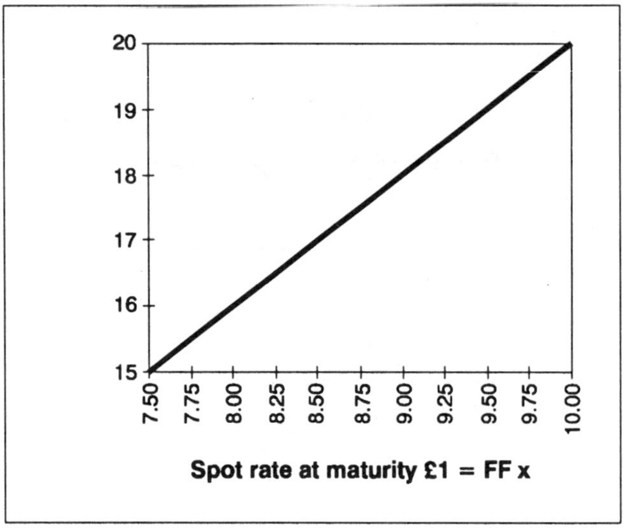

It should be pointed out that the reason Figure 7.5 is upward sloping to the right, and Figure 7.1 is downward sloping to the right, is not that Figure 7.5 relates to exports and Figure 7.1 relates to imports. Figure 7.5 has a positive slope because the proceeds are expressed in terms of the terms currency. Figure 7.1 has a negative slope because the cost is expressed in terms of the commodity currency. If Example 7.2 referred to a British exporter measuring the pound proceeds of the sale of French francs, then Figure 7.5 would be downward sloping to the right. Similarly, if Example 7.1 referred to a Japanese importer measuring the yen cost of buying the dollar, Figure 7.1 would be upward sloping to the right.

Fortunately, the analysis is unaffected whichever way the figures are drawn. This is merely pointed out to avoid confusion on the part of the reader.

Market rates are:

Spot rate	£1 = FF8.7050	8.7090
2 month forward margin	+ .0060	+ .0080
2 month forward rate	£1 = FF8.7110	8.7170

The French exporter could hedge by selling £2,000,000 forward at the market bid rate of £1 = FF8.7110.

The FF proceeds if hedged = 2,000,000 × 8.7110 = FF17,422,000.

Figure 7.6

Hedged exports

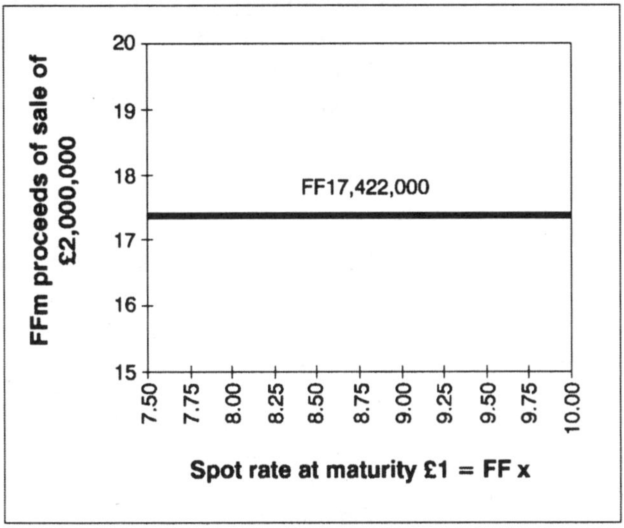

Once hedged, the exporter knows with certainty that he or she will receive FF17,422,000 for the wine regardless of the spot rate in two months time. By hedging, the exporter has eliminated the exposure to the exchange rate.

Figure 7.7

Hedged and unhedged exports

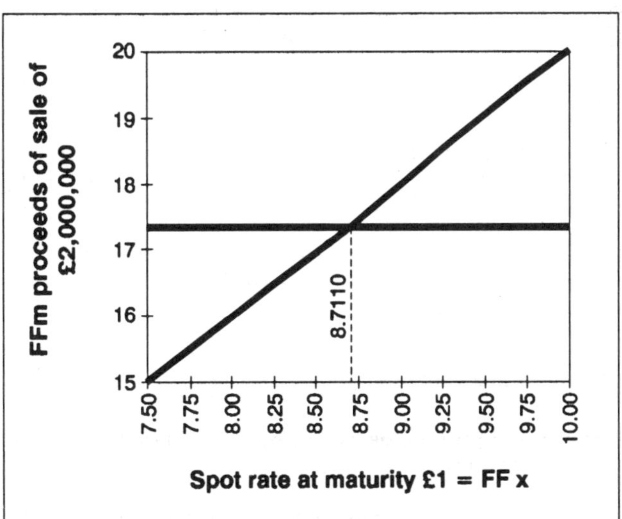

The forward rate £1 = FF8.7110 represents the break-even rate between being hedged and unhedged.[2] If at maturity the spot rate is greater than 8.7110, the exporter would be better off unhedged than hedged. For example, if the spot rate at maturity is 9.0000, he or she would receive FF18,000,000 for the wine if unhedged and FF17,422,000 if hedged. On the other hand, if at maturity the spot rate is less than 8.7110, the exporter would be better off hedged than unhedged and at 8.5000, for example, would receive FF17,422,000 if hedged and FF17,000,000 if unhedged.

Effective exchange rates

It is possible to draw the above diagrams with the effective exchange rate as the vertical axis. This is often helpful for the exporters and importers who set their objectives in terms of an exchange rate level rather than a dollar amount. Figure 7.3 could be redrawn as in Figure 7.8. Notice that changing the units of measurement from the dollar cost of purchasing the imports to the effective exchange rate at which the imports will be purchased changes the unhedged line from downward sloping to upward sloping.

Figure 7.8

Effective exchange rates

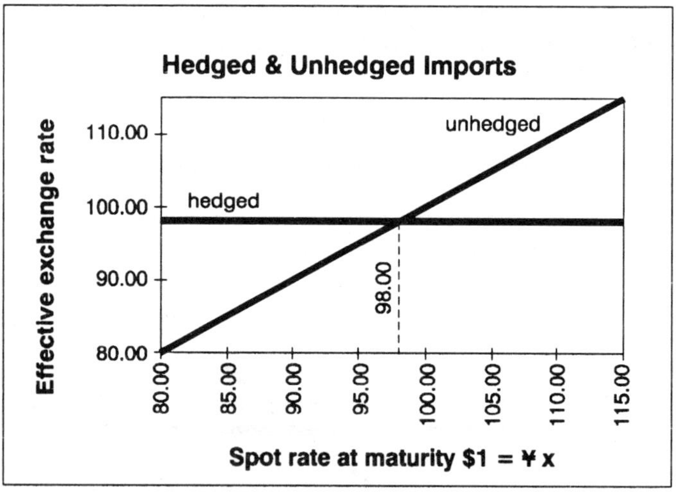

2. At the break-even rate, proceeds if hedged = proceeds if unhedged

$$\text{ie} \quad 2{,}000{,}000 \times f = 2{,}000{,}000 \times b$$

$$\therefore \quad b = f$$

$$= 8.7110$$

Benefits and Costs of Premiums and Discounts

In the above examples, the importer would pay a cost equal to the forward discount to hedge the yen payables and the French exporter would receive a benefit equal to the forward premium to hedge the pound receivables.

If the commodity is at a discount, the buyer enjoys the benefit and the seller incurs the cost of the discount. If the commodity is at a premium, the buyer pays the cost and the seller enjoys the benefit of the premium.

The benefit or cost of hedging will reflect the forward premium or discount.

Cost to buy ¥1,000,000,000 spot at 100.00	$10,000,000.00
Cost to buy ¥1,000,000,000 forward at 98.00	$10,204,081.63
∴ Cost of hedging ¥1,000,000,000 payables	$ 204,081.63

Cost of hedging yen payables in dollar terms:

$$= \frac{1{,}000{,}000{,}000}{98.00} - \frac{1{,}000{,}000{,}000}{100.00}$$

$$= \$204{,}081.63$$

Proceeds of selling £2,000,000 spot at 8.7050	FF17,410,000.00
Proceeds of selling £2,000,000 forward at 8.7110	FF17.422.000.00
∴ Benefit of hedging £2,000,000 receivables	FF 12,000.00

Benefit of hedging sterling receivables in FF terms:

$$= 2{,}000{,}000 \times 8.7110 - 2{,}000{,}000 \times 8.7050$$

$$= 2{,}000{,}000\ (8.7110 - 8.7050)$$

$$= 2{,}000{,}000 \times 0.0060$$

$$= \text{FF } 12{,}000.00$$

When the terms currency amount is constant, the cost or benefit of hedging cannot be determined directly from the forward margin. This is because forward margins are not exchange rates; they are differentials between exchange rates.

Hedging Foreign Currency Borrowings

Borrowing a foreign currency does not create a net exchange position. However, if the foreign currency borrowed is sold for another currency, usually the local currency, the sale of the foreign currency creates an exchange rate exposure. The local currency cost of repaying the loan rises as the local currency depreciates against the foreign currency and falls as the local currency appreciates against the foreign currency.

Example 7.3

A company borrows SF10,000,000 for six months at an interest rate of 3.50% pa and converts the Swiss francs into pounds by selling them at a spot rate of £1 = SF2.0000. The loan provides initial proceeds of £5,000,000.

The borrower has an obligation to pay SF10,175,000, being principal plus interest, in six months time. This obligation constitutes a net exchange position similar to that of the importer with an obligation to pay foreign currency in the future. Note that the net exchange position includes the future obligation to pay interest (FOTPI), not just the principal amount.

Figure 7.9

Unhedged SF borrowing

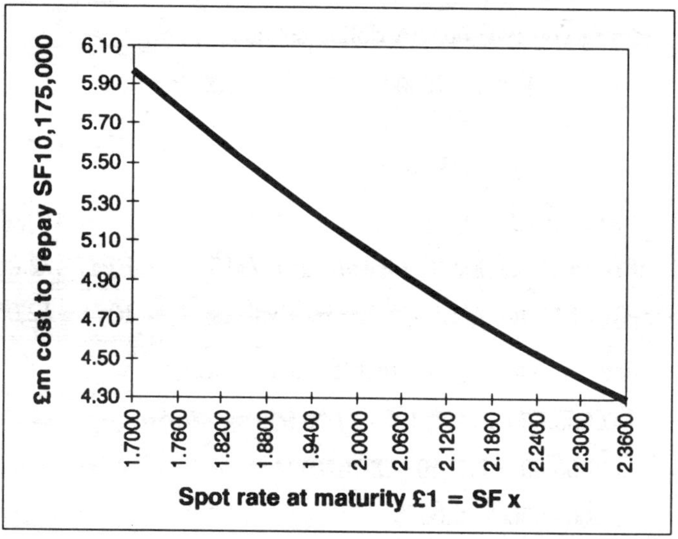

If the borrower remains unhedged, the sterling cost of repaying the Swiss franc loan will fluctuate with the exchange rate. As the pound strengthens against the Swiss franc, the cost of buying the SF10,175,000 necessary to repay the loan will fall. Similarly, as the pound weakens against the Swiss franc, the cost of buying the SF10,175,000 necessary to repay the loan will rise.

> Borrowers gain by borrowing currencies which will weaken and lose by borrowing currencies which will strengthen.

If the borrower expects the pound to depreciate against the Swiss franc, the foreign exchange exposure can be hedged (ie eliminated) by purchasing SF10,175,000 forward.

Market rates are:

Spot rate	£1	=	SF2.0000
6 month forward margin		–	0.0500
6 month forward rate	£1	=	SF1.9500

The borrower could hedge by buying SF10,175,000 at the forward rate £1 = SF1.9500.

$$\text{The sterling cost if hedged} = \frac{10{,}175{,}000}{1.9500} = £5{,}217{,}948.72$$

Exhibit 7.1

Cash flow representation of a hedged SF loan

£		Spot	SF	
5,000,000		2.0000		10,000,000
		3.50%	+10,000,000	
			10,000,000	10,000,000
£		**6 months**	**SF**	
	– 5,217,948.72	1.9500	+10,175,000	
		P + I		–10,175,000
			10,175,000	10,175,000

Figure 7.10

Hedged SF loan

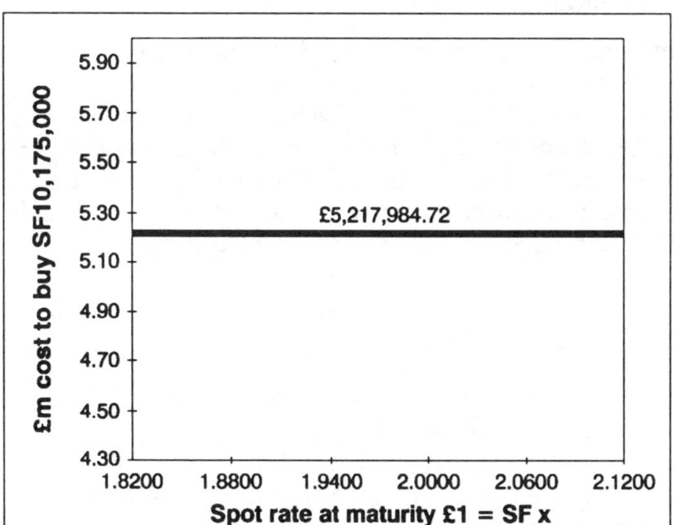

Once hedged, the borrower knows that it will cost £5,217,948.72 to repay the Swiss franc loan principal plus interest in six months time. By hedging, the borrower has eliminated the exposure to exchange rate changes.

Figure 7.11

Hedged and unhedged SF loan

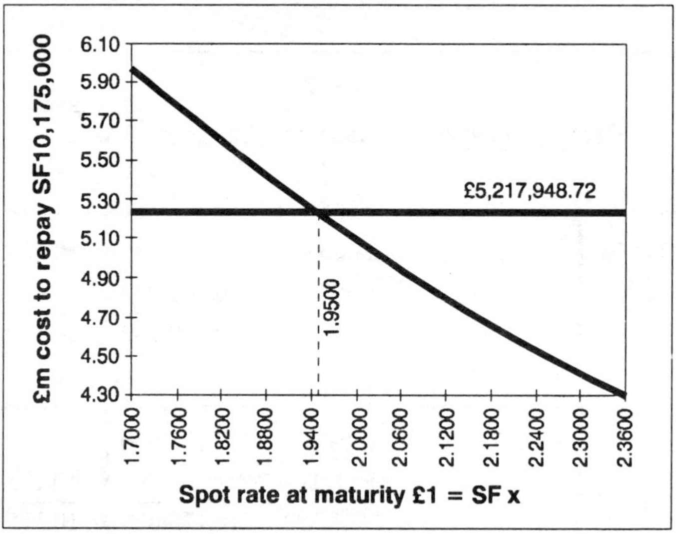

The forward rate £1 = SF1.9500 represents the break-even rate between being hedged and unhedged.[3]

If at maturity the spot rate is less than 1.9500, the borrower would be better off hedged than unhedged. For example, if the spot rate at maturity is 1.9000, the cost of repayment would be £5,217,948.72 if hedged and £5,355,263.16 if unhedged. On the other hand, if at maturity the spot rate is greater than 1.9500, the borrower would be better off unhedged than hedged. For example, if the spot rate at maturity is 1.9800, the cost of repayment would still be £5,217,948.72 if hedged but only £5,138,888.89 if unhedged.

3. At the break-even rate, cost if hedged = cost if unhedged

$$\text{ie} \quad \frac{10{,}175{,}000}{f} = \frac{10{,}175{,}000}{b}$$

$$\therefore \quad b = 1.9500$$

Effective Cost of Hedged Foreign Currency Borrowings

By hedging the Swiss franc principal plus interest at the forward rate of £1 = SF1.9500, the borrower knows it will cost exactly £5,217,948.72 to repay a loan which had proceeds of £5,000,000.

$$\text{Effective interest} = £5{,}217{,}948.72 - 5{,}000{,}000$$
$$= £217{,}948.72$$

$$\text{Effective interest rate \% pa} = \frac{\text{interest}}{\text{principal}} \times \text{time factor} \times 100$$
$$= \frac{217{,}948.72}{5{,}000{,}000} \times \frac{365}{180} \times 100$$
$$= 8.84\ \%\ \text{pa (365 dpy basis)}$$

Equation 6.3 provides an algebraic means of calculating the effective borrowing cost of a fully hedged foreign currency loan.

$$f = \frac{s\,(1 + r_T t)}{(1 + r_C t)}$$

In Example 7.3

$$f = 1.9500$$
$$s = 2.0000$$
$$r_T = 0.035$$
$$r_C = ?$$
$$d = 180$$

Hence

$$1.9500 = \frac{2.0000\,(1 + 0.035 \times 180/360)}{(1 + r_C \times 180/365)}$$

$$\therefore\quad (1 + r_C \times 180/365) = \frac{2.0000}{1.9500}(1.0175)$$
$$= 1.043590$$

$$\therefore\quad r_C = 0.0884$$

Figure 7.12

Effective borrowing cost

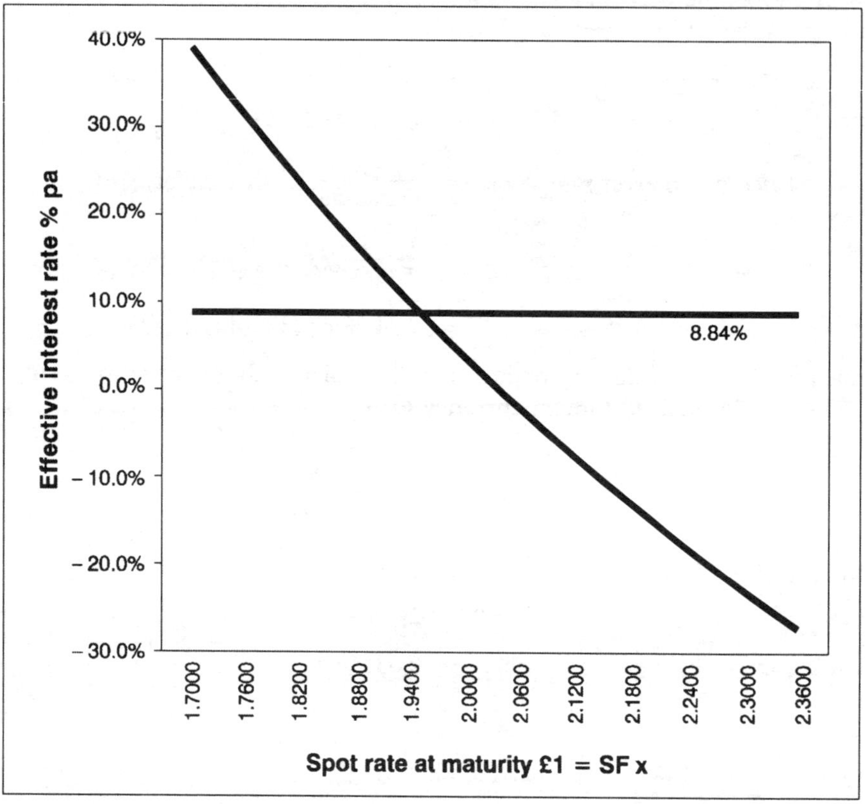

Example 7.4

A US corporation borrows £7,000,000 for 38 days at an interest rate of 10.50% pa (365 dpy) and sells the proceeds spot at an exchange rate of £1 = $1.7420. The corporation hedges by purchasing principal plus interest forward for the repayment date at a rate of £1 = $1.7380. What is the effective interest rate?

$$s = 1.7420$$

$$f = 1.7380$$

$$r_T = ?$$

$$r_C = 0.1050$$

$$d = 38$$

$$dpy_T = 360$$

$$dpy_C = 365$$

Using Equation 6.4,

$$f = s\,\frac{(1 + r_T d/dpy_T)}{(1 + r_C d/dpy_C)}$$

$$1.7380 = \frac{1.7420\,(1 + r_T \times 38/360)}{(1 + 0.1050 \times 38/365)}$$

$$\therefore \quad (1 + r_T \times 38/360) = \frac{1.7380}{1.7420}\,(1.010932)$$

$$= 1.008610$$

$$\therefore \quad r_T = 0.0816 = 8.16\ \%\ \text{pa}$$

Cost of Hedging Foreign Currency Borrowings

The difference between the effective rate of a hedged foreign currency loan and the nominal foreign currency interest rate represents the cost or benefit of hedging.

Continuing Example 7.3,

	Effective interest rate of hedged SF loan	8.84% pa
	Nominal interest rate of SF loan	3.50% pa
∴	Cost of hedging	5.34% pa

In this case, hedging means buying Swiss francs forward at a premium (ie selling pounds forward at a discount). The decision to hedge, therefore, involves a cost equivalent to adding 5.34 % pa to the nominal interest rate. This cost reflects the forward margin of 500 exchange points. That is, in this example 500 exchange points are equivalent to 534 basis points.

Because the forward margin reflects the prevailing interest differential between the two currencies, the effective interest rate on a fully hedged foreign currency borrowing should be equal to the equivalent local currency borrowing rate.

> A fully hedged foreign currency loan is equivalent to a local currency loan.

In practice, the effective interest rate on a fully hedged foreign currency loan will normally be marginally higher than the local borrowing rate. Borrowing a foreign currency may mean incurring additional costs such as interest withholding tax. Hedging may involve paying a bid-offer spread etc. In some cases, it is possible to generate local currency liquidity more cheaply through a fully hedged borrowing than by borrowing the local currency through the domestic money market. This is examined further in Chapter 8 in the section dealing with covered interest arbitrage.

Effective Cost of Unhedged Foreign Currency Borrowings

Returning to Example 7.3, it is only possible to calculate the effective interest rate when the exchange rate at which the Swiss franc principal and interest will be purchased is known. If the borrower remains unhedged and purchases SF10,175,000 at the prevailing spot rate at maturity, the effective borrowing cost will not be known until maturity. However, it is possible to calculate what the effective interest rate would be if the spot rate at maturity turns out to have a particular value. For example, if at maturity the spot rate at which the borrower could purchase Swiss francs is 1.9700, then the effective borrowing cost will be 6.69 % pa.

This is calculated by again using the relationship

$$f = s\frac{(1 + r_T t)}{(1 + r_C t)}$$

where f represents the future spot rate rather than the current forward rate.

Solving for r_C,

$$f = 1.9700$$

$$s = 2.0000$$

$$r_T = 0.035$$

$$t = 180$$

$$\therefore \quad 1.9700 = \frac{2.0000\ (1 + 0.035 \times 180/360)}{(1 + r_C \times 180/365)}$$

$$\therefore \quad r_C = 0.0669 = 6.69\%\ \text{pa}$$

By allowing f to take different values, it is possible to calculate the effective interest rates which would result from an unhedged borrowing for different possible future spot rates.

The unhedged borrower loses if the exchange rate falls. For example, if at maturity the spot rate has fallen to 1.9000, the effective interest rate would have risen to 14.41% pa. Conversely, the unhedged borrower gains if the exchange rate rises. For example, if at maturity the spot rate has risen to 2.1000, the effective interest rate would have fallen to – 6.28% pa. The borrower's foreign exchange gain would exceed the nominal interest cost so that the borrower ends up repaying less than the proceeds obtained at drawdown, thereby enjoying a negative effective interest rate.

Borrowers may hedge at any time during the life of the loan. For example, they may remain unhedged for a month hoping that the exchange rate will rise and then hedge for the remaining period. Suppose a borrower targets a borrowing rate of 7% pa for the period. What would the 5 month forward rate at the end of the first month need to be for the borrower to be able to hedge the principal plus interest at an effective rate of 7% pa?

$$s = 2.0000$$
$$f = ?$$
$$r_T = 0.035$$
$$r_C = 0.07$$

Again using Equation 6.3:

$$f = s\frac{(1 + r_T t)}{(1 + r_C t)}$$
$$= \frac{2.0000\,(1 + 0.035 \times 180/360)}{(1 + 0.07 \times 150/365)}$$
$$= 1.9781$$

Figure 7.13

Locking in 7% pa borrowing cost

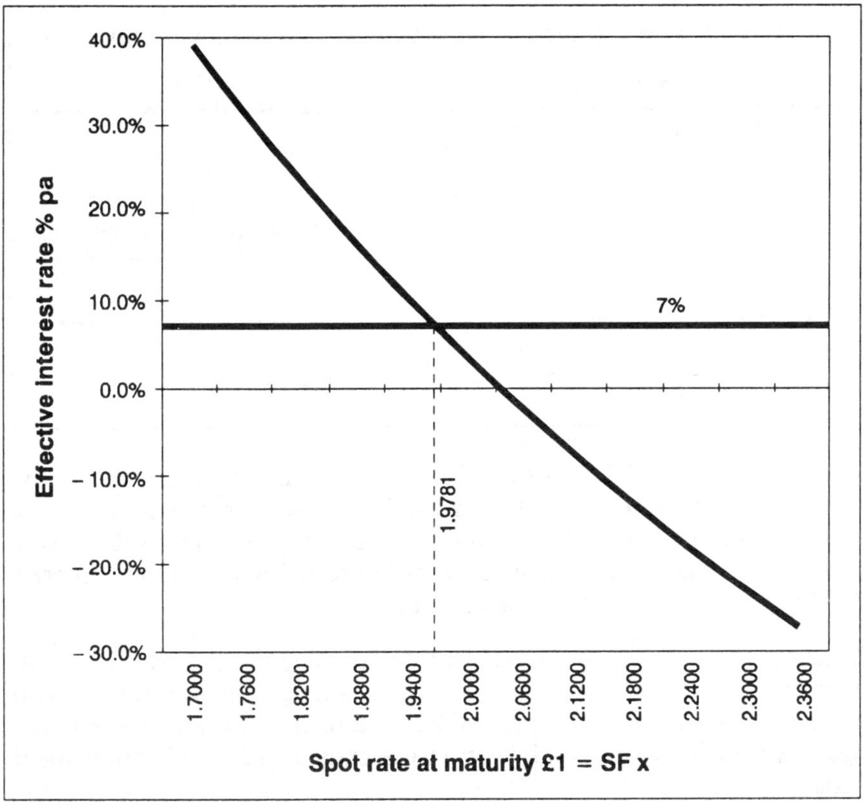

It should be pointed out that the borrower might not have the opportunity to purchase Swiss francs at a forward rate of 1.9781. However, he or she knows that if the forward rate reaches 1.9781, then it is possible to lock in an effective borrowing cost for the period equal to the 7% pa objective.

Hedging Foreign Currency Investments

Investing in a foreign currency does not in itself create a net exchange position. However, *purchasing* the foreign currency so that it can be invested does create an exchange rate exposure. The local currency return on a foreign currency investment rises as the foreign currency appreciates against the local currency and falls as the foreign currency depreciates against the local currency.

Example 7.5

An investor has $10,000,000 to invest. The $10,000,000 is used to purchase DG15,000,000 at a spot rate of $1 = DG1.5000 and the Dutch guilders are invested for 60 days at an interest rate of 4% pa (360 dpy).

Exhibit 7.2

Cash flow representation of an unhedged DG investment

$			DG	
		Spot		
	− 10,000,000	1.5000	+ 15,000,000	
		4%		− 15,000,000
			15,000,000	15,000,000

$			DG	
		60 days		
		P + I	+ 15,100,000	

The investment will be worth DG15,100,000 at maturity. Assuming the investor intends to sell these Dutch guilders for dollars, the net exchange position is similar to that of an exporter with Dutch guilder receivables. Note that the net exchange position includes the future obligation to receive interest (FOTRI) as well as the principal amount.

If the investor remains unhedged, the dollar value of the investment will fluctuate with the exchange rate. As the dollar strengthens against the Dutch guilder, the value of the Dutch guilder investment falls and as the dollar weakens against the Dutch guilder, the value of the Dutch guilder investment rises.

Investors gain by investing in currencies which will appreciate and lose by investing in currencies which will depreciate.

Figure 7.14
Unhedged DG investment

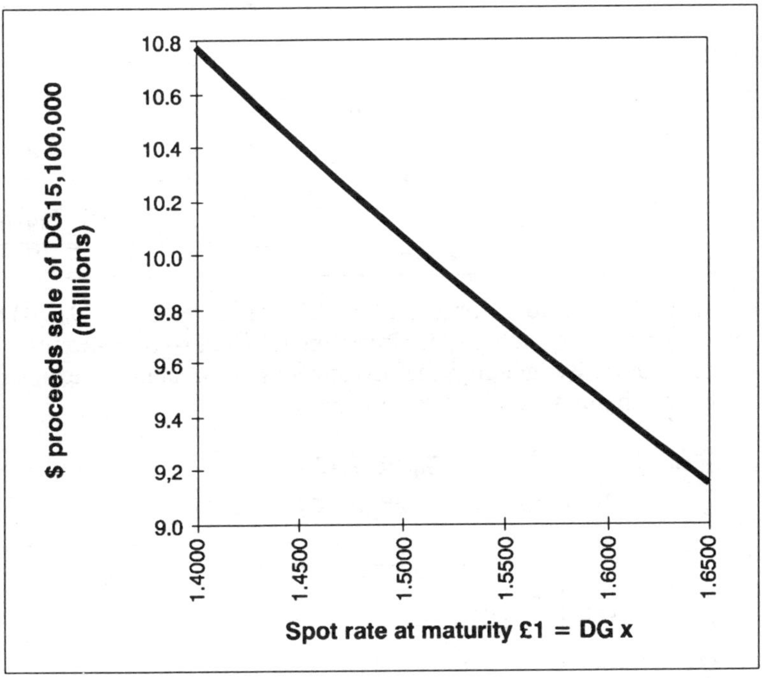

If the investor expects the dollar to appreciate against the Dutch guilder, he or she can hedge (ie eliminate) the foreign exchange exposure by selling DG15,100,000 forward.

Market rates are:

Spot rate	$1	=	DG 1.5000
2 month forward margin			– 0.0200
2 month forward rate	$1	=	DG 1.4800

The investor could hedge by selling DG15,100,000 at the forward rate $1 = DG1.4800.

The dollar proceeds if hedged:

$$\frac{15{,}100{,}000}{1.4800} = \$10{,}202{,}703$$

Exhibit 7.3

Cash flow representation of a hedged DG investment

$			DG	
		Spot		
	10,000,000	1.5000	+15,000,000	
		4%		−15,000,000
			15,000,000	15,000,000
$			**DG**	
		60 days		
+10,202,703		1.5100		−15,100,000
		P + I	+15,100,000	
			15,100,000	15,100,000

Once hedged, the investor knows that he or she will receive $10,202,703 from the conversion of the Dutch guilder investment principal plus interest at the end of the 60 days. By hedging, the investor has eliminated the exposure to exchange rate changes.

Figure 7.15

Hedged and unhedged DG investment

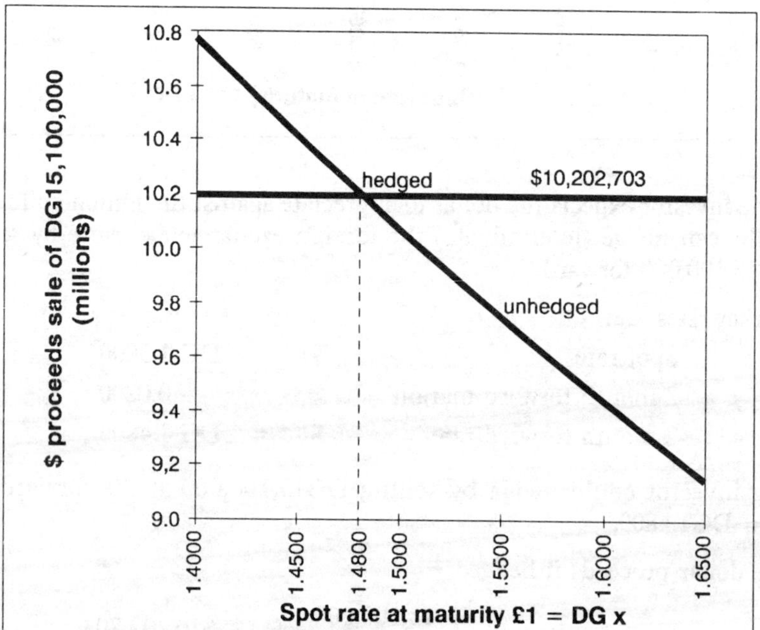

The forward rate $1 = DG1.4800 represents the break-even rate between being hedged and unhedged.[4] If at maturity the spot rate is less than 1.4800, the investor would be better off unhedged than hedged. For example, if the spot rate at maturity is DG1.4000, the proceeds would be worth $10,785,714 if unhedged and $10,202,703 if hedged. On the other hand, if at maturity the spot rate is greater than 1.4800, the investor would be better off hedged than unhedged. For example, if the spot rate at maturity is DG1.5000, the proceeds would be worth $10,202,703 if hedged and $10,000,000 if unhedged.

Effective Yield on Hedged Foreign Currency Investments

By hedging the Dutch guilder principal plus interest at the forward rate of $1 = DG1.4800, the investor knows he or she will receive exactly $10,202,703 from an initial investment of $10,000,000.

$$\begin{aligned}\text{Effective interest earned} &= \$10{,}202{,}703 - 10{,}000{,}000\\ &= \$202{,}703\\ \text{Effective yield \% pa} &= \frac{\text{interest}}{\text{principal}} \times \text{time factor} \times 100\\ &= \frac{202{,}703}{10{,}000{,}000} \times \frac{360}{60} \times 100\\ &= 12.16\% \text{ pa (360 dpy basis)}\end{aligned}$$

The difference between the nominal and effective yield on a foreign currency investment represents the benefit or cost of hedging.

Continuing Example 7.5,

	Effective yield on hedged DG	12.16% pa
	Nominal yield on DG	4.00% pa
∴	Benefit of hedging	8.16% pa

In this case, hedging means selling Dutch guilders at a forward premium (ie buying dollars at a forward discount). The decision to hedge, therefore, involves a benefit equivalent to adding 8.16% pa to the nominal yield.

Because the forward margin reflects the prevailing interest differential between the two currencies, the effective yield on a fully hedged foreign currency investment should be equal to the yield on the local currency.

> A fully hedged foreign currency investment is equivalent to a local currency investment.

4. At the break-even rate, proceeds if hedged = proceeds if unhedged

$$\frac{15{,}100{,}000}{f} = \frac{15{,}100{,}000}{b}$$

$$\therefore\ b = f = 1.4800$$

In practice, the effective yield on a fully hedged foreign currency investment will normally be marginally less than the corresponding local currency yield. This may be because the foreign investment attracts interest-withholding tax or because hedging involves paying an additional bid-offer spread. However, it is sometimes possible to engineer a higher effective yield through a hedged foreign currency investment than by investing directly through the local money market.

Effective Yield on Unhedged Foreign Currency Investments

An investor may purchase a foreign currency or invest through the Eurodollar deposit market without hedging. If the investor in Example 7.4 remains unhedged until maturity when DG15,100,00 are sold spot, he or she will not know the effective yield until the rate at which the Dutch guilders are sold is known. However, it is possible to calculate what the effective yield would be for different values of the spot rate at maturity. For example, if at maturity the spot rate turns out to be DG 1.4500, then the effective yield will be 24.8% pa.

Again using the relationship

$$f = \frac{s\,(1 + r_T\,t)}{(1 + r_C t)}$$

$$f = 1.4500$$

$$s = 1.5000$$

$$r_T = 0.04$$

$$t = 60/360$$

Solving for r_C,

$$1.4500 = 1.5000\,(1 + 0.04 \times 60/360)/(1 + r_C \times 60/360)$$

$$\therefore \quad r_C = 0.248 = 24.8\,\%$$

By allowing f to take different values, it is possible to calculate the effective yield on an unhedged investment for different possible future spot rates.

The unhedged investor gains as the exchange rate falls and loses as it rises. For example, if at maturity the spot rate is 1.5100, the effective yield would be zero. The investor's exchange loss would exactly offset the 4 % pa nominal yield. At maturity, the investor would retrieve the principal without earning any interest. If the spot rate at maturity is higher than 1.5100, the yield will be negative, ie the investor will not only earn no interest but will also lose some of the principal. This demonstrates the risk of unhedged foreign currency investments.

An investor may hedge at any time during the life of the investment. For example, the investor may remain unhedged for the first month, hoping that the forward exchange rate will fall, and then hedge for the remaining period.

Figure 7.16

Effective yields on unhedged DG investment for different spot rates at maturity

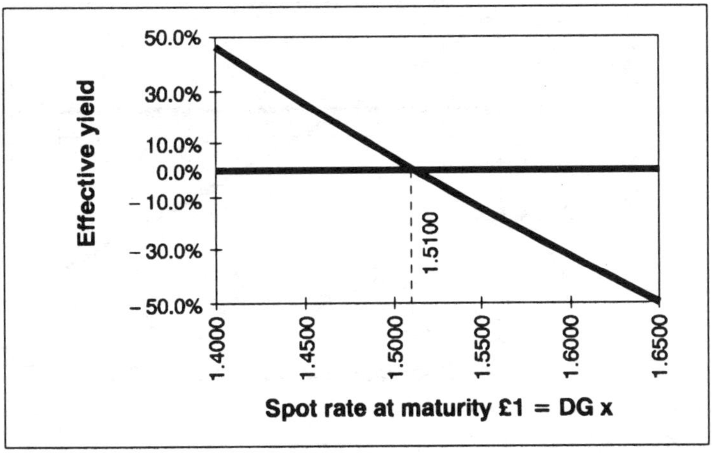

Example 7.6

Suppose the investor hopes to achieve an effective yield of 10% pa for the period. What would the forward rate need to be for the investor to be able to hedge the principal plus interest at an effective yield of 10% pa?

$$s = 1.5000$$

$$f = ?$$

$$r_T = 0.04$$

$$r_C = 0.10$$

$$t = 60/360$$

Solving for f,

$$f = s\frac{(1 + r_T t)}{(1 + r_C t)}$$

$$= \frac{1.5000\,(1 + 0.04/6)}{(1 + 0.10/6)}$$

$$= 1.4852$$

Figure 7.17

Locking in 10% pa effective yield

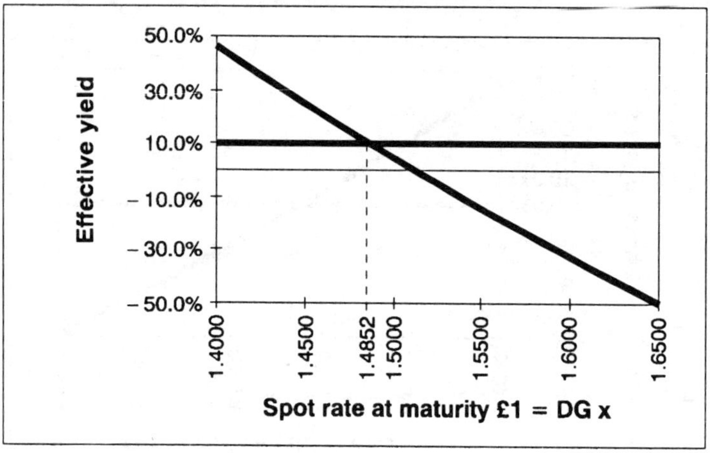

Of course, the investor may never have the opportunity to sell Dutch guilders at a forward rate of 1.4852. However, the investor knows that if the forward rate reaches 1.4852, then an effective yield can be locked in for the period that meets the 10% pa target.

The effective yield on a foreign currency investment can be derived from Equation 6.3,

$$f = s\frac{(1 + r_T t)}{(1 + r_C t)}$$

In Example 7.6,

$$f = 1.4800$$

$$s = 1.5000$$

$$r_T = 0.04$$

$$r_C = ?$$

$$t = 60/360$$

Hence,

$$1.4800 = \frac{(1 + 0.04/6)}{(1 + r_C/6)}$$

$$\therefore \quad r_C = 12.16\% \text{ pa}$$

Example 7.7

A New Zealand exporter has US$5,000,000 income due each year for five years. He could sell forward these US dollars at the prevailing market exchange rates to lock in the following future New Zealand dollar proceeds.

Year	US$ sales	Forward rate	NZ$ proceeds
1	5,000,000	0.6660	7,507,508
2	5,000,000	0.6600	7,733,952
3	5,000,000	0.6450	7,917,656
4	5,000,000	0.6380	8,064,516
5	5,000,000	0.6300	8,143,222
	25,000,000		**39,366,955**

The exporter may prefer to sell all five years of US dollar receivables at the same (par forward) rate. Costs are presumably fairly constant in New Zealand dollar terms so it suits the exporter to have more even cash flows. The exporter may have a budgeted exchange rate for the 5 years. By doing a par forward, the exporter may be able to achieve a better than budget rate every year.

The unadjusted average forward rate

$$= \frac{25{,}000{,}000}{39{,}366{,}955} = 0.6351$$

If the bank agreed to buy the US$5,000,000 from the exporter at 0.6351 each year for five years, the exporter would receive equal proceeds of NZ$7,872,776 each year. The exporter would be better off than if hedging at the outright forward rates because he or she would be receiving more of the higher interest rate currency (NZ$), sooner.

For example, at the end of the first year, the exporter would receive NZ$7,872,776 under the unadjusted par forward versus NZ$7,507,508 under an outright forward. The bank is effectively lending the exporter NZ$365,268. Similarly, at the end of the second year, by providing the exporter with a more favourable rate, the bank effectively advances cash to the exporter. In the third, fourth and fifth years the par forward rate is worse than the outright forward rate, so the exporter repays the cash to the bank.

The bank charges interest by adjusting the par forward rate upwards to the point where the NPV of the New Zealand dollar cash flows under the (adjusted) par forward rate equals the New Zealand dollar cash flows of the five separate (outright) forwards.

If the yield curves are as in Exhibit 7.4, this is achieved if the par forward rate equals 0.6373.

Exhibit 7.4

Cash flows par forward transaction as in Example 7.7

Year	NZ$ rate	US$ rate	Outright forward	NZ$ PV	Par forward	NZ$ PV
1	9.5%	5.7%	0.6660	6,856,171	0.6373	7,164,930
2	9.4%	5.9%	0.6465	6,461,998	0.6373	6,555,283
3	9.3%	6.1%	0.6315	6,063,678	0.6373	6,008,494
4	9.2%	6.3%	0.6200	5,671,367	0.6373	5,517,413
5	9.0%	6.5%	0.6140	5,292,601	0.6373	5,099,101
Total NPV				30,345,816		30,342,221

The difference (NZ$3,595) between the two NPV amounts is a rounding difference which represents profit to the bank. The bank is giving the exporter a set of New Zealand dollar cash flows of lower value than under the outright forwards. Depending on the creditworthiness of the exporter and the ease with which the bank can hedge its cash flow position, it may need to adjust the par forward rate above 0.6373 to be commercial.

Figure 7.18

Par forward

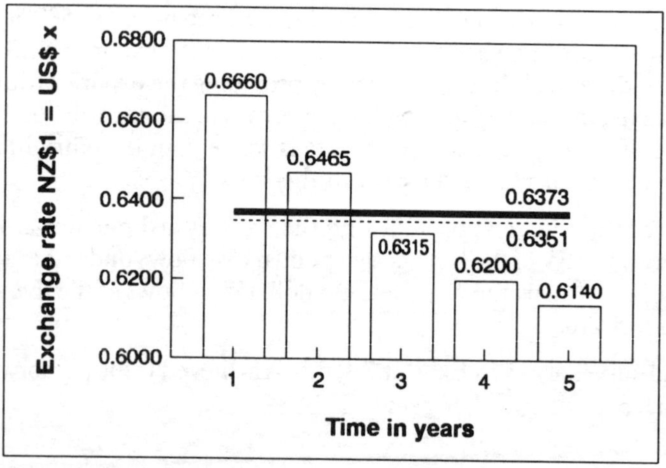

Practice Problems

7.1 Hedging export receivables

A New Zealand exporter is due to receive US$4,560,000 in 62 days from spot.

The exporter considers the alternatives of remaining unhedged and selling the US dollars spot upon receiving them, or hedging by forward selling the US dollar receipts.

Spot rate	NZ$1 = US$ 0.6500
62 day NZ$ rate	9.75 % pa (365 dpy)
62 day US$ rate	5.75 % pa (360 dpy)

(a) Calculate the 62 day forward rate at which the exporter could hedge

(b) If the expectation is that in 62 days time the spot rate will be NZ$1 = US$0.6350, should the exporter hedge or remain unhedged?

(c) What is the break-even rate between being hedged and unhedged?

7.2 Hedged and unhedged foreign currency borrower

A company requires $8,000,000 for 274 days. Two alternatives are considered:

1. borrowing dollars domestically at an interest rate of 9.5% pa (360 dpy);
2. borrowing deutschemarks at an interest cost of 4.5% pa (360 dpy).

(a) Calculate the effective borrowing cost if the spot rate at drawdown is $1 = DM1.4650, and at repayment of principal and interest is $1 = DM1.4540.

(b) Calculate the forward rate at which the company could hedge the deutschemark loan.

(c) Which of the alternatives involves the lower cost?

7.3 Hedged and unhedged foreign currency investments

A funds manager has dollars to invest for six months.

Spot rates

$1 = ¥100
£1 = $1.5000

The funds manager considers three alternatives:

1. Investing the dollars directly at 6 % pa;
2. Selling the dollars to buy yen to invest unhedged at 2% pa;

3. Selling the dollars to buy pounds to invest unhedged at 9% pa.
   - (a) Calculate the effective yield on the unhedged yen and unhedged pound investments if the spot rates at maturity turn out to be \$1 = ¥90 and £1 = \$1.4750.
   - (b) Which of the three alternatives would have yielded the highest return on the investment?

7.4 Break-even rate on unhedged investment

Spot rate	\$1 =	¥106.50	106.60
6 month dollars		6.00%	6.25% pa
6 month yen		2.00%	2.50% pa

A funds manager has dollars to invest for six months.

- (a) If the funds manager elects to use the dollars to buy yen for an offshore investment, what is the break-even rate for the future spot rate?
- (b) If at maturity of the yen investment, the spot rate turns out to be \$1 = ¥103.30/103.40, calculate the effective yield.

Supplementary Questions

7.5 Hedged and unhedged imports

A Pesoland importer has an obligation to pay C10,000,000 in a week's time.

Spot	C1 = P1.5200 / 1.5210
1 week Crowns	8.00% / 8.25%
1 week Pesos	6.50% / 7.00%

- (a) At what rate can the importer hedge the crown liability?
- (b) What would be the cost of the imports in peso terms if the importer decides to hedge?
- (c) If the importer elected not to hedge and he has to buy C10,000,000 at the end of the week at the then spot rate of C1 = P1.5170 / 1.5180, what would be the peso cost of the imports?

7.6 Hedged and unhedged exports

An Australian exporter will receive US\$5,000,000 in one year.

Spot	A\$1 = US\$0.7720 / 25
1 year swap	50 / 45

- (a) What will be the Australian dollar proceeds if it is hedged?

If at the end of the year spot is A$1 = US$ 0.7625 / 30

(b) What would the Australian dollars proceeds be if it is unhedged?

(c) Would the exporter be better off hedged or unhedged?

7.7 Unhedged foreign currency borrowing

A borrower requires Singapore dollars for a year.

Spot	US$1 = S$	1.4100 / 1.4120
1 year US dollars		5.5% / 6.0%
1 year Singapore dollars		2.5% / 3.0%

What would be the effective cost in % pa of raising Singapore dollars today unhedged if the spot rate at the end of the year is US$1 = S$1.4000 / 1.4020?

7.8 Unhedged foreign investment

Spot	$1 = Yen	104.90 / 105.00
6 month dollars		5.5% / 5.75%
6 month yen		0.5% / 1.0%

An investor has dollars to invest. What is the break-even exchange rate for an unhedged investment in yen?

7.9 Unhedged foreign investment

A fund manager has dollars to invest for 6 months.

1 January

Spot	US$1	=	Yen	110.00
	£1	=	US$	1.5000
6 month dollars				5.5%
6 month yen				1.0%
6 month pounds				6.0%

30 June

Spot	US$1	=	Yen	100
	£1	=	US$	1.4750

Three alternatives are considered:

1. Investing in US dollars;
2. Buying yen and investing in yen unhedged;

3. Buying pounds and investing in pounds unhedged.

(a) Calculate the effective yield on each alternative.

(b) Which alternative would have yielded the highest return?

8

Currency Swaps

In this chapter, the concept of the currency swap is introduced. Swaps provide a powerful tool for manipulating cross-currency cash flows without creating a net exchange position. Swaps can be used to roll foreign exchange positions, simulate foreign currency loans or investments and for covered interest arbitrage.

Definition

A *currency swap* is the simultaneous purchase and sale of equivalent amounts of one currency against another currency for different maturities. A swap does not create a net exchange position but it does create mismatched cash flows for a period of time.

A swap is equivalent to two money market transactions.

To illustrate this point, consider the cash flows involved when someone buys Australian dollars spot against US dollars and sells Australian dollars three months forward against US dollars.

Exhibit 8.1

Cash flow representation of a currency swap

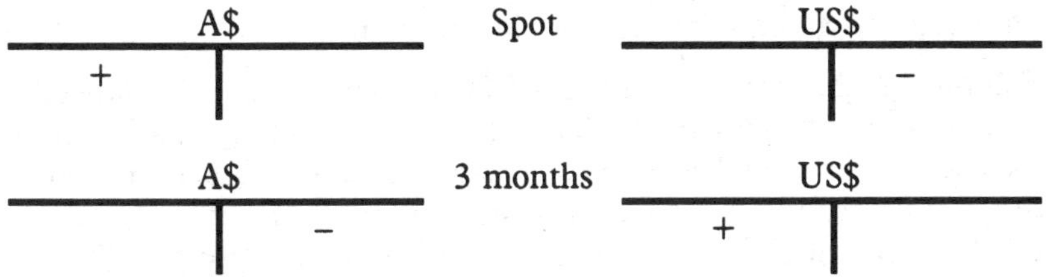

The cash flows are the same as when borrowing Australian dollars for three months and lending US dollars for three months. The pricing of the swap must therefore reflect the interest rates applicable to these money market transactions.

The direction of the cash flows in the second leg of the swap is the opposite of those in the first leg of the swap. Consequently, as with money market transactions, currency swaps create only a temporary mismatch in cash flows. They do not create a net exchange position.

Types of Currency Swaps

A ***pure swap*** is a swap in which both the spot and forward transactions are done simultaneously with the *same* counterparty.

An ***engineered swap*** is a swap in which the spot and forward transactions are done with *different* counterparties.

Swap Rates

Swap rates (previously referred to as forward margins) reflect the difference between spot rates and forward rates.

Swap rate = forward rate − spot rate **Equation 8.1**

Swap rates are not exchange rates. They are merely differentials. Technically they should not be referred to as "rates" (ie ratios). However, the term "swap rate" is used here to conform with common practice.

Exhibit 8.2

Swap rates are differentials not exchange rates

			Bid	Offer
Spot rates	A$1	=	US$0.7700	0.7705
3 month swap rates			– 0.0032	– 0.0022
3 month forward rates	A$1	=	US$0.7668	0.7683

The ***swap bid rate*** is the *differential* at which the quoting bank is willing to buy forward the commodity currency in the swap.

In Exhibit 8.2, the swap bid rate is – 0.0032, showing that the Australian dollar is at a forward *discount* of 32 points. A bank quoting a swap bid rate of – 0.0032 is willing to sell Australian dollars spot and buy Australian dollars three months forward at a differential of 32 points. By buying Australian dollars forward at 0.7668 and selling Australian dollars spot at 0.7700, the bank *receives* the benefit of the 32 points forward discount.

The ***swap offer rate*** is the *differential* at which the quoting bank is willing to sell forward the commodity currency in the swap.

In Exhibit 8.2, the swap offer rate is – 0.0022, showing that the Australian dollar is at a forward *discount* of 22 points. A bank quoting a swap offer rate of – 0.0022 is willing to buy Australian dollars spot and sell Australian dollars three months forward at a differential of 22 points. By buying Australian dollars spot at 0.7705 and selling Australian dollars forward at 0.7683, the bank *pays* the 22 points forward discount.

The quoting bank will quote its bid and offer swap rates such that it receives the greater benefit or pays the lesser cost. It will buy the commodity currency at a higher forward discount (or swap benefit) and it will sell the commodity currency at a lower forward discount (or swap cost).

In bid-offer quotations, it is not necessary to show the sign of swap rates to identify them as forward premiums or discounts. If the swap bid rate is a larger number than the swap offer rate, it is a negative number implying that the commodity currency is at a forward discount. On the other hand, if the swap bid rate is a smaller number than the swap offer rate (ie it looks like an exchange rate quotation, in that the bid rate is less than the offer rate), then the swap rate is a positive number implying that the commodity currency is at a forward premium.

Exhibit 8.3

Swap rates reflect forward premiums and discounts

3 month swap rates

A$ commodity currency, US$ terms currency

Bid	Offer	
		A$ is at forward discount
32	22	A$ interest rate is higher than US$ interest rate

US$ commodity currency, Italian lira terms currency

Bid	Offer	
		US$ is at forward premium
27	33	US$ interest rate is lower than lira interest rate

Determining the Spot Rate in a Swap

The spot rate on which a pure swap is based is virtually irrelevant within a reasonably close range. It is the swap rate reflecting the interest differential which determines the benefit or cost of the swap. Consider a swap where the quoting bank sells A$1,000,000 spot and buys A$1,000,000 at a three month forward discount of 32 points based on slightly different spot rates 0.7700 and 0.7705.

The forward discount of 32 points is worth US$3,200 per A$1,000,000 of the swap, regardless of the spot rate upon which the swap is based. The quoting bank would marginally prefer the spot deal to be done at 0.7705 as it would have the use of an additional US$500 for three months. However, the incremental benefit is trivial (US$7.50, assuming the US$500 can be invested for three months at 6.0% pa). In practice, the parties to the swap generally agree on a mutually acceptable spot rate. The quoting bank usually suggests which spot rate should be used. This is commonly the mid rate at the time.

Exhibit 8.4

Cash flows in a swap using slightly different spot rates

Based on spot 0.7700

A$		Spot	US$	
	− 1,000,000	0.7700	+ 770,000	

A$		3 months	US$	
+ 1,000,000		0.7668		− 766,800

Benefit of swap = US$ (770,000 – 766,800) = US$ 3,200

Based on spot 0.7705

A$		Spot	US$	
	− 1,000,000	0.7705	+ 770,500	

A$		3 months	US$	
+ 1,000,000		0.7673		− 767,300

Benefit of swap = US$ 770,500 – 767,300 = US$ 3,200 (again)

Pure Swaps and Engineered Swaps

In a pure swap, both legs of the swap are based on the same spot rate. In an engineered swap, because the two legs of the swap are transacted with different counterparties, the two deals will generally be based on different spot rates. Consequently, the calling bank or customer will normally find it more economical to enter into pure swaps rather than engineered swaps.

If the bid-offer spread is 5 points, the engineered swap will cost the customer an additional five points because he or she will have to pay the spot bid-offer spread. In a pure swap, the customer avoids the need to pay the spot bid-offer spread.

Exhibit 8.5

Pure swaps and engineered swaps

				Bid	Offer
Spot rates	A$1	=	US$	0.7700	0.7705
3 month swap rates				0.0032	0.0022
3 month forward rates	A$1	=	US$	0.7668	0.7683

A customer wants to buy A$1,000,000 spot and sell A$1,000,000 three months forward.

	Pure swap			Engineered swap
Buy A$ spot	0.7700	or	0.7705	0.7705
Sell A$ forward	0.7668		0.7673	0.7668
Cost of swap	**0.0032**		**0.0032**	**0.0037**

Short Dated Swaps

Swaps where one or both of the transactions are value today or tomorrow are known as ***short dated swaps***. The swap from today until tomorrow is known as the overnight swap and from tomorrow to the spot value date is called the tom/next swap. The swap rate from today until spot is determined by adding together the overnight and tom/next swap rates.

Short dated swap rates are often quoted with the offer rate before the bid rate. This is an unfortunate convention. To avoid confusion, it should be remembered that the quoting bank always quotes so that the points are in its favour. If the customer or calling bank is getting the benefit of the points, the smaller number of points will apply. However, if the customer or the calling bank are paying the (cost of the) points, the larger number will apply.

Suppose that today is Friday 6 September and spot value is Tuesday 10 September.

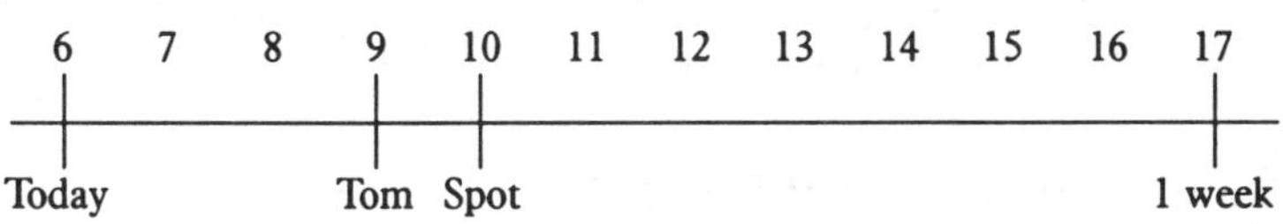

A bank is quoting:

Spot $1 = DM 1.5292 / 1.5302

Swap Rates:	
Overnight	8.4 / 8.1
Tom/next	2.8 / 2.7
1 week	13.0 / 12.5

At what rate can a customer *buy* dollars outright value tomorrow (9 September)?

The customer will buy dollars at the offer rate so the quote will be based on the spot offer rate 1.5302. The dollar is the high interest currency and so at a forward discount. It will, therefore, be at a short dated premium. The one week forward rate would be 12.5 points below the spot rate so the value tomorrow rate must be some number of points above the spot rate. Should that number be 2.8 or 2.7? The quoting bank will be better off it it sells dollars value tomorrow at a higher rate, so it will charge the customer 2.8 points premium. The bank would quote:

Value Tom = 1.5302 + 0.00028 = 1.53048

By buying dollars value tomorrow, the customer will be getting the use of the higher interest currency first. So the customer will have to buy the dollars at a worse (ie higher) exchange rate. Therefore, the swap points need to be added to the spot rate and the higher number of points will apply.

At what rate can a customer *sell* dollars outright value today (6 September)?

To determine the outright value today rate, it is necessary to add the appropriate overnight and tom/next swap rates together.

The customer will sell dollars at the bid rate so the quote is based on the spot bid rate 1.5292. Because the customer is giving up the use of the high interest currency, he or she will earn the benefit of the swap points by selling dollars value today at a rate higher than the spot rate. The quoting bank would give the customer the fewer number of swap points, namely, 2.7 for overnight and 8.1 for the tom/next 3 day run. The bank would quote:

Value Today = 1.5292 + 0.00027 + 0.00081 = 1.53028

It is possible to have a pure swap from a short date until a forward date. For example, a customer might want to buy dollars value 17 September and sell dollars value today (6 September). The quoting bank would give the customer the smaller number of points benefit.

Benefit of swap 17 September over 6 September = 12.5 + 2.7 + 8.1 = 23.3 points

Assuming the pure swap is based on a spot rate of 1.5300, the customer would sell dollars value today at 1.5300 + 0.00027 + 0.00081 = 1.53108 and buy dollars value 17 September at 1.5300 – 0.00125 = 1.52875.

Note: 1.53108 – 1.52875 = 0.00233.

Applications of Currency Swaps

Currency swaps provide a powerful tool for manipulating cross currency cash flows without creating a net exchange position. The applications of swaps include:

- rolling foreign exchange positions
- simulated foreign currency loans
- simulated foreign currency investments
- covered interest arbitrage.

Swaps can also be used to open and close gaps. This is covered in Chapter 9.

Rolling a Foreign Exchange Position

Swaps can be used to extend or shorten the maturity date of a foreign exchange position. The swap may be based either on current market or historic rates.

Example 8.1

Three months ago, an Australian importer purchased US$10,000,000 three months forward at an outright rate of 0.7500 to hedge expected US dollar payments. The original forward contract is maturing in two days time, ie today's spot value date. The ship has been delayed and the importer will not be required to make the US dollar payment for a further month. The current interbank rate scenario is:

Spot rate	A$1 =	US$0.7500	0.7505
1 month (30 days) Australian dollars		7.50%	7.75 % (365 dpy)
1 month (30 days) US dollars		6.00%	6.25 % (360 dpy)
1 month swap rate		10	7

It is initially assumed that, coincidentally, the spot rate is the same as the original outright forward rate (0.7500). This is highly unlikely in practice but nevertheless possible.

One alternative would be for the importer to take delivery of the US dollars and to place them on the money market for one month. The importer would need to borrow Australian dollars for one month to fund the purchase of the US dollars. Assuming the importer could borrow Australian dollars at 7.75% pa and deposit US dollars at 6.0% pa, the resulting cash flows would be as in Exhibit 8.6.

Exhibit 8.6

Rolling an exchange position through the money market

Importer's cash flows

A$		Spot	US$	
	− 13,333,333	0.7500	+ 10,000,000	
+ 13,333,333		**7.75%**		
13,333,333	13,333,333	**6.0 %**		**− 10,000,000**
			10,000,000	10,000,000

A$		1 month	US$	
	− 13,418,231		**+ 10,050,000**	

$$\text{Effective forward rate} = \frac{10{,}050{,}000}{13{,}418{,}231} = 0.7490$$

A second alternative would be for the importer to roll the position through a swap. This would require selling US dollars spot and buying US dollars one month forward. Thinking in terms of the commodity currency, the importer would buy Australian dollars spot and sell Australian dollars one month forward. Assuming the importer deals at the above market rates and the pure swap is based on the spot rate 0.7500, the importer would buy Australian dollars spot at 0.7500 and sell Australian dollars one month forward at 0.7500 – 0.0010 = 0.7490. The cash flows would be as in Exhibit 8.7

Exhibit 8.7

Rolling an exchange position through market swap

Importer's cash flows

A$		Spot	US$	
	– 13,333,333	**0.7500**	+ 10,000,000	
+ 13,333,333		**0.7500**		**– 10,000,000**
13,333,333	13,333,333		10,000,000	10,000,000

A$		1 month	US$	
	– 13,351,135	**0.7490**	**+ 10,000,000**	

$$\text{Effective forward rate} = \frac{10{,}000{,}000}{13{,}351{,}135} = 0.7490$$

Rolling the outright forward exchange position through a swap produces the same outcome as rolling it through two money market transactions. Both methods involved an effective new forward rate of A$1 = US$0.7490.

In practice, the importer would probably not be able to borrow at the interbank offer rate. The importer would have to borrow at a margin above the interbank offer rate. Depending on the importer's credit rating, this margin might be, say, 50 basis points. In that case, the importer would borrow the A$13,333,333 at 8.25% pa (ie 7.75% + 0.50%). However, the importer may be able to access the interbank borrowing rate if the position is rolled through a swap. So rolling through a swap will generally be more economical than rolling through two money market transactions.

If the importer had to borrow the Australian dollars at 8.25%, the cash flows would be as in Exhibit 8.8. The additional 50 basis points would worsen the effective forward rate by 4 exchange points to A$1 = US$0.7486.

Exhibit 8.8

Rolling an exchange position through the money market

Importer's cash flows with 50 basis point credit margin

A$	A$	Spot	US$	US$
	− 13,333,333	0.7500	+ 10,000,000	
+ 13,333,333		8.25%		
		6.0%		− 10,000,000
13,333,333	13,333,333		10,000,000	10,000,000

A$	A$	1 month	US$	US$
	− 13,425,000		+ 10,050,000	

$$\text{Effective forward rate} = \frac{10,050,000}{13,425,000} = 0.7486$$

Rolling an exchange position through a swap also has the advantage that it is off balance sheet and will use less credit lines and capital.

A further complication exists if the spot rate at the time does not coincide with the original forward outright rate. Suppose, for example, that at the time of doing the rollover the spot rate has risen to A$1 = US$0.8000. The cash flows for a market rate swap would be as in Exhibit 8.9.

Exhibit 8.9

Rolling an exchange position through market swap with spot 0.8000

Importer's cash flows

A$	A$	Spot	US$	US$
	− 13,333,333		+ 10,000,000	
+ 12,500,000		0.8000		− 10,000,000
+ 833,333		8.25 %		
13,333,333	13,333,333		10,000,000	10,000,000

A$	A$	1 month	US$	US$
	− 12,515,645	0.7990	+ 10,000,000	
	− 839,062			
	13,354,707			

Selling US$10,000,000 value spot at a rate of A$1 = US$0.8000 will generate A$ 12,500,000. This is insufficient to meet the obligation to pay A$13,333,333 under the forward contract maturing at the rate of A$1 = US$0.7500. The importer will need to borrow the A$833,333 shortfall to clear his or her obligation. Assuming this is borrowed at 8.25%, the Australian dollar obligation due at the new forward date will be A$12,515,645 (US$10,000,000 at 0.7990) plus A$839,062 (ie 833,333 × (1 + 0.0825 × 1 /12) making a total of A$13,354,707.

$$\text{Effective forward rate} = \frac{10{,}000{,}000}{12{,}515{,}645 + 839{,}062} = 0.7487$$

The effective forward rate in the case where the spot has risen to A$1 = US$0.8000 is 3 points worse than if the spot rate was A$1 = US$0.7500. The 3 points reflect the interest cost of borrowing the A$833,333 cash shortfall for the month.

If the spot rate at the time of rolling was below the original forward rate, the effective forward rate would be improved because the spot movement would generate a positive cash flow at the original maturity date which could be invested and earn interest.

This issue is likely to be most significant if there has been a large spot movement or the time period is long and if the interest rate in the currency in which the cash flows occur is high.

Historic Rate Rollovers

A third alternative is for the importer to do an ***historic rate rollover***. If the swap is based on a spot rate which is set equal to the historic rate, there will be no net cash flow on the spot date.

Exhibit 8.10

Historic rate rollover

Importer's cash flows

A$		Spot	US$	
	− 13,333,333	0.7500	+ 10,000,000	
+ 13,333,333		**0.7500**		**− 10,000,000**
13,333,333	13,333,333		10,000,000	10,000,000
A$		**1 month**	**US$**	
	?	?	**+ 10,000,000**	

How is the forward rate determined in an historic rate rollover?

It would be incorrect to merely apply the market swap rate – 0.0010 to the historic rate 0.7500 to arrive at an historic forward rate of 0.7490. To do so would be to overlook two issues. First, as the terms currency amount is being held constant, the value of 10 points is worth considerably more at 0.7500 than at 0.8000. Secondly, while banks commonly deal at historic rates for their corporate customers, they only deal interbank at market rates. Consequently, the bank will do an historic rate swap with the importer and a market rate swap with another bank. The bank's cash flows would be as in Exhibit 8.11.

Exhibit 8.11

Historic rate rollover matched by market rate swap

Bank's cash flows

A$		Spot	US$	
	– 13,333,333	0.7500	+ 10,000,000	
+ 12,500,000		0.8000		– 10,000,000
+ 833,333		7.75%		
13,333,333	13,333,333		10,000,000	10,000,000

A$		3 months	US$	
+ 13,354,701		0.7488		– 10,000,000
	– 12,515,645	0.7990	+ 10,000,000	
	– 838,715	P + I		
	341	Profit[1]		
13,354,701	13,354,708		10,000,000	10,000,000

$$\text{Effective forward rate} = \frac{10{,}000{,}000}{12{,}515{,}645 + 838{,}715} = 0.7488$$

On the spot date, the bank will experience a cash shortfall of A$833,333. In effect, the bank inherits the importer's loss temporarily. By funding this loss at 7.75% pa, the bank incurs an incremental cost of A$838,715 payable at the final maturity date.

The effective forward rate 0.7488 will be marginally better for the importer than if rolled at market rates 0.7487. This reflects the difference between funding the cash flow difference at 8.25% pa for the importer and 7.75% pa for the bank. The bank might well be justified in arguing that the importer's

1. The rounding difference of A$341 constitutes profit to the bank.

borrowing rate of 8.25% pa should be used to calculate the historic forward rate, as the bank is taking a credit risk on the importer by the extension of credit for the additional month. If this is the case, the forward rate in the historic rate rollover will be equal to the effective rate for a market rate swap. In practice, however, banks are not inclined to make such adjustments.

The Central Banks of a number of countries have prohibited the use of historic rate rollovers because they have been used to conceal losses which have resulted from foreign exchange trading. Where they are permitted, historic rate rollovers can be used as a convenient way of extending hedge cover without having to manage the residual cash flows on the rollover date. Companies using HRRs should ensure that they are priced correctly as explained above. A good control to avoid inappropriate use of HRRs is to require management sign-off before they can be transacted.

Early Take-ups

Swaps can also be used to shorten the maturity date of a foreign exchange position. As when extending the maturity date, the swap may be based on current or historic rates. A swap based on historic rates which shortens the maturity of a foreign exchange contract is known as an ***early take-up*** or ***pre-delivery***. As with historic rate rollovers, the pricing of an early take-up should take account of the funding cost or investment benefit of bringing profits or losses forward.

Example 8.2

Three months ago, a New Zealand exporter sold US$6,700,000 six months forward at an outright rate of 0.6700 to hedge future US dollar receivables. The contract has three months to run, but the exporter now finds she will be receiving the US$6,700,000 value spot. The exporter would like to bring the maturity of the forward contract back into line with the actual cash flows.

The current market rates are:

Spot rate	NZ$1	=	US$0.6795	0.6805
3 month NZ dollars			9.5 %	9.6 %
3 month US dollars			6.0 %	6.1 %
3 month swap rate			– 60	– 57

The exporter could enter into a market rate swap in which US$6,700,000 would be sold spot at the mid rate 0.6800 and US$6,700,000 bought one month forward at 0.6800 – 0.0060 = 0.6740. The cash flows would be as in Exhibit 8.12. The exporter would have disposed of the US$6,700,000 which she will receive value spot, but will be left with a cash flow surplus of NZ$59,757.65 at the 3 month date. The exporter could square the 3 month cash flows by borrowing NZ$58,357.08 for 3 months at 9.6% pa.

$$\text{PV (NZ\$ 59,757.65)} = \frac{59{,}757.65}{(1 + 0.096 \times 3/12)} = \text{NZ\$ 58,357.08}$$

Exhibit 8.12

Swap at market rates
Exporter's cash flows

NZ$		Spot	US$	
+ 9,852,941.18		0.6800		– 6,700,000.00
+ 58,357.08		**9.6 %**		
9,911,298.26		**0.6760**		6,700,000

NZ$		3 months	US$	
10,000,000.00		0.6700		6,700,000.00
	– 9,940,242.35	0.6740	+ 6,700,000.00	
	– 59,575.65			
10,000,000.00	10,000,000.00		6,700,000.00	6,700,000.00

$$\text{Effective spot rate} = \frac{6,700,000.00}{9,852,942.18 + 58,357.08} = 0.6760$$

Alternatively, the exporter could do an early take-up. Under an early take-up, the forward rate is set equal to the original forward rate so that no cash flow occurs at the forward date. The spot rate is determined by adjusting the historic forward rate for the interest cost or benefit of squaring the forward cash flows through the money market.

Exhibit 8.13

Early take-up
Exporter's cash flows

NZ$		Spot	US$	
9,911,242.60		0.6760		– 6,700,000.00

NZ$		3 months	US$	
10,000,000.00		0.6700		– 6,700,000.00
	– 10,000,000.00	0.6700	+ 6,700,000.00	
10,000,000.00	10,000,000.00		6,700,000.00	6,700,000.00

The spot rate for the early take-up is equal to the effective spot rate calculated in Exhibit 8.12. There is a minor difference in the New Zealand dollar amount on the spot date due to rounding.[2]

Simulated Foreign Currency Loans

Currency swaps provide a means of generating liquidity in another currency. A borrower may wish to borrow Hong Kong dollars for three months. Perhaps the borrower has no facility in place through which either the local Hong Kong dollar or Euro-Hong Kong dollar money markets can be accessed.

Provided he or she can borrow another currency, say US dollars, and enter into a US$/HK$ swap, the means exist to generate the Hong Kong dollars required. Generating liquidity in one currency by borrowing another currency and entering into a currency swap is known as a ***simulated loan.***

The cash flows are equivalent to borrowing Hong Kong dollars for the period.

Exhibit 8.14

Simulated HK$ loan

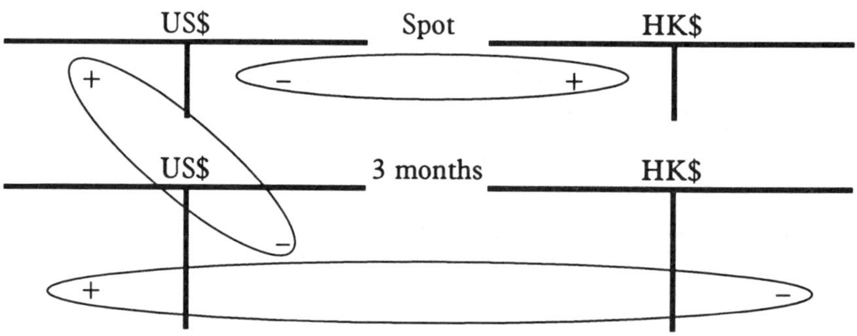

Step 1. Borrow US$ for 3 months.

Step 2. Sell US$ and buy HK$ spot.
Buy US$ and sell HK$ 3 months forward.

The borrower has borrowed US dollars and swapped them into Hong Kong dollars.

2. NZ$ 9,911,242.60 – 9,911,298.26 = NZ$ 55.66

Example 8.3

Spot rate	US$1 = HK$ 7.8000		7.8020
3 month (90 days) US dollars		6.75% pa	7.00% pa (360 dpy)
3 months swap rate		280	300

At what effective interest rate can the borrower generate Hong Kong dollars for three months through a simulated loan?

To generate Hong Kong dollars, the borrower should:

Step 1. Borrow US dollars at 7.00% pa

Step 2. Swap US dollars for Hong Kong dollars for three months, ie sell US dollars spot at 7.8010 (mid rate) and buy US dollars forward at 7.8310 (ie 7.8010 – 0.0300).

$$s = 7.8010$$

$$r_C = 0.07$$

$$r_T = ?$$

$$t = 90/360$$

$$f = 7.8310$$

$$f = s\frac{(1 + r_T t)}{(1 + r_C t)}$$

$$\therefore \quad 7.8310 = 7.8010\,\frac{(1 + r_T/4)}{(1 + 0.07/4)}$$

$$\therefore \quad r_T = 8.57\% \text{ pa}$$

The cash flows in the Hong Kong dollar borrowing are uneven. The repayment amount (principal plus interest) will be more than the amount borrowed (principal only). Consequently, to generate Hong Kong dollars through a simulated loan the swap needs to be for unequal amounts of Hong Kong dollars. The spot amount of Hong Kong dollars is determined by the required Hong Kong dollar principal. The principal amount of the US dollar loan is determined by converting the required number of Hong Kong dollars at the spot rate. The forward amount of Hong Kong dollars is determined by converting the forward amount of US dollars (principal plus interest) at the forward exchange rate.

Exhibit 8.15

Simulated loan HK$10,000,000 for 3 months

US$		Spot	HK$	
	−1,281,887	7.8010	+ 10,000,000	
+ 1,281,887		7.0%		
1,281,887	1,281,887			

US$		3 months	HK$	
	− 1,304,320	P + I		
+ 1,304,320		7.8310		− 10,214,130
1,304,320	1,304,320			

The effective interest rate of the simulated Hong Kong dollars loan

$$= \frac{\text{Interest}}{\text{Principal}} \times \text{time}$$

$$= \frac{(10{,}214{,}130 - 10{,}000{,}000)}{10{,}000{,}000} \times \frac{1200}{4}$$

$$= 8.57\% \text{ pa}$$

The effective cost of borrowing a currency through a simulated loan may be less than the cost of borrowing it directly through the money market. Borrowing a foreign currency may attract interest withholding tax which adds to the effective interest cost. It may be possible to avoid incurring interest withholding tax if the company generates the foreign currency through a simulated loan involving a local currency borrowing.

In some cases, exchange control restrictions may prevent non-residents from borrowing the currency at all. Provided a swap market exists, it is possible to generate liquidity in the restricted currency.

It is possible to raise local currency by borrowing a foreign currency and swapping it into local currency. This would be appropriate when the effective interest cost of local currency through a swap is cheaper than the domestic cost of funds or when domestic funds are not easily accessed.

Example 8.4

A borrower requires deutschemarks for three months and considers two alternatives:

1. Borrowing deutschemarks directly through the Euro-deutschemark market; or
2. Borrowing dollars domestically and swapping them into deutschemarks.

Spot rate	US$1	=	DM 1.4740	1.4750
3 month DM			3.00% pa	3.25% pa
3 month US$			5.50% pa	5.625% pa
3 month swap rates			95	81

Alternative 1. Borrowing deutschemarks directly attracts 10% interest withholding tax.

Therefore,

$$\text{Effective cost of borrowing DM directly} = 3.25 \times 1.1$$
$$= 3.575\% \text{ pa}$$

Alternative 2. Borrowing dollars at 5.625% pa and selling the dollars spot at 1.4745 then buying dollars forward at 1.4745 – 0.0081 = 1.4664. (Swap based on spot mid rate)

Exhibit 8.16

Cash flows of simulated DM loan

US$		Spot	DM	
	– 678,196.00	1.4745	+ 1,000,000	
+ 678,196.00				
678,196.00	678,196.00			

US$		3 months	DM	
	– 687,733.13	P + I		
+ 687,733.13		1.4664		– 1,008,475
687,733.13	687,733.13			

$$\text{Effective DM rate} = \frac{(1{,}008{,}475 - 1{,}000{,}000)}{1{,}000{,}000} \times \frac{1200}{3}$$
$$= 3.39\ \%\ \text{pa}$$

$$s = 1.4745$$
$$f = 1.4664$$
$$r_C = 0.05625$$
$$t = 90/360$$
$$f = \frac{s(1 + r_T t)}{(1 + r_C t)}$$
$$\therefore \quad 1.4664 = 1.4745 \frac{(1 + r_T/4)}{(1 + 0.05625/4)}$$
$$\therefore \quad r_T = 3.39\% \text{ pa}$$

Alternative 2 provides a cheaper means of raising deutschemarks than Alternative 1. That is, in this example it turns out to be cheaper to raise deutschemarks through a simulated loan than borrowing deutschemarks directly and paying interest withholding tax.

Simulated Foreign Currency Investments

Currency swaps provide the means to simulate foreign currency investments. Consider an investor with yen to place for three months. It may be possible to place them directly through the domestic yen money market or invest them in a Euro-yen deposit. Alternatively, the investor can enter into a yen/dollar swap and invest the dollars in the domestic deposit market. Investing a foreign currency indirectly through a swap and a domestic placement is known as a ***simulated foreign currency investment.***

Exhibit 8.17

Simulated investment

Step 1. Swap yen for dollars for 3 months ie buy dollars and sell yen spot, and sell dollars and buy yen forward.

Step 2. Invest dollars for 3 months.

The cash flows are equivalent to investing yen for three months.

Example 8.5

A fund manager has ¥100,000,000 to invest for 3 months. Calculate the effective yield of swapping into dollars and investing the dollars. Assume no interest withholding tax is payable.

Spot rate	$1	=	¥104.90	105.00
3 month dollars			5.5% pa	5.625% pa
3 month yen			1.25% pa	1.50% pa
3 month swap rate			– 1.13	– 1.04

Alternative 1. Invest yen directly through the money market. Effective yield from investing yen directly = 1.25% pa.

Alternative 2. Swap yen into dollars by buying dollars spot at 104.95 and selling dollars forward at 104.95 – 1.13 = 103.82, and then investing the dollars at 5.5% pa.

Exhibit 8.18

Simulated yen investment

$		Spot	¥	
+ 952,834.68		104.95		– 100,000,000
	– 952,834.68	5.5%		
952,834.68	952,834.68			

$		3 months	¥	
+ 952,834.18		Principal		
+ 13,101.48		Interest		
	– 965,936.16	103.82	+ 100,282,108	
965,936.16	965,936.16			

$$\text{Effective yield} = \frac{(100{,}282{,}108 - 100{,}000{,}000)}{100{,}000{,}000} \times \frac{1200}{3} = 1.13\ \%\ \text{pa}$$

$$s = 104.95$$
$$f = 103.82$$
$$r_C = 0.055$$
$$t = 3/12$$
$$f = \frac{s\,(1 + r_T t)}{(1 + r_C t)}$$
$$\therefore\quad 103.82 = \frac{104.95\,(1 + r_T \times 3/12)}{(1 + 0.055 \times 3/12)}$$
$$\therefore\quad r_T = 1.13\%\ \text{pa}$$

That is, the effective yield from the simulated yen investment is 1.13% pa. Alternative 1 provides a higher yield than Alternative 2. That is, in this example the yield on the direct yen placement is higher than on the simulated yen investment.

Notice it is not the case that the more involved structure is better. In Example 8.4, borrowing deutschemarks indirectly through the swap market turned out to be cheaper because it avoided interest withholding tax. However, in general, unless some artificial constraint such as capital controls or withholding tax exists it is more economical to use the structure which crosses the least number of bid-offer spreads.

Covered Interest Arbitrage

If swap rates are inconsistent with the prevailing spot rate and interest rates, it may be possible to profit from a risk-free set of transactions by taking advantage of the inconsistent set of rates in the market.

Example 8.6

Spot rate	US$1	=	DM1.4740	1.4750
3 month US$			5.50%	5.625% pa
3 month DM			3.00%	3.25% pa
3 month swap rate			95	81

With an announcement of an increase in the dollar discount rate, a dealer checked the money market rates and observed that the three month Eurodollar had increased to 6.0/6.125% pa, while the three month dollar/deutschemark swap rate remained unchanged at 95/81. What should the dealer do to immediately profit from the situation?

Exhibit 8.19

Covered interest arbitrage

	Before		**After**	
	Bid	Offer	Bid	Offer
3 month dollar rate	5.5% pa	5.625% pa	6.0% pa	6.125% pa
3 month DM rate	3.0% pa	3.25% pa	3.0% pa	3.25% pa
Available				
3 month swap rate	95	81	**95**	81
Equilibrium				
3 month swap rate	95	81	113	**100**

Because the swap rates have not yet moved to reflect the prevailing market interest rates, the swap rates available after the announcement are less than the equilibrium swap rates implied by the prevailing interest rates. In the swap market, the dollar is temporarily available at a smaller than market discount. The arbitrage opportunity lies in selling forward the dollar at the below equilibrium swap rate and covering through the money market.

Exhibit 8.20

Covered interest arbitrage

via two money market deals

Action in the swap market

1. Buy dollars spot at 1.4745
2. Sell dollars forward at 1.4650 — Cost = 95 points

Action in the money market

3. Lend dollars 3 months at 6.0% pa — Benefit = 100 points
4. Borrow DM 3 months at 3.25% pa

Net gain = 5 points

$		Spot	DM	
+ 1,000,000		**1.4745**		**– 1,474,500**
	– 1,000,000		+ 1,474,500	
1,000,000	1,000,000		1,474,500	1,474,500

$		3 months	DM	
	– 1,015,000	**1.4650**	**+ 1,486,975**	
+ 1,015,000				– 1,486,480
		Profit		495
1,015,00	1,015,000		1,486,975	1,486,975

Profit = DM1,486,975 – 1,486,480 = DM495[3] (ie 5 points)

To crystallise the profit in deutschemarks, it is necessary to do an uneven swap for a spot amount of $1,000,000 (principal) and a forward amount of $1,015,000 (principal + interest).

It is likely that some swaps price makers will immediately adjust their swap rates to reflect the now prevailing interest rates. If so, it would be possible to arbitrage the swap rates of those dealers who have not yet adjusted their prices.

3. The DM 5 difference between the profit calculated using two money market deals and that using two swaps is merely due to rounding.

	Bid	Offer
Unadjusted swap rates	**95**	81
Adjusted swap rates	113	**100**

An arbitrage opportunity exists because there is a bid rate which is higher than the offer rate. Remember, swap rates are differentials. These are negative numbers: – 0.95 > –1.00.

Exhibit 8.21

Covered interest arbitrage via two swap deals

Action in the unadjusted swap market

1.	Buy dollars spot at	1.4745			
	Sell dollars forward at	1.4650	Cost	=	95 points

Action in the adjusted swap market

2.	Sell dollars spot at	1.4745			
	Buy dollars forward at	1.4645	Benefit	=	100 points
			Net gain	=	5 points

Assuming the above set of transactions is done for a principal amount of \$1,000,000, the profit from the arbitrage would be equal to DM1,000,000 × 0.0005 = DM500.

\$		Spot	DM	
+ 1,000,000		1.4745		– 1,474,500
	– 1,000,000	1.4745	+ 1,474,500	
1,000,000	1,000,000		1,474,500	1,474,500

\$		3 months	DM	
	– 1,000,000	1.4650	+ 1,465,000	
+ 1,000,000		1.4645		– 1,464,500
		Profit		**500**
1,000,000	1,000,000		1,465,000	1,465,000

Profit = DM 500[4] (ie 5 points)

4. The DM 5 difference between the profit calculated using two money market deals and that using two swaps is merely due to rounding.

As there is no market risk involved in covered interest arbitrage, the amount of profit to be made is merely a function of the volume of the transaction. If the arbitrage could be performed with a principal amount of $100,000,000, the profit would be DM50,000. The market rates will quickly adjust toward equilibrium levels so that the arbitrage opportunity will be short lived. In practice, it may only exist for a matter of seconds. A market risk exists to the extent that, unless all legs of the arbitrage can be done simultaneously, there is a risk that one or more of the rates will move so that the transaction is no longer profitable. Arbitrageurs who endeavour to perform the arbitrage on too large a volume may find that bid-offer spreads widen against them or that they cannot get set for the full amount in all legs of the deal and are caught running a position which moves against them.

The forces of equilibrium will tend to push swap rates up towards 113 / 100 as they are hit on the bid or to push dollar interest rates down towards 5.5 / 5.625 as they are hit on the bid or some combination of the above. In practice, the adjustment would probably occur mostly in the swap rates.

As arbitrageurs borrow deutschemarks, there may even be an upward impact on deutschemark interest rates. If the full adjustment to equilibrium were to occur through deutschemark interest rates, to what level would deutschemark rates need to rise?

$$
\begin{aligned}
s &= 1.4745 \\
f &= 1.4645 \\
r_C &= 0.06 \\
r_T &= ? \\
d &= 90 \\
dpy &= 360
\end{aligned}
$$

Solving Equation 6.3 for r_T,

$$r_T = 3.25\% \text{ pa}$$

Precisely which rates move to bring the market back into equilibrium will depend on market conditions at the time.

In the absence of regulations preventing one or more of the arbitrage transactions taking place, rates will quickly return to equilibrium.

Central Bank Swaps

Central Banks can use currency swaps to temporarily inject or withdraw liquidity from the local money market without creating a net exchange position. By offering a better than market swap rate, the Central Bank can entice commercial banks to enter into swaps which will have the desired effect on liquidity.

Example 8. 7

The Central Bank of Crownland wishes to inject liquidity into the local money market. It could add to the Crownland money supply by purchasing foreign currency from residents. However, an outright sale of crowns would have an undesirable effect on the exchange rate. To inject liquidity without affecting the exchange rate, the Central Bank would encourage banks to buy crowns spot from the Central Bank and to sell crowns forward.

If crowns are available in the market at a forward discount of 85 points, by offering to buy crowns in a swap at a forward discount of only 80 points, the Central Bank gives the commercial banks the opportunity to arbitrage its swap rate with the market.

Exhibit 8.22

Central Bank swap

Benefit of swap with market	85 points
Cost of swap with Central Bank	80 points
Gain from Central Bank swap arbitrage	5 points

The commercial banks can lay off the swap position with the market through a reverse swap or through the money market at a profit of five points. As deals between commercial banks and other market participants do not affect money supply (they merely transfer ownership), the Central Bank will achieve its objective of temporarily injecting liquidity.

Covering an Outright Forward Exchange Position

The interaction between swap rates and interest rates is well illustrated by examining the different ways of squaring an outright forward exchange position.

Example 8.8

Market rates are

1 month A$ interest rates		7.25% pa	7.50% pa
1 month US$ interest rates		5.75% pa	6.25% pa
Spot rate	A$1 = US$	0.7720	0.7730
1 month swap rates		– 0.0012	– 0.0006
1 month forward rates	A$1 = US$	0.7708	0.7724

A customer calls a bank late in the afternoon and asks for a rate at which to sell Australian dollars one month forward. Hoping to make one point profit, the bank quotes a forward bid rate A$1 = US$0.7707. The customer agrees to deal and sells the bank A$10,000,000. The bank is now long A$10,000,000/ short US$7,707,000 and has mismatched cash flows one month from now.

Exhibit 8.23

Outright forward exchange position

Bank is long A$10,000,000 1 month forward

A$	Cash flows	US$	Net exchange position
A$	Spot	US$	
A$	1 month	US$	
+10,000,000	0.7707	−7,707,000	Short US$ 7,707,000 Long A$ 10,000,000

The bank has at least three ways of squaring its net exchange and mismatched cash flow positions.

1. It could do the exact opposite outright forward transaction.
2. It could cover the net exchange position spot and square the mismatched cash flow positions through the money market.
3. It could cover the net exchange position spot and square the mismatched cash flow positions through a reverse swap.

If the bank is able to use Method 1, it would need to sell A$10,000,000 one month forward. Assuming it could deal at the market bid rate 0.7708, the bank would square its net exchange position at a one point profit.

Exhibit 8.24

Covering a forward exchange position

Method 1: Do the opposite forward transaction

A$ (debit)	A$ (credit)	Spot	US$ (debit)	US$ (credit)

A$ (debit)	A$ (credit)	1 month	US$ (debit)	US$ (credit)
10,000,000		0.7707		− 7,707,000
	− 10,000,000	**0.7708**	+ 7,708,000	
		Profit		1,000
10,000,000	10,000,000		7,708,000	7,708,000

Profit = US$1,000 (ie 1 point) = A$1,297.35 (at 0.7708)

Net exchange position is *square* except for US$1,000 profit.

In practice, banks do not quote one another outright forward exchange rates, so Method 1 is not a realistic alternative. To eliminate its exchange risk, the bank should cover itself in the spot market by selling A$10,000,000 spot at the market's bid rate 0.7720.

Exhibit 8.25

Covering a forward exchange position in the spot market

A$		Spot	US$	
	– 10,000,000	0.7720	+ 7,720,000	

A$		1 month	US$	
10,000,000		0.7707		7,707,000

Net exchange position is square but the A$ and US$ cash flows are mismatched.

By selling Australian dollars spot and buying Australian dollars forward, the bank has engineered a swap. The spot purchase of US dollars will square the net exchange position, leaving a mismatched cash flow position. The mismatched cash flow position can be covered through either the money market or a swap. If the bank intends to cover the forward exchange position through the money market, what amount should it cover spot?

The money market transactions necessary to give matched cash flows would be:

1. borrow Australian dollars for one month; and
2. lend U.S.dollars for one month.

The US dollar amount to cover spot would be that amount which if invested for one month at 5.75% pa would accumulate to a future value of US$7,707,000.

$$\text{PV(US\$7,707,000)} = \frac{7{,}707{,}000}{1 + 0.0575 \times 30/360} = \text{US\$7,670,246.73}$$

Consequently, the bank should purchase US$7,670,246.73 at the spot rate 0.7720, by selling A$9,935,552.76. The bank would then need to borrow A$9,935,552.76 for one month at 7.75% pa. This would require a repayment of 9,935,552.76 × (1 + 0.0775 × 30/365) = A$9,998,840.87.

Exhibit 8.26

Covering a forward exchange position

Method 2: Spot deal and two money market deals

A$		Spot	US$	
	9,935,552.76	0.7720	7,670,246.73	
		5.75 %		**- 7,670,246.73**
+ 9,935,552.76		7.75 %		
9,935,552.76	9,935,552.76		7,670,246.73	7,670,246.73

A$		1 month	US$	
10,000,000		0.7707		- 7,707,000
			+ 7,707,000	
	- 9,998,840.87			
	1,159.13	Profit		
10,000,000.00	10,000,000.00		7,707,000	7,707,000

Profit = 10,000,000 – 9,998,840.87 = A$1,159.13 (ie 1 point)

Net exchange position is *square.*

To cover the mismatched Australian dollar cash position, the bank should borrow A$9,935,552.76 for one month at 7.75% pa. The future value of this borrowing is A$9,998,840.87 yielding a profit of A$1,159.13. The profit generated by covering the forward position through the money market is marginally greater (A$1,159.13 for Method 2 versus A$1,297.35 for Method 1). This difference is trivial and merely reflects rounding in quoting the forward rate as 0.7708 rather than 0.770789344.

If the bank elects to cover the forward exchange position through a spot deal and a swap, the swap required is the reverse of that which was engineered through the forward sale of US dollars to the customer and the purchase of US dollars from its spot counterparty. The reverse swap would be:

1. Sell US dollars spot at 0.7720; and
2. Buy US dollars forward at 0.7708.

Exhibit 8.27

Covering a forward exchange position

Method 3: Spot deal and a reverse swap

A$		Spot	US$	
	9,935,552.76	0.7720	7,670,246.73	
+ 9,935,552.76		**0.7720**		**– 7,670,246.73**
9,935,552.76	9,935,552.76		7,670,246.73	7,670,246.73

A$		1 month	US$	
10,000,000.00		0.7707		– 7,707,000
	– 9,998,702.65	**0.7708**	**+ 7,707,000**	
	1,297.35	Profit		
10,000,000.00	10,000,000.00		7,707,000	7,707,000

Profit = A$10,000,000 – 9,998,702.65 = A$1,297.35 (ie 1 point)
Net exchange position is *square*.

Provided the rates are consistent, all three methods will yield the bank the same profit with no net exchange position except for rounding differences.

Practice Problems

8.1 Pure swaps and engineered swaps

Spot rates	$1	=	SF1.2735	1.2740
1 month swap rates			0.0030	0.0025

(a) What is the one month outright bid rate?
(b) What is the one month outright offer rate?

A customer wants to buy dollars spot and sell dollars one month forward

(c) What is the benefit or cost to the customer of an engineered swap?
(d) What is the benefit or cost to the customer of a pure swap?

8.2 Calculating swap rates

Spot rate	Cl	=	Pl.4860	
1 week crowns			7% pa	8% pa (3 wpy)
1 week pesos			4% pa	5% pa (3 wpy)

Calculate the break-even one week bid and offer swap rates.

8.3 Simulated foreign currency loan

A company requires Singapore dollars for one year.

Spot rate	US$1	=	S$1.4100
1 year forward	US$1	=	S$1.3570
1 year US dollar interest rate			6.00% pa

Calculate the effective cost of generating Singapore dollars for one year.

8.4 Simulated foreign currency investment

A funds manager has deutschemarks to invest for three months and considers two alternatives:

1. investing deutschemarks directly at 2.4% pa; or
2. swapping deutschemarks into dollars and investing dollars.

Which alternative provides the higher effective yield given the prevailing market rates.

Spot	$1	=	DM1.5060	
3 month $			5.5% pa	5.625% pa
3 month swap			115	110

8.5 Short dated swaps

Today is Friday 5 July.

Spot rate	$1	=	DM1.4780	1.4785

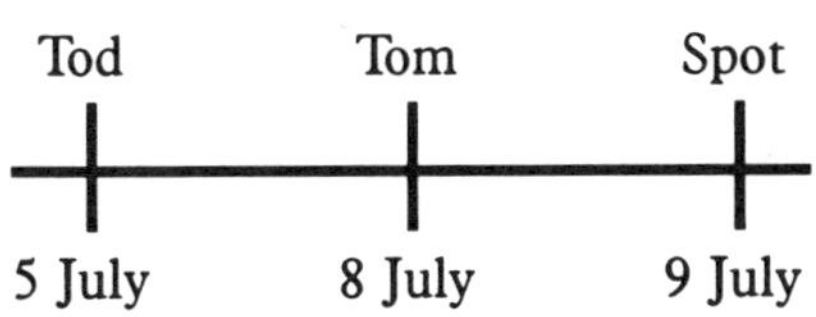

Margins	Bid	Offer
Overnight	+ 4.2	+ 3.3
Tom/Next	+ 1.4	+ 1.1
1 week	– 10.0	– 8.0

(a) At what rate can a customer sell dollars outright value tom ?

(b) At what rate can a customer buy dollars outright value today ?

(c) At what rate could a customer buy dollars value one week over tom (8 July)?

Supplementary Questions

8.6 Pure swaps and engineered swaps

Spot	$1 =	¥121.30	121.35
1 year swap		5.17	5.01

(a) At what rate can a customer buy yen outright 1 year forward?

(b) What is the benefit or cost to a customer of buying dollars 1 year forward and selling dollars spot in a pure swap?

(c) At what rates would a customer deal if it bought dollars 1 year forward and sold dollars spot in an engineered swap?

8.7 Simulated foreign currency borrowing

An American company wants to borrow Canadian dollars for 6 months

Spot	US$1 =	C$1.3540	1.3550
6 months US dollars		5.50%	5.75% pa
6 months Canadian dollars		8.00%	8.50% pa
6 month swap rate		148	168

Is it is cheaper to borrow the Canadian dollars directly or to borrow US dollars and swap them into Canadian dollars?

9

The Swaps Curve and Gapping in the Foreign Exchange Market

In this chapter, the concept of the swaps curve is introduced. Gapping in the foreign exchange market provides a means of taking advantage of expected changes in swap rates. The profitability of a gap opened and closed in the swaps market depends primarily on the change in interest differentials as reflected in the swap rates.

The Swaps Curve

At any point of time, there will be a set of swap rates which applies to a particular currency pair for various tenors. The curve obtained when swap rates are plotted against tenors is known as the ***swaps curve.***

For example, based on a spot rate of $1 = ¥107.00, the following swap rates applied for the dollar against the yen on 23 August 1996:

Tenor	Swap rate
tom next	+ 0.014
spot	0.00
1 week	– 0.10
2 weeks	– 0.21
3 weeks	– 0.33
1 month	– 0.45
2 months	– 0.90
3 months	– 1.36
4 months	– 1.82

Tenor	Swap rate
5 months	– 2.26
6 months	– 2.73
7 months	– 3.16
8 months	– 3.59
9 months	– 4.02
10 months	– 4.45
11 months	– 4.88
12 months	– 5.30

Plotting these points produces the swaps curve shown in Figure 9.1.

Figure 9. 1

Swaps curve dollar/yen

23 August 1996 Spot $1 = ¥107.00

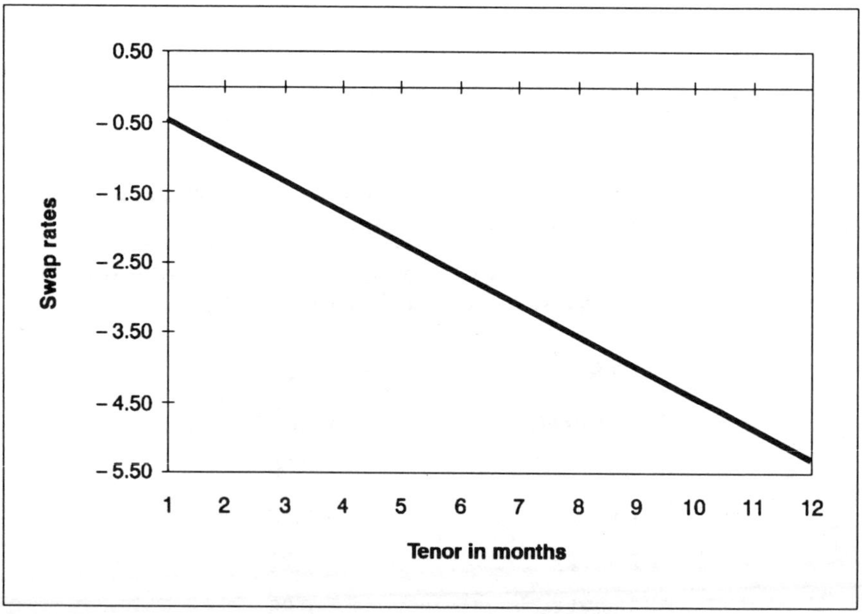

The negative swap rates reflect the fact that the commodity currency (dollar) is at a forward discount against the terms currency (yen). Positive swap rates would indicate that the commodity currency is at a forward premium against the terms currency.

The shape of the swap curve reflects the relationship between the respective yield curves of the two currencies. Parallel yield curves implying constant interest differentials will generate a swaps curve as shown in Figure 9.2. Incidentally, the swaps curve is non-linear.

Figure 9.2

Parallel yield curves

Constant interest rate differential swaps curve

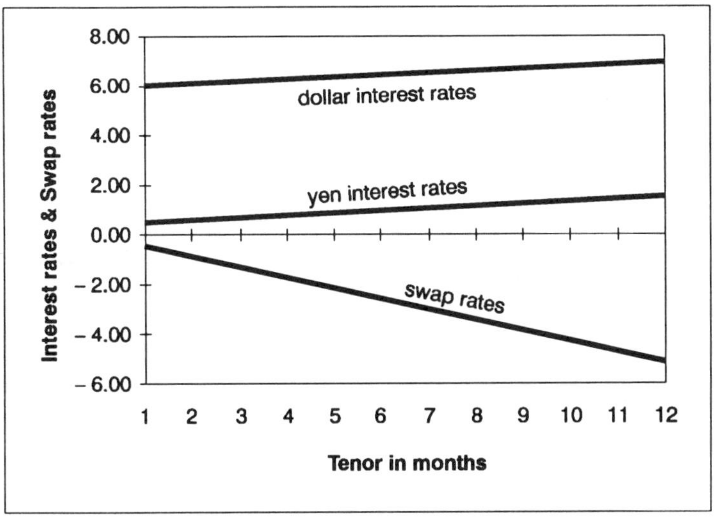

The constant interest differential swaps curve is non-linear because the swap rate is not a linear function of time.

$$\begin{aligned}
\text{Swap rate} &= f - s \\
&= \frac{s\,(1 + r_T t)}{(1 + r_C t)} - s \\
&= s\,\frac{(1 + r_T t) - (1 + r_C t)}{(1 + r_C t)} \\
&= \frac{s\,(r_T - r_C)t}{(1 + r_C t)}
\end{aligned}$$

If the interest differential is constant,

$$\begin{aligned}
r_T - r_C &= k \\
\therefore \quad \text{Swap rate} &= \frac{skt}{(1 + r_C t)} \\
\therefore \quad \frac{d}{dt}\,(\text{Swap rate}) &= \frac{skt}{(1 + r_C t)^2}
\end{aligned}$$

As the first derivative of the swap rate is a function of time, the swaps curve is not linear.

If the yield curves diverge, the interest differential widens as the tenor lengthens. This will imply a swaps curve which is *convex* from above.

Figure 9.3

Diverging yield curves

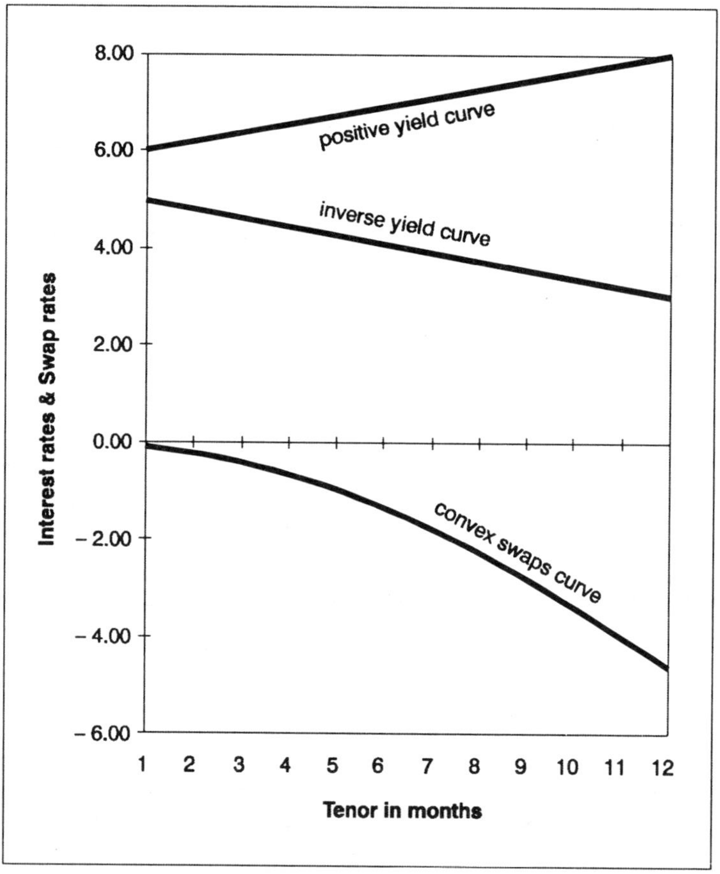

If the yield curves converge, the interest differential narrows as the tenor lengthens. This will imply a swaps curve which is *concave* from above.

Figure 9.4

Converging yield curves

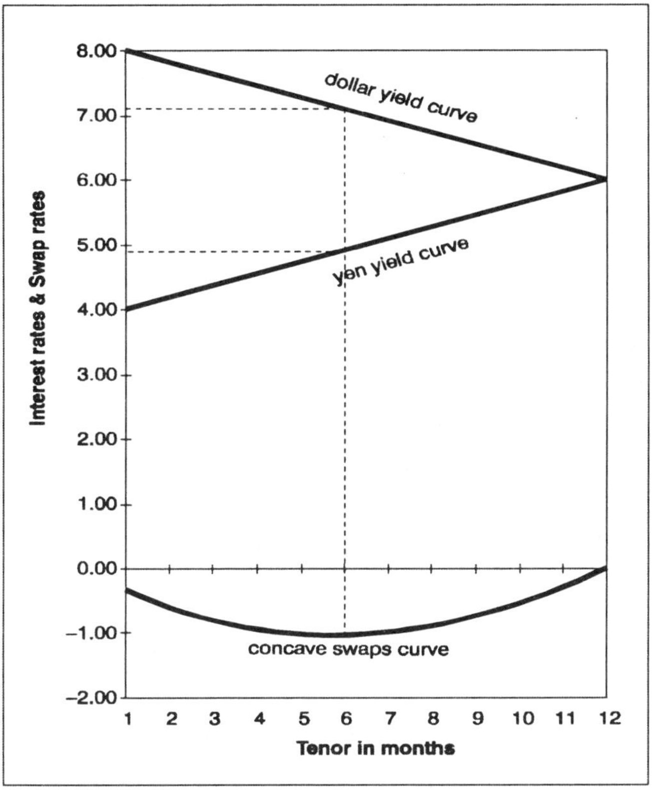

If the yield curves intersect, the swap rate and therefore the interest differential at the point of intersection must be zero. The swaps curve will go from negative to positive.

Figure 9.5

Intersecting yield curves

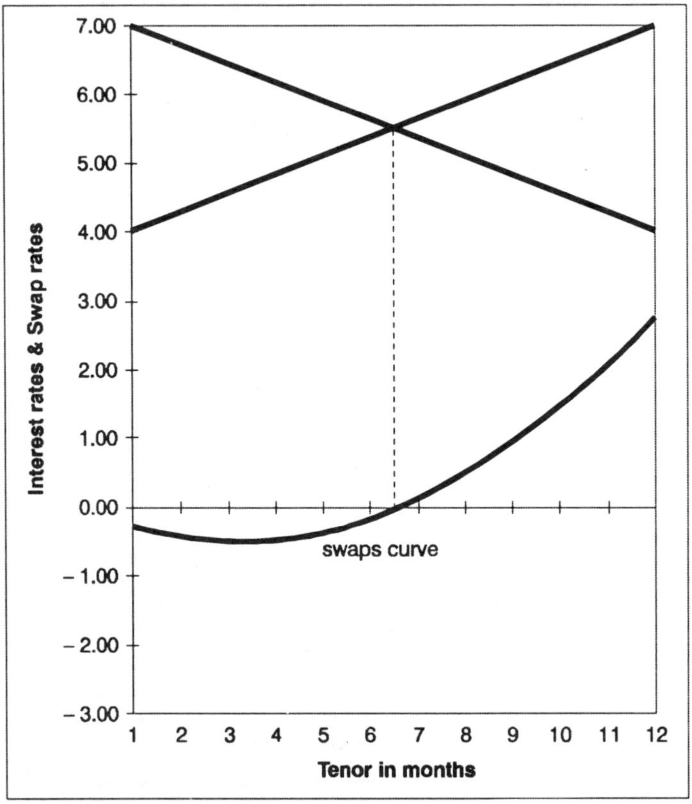

Movements of the Swaps Curve

It is convenient to distinguish between parallel shifts and rotations of the swaps curve. A parallel shift of the swaps curve would reflect an equal increase or decrease in the swap rate for a range of tenors. The slope of the swaps curve is unchanged; it merely moves up or down.

Parallel shift of the swaps curve

Tenor in months	Swap rate before shift	Swap rate after shift	Change in swap rate
1	– 0 45	– 0.15	+ 0.30
2	– 0.90	– 0.60	+ 0.30
3	– 1.35	– 1.05	+ 0.30
4	– 1.80	– 1.50	+ 0.30
5	– 2.25	– 1.95	+ 0.30
6	– 2.70	– 2.40	+ 0.30

Figure 9.6
Parallel shift of the swaps curve

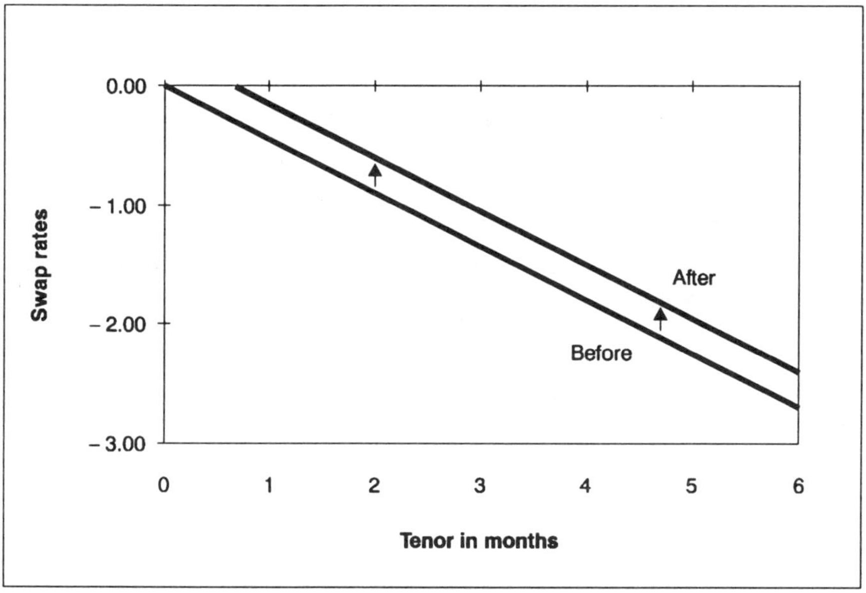

Rotation of the swaps curve

A rotation of the swaps curve would reflect a proportional increase or decrease in swap rates resulting in a change in the slope of the swaps curve.

Tenor in months	Swap rate before rotation	Swap rate after rotation	Change in swap rate
1	– 0.45	– 0 30	+ 0.15
2	– 0.90	– 0.60	+ 0.30
3	– 1.35	– 0.90	+ 0.45
4	– 1.80	– 1.20	+ 0.60
5	– 2.25	– 1.50	+ 0.90
6	– 2.70	– 1.80	+ 1.20

Figure 9. 7

Rotation of the swaps curve

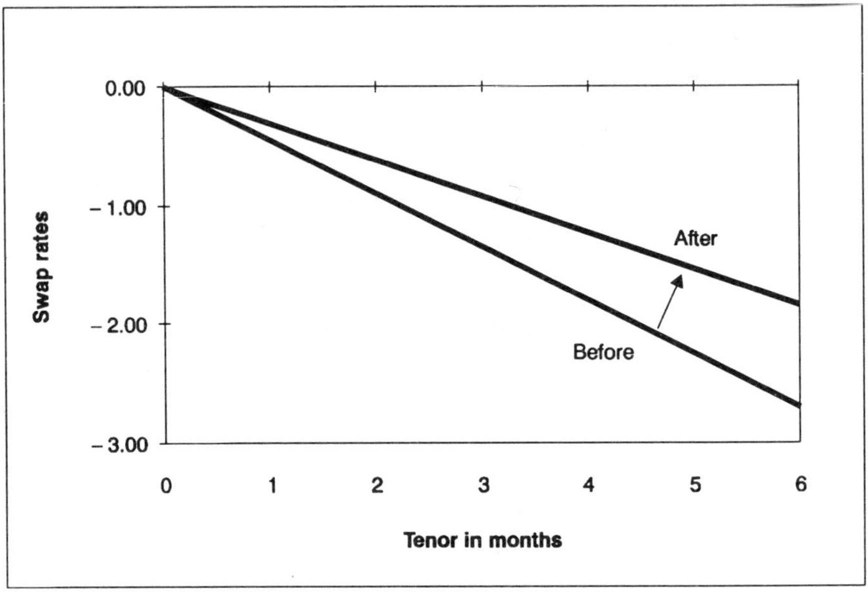

In practice, movements in the swaps curve will involve various combinations of shifts and rotations.

Gapping in the Foreign Exchange Market: How to Profit from Expected Changes in Interest Rate Differentials

Just as it is possible to take advantage of an expected change in a single interest rate by opening and closing gaps through the money market, it is possible to use swaps to take advantage of expected changes in interest rate differentials by opening and closing gaps in the foreign exchange market. The profit or loss generated by opening and closing a gap through swaps will depend on the movement of the swaps curve, the shape of the swaps curve and changes in the spot exchange rate.

Example 9. 1

Dollar interest rates are expected to fall relative to yen interest rates with the parallel shift, as shown in Figure 9.6. Assume the spot rate is $1 = ¥100.00.

It is possible to take advantage of the expected drop in the interest differential by buying dollars forward before the forward discount falls. An outright forward purchase of dollars would earn the benefit of the swap points, but it would also create a net exchange position. Assuming a net exchange position is not desired, it would be possible to open a gap to take advantage of the expected fall in interest differentials by doing a swap.

To open the desired gap, it would be necessary to buy the discount currency (dollar) for a longer tenor (eg, 6 months) and sell the discount currency (dollar) for a shorter tenor (eg, 1 month).

Using a swap to open a gap creates a swap position. If swap rates fall because, as expected, dollar interest rates fall relative to yen interest rates, a profit will result. However if, contrary to expectations, swap rates rise reflecting a rise in dollar interest rates relative to yen interest rates, a loss will result.

Exhibit 9.1

Opening a gap with a swap

$		Spot	¥	
	– 1,000,000	100.00	+ 100,000,000	
+ 1,000,000		100.00		– 100,000,000
1,000,000	1,000,000		100,000,000	100,000,000

$		1 month	¥	
	– 1,000,000	99.55		+ 99,550,000

$		6 months	¥	
+ 1,000,000		97.30		– 100,000,000

Opening the gap provides a benefit of 225 points or ¥2,250,000 per $1,000,000. This does not represent profit because there is an open swap position. If swap rates fall, an unrealised profit will exist. If the gap is closed through a reverse swap after swap rates have fallen, then a profit will be realised.

The gap can be closed at any time through a reverse swap. To close the gap one month later, it would be necessary to buy $1,000,000 spot and sell $1,000,000 five months forward to match the dates of the cash flow. Assuming that swap rates have fallen, the gap could be closed at a profit. For simplicity, it is initially assumed that the spot rate has fallen to the original one month outright rate of $1 = ¥99.55.

Swaps curve becomes less negative

	When gap is opened		*When gap is closed (1 month later)*	
Tenor (months)	Swap rates	Exchange rates	Swap rates	Exchange rates
Spot		100.00		**99.55**
1	– 0.45	**99.55**	– 0.30	99.25
2	– 0.90	99.10	– 0.60	98.95
3	– 1.35	98.65	– 0.90	98.65
4	– 1.80	98.20	– 1.20	98.35
5	– 2.25	97.75	– 1.50	**98.05**
6	– 2.70	**97.30**	– 1.80	97.75

Exhibit 9.2

Closing the gap when the swaps curve has become less negative

One month later ...

$		Spot	¥	
	1,000,000	99.55	99,550,000	
+ 1,000,000		**99.55**		**– 99,550,000**
1,000,000	1,000,000		99,550,000	99,550,000

$		5 months	¥	
1,000,000		97.30		97,300,000
	– 1,000,000	**98.05**	**+ 98,050,000**	
		Profit		750,000
1,000,000	1,000,000		98,050,000	98,050,000

Profit = ¥98,050,000 – 97,300,000 = ¥750,000

Closing the gap would involve buying $1,000,000 spot at ¥99.55 and selling $1,000,000 five months forward at ¥98.05. This would realise a profit of

¥750,000 as shown in Exhibit 9.2.

Benefit of opening gap	= 99.55 – 97.30	= 225 points	=	¥2,250,000
Cost of closing gap	= 99.55 – 98.05	= 150 points	=	¥1,500,000
Profit from gap		= 75 points	=	¥ 750,000

Consider instead the case where, contrary to expectations, dollar interest rates rise relative to yen interest rates. The interest differential widens and the swaps curve becomes more negative (that is, the forward discount becomes larger). If the gap were closed using the higher swap rate, a loss would be realised.

Swaps curve becomes more negative

	When gap was opened		*When gap is closed (1 month later)*	
Tenor (months)	Swap rates	Exchange rates	Swap rates	Exchange rates
Spot		100.00		**99.55**
1	– 0.45	99.55	– 0.60	98.95
2	– 0.90	99.10	– 1.20	98.35
3	– 1.35	98.65	– 1.80	97.75
4	– 1.80	98.20	– 2.40	97.15
5	– 2.25	97.75	– 3.00	**96.55**
6	– 2.70	97.30	– 3.60	95.95

Exhibit 9.3

Closing the gap when the swaps curve has become more negative

One month later ...

$		Spot	¥	
	– 1,000,000	99.55	+ 99,550,000	
+ 1,000,000		**99.55**		**– 99,550,000**
1,000,000	1,000,000		99,550,000	99,550,000

$		5 months	¥	
+ 1,000,000		97.30		– 97,300,000
	– 1,000,000	**96.55**	**+ 96,550,000**	
		Loss	750,000	
1,000,000	1,000,000		97,300,000	97,300,000

Loss = ¥97,300,000 – 96,550,000 = ¥750,000

Closing the gap would involve buying $1,000,000 spot at ¥99.55 and selling $1,000,000 five months forward at ¥96.55. This would realise a *loss* of ¥750,000.

Cost of closing gap	= 99.55 – 96.55	= 300 points	=	¥3,000,000
Benefit of opening gap	= 99.55 – 97.30	= 225 points	=	¥2,250,000
Loss from gap		= 75 points	=	¥ 750,000

The gap will yield a profit if the swap rate falls and will result in a loss if the swap rate rises.

Riding the Swaps Curve

The shape of the swaps curve may make it attractive to open a gap. The more non-linear the swap curve is, the greater will be the bias towards a swap making or losing money.

For example, given a U-shaped swaps curve as in Figure 9.4, there is an incentive to open a gap which will earn the largest possible proportional benefit. By buying dollars 6 months forward and selling them 12 months forward, it is possible to earn a net forward discount of 97 points. Assuming the six month swap rate remains at 97 points discount, the gap could be closed for a further benefit of 97 points. The gap would generate a profit of 194 points.

Opening the gap	Benefit (+)/cost (–) in points
Buy dollars 6 months forward	+ 97
Sell dollars 12 months forward	0
Benefit of opening the gap	+ 97
Benefit of closing the gap	+ 97
Profit from the gap	+ 194

The gap would break-even if the six month swap rate changed from -0.97 to +0.97. For the gap to lose money, the six month swap rate would have to rise by more than 194 points (ignoring movements in the spot rate, which are discussed in the following section). For this change in the swap rate to occur, the six month dollar interest rate would need to fall from 7% pa to 4% pa if the yen rate remained at 5% pa. Assuming that such an outcome is considered unlikely, opening the above gap would be considered a "good bet".

Opening gaps to take advantage of the shape of the swaps curve is known as ***"riding the swaps curve"***.

Cash Flow Implications of Spot Rate Changes

Movements in the spot rate between when the gap is opened and closed can have a significant impact on the profitability of the gap because of timing differences in the cash flows which occur at each end of the gap.

Consider the gap opened in Example 9.1. To illustrate the impact of spot rate changes, suppose that during the month in which the gap is opened the spot rate rises from ¥100.00 to ¥105.00 while the swaps curve remains as it was when the gap was opened. If the spot rate changes but the swap rates do not, it might be expected that as a gap represents a swap position rather than a net exchange position, spot rate changes would have no impact on the profitability of the gap.

Spot rate rises while swap rate is unchanged

	When gap is opened		***When gap is closed (one month later)***	
Tenor (months)	Swap rates	Exchange rates	Swap rates	Exchange rates
Spot		100.00		**105.00**
1	– 0.45	**99.55**	– 0.45	104.55
2	– 0.90	99.10	– 0.90	104.10
3	– 1.35	98.65	– 1.35	103.65
4	– 1.80	98.20	– 1.80	103.20
5	– 2.25	97.75	– 2.25	**102.75**
6	– 2.70	**97.30**	– 2.70	102.30

Benefit of opening gap	= 99.55 – 97.30 =	225 points	=	¥2,250,000
Cost of closing gap	= 105.00 – 102.75 =	225 points	=	¥2,250,000
Loss from gap	=	0 points	=	¥ 0

However, this calculation overlooks the timing of cash flows. Closing the gap would involve buying $1,000,000 spot at 105.00 and selling $1,000,000 five months later at 102.75. This would create the cash flows as shown in Exhibit 9.4.

Exhibit 9.4

Closing the gap after spot movement

One month later:

$		Spot	¥	
	– 1,000,000	99.55	+ 99,550,000	
+ 1,000,000		**105.00**		**– 105,000,000**
		1 %	+ 5,450,000	
1,000,000	1,000,000		105,000,000	105,000,000

$		5 months	¥	
+ 1,000,000		97.30		– 97,300,000
	– 1,000,000	**102.75**	**+ 102,750,000**	
		P + I		– 5,472,708
		Loss	22,708	
1,000,000	1,000,000		102,772,708	102,772,708

Loss = ¥97,300,000 + 5,472,708 – 102,750,000 = ¥22,708

The loss represents the interest cost of funding the cash shortfall of ¥5,450,000 for five months at 1% pa.[1] This cash shortfall is a direct consequence of the difference between the original one month outright rate of ¥99.55 and the spot rate at the time of closing the gap which was ¥105.00. If the spot rate at maturity is greater than ¥99.55, there will be a negative cash balance which will require funding at a cost. On the other hand, if the spot rate at maturity is less than ¥99.55, there will be a positive cash balance, which can be invested for a benefit. If the exchange rate movement is dramatic or the duration of the gap is long, the interest impact of the cash flow effect of spot rate changes may be substantial. Indeed it can be more than sufficient to offset the gain or loss resulting from movements in the swap rate.

Calculating Break-even Rates

In practice, spot rates and swap rates are continually changing. Continuing the above example, what is the break-even forward rate if at the maturity of the gap, the spot rate is 105.00?

1. ¥5,450,000 × 0.01 × 5/12 = ¥22,708

At the break-even forward rate b,

$$\text{cash flow at spot date} = \text{PV(cash flow at forward date)}$$

$$1{,}000{,}000\ (99.55 - 105.00) = \frac{1{,}000{,}000\ (b - 97.30)}{(1 + 0.01 \times 5/12)}$$

$$\therefore \quad b = 102.77$$

In general,

$$f_1 - s = \frac{b - f_2}{1 + rt} \qquad \textbf{Equation 9.1}$$

where b is the break-even forward rate for the far maturity date at the duration of the gap, that is when the near maturity date becomes spot.

The break-even rate is effectively that rate which offsets the swap points earned (or paid) when the gap was opened and adjusted for the interest cost (or benefit) from the cash flow created by the change in spot rate. Observing the cash flows in Exhibit 9.4:

Dollar	Yen	Rate	
1,000,000	102,750,000	102.75	
	22,708	0.02	Interest equivalent
1,000,000	102,772,708	102.77	

It can be seen from the cash flows that the break-even rate is ¥102.77.

Rearranging Equation 9.1,

$$b = f_2 + (f_1 - s)(1 + rt)$$

The break-even rate is a direct function of (1 + rt). If the interest rate is higher or the period of the gap longer, then the break-even rate will tend to be farther from the forward rate of the near leg of the swap (f_1).

Figure 9.8

Break-even rate

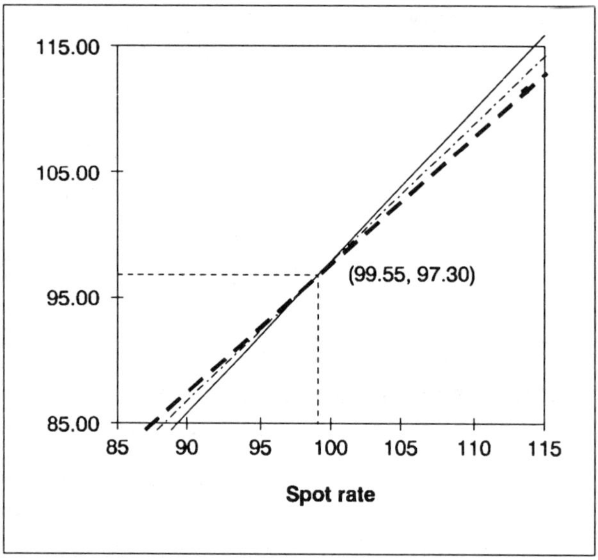

The concurrent point is at (f_1, f_2), which in this example is (99.55, 97.30).

The break-even rate will vary with the spot rate at the time of closing the gap and the value of (1 + rt).

Spot rate when closing gap	1 + rt = 1.01	1 + rt = 1.10	1 + rt = 1.20
95.00	92.70	92.30	91.84
105.00	102.78	103.30	103.84

Forward Exchange Agreements (FXA)

A *forward exchange agreement* **(FXA)** is a non-deliverable currency swap. Under the FXA agreement on contract date, a notional gap is opened across a period from a near date maturity to a far date maturity. The gap is subsequently closed at a time not later than the near maturity date. It may be closed through a reversing forward swap prior to the spot date for the near maturity. The parties to the FXA agree to settle for an amount which reflects the profit or loss from the gap. Settlement is generally for value the near maturity date.

Example 9.2

A corporation expects dollar interest rates to fall relative to yen interest rates.

On 12 June, it enters into an FXA to notionally sell $10,000,000 at ¥99.55 value 12 July and to notionally buy $10,000,000 at ¥98.65 value 12 September.

On 22 June, the corporation decides to close the gap by notionally buying \$10,000,000 for value 12 July at ¥102.30 and notionally selling \$10,000,000 for value 12 September at ¥102.10.

Calculate the settlement in yen for value 12 July given that the yen interest rate for the period from 12 July to 12 September is 1% pa.

$$\text{Settlement in terms currency} = P\left[(f_{0/1} + f_{1/1}) + \frac{(f_{0/2} + f_{1/2})}{(1 + r_{1/2}t)}\right] \qquad \textbf{Equation 9.2}$$

where:

P	=	principal amount in commodity currency	=	10,000,000
$f_{0/1}$	=	forward rate for near date maturity on contract date	=	+ 99.55
$f_{0/2}$	=	forward rate for far date maturity on contract date	=	– 98.65
$f_{1/1}$	=	forward rate for near date maturity on closing date	=	– 102.30
$f_{1/2}$	=	forward rate for far date maturity on closing date	=	+ 102.10
$r_{1/2}$	=	terms currency interest rate from near date maturity to far date maturity	=	1% pa
t	=	period from near date maturity to far date maturity	=	62 days
$f > 0$		for the seller of the commodity currency		
$f < 0$		for the buyer of the commodity currency		

Exhibit 9.5

FXA value dates

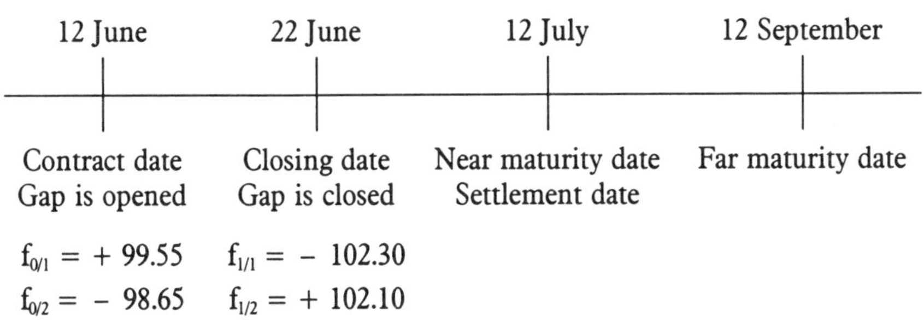

$$\text{Settlement in yen} = 10{,}000{,}000\left[(99.55 - 102.30) + \frac{(-98.65 + 102.10)}{(1 + 0.01 \times 62/360)}\right]$$

$$= +\,¥6{,}940{,}685$$

A positive settlement implies that the corporation receives the settlement, that is, it has made a profit of from the gap.

The settlement can be converted to a dollar amount at the forward exchange rate $f_{1/1}$.

$$\text{Settlement in commodity currency} = P/f_{1/1}\,[(f_{0/1} + f_{1/1}) + \frac{(f_{0/2} + f_{1/2})]}{(1 + r_{1/2}t)} \qquad \textbf{Equation 9.3}$$

$$= \frac{\$6{,}940{,}685}{102.10}$$

$$= +\ \$67{,}979.29$$

The benefit of an FXA over gapping deliverable currency swaps is that the FXA utilises much less credit. Delivery risk is avoided. In addition, the rate risk is only the interest rate differential risk, not the spot risk on one or both legs of the swaps.

In practice, FXAs are rarely used, because the banks that engage actively in gapping through the FX market tend to have ample credit lines for each other and find full flow of funds easier to administer than cash settlements. This situation is only likely to change if credit pressures necessitate it.

Practice Problems

9.1 Parallel shift in a positive swaps curve

The spot exchange rate is currently $1 = ₤1550.

Dollar interest rates are below lira rates so the swaps curve is positive. Dollar interest rates are expected to rise relative to lire rates and the dollar is expected to appreciate against the lira.

	Current rates		***Expected rates (1 month from now)***	
Tenor (months)	Swap rates	Exchange rates	Swap rates	Exchange rates
Spot		1550		1600
1	+ 4	1554	+ 2	1602
2	+ 8	1558	+ 6	1606
3	+ 12	1562	+ 10	1610

(a) What gap (three months against one month) should be opened to take advantage of the expected movement in rates?

(b) How much profit would be generated on a principal amount of $1,000,000 if rates move according to expectation?

(c) Calculate the profit for value at three months, assuming that one month from now the two month lira interest rate will be 9.5% pa.

9.2 Rotation of a negative swaps curve

A corporation expects the New Zealand dollar yield curve to become more inverse and the dollar yield curve to become more positive.

	Current interest rates		***Expected interest rates (1 month later)***	
Tenor (months)	NZ$	US$	NZ$	US$
1	9.5	5.5	10.0	5.0
5	9.1	5.9	8.4	6.8
6	9.0	6.0	8.0	7.0

(a) The spot exchange rate is NZ$1 = US$0.6900 and it is expected that in one month's time, the spot rate will be NZ$1 = US$0.7000. These rates imply the following swaps curves:

	Current rates		***Expected rates (1 month later)***	
Tenor (months)	Swap rates	Exchange rates	Swap rates	Exchange rates
Spot		0.6900		**0.7000**
1	– 0.0023	**0.6877**	– 0.0029	0.6971
5	– 0.0089	0.6811	– 0.0044	**0.6955**
6	– 0.0099	**0.6801**	– 0.0034	0.6966

To benefit from the expected narrowing of the interest differential, the corporation opens a gap by selling NZ$1,000,000 one month forward at 0.6877 and buying NZ$1,000,000 six months forward at 0.6801. Assuming that after one month the rates have moved as expected and the gap is closed by buying NZ$1,000,000 spot and selling NZ$1,000,000 five months forward, how much profit would the corporation make?

(b) Calculate the profit resulting from opening and closing the same gap if after one month the spot rate is 0.6800 and the 5 month swap rate is – 0.0044.

Supplementary Question

9.3 Parallel shift in a negative swaps curve

Dollar interest rates are higher than yen rates so the swaps curve is negative. Over the next month, dollar interest rates are expected to rise relative to yen rates and the dollar is expected to appreciate against the yen.

	Current rates		Expected rates (1 month from now)	
Tenor (months)	Swap rates	Exchange rates	Swap rates	Exchange rates
Spot		107.00		109.00
1	– 0.45	106.55	– 0.55	108.45
2	– 0.90	106.10	– 1.00	108.00
3	– 1.36	105.64	– 1.50	107.50

(a) What gap (three months against one month) should be opened to take advantage of the expected movement in rates?

(b) How much profit would be made on a principal amount of $1,000,000 if rates move as expected? Assume that when the gap is closed, the 2 month yen interest rate is 1% pa.

10

Currency Options – Pricing

This chapter introduces the concept of currency options and examines the factors which influence the price of options. Options pricing is explained intuitively using a binomial model but can alternatively be determined using closed form mathematical formulae such as the Black-Scholes model.

Definitions and Concepts

The terminology used to describe currency options is essentially the same as that used to describe stock options.

A ***currency option*** is the right, without the obligation, to buy or sell one currency against another currency at a specified price at a specified time.

Calls and puts

A ***call*** is the right, without the obligation, to *buy* a currency. A ***put*** is the right, without the obligation, to *sell* a currency.

In every foreign exchange transaction, one currency is purchased and another currency sold. Consequently, every currency option is both a call and a put. An option to buy dollars against yen is both a dollar call and a yen put. For consistency in this book, unless otherwise stated, calls will refer to commodity currency calls and puts will refer to commodity currency puts.

Parties to an option

There are two parties to an option – the buyer and the seller. The ***buyer*** of the option enjoys the right to exercise the option and the right to *not* exercise the option (ie to let it lapse). The ***seller*** of the option has the obligation to deal at the contracted rate if the buyer elects to exercise the option. The seller is also known as the writer or grantor of the option.

Option premium

The price of the option is known as the ***option premium***. The buyer pays the premium to the seller as compensation for the risk involved in writing the option. The premium is normally paid on the spot value date from the date on which the option is contracted.

Value terms

The ***strike price*** or ***strike rate*** is the exchange rate at which the option will be exercised if the buyer elects to exercise the option.

In-the-money (ITM) describes an option for which the strike price is better than the market price. ***Out-of-the-money*** (OTM) describes an option for which the strike price is worse then the market price. ***At-the-money*** (ATM) describes an option for which the strike price is the same as the market price. For European options the at-the-money strike price is the forward rate.

Exhibit 10. 1

Calls and puts: ATM/ITM/OTM matrix

			Call	Put
Strike	<	forward rate	ITM	OTM
Strike	=	forward rate	ATM	ATM
Strike	>	forward rate	OTM	ITM

The premium will be higher if the option is in-the-money and lower if the option is out-of-the-money.

Maturity of the option

The ***expiration date*** or ***expiry date*** refers to the date on which the buyer's right to exercise the option ends. In practice, a specific expiry time (eg 3 pm New York time on the expiry date) is agreed. If an option is exercised on the expiry date, the cash flows will occur on the then spot value date.

An ***American option*** refers to an option which can be exercised for spot value on any date between the contract date and the expiry date. A ***European option*** refers to an option which, theoretically, can only be exercised for spot value on the expiry date. In practice, writers of European options allow buyers to give notice prior to the expiry date that they will exercise the option. If a European option is "exercised" prior to expiry date, the cash flows will occur on the spot value date following the expiry date.

Exhibit 10.2

Currency option value dates

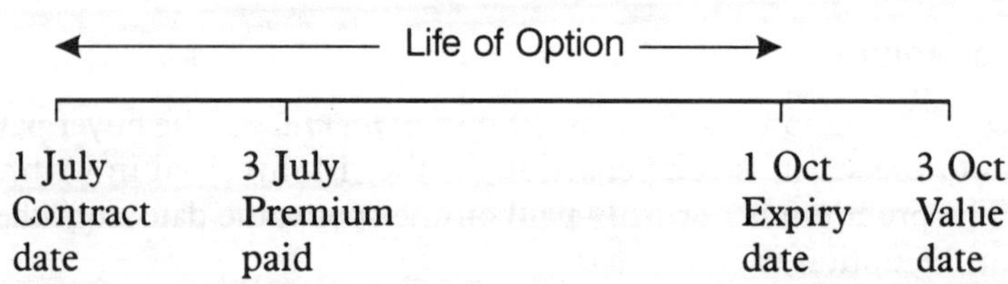

Sources of options

Exchange-traded options refer to contracts traded through certain stock, futures or commodity exchanges. These contracts have strictly defined characteristics such as standard amounts, standard expiry dates and standard strike prices. ***Over-the-counter* (OTC) *options*** refer to options written by banks and other institutions but not traded through public exchanges. Over-the-counter options can be tailored to suit the exact needs of the option buyer. The options referred to in this book are generally over-the-counter European options.

Calculating Option Premiums

It is common for option premiums to be expressed as either a *flat* percentage of the face value or as a fixed number of exchange points. It is possible to express the premium in terms of any currency. The dollar amount of an option premium can be determined from either the percentage of strike or number of points.

Example 10.1

An option pricing model expresses the option premium of a three month dollar call/yen put as 1.25% or 145 points.

Spot rate	$1	=	¥116.00
Strike price	$1	=	¥115.00

Calculate the dollar value of the premium for an option with face value of $20,000,000.

$$\text{Premium} = \$20{,}000{,}000 \times \frac{1.25}{100} = \$250{,}000$$

The premium is paid up-front so to express the premium in yen, it is necessary to convert at the spot rate.

$$\text{Premium} = \$250{,}000 \times 116.00 = ¥29{,}000{,}000$$

Alternatively,

$$\text{Premium} = \$20{,}000{,}000 \times 1.45 = ¥29{,}000{,}000$$

$$= \frac{\$29{,}000{,}000}{116.00} = \$250{,}000$$

Profit Profiles: Naked Options

An option which is bought or sold without any underlying foreign exchange exposure is called a ***naked option.***

Bought call

Example 10.2

A person buys a dollar call/yen put for face value $10,000,000 with a strike price of ¥110.00 and expiry date three months for a premium of 2.00% (flat). If the spot rate is ¥112.00 and the three month dollar interest rate is 5% pa, calculate in future value terms the profit outcome if, at expiry, the exchange rate is:

a) 120.00
b) 110.00
c) 100.00

Premium	=	$10{,}000{,}000 \times 0.02$
	=	$200,000
FV (Premium)	=	$200{,}000\ (1 + 0.05 \times 3/12)$
	=	$202,500

The buyer of the option pays the premium and has the right to buy $10,000,000 and sell ¥1,100,000,000 at an exchange rate $1 = ¥110.00.

(a) If at expiry the exchange rate is above the strike price, the dollar call will be in-the-money, so the option owner will exercise the option by selling ¥1,100,000,000 for $10,000,000. If the exchange rate at expiry is ¥120.00, the option owner could simultaneously buy ¥1,100,000,000 in the market for $9,166,666.67.

Profit from option

=	proceeds of sale of ¥1,100,000,000 through option	–	cost of purchase of ¥1,100,000,000 through market	–	FV (Premium)
=	10,000,000	–	9,166,667	–	202,500
=	$630,833				

(b) If at expiry the exchange rate is at the strike price of ¥110.00, the dollar call will be at-the-money. The option owner will allow the option to lapse because there would be no benefit in buying dollars through the option and selling them through the market at the same rate.

Profit from option	=	– FV (Premium)
	=	– \$202,500

(c) If at expiry the exchange rate is less than the strike price, the dollar call will be out-of-the-money so the option owner will allow the option to lapse.

Profit from option	=	– FV (Premium)
	=	– \$202,500

Figure 10.1

Profit profile: bought dollar call strike ¥110.00

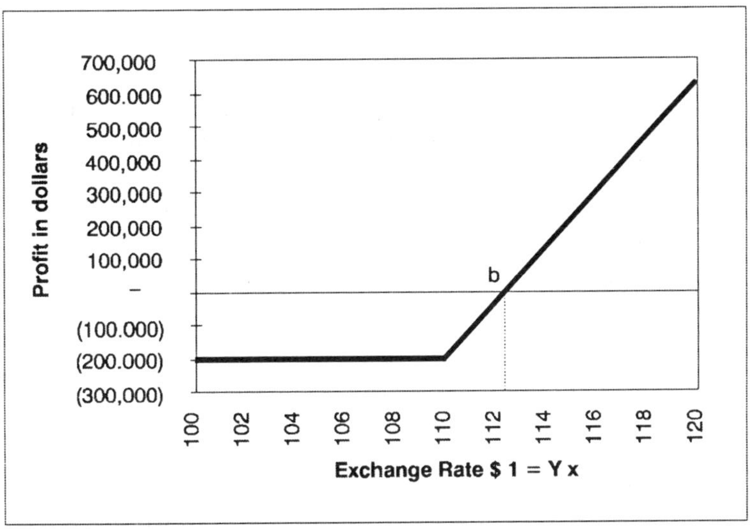

This shape represents the typical profit profile of a bought call.

The break-even rate b is the exchange rate at which the option will produce a zero profit. That is, the profit from exercising the option will be just sufficient to offset the premium.

proceeds of sale	–	cost of purchase	=	FV (Premium)
of ¥1,100,000,000		of ¥1,100,000,000		
through option		through market		

$$\therefore \quad \frac{1,100,000,000}{110.00} - \frac{1,100,000,000}{b} = 202,500$$

$$\therefore \quad 10,000,000 - \frac{1,100,000,000}{b} = 202,500$$

$$\therefore \quad - \frac{1,100,000,000}{b} = 202,500 - 10,000,000$$

$$\therefore \quad b = \frac{1,100,000,000}{10,000,000 - 202,500}$$

$$= 112.27$$

Bought put

Example 10.3

A person buys a dollar put/DM call for a face value of $10,000,000 with a strike price of 1.5000 and expiry date three months for a premium of 3.00% flat. If the three month dollar interest rate is 5% pa, calculate in future value terms the profit outcome if at expiry the exchange rate is:

a) 1.4000

b) 1.5000

c) 1.6000

$$\text{Premium} = 10,000,000 \times 0.03$$

$$= \$300,000$$

$$\text{FV (Premium)} = 300,000 \times (1 + 0.05 \times 3/12)$$

$$= \$303,750$$

The buyer of the option pays the premium and has the right to sell $10,000,000 and buy DM 15,000,000 at an exchange rate $1 = DM1.5000

(a) If at expiry the exchange rate is below the strike price, the dollar put will be in-the-money so the option owner will exercise the option, thereby buying DM15,000,000 for $10,000,000. If the exchange rate at expiry is 1.4000, the option owner could simultaneously sell DM15,000,000 in the market for $10,714,285.71.

Profit from option

=	proceeds of sale of DM15,000,000 through market	–	cost of purchase of DM15,000,000 through option	–	FV (Premium)
=	10,714,285.71	–	10,000,000	–	303,750
=	$410,535.71				

(b) If at expiry the exchange rate is 1.5000, the dollar put will be at-the-money. The option-owner will allow the option to lapse because there would be no benefit in selling dollars through the option and buying them through the market at the same rate.

Profit from option	=	– FV (Premium)
	=	– $303,750

(c) If at expiry the exchange rate is 1.6000, the dollar put will be out-of-the-money so the option owner will allow it to lapse.

Profit from option	=	– FV (Premium)
	=	– $303,750

The profit profile of a bought dollar put is shown in Figure 10.2.

Figure 10.2

Profit profile: bought dollar put strike DM 1.5000

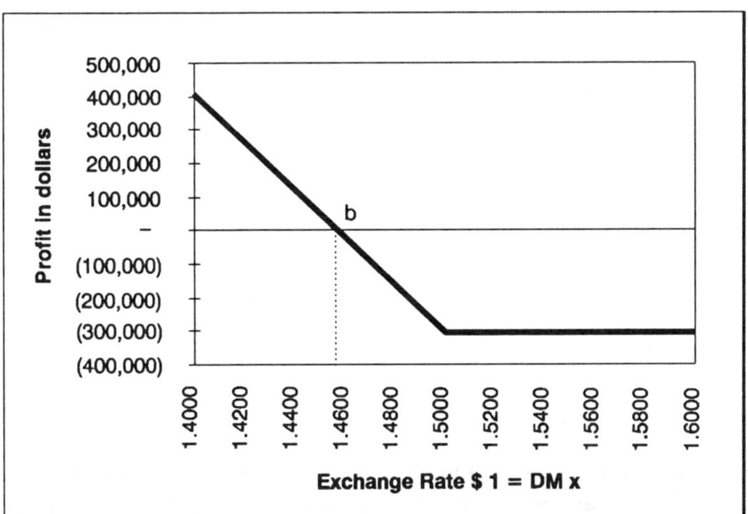

This shape represents the typical profit profile of a bought put.

The break-even rate b is the exchange rate at which the option will produce a zero profit.

proceeds of sale of DM15,000,000 through market	–	cost of purchase of DM15,000,000 through option	=	FV (Premium)

$$\therefore \quad \frac{15,000,000}{b} - \frac{15,000,000}{1.5000} = 303,750$$

$$\therefore \quad b = \frac{15,000,000}{10,000,000 + 303,750}$$

$$= 1.4558$$

Sold call

Example 10.4

A person writes a dollar call/yen put for a face value of $10,000,000 with a strike price of 110.00 and expiry date of three months for a premium of 2.00% flat. If the three month dollar interest rate is 5% pa, calculate in future value terms the profit outcome if at expiry the exchange rate is:

a) 120.00
b) 110.00
c) 100.00

As in Example 10.1, FV (Premium) = $202,500. The writer of the option receives the premium.

(a) If at expiry the exchange rate is above the strike price, the dollar call will be in-the-money, so the buyer of the option will exercise the option. If the dollar call is exercised, the writer is obliged to sell $10,000,000 for ¥1,100,000,000. To square the net exchange position, the writer will have to sell ¥1,100,000,000 in the market. If at expiry the market rate is ¥120.00, the writer will buy ¥1,100,000,000 through the option and sell ¥1,100,000,000 for $9,166,666.67.

Profit from option

=	proceeds of sale of ¥1,100,000,000 through market	–	cost of purchase of ¥1,100,000,000 through option	+	FV (Premium)
=	9,166,666.67	–	10,000,000	+	202,500
=	– $ 630.833.33				

(b) If at expiry the exchange rate is at the strike price of ¥110.00, the owner of the dollar call will allow it to lapse so the writer merely keeps the premium.

Profit from option = FV (Premium)

= + \$202.500

(c) If at expiry the exchange rate is less than the strike price, the owner of the dollar call will allow it to lapse.

Profit from option = FV (Premium)

= + \$202,500

Figure 10.3

Profit profile: sold dollar call strike ¥ 110.00

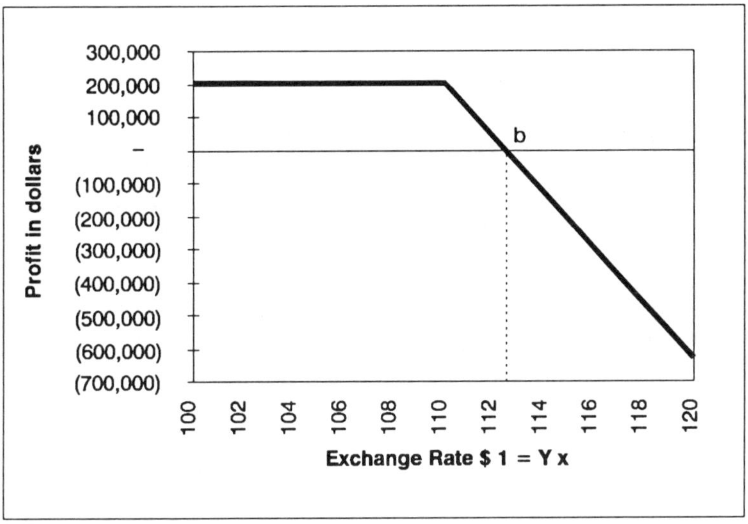

This shape represents the typical profit profile of a sold call.

The break-even rate b is the exchange rate at which the option will produce zero profit. That is, the future value of the premium received will be just sufficient to offset the loss from writing the option.

cost of purchase of ¥1,100,000,000 through option	–	proceeds of sale of ¥1,100,000,000 through market	=	FV (Premium)
$\therefore \dfrac{1{,}100{,}000{,}000}{110.00}$	–	$\dfrac{1{,}100{,}000{,}000}{b}$	=	202,500
b			=	$\dfrac{1{,}100{,}000{,}000}{10{,}000{,}000 - 202{,}500}$
			=	112.27

Sold put

Example 10.5

A person writes a dollar put/DM call for face value of $10,000,000 with a strike price of 1.5000 and expiry date three months for a premium of 3.00% flat. If the three month interest rate is 5% pa, calculate in future value terms the profit outcome if at expiry date the exchange rate is:

(a) 1.4000;
(b) 1.5000;
(c) 1.6000.

As in Example 10.2, FV (Premium) = $303,750: the writer receives the premium.

(a) If at expiry the exchange rate is below the strike price, the dollar put will be in-the-money so the buyer of the option will exercise the option. If the option is exercised, the writer is obliged to buy $10,000,000 for DM15,000,000. To square the net exchange position, the writer will have to buy DM15,000,000 in the market. If at expiry the market rate is 1.4000, the writer will sell DM15,000,000 through the option and buy DM15,000,000 for $10,714,285.71.

Profit from option

= proceeds of sale of DM15,000,000 through option − cost of purchase of DM15,000,000 through market + FV (Premium)

$$= \frac{15,000,000}{1.5000} - \frac{15,000,000}{1.4000} + 303,750$$

= − $410,535.71

(b) If at expiry the exchange rate is at the strike price of 1.5000, the owner of the dollar call will allow it to lapse so the writer merely keeps the premium.

Profit from option = FV (Premium)
= + $303,750

(c) If at expiry the exchange rate is above the strike price, the dollar put will lapse.

Profit from option = FV (Premium)
= + $303,750

Figure 10.4

Profit profile: sold dollar put strike DM 1.5000

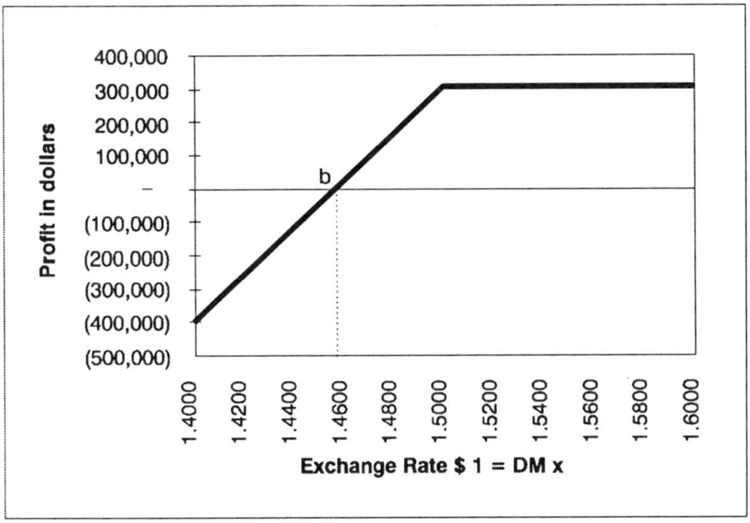

This shape represents the typical profit profile of a sold put.

The break-even rate b is such that the future value of the premium received will be just sufficient to offset the loss from writing the option.

cost of purchase of DM15,000,000	–	proceeds of sale of DM15,000,000	=	FV (Premium)
$\frac{15{,}000{,}000}{b}$	–	$\frac{15{,}000{,}000}{1.5000}$	=	303,750

$$\therefore \quad b = \frac{15{,}000{,}000}{10{,}000{,}000 + 303{,}750}$$

$$= 1.4558$$

Option Pricing

The fair value option premium is the present value of the expected pay-out.

Example 10.6

Calculate the premium for a six month dollar call/yen put with strike price ¥100.00 and face value $1,000,000.

The pay-out of the option will be a function of where the spot rate is at expiry relative to the strike price. If, for example, the spot rate at expiry is ¥106.00, then the pay-out would be ¥6,000,000.

$$\text{Pay-out} = 1{,}000{,}000 \times (106.00 - 100.00) = ¥\ 6{,}000{,}000$$

The expected pay-out will depend on the probability of the spot rate at expiry being at various levels.

A binomial tree can be used to show the set of possible outcomes. Assuming the spot rate at the start of the option period is ¥100.00 and that each month there is equal probability that the rate could move up or down, say 3 yen, then the possible paths which the rate could follow during the 6 month option period are as set out in Exhibit 10.3.

Exhibit 10.3
Binomial tree

End of Month	0	1	2	3	4	5	6
							118
						115	
					112		112
				109		109	
			106		106		106
		103		103		103	
	100		100		100		100
		97		97		97	
			94		94		94
				91		91	
					88		88
						85	
							82

At the end of the first month, the price will be either 100 + 3 = 103 or 100 – 3 = 97.

At the end of the second month, the price could be one of:

103 + 3 = 106	Probability = 1/2 × 1/2 = 1/4	
103 – 3 = 100	Probability = 1/2 × 1/2 = 1/4	} 1/2
97 + 3 = 100	Probability = 1/2 × 1/2 = 1/4	}
97 – 3 = 94	Probability = 1/2 × 1/2 = 1/4	

It is twice as probable that at the end of the second month, the price will be 100 than either 94 or 106.

Possible Outcomes	# Paths	Probability
106	1	1/4
100	2	2/4 = 1/2
94	1	1/4
Total	4	4/4 = 1

And so on.

By the end of the sixth month, there will be seven possible outcomes, with probabilities reflecting the number of paths which get to those outcomes. There are 64 possible paths which the price could follow. (Note: $2^6 = 64$). Twenty of them have a final value of 100. Only one of the 64 paths ends at 118 (the rate has to go up every month for 6 months in a row). Similarly, only one path ends at 82 (the rate has to go down every months for 6 months in a row).

Possible Outcomes	# Paths	Probability
118	1	1/64
112	6	6/64
106	15	15/64
100	20	20/64
94	15	15/64
88	6	6/64
82	1	1/64
Total	64	64/64 = 1

Given that the stike price is 100, the pay-out for each of the possible outcomes would be:

Possible Outcomes	Pay-out in yen
118	18,000,000
112	12,000,000
106	6,000,000
100	0
94	0
88	0
82	0

If the price at expiry is 100 or less, the owner of the option will choose not to exercise so the pay-out will be zero.

The expected pay-out can be calculated by multiplying the pay-out associated with each of the possible outcomes by the probability of that outcome.

Possible Outcomes	Pay-out in yen	Probability	Expected Pay-Out
118	18,000,000	1/64	281,250
112	12,000,000	6/64	1,175,000
106	6,000,000	15/64	1,486,250
100	0	20/64	0
94	0	5/64	0
88	0	6/64	0
82	0	1/64	0
	Total	1	**2,812,500**

The expected pay-out of the option is ¥2,812,500 = $28,125.00 (at spot $1 = ¥100)

If the option premium were paid at expiry, this would be its fair value. In practice, the option premium is generally paid up-front. The fair value option premium is the present value of the expected pay-out at expiry. If the 6 month dollar interest rate is 5% pa, the up-front premium would be:

$$\frac{\$28,125.00}{1 + 0.05 \times 6/12} = \$27,439.02$$

The distribution which shows the probability of each of the possible outcomes is known as the ***probability density function***.

Figure 10.5

Probability density function

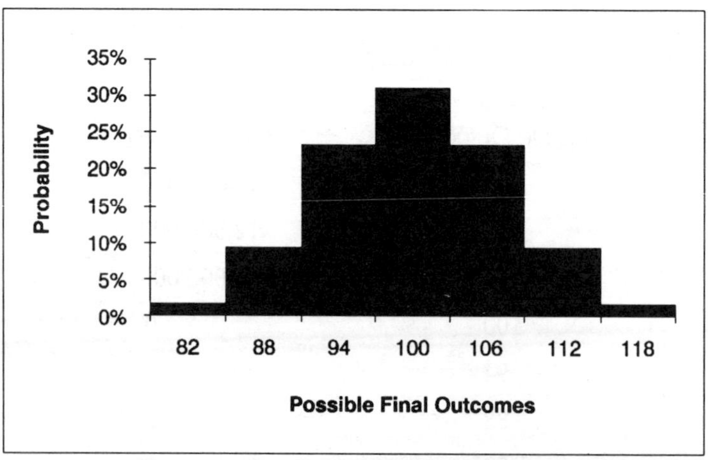

If the option has a different strike price, it will command a different premium. The binomial tree and the probabilities will not change but the expected pay-out will.

Example 10.7

If the strike price were set at 105.00, then the expected pay-out would fall to:

Possible Outcomes	Pay-out in yen	Probability	Expected Pay-out
118	13,000,000	1/64	203,125
112	7,000,000	6/64	656,250
106	1,000,000	15/64	234,375
100	0	20/64	0
94	0	5/64	0
88	0	6/64	0
82	0	1/64	0
	Total	1	**1,093,750**

The expected pay-out would now be ¥1,093,750 = $10,937.50

The up-front premium would be $\frac{\$10{,}937.50}{(1 + 0.05 \times 6/12)} = \$10{,}670.73$

If the up-down factor changes, the option will have a different premium. The pay-out for any given outcome will be the same but the probabilities will change.

Example 10.8

If the up-down factor was ¥2 per month, then the binomial tree would be as in Exhibit 10.4.

Exhibit 10.4

Binomial Tree with Up-Down Factor = ¥ 2

End of Month	0	1	2	3	4	5	6
							112
						110	
					108		108
				106		106	
			104		104		104
		102		102		102	
	100		100		100		100
		98		98		98	
			96		96		96
				94		94	
					92		92
						90	
							88

The expected pay-out for a dollar call with strike price at 100 would be:

Possible Outcomes	Pay-out in yen	Probability	Expected Pay-out
118	13,000,000	1/64	203,125
112	7,000,000	6/64	656,250
106	1,000,000	15/64	234,375
100	0	20/64	0
94	0	5/64	0
88	0	6/64	0
82	0	1/64	0
	Total	1	**1,093,750**

The expected pay-out would now be ¥1,875,000 = $18,750.00

The up-front premium would be $18,292.68

A smaller up-down factor means less volatility. The spread of possible outcomes is less when the up-down factor is ¥2 than when it was ¥3. It can be shown that an up-down factor of ¥3 represents volatility of 10.4% pa and an up-down factor of ¥2 represents volatility of 6.9% pa.[1]

In general, the factors determining the price of a currency option include:

- the strike price in relation to the market rate
- the time to expiry
- the expected volatility
- the risk free interest rate.

Relationship Between the Strike Price and Market Rate

The relationship between the strike price and the market rate will determine whether the option is at-the-money, in-the-money or out-of-the-money in accordance with Exhibit 10.1. An option which is in-the-money has value by virtue of the fact that it is in-the-money. This is referred to as ***intrinsic value.*** The further an option is in-the-money, the greater will be its intrinsic value. By definition, an out-of-the-money option has no intrinsic value.

1. Refer to Example 10.10 to see how volatility is calculated.

Figure 10.6

Intrinsic value: dollar call strike ¥ 110.00

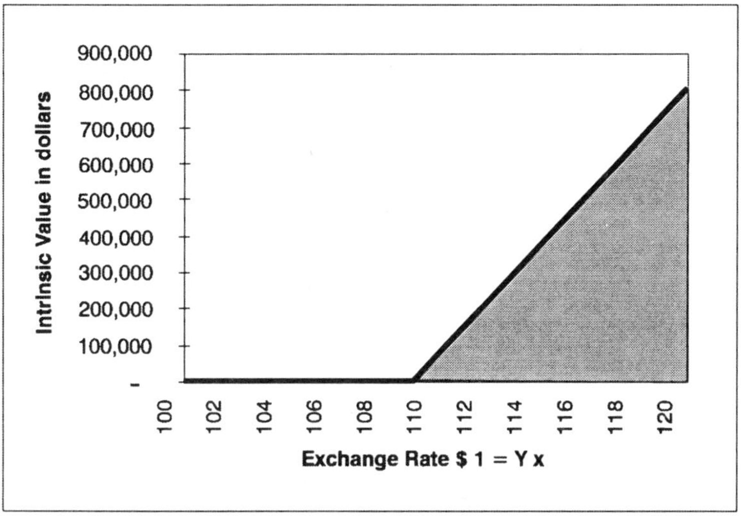

During the life of an option, its intrinsic value will vary as the market rate takes the strike price further into-the-money or out-of-the-money. For example, a dollar call with a strike price of ¥110.00 will have more intrinsic value when the market exchange rate is ¥115.00 than when it is ¥114.00. If the face value of the option is $10,000,000, its intrinsic value in yen terms will be:

at 115.00, intrinsic value = 10,000,000 (115.00 – 110.00) = ¥ 40,000,000;

at 114.00, intrinsic value = 10,000,000 (114.00 – 110.00) = ¥ 30,000,000.

If the market exchange rate falls below the strike price of ¥110.00, its intrinsic value will be zero.

Figure 10.7

Intrinsic value: dollar put strike DM 1.5000

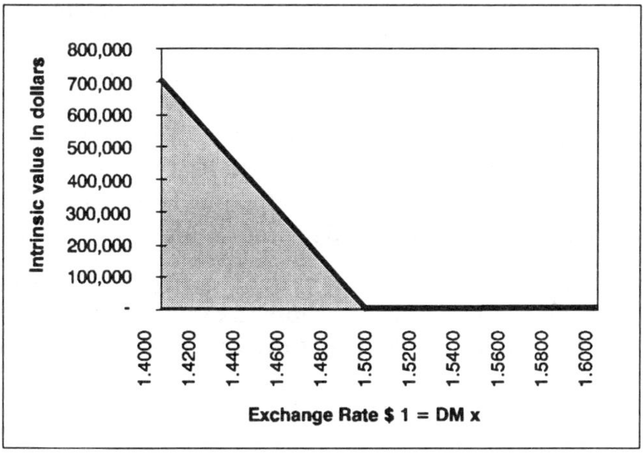

Time to Expiry

An option which has not yet expired has ***time value***. An option which is at-the-money or out-of-the-money has value because it might move into-the-money before expiry. An option which is in-the-money has time value because it might move further in-the-money. The closer the option is to expiry, the lower its time value.

Figure 10.8

Time decay of an at-the-money option

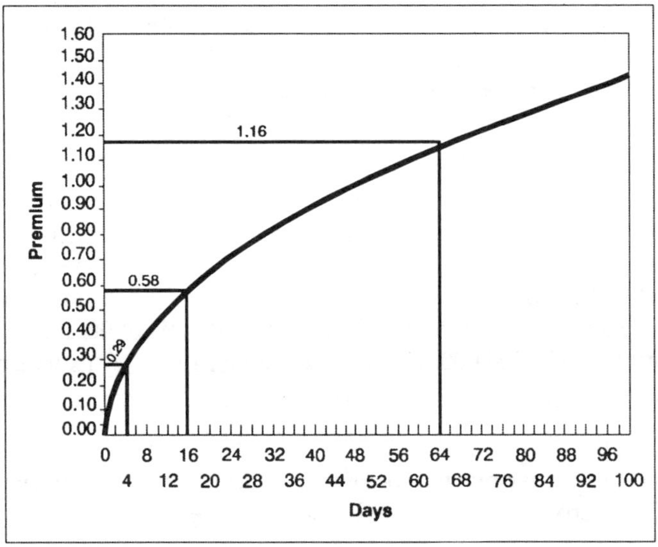

The time value of an option declines as it approaches expiry. An option which is close to at-the-money value declines at an accelerating rate as it approaches expiration. At expiry, time value equals zero. The decline in the time value of an option as it approaches expiry is known as ***time decay***. The time value is a function of the square root of time until expiry. For example, the time value of an at-the-money option with four days until expiry will be half that of the same option with 16 days until expiry. That is, the decay of time value in the final four days will equal that of the previous 12 days which in turn will equal that of the previous 48 days and so on.

The time value of an option will vary as the exchange rate changes. An option which is well out-of-the-money and close to expiry cannot command a high premium because it is unlikely that the option will be in-the-money at expiration.

The time value on an out-of-the-money option declines as the exchange rate takes it further out-of-the-money. For example, a dollar call with strike price at ¥110.00 is further out-of-the-money at ¥105.00 than at ¥109.00. If the at-the-money premium is 2.00% (when the spot rate is ¥112.00), the premium might be 1.90% at ¥109.00 and 0.67% at ¥105.00.

Time value is always positive until the expiration date. It is maximised at the at-the-money strike price where the uncertainty as to whether it will be in or out-of-the-money is greatest.

Figure 10.9

Time value of an option

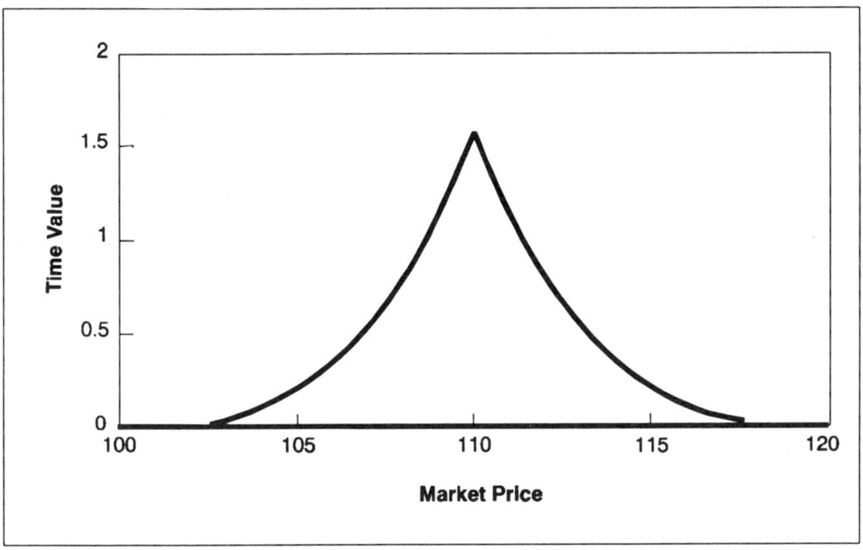

The overall price of an option is the sum of its intrinsic value and time value.

Option premium = intrinsic value + time value	**Equation 10.1**

Figure 10.10

Premium = intrinsic value + time value: dollar call

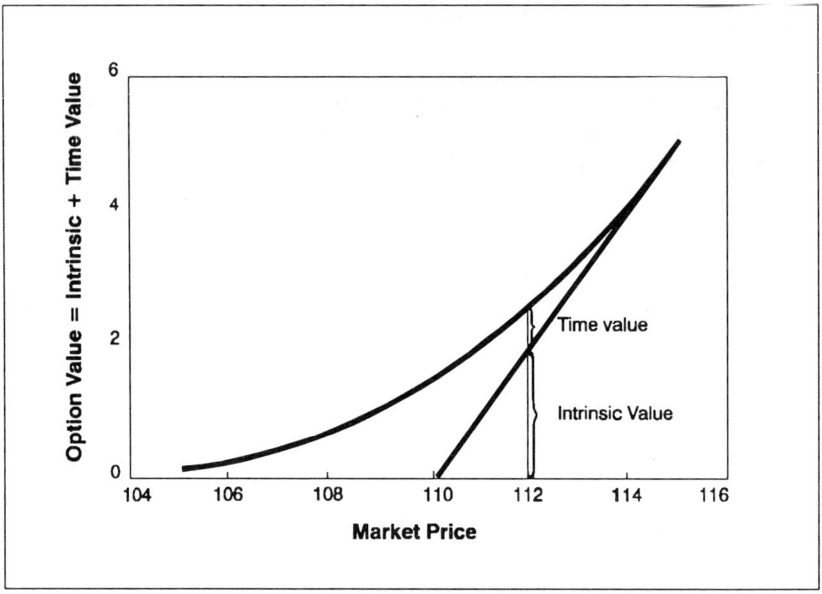

Figure 10.11

Premium = intrinsic value + time value: dollar put

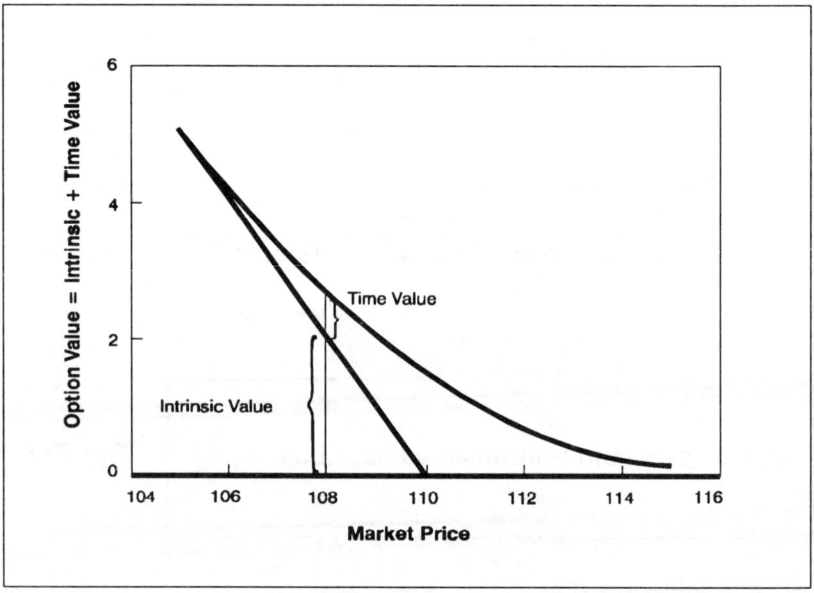

Volatility

The greater the expected volatility of the exchange rate, the higher the option premium will be. The more volatile the exchange rate, the higher the probability that the option will move further into-the-money before expiry and therefore, the greater the risk on the option writer and accordingly, the higher the option premium. Expected volatility is set by the market and is generally a function of recent historical volatility and market expectations. Historic volatility is measured as one standard deviation of exchange rate changes.

$$\sigma_t = \sqrt{\sum p_i(x_i - \overline{x})^2}$$ ***Equation 10.2***

where σ_t = volatility for tenor

x_i = each of the possible exchange rates at expiry

$\overline{x}$ = expected exchange rate at expiry = forward rate

p_i = probability of outcome

The higher the volatility, the larger is a standard deviation. If the exchange rate is more volatile, there is a higher probability that it will move from the current rate of ¥110.00 to, say, ¥115.00 than if the exchange rate is less volatile. Accordingly, the time value is greater the higher the volatility.

Figure 10.12

Time value is a function of volatility

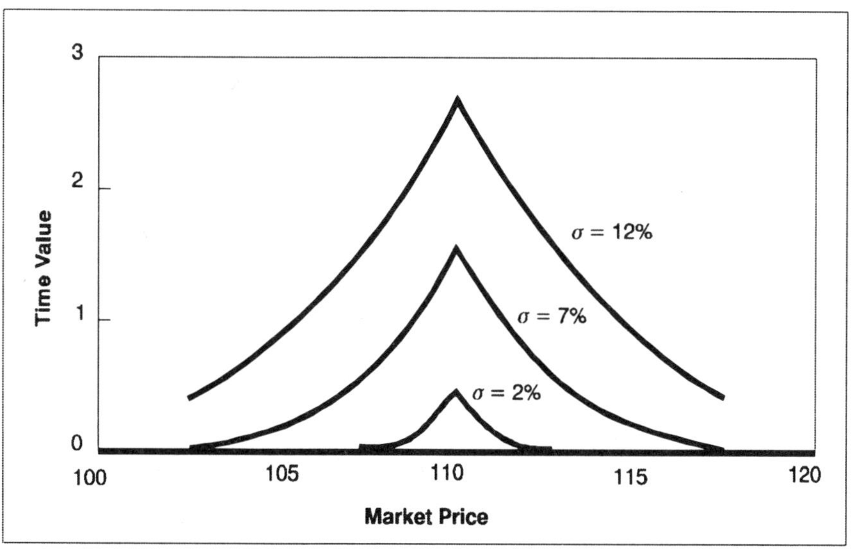

Like interest rates, volatilities are normally expressed in terms of percentage per annum. To convert an annual volatility rate to a volatility rate for a different period, multiply by the square root of time.

$$\sigma_t = \sigma_A \sqrt{t}$$ ***Equation 10.3***

where σ_t = volatility for tenor

σ_A = annual volatility

t = time in years

Example 10.9

Annual volatility is 10% pa. Calculate the volatility for tenors of:

a) three months

$$t = 1/4$$

$$\sigma_t = 10\sqrt{(1/4)} = 10 \times 1/2 = 5\%.$$

b) two years

$$t = 2$$

$$\sigma_t = 10\sqrt{2} = 14.1\%$$

Example 10.10

Calculate (annual) volatility for the distribution in Example 10.6.

Outcome	$(x - \bar{x})$	$(x - \bar{x})^2$	Probability(p)	$p(x - \bar{x})^2$
118	18	324	1/64	5.0625
112	12	144	6/64	13.500
106	6	36	15/64	8.4375
100	0	0	20/64	0
94	6	36	15/64	8.4375
88	12	144	6/64	13.500
82	18	324	1/64	5.0625
		Total	64/64	54.000

$$\therefore \sigma_t = \sqrt{54} = 7.348469$$

Expressed as a percentage of the forward rate $= \frac{7.348469}{100} = 7.348469\%$

Annualised $\sigma_A = \frac{\sigma_t}{\sqrt{6/12}} = \frac{7.348469}{0.707107} = 10.4\%$ pa

Expectations are subjective. Consequently, expected volatility is likely to vary from one market participant to another. In fact, volatility is such an important determinant of options pricing that in practice option dealers simply quote bid and offer volatilities.

Risk-Free Interest Rate

The price of an option also depends on the risk-free interest rate. As the option premium is paid up-front, but the currency is not delivered until the value date for which the option is exercised, the option writer has the use of the premium. The writer will adjust the premium downwards to reflect its time value. The interest rate used to discount the premium to adjust for its time value is known as the ***risk-free interest rate***, because it is assumed that there is no credit risk involved in discounting the premium. The relative importance of the risk-free interest rate tends to increase the longer the term of the option.

Put-Call Parity

Calls and puts are closely related. If a person bought a dollar call/yen put and sold a dollar put/yen call with the same strike price for the same amount and with the same expiry, he or she would have the same profit outcome at expiry as if dollars had been bought forward against yen.

Example 10.11

A trader bought a 6 month dollar call/yen put with strike price $1 = ¥110.00 and sold a 6 month dollar put/yen call also with a strike price of $1 = ¥110.00. The pay-out at the end of the 6 month period will be the same as if the trader had purchased dollars forward against yen at an outright rate of ¥110.00 as set out below:

Spot rate at expiry	Pay-out from bought $ call	Pay-out from sold $ put	Combined Pay-out
105.00	0	– 5.00	– 5.00
106.00	0	– 4.00	– 4.00
107.00	0	– 3.00	– 3.00
108.00	0	– 2.00	– 2.00
109.00	0	– 1.00	– 1.00
110.00	0	0	0
111.00	+ 1.00	0	+ 1.00
112.00	+ 2.00	0	+ 2.00
113.00	+ 3.00	0	+ 3.00
114.00	+ 4.00	0	+ 4.00
115.00	+ 5.00	0	+ 5.00

The relationship that a bought call and a sold put equals a long forward is known as ***put-call parity.***

Bought Call + Sold Put = Bought Forward[3] *Equation 10.4*

It follows that a sold call and a bought put produces the same outcome as a short forward position.

Put-Call Arbitrage

Put-call parity means that there is a unique relationship between the call premium and the put premium for a given strike. If the call premium and put premium are not in accordance with put-call parity, then an arbitrage opportunity exists.

Example 10.12

Spot	$1	=	¥110.00
6 month forward	$1	=	¥109.00
Premium of 6 month options with strike ¥108.00:			
Dollar call			¥2.00
Dollar put			¥1.10

By buying a ¥108 dollar call and selling a ¥108 dollar put, it is possible to engineer a long dollar position against the yen at an effective exchange rate

3. Applies to European options only.

$1 = ¥108.00. This position could be covered by selling dollars 6 months forward at the forward rate $1 = ¥109.00, for a gain of ¥1.00. The net premium paid would be ¥0.90 (ie ¥2.00 to buy the dollar call less ¥1.10 from selling the dollar put). This represents the cost of engineering the long dollar position at 108.00. The 10 points difference between the ¥1.00 gain and the ¥0.90 net premium constitutes profit from the arbitrage.

Steps to arbitrage put-call disparity

		Premium
Buy 108 dollar call		– ¥2.00
Sell 108 dollar put		+ ¥1.10
Long dollars forward at	108.00	– ¥0.90
Sell dollars forward at	109.00	
Gain from closing	¥1.00	
Net premium	– ¥0.90	
Profit	¥0.10	

To be more precise, the future value of the ¥0.90 net premium should be compared to ¥1.00 settlement which will occur at the end of the 6 month period. However, if the 6 month yen interest rate is as low as, say, 0.5% pa, the difference is trivial.

Put-call parity can be restated as:

Equation 10.5

forward rate – strike rate = FV(call premium – put premium)

People would exploit this arbitrage opportunity until put-call parity is resumed. In practice, the arbitrage process will ensure that the put-call parity relationship applies.

For an option pricing model to be arbitrage-free, the at-the-money strike price must equal the forward rate. It follows from Equation 10.5 that the call premium will equal the put premium for at-the-money options.

The binomial model can be made arbitrage-free by centering the possible outcomes at expiry around the forward rate by assuming that the spot rate drifts from its current level towards the forward rate during the life of the option. This means that the up-factor will have a different value from the down-factor by twice the amount of drift.

Revisiting the binomial model to price a 6 month dollar call/yen put when the spot rate is $1 = ¥100.00 and the 6 month forward rate is $1 = ¥99.00, the binomial tree would be as in Exhibit 10.5 where the up-down factor is ¥3 +/– the allowance for drift towards the forward rate.

$$\text{Monthly drift} = \frac{\text{forward rate} - \text{spot rate}}{\text{number of months}} = \frac{99.00 - 100.00}{6} = -¥0.17$$

The up outcome for month 1 = 100.00 + 3.00 – 0.17 = ¥102.83

The down outcome for month 1 = 100.00 – 3.00 – 0.17 = ¥96.83

In general,

Up outcome in month x = outcome in month (x – 1) + up factor + drift

Down outcome in month x = outcome in month (x – 1) – down factor + drfit

Exhibit 10.5

Binomial tree centered around forward rate $1 = ¥ 99.00

End of Month	0	1	2	3	4	5	6
							117.00
						114.17	
					111.33		111.00
				108.50		108.17	
			105.67		105.33		105.00
		102.83		102.50		102.17	
	100.00		99.67		99.33		**99.00**
		96.83		96.50		96.17	
			93.67		93.33		93.00
				90.50		90.17	
					87.33		87.00
						84.17	
							81.00

The description of intrinsic value can be qualified to be the extent to which the *forward* rate is better than the strike price.

Interest Rate Differentials

The price of a currency option is therefore related to the interest rates of the two currencies.

The writer of the option has a potential net exchange position. For example, if writing a dollar put/deutschemark call, the writer has a risk that if the dollar depreciates, the option will be exercised and he or she will tend to lose money. To avoid this, the writer may choose to hedge all or part of the potential position by selling dollars forward before the exchange rate falls. It is common practice to hedge a variable portion of the potential position. This is known as ***delta hedging*** and is discussed in Chapter 14.

As the interest rate differential changes, the benefit or cost of delta hedging or unhedging will change. Consequently, the interest rate differential is a determinant of the option price.

The relative importance of the interest differential tends to increase the longer the term of the option.

American Versus European Options

An American-style option will command a higher premium than the equivalent European-style option, provided the call currency is the higher interest rate currency. For example, if dollar interest rates are higher than yen interest rates, the premium on an American-style dollar call/ yen put would be higher than on a European-style dollar call/yen put with the same strike price and expiry date. This is because the holder of an American-style dollar call can exercise for spot value prior to the expiry date, thereby receiving the higher interest currency and paying the lower interest currency early. The writer raises the premium on the American option to provide for this possibility.

The premium on an American-style option is never less than the equivalent European-style option. If the call currency is the lower interest rate currency, it will command the same premium as the holder of the American option will tend not to exercise early for spot value because of the need to fund the higher interest currency until the expiry date.

Black-Scholes model

The binomial model provides a more accurate calculation of the option premium when the time interval between steps in the binomial tree is smaller and the number of possible outcomes at expiry is larger. In 1973, Fisher Black and Myron Scholes developed a mathematical model for pricing stock options.

$$C = S.N(d_1) - K.e^{-rt}.N(d_2)$$ *Equation 10.6*

where:

C	=	call premium
S	=	security price
K	=	strike price
r	=	risk-free interest rate (expressed as a continuous compounding rate)
t	=	time to expiry in years
N( )	=	Cumulative normal distribution function[4]
d_1	=	$\dfrac{\log\left(\frac{S}{K}\right) + r + \frac{1}{2}\sigma t}{\sigma\sqrt{t}}$
d_2	=	$d_1 - \sigma\sqrt{t}$
σ	=	expected volatility

The put-call parity relationship makes it possible to calculate the premium of puts.

$$P = C + e^{-rt}.K - S$$ *Equation 10.7*

While the Black-Scholes formula may look complicated, it can easily be seen that the call premium depends upon the strike price relative to the price of the security, expected volatility, time to expiry and the risk-free interest rate – the same factors which determined the option premium in the binomial model.

In effect, the Black-Scholes model is the continuous case of the binomial model. There are an infinite number of paths. The probability density function as shown in Figure 10.5 becomes a normal distribution as shown in Figure 10.13.

4. Cumulative normal distribution tables are readily available (see Appendix) or use NORMAL function on calculator or spreadsheet.

Figure 10.13

Normal probability density function

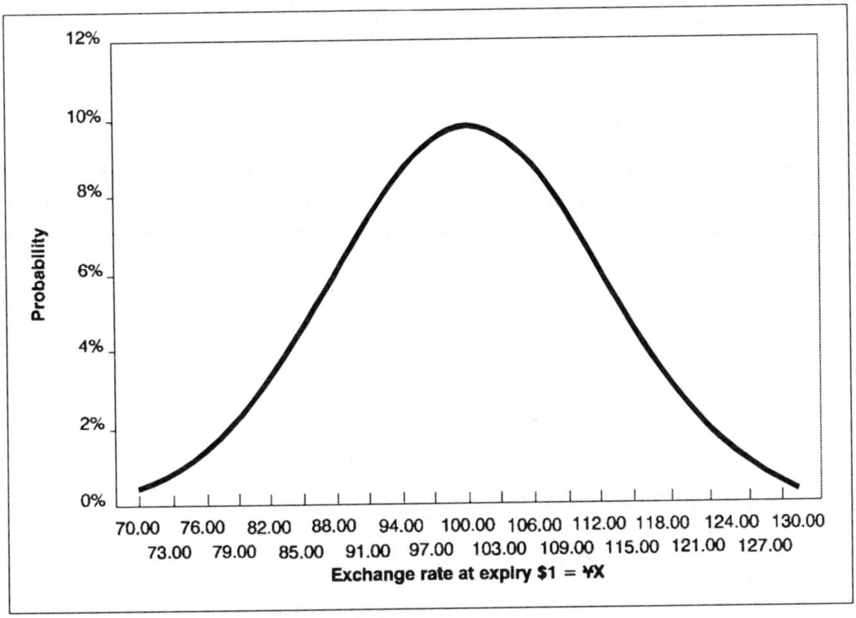

The Black-Scholes model has been adapted for currency options to provide for the fact that the forward rate is generally different from the spot rate because the interest rates of the two currencies are not normally equal.

$$C = \frac{s\,N(d_1)}{(1+r_C t)} - \frac{k\,N(d_2)}{(1+r_T t)}$$

Equation 10.8

where:

s	=	spot rate
k	=	strike price
r_T	=	terms currency interest rate
r_C	=	commodity currency interest rate
t	=	time to expiry in years
$N(\ )$	=	Cumulative normal distribution function
d_1	=	$\dfrac{\log_e(s/k) + (r_T - r_C + \frac{1}{2}\sigma)t}{\sigma\sqrt{t}}$
d_2	=	$d_1 - \sigma\sqrt{t}$
σ	=	expected volatility

$$P = C - \frac{S}{(1 + r_C t)} + \frac{K}{(1 + r_T t)}$$ *Equation 10.9*

Example 10.13

Calculate the premium for a 3 month dollar call/yen put with strike price ¥108.00 given the current spot rate is $1 = ¥110.00, 3 month dollar and yen interest rates are 5.0% and 1% pa respectively and assuming volatility will be 10% pa.

$$s = 110.00$$

$$k = 108.00$$

$$t = 3/12 = 0.25$$

$$\sigma = 10\% \text{ pa} = 0.10$$

$$r_T = 1.0\% \text{ pa} = 0.01$$

$$r_C = 5.0\% \text{ pa} = 0.05$$

Hence,

$$d_1 = \frac{\ln(110/108) + (0.01 - 0.05 + ½(0.10)) \times 0.25}{0.1\sqrt{0.25}}$$

$$= \frac{0.018349 - 0.00875}{0.05}$$

$$= 0.191983$$

$$d_2 = 0.191983 - 0.05$$

$$= 0.141983$$

$$N(d_1) = 0.576122$$

$$N(d_2) = 0.556453$$

$$\therefore C = 110/(1+0.05/4) \times 0.576122 - 108/(1+0.01/4) \times 0.556453$$

$$= 2.64$$

As the forward rate is $f = \frac{s(1 + r_T t)}{(1 + r_C t)} = 108.92,$

it can be shown that the call premium formula can be expressed as:

$$C = \frac{f.N(d_1) - k.N(d_2)}{(1 + r_T t)}$$

Equation 10.10

$$= \frac{108.92 \times 0.576122 - 108 \times 0.556453}{1 + 0.01 \times 3/12}$$

$$= 2.64$$

Lognormal Model

One limitation of the normal binomial model and therefore the Black-Scholes model is that if volatility is large enough, it can generate outcomes with negative values. In reality, negative exchange rates are nonsensical. The lognormal model overcomes this problem by generating a binomial tree using up-down factors which are constant percentage changes rather than absolute amounts. The continuous case produces what is known as a ***lognormal*** distribution. In most cases, the normal binomial and adapted Black-Scholes models are a good approximation for the lognormal model.

Practice Problems

10.1 Pricing a put using a binomial model

Use a simple binomial model to calculate the premium for a 3 month dollar put/yen call given:

Spot rate	s	$1	= ¥110.00
Strike price	k	$1	= ¥112.00
Face value			$10,000,000
3 month yen interest rate			1.0% pa
3 month dollar interest rate			5.0% pa
Hence, forward rate	f	$1	= ¥108.92
Up-down factor			= ¥2.00 per month +/– drift

10.2 Volatility

Calculate the (annual) volatility in Practice Problem 10.1.

10.3 Pricing put using the Black-Scholes formula

Use the adapted Black-Scholes formula and put-call parity to calculate the premium for the same dollar put as in Practice Problem 10.1. Use volatility as calculated in Practice problem 10.2.

10.4 Put-Call Arbitrage

Identify the arbitrage opportunity available given the following prices. Articulate the actions which need to be taken to profit through the above arbitrage. Calculate the profit which could be made on a face value of $10,000,000.

Spot rate	$1	=	DM1.5000
1 year forward rate	$1	=	DM1.4800
1 year dollar call(k = 1.5200) premium		=	DM0.0100
1 year dollar put (k = 1.5200) premium		=	DM0.0450
1 year deutschemark interest rate			3.0% pa

Supplementary Questions

10.5 Pricing a call using binomial model

Use a binomial model to calculate the premium of a 3 month sterling call/ dollar put given:

Spot rate	s	=	1.7000
Forward rate	f	=	1.6970
Strike price	k	=	1.7200
Face value			£1,000,000
3 month dollar interest rate		=	6.0% pa
3 month sterling interest rate		=	6.7% pa
Up-down factor		=	$0.0400 per month +/– drift

10.6 Volatility

Calculate the (annual) volatility in Supplementary Question 10.5.

10.7 Pricing a call using the Black-Scholes model

Use the adapted Black-Scholes formula to calculate the premium for the same sterling call as in Supplementary Question 10.5.

11

Applications of Currency Options

Options have many practical applications for exporters, importers, borrowers, investors and traders. This chapter examines a number of applications which involve the use of standard options. By varying one or more of the number and type of option, the strike prices, and the face value of the options, it is possible to tailor a variety of outcomes to suit the particular risk profile desired for a foreign currency exposure.

Options provide a person with a foreign exchange exposure with an extremely flexible tool for manipulating potential cash flows and the associated risk.

Natural Options

An option which is bought or sold with an underlying foreign exchange exposure is called a ***natural option***.

Importer

Example 11.1

An importer, who has an obligation to pay DM10,000,000 in one month's time, considers three scenarios:

1. Remaining unhedged and purchasing the deutschemarks at the prevailing spot rate one month from now;
2. Hedging by buying deutschemarks forward; or
3. Hedging by buying a dollar put/ deutschemark call.

The prevailing market rates are:

Spot rate	$1 = DM1.5100
1 month forward rate	$1 = DM1.5070
1 month dollar interest rate	5% pa
1 month dollar put (strike 1.5100)	1%

(a) Calculate the premium payable in dollars.

$$\begin{aligned} \text{Premium} &= \text{DM}10{,}000{,}000 \times 1/100 \\ &= \text{DM}100{,}000 \\ &= \$66{,}225.17 \text{ (at spot rate 1.5100)} \\ \text{FV (Premium)} &= \$66{,}225.17 \times (1 + 0.05 \times 1/12) \\ &= \$66{,}501.11 \end{aligned}$$

(b) Calculate the cost of buying DM10,000,000 for value the forward date for each of the three scenarios if at maturity the spot rate is:

(i) 1.4800;

(ii) 1.5100;

(iii) 1.5400.

1. The dollar cost of the imports if unhedged

$$= \frac{10{,}000{,}000}{x} \quad \text{where x = spot rate at maturity.}$$

(i) $x = 1.4800, \text{ cost } = \dfrac{10{,}000{,}000}{1.4800} = \$6{,}756{,}756.76$

(ii) $x = 1.5100, \text{ cost } = \dfrac{10{,}000{,}000}{1.5100} = \$6{,}622{,}516.56$

(iii) $x = 1.5400, \text{ cost } = \dfrac{10{,}000{,}000}{1.5400} = \$6{,}493{,}506.49$

2. The dollar cost of the imports if hedged with a forward

(i) $x = 1.4800, \text{ cost } = \dfrac{10{,}000{,}000}{1.5070} = \$6{,}635{,}700.07$

(ii) $x = 1.5100, \text{ cost } = \dfrac{10{,}000{,}000}{1.5070} = \$6{,}635{,}700.07$

(iii) $x = 1.5400, \text{ cost } = \dfrac{10{,}000{,}000}{1.5070} = \$6{,}635{,}700.07$

3. The dollar cost of the imports if hedged with a bought dollar put

$$= \frac{10{,}000{,}000}{x} + \text{FV (Premium) if } x \geq 1.5100 \text{ (strike price), or}$$

$$\frac{10{,}000{,}000}{1.5100} + \text{FV (Premium) if } x < 1.5100 \text{ (strike price).}$$

(i) $x = 1.4800, \text{ cost } = \dfrac{10{,}000{,}000}{1.5100} + 66{,}501.11 = \$\ 6{,}689{,}017.67$

(ii) $x = 1.5100, \text{ cost } = \dfrac{10{,}000{,}000}{1.5100} + 66{,}501.11 = \$\ 6{,}689{,}017.67$

(iii) $x = 1.5400, \text{ cost } = \dfrac{10{,}000{,}000}{1.5400} + 66{,}501.11 = \$\ 6{,}560{,}007.60$

Figure 11.1
Imports hedged with bought dollar put

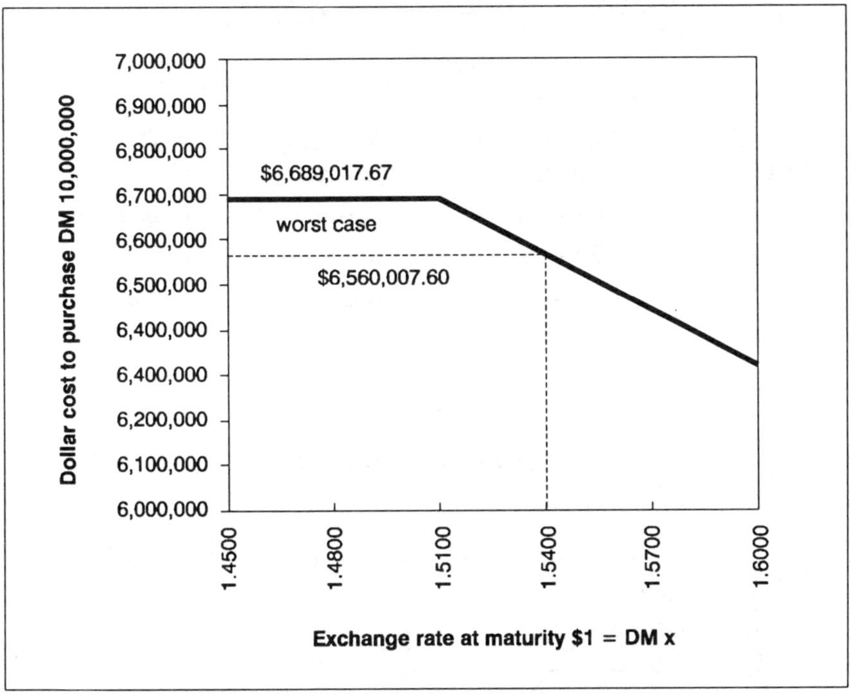

The effect of buying the dollar put is to place a ceiling on the cost of the imports without limiting the potential benefit if the spot rate rises. The importer limits the cost to a maximum of $6,689,017.67 without limiting the minimum.

(c) Calculate the break-even rates between being:

- (i) unhedged and hedged with a forward;
- (ii) unhedged and hedged with a bought put;
- (iii) hedged with a forward and hedged with a bought put.

(i) The break-even rate b_1 occurs where:

cost if unhedged = cost if hedged with a forward

$$\text{ie} \quad \frac{10{,}000{,}000}{b_1} = \frac{10{,}000{,}000}{1.5070}$$

$$\therefore \quad b_1 = 1.5070$$

(ii) The break-even rate b_2 occurs where:

cost if unhedged = cost if hedged with put

$$\text{ie} \quad \frac{10{,}000{,}000}{b_2} = \frac{10{,}000{,}000}{1.5100} + 66{,}501.11$$

$$\therefore \quad b_2 = 1.4950$$

(iii) The break-even rate b_3 occurs where:

cost with forward = cost with put

$$\text{ie} \quad \frac{10{,}000{,}000}{1.5070} = \frac{10{,}000{,}000}{b_3} + 66{,}501.11$$

$$\therefore \quad b_3 = 1.5223$$

Spot rate at maturity	Lowest cost strategy	Mid cost strategy	Highest cost strategy
$x < b_2$	forward	option	unhedged
$b_2 < x < b_1$	forward	unhedged	option
$b_1 < x < b_3$	unhedged	forward	option
$x > b_3$	unhedged	option	forward

Figure 11.2

Importer's alternatives

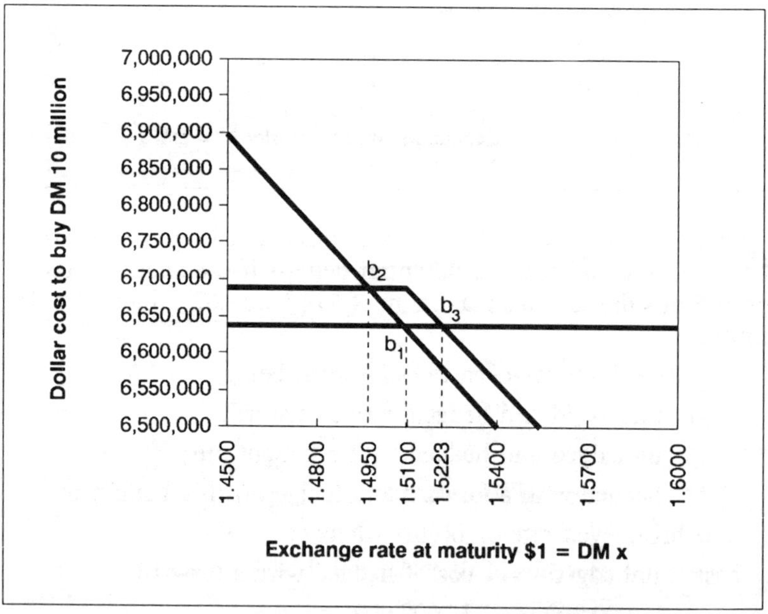

Exporter

Example 11.2

An exporter will receive DM1,000,000 in three months time and considers three scenarios:

1. Remaining unhedged and selling the deutschemarks at the prevailing spot rate three months from now;

2. Hedging by selling the deutschemarks forward; or
3. Hedging by buying a dollar call /deutschemark put.

The prevailing market rates are:

Spot rate	$1 =	DM1.5100
3 month forward rate	$1 =	DM1.5000
3 month dollar interest rate		5.0% pa
3 month dollar call (strike 1.5000)		1.5%

(a) Calculate the premium payable in dollars.

Premium = DM1,000,000 × 1.5/100
= DM15,000
= $9,933.77 (at spot rate 1.5100)

FV (premium) = 9,933.77 × (1 + 0.05/4)
= $10,057.94

(b) Calculate the proceeds from selling DM1,000,000 for each of the three scenarios for the forward value date if at maturity the spot rate is:

(i) 1.4500;
(ii) 1.5000;
(iii) 1.5500.

1. The dollar proceeds of the exports if unhedged

$$= \frac{1{,}000{,}000}{x} \quad \text{where } x = \text{spot rate at maturity}$$

(i) $x = 1.4500$, proceeds $= \dfrac{1{,}000{,}000}{1.4500} =$ \$689,655.17

(ii) $x = 1.5000$, proceeds $= \dfrac{1{,}000{,}000}{1.5000} =$ \$666,666.67

(iii) $x = 1.5500$, proceeds $= \dfrac{1{,}000{,}000}{1.5500} =$ \$645,161.29

2. The dollar proceeds of the exports if hedged with a forward

$$= \frac{1{,}000{,}000}{f} \quad \text{where } f = \text{forward rate}$$

(i) $x = 1.4500$, proceeds $= \dfrac{1{,}000{,}000}{1.5000} =$ \$666,666.67

(ii) $x = 1.5000$, proceeds $= \dfrac{1{,}000{,}000}{1.5000} =$ \$666,666.67

(iii) $x = 1.5500$, proceeds $= \dfrac{1{,}000{,}000}{1.5000} =$ \$666,666.67

3. The dollar proceeds of the exports if hedged with a bought dollar call

$$= \frac{1{,}000{,}000}{x} \quad - \quad \text{FV (Premium) if } x \leq 1.5000 \text{ (strike price); or}$$

$$= \frac{1{,}000{,}000}{1.5000} \quad - \quad \text{FV (Premium) if } x > 1.5000 \text{ (strike price).}$$

(i) $x = 1.4500$, proceeds $= \frac{1{,}000{,}000}{1.4500} - 10{,}057.94 = \$679{,}597.23$

(ii) $x = 1.5000$, proceeds $= \frac{1{,}000{,}000}{1.5000} - 10{,}057.94 = \$656{,}608.73$

(iii) $x = 1.5500$, proceeds $= \frac{1{,}000{,}000}{1.5000} - 10{,}057.94 = \$656{,}608.73$

Figure 11.3

Exports hedged with bought dollar call

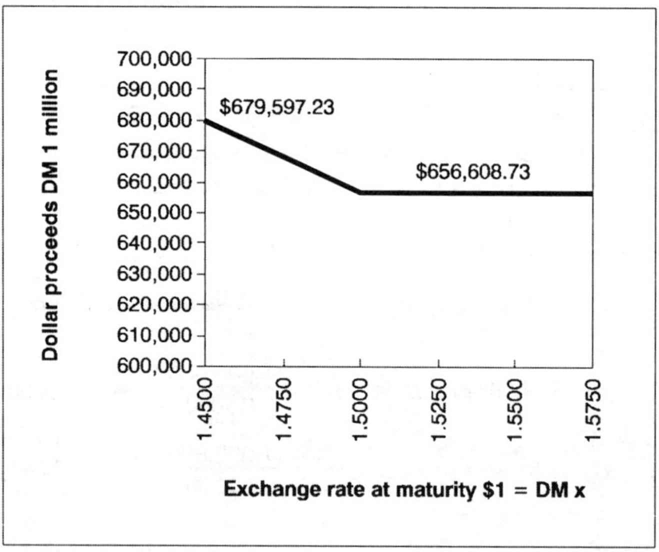

The effect of buying the dollar call is to limit the worst case dollar proceeds to $656,608.73 without limiting the potential benefits if the spot rate falls.

(c) Calculate the break-even rates between being:

(i) unhedged and hedged with a forward;

(ii) unhedged and hedged with a bought call;

(iii) hedged with a forward and hedged with a bought call.

(i) The break-even rate b_1 occurs where:

$$\text{proceeds if unhedged} = \text{proceeds if hedged}$$

$$\text{ie} \quad \frac{1{,}000{,}000}{b_1} = \frac{1{,}000{,}000}{1.5070}$$

$$\therefore \quad b_1 = 1.5070 \text{ (ie the forward rate)}$$

(ii) The break-even rate b_2 occurs where:

$$\text{proceeds if unhedged} = \text{proceeds with option}$$

$$\text{ie} \quad \frac{1{,}000{,}000}{b_2} = \frac{1{,}000{,}000}{1.5000} - 10{,}057.94$$

$$\therefore \quad b_2 = 1.5230$$

(iii) The break-even rate b_3 occurs where:

$$\text{proceeds if hedged} = \text{proceeds with option}$$

$$\text{ie} \quad \frac{1{,}000{,}000}{1.5070} = \frac{1{,}000{,}000}{b_3} - 10{,}057.94$$

$$\therefore \quad b_3 = 1.4845$$

Figure 11.4(a)

Exporter's alternatives

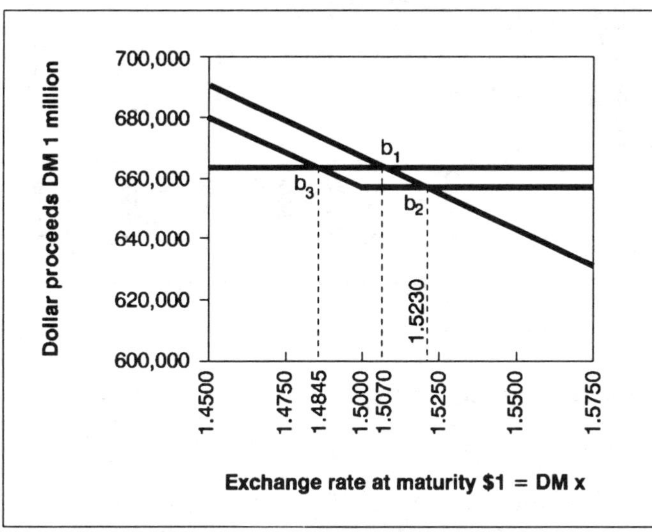

The relative merit of the three strategies can be ranked depending on what the spot rate turns out to be at maturity.

Spot rate at maturity	Highest proceeds strategy	Mid range strategy	Lowest proceeds strategy
$x < b_3$	unhedged	option	forward
$b_3 < x < b_1$	unhedged	forward	option
$b_1 < x < b_2$	forward	unhedged	option
$x < b_2$	forward	option	unhedged

Effective Exchange Rate

People sometimes like to review the possible outcomes of different strategies in terms of their effective exchange rates rather than as the dollar proceeds or costs. Diagrams such as Figure 11.4(a) can be redrawn with the effective exchange rate as the vertical axis as shown in Figure 11.4(b).

Figure 11.4(b)
Effective exchange rate

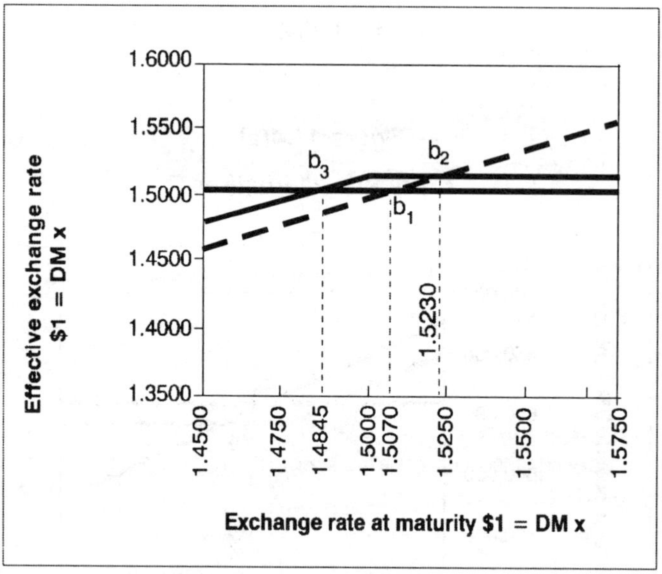

Foreign Currency Borrower

Example 11.3

A real estate developer requires $20,000,000 for six months. Upon electing to borrow Swiss francs for the period at an interest rate of 3% pa interest in arrears, the developer considers four scenarios:

1. Remaining unhedged and purchasing the required Swiss francs (principal plus interest) at the prevailing spot rate at maturity;
2. Hedging by buying forward Swiss francs (principal plus interest);

3. Hedging by buying a dollar put/Swiss franc call; or
4. Hemaining unhedged but writing a dollar call/Swiss franc put.

The prevailing markets rates are:

Spot rate	\$1 = SF1.2500	1.2510
6 month forward rate	\$1 = SF1.2370	1.2390
6 month dollar interest rate	5.0% pa	
6 month dollar put/SF call (strike 1.2500)	3.8%	4.0%
6 month dollar call/SF put (strike 1.2500)	2.8%	3.0%

(a) Calculate the Swiss franc liability due in six months.

SF Principal	= 20,000,000 × 1.2510	=	SF25,020,000
SF Interest	= 25,020,000 × 0.03/2	=	SF 375,300
SF (Principal + Interest) =		=	SF25,395,300

(b) Calculate the dollar premium required to buy a dollar put to cover this liability and the dollar premium received from selling a dollar call for the same face value.

Premium paid for dollar put $= \frac{25{,}395{,}300}{1.2500} \times \frac{4.0}{100} = \$812{,}649.60$

FV (Premium) paid $= 812{,}649.60\ (1 + 0.05/2) = \$832{,}965.84$

Premium received from dollar call $= \frac{25{,}395{,}300}{1.2500} \times \frac{2.8}{100} = \$568{,}854.72$

FV (Premium) received $= 568{,}854.72 \times (1 + 0.05/2) = \$583{,}076.09$

(c) Calculate the dollar cost of repaying the Swiss francs (principal + interest) under each of the four scenarios if the spot rate at maturity is:

(i) 1.1000

(ii) 1.2500

(iii) 1.4000

1. Unhedged

$= \frac{25{,}395{,}300}{x}$ where x = spot bid rate at maturity.

2. Hedged with a forward

$= \frac{25{,}395{,}300}{f}$ where f = forward bid rate.

3. Hedged with a bought dollar put

$$= \frac{25,395,300}{x} + 832,965.84 \quad \text{if } x \geq 1.2500, \text{ or}$$

$$= \frac{25,395,300}{1.2500} + 832,965.84 \quad \text{if } x < 1.2500.$$

4. Unhedged with a sold dollar call

$$= \frac{25,395,300}{1.2500} - 583,076.09 \quad \text{if } x > 1.2500, \text{ or}$$

$$= \frac{25,395,300}{x} - 583,076.09 \quad \text{if } x \leq 1.2500.$$

Figure 11.5

SF borrower's alternatives

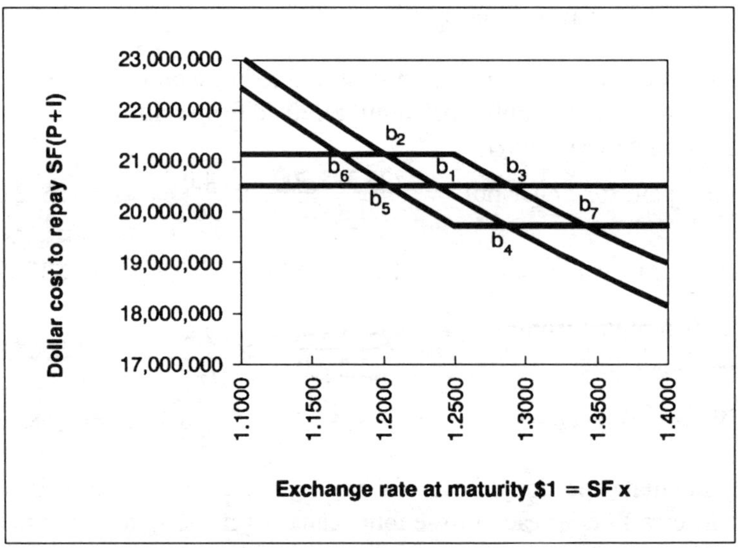

Dollar cost of purchasing SF 25,395,300

Spot rate at maturity:	1.1000	1.2500	1.4000
1. Unhedged	23,086,636.36	20,316,240.00	18,139,500.00
2. Hedged with a forward at 1.2370	20,529,749.39	20,529,749.39	20,529,74.39
3. Hedged with bought dollar put strike 1.2500	21,149,205.84	21,149,205.84	18,972,465.84
4. Unhedged with a sold dollar call strike 1.2500	22,503,560.27	19,733,163.91	19,733,163.91

(d) Calculate the effective borrowing cost under each of the above four scenarios.

$$\text{Effective borrowing cost} = \frac{\$\ \text{cost to repay SF (P + I)} - 20{,}000{,}000}{20{,}000{,}000} \times 200$$

Spot rate at maturity:	1.1000	1.2500	1.4000
	Effective borrowing cost % pa		
1. Unhedged	30.9%	3.2%	–18.6%
2. Hedged with a forward at 1.2370	5.3%	5.3%	5.3%
3. Hedged with a bought dollar put strike 1.2500	11.5%	11.5%	–10.3%
4. Unhedged with a sold dollar call strike 1.2500	25.0%	– 2.7%	– 2.7%

Figure 11.6
Effective borrowing costs

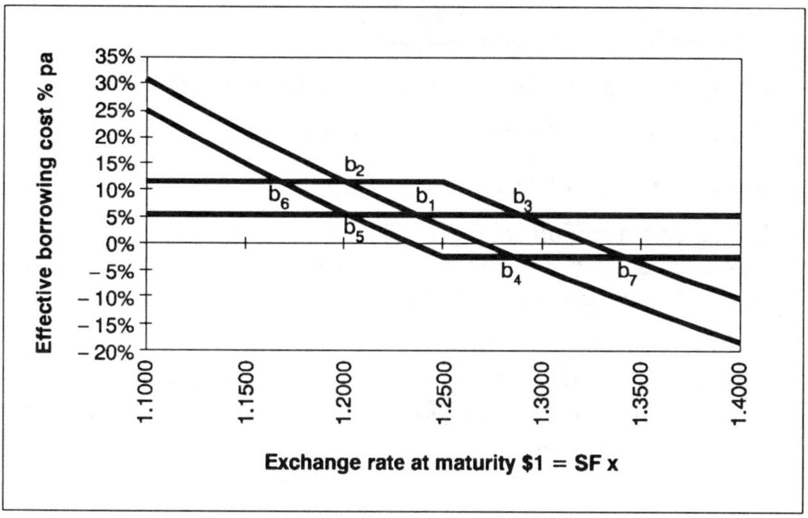

(e) Determine the break-even rates between being:

(i) unhedged and hedged with a forward, b_1;

(ii) unhedged and hedged with a bought dollar put, b_2;

(iii) hedged with a forward and hedged with a bought dollar put, b_3;

(iv) unhedged and unhedged with a sold dollar call, b_4;

(v) hedged with a forward and unhedged with a sold dollar call, b_5;

(vi) hedged with a bought dollar put and unhedged with a sold dollar call, b_6 and b_7.

The break-even rates are:

	Exchange rate	\$ cost of SF (P + I)	Effective interest rate % pa
b_1	1.2370	20,529,749.39	5.3 %
b_2	1.2008	21,149,205.84	11.5 %
b_3	1.2893	20,529,749.39	5.3 %
b_4	1.2869	19,733,163.91	– 2.7 %
b_5	1.2028	20,529,749.39	5.3 %
b_6	1.1686	21,149,205.84	11.5 %
b_7	1.3437	19,733,163.91	– 2.7 %

Foreign Exchange Trader

Example 11.4

One month ago, a foreign exchange trader bought \$10,000,000 against deutschemarks at an outright three month forward rate of 1.4800. The spot rate has since risen to 1.5150 and the two month forward rate is now 1.5100. The two month dollar interest rate is 5% pa. The trader considers three strategies for taking profits:

1. selling dollars two months forward;
2. buying a dollar put (strike 1.5100) premium 2.0%; or
3. writing a dollar call (strike 1.5150) premium 1.7%.

Determine the profit outcome of each of the strategies.

1. The original position is long \$10,000,000 and short DM14,800,000. To square the position through a forward contract, the trader needs to buy DM14,800,000 at a rate of 1.5100.

   Profit = dollar proceeds of sale of DM14,800,000 through original position – dollar cost to purchase DM14,800,000 through reversing forward

   $$= 10{,}000{,}000 - \frac{14{,}800{,}000}{1.5100}$$

   $$= \$198{,}675.50$$

2. To square the position through a bought dollar put for face value DM14,800,000 and gain the right to buy back the dollars that were sold in opening the position.

   $$\text{Premium paid for dollar put} = \frac{14{,}800{,}000}{1.5150} \times \frac{2.0}{100} = \$195{,}379.54$$

   $$\text{FV (Premium)} = \$195{,}379.54 \times (1 + 0.05 \times 2/12)$$
   $$= \$197{,}007.70$$

Profit	=	dollar proceeds of sale of DM14,800,000 through original position	–	dollar cost of purchase of DM14,800,000 through option

$$= 10{,}000{,}000 - \begin{cases} \dfrac{14{,}800{,}000}{x} + 197{,}007.70 & \text{f } x \geq 1.5100 \\ \text{or} & \\ \dfrac{14{,}800{,}000}{1.5100} + 197{,}007.70 & \text{if } x < 1.5100 \end{cases}$$

The trader effectively gives up $197,007.70 of the unrealised profit to buy the option which eliminates the possibility of further loss (if the exchange rate falls) but leaves open the opportunity for further gain if the exchange rate rises above 1.5100.

3. Another alternative is for the dealer to write a dollar call which, if exercised, will lock in the profit. Writing the option will earn a premium which will add to the potential profit. However, writing the option does *not* hedge the net exchange position. If the exchange rate subsequently falls before the maturity date, the trader will lose some or all of the unrealised profit. The premium received acts as an additional buffer against a possible adverse exchange rate movement.

$$\text{Premium received for dollar call} = \frac{14{,}800{,}000}{1.5150} \times \frac{1.7}{100}$$

$$= \$166{,}072.61$$

$$\text{FV (Premium)} = \$166{,}072.61 \times (1 + 0.05 \times 2/12)$$

$$= \$167{,}456.55$$

Profit	=	dollar proceeds of sale of DM14,800,000 through original position	–	dollar cost of purchase of DM14,800,000 with sold option

$$= 10{,}000{,}000 - \begin{cases} \dfrac{14{,}800{,}000}{x} - 167{,}456.55 & \text{if } x \leq 1.5150 \\ \text{or} & \\ \dfrac{14{,}800{,}000}{1.5150} - 167{,}456.55 & \text{if } x > 1.5150 \end{cases}$$

If the exchange rate falls below the break-even rate b, the trader will incur a loss. The value of b is calculated by solving the profit equation with profit equal to zero.

$$\text{Profit} = 10{,}000.000 - (14{,}800{,}000/b - 167{,}456.55)$$

$$\therefore\ 0 = 10{,}000{,}000 - (14{,}800{,}000/b - 167{,}456.55)$$

$$\therefore\ b = 1.4556$$

Foreign Currency Investor

Example 11.5

A funds manager wishes to maximise the yield on an investment of $10,000,000 available for investing for 365 days. Instead of investing in the dollar money market at 5% pa (360 days per year), the funds manager elects to sell the dollars to buy ¥1,100,000,000 and to invest the yen at 1.0% pa (360 days per year). The funds manager considers two alternatives:

- Remaining unhedged and selling the ¥1,111,152,778 (principal plus interest) at the prevailing spot rate at maturity; or
- Buying a dollar call/yen put at ¥110.00 for ¥1,111,152,778 for a premium of 3.25%.

(a) Calculate the effective yield % pa (365 dpy basis) for each alternative if the spot rate at maturity is:

(i) 100.00;

(ii) 110.00;

(iii) 120.00.

Unhedged

Dollar proceeds from the yen investment

$$= \frac{1,111,152,778}{x} \quad \text{where } x = \text{exchange rate at maturity}$$

(i) x = 100.00, proceeds = $11,111,527.78

(ii) x = 110.00, proceeds = $10,101,388.89

(iii) x = 120.00, proceeds = $9,259,606.48

$$\text{Yield \% pa} = \frac{\$\text{ proceeds} - 10,000,000}{10,000,000} \times \frac{365}{365} \times 100$$

(i) $x = 100.00, \text{ yield \%} = \frac{1,111,527.78}{10,000,000} = 11.1\%$

(ii) $x = 110.00, \text{ yield \%} = \frac{101,388.89}{10,000,000} = 1.0\%$

(iii) $x = 120.00, \text{ yield \%} = -\frac{740,393.52}{10,000,000} = -7.4\ \%$

Bought Dollar Call

$$\text{Premium} = \frac{1{,}111{,}152{,}778}{110.00} \times \frac{3.25}{100} = \$328{,}295.14$$

$$\text{FV(Premium)} = 328{,}295.14 \times (1 + 0.05 \times \frac{365}{360}) = \$344{,}937.88$$

Dollar proceeds from the yen investment

$$= \frac{1{,}111{,}152{,}778}{x} - 344{,}937.88 \quad \text{if } x \leq 110.00$$

$$= \frac{1{,}111{,}152{,}778}{110.00} - 344{,}937.88 \quad \text{if } x > 110.00$$

(i) x = 100.00, proceeds = \$10,766,214.90

(ii) x = 110.00, proceeds = \$ 9,756,451.01

(iii) x = 120.00, proceeds = \$ 9,756,451.01

(i) x = 100.00, yield % $= \frac{766{,}214.90}{10{,}000{,}000} =$ 7.66%

(ii) x = 110.00, yield % $= -\frac{243{,}548.99}{10{,}000{,}000} =$ – 2.4 %

(iii) x = 120.00, yield % $= -\frac{243{,}548.99}{10{,}000{,}000} =$ – 2.4 %

(b) Calculate the break-even rate between being unhedged and holding the bought dollar call.

The break-even rate b occurs where:

proceeds if unhedged = proceeds with bought dollar call

ie $$\frac{1{,}111{,}152{,}778}{b} = \frac{1{,}111{,}152{,}778}{110.00} - 344{,}937.88$$

$\therefore$ b = 113.89

(c) Calculate the spot rate at maturity required for the effective yield to be 10% pa with the bought dollar call.

Effective yield = 10% pa when:

Proceeds with bought dollar call = 1.1 × \$10,000,000

ie $$\frac{1{,}111{,}152{,}778}{x} - 344{,}937.88 = 11{,}000{,}000$$

$\therefore$ x = 97.94

Varying the Strike Price

Consider the importer in Example 11.1. Three scenarios have already been examined:

1. Remaining unhedged;
2. Hedging by buying deutschemarks forward;
3. Hedging by buying a dollar put/deutschemark call with a strike price of 1.5100.

Many additional outcomes may become available by varying the strike price of the bought dollar put.

	Strike	Premium	FV (Premium)
Alternative 3.	1.5100	1.00%	66,501.11
Alternative 3a.	1.5400	1.90%	126,352.11
Alternative 3b.	1.4800	0.48%	19,950.33

The dollar cost of the imports hedged with a bought dollar put with strike price y,

$$= \frac{10{,}000{,}000}{x} + \text{FV(Premium)} \quad \text{if } x \geq y \text{, or}$$

$$= \frac{10{,}000{,}000}{y} + \text{FV (Premium)} \quad \text{if } x < y$$

Figure 11.7

Imports hedged with dollar puts at different strike prices

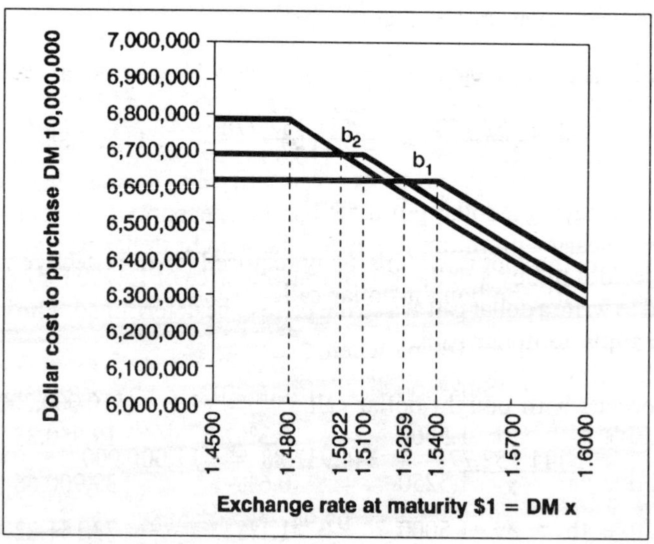

By buying an option which is further in-the-money, the importer will pay more to buy DM10,000,000 if the exchange rate at expiry exceeds the higher strike price (1.5400), because of the larger premium payable on the more in-the-money option. On the other hand, the importer will be better off with the more in-the-money option if the exchange rate at expiry is less than the lower strike price (1.5100), because the strike price at which the deutschemarks will be bought will be more favourable. There is a break-even rate b_1 between 1.5100 and 1.5400, at which the benefit of the higher strike price is just offset by the cost of paying the higher premium.

The unhedged line represents the limiting case of an out-of-the-money option. As the strike price is set further out-of-the-money, the option approaches the unhedged line.

To calculate b_1:

Cost without exercise at strike 1.5100 = cost with exercise at strike 1.5400

$$\frac{10{,}000{,}000}{b_1} + 66{,}501.11 = \frac{10{,}000{,}000}{1.5400} + 126{,}501.11$$

$$\therefore \quad b_1 = 1.5259$$

By buying an option which is further out-of-the-money, the importer will pay less if the option lapses because of the lower premium payable, but will pay more if the option is exercised because of the less favorable strike price. There is a break-even rate, b_2, between 1.4800 and 1.5100, at which the benefit of the lower premium is just offset by the lower strike price.

To calculate b_2:

Cost without exercise at strike 1.4800 = cost with exercise at strike 1.5100

$$\frac{10{,}000{,}000}{b_2} + 31{,}920.54 = \frac{10{,}000{,}000}{1.5100} + 66{,}501.11$$

$$\therefore \quad b_2 = 1.5022$$

Collars

Another set of alternatives can be generated by considering the case where, in addition to buying a dollar put to hedge the exposure, the importer writes a dollar call to earn a premium to pay for the bought dollar put. Suppose the importer decides to buy a dollar put at a strike price of 1.4700 for a premium of 0.3% and to write a dollar call at a strike price to be determined. The following premiums apply to dollar calls:

	Strike price	Premium	FV (Premium)
Alternative 4.	1.5500	0.3%	19,950.33
Alternative 4a.	1.5250	0.6%	39,900.66
Alternative 4b.	1.5000	1.1%	73,151.22

Zero premium collar

Alternative 4

If the importer writes a dollar call with a strike price of 1.5500 for a premium of 0.3%, then he or she would receive a premium just sufficient to allow the payment of the premium on the bought dollar put.

FV (Net premium) = FV (Premium received) – FV (Premium paid)
= 19,950.33 – 19,950.33
= 0

If at expiry the exchange rate is less than 1.4700, the dollar put (strike 1.4700) will be in-the-money and the dollar call (strike 1.5500) will be out-of-the-money. The importer will exercise the bought dollar put and will find that the sold dollar call will lapse. The importer will buy DM10,000,000 at a worse case rate of 1.4700 for a cost of $6,802,721.09.

Figure 11.8

Zero premium collar hedging imports

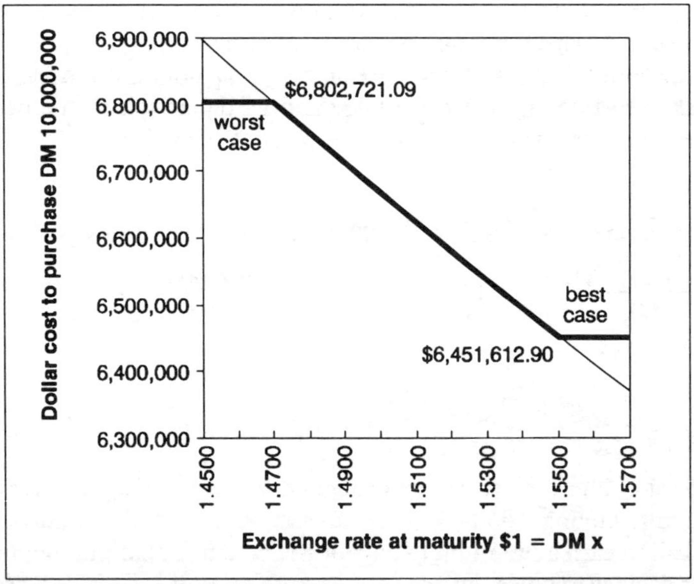

If at expiry the exchange rate is more than 1.5500, the dollar call (strike 1.5500) will be in-the-money and the dollar put (strike 1.4700) will be out-of-the-money. The importer will be exercised on the dollar call and will abandon the dollar put. As a result of the dollar call being called, the importer will buy DM10,000,000 at a best rate case of 1.5500 for a cost of $6,451,612.90.

If at expiry the exchange rate is between 1.4700 and 1.5500, both options will be out-of-the-money and so both will lapse. The importer will buy

DM10,000,000 at the market exchange rate. For example, if at expiry the exchange rate is 1.5000, the cost of buying DM10,000,000 will be:

10,000,000/ 1.5000 = \$6,666,666.67.

This strategy is known as a ***zero premium collar.*** It is also referred to as a cylinder, range forward or fence. Different banks tend to use different names but the concept is the same. The importer buys an out-of-the-money option which, if exercised, determines the worst case. The importer is hedged because he or she has a limited downside. The importer also writes that option which, if exercised, will provide the currency required to meet the foreign currency obligation, namely a dollar call. Provided the strike price of the dollar call is higher than the strike price of the dollar put, at most, one of the options will be exercised at expiry.

In effect, the importer gives up the possible benefit of the exchange rate rising above 1.5500 to avoid paying the premium on the bought dollar put. This may represent a less painful sacrifice because it requires no initial outlay of cash and while 1.5500 is not the best possible rate, it nevertheless is a good rate.

The above zero premium collar was constructed using a bought dollar put and a sold dollar call with premiums equal to 0.3%. Similar zero premium collars can be constructed, based on strike prices which imply equal offsetting premiums at other levels. The lower the premium, the wider will be the collar. For example, a premium of 0.2% might buy a dollar put with strike price 1.4600 and a dollar call with strike price 1.5600. A premium of 0.5% might buy a dollar put with strike price 1.4825 and a dollar call with strike price 1.5325 and so on.

Figure 11.9

Zero premium collars

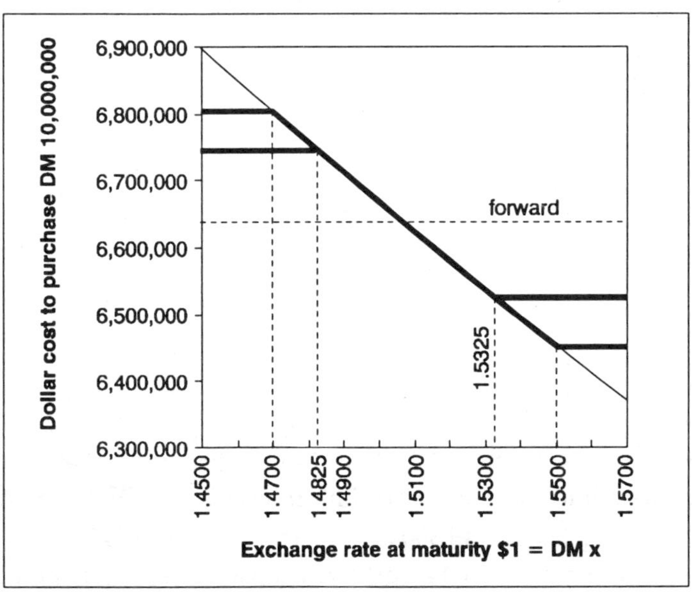

Ignoring bid-offer spread, the zero premium collars will lie symmetrically between the unhedged line and the forward rate. Indeed, it can be seen that the forward rate is the limiting case of a collar where the strike price of the put equals the strike price of the call. The unhedged line is the other limiting case where the put and the call are so far out-of-the-money that their premiums are effectively zero.

In practice, bid-offer spreads will skew the collar slightly against the price-taker and in favour of the price-maker.

Debit collar

Alternative 4a

If the premium received from the sold option is less than the premium paid for the bought option, the collar buyer will effectively pay a net premium. This is called a ***debit collar.***

Figure 11.10

Debit collar hedging imports

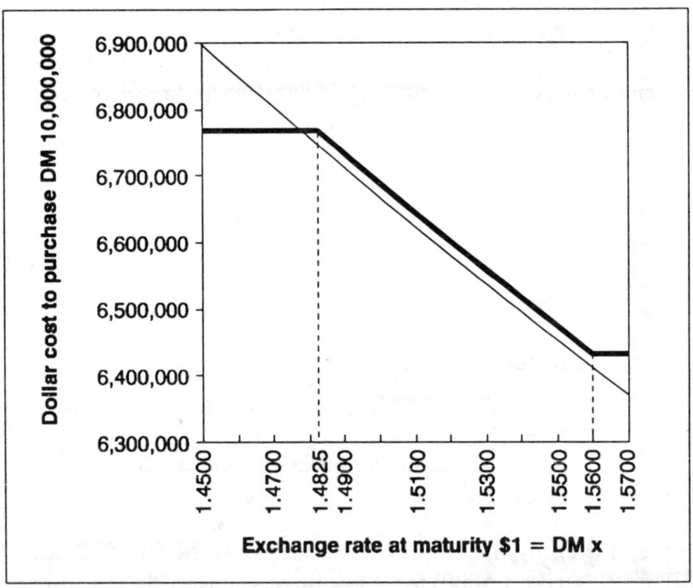

For example, if the importer bought a dollar put (strike 1.4825) for 0.5% and sold a dollar call (strike 1.5600) for 0.2%, he or she would pay a smaller net premium than if the importer had simply bought the dollar put.

FV (Net premium)	=	FV (Premium received)	–	FV (Premium paid)
	=	13,300.22	–	33,250.56
	=	– 19,950.34		

The worst case under a debit collar will be worse than the zero premium collar worst case by the amount of the net premium payable. The best case under the debit collar will be better than the zero premium collar best case because the dollar call is written at a higher strike price. The debit collar is not symmetrical about the zero cost cylinder because of the leverage generated by a change in premium bringing about a proportionally greater change in strike price.

Credit collar

Alternative 4b

If the premium received from the sold option is greater than the premium paid for the bought option, the collar buyer will effectively receive a net premium. This is called a ***credit collar.***

Figure 11.11

Credit collar hedging imports

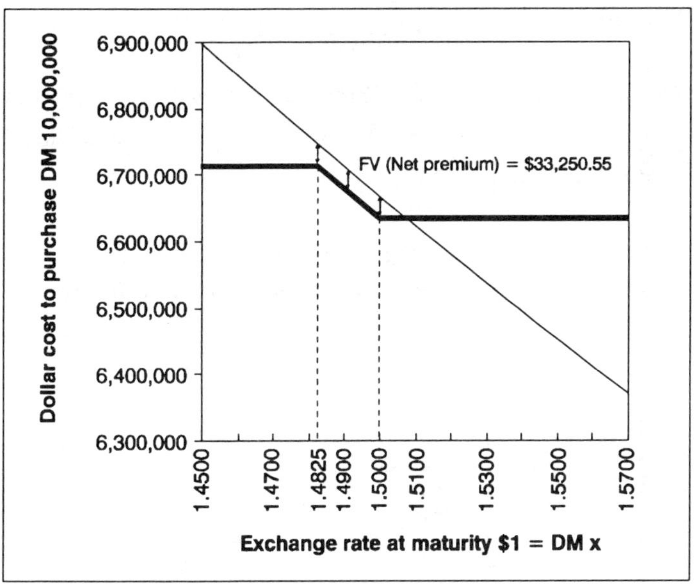

For example, if the importer bought a dollar put (strike 1.4825) for 0.5% and sold a dollar call (strike 1.5000) for 1.1%, he or she would earn a net premium of 0.6%.

FV (Net premium)	=	FV (Premium received)	–	FV (Premium paid)
	=	73,151.22	–	39,900.67
	=	+ 33,250.55		

The worst case under a credit collar will be better than the zero premium collar worst case by the amount of the net premium received. The best case under the credit collar will be worse than under the zero premium collar because the dollar call is written at a lower strike price.

Participating Options

Alternative 5

Another set of strategies can be generated by buying and writing the opposite types of option with the same strike price, but for different face values. These are called ***participating options***. They are also known as participating forwards, percentage forwards and various other names.

Given that the premium to purchase a dollar put with strike price 1.4825 is 0.5% and the premium for selling at dollar call with the same strike price is 1.5%, the importer could hedge with a zero premium participating option by buying a dollar put (strike 1.4825) for face value DM10,000,000 and writing a dollar call (strike 1.4825) for face value DM3,333,333.

$$\text{FV (Premium received)} = \frac{3{,}333{,}333}{1.5100} \times \frac{1.5}{100} \times \left(1 + \frac{0.05}{12}\right) = \$33{,}250.55$$

$$\text{FV(Premium paid)} = \frac{10{,}000{,}000}{1.5100} \times \frac{0.5}{100} \times \left(1 + \frac{0.05}{12}\right) = \$33{,}250.55$$

$$\begin{aligned}\therefore \text{FV (Net premium)} &= \text{FV (Premium received)} - \text{FV(Premium paid)} \\ &= 33{,}250.55 - 33{,}250.55 \\ &= 0\end{aligned}$$

Figure 11.12

Zero premium participating option hedging imports

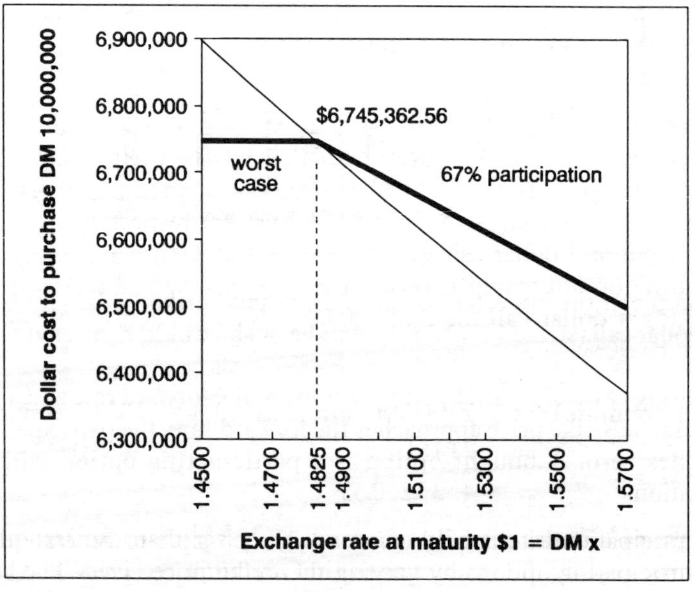

If at expiry the exchange rate is below the strike price (1.4825), the dollar put will be in-the-money and the dollar call will be out-of-the-money. The importer will exercise the bought dollar put, thereby buying DM10,000,000 at the worst case rate of 1.4825 for $6,745,362.56. The dollar call will be allowed to lapse.

If at expiry the exchange rate is above the strike price (1.4825), the dollar put will be out-of-the-money and the dollar call will be in-the-money. The importer will abandon the dollar put. The importer's counterparty will exercise the dollar call. As a result, the importer will buy DM3,333,333 at the strike price 1.4825 and then buy the remaining DM6,666,667 at the prevailing market exchange rate, which is higher and therefore better than 1.4825.

By buying a participating option, the importer hedges against the downside risk of a falling exchange rate and at the same time is positioned to be able to enjoy part of the benefit of a rising exchange rate. In this case, if the exchange rate falls, the importer is effectively 100% hedged but if the exchange rate rises, he or she is effectively 67% unhedged. The ***participation rate*** is 67%.

In general, the participation rate is a function of the amounts of the two options.

Participation rate %

$$= \frac{\text{amount of bought option} - \text{amount of sold option}}{\text{amount of bought option}} \times 100 \qquad \textbf{Equation 11.1}$$

$$= \frac{10{,}000{,}000 - 3{,}333{,}333}{10{,}000{,}000} \times 100$$

$$= 67\%$$

In effect, the importer pays the premium to buy an out-of-the-money dollar put by writing an in-the-money dollar call for a lesser amount at the same strike price.

Similar zero premium participating options can be generated at different strike prices. The lower the strike price, the higher will be the participation rate. In the example above, setting the strike price at 1.4825 produces a participation rate of 67%. If the strike price was set at 1.4600, the respective premiums on the dollar put and dollar call would be 0.2% and 2.0%. The zero premium participating option would involve buying a dollar put for DM10,000,000 and writing a dollar call for DM1,000,000. The participation rate would therefore be 90%.

The limiting cases of a participating option are the forward rate and a bought option. As the strike price approaches the forward rate, the participation rate approaches zero. A bought option is a participating option with 100% participation.

If the participation rate is held constant, it is possible to generate debit or credit participating options by varying the strike price.

Participating Collars

Alternative 6

Another set of strategies can be generated by writing and buying opposite types of options with different strike prices and different face values. These are known as ***participating collars.***

The importer could hedge with a zero premium participating collar by buying a dollar put (strike 1.4700) for face value DM10,000,000 and writing a dollar call (strike 1.5325) for face value DM6,000,000.

$$\text{FV (Premium paid)} = \frac{10,000,000}{1.5100} \times \frac{0.3}{100} \times (1 + 0.05/12) = \$19,950.33$$

$$\text{FV (Premium received)} = \frac{6,000,000}{1.5100} \times \frac{0.5}{100} \times (1 + 0.05/12) = \$19,950.33$$

$$\text{FV (Net premium)} = 0$$

Figure 11.13

Participating collar hedging imports

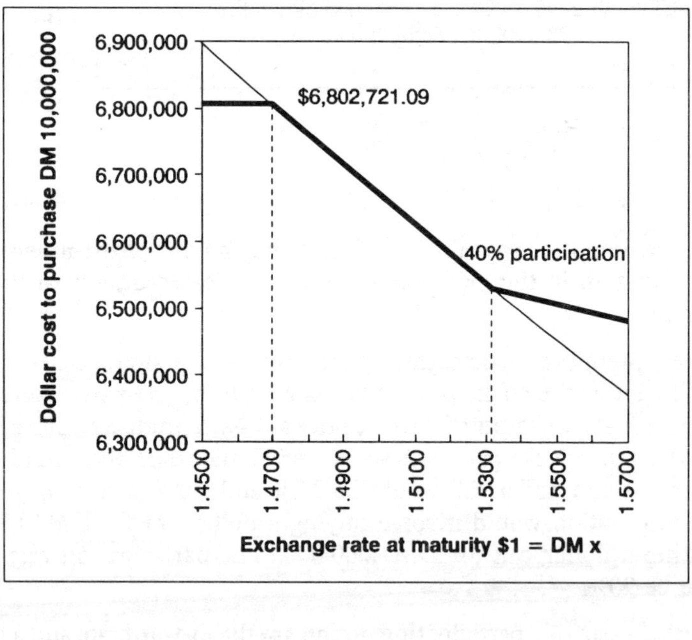

If at maturity the exchange rate is below 1.4700, the importer exercises the bought dollar put and the sold dollar call lapses. In the worst case, the importer buys DM10,000,000 at 1.4700 for $6,802,721.09. If at maturity the exchange rate is in the range 1.4700 to 1.5325, the DM10,000,000 is purchased at the market rate. If the exchange rate is above 1.5325, the sold dollar call will be exercised. The importer will buy DM6,000,000 at 1.5325 through the dollar call and the remaining DM4,000,000 at the prevailing market rate, thereby enjoying 40% participation in any rise in the exchange rate above 1.5325.

By choosing different strike prices, the importer can generate different outcomes. By varying the strike price of the bought dollar put, he or she can raise or lower the worst case rate. However, the strike price of the bought option can be no better than the forward rate (in which case the participating collar reduces to a forward). The importer can vary the participation rate by raising or lowering the strike price of the sold option. As with the participating option, there is a trade-off between the turning point and the participation rate. The importer can enjoy a higher participation rate only by dropping 100% participation earlier.

Again, it is possible to create debit or credit participating collars.

There are a very large number of possible strategies which can be generated with various combinations of option products. This gives the person with a foreign currency exposure enormous flexibility in tailoring a risk profile to suit his particular views and needs.

Applications of option combinations for exporters, foreign currency borrowers and investors are covered in the Practice Problems.

Practice Problems

11.1 Exporter

An exporter with the same exposure as in Example 11.2 enters into a participating collar to hedge the deutschemark receivables. The exporter buys a dollar call/deutschemark put with the strike of 1.5000 for DM1,000,000 at a premium of 1.5% and writes a dollar put/deutschemark call with the strike of 1.4800 for DM600,000 at a premium of 1.5%.

(a) Calculate the future value of the net premium payable in dollars.

(b) Calculate the proceeds from selling DM1,000,000 if the spot rate at maturity is:
   (i) 1.4500;
   (ii) 1.4900;
   (iii) 1.5500.

(c) Calculate the break-even rate between the participating collar and the unhedged position.

11.2 Foreign currency borrower

A foreign currency borrower with the same exposure as in Example 11.3 constructs a participating option to hedge Swiss franc liabilities. The borrower buys a dollar put/Swiss franc call for SF25,395,300 with a strike of 1.2300 at a premium of 3.0% and writes a dollar call/Swiss franc put for SF12,697,650 with a strike 1.2300 at a premium of 2.4%.

(a) Calculate the future value of the net premium payable in dollars.

(b) Calculate the dollar cost of repaying the Swiss franc loan principal plus interest if the spot rate at maturity is:

- (i) 1.2000;
- (ii) 1.2400;
- (iii) 1.3000.

(c) Calculate the effective borrowing cost in percent per annum of the Swiss franc loan if the spot rate at maturity is:

- (i) 1.2000;
- (ii) 1.2400;
- (iii) 1.3000.

(d) Calculate the break-even rate with borrowing dollars.

11.3 Foreign currency investor

A funds manager with the same exposure as in Example 11.5 buys a collar by buying a dollar call at 110.00 for ¥1,111,152,778 at a premium of 3.25% and writing a dollar put at 109.00 for ¥777,806,945 at a premium of 2.00%.

(a) Calculate the effective yield if the spot rate at maturity is:

- (i) 100.00;
- (ii) 110.00;
- (iii) 120.00.

(b) If the spot rate at maturity is ¥114.00, calculate the effective yield percent per annum versus being:

- (i) unhedged;
- (ii) invested in dollars;
- (iii) hedged with a bought dollar call (strike ¥110.00).

Supplementary Question

11.4 Foreign exchange trader – 2 for 1 strategy

A trader with the same exposure as in example 11.4 buys a dollar put (strike 1.5100) premium 2.0% for face value DM14,800,000 and sells a dollar call (strike 1.5150) premium 1.7% for twice the face value (ie DM29,600,00).

(a) Calculate the future value of the net premium in dollars.

(b) Calculate the profit if the spot rate at expiry is

(i) 1.4500

(ii) 1.5000

(iii) 1.5500

(c) Draw the profit profile showing profit against various possible exchange rates at expiry.

12

Option Derivatives

This chapter examines the pricing and applications of option derivative products, such as digital options, barrier options and several other types of "exotic" options, as well as other structures which take advantage of the correlation between different variables. Options give greater choice to people with currency exposures. Option derivative products provide even greater flexibility over how the exposure can be managed.

Digital Options

A digital option has a fixed pay-out regardless of how far it is in-the-money. Digital options are also known as binary options.

An ***at-expiry*** digital has its pay-out determined by the market price at its expiry. A ***one-touch*** digital pays-out if the market price ever reaches the strike price during the life of the option. The pay-out for a one-touch option can occur at either the time of touching or at expiry depending on the terms of the contract.

Betting on the outcome of a toss of a coin is a simple everyday example of a digital option. By betting on heads, a person agrees to pay a specified amount (premium), eg $100, if the result is tails and to receive the same amount if the result is heads.

Figure 12.1
Digital option
Heads or tails

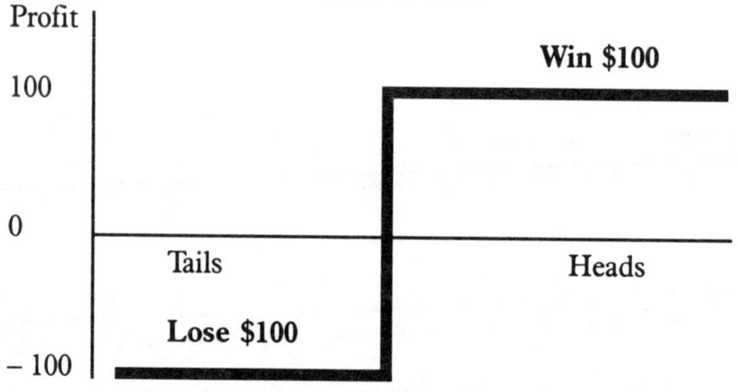

Figure 12.1 shows the pay-off diagram for a person who has bet $100 on heads. The vertical line is a typical element of the pay-off for a digital option.

If two coins are tossed there are three possible outcomes – two heads (probability ¼), two tails (probability ¼) and a head and a tail (probability 2/4). The pay-off for a person who bets $100 on two heads would be as in Figure 12.2.

Figure 12.2

Digital option

Two heads

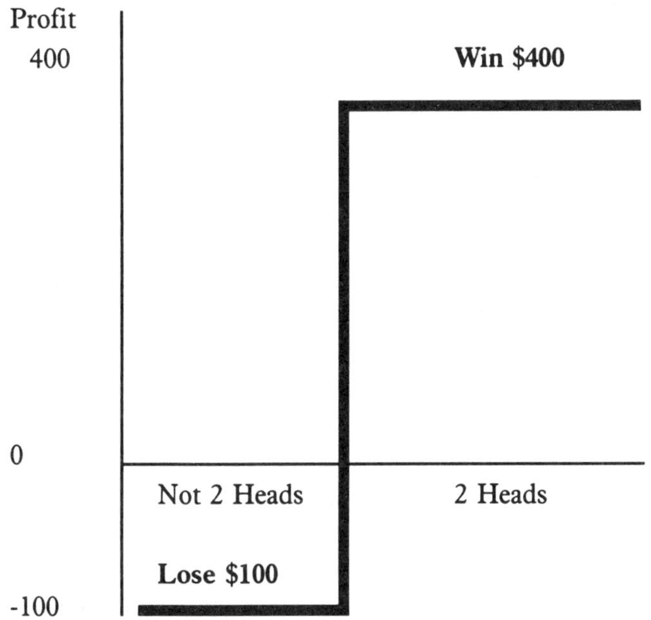

The pay-out reflects the probability of the outcome occurring. Conversely, the premium is the (present value of the) expected pay-out.

Outcome	Pay-out	Probability	Expected Value
2 Heads	400	¼	100
2 Tails	0	¼	0
1 Head, 1 Tail	0	½	0
		Total	**100**

Pricing an At-expiry Digital

At-expiry digital options can be priced using the same technique as standard calls and puts. The premium is the present value of the expected pay-out.

Example 12.1

Calculate the premium for a 6 month dollar call/ yen put which pays $1,000,000 if at expiry spot dollar/yen is 110 or above given the same scenario as in Example 10.6.

The binomial tree and probabilities of each possible outcome will be the same as in Figure 10.7 but the pay-out for the digital option will be different from those in Example 10.6.

Possible Outcomes	Probability	Pay-out	Expected Value
118	1/64	1,000,000	15,625.00
112	6/64	1,000,000	93,750.00
106	15/64	0	0
100	20/64	0	0
94	15/64	0	0
88	6/64	0	0
82	1/64	0	0
		Total	**109,375.00**

The expected pay-out of the option is $109,375.00. If the premium were paid at expiry, this would be its fair value. The general practice is for the premium to be paid up-front for digital options as well as for standard calls and puts. If the 6 month dollar interest rate is 5% pa, the up-front premium would be:

$$\frac{\$109{,}375.00}{1 + 0.05 \times 6/12} = \$106{,}707.32$$

Reverse Binomial Pricing Method

Alternatively, the premium of the digital call in Example 12.1 could be priced using the reverse binomial method. This involves starting with the pay-out for each of the possible outcomes at expiry and working backwards through the binomial tree to determine the expected value at inception.

Figure 12.3

Reverse binomial method

Month	0	1	2	3	4	5	6	Outcome
							1,000,000	118
						1,000,000		
					750,000		1,000,000	112
				500,000		500,000		
			312,500		250,000		0	106
		187,500		125,000		0		
	109,375		**62,500**		0		0	100
		31,250		0		0		
			0		0		0	94
				0		0		
					0		0	88
						0		
							0	82

If at the end of the 6 months spot is $1 = ¥118 or ¥112, the pay-out would be $1,000,000. It follows that if there is equal probability that the price will move up or down ¥3 in the final month, if the price is ¥115 at the end of the 5th month then the value of the option at that time must be $1,000,000.

Similarly, because the pay-out at the end of the 6 months would be $1,000,000 at ¥112 and zero at ¥106, it follows that the value of the option at the end of the 5th month must be $500,000 if the price is ¥109.

By working backwards through the binomial tree it can be seen, as in Figure 12.3, that the future value of the premium is $109,375 and so the premium is $106,707.32.

The reverse binomial method is useful because it shows the at-expiry value of the option at each stage of the tree. For example, if at the end of the 2nd month the price is ¥100, then the (future) value of the option would be $62,500. It also provides a means for pricing path dependent options such as one-touch digitals.

Pricing One-touch Digitals

Example 12.2

Calculate the premium of a 6 month dollar call/yen put which pays $1,000,000 if the spot rate touches or exceeds ¥110 at any time during the life of the option, given the same parameters as in Example 12.1.

The one-touch digital will pay \$1,000,000 at expiry if the price at the end of the 4th month is ¥112 (because it exceeds ¥110). Accordingly, the value in the reverse binomial tree at the 4th month, ¥112 outcome which could be designated as the (4,112 node) must be \$1,000,000. It follows that the values of nodes (3,109), (2,106), (1,103) and (0,100) would be \$625,000; \$375,000; \$218,750 and \$125,000 respectively as shown in Figure 12.4.

Figure 12.4
Reverse binomial method
Pricing one-touch digital

Month	0	1	2	3	4	5	6	Outcome
							1,000,000	118
						1,000,000		
					1,000,000		1,000,000	112
				625,000		500,000		
			375,000		250,000		0	106
		218,750		125,000		0		
	125,000		62,500		0		0	100
		31,250		0		0		
			0		0		0	94
				0		0		
					0		0	88
						0		
							0	82

$$\text{Premium} = \text{PV}(125{,}000) = \frac{125{,}000.00}{(1+0.05 \times 6/12)} = \mathbf{\$121{,}951.12}$$

The premium of the one-touch digital is higher than that of the corresponding at-expiry digital because the expected pay-out is higher, to the extent that it is possible for the price to touch the strike during the life of the option but to expire below it. The difference between \$121,951.12 and \$106,707.32 dimensions the extra value of the one-touch feature.

Closed Form Pricing Formula

Mathematicians have worked out formulae for pricing digital options. The formula for at-expiry digitals is simpler than the Black-Scholes formula because the pay-out is a fixed amount and the probabilities are the same as for standard calls and puts.

$$C = \frac{X\,N(d_2)}{(1+r_T t)}$$ **Equation 12.1**

where X is the fixed pay-out from a digital call and the other notation is as in Equation 10.9.

One-touch digitals are more complicated to price because the probability of being exercised must take account of the possibility of the trigger being touched.

Applications of Digital Options

Digital options have a number of powerful applications for people managing currency exposures.

Pay later option

A ***pay-later option*** is one for which the premium is only paid if the option expires in-the-money. These are also known as contingent premium options. If paid, the premium must be larger than the up-front premium of the corresponding standard option.

The importer in Example 11.1 could reshape his exposure by selling or buying digital options. For example, the importer could sell an at-expiry digital which would pay DM200,000 if, but only if, the spot rate at expiry is 1.5300 or above to earn the DM100,000 premium required to buy a dollar put/ deutschemark call with strike 1.5100.

Figure 12.5
Pay later put
Protecting importer

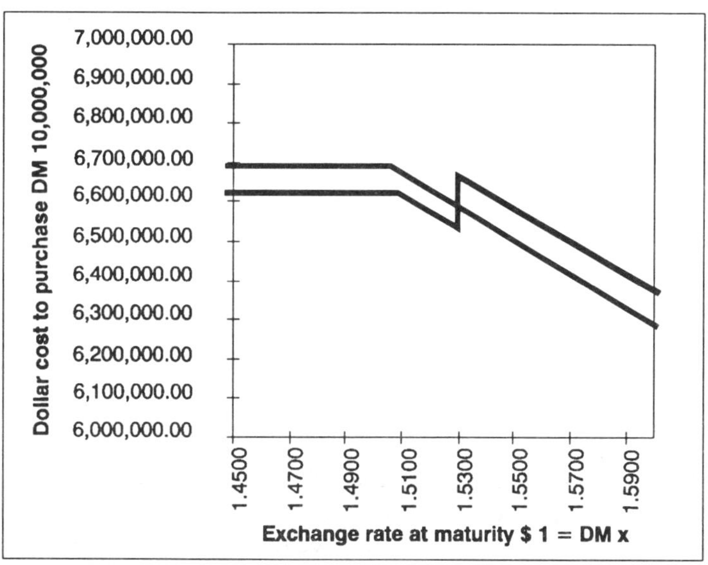

If at expiry the spot rate is less than 1.5100, it would cost the importer only $6,622,516.56 to buy the DM10,000,000 to pay for the imports. This is $66,501.11 cheaper than with the straight bought 1.5100 dollar put because the importer would gain the benefit of receiving the premium from the sold digital option. Between 1.5100 and 1.5299, the importer would also be better off by the future value of the premium saved.

If at expiry the spot rate is 1.5300 or higher, the importer will be DM200,000 worse off than with the bought dollar put. The worst case would be $6,666,666.67 which would occur if the spot rate at expiry is exactly 1.5300. The importer may prefer the pay-later put because the premium only has to be paid when the rate has moved in his favour and the worst case is not as bad as with the straight bought dollar put.

Many variations of this structure are possible. The importer could sell digitals at other strike prices. For example, instead of selling the 1.5300 digital, the importer might fund the premium of the bought 1.5100 put by selling a digital which would pay DM150,000 at 1.5300 and another which would pay DM150,000 at 1.5500. This would put two steps in the pay-off and would not be significantly worse than the straight dollar put until 1.5500, as shown in Figure 12.6.

Figure 12.6

Pay later put with 2 sold digitals

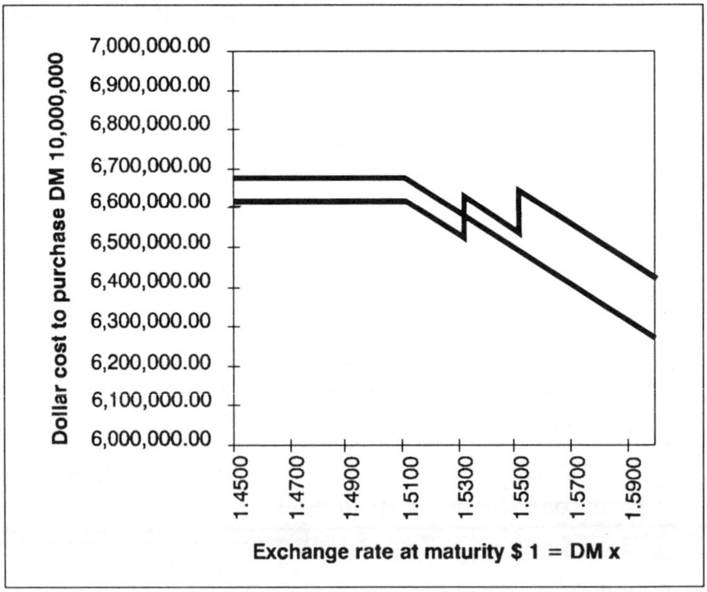

Currency linked note

A ***currency linked note*** is an instrument for which the yield is a function of the exchange rate. Many structures are possible. A popular one gives the investor a better than market yield provided the exchange rate remains within a specified range but a lower than market yield if it moves outside that range.

If the 6 month dollar interest rate is 5% pa when spot dollar/yen is 110.00, an investor might be able to purchase a currency linked note for which the yield will be 10% pa provided the dollar remains within a range of 100.00 to 120.00 for the entire 6 months but only 2% pa if at any time the spot rate touches or moves above 120.00 or below 100.00.

The currency linked note would normally be packaged by the bank as a single product. To construct it, the bank would merely sell two one-touch digitals. The future value of the premium received would be sufficient to lift the yield to 10% pa provided neither level is touched. The pay-out would be such that the yield is reduced to 2% pa if either digital is exercised.

This sort of product appeals to many investors, because their capital is guaranteed and they are assured a minimal acceptable return with the possibility of a yield which is much higher than otherwise available. The investor is effectively betting that the exchange rate will be less volatile than the rate which is priced into the options.

Figure 12.7
Currency linked note

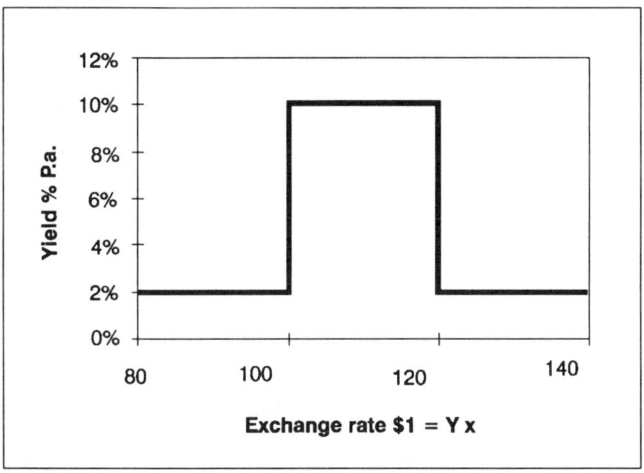

Barrier Options

Path dependent options are those whose pay-off depend on the path the market price follows through the life of the option.

Standard calls and puts as well as at-expiry digitals are not path dependent because their pay-out depends only on where the market price is at expiry versus the strike price.

One-touch digital options are one example of path dependent options. The most common group of path dependent options is known as barrier options. Other examples of path dependent options include average rate or average strike options and look-back options.

Barrier options are options which can be knocked-out or which only kick-in if the market price reaches a specified level.

Knock-out and kick-out options have a zero pay-out if the barrier level is reached even if the market price at expiry is better than the strike price. ***Kick-in and knock-in options*** have zero pay-out unless the option expires in-the-money (ie the market price at expiry is better than the strike price *and* at sometime during the life of the option the market price has reached the barrier level). Options "knock" in or out at barrier levels which are out-of-the-money and "kick" in or out at barrier levels which are in-the-money.

Figure 12.8

Kick-out dollar call/yen put

Strike = ¥102, Kick-out = ¥108

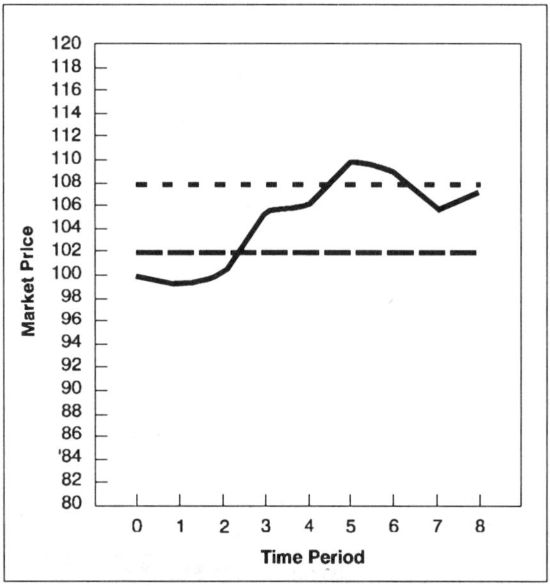

The option portrayed in Figure 12.8 is an 8 month dollar call/yen put with strike price at ¥102.00 but which kicks-out at ¥108.00. The solid line shows one of the many possible paths which the market price could follow during the life of the option. At inception, the spot rate was ¥100.00. At expiry, it was ¥107.90. This particular option would have been knocked-out during the fourth month when the spot rate went through ¥108.00. So, even though the spot rate at expiry was well above the ¥102.00 strike price, the pay-out would be zero.

If instead the option in Figure 12.8 had been a kick-in at ¥108.00, the pay-out would have been:

Pay-out	=	Expiry price	−	Strike price
	=	107.90	−	102.00
	=	¥5.90		

The sum of the pay-out for the kick-out and the pay-out for the kick-in will equal the pay-out for the standard option with the same strike price provided the barriers are at the same level. Only one of the kick-out and kick-in can be exercised if the barrier level is the same for both. In the case above, the pay-out from the kick-out is zero and the pay-out from the kick-in is ¥5.90. The sum of the two equals the pay-out from the standard call which would be ¥5.90.

It follows that the sum of premiums for the kick-out and the kick-in will equal the premium for the standard call provided the barrier level is the same and the options have the same strike price.

Kick-out premium + Kick-in premium = Call premium **Equation 12.2**

Pricing Knock-outs and Kick-outs

The reverse binomial method can be used to price the standard dollar call/yen put in Example 10.6.

Figure 12.9

Dollar call strike = ¥100

Month	0	1	2	3	4	5	6	Outcome
							18,000,000	118
						15,000,000		
					12,000,000		12,000,000	112
				9,000,000		9,000,000		
			6,375,000		6,000,000		6,000,000	106
		4,312,500		3,750,000		3,000,000		
	2,812,500		2,250,000		1,500,000		0	100
		1,312,500		750,000		0		
			375,000		0		0	94
				0		0		
					0		0	88
						0		
							0	82

Premium = PV(¥ 2,812,500) = ¥2,743,902

The reverse binomial method can also be used to price kick-out options.

Example 12.3

Calculate the premium of a 6 month dollar call/yen put with strike price ¥100.00 which kicks-out at ¥112.00 given a monthly up-down factor of ¥ 3.

The binomial tree will be similar to that in Figure 12.9 but all nodes at ¥112 or above will have zero value because these will be kicked-out. The revised binomial tree will be as in Figure 12.10 yielding a premium for the kick-out call of ¥1,280,488.

Figure 12.10

Dollar call strike = ¥ 100, kick-out = ¥ 112

Month	0	1	2	3	4	5	6	Outcome
							0	118
						0		
					0		0	112
				1,500,000		3,000,000		
			1,875,000		3,000,000		6,000,000	106
		1,687,500		2,250,000		3,000,000		
	1,312,500		1,500,000		1,500,000		0	100
		937,500		750,000		0		
			375,000		0		0	94
				0		0		
					0		0	88
						0		
							0	82

Premium = PV(¥1,312,500) = ¥1,280,488

The premium of the ¥100 call which kicks-out at ¥112 is less than half the premium of a standard ¥100 call. The kick-out option is much cheaper but it provides much less value. The branches of the binomial tree which are kicked-out have considerable value. Furthermore, some of the branches which were not kicked-out also lost value because as the spot price approaches the ¥112 kick-out level, the probability of being kicked-out increases.

Pricing Kick-ins and Knock-ins

The relationship in Equation 12.2 can be used to price kick-in and knock-in options. If the premium for a standard ¥100 call is ¥2,743,902 and the premium for the ¥100 call which kicks-out at ¥112 is ¥1,280,488, then the premium for a ¥100 call which kicks-in at ¥112 must be:

Premium of kick-in	=	Premium of call	–	Premium of kick-out
	=	2,743,902	–	1,280,488
	=	¥ 1,463,414		

It follows from Equation 12.3 that options which may knock or kick in or out always have lower premiums than their corresponding standard option. The barrier options only have value some of the time that the standard option does, so they command a lower premium.

Closed Form Solutions

Knock-outs and kick-ins can also be priced using formulae. These formulae look complicated because in addition to the variables involved in pricing standard options they also need to incorporate the barrier level and whether the barrier is triggered in an upward or downward direction. The options priced in Example 12.3 are an up-and-out dollar call and an up-and-in dollar call because the barrier is triggered if the spot rate moves *up* from its current level. It is also possible to have down-and-out and down-and-in options which are triggered if the spot rate *falls* to the barrier level.

The various formulae for up/down, in/out, calls and puts are not provided here but are readily available for readers who are interested.[1]

Applications of Barrier Options

Example 12.4

The exporter in Example 11.2 could purchase a 3 month up-and-out dollar call/deutschemark put with a strike price of 1.5000 which kicks-out at 1.6000 for a premium of 0.5% versus 1.5% for the standard dollar call with the same strike price.

The advantage of the kick-out over the standard dollar call is the lower premium. The premium payable would be only DM5,000 versus DM15,000 for the standard call.

The disadvantage of the kick-out option is that if the spot rate rises to 1.6000 or above at any time during the three months, the exporter loses the hedge. The exporter could become unhedged when the exchange rate is high and so at an attractive level to be hedged.

The exporter might be prepared to risk having the hedge kicked-out at 1.6000 to save some of the premium if he or she feels that the spot rate is unlikely to reach 1.6000 during the period. Buying a standard 1.5000 dollar call protects the exporter against the exchange rate rising to any level during the three months. If he or she is confident that the rate will not exceed 1.6000 more premium would be paid than is necessary if the standard call is bought.

Alternatively, the exporter could purchase a three month up-and-in dollar

1. S Das, *Exotic Options* (LBC Information Services, Sydney, 1996)

call/deutschemark put with a strike price of 1.5000 which kicks-in at 1.6000 for a premium of 1.0%.

Again, the advantage of the kick-in over the standard dollar call is the lower premium. In this case, the premium for the kick-in call would be DM10,000, which is DM5,000 cheaper than the standard call and DM5,000 dearer than the kick-out call.

The exporter will be better off with the kick-in than with the kick-out if the spot rate ever reaches 1.6000 during the three month period, but worse off if it does not. With the kick-in, the exporter will be hedged when it is needed most (ie above 1.6000). The exporter's business might be able to absorb the loss of revenue if the spot rate is between 1.5000 and 1.6000 but not if it is above 1.6000. The kick-in provides disaster insurance. A similar outcome could be achieved by buying a standard dollar call with strike at 1.6000. The pay-out from the dollar call which kicks-in at 1.6000 will be greater than the standard. It would pay the difference between the price at expiry and 1.5000, whereas the standard 1.6000 call would only pay the amount in excess of 1.6000. Accordingly, the kick-in would command a higher premium.

There is no best strategy before the event. The point is simply that more options provide the hedger with greater choice. Barrier options add to the flexibility available to hedgers. By varying the strike price and/or barrier level, the hedger can pay for what he or she wants and no more.

Knock-out Forwards

The put-call parity relationship (Equation 10.4) applies to barrier options.

Knock-out Call – Knock-out Put = Knock-out Forward	**Equation 12.3**

The strike prices and the knock-out level must correspond.

This makes it possible to create structures such as the ***knock-out forward***. This enables a person to enter into a better than market forward rate which knocks-out if the spot rate breaches the barrier level. For example, if the premium of a 1.4800 call which knocks-out at 1.5500 is equal to the premium of a 1.4800 put which knocks-out at 1.5500, then it would be possible to construct a (zero premium) knock-out forward which would enable the exporter to sell the deutschemark receivables at 1.4800 unless the spot rate reaches 1.5500 during the three month period. If the spot rate stays below 1.5500, the exporter achieves a forward rate which is 200 points better than the market forward rate of 1.5000 and no premium is payable.

The risk with using a knock-out forward is that the exporter may become unhedged with the exchange rate above 1.5500 where he or she would most like to be hedged. However, in many cases, the exporter's alternative course of action in a rising exchange rate environment would be to remain unhedged, hoping for the exchange rate to fall to a more attractive level. If so, the exporter would be better off with the knock-out forward.

Reset options are options for which the strike price may change during the life of the option. ***Ladder options*** are reset options with multiple triggers which lock-in a new minimum amount of profit each time a trigger is reached. These are also known as ratchet, cliquet or lock-in options. These options are popular with traders who want to let profitable positions run, but also want to avoid seeing their unrealised profits eroded or turn into losses if the rate moves against them.

Reset and ladder options are constructed by buying a series of better and better kick-in options which kick-in as the market moves further in the trader's favour, and selling a series of kick-outs which kick-out as the new options kick-in.

For example, a trader who expects the dollar to strengthen against the deutschemark buys a dollar call with strike price DM1.5000. To turn the dollar call into a reset option, it is necessary to also buy a dollar call with a better strike price (say 1.4800) which kicks-in at say, 1.5500 and to sell a 1.5000 call which kicks-out at 1.5500. In this case, once the spot rate reaches 1.5500, the original 1.5000 call is effectively replaced with a 1.4800 call.

The process is repeated to create a ladder option. By buying another kick-in call with strike of, say, 1.4600 which kicks-in at, say, 1.6000, and selling a 1.4800 kick-out call which kicks-out at 1.6000, it is possible to construct a second step in the ladder.

The additional premium required to turn a standard option into a reset or ladder option is not usually very much if the kick-in level is far enough away from the starting rate and because the premium received from writing the kick-outs partly defrays the premium needed to buy the kick-ins.

Combinations

There is an unlimited number of possible combinations of standard calls and puts, knock-out, kick-out, knock-in, kick-in and digital options which can be used to shape the profile that best suits the person's view. No structure is best in all cases. There are always trade-offs. Finding the "best" strategy is a matter of identifying a structure that best fits the needs and views of the person. It is always necessary to give up something to get something else. A lower premium can be obtained by accepting a worse strike price, by setting a knock-out level closer to the current rate or by selling some option and so on. Digital and barrier options add to the bag of tricks available to the hedger. It may never be necessary but it is worth knowing how to use them in particular circumstances.

Other Path Dependent Options

Path dependent options include average rate, average strike and look-back options.

An ***average rate option*** is one where the pay-off equals the difference between the average rate and the strike price or zero whichever is higher. These are also known as Asian options.

The average rate is a function of the path which the exchange rate takes over the life of the option. It is usually calculated as the arithmetic average of daily rates taken at a specified time of day. If the spot rate follows the path shown in Figure 12.11, the average rate would be ¥104.00. The pay-out on a dollar call with strike price of ¥102.00 would be ¥2.00.

Pay-out	=	Average rate	–	Strike price
	=	104.00	–	102.00
	=	¥2.00		

Figure 12.11

Average rate dollar call strike ¥102.00

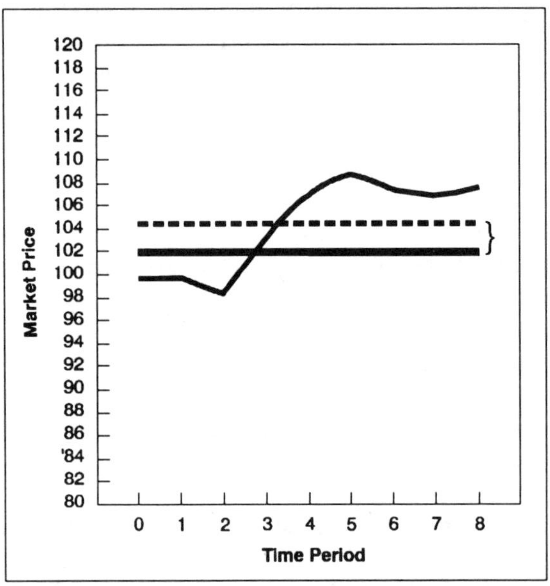

An ***average strike option*** is one for which the strike price is the average rate. If the spot rate follows the path shown in Figure 12.11 so that the average rate is ¥104.00 and the spot rate at expiry is ¥107.00, then the pay-out of an average strike call would be ¥3.00.

Pay-out	=	Expiry rate	–	Average rate
	=	107.00	–	104.00
	=	¥3.00		

The sum of the pay-out from the average rate call and the corresponding average strike call equals the pay-out from the standard call with the same strike price. Similarly, the sum of the premiums of the average rate and corresponding average strike call will equal the premium of the standard call. It follows that average rate and average strike options have lower premiums than their corresponding standard options. This is to be expected because the volatility of the average must be lower than the volatility of the underlying spot rate.

Average rate and average strike options can, therefore, provide economical hedges for companies who have contractual arrangements with receipts or payments based on average exchange rates. For example, a newspaper company buys newsprint from a mill. Like most commodities, paper is priced in US dollars. The newspaper company (the importer) and the mill (the exporter) have equal and opposite exchange rate exposures. They may agree that the price paid for the paper will reflect the average exchange rate during the period of shipment. If so, both would have exposure to the average exchange rate which is less volatile than the spot rate. Both parties could use average rate or average strike options to economically and efficiently hedge their exposures.

A ***look-back option*** is one for which the pay-out is the peak difference between the strike price and the market price during the life of the option.

If the spot rate follows the path shown in Figure 12.12, the pay-out on a look-back dollar call with strike price ¥102.00 would be ¥10.00.

Pay-out	=	Maximum value	–	Strike price
	=	112.00	–	102.00
	=	¥10.00		

Figure 12.12

Look-back dollar call strike ¥102.00

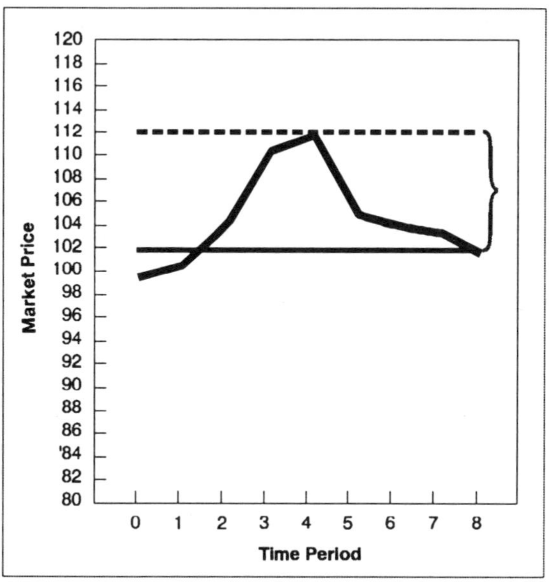

Even though the spot rate at expiry in this example was ¥101.70 which is less than the strike price, the look-back call would pay-out ¥10.00.

Look-back options provide traders with the benefit of hindsight. They can achieve the best possible rate which occurred during the period. This makes look-back options sound very attractive. However, they are not used much in practice because the premium required to buy look-back options is typically large. Remember, the premium is the present value of the expected pay-out. Because the expected pay-out is high, the premium will be high.

A ***shout option*** gives its owner the right to lock-in a minimum pay-out equal to the intrinsic value at the time by "shouting", ie declaring an intention to do so. A Japanese exporter buys a dollar call with strike price ¥102.00 to hedge US dollar receivables which are due in eight months. If the spot rate moves as in Figure 12.13, the exporter enjoys seeing the dollar rise during the first four months. In the fifth month the dollar starts to fall sharply. When the rate falls to ¥107.50, the exporter shouts. If the spot rate continues to fall as in Figure 12.13, the pay-out from the option would be ¥5.50. On the other hand, if the rate at expiry is greater than ¥107.50, the pay-out would be as for a standard dollar call.

Pay-out	=	min (shout level – strike, expiry rate – strike)		
	=	107.50	–	102.00
	=	¥5.50		

Figure 12.13

Shout option

Dollar call with strike ¥102.00 shouted at ¥107.50

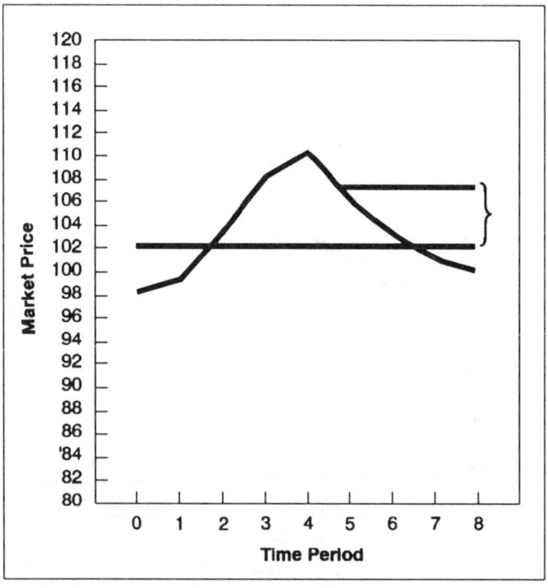

The premium for the shout option will be considerably less than for the look-back call because the expected pay-out is less. The owner of the shout option would only obtain the same pay-out as the look-back option if he or she shouts at exactly the peak of the market. If the shout is early, an opportunity to shout later at a higher level may be missed. On the other hand, if the shout is late, the opportunity to lock-in a better rate than will be achieved again may be missed.

Other non-path dependent options

There are other types of options, most of which are not used much in practice.

A ***compound option*** is an option on an option. The buyer of a compound option has the right, but not the obligation, to enter into an option with a specified strike price for a specified premium at a specified future date. Compound options are useful for companies bidding on contracts which, if won, will result in a future foreign currency exposure.

A British company bidding on a French contract will not know if it will have French franc exposure until the contract is awarded in three months. If its bid is successful, it will have French franc income after a further year. Its bid is based on prevailing exchange rates. If after three months it is awarded the bid but by then the pound has appreciated against the franc, the project will not be as profitable as budgeted. The rate may even have moved so far that winning the bid could mean locking in a loss.

The company could purchase a 15 month franc put/sterling call for say, 5% premium. This would involve a considerable cash outlay which would be unnecessary if the contract is lost. If the contract is lost, the company could sell a 12 month franc put/sterling call at the time to recover some of the 5% premium. However, the premium may be considerably lower, say 3%, because there has been 3 months' time decay, the pound may have appreciated against the franc and volatility may have fallen.

Instead, the company could purchase a compound option to enter into a 12 month franc put/sterling call with a premium of 4.5% in three months for a premium of only, say, 1% today. The initial cash outlay is 1% as opposed to 5%. If the company wins the contract, it can purchase the 12 month franc put/sterling call for a further 4.5%. If the then premium for the 12 month franc put/sterling call is less than 4.5%, the company could allow the compound option to lapse and purchase the cheaper 12 month option in the market. If the company loses the contract, it can allow the compound option to lapse, or if the then premium on the franc put is greater than 4.5%, it could exercise the compound option and then sell a 12 month franc put to realise a profit which would offset all or part of the premium paid to buy the compound option.

Compound options give companies the ability to achieve the bought option profile at relatively little cost. They only have to pay for the bulk of the cover when they know they need it and can most afford to pay for it.

Chooser options are options which have a defined strike price and on a specified date the buyer can choose whether the option is a call or a put. They are also known as preference or double options.

Buying chooser options provides a hedge against extreme volatility. A person who is worried that the exchange rate could rise or fall dramatically without knowing in which direction could purchase a chooser option. If the price rises, he or she elects that the option is a call. If it falls, the option can be elected to be a put. Chooser options are cheaper than bought straddles because they only involve the purchase of a single option.

An ***instalment option*** has the premium paid periodically. The owner of the option pays the premium in instalments, usually at regular intervals, and may elect to terminate the option at any time. Once terminated, there is no obligation to pay the remaining instalments.

A six month option with an up-front premium of 500 points could be purchased in monthly instalments of 100 points. If the owner of the option holds it until maturity a total of 600 points in premium will be paid. However, if after, say, two months, the exchange rate has moved so that the option is well out-of-the-money, he or she may elect to cancel the option and will have paid only 200 points premium.

Instalment options are also known as rental options or pay-as-you-go options.

Power options have pay-outs which are a function of the difference between the strike price and the rate at expiry raised to a power greater than one. The pay-out on a standard dollar call with strike price ¥100.00 which expires with the spot rate at ¥102.00 would be ¥2.00. A power option with pay-out equal to $(x - 100)^2$ if the expiry rate, x, is greater than 100 would have a pay-out of ¥4.00 if the spot rate at expiry is ¥102.00.

Spot rate at expiry	Pay-out for standard call	Pay-out for power option
95	0	0
100	0	0
102	2	4
104	4	16
110	10	100

Power options involve leverage. The risk taken by the seller of power options is substantially greater than that for a standard option.

Contingent options kick-in if a specified, possibly unrelated, event occurs. For example, a currency option might kick-in if interest rates reach a certain level.

Quanto options are options for which the quantity of the face value varies with some other variable. A dollar-based fund manager investing in Japanese equities has a foreign exchange exposure which varies in size with the yen value of the portfolio.

Example 12.5

A US fund manager purchases $10,000,000 of Japanese equities when the spot exchange rate is $1 = ¥100.00 and the Nikkei 225 index is 20,000. The yen value of the portfolio would be initially ¥1,000,000,000 (10,000,000 × 100.00) and will vary as the prices of the equities rise or fall. Assuming that the particular basket of stocks varies approximately with the Nikkei index, if the N225 rises to 21,000, the portfolio would then be worth about ¥1,050,000,000. On the other hand, if the N225 falls to 19,000, the portfolio would be worth ¥950,000,000. Buying a standard yen put/dollar call for face value ¥1,000,000,000 would provide an imperfect hedge of the currency risk. If N225 is 21,000, the investor would be underhedged; if N225 is 19,000 he or she would be overhedged. A quanto option for which the yen face value varies with the N225 index would provide a better hedge. It would not be perfect to the extent that the specific portfolio may outperform or underperform the index but it is likely to be superior to a standard (ie constant volume) option.

Correlation

The price of contingent options and quantos is affected by the correlation between the exchange rate and the related variable.

Correlation describes how closely two sets of variables are related. Correlation can be measured using the following formula:

$$\rho = \frac{n\Sigma xy - \Sigma x \Sigma y}{\sqrt{[n\Sigma x^2 - (\Sigma x)^2][n\Sigma y^2 - (\Sigma y)^2]}} \qquad \textbf{Equation 12.4}$$

If the correlation coefficient ρ is positive, then when variable x rises, variable y also tends to rise. If the correlation coefficient is negative, then when x rises, y tends to fall. If the correlation coefficient equals +1, then x and y are perfectly correlated ie y always rises or falls with x. If the coefficient equals −1, then x and y are perfectly negatively correlated ie when x rises y always falls and vice versa. If $\rho = 0$, then x and y are independent.

Example 12.6

Over a period of 10 months, the dollar yen and dollar mark moved as shown in Exhibit 12.1. Calculate the correlation between the two exchange rates over this period.

Exhibit 12.1

Calculating correlation

Month	$ / Yen	$ / DM
1	105.60	1.5150
2	106.00	1.5230
3	107.25	1.5360
4	104.40	1.5570
5	106.20	1.5540
6	108.40	1.5680
7	107.75	1.5790
8	108.25	1.5660
9	109.00	1.5890
10	109.10	1.5995

Applying Equation 12.4, $\rho = +0.72$

The higher the correlation coefficient, the closer the relationship between the two exchange rates. A correlation of 0.72 is high. Over the period, the dollar was mostly rising against both the yen and the deutschemark. In some months, the dollar rose more against the yen than it did against the deutschemark. In other months, it rose more against the deutschemark than the yen. In month 4, the dollar fell against the yen but continued rising against the deutschemark whereas in month 8, it fell against the deutschemark but rose against the yen.

Considerations in the Japanese economy may affect the yen but not the deutschemark, and some factors in Germany may affect the deutschemark but not the yen. Other factors (eg developments in the US economy) will affect both exchange rates.

The correlation between two exchange rates will vary over time. However, if a sufficient number of observations are taken over a long enough time, consistent relationships between exchange rates will be reflected.

Cross Rate Volatility

The volatility of a cross rate can be derived from the volatilities of the two exchange rates and the correlation between them.

If the cross rate is the ratio of the two exchange rates:

$$\sigma_{12}^2 = \sigma_1^2 + \sigma_2^2 - 2\rho\sigma_1\sigma_2 \qquad \textbf{Equation 12.5(a)}$$

If the cross rate is the product of the two exchange rates:

$$\sigma_{12}^2 = \sigma_1^2 + \sigma_2^2 + 2\rho\sigma_1\sigma_2$$

Equation 12.5(b)

where

σ_{12} = cross rate volatility
σ_1 = volatility of exchange rate 1
σ_2 = volatility of exchange rate 2
ρ = correlation between currency 1 and currency 2

Example 12.7

If $\sigma_{\$/¥}$ = 12.5%
$\sigma_{\$/DM}$ = 10.0%
ρ = 0.72

then, $\sigma^2_{¥/DM} = \sigma^2_{\$/¥} + \sigma^2_{\$/DM} - 2\rho\,\sigma_{\$/¥}\;\sigma_{\$/DM}$

$= (0.125)^2 + (0.1)^2 \; - 2(0.72)(0.125)(0.1)$

$= 0.15625 + 0.01 - 0.18$

$= 0.007625$

$\therefore \quad \sigma_{¥/DM} = \sqrt{0.007625} = 0.087 = 8.7\%$

If the cross rate volatility is not as implied by Equation 12.5, an arbitrage opportunity exists. Arbitrageurs will buy options with below equilibrium volatility and sell options with above equilibrium volatility until the cross volatility relationship is restored.

Basket Options

A ***basket option*** is an option for which the underlying is a basket of currencies.

Provided all of the currencies in the basket are not perfectly correlated, the volatility and so the premium of the basket will be less than the weighted average of the volatilities and premiums of the component currencies.

Example 12.8

A fund manager invests $60,000,000 in Japanese assets and $40,000,000 in German assets when the respective exchange rates are ¥110.00 and DM1.5000. He could hedge against currency risk by purchasing a dollar call/yen put and a dollar call/deutschemark put. Alternatively, he could purchase a dollar call/basket put.

The basket would be comprised of ¥6,600,000,000 and DM60,000,000 as shown in Exhibit 12.2.

Exhibit 12.2
Basket of currencies

Currency	Amount in dollars	Weight	Exchange rate	Currency
Yen	$60,000,000	0.6	110.00	¥6,600,000,000
DM	$40,000,000	0.4	1.5000	DM 60,000,000
Total	$100,000,000	1.0		

Note: Sum of the weights = 1

The pay-out for the basket option will be a function of an index. The index is a number which reflects the value of the basket of currencies. The index is usually given a base number equal to 100 at the start of the option period. The value of the index can then be calculated for any set of exchange rates. For example, if the dollar has risen to ¥115.00 and DM1.6000, then the index will have fallen to 94.9. The basket of currencies is only worth 94.9% of what it was previously worth.

Exhibit 12.3
Currency index

Currency amount	Exchange rate	Dollar value	Index value
¥6,600,000,000	115.00	57,391,304	57.4
DM60,000,000	1.6000	37,500,000	37.5
Total		94,891,304	**94.9**

An index value can be computed for a set of strike prices. For example, if the strike prices for the basket option are ¥115.00 and DM1.6000, the strike index would be 94.9.

The basket put will pay-out if the basket index at expiry is less than the strike index. For example, if at expiry the dollar is ¥120.00 and DM1.7000, the pay-out would be $4,600,000.

Pay-out = Principal (strike index – expiry index)
= 100,000,000 (94.9 – 90.3)
= $4,600,000

Exhibit 12.4
Index at expiry

Currency amount	Exchange rate	Dollar value	Index value
Y6,600,000,000	120.00	55,000,000	55.0
DM60,000,000	1.7000	35,294,118	35.3
Total		90,294,118	**90.3**

The pay-out from a basket option can be less than the sum of the pay-outs of the individual options. For example, if the exchange rates at expiry were ¥120.00 and DM1.5500, then the pay-out from the basket put would be $1,200,000 as opposed to $2,400,000 from the yen put on its own.

Exhibit 12.5
Index at expiry

Currency Amount	Exchange rate	Dollar value	Index value
Y6,600,000,000	120.00	55,000,000	55.0
DM60,000,000	1.5500	38,709,677	38.7
Total		93,709,677	**93.7**

Pay-out from basket put = 100,000,000 (94.9 – 93.7) = $1,200,000

Pay-out from yen put $= \frac{6,600,000,000}{115.00} - \frac{6,600,000,000}{120.00}$ = $2,400,000

The investor might not particularly mind that he or she has not maximised the pay-out from the option. The motivation for wanting a pay-out is to limit the amount that can be lost from the *general* weakening of the invested foreign currencies. The basket option achieves this objective. The investor may prefer to pay a lower premium for the basket option than for a separately purchased yen put and a DM put, even if the possible pay-out is less.

The premium for the basket option will be less than the sum of the premiums of the individual puts because the basket index will be less volatile than the weighted average of the volatilities of the separate exchange rates.

The volatility of the basket can be calculated using Equation 12.6.

$$\sigma_{basket} = \sqrt{\Sigma w_i w_j \sigma_i \sigma_j \rho_{ij}}$$ **Equation 12.6**

If dollar yen volatility is 12.5%, dollar mark volatility 10.0% and the correlation between dollar yen and dollar mark 0.72, then

$$\sigma_{basket} = \sqrt{(0.6\times0.6\times0.125\times0.125)+(0.6\times0.4\times0.125\times0.1\times0.72)+(0.4\times0.6\times0.1\times0.125\times0.72)+(0.4\times0.4\times0.1\times0.1)}$$

$$= 0.107 = 10.7\%$$

The weighted volatility of the separate yen and DM puts would be:

$(0.6 \times 0.125) + (0.4 \times 0.10) = 0.115 = 11.5\%$

It follows that the premium for the basket option will be less than the sum of the premiums of the separate yen and deutschemark puts.

It should be pointed out that it is possible to calculate the premium of the basket put because the market price (current value of the index), strike price (strike index) and volatility are all known.

In practice, basket options are normally based on a basket of three to five currency pairs. This typically generates a significant saving in premium without becoming too cumbersome to operate. Fund managers with exposures in many currencies tend to group them together into like sets, eg they might use deutschemarks as a proxy for other European currencies.

It is possible to construct collars, knock-outs digitals etc with basket options.

Hybrids

Hybrids are derivatives which establish a price based on the relationship between the two variables which might not normally be associated with each other.

Example 12.8

An Australian nickel producer has exposure to both the price of nickel and the A$/US$ exchange rate. Profit rises with the price of nickel and falls when the exchange rate rises.

The company produces 60,000,000 pounds of nickel per year. Nickel is priced in US dollars. Its annual revenue is therefore 60,000,000 × P where P = price of nickel per pound.

Revenue = 60,000,000 × P

The company has costs of US$25,000,000 per year. It estimates that it has an additional A$110,000,000 in expenses.

The company would like to hedge its currency risk without having to hedge its nickel price risk. How many US dollars should the company sell forward to eliminate its exchange rate risk?

US dollar exposure = 60,000,000 × P – 25,000,000

The amount can vary dramatically with the volatile price of nickel. Average annual volatility has been over 30%. The price is currently $3.75 per pound but over the past few years, it has been as low as $1.80 and as high as $4.55. The price reached $8.15 in 1989. Exhibit 12.6 shows how the company's foreign exchange risk varies with the price of nickel.

Exhibit 12.6

Currency risk at different nickel prices

Price of nickel	US$ exposure
1.75	80,000,000
2.76	140,000,000
3.77	200,000,000
4.78	260,000,000
5.79	320,000,000

If the company sells US$200,000,000, it takes the risk that it will overhedge. For example, if the price of nickel then falls to, say, $2.75, it will have sold US$60,000,000 more than it will have. It needs a forward exchange contract with a quanto like feature – that is, the number of US dollars it sells forward will vary with the nickel price.

The fact that historically there has been a high positive correlation between the price of nickel and the exchange rate provides something of a natural hedge – if the price of nickel falls, then it is likely that the exchange rate will also fall. This would imply that the producer should do nothing. However, the correlation is far from perfectly negative. It will lose much more from a fall in the nickel price than it will make from the associated likely fall in the exchange rate. Exhibit 12.7 is a matrix which shows the expected pre-tax profit in Australian dollars for various possible combinations of the nickel price and exchange rate.

Exhibit 12.7

Nickel producer's pre-tax profit in A$ million

Nickel Price	1.75	2.75	3.75	4.75	5.75
Exchange rate					
0.5000	50	170	290	410	530
0.6000	23	123	223	323	423
0.7000	4	90	176	261	347
0.8000	– 10	65	140	215	290
0.9000	– 21	46	112	179	246

The positive correlation between the nickel price and the exchange rate means that combinations in the top right hand corner (eg $5.75 and 0.5000) and bottom left hand corner (eg $1.75 and 0.9000) are very unlikely. The surface in Figure 12.14 shows how the correlation between the nickel price and the exchange rate affects the probability of different possible outcomes.

Figure 12.14

Probabilities of combinations of nickel prices and exchange rates given + 0.30 correlation

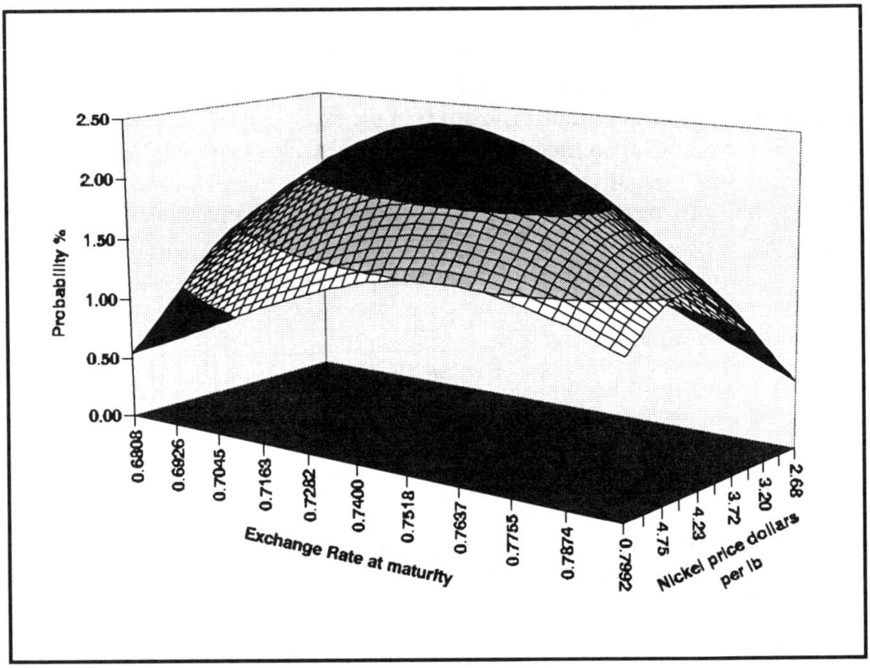

It was possible to use this three dimensional probability density function to construct a hybrid to allow the producer to hedge by selling forward the variable number of US dollars each quarter for three years at an exchange rate which varies with the average price of nickel for the quarter according to the following relationship:

$$\text{Exchange rate} \quad = \quad 0.3325 + 0.1 \times \text{Price of nickel}$$

Exhibit 12.15 shows the exchange rate generated by this formula and the resultant pre-tax profit in Australian dollars for various possible nickel prices.

Exhibit 12.15

Nickel correlated currency hedge

Nickel price	US$ sold	Exchange rate	Pre-tax profit
1.75	80,000,000	0.5075	48,000,000
2.76	140,000,000	0.6075	120,000,000
3.77	200,000,000	0.7075	173,000,000
4.78	260,000,000	0.8075	212,000,000
5.79	320,000,000	0.9075	243,000,000

In addition to avoiding the possibility of overhedging, the hybrid structure enables the nickel producer to totally eliminate exchange rate risk but continue to benefit from any rise in the price of nickel.

Summary

Options increase the choices available to hedgers. Option derivatives and hybrids add to the number of choices. It is possible to design a structure which suits the needs and views of the person or organisation with the exposure.

The set of options presented above is not definitive. All sorts of possible structures can be created. Some of the more exotic options are not widely used in practice. However, option derivatives such as digitals, barriers and baskets are very popular.

There is no doubt that additional products will be developed in the future and further combinations and applications of existing products will be used. Once a basic understanding of the concepts is acquired, the only real constraint is imagination.

Practice Problems

12.1 Pricing an at-expiry digital call

Use the reverse binomial method to calculate the premium of a 4 month Australian dollar call which pays US$ 100,000 if the spot rate at-expiry is 0.7800 or higher. Given the current spot rate is 0.7500, the 4 month forward rate is 0.7520, the 4 month US dollar interest rate is 6.0% pa. and assuming an up-down factor of 0.0150 per month.

12.2 Pricing a power option

Calculate the premium of a dollar call with face value $10,000,000 which pays (X - 105.00)2 assuming the binomial tree as shown in Exhibit 10.3. The 6 month yen interest rate is 1% pa and the current spot rate is $1 = ¥ 100.00.

There is no supplementary problem for Chapter 12.

13

Factors Affecting Exchange Rates

There are many factors which influence exchange rates and they assume different significance at different times. This chapter attempts to build a framework for examining the main factors which affect exchange rates and to provide guidelines for people managing currency exposures.

Theories of Exchange Rate Determination

None of the numerous theories of exchange rate determination is sufficiently comprehensive or dynamic to explain exchange rate movements on its own, let alone accurately predict the future direction and level of exchange rates. Nonetheless, there are important elements in most of the theories. Examining a few of the most popular theories is a good starting point for building a framework to analyse exchange rate changes. Understanding why a theory fails provides further insight into the complex issue of exchange rate determination.

Current Account Balance

The balance of payments is a record of a country's transactions with the rest of the world. The current account records exports and imports of goods and services. If more money is received from the sale of exports than is paid for imports, there is a ***current account surplus***[1]. On the other hand, if more is spent purchasing imports than is received from selling exports, there is a ***current account deficit***[1]. Classical economic theory says that currencies with increasing current account surpluses or decreasing current account deficits tend to strengthen against currencies with decreasing current account surpluses or increasing current account deficits.

The capital account records cross border borrowing and investment. As a general rule, countries with current account deficits need to borrow (or obtain investment) from countries with current account surpluses.

---

1. Interest and dividend flows associated with capital flows into and out of the country are also included in the current account. Interest and dividends received from offshore are credits (like export receipts). Interest and dividends paid offshore are debits (like import payments).

The currency of a country with a current account surplus will tend to appreciate against the currency of a country with a current account deficit. If Country A has a current account surplus and Country B a current account deficit, then Currency A will tend to appreciate against Currency B. To purchase Country A's exports, a foreigner needs to buy Currency A. The citizens of Country A need to sell Currency A to buy foreign currencies to purchase their imports. If exports exceed imports, there will be greater demand to buy Currency A than to sell it. The exchange rate which is the price of Currency A will appreciate to reflect relatively high demand for the currency.

Conversely, the currency of a country with a current account deficit will tend to depreciate against the currency of a country with a current account surplus. If imports exceed exports as in Country B, then there will be more interest in selling Currency B than in buying it. So the price of Currency B will tend to fall.

It should be emphasised that it is the *change* in the current account deficit which is relevant. If a country has a diminishing current account surplus, its currency will tend to depreciate whereas in a country with a shrinking current account deficit, it will tend to appreciate. If less exports or more imports are being purchased than previously, then the demand for the currency and so the exchange rate will tend to decline.

In practice, exchange rates do not always move to reflect relative current account figures. Over time, the relationship generally holds true but there can be sustained periods during which exchange rates move in the opposite direction.

However, the current account is *an* important determinant of exchange rates.

Purchasing Power Parity Theory

The ***purchasing power parity theory*** states that in the long run exchange rates tend to reflect relative inflation rates.

Purchasing power refers to the ability of money to buy goods and services. Over time, prices tend to rise. The inflation rate measures the rate of change of prices over a period of time. Purchasing power declines with inflation. The same amount of money buys fewer goods after prices have risen than it did before they rose.

Purchasing power parity asserts that exchange rates should change so as to reflect the relative purchasing power of the two currencies. If Country A has a higher inflation rate than Country B, then over time Country A's exports will become less competitive and Country B's exports will become more competitive so the exchange rate must adjust to keep the real (ie inflation adjusted) exchange rate constant.

The Economist published an article[2] which used the example of Big Mac hamburgers to illustrate purchasing power parity. A Big Mac is a homogeneous

2. April 1992.

product – it is identical whether you buy it in New York, London, Frankfurt or Tokyo – and so, it could be expected to be the same price wherever it is sold.

The exchange rate implied by the purchasing power parity theory is that reflecting the relative price of a Big Mac. For example, if a Big Mac costs $2.19 in New York and £1.74 in London, the implied exchange rate = 1.74/1.29 = 1.2586.

In practice, it is little more than coincidence if actual exchange rates are at the levels implied by purchasing power parity. Figure 13.1 shows how actual exchange rates differed from the PPP level on 7 April 1992. In fact, in the five years since then, none of these exchange rates has reached the PPP level and for much of the time, the exchange rates moved away from the purchasing power parity levels.

Exhibit 13.1
Big Mac Parity

Country	Price in local currency	Implied (PPP) Exchange rate	Exchange Rate 7 April 1992
US	2.19	1.00	1.00
UK	£1.74	1.2586	1.7500
Germany	DM4.50	2.0500	1.6400
Japan	¥380.00	174.00	133.00

One reason that purchasing power parity does not work is that geographical separation denies people the means to arbitrage inconsistent prices. If a person on a trans-Pacific flight was given the opportunity to buy a hamburger for either $2.19 or ¥380.00 when the exchange rate was $1 = ¥133.00, he or she would choose to pay in dollars rather than yen. Because people would always be better off paying in dollars, the exchange rate would *tend* to change from 133.00 towards 174.00 at which rate the arbitrage opportunity would disappear.

A person in Tokyo would not consider going to New York to buy a Big Mac more cheaply. The time and cost would be much too great. So, the relative price of a Big Mac can remain substantially different from the PPP exchange rate indefinitely. Barriers to free trade, eg import tariffs, are another source of sustainable disparity in relative prices.

Another problem with purchasing power parity is that while there is a single exchange rate between two currencies at any point of time, the relative price may vary greatly depending on which goods and services are being considered. For example, a car which costs $21,900 in the US (ie 10,000 times as much as a Big Mac) might cost ¥4,560,000 in Japan (ie 12,000 times as much as a Big Mac). The relative price of cars implies a PPP exchange rate of 208.22 whereas the relative price of Big Macs implied 174.00.

This problem is typically addressed by assuming that exchange rate parity will reflect relative inflation rates where inflation is measured as the change in prices *generally*. Price indices such as the CPI (Consumer Price Index) are used to estimate general price changes. Measuring variables such as CPI is extremely difficult and is subject to substantial errors of aggregation and measurement. It is important to realise that while inflation may be reported to the first decimal place of 1% per annum, the measure is nowhere that precise.

Empirical evidence on purchasing power parity is unconvincing except for countries which have had very high rates of inflation. Countries such as some of those in Latin America have typically had rapidly depreciating currencies associated with their very high inflation rates. Generally speaking, however, exchange rates do not reflect relative inflation rates although there are some periods for which the relationship holds reasonably well.

The thing to remember about the purchasing power parity theory is that the relative inflation rate is another of the important factors which influence exchange rates.

Interest Rate Parity Theory

Interest rate parity theory states that in the long run exchange rates tend to reflect relative interest rates.

Capital tends to flow between countries such that over time, high interest rate currencies depreciate against low interest rate currencies. For example, over the past 15 years, US interest rates have generally been significantly higher than Japanese interest rates. This has corresponded with a general weakening of the dollar against the yen.

Because the forward exchange rate reflects the interest rates of the two currencies, interest rate parity implies that over time, the forward rate will be the best predictor of the future spot rate. Empirically, the forward rate has not been a good predicter of where the spot rate would go. Over some periods, the spot rate has moved well beyond where the forward rate had been. In other periods, it has moved in the opposite direction.

In practice, the relationship between relative interest rates and exchange rates is much more complex than implied by the interest rate parity theory. In the short term, capital tends to flow out of the low interest rate currency and into the high interest rate currency causing the low interest rate currency to lose value against the high interest rate currency. This is the opposite of what is supposed to happen according to interest rate parity theory.

Example 13.1

	Interest Rate
Currency A	6% pa
Currency B	3% pa

In the short term, people will be inclined to borrow Currency B at 3% pa, sell it to buy Currency A and to invest in Currency A at 6% pa. Because people will be selling Currency B and buying Currency A, Currency B will tend to depreciate against Currency A.

Whether or not this strategy turns out to be profitable will depend on what happens to the exchange rate. If the exchange rate remains unchanged or if Currency B depreciates by less than the interest differential, then the strategy will prove profitable. On the other hand, if Currency B depreciates by more than the interest differential, the strategy will result in a loss (ie the exchange rate loss will exceed the gain in the interest rate markets).

Interest rate parity theory asserts that the relative interest rates reflect the market's exchange rate expectations. If Currency A has a higher interest rate than Currency B, it means that Currency A *needs* to have a higher interest rate to induce investors to take the currency risk to invest in Currency A rather than Currency B.

It is important to understand that according to interest rate parity theory, it is changes in *relative* interest rates which matters. If, for example, the interest rate of Currency A fell to 5% pa and that of Currency B rose to 4% pa, that would constitute a fall in Currency A's interest rate *relative* to Currency B's. Accordingly, Currency A will tend to appreciate against Currency B.

The above argument is plausible and, in general, empirical evidence supports interest rate parity theory in direction if not by degree, but it is highly time period dependent. There are lengthy periods in which exchange rates move in the opposite direction to that implied by interest rate parity.

The weakness in the interest rate parity argument is that in general interest rates are not determined by the investor market. Central Banks actively manage interest rates and their primary objective is not usually exchange rate management. Central Bank objectives may vary from country to country and they tend to change over time. In recent history (ie since the break-down of the Bretton Woods agreement in the early 1970s), Central Banks have generally managed interest rates to control inflation and to foster economic growth rather than to influence exchange rates.

The lesson to take from the interest rate parity theory is that relative interest rates and exchange rate expectations are important factors which influence exchange rates.

Factors Affecting Interest Rates

Saying that interest rate levels affect exchange rates begs the question, what factors affect interest rates?

Interest rates are determined by supply and demand. However, in most countries the Central Bank intervenes actively to manage interest rates.

Central Banks tend to use interest rates to control the level of economic activity. If the economy is buoyant, the demand for goods and services and so the demand for money will be high. The economy will grow quickly but inflation is likely to be rising. If the economy is sluggish, the demand for goods and services and so the demand for money will be low. The economy will be growing slowly. It may even be in recession (ie negative growth). Unemployment is likely to be high.

The ***business cycle*** describes the pattern of alternate periods of high and low or negative growth.

Figure 13.1

Business cycle

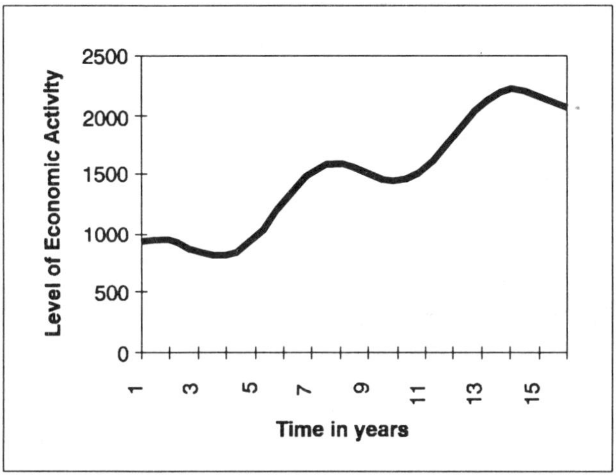

During periods of recession, monetary authorities are likely to lower interest rates to stimulate economic activity. During periods of high growth, authorities are inclined to raise interest rates to contain inflation.

In practice, measuring the level of economic activity is not a simple task. Many economic measures are used to indicate the level of activity. Some of these are what is known as specific indicators which measure one aspect of economic activity. Others are general indicators which attempt to dimension the overall level of economic activity.

<u>Examples of Specific Indicators</u>

Retail sales
Housing starts
Motor vehicle registrations
Durable goods orders
Industrial production
Personal income
Unemployment rate

<u>Examples of General Economic Indicators</u>

GDP (Gross Domestic Product)
National income
Economic growth rate (real GDP per capita)

No one measure on its own provides a complete picture. However, by observing a whole range of general and specific indicators, it is possible to piece together a reasonable picture of how the economy is performing. Policy makers typically review as much economic data as is available before taking decisions to tighten (ie raise) or ease (ie lower) interest rates.

Whichever economic indicators are used, the business cycle does not follow a smooth curve as in Figure 13.1. The fact is that the economy is complex and measuring economic aggregates is prone to error. Furthermore, there are inevitable lags. It may take months to collect and aggregate data so that by the time the data is released, the level of economic activity may have changed.

Some economists calculate indices which incorporate a range of specific indicators. The most popular of these is known as the index of leading indicators, which attempts to show the direction in which the economy is heading rather than merely looking at where it has been.

There is a continual release of statistics on the economy which helps anticipating likely changes in interest rates.

It was pointed out in Chapter 4 that the shape of the yield curve reflects where the market generally expects interest rates to be in the future.

Interrelationship Between Interest Rates and Exchange Rates

Changes in interest rates affect exchange rates. Changes in exchange rates can also affect interest rates. When a currency depreciates, the cost of imports rises. If imports represent a significant component of the economy, this can adversely impact the inflation rate. Monetary authorities can tighten interest rates to dampen the inflationary effect of a weakening currency.

Sometimes Central Banks consider exchange rate stability to be an important economic objective. If so, they may use monetary policy to help achieve their exchange rate targets. Raising interest rates will tend to attract capital, thereby supporting the exchange rate.

Time Horizon

Corporations wishing to manage the exchange rate risk associated with their business generally take a long term perspective. Their business naturally has net exchange positions for extended periods. Their profitability depends on what happens to exchange rates over a period of months or years. Accordingly, their time horizon is medium or long term.

Foreign exchange traders who are market making will have a very short time horizon. They make money by carrying positions for very short periods – hours, minutes or even seconds.

Different factors affect exchange rates in the short term than those which are relevant over a longer time horizon.

As the factors considered above have longer term relevance, this is a convenient point to draw together a framework analysing the long term exchange rate outlook.

Framework – Long Term Outlook

Factor	Considerations	Implications
Current account	Widening surplus or narrowing deficit	stronger currency
	Narrowing surplus or widening deficit	weaker currency
Inflation rates	Relatively low inflation	stronger currency
	Relatively high inflation	weaker currency
Interest rates	Relatively low interest rate	stronger currency
	Relatively high interest rate	weaker currency

The above factors are sometimes referred to as the ***fundamental factors.***

The *direction* in which exchange rates are likely to move over an extended period is likely to be predominantly determined by the fundamental factors. If all three factors point in the same direction, there is a high probability that exchange rates will trend in that direction. For example, a country with a widening current account deficit with a high relative inflation rate and high relative interest rates is very likely to have a weakening currency.

The *extent* to which exchange rates can be expected to move is more difficult to predict. The more the current account imbalance, the relative inflation rate and interest rates change, the further the exchange rate is likely to move. Forward rates are one indicator but should be used with caution. All variables keep changing and the measures are imprecise. The relative importance of the fundamental factors can change over time depending on the current policy slant and even "fashion".

The recommended approach is to systematically review the fundamental factors asking how each is likely to change and *roughly* what impact that would be expected to have on exchange rates. Forecasting a range within which the exchange rate is expected to be often makes more sense than point forecasting. This process should be reviewed regularly as new information comes to hand.

It is worth remembering that the shape of the yield curve and forward exchange rates embody the market's expectations for interest rates and exchange rates. It is also true that market volatilities used in option pricing embody the market's expectations for how volatile rates will be. If your forecast differs significantly from the forward rate, it is worth analysing why your outlook differs from the market.

Short Term Factors

The fundamental factors are normally very poor predictors of short term exchange rate movements. In the short term, exchange rates tend to be affected by a different set of factors.

Various factors influence spot rates in the short term, primarily through how they affect market *expectations*.

Market flows

Dealers see the transactions being done with their customers and the orders which they are asked to watch. If on a particular day dealers observe that their customers are predominantly buying a particular currency, it is reasonable for them to expect that currency to strengthen. The logical action for them to take is to go long that currency. The combined impact of both the customers and the banks wanting to buy the currency is likely to push the exchange rate up at least for a short time.

Many billions of dollars of foreign exchange transactions are done every day. It is not the actual volume which matters as much as the perceptions which are created. For every buyer there is a seller. On some days, massive volumes are transacted with very little price movement. On other days, the rate can move a long way on the back of relatively small turnover. The more closely aligned market participants become in the view of which direction the exchange rate is likely to move next, the further it is likely to move. Large transactions done by prominent players (eg global fund managers) tend to have the greatest impact on perceptions.

Central Bank intervention

One group of prominent players is the Central Banks. At certain times, they enter the market with the intention of moving exchange rates in a particular direction. Central Bank intervention relies on the expectation that the banks will follow their lead. If the Central Bank buys the local currency, it will be hoping that the commercial banks follow suit thereby causing the currency to strengthen. Sometimes Central Banks "jaw-bone", which means talking the exchange rate up (or down). By publicly saying that they intend to purchase the currency, they hope to lead the market into doing so.

Central Bank intervention can back-fire. On occasions, the market interprets the intervention as an indication that there is a problem. In the early 1980s, the French Central Bank intervened by buying French francs when the franc was close to the lower band within which the EMS operated. The banks took this as a signal to sell the franc and on a number of occasions forced a devaluation. After four or five unsuccessful attempts to hold the franc within the EMS band, the Central Bank changed its approach and instead of intervening through the foreign exchange market, it used the money market. It tightened to the point where the overnight franc interest rate was 500% pa. This made it very expensive to carry a short franc position and proved successful at keeping the exchange rate within the band.

These days, Central Bank intervention is most successful when Central Banks intervene or jaw-bone on a concerted basis. If the market observes the Federal Reserve, Bundesbank, Bank of Japan and Bank of England all buying dollars, it is most unlikely to "take them on" by selling dollars.

Release of economic statistics

The market knows in advance when various statistics will be reported. Economists put considerable effort into predicting what the figures will be. Sometimes people survey these forecasts and publish them. When the figure is released, dealers are ready to pounce. If the figure is significantly different from what was expected, they will have planned to buy or sell the currency in anticipation of a change in the exchange rate. This type of behaviour tends to be self-fulfilling in the short term.

Market sentiment

There is a tendency for market sentiment to develop. Certain themes become popular with market commentators. News reports tend to focus on certain issues. For this reason, rates tend to overshoot. When market sentiment changes, there is often a sudden adjustment or correction in the rate. Sentiment changes may occur as a result of a surprise piece of information or they may result from a band wagon effect.

The timing of changes in market sentiment is very difficult to predict. However, it is good practice to try to estimate to what extent expected information is incorporated (or "discounted") into the rate.

Technical analysis

Technical analysis involves the use of empirical information to predict future price movements. Even though the author favours fundamental analysis over technical analysis, it is worth being aware of critical chart points. Because many traders use technical analysis, there can be considerable market impact when support or resistance levels are broken.

The common thread through all of the short term factors is that they work through expectations and change of perception. These are "soft" variables. They are difficult if not impossible to measure and they can change quickly. There is no time for the sort of thorough analysis which is recommended for people to manage their long term currency risk and even if there was, it would not work. Consequently, spot traders rely on their ability to "read" the market and to react accordingly to be profitable.

Summary

Different types of factors affect exchange rates in the short term to those that affect them in the longer term. Consequently, a different approach is required. It is important to understand when different factors are relevant. It is recommended that the framework of fundamental factors is used for longer term analysis.

Practice Problems

There are no practice problems for Chapter 13.

14

Value at Risk

In mathematics, risk exists whenever there is uncertainty. A change in the value of one variable can lead to an increase or decrease in the value of a second variable. In finance, risk is taken to be the risk that the monetary value of an asset will fall as a result of a change in some factor. The risk that the monetary value of the asset will increase is considered opportunity.

In the real world, uncertainty exists all the time. Financial risk and opportunity are always present. In this chapter, the three major categories of financial risk are examined – market price risk, credit risk and liquidity risk. These three categories of risk are separate but interdependent. Techniques to measure the value at risk and to manage each of these types of risk are discussed.

Market Price Risk

Market price risk is the risk that an asset or portfolio of assets will lose value as a result of a change in the price of a market factor. A rise in interest rates will reduce the value of a bond. A change in exchange rates may cause a foreign exchange position to result in a loss. An increase in volatility will tend to reduce the value of a short option strategy and so on.

Interest rates, exchange rates, volatility and time are referred to as ***market factors***. Other examples of market factors include equity and commodity prices and spreads or the correlation between different factors.

Factor Sensitivities

Factor sensitivities measure the extent to which a change in a market factor by a specified amount would result in a gain or loss.

Suppose, for example, that a dollar based company has a net short exchange position of \$100,000,000 against deutschemarks. A 1% increase in the \$/DM rate from 1.5000 to 1.5150 would lead to a loss of \$1,000,000.

$$\text{Factor sensitivity} = \frac{\text{Change in Value}}{\text{Change in Market Factor}} \qquad \textbf{Equation 14.1}$$

$$= 100{,}000{,}000\ (1.5000 - 1.5150)$$

$$= \text{DM}1{,}500{,}000 = \$1{,}000{,}000$$

How large a change in the market factor is appropriate? Should factor sensitivities be calculated for a 1% change, a 5% change or some other amount? The answer depends on the period of time for which the position is expected to remain open (known as the ***defeasance period***), the tolerance to absorb losses and the expected volatility of the market factor.

A spot trader who continually jobs the market may have a defeasance period of a few minutes. In the other extreme, a corporation may carry an exchange or interest rate position for several years. Factor sensitivities should be calculated for defeasance periods which match the circumstances.

Duration

Duration is the time weighted average life to maturity. It reflects the sensitivity of a portfolio of cash flows to a change in interest rates.

Consider a five year bond in a 5% rate environment. It has the following cash flows with present values as shown below:

End of Year (t)	Cash flow	Present Value	PV × t
1	5,000,000	4,761,905	4,761,905
2	5,000,000	4,535,147	9,070,295
3	5,000,000	4,319,188	12,957,564
4	5,000,000	4,113,512	16,454,050
5	5,000,000	3,917,631	19,588,154
	100,000,000	78,352,617	391,763,083
		100,000,000	454,595,051

$$\text{Duration} = \frac{\Sigma\ PV \times t}{P} = \frac{454{,}595{,}051}{100{,}000{,}000} = 4.546 \text{ years}$$

$$\text{Modified Duration} = \frac{\text{Duration}}{(1 + i)} = \frac{4.546}{1.05} = 4.25 \text{ years}$$

$$\Delta P \doteqdot \Delta i \times MD \times P$$

Equation 14.2

A 1 percentage point increase in rates (from 5% to 6%) would reduce the value of the bond by approximately $4,250,000 from $100,000,000 to $95,750,000. Similarly, a 1 percentage point fall in rates (to 4%) would increase the value of the portfolio of cash flows by approximately $4,250,000 to $104,250,000.

Value at Risk

Value at Risk (VaR) quantifies the risk associated with a prescribed adverse price movement in the same way that modified duration dimensions the risk inherent in a 1 percentage point change in interest rates.

It is possible to use distribution theory to develop measures of market price risk. It is usually reasonable to assume that prices are normally distributed. (For prices for which negative values are nonsensical, log normal distributions may be used.)

Distribution theory makes it possible to identify the probability that the market price will be at, above or below a specific level at a specified time in the future, given that the current market price is known and making an assumption about the expected volatility of the distribution.

For example, if the current exchange rate is \$1 = DM1.4750, volatility is expected to be 12% per annum and exchange rate changes are assumed to be normally distributed, then it is possible to say that there is a 15.9% chance that in one year the spot rate will be below 1.2980, a 10% chance that it will be below 1.2480 and a 5% chance that it will be below 1.1830.

It is a property of a normal distribution that 15.9% will lie below one standard deviation below the mean.

Given that $\sigma = 12\%$, one standard deviation $= 1.4750 \times 0.12 = 0.1770$.

Thus there is a 15.9% probability that the spot rate in 12 months' time will be below $1.4750 - 0.1770 = 1.2980$.

It is also the case that 10% will lie below 1.2825 standard deviations and 5% below 1.6497 standard deviations and so on. As one standard deviation is DM 0.1770 it follows that there is:

- 10% chance that the rate will be below $1.4750 - 1.2825 \times 0.1770 = 1.2480$, and
- 5% chance that the rate will be below $1.4750 - 1.6497 \times 0.1770 = 1.1830$.

Note that to avoid arbitrage, the mean of the distribution in Figure 14.1 must be the forward exchange rate.

Figure 14.1
Probability distribution 1 year's time
A one standard deviation movement

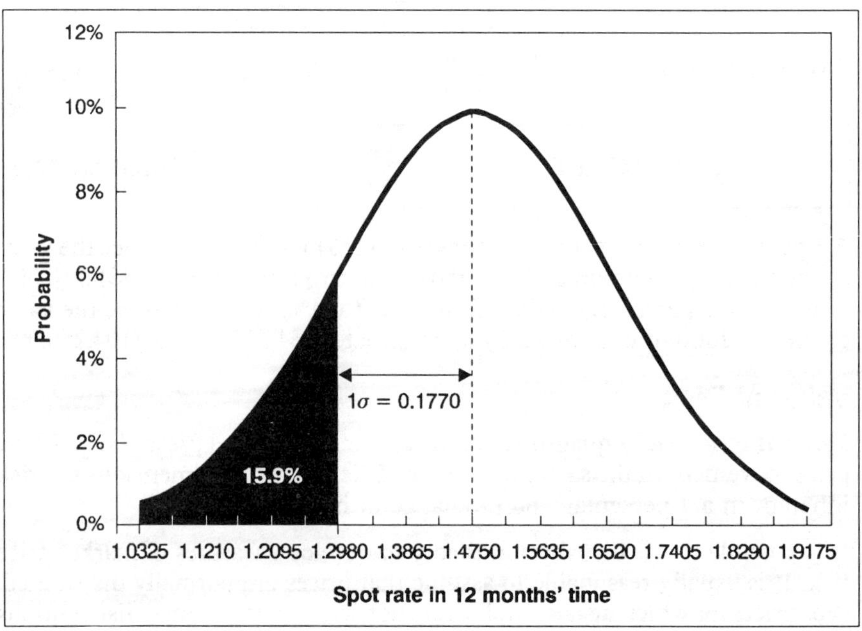

It is simple to calculate the loss which would result from a specified adverse movement in the exchange rate.

A trader who is long $10,000,000 against the deutschemark at 1.4750 would lose DM1,770,000 if the spot rate at the end of the year is 1.2980. The trader would lose DM2,270,000 if the rate turns out to be 1.2480 and DM2,920,000 at 1.1830. So it can be said that there is a 15.9% chance that the loss will be more than DM1,770,000, a 10% chance of losing more than DM2,270,000 and a 5% chance of losing more than DM2,920,000.

Exhibit 14.1
Value at Risk

Tolerance level	"Worst" case exchange rate	Loss on $10,000,000 position
15.9% (1σ)	1.2980	DM1,770,000 = $1,363,636
10% (1.2825σ)	1.2490	DM2,270,000 = $1,817,454
5% (1.6497σ)	1.1830	DM2,920,000 = $2,468,301

Equation 10.3[1] determines how the value at risk changes for longer or shorter periods. There is 15.9% (one standard deviation) probability that the rate will be below 1.2247 in two years or below 1.3498 in six months. There is a 2.3% (two standard deviations) probability that it will be below 0.9744 in two years or below 1.2247 in six months and so on.

Figure 14.2
Value at Risk
15.9% tolerance

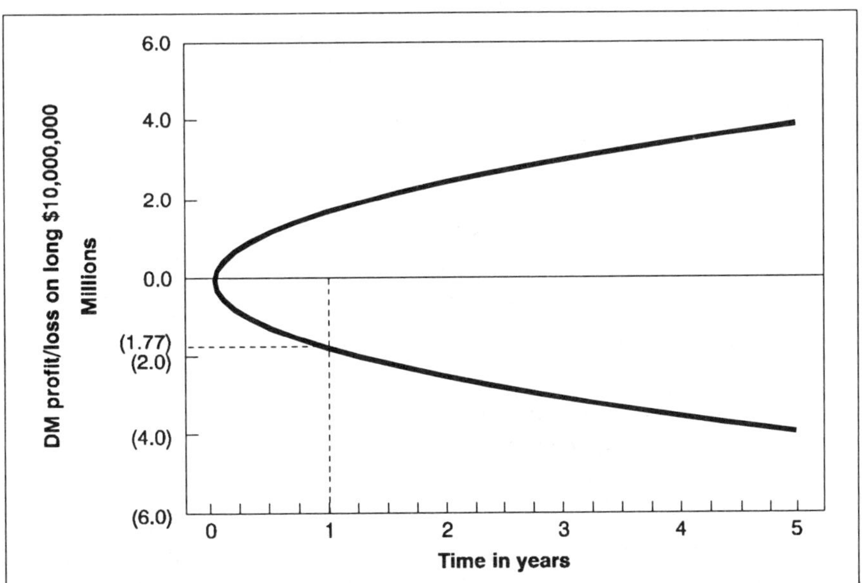

1. $\sigma_t = \sigma_A\sqrt{t}$

How many standard deviations are sufficient?

A one standard deviation adverse price movement can be expected to occur every six periods and a two standard deviations adverse movement every 44 periods. If the defeasance period is one year as in the above example and the exchange rate exhibits 12% annual volatility as expected, then it should be expected that in one year out of six the rate would fall below 1.2980 and in only one year in 44, to below 1.1210 starting from its current level of 1.4750.

In most circumstances, measuring factor sensitivities to one or two standard deviations is more than adequate. Many organisations are content to operate at tolerance levels of 5% or 10%. The financial capacity of the individual or organisation to absorb losses should be taken into account. It is not prudent to "bet the farm" against a one or two standard deviation movement. The one day movement in the US$/£ rate on the day that sterling left the ERM was a 12 standard deviation event. So it should be remembered that, while highly improbable, such massive price changes can occur.

Multiple Factors

Many transactions are subject to changes in more than one market price. For example, a forward exchange contract changes value both with changes to interest rates and to the spot exchange rate. It is possible to dimension the sensitivity to several market factors.

When spot $/DM is 1.5180 and one year dollar and DM interest rates are 6% and 3% respectively, the one year forward exchange rate will be 1.4750. The sensitivity of a one standard deviation movement on a $10,000,000 position over one year would be:

Price	Volatility	Factor Sensitivity		
$/DM	12%	10,000,000 × (1.4750 – 1.2980)	=	$1,363,636
$ rate	18%	10,000,000 × (0.06 – 0.0492)	=	$108,000
DM rate	15%	10,000,000 × (0.03 – 0.0255)	=	$45,000

It is often the case that, as in the above example, one market factor is dominant. In this case, it is the spot rate. As a general rule, the longer the tenor of the transaction, the greater the sensitivity to changes in interest rates.

Note that the volatilities of the individual market factors are different.

A superior measure of factor sensitivities is the change in the NPV of the future cash flows. This is particularly true for longer tenor transactions. However, for transactions out to a year, calculating factor sensitivities on the face value is a reasonable approximation.

Example 14.1

Using the NPV method, calculate the factor sensitivity for a 1% increase in spot $/DM on a 5 year short $1,000,000 position given the following market rate scenario:

Spot	$1 =	DM1.5000
5 year dollars		5% pa (annually compounding)
5 year marks		3% pa (annually compounding)

When $s = 1.5000$,

$$f = 1.5000\,\frac{(1.03)^5}{(1.05)^5} = 1.3625$$

Cash flows at 5 year date:	– $1,000,000	=	+ DM1,362,500
PV($ cash flows)			– $783,526.17
PV(DM cash flows)	+ DM1,175,304.45	=	+ $783,526.17
NPV			0.00

When $s = 1.5150$, (ie 1.5000×1.01)

$$f = 1.5150\,\frac{(1.03)^5}{(1.05)^5} = 1.3761$$

Cash flows at 5 year date:	– $1,000,000	=	+ DM1,376,100
PV($ cash flows)			– $783,526.17
PV(DM cash flows)	+ DM 1,175,304.45	=	+ $775,778.51
NPV		=	+ $7,747.66

A 1% increase in the spot exchange rate would reduce the net present value of the 5 year outright position by $7,747.66.

Theta

The sensitivity to changes in time to maturity is known as ***theta***.

$$\text{Theta} = \frac{\text{Change in Value}}{\text{Change in Time to Maturity}} \qquad \textbf{Equation 14.3}$$

$$= \frac{V_2 - V_1}{t_2 - t_1}$$

Example 14.2

Calculate theta for a one day change in time to maturity for a three month forward long $10,000,000 position.

Market rate scenario:

Spot	$1	=	¥100.00		
3 month dollars			5% pa		
3 month yen			1% pa		
At t = 90 days,	f_{90}	=	$100 \dfrac{(1 + 0.01 \times 90/360)}{(1 + 0.05 \times 90/360}$	=	99.01
At t = 89 days,	f_{89}	=	$100 \dfrac{(1 + 0.01 \times 89/360)}{(1 + 0.05 \times 89/360)}$	=	99.02
Theta (T)		=	$\dfrac{99.01 - 99.02}{90 - 89}$	=	– 0.01

For every day of time value, the position increases by 1 point (ie ¥100,000 or $1,000 on a face value of $10,000,000).

For an option,

$$\text{Theta} = \frac{\text{Change in Premium}}{\text{Change in Time to Expiry}} \qquad \textbf{Equation 14.4}$$

$$= \frac{P_2 - P_1}{t_2 - t_1}$$

The premium of an at-the-money (f = k =100.00) dollar call/yen put varies with the number of days to expiry as follows:

Days to Expiry	Premium
64	$1.16
16	$0.58
4	$0.29

Figure 14.3
Time decay ATM option

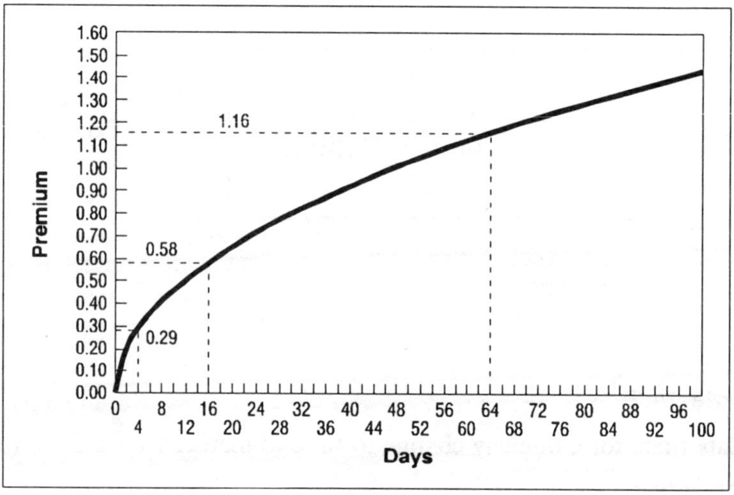

This is the typical shape of time decay for an at-the-money option. As the option approaches expiry, it loses value faster and faster until at expiry it has zero value. The premium halves as the time to expiry reduces by a factor of four.

For out-of-the-money and in-the-money options, the time decay occurs earlier than for an at-the-money option. If with, say, 20 days to go the market price is well above or below the strike price, the outcome is pretty much known so the time value will be close to zero. The in-the-money option will decay towards its intrinsic value.

Figure 14.4

Time decay out-of-the-money option

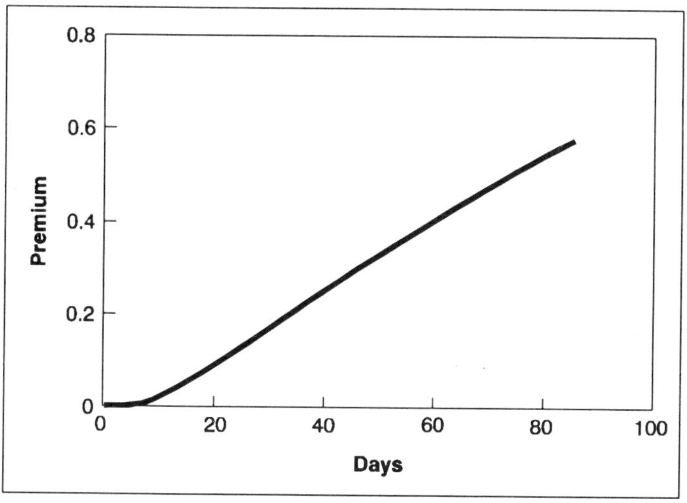

Figure 14.5

Time decay In-the-money option (intrinsic value = 2)

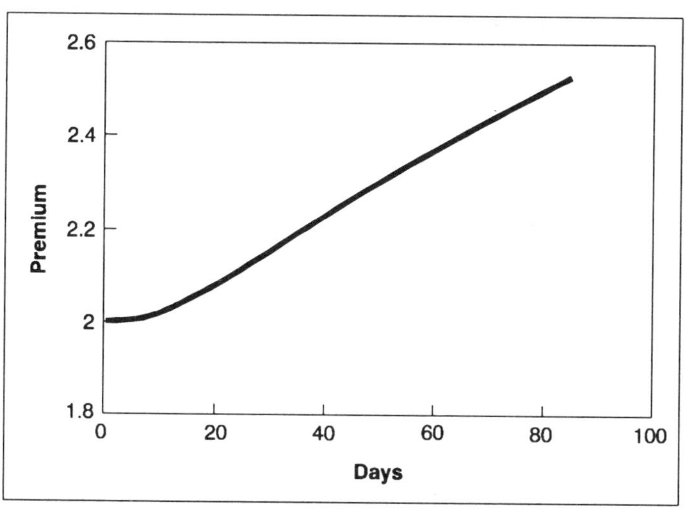

Delta

Delta is the change in (present) value for a given change in the market price. This is the same concept as factor sensitivity. Delta is mostly used in relation to options.

$$\text{Delta } (\Delta) = \frac{\text{Change in Premium}}{\text{Change in Market Price}} \qquad \textbf{Equation 14.5}$$

$$= \frac{P_2 - P_1}{M_2 - M_1}$$

The premium of an at-the-money dollar call yen put with strike k = 100.00 with 90 days to expiry varies as follows:

Market Price	Premium
95.00	$0.09
96.00	$0.18
97.00	$0.33
98.00	$0.56
99.00	$0.89
100.00	$1.33
101.00	$1.89
102.00	$2.55
103.00	$3.31
104.00	$4.14
105.00	$5.03

Between 96 and 97, $\Delta = \frac{0.33 - 0.18}{97 - 96} = 0.15$

Between 104 and 105, $\Delta = \frac{5.03 - 4.14}{105 - 104} = 0.89$

Figure 14.6
Delta

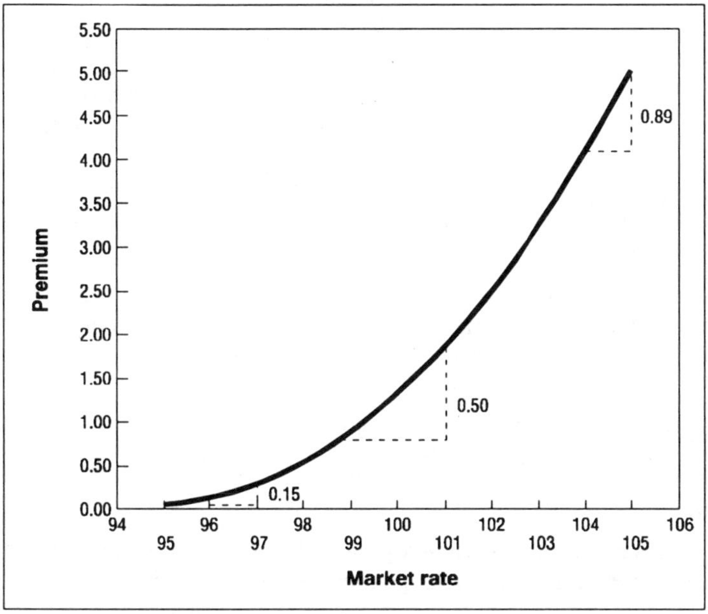

At-the-money, eg between 99 and 101,

$$\Delta = \frac{1.89 - 0.89}{101 - 99} = \frac{1.00}{2} = 0.5$$

Figure 14.7
Delta

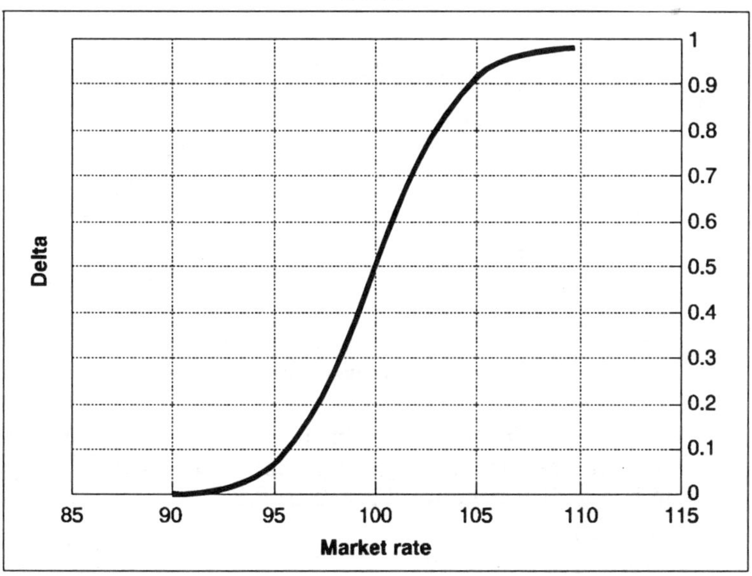

Geometrically, delta is the slope of the pay-off diagram. It can be seen in Figure 14.7 that delta varies from approaching zero well out-of-the-money to approaching one well in-the-money and equals 0.5 at-the-money.

Delta is the equivalent of the spot position. Purchasing $10,000,000 outright forward against yen would create a long $10,000,000 net exchange position. Purchasing $10,000,000 of at-the-money dollar calls creates an equivalent spot position of long $5,000,000 because for an at-the-money call, delta equals 0.5.

A 1% increase in the market price from 100.00 to 101.00 would increase the value of the long dollar position by $100,000. The same 1% increase in the market price from 100.00 to 101.00 would increase the value of the long dollar call by $50,000.

Delta, therefore, shows the percentage of an option which needs to be hedged against possible spot movements. If $\Delta = 0.5$, it is possible to hedge a $10,000,000 short dollar call against changes in the spot rate by buying $5,000,000 spot.

If the spot rate rises from 100 to 101,

Loss from short $10,000,000 call	=	$50,000
Gain from long $5,000,000 hedge	=	$50,000
Net gain or loss	=	$ 0

This process is known as ***delta hedging*** and is common practice among option traders who typically want to hedge themselves against potential spot changes.

Figure 14.8
Delta hedging

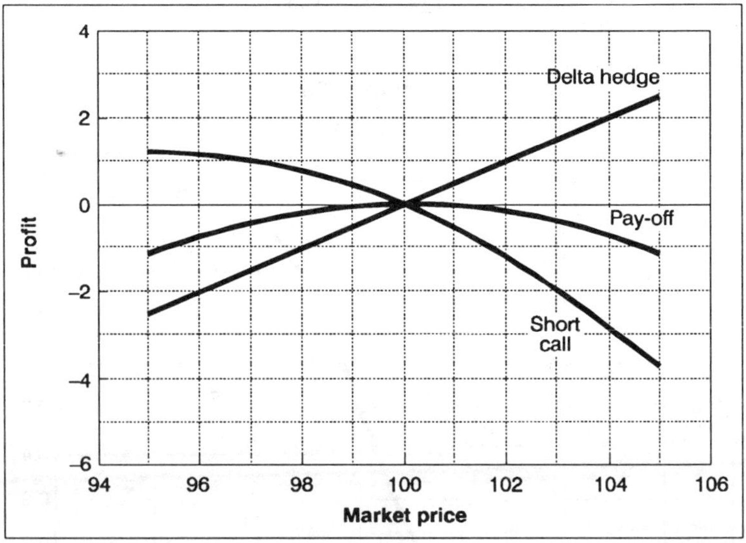

Because delta changes with the underlying market rate, the option trader will need to continually readjust the hedge to remain ***delta neutral***. If the spot rate continues to rise to 102, delta would then be 0.61.

$$\Delta = \frac{2.55 - 1.33}{102 - 100} = \frac{1.22}{2} = 0.61$$

If the hedge was unchanged,

Loss from short \$10,000,000 call	=	10,000,000 (2.55 – 1.33)	=	\$122,000
Gain from long \$5,000,000 hedge	=	5,000,000 (102 – 100)/102	=	\$ 98,039
Net loss			=	\$ 23,961

A \$5,000,000 hedge which was appropriate at 100 when $\Delta = 0.5$ is not sufficient at 102 because Δ is now 0.61. The short dollar call is underhedged or ***delta short***. To restore a delta neutral hedge, the trader would need to adjust the delta hedge by buying an additional \$1,100,000 spot so that the hedge ratio is again equal to delta.

Gamma

Gamma measures how quickly delta changes and so how often the hedge needs rebalancing.

$$\text{Gamma (X)} = \frac{\text{Change in Delta}}{\text{Change in Market Rate}} \qquad \textbf{Equation 14.6}$$

$$= \frac{\Delta_2 - \Delta_1}{P_2 - P_1}$$

Figure 14.9

Delta and gamma

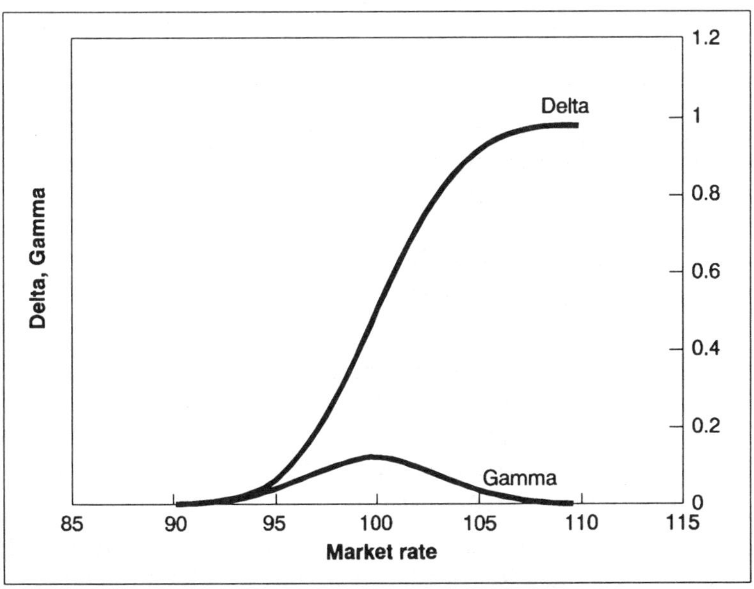

As options approach expiry, gamma tends to become large around the strike price. If the market price is below the strike price, the probability of the call being exercised is low so the delta (ie the amount needing to be hedged) is small. On the other hand, if the market price is above the strike price, the probability of the call being exercised is high so the delta is high. A small change in the market price from just below the strike to just above the strike can require a large change in the hedge.

Figure 14.10

Gamma at t = 1 day

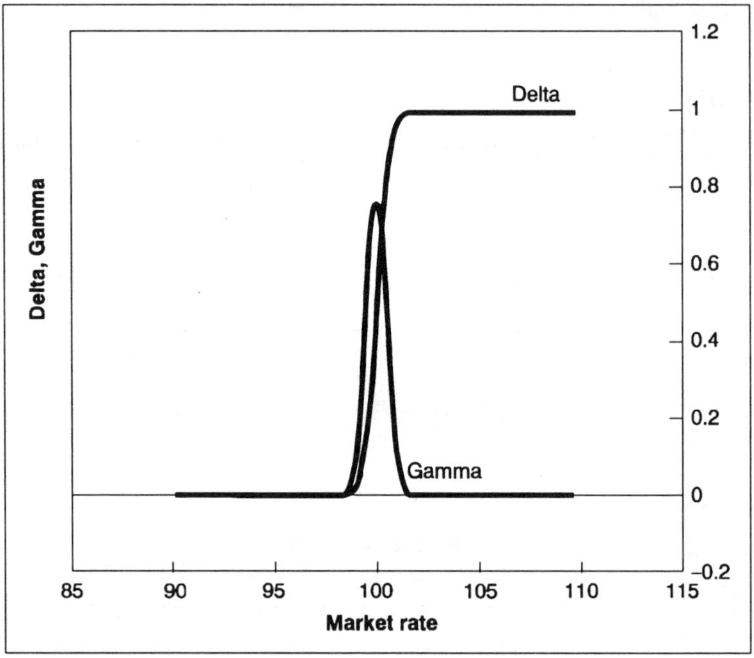

Traders who have purchased options have ***long gamma*** positions. They tend to gain from changes in the market price. Traders who have sold options have ***short gamma*** positions. They tend to lose from changes in the market price. Option traders try to avoid having large negative gamma positions because they expose themselves to possible large losses if the underlying market price moves. Negative gamma positions can be reduced by buying options. Buying short dated options has the most impact on reducing negative gamma.

Another technique is to avoid strike price concentration. By structuring the book so that the options which have been written are at a wide range of strike prices, an option trader can be confident that even if he or she is exposed to high gamma risk at a certain rate, the portfolio of sold options as a whole has only a relatively small gamma risk.

The option writer will realise a loss every time the delta hedge is adjusted. In the above example, a loss of $23,961 would be realised when the hedge is increased from 0.5 to 0.61 when the exchange rate reached 102. If volatility turns out to equal the volatility which was used to price the option, then over the course of continually delta hedging the sold option, the cumulative loss from adjusting the delta hedge would exactly equal the premium received for writing the option.

There is a trade-off between time decay, which works in favour of the option seller, and the expected hedging cost of following a delta neutral strategy. If actual volatility turns out to be higher than the volatility used to price the option, the option writer will lose more from delta hedging than was collected as premium. On the other hand, if actual volatility turns out to be less than the volatility used to price the option, then the cost of delta hedging will be less than the premium collected.

Traders running option portfolios, therefore, are predominantly concerned with managing their volatility risk.

Vega

The sensitivity of a change in the price of an option to changes in volatility is known as ***vega***.

$$\text{Vega} = \frac{\text{Change in Premium}}{\text{Change in Volatility}} \qquad \text{Equation 14.7}$$

$$= \frac{P_2 - P_1}{\sigma_2 - \sigma_1}$$

A trader who has net purchased options will be ***long vega***, and will stand to gain if volatility rises and lose if volatility falls. A trader who has net sold options will be ***short vega***, and will stand to gain if volatility falls and lose if volatility rises.

Hybrid transactions for which the pay-out is a function of a different market factor also have sensitivity to changes in the correlation between the two market factors.

Factor Sensitivity Limits

Organisations control the extent of market price risk by approving ***limits*** which specify the maximum exposure permitted. Factor sensitivity limits can be set for as many market factors as are considered relevant. They can be set for the entire organisation or for an individual dealer or both.

A foreign exchange trader dealing in $/DM may use a variety of products to open and hedge positions – spot, forwards, swaps, bonds, futures, FRAs, and so on. The trader will have exposure to the exchange rate and interest rates in both currencies.

Management may want the forwards trader to carry only a small amount of exchange rate risk, with exposure predominantly to the interest rate differentials. The following limit structure might be approved to constrain the risks which the dealer may take:

\$/DM spot	\$ 10,000	per 1% change in rate
\$ interest rates	\$100,000	per 1 basis point
DM interest rates	\$100,000	per 1 basis point

These limits may be further broken down into tenor buckets. For example, the full \$100,000 interest rate sensitivity may be used out to 1 year where liquidity is good but only \$10,000 may be used for transactions maturing beyond 1 year.

It is possible to establish a full set of factor sensitivity limits to cover whatever market price risks are relevant for the business. These can be specified by individual dealer or by business unit to suit the structure of the business.

The Problem with Stop-losses

Stop-losses are instructions to close out an open position if a market trades through a specified level. Stop-losses are often used to attempt to limit the amount which can be lost on a position.

Stop-losses orders work fairly well for positions which are pure trading positions. They can be closed out and are finished with. However, for banks which conduct market making activities and corporations who have recurring exposures, stop-losses do not serve to limit potential losses.

A better approach is to establish **management action triggers**. These require management attention whenever accumulated losses reach a predetermined level. Once this level is triggered, management reviews the causes of the adverse price movement and ascertains the likelihood of further such changes, weighs these up against their appetite for risk and decides upon a next course of action – perhaps closing or reducing the position or possibly setting a new, higher trigger. Management action triggers provide a more dynamic approach to risk management than stop-losses.

Portfolio Value at Risk

It is convenient to have a measure of the overall market price risk for an entire portfolio or business.

Portfolio Value at Risk measures how much would be lost if all market factors moved adversely to a prescribed level of tolerance (eg 10% or 2 standard deviations) usually over a 1 day time horizon.

Because many of the market factors are likely to be closely correlated, portfolio value at risk should be calculated on a covaried basis.

For example, there is a high positive correlation between $/DM and $/DG. If the dollar strengthens against the deutschemark, it is also likely to strengthen against the guilder. If a dealer is long $10,000,000 against DM and short $10,000,000 against DG, the two risks will largely offset one another. If the correlation factor is + 0.95, then the covaried factor sensitivity to a 1% increase in dollar exchange rates for the portfolio of exposures would be only $5,000. That is, the expected loss from a 1% increase in $/DM and $/DG together is $5,000.

If the volatilities of the two exchange rates are such that two standard deviations was, say, a 3% movement over a one day period, then value at risk would be $15,000.

In a large dealing room, there are likely to be hundreds of different market factors to address. However, with reasonable systems, it is a simple matter to calculate a covaried value at risk for the entire room's exposure.

A ***Value at Risk Limit*** is a limit set by management (or possibly a regulator) which limits the size of the permissible value at risk exposure.

Stress tests

Occasionally, very large price movements happen. It is advisable to periodically conduct stress tests that dimension the possible loss which would result from an extreme price shock, eg a 4 standard deviation event.

Credit Risk

Credit risk is the risk that a counterparty will be unwilling or unable to pay.

Credit risk is comprised of settlement risk and pre-settlement risk.

Settlement risk is the risk that a counterparty takes delivery but fails to pay. Settlement risk occurs when there is a non-simultaneous exchange of items of equivalent value between counterparties. If a customer of a firm takes delivery of a consignment of goods worth $10,000,000 and fails to pay immediately or in advance, the firm has $10,000,000 settlement risk (or delivery risk) on the customer. If the customer fails to pay, the firm loses $10,000,000. If the customer is late in paying eg pays the $10,000,000 for the goods but not until one year later, the firm loses the interest on $10,000,000 for the year. If interest rates are 5%, the loss due to late settlement would be $500,000.

For foreign exchange transactions, settlement risk applies from the time payment of one currency is made to the counterparty until good funds are received from the counterparty in the other currency. Because payments are made into bank accounts which will be in other countries, and possibly in different time zones, it is frequently the case that payments cannot be made simultaneously. For example, if a company in Japan sells NZ dollars against US dollars to a British counterparty, the NZ dollars will be paid into the

British company's account with a bank in New Zealand before the close of business in New Zealand, but it cannot receive the US dollars into its bank account in the US until New York business hours. There is at least an eight hour delay. Further, by the time the US dollars are credited to the Japanese company's New York account, it will be well into the Japanese night. People in the company in Japan are not likely to be aware that they have received good funds until the next morning their time. If there is a time lag between when funds are received and confirmation that they have been received (eg they may not receive a statement showing that the US dollars have been received until the following day), then the settlement risk applies for a longer period.

Settlement risk is predominantly operational risk. Good systems enable an organisation to know at the earliest possible time that it has received payment from its counterparty.

Settlement risk on a particular counterparty can be limited by using ***settlement risk limits***. For example, the credit department may limit the settlement risk which can be taken on the specified counterparty to say, $5,000,000, on any day. Dealers would be permitted to enter into transactions with the counterparty provided the settlement risk carried on that counterparty does not exceed $5,000,000 on any settlement date. If the process for receiving confirmation of settlements takes more than a day, that would further restrict the permitted transactions.

Various techniques exist to reduce settlement risk.

Customers may be required to pay in advance. For example, if a foreign exchange transaction is for value 17 May, the bank may require the customer to settle its side of the deal value 16 May before releasing funds to the customer on 17 May. Normally, the bank would give good value, ie pay the customer a day's interest. A variation is to require the customer to post collateral.

Another technique to reduce settlement risk is to spread the settlement dates of a large transaction over a number of days. For example, a customer with a settlement risk limit of $5,000,000 per day could do a $20,000,000 transaction by agreeing to stagger the settlement over four days. This would enable both counterparties to hold back payments to the other party until they know the settlement due the previous day has occurred.

Yet another technique is to use a creditworthy intermediary. If a bank has no settlement risk lines available for a customer that wishes to enter into a $10,000,000 transaction, it may be able to find another bank with whom it has lines which is prepared to stand in between the original bank and the customer. The second bank would generally expect to receive some compensation from the first bank for taking the settlement risk on the customer. This could take the form of a small difference in the rates at which the second bank deals with the customer on the one hand and the first bank on the other.

Pre-settlement Risk

Pre-settlement risk occurs when a counterparty defaults on a contractual obligation prior to settlement. The necessary condition for a credit loss to result from pre-settlement risk is that the counterparty defaults *and* the set of transactions with the counterparty has a positive replacement value.

Pre-settlement risk comprises the replacement cost and an estimate of potential exposure.

PSR = Replacement Cost + Potential Exposure	Equation 14.8

Replacement cost is the difference between the value of the transaction as contracted and what it would be worth if transacted at current market rates for the original value dates. Replacement cost is also known as the ***mark-to-market value***. It dimensions the current exposure on the counterparty.

Example 14.3

Three months ago, a customer bought ¥1,000,000,000 by selling $10,000,000 to a bank one year forward at a then forward exchange rate of $1 = ¥100.00. Today the 9 month forward rate is $1 = ¥105.00. If the customer defaulted, the bank would have to sell ¥1,000,000,000 at 105.00 to reinstate its position. The bank would receive a replacement value of only $9,523,809.52 which is $476,190.48 less than the $10,000,000 which it is due to receive from the customer.

In terms of market risk, the bank is $476,190.48 in-the-money and the customer is $476,190.48 out-of-the-money. In terms of *credit* risk, the bank stands to lose $476,190.48 if its customer defaults. The bank has credit risk because the market value of its position is in-the-money and the market value of its customer's position is out-of-the-money.

From the bank's perspective, its mark-to-market value of its contract with the customer is:

$$\begin{aligned} \text{MTM} &= \frac{1{,}000{,}000{,}000}{100.00} - \frac{1{,}000{,}000{,}000}{105.00} \\ &= 10{,}000{,}000.00 - 9{,}523{,}809.52 \\ &= \$476{,}190.48 \end{aligned}$$

Note: A positive mark-to-market value indicates that the market value of the *position* is in-the-money and so there is a positive replacement cost and, therefore, a credit risk on the counterparty.

From the customer's perspective, there is no credit risk on the bank. If the bank defaulted for some reason, which is difficult to imagine, the customer could now buy the ¥1,000,000,000 more cheaply, which would not be a problem. The customer's mark-to-market value is negative so it would have a replacement benefit and, therefore, no credit risk on the bank.[2]

NPV Method

A superior method of measuring replacement cost is the present value of the mark-to-market amount. This brings the value of the replacement cost into today's terms which makes more sense than using future value terms, particularly if the time period is long or interest rates are high. If the 9 month dollar interest rate is 5% pa, the mark-to-market value in present value terms would be $458,978.78.

$$PV(476{,}190.48) = \frac{476{,}190.48}{(1+0.05 \times 9/12)} = 458{,}978.78$$

For bought options, the replacement cost is the mark-to-market value of the option which is the current premium. There is no pre-settlement risk on sold options unless the payment of the premium is deferred, in which case it equals the present value of the deferred premium.

Potential Exposure

Continuing Example 14.3, the bank has additional credit risk on the customer because in the 9 months still to go before the contract settles it is possible that the replacement cost will increase further. This would happen if the exchange rate rises above 105.00.

Potential exposure represents a provision against a possible increase in replacement cost.

It is possible to use distribution theory to estimate potential exposure. If the expected volatility of the dollar/yen exchange rate is, say, 12% pa, then over the 9 months remaining a one standard deviation movement would be ¥10.91. A 1.2825 standard deviation adverse movement which could be expected to occur 10% of the time would involve the exchange rate rising from 105.00 to 119.00. If the bank is comfortable having less than 10% chance of underestimating its credit loss, it could dimension its potential exposure on the customer as the difference between ¥1,000,000,000 at 105.00 and ¥1,000,000,000 at 119.00:

$$\begin{aligned} FV(\text{Potential Exposure}) &= \frac{1{,}000{,}000{,}000}{105.00} - \frac{1{,}000{,}000{,}000}{119.00} \\ &= 9{,}523{,}809.52 - 8{,}403{,}361.35 \\ &= \$1{,}120{,}448.17 \end{aligned}$$

$$\therefore \text{ Potential Exposure} = \frac{1{,}120{,}448.17}{(1+0.05 \times 9/12)} = \$1{,}079{,}950.04$$

2. In fact the customer has potential exposure but no current exposure.

Pre-settlement risk equals replacement cost plus the estimate of potential exposure.

$$\begin{aligned} \text{PSR} &= \text{Replacement Cost} + \text{Potential Exposure} \\ &= 458{,}978.78 + 1{,}079{,}950.04 \\ &= \$1{,}538{,}928.82 \end{aligned}$$

The bank could consider itself as having $1,538,928.82 credit risk on the customer as a result of having sold □1,000,000,000 to the customer at a one year forward rate of 100.00 three months ago.

If the mark-to-market value is negative (ie if the customer's position is in-the-money and the bank's position is out-of-the-money), then the bank clearly has less pre-settlement risk on the customer.

For example, if instead after three months the then 9 months forward rate was 95.00,

$$\begin{aligned} \text{FV(MTM)} &= \frac{1{,}000{,}000{,}000}{100.00} - \frac{1{,}000{,}000{,}000}{95.00} \\ &= 10{,}000{,}000.00 - 10{,}526{,}315.79 \\ &= -\$526{,}315.79 \end{aligned}$$

$$\therefore \quad \text{MTM} = \frac{-526{,}315.79}{(1 + 0.05 \times 9/12)} = -\$507{,}292.33$$

$$\begin{aligned} \text{Potential Exposure} &= \$1{,}079{,}950.04 \text{ (as previously)} \\ \text{So, PSR} &= -507{,}292.33 + 1{,}079{,}950.04 \\ &= \$\ 572{,}657.71 \end{aligned}$$

Credit Risk Factors

A ***credit risk factor*** is a number which can be multiplied by the principal amount of the transaction to provide the deemed amount of potential exposure.

$$\text{Potential Exposure} = \text{CRF} \times \text{Principal} \qquad \textbf{Equation 14.9}$$

Continuing Example 14.3,

$$\text{CRF} = \frac{1{,}079{,}950.04}{10{,}000{,}000.00} = 10.8\%$$

It is possible to generate tables of credit risk factors for different tenors for exchange rates with different expected volatilities. Such tables make it easy for dealers to establish how much pre-settlement risk will be associated with a transaction. The credit risk factor will be a function of expected volatility and the square root of time to maturity.

Figure 14.11
Credit risk factors

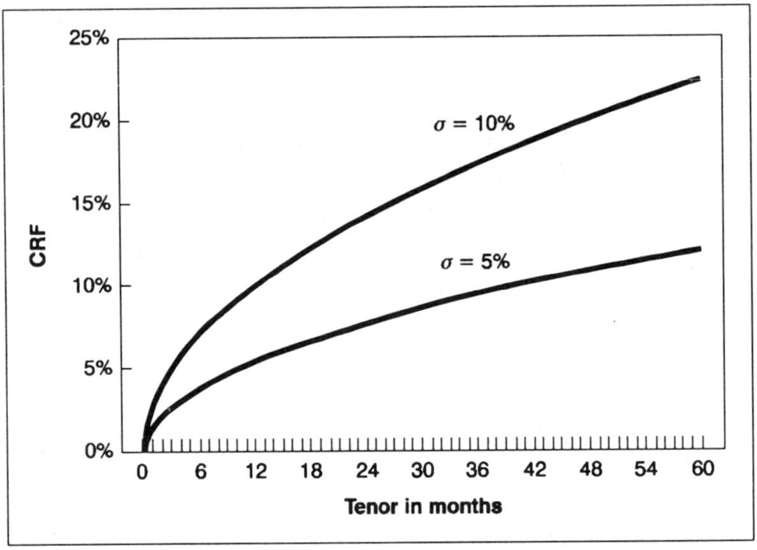

Credit risk factors increase with the tenor of the transaction and expected volatility. The longer the transaction has till maturity, the greater will be the potential risk. In Figure 14.11, the higher curve shows the credit risk factors for currency pairs for which expected volatility is deemed to be 10% pa and the lower curve where expected volatility is deemed to be 5% pa.

The 10% CRF curve shows the following credit risk factors:

Tenor	CRF
1 month	2.9%
3 months	5.0%
6 months	7.1%
1 year	10.1%
2 years	14.2%
5 years	22.5%

If dollar/mark is assumed to have 10% pa expected volatility, then the credit risk factor for a contract with six months to maturity would be 7.1%. The estimate of potential exposure on a $10,000,000 transaction would be calculated as follows:

Estimate of Potential Exposure	=	CRF	×	P
	=	0.071	×	10,000,000
	=	$710,000		

Example 14.4

A dealer buys \$5,000,000 one year forward against yen at an outright rate of \$1 = ¥106.75.

(a) If the credit risk factor for 1 year dollar/yen is 10.1%, what is the pre-settlement risk of the transaction when it is done, given that dollar interest rates are 6.0% pa?

$$\begin{aligned}
\text{PSR} &= \text{MTM} + \text{Potential Exposure} \\
\text{MTM} &= 0 \qquad \text{(because deal is done at market rates)} \\
\text{FV(Potential Exposure)} &= \text{CRF} \times \text{P} \\
&= 0.101 \times 5{,}000{,}000 \\
&= \$505{,}000 \\
\therefore \quad \text{Potential Exposure} &= \frac{505{,}000}{(1 + 0.06)} = \$476{,}415.09 \\
\therefore \text{PSR} &= \$476{,}415.09
\end{aligned}$$

(b) One month later, the 11 month rate is \$1 = ¥107.50 and dollar interest rates are still 6.0% pa, calculate the pre-settlement risk if the 11 month CRF = 9.2%.

$$\begin{aligned}
\text{FV(MTM)} &= 5{,}000{,}000\ (106.75 - 107.50) \\
&= \frac{-\,3{,}750{,}000}{107.50} \\
&= -\ \$34{,}883.72 \\
\therefore \quad \text{MTM} &= \frac{-\,34{,}883.72}{(1 + 0.06 \times 11/12)} = -\ 33{,}065.14 \\
\text{Potential Exposure} &= \frac{5{,}000{,}000}{(1 + 0.06 \times 11/12)} \times 0.092 \\
&= \$436{,}018.96 \\
\therefore \quad \text{PSR} &= -\ 33{,}065.14 + 436{,}018.96 \\
&= \$402{,}953.82
\end{aligned}$$

Pre-settlement Risk Limits

Pre-settlement risk on a particular counterparty can be limited by using ***pre-settlement risk limits***. For example, the credit department may limit the pre-settlement risk which can be taken on the specified counterparty to say, \$50,000,000. Dealers would be permitted to enter into transactions with the counterparty provided the pre-settlement risk carried on that counterparty never exceeds \$50,000,000. The size of the limit generally depends on the creditworthiness of the counterparty as reflected by its credit rating. Separate limits may be set for different tenors. For example, a particular counterparty may be allocated a limit of \$50,000,000 for transactions out to two years but only \$20,000,000 for transactions beyond two years. The reason for the smaller limit for longer tenors is that there is greater uncertainty that the counterparty will be creditworthy or even in existence.

Techniques to Reduce PSR

Credit is a scarce resource. Various techniques can be used to minimise the usage of pre-settlement risk credit lines.

Netting PSR

It is often the case that an organisation will have multiple transactions with the same counterparty. The aggregate credit exposure could be calculated by simply adding together the pre-settlement risk for all of the individual transactions. However, provided a legally enforcable netting agreement is in place, the aggregate exposure may be substantially less than the sum of the individual PSRs.

A portfolio of three forward foreign exchange contracts with the same counterparty but different times to maturity has less exposure than the sum of the pre-settlement risks of the three contracts.

Example 14.5

A firm has the following three foreign exchange transactions with a particular counterparty:

Transaction	$ Amount	Maturity	Pre-settlement Risk	
A	+ 4,000,000	6 months	244,949	+ 244,949
B	– 3,000,000	1 year	259,808	– 259,808
C	+ 1,000,000	2 years	122,474	+ 122,474
Total without netting:			627,231	
Total with netting:				107,616

Figure 14.12

Pre-settlement risk on three separate transactions

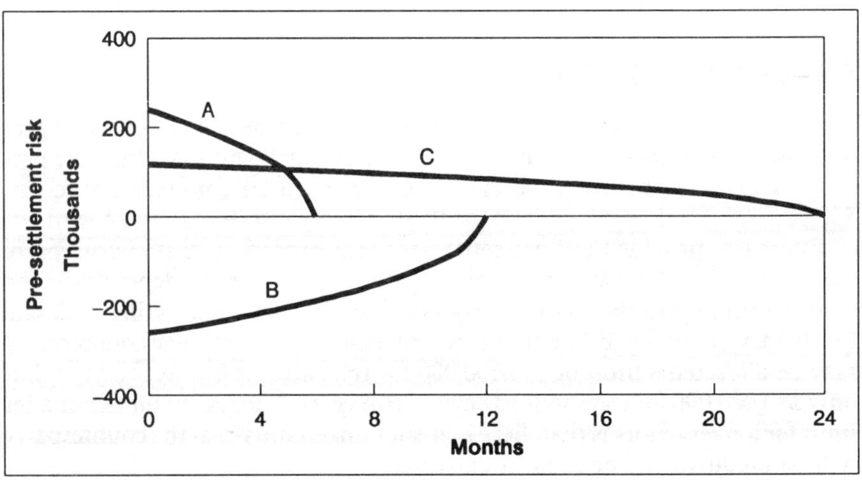

Figure 14.13
Pre-settlement risk with and without netting

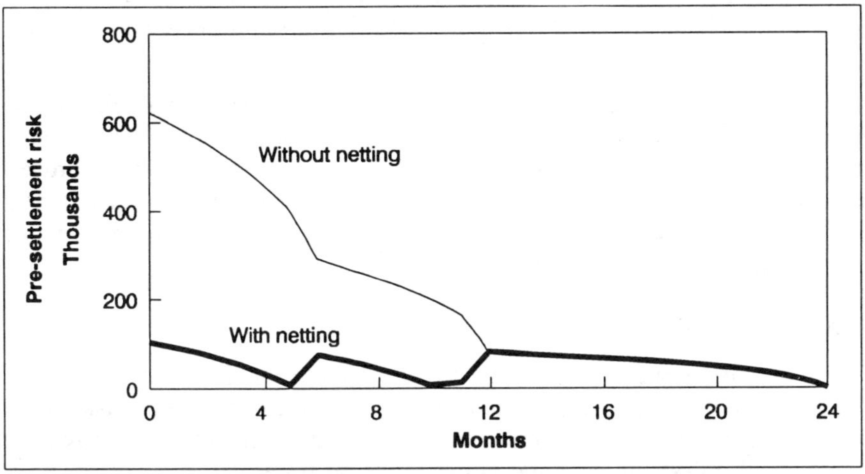

For each of the three transactions, the pre-settlement risk declines as the contract approaches maturity. Because the transaction with one year to maturity is opposite in sign to the other two, the aggregate exposure with netting is significantly less than without netting. In this case, it is less than one sixth of what it would have been without netting.

In some jurisdictions, liquidators are allowed to ***cherry-pick,*** ie collect on transactions which are in-the-money without having to pay out on transactions which are out-of-the-money. When this is the case, there is no benefit in netting. Clearly, from the point of view of reducing credit risk, netting is preferable when it is enforceable.

Allowing for correlation

There may be a reduction in credit risk even if the transactions with a particular counterparty are not all in the same currency pair. There is a high positive correlation between dollar/guilder and dollar/mark. Suppose it is 0.95. A portfolio with a long dollar position against the guilder and a short dollar position against the deutschemark will have some natural offset. The loss resulting from the dollar rising against the deutschemark is very likely to be largely offset by the dollar also rising against the guilder. If the two exposures are of roughly equal size, the risk on the portfolio will be only a small fraction of the risk on either leg.

Indeed, a superior method of dimensioning credit risk for a portfolio of transactions with a counterparty is to run a Monte Carlo simulation on the entire portfolio. Input into the simulation includes the set of transactions (currencies, amounts, sides, maturities) and a variance-covariance matrix (assumed volatilities and correlations for each currency pair).

It is possible to estimate the potential change in the value of the counterparty's portfolio as a time varying amount of risk over the life of the portfolio with a peak at some point in time. It is typically measured to two standard deviations assuming a tolerance level of 97.7% and that volatilities and correlations behave as expected.

It must be understood that in practice assumptions about volatilities and correlations do not always to turn out to be correct but provided the tolerance level is conservative, there will be little risk of credit losses exceeding approved limits. A second level of protection lies in the fact that for an organisation to suffer a credit loss, the counterparty must not only be out-of-the-money but it must also choose not to pay.

Market reset payments

Documentation can provide for payments equal to the then mark-to-market amount to be made at pre-specified periods. This limits the credit risk on the counterparty to the amount implied by the period at which the reset payment is required unless the payment is not made on time.

Right to break (early termination) clauses

Credit departments typically set a maximum tenor for transactions with certain counterparties reflecting uncertainty over the possible creditworthiness of the counterparty beyond that time.

Either or both parties can be given the right to terminate contracts at specified times. This enables transactions to be done with counterparties for tenors longer than their tenor limit.

For example, if transactions with a particular customer are limited to a maximum of two years, it is possible to enter into a five year forward with a right to break after two years. Provided the customer is still considered creditworthy after the first two years, the transaction will continue with another right to break at the four year point. If, on the other hand, the customer is no longer considered creditworthy at the time of the right to break, then the transaction can be unwound. The right to break need not require an event of default.

Margining

The counterparty may be required to lodge cash as a margin to provide a buffer against potential credit losses. This mechanism is widely used for exchange traded products and is commonly used in over-the-counter transactions as well.

Typically, the customer is required to lodge an initial margin amount (eg 5% of face value) and to top-up whenever the mark-to-market exposure reaches or exceeds a pre-specified level. If the party fails to make a margin payment on time, outstanding contracts are closed out.

Margining limits the credit risk to the trigger level at which the margin call will be made. There is actually an incremental amount of risk involved because the market could move further against the counterparty between the trigger being hit and the margin being received. Provided the process is efficient this will be a relatively small amount and a provision for it is often built into the margining requirements.

Collateral

The counterparty may be permitted to lodge some asset other than cash as collateral against potential credit risk. Typically, collateral is in the form of stocks or bonds but any asset which is acceptable to the organisation taking the credit risk can be used. Because the value of the collateral is likely to change over time, there needs to be a process to revalue the collateral at regular intervals in case a top-up of collateral is required to maintain adequate cover of the mark-to-market exposure.

Liquidity Risk

There are two types of liquidity risk.

Funding liquidity is the ability to make payments on time. ***Funding liquidity risk*** is the risk of not having access to sufficient cash to be able to make payments on time. It is most important to confine funding liquidity risk, not only because there are likely to be severe interest penalties, but also because counterparties may refuse to deal with an organisation which fails to meet its cash flow obligations. Even if the organisation has substantial unrealisable assets, if it has not managed its cash flow so as to be able to make a payment, confidence in its business can be undermined.

Market liquidity describes the volumes which can readily be transacted in the market. ***Market liquidity risk*** is the risk that it may not be possible to do the full amount of a transaction without seriously impacting the market price. Spot foreign exchange in the major currencies are some of the deepest (ie most liquid markets) in the world. Literally billions of dollars of transactions are done every day in dollar/mark, dollar/yen and cable. However, exotic currencies can be very thin or illiquid. It can be quite difficult to find a counterparty to quote even $10,000,000 in some South American, African or Eastern European currencies. Even in the major currencies, liquidity can be scarce at certain times. At 6 pm New York time, which is three hours after New York interbank trading closes and two or three hours before the Asian market opens, it can be difficult to obtain a quote in mark/lira, which is a very liquid market during European hours.

Market liquidity is generally reflected in the bid-offer spread. If there are many banks prepared to quote two-way prices in the currency at that time of day, the bid-offer spread will be narrow. However, if there are only a couple of banks quoting the currency, and/or if the amount is relatively large, the bid-offer spread will be wider. If a news release which could have a significant impact on the market price is due out in a minute's time, liquidity may tend to dry up temporarily.

Like funding liquidity risk, it is important to understand and manage market liquidity risk. A dealer who trades profitably all month can have the month's profitability spoilt by having a position which he or she cannot get out of without taking a big loss because of lack of market liquidity.

Managing Funding Liquidity Risk

Liquidity squeezes occur from time to time. Sometimes they are deliberately engineered by the Central Bank. Even when the market generally is liquid, a particular party may find itself with a liquidity problem. This could be the consequence of its credit position deteriorating or simply a function of poor management.

Managing funding liquidity risk means ensuring that there will always be sufficient cash or credit facilities available to meet payment obligations.

Maximum cumulative outflow is the largest negative cash outflow position which will accumulate from existing commitments.

If an organisation has a zero cash balance in its dollar bank account at the start of the week and has existing commitments which will cause the following cash flows during the week, then its maximum cumulative outflow would be 30 which would occur on Tuesday.

	Inflows	Outflows	Balance
Monday opening			0
Monday	+ 10	– 20	– 10
Tuesday	+ 30	– 50	– **30**
Wednesday	+ 50	– 20	0
Thursday	+ 40	– 10	+ 30
Friday	+ 20	– 30	+ 20

A ***maximum cumulative outflow limit*** is a limit to the permitted value of the maximum cumulative outflow. The organisation may know from experience that it can easily raise say $100,000,000 on any day by borrowing from banks with whom it has standby credit facilities or by selling other currencies or liquid securities. If so, its management would probably approve an MCO limit of up to $100,000,000.

It is generally the case that it is possible to raise more money over a longer period of time. Consequently, there may be a larger MCO limit set for the first month than for the first week and so on.

The organisation should have an MCO limit in every currency in which it has cash flows except for those currencies for which it follows a policy of always squaring off cash flows in the currencies, in which case it effectively has a zero MCO limit in those currencies.

MCO limits should be reviewed regularly (eg at a monthly meeting) and when liquidity is tight, the limits may be reduced or reviewed more regularly (eg every day).

It is good practice to also prepare a contingency funding plan which sets out what actions (eg selling specific assets and arranging additional sources of funds) would be taken in the event of a liquidity problem arising.

Another good practice is to diversify funding sources so that if a particular provider of funds or class of funds provider dries up, there will be sufficient cash flow available for business to proceed as usual. Management and Central Banks often require information on large funds providers. For example, the Central Bank may require a bank to report all cases where it obtains more than say 10% of its funding from a single entity, or management may impose limits or triggers on the percentage of funds sourced through a particular program (eg issuing commercial paper) or from a particular customer segment (eg consumer deposits). The limits or trigger levels will depend on the nature of the business.

Managing market liquidity relies on having experienced leaders who can guide junior dealers in how to quote (ie how much bid-offer spread) and what size positions to carry in particular currencies at certain times. Because market liquidity tends to vary dramatically over time, it is usually better to have the flexibility of allowing middle management judgement to react to the circumstances than to prescribe firm rules or limits. The most important thing is to know that people who understand market liquidity are always present and focused on the issue.

Interdependence of Market, Credit and Liquidity Risks

While it is meaningful to measure and manage the different types of risk separately, it is important to appreciate that they are closely interrelated. Less liquidity almost certainly means greater price risk. If volatility is high, then both price risk and credit risk will be greater. Reducing credit limits with particular counterparties will reduce liquidity and so will increase price risk and so on. The full set of risks should be viewed together as well as separately.

Other Types of Financial Risks

Other types of risk also apply to foreign exchange and other financial transactions.

Legal or documentation risk

Both parties to a transaction should have signed mutually acceptable and legally enforceable documentation and an effective process needs to be in place to confirm the details of transactions as they are done.

Operational risk

The back-office needs to be thorough and efficient in confirming, booking and settling transactions as well as following up on any outstanding issues.

Tax and accounting risk

It is important to be aware of the tax and accounting implications of transactions. Treatment frequently varies from country to country. Even within the same country, the treatment for tax may be different than for accounting. Failure to understand the tax or accounting implications of transactions or penalties for incorrect reporting can be very expensive.

Selling risk

Organisations which market financial products have a duty of care to ensure that their products are suitable for their clients and that their clients understand the risks of entering into the transaction. The more complex the transaction and the less sophisticated the client, the greater is the obligation on the selling organisation. The risk is that a client may sue the bank if the bank has failed to properly identify the risks of it entering into the transaction.

As with market risk, credit risk and liquidity risk, other risks such as legal, operational, accounting and selling risk are best mitigated by having people who understand what risks are involved in the transactions and knowing how to manage them effectively. If the people are experienced, there is a continuing program of education and a culture of compliance, then the likelihood of losses in excess of tolerable levels will be minimised.

Practice Problems

14.1 Value at Risk

A dealer purchased $10,000,000 against French francs 2 years forward at an outright rate of $1 = FF 4.8308 and has not covered the position. The prevailing market rates are:

Spot	$1	=	FF 5.0000
2 year dollars			5.5 % pa
2 year francs			3.7 % pa

Note: $5.0000 \times \dfrac{(1 + 0.037)^2}{(1 + 0.055)^2} = 4.8308$

(a) Calculate the factor sensitivity in NPV terms to a 100 point increase in the spot rate?

(b) If $\sigma = 12\%$ pa for dollar/Paris, calculate the value at risk for a 1.65 standard deviation movement over a 2 year time horizon.

14.2 Credit risk

Two months ago counterparty XYZ sold $10,000,000 against deutschemarks value 5 months from then at a forward rate of $1 = DM 1.5170.

The prevailing rates today are:

Spot	$ 1	=	DM 1.6455
3 month swap rate			– 0.0095
3 month dollars			5.0 % pa

The Credit Risk Factor for 3 month $/DM is 7.0 %.

Calculate in dollar NPV terms:

(a) The mark-to-market exposure

(b) The estimated potential exposure on XYZ over the remaining 3 months

(c) Today's presettlement risk on XYZ

(d) dealer purchased value 3 months, how large a deal can be done with them?

There is no Supplementary Question for Chapter 14.

Answers to Practice Problems

Chapter 1

1.1 Reciprocal rates

(a) $FF1 = US\$ \frac{1}{4.5420} = US\$0.2202$

(b) $A\$1 = £ \frac{1}{2.0465} = £0.4886$

(c) $US\$1 = NZ\$ \frac{1}{0.6520} = NZ\$1.5337$

1.2 Cross rates

(a)

$$\begin{aligned} DM? &= £1 \\ £1 &= US\$\ 1.5560 \\ US\$1 &= DM\ 1.4525 \\ \hline \therefore £1 &= DM \frac{1 \times 1.5560 \times 1.4525}{1 \times 1} = DM2.2601 \end{aligned}$$

(b)

$$\begin{aligned} ¥? &= DM1 \\ DM\ 1.4525 &= US\$1 \\ US\$1 &= ¥103.25 \\ \hline \therefore DM1 &= ¥ \frac{1 \times 1 \times 103.25}{1.4525 \times 1} = ¥\ 71.08 \end{aligned}$$

(c)

$$\begin{aligned} \text{A\$?} &= \text{DM1} \\ \text{DM1.4525} &= \text{US\$1} \\ \text{US\$0.7420} &= \text{A\$1} \\ \therefore \text{DM1} &= \text{A\$}\ \frac{1 \times 1 \times 1}{1.4525 \times 0.7420} = \text{A\$0.9279} \end{aligned}$$

(d)

$$\begin{aligned} \text{A\$?} &= ¥1 \\ ¥103.25 &= \text{US\$1} \\ \text{US\$0.7420} &= \text{A\$1} \\ \therefore ¥1 &= \text{A\$}\ \frac{1 \times 1 \times 1}{103.25 \times 0.7420} = \text{A\$0.0131} \end{aligned}$$

1.3 Calculating profits & losses

(a)

$$\begin{aligned} \text{Profit} &= \text{Proceeds of sale} - \text{Cost of purchase} \\ &= 8{,}540{,}000 \times 1.4675 - 8{,}540{,}000 \times 1.4870 \\ &= 12{,}532{,}450 - 12{,}698{,}980 \\ &= -\text{P } 166{,}530 \end{aligned}$$

(b)

$$\begin{aligned} \text{Unrealised Profit} &= \text{Proceeds of sale} - \text{Cost of purchase} \\ &= \frac{17{,}283{,}945}{0.5072} - \frac{17{,}283{,}945}{0.4980} \\ &= \text{R}34{,}077{,}178.63 - 34{,}706{,}716.87 \\ &= -\text{R}629{,}538.24 \\ &= -\text{P}629{,}538.24 \times 0.5072 \\ &= -\text{P}319{,}301.80 \end{aligned}$$

1.4 Reciprocal rates

(a) $\text{FF1} = \text{US\$}\dfrac{1}{5.6830} = \text{US\$0.1760}$

(b) $\text{DM1} = \text{US\$}\dfrac{1}{1.6670} = \text{US\$0.5999}$

(c) $\text{US\$1} = \text{NZ\$}\dfrac{1}{0.5920} = \text{US\$1.6892}$

1.5 Realised profit

$$\begin{aligned}\text{Profit} &= \text{Proceeds of sale} - \text{Cost of purchase}\\ &= 9{,}360{,}000 \times 1.4620 - 9{,}360{,}000 \times 1.4510\\ &= \text{P}13{,}684{,}320 - 13{,}581{,}360\\ &= +\text{P}102{,}960\end{aligned}$$

1.6 Unrealised profit

$$\begin{aligned}\text{Profit} &= \text{Proceeds of sale} - \text{Cost of purchase}\\ &= \frac{17{,}283{,}945}{0.4860} - \frac{17{,}283{,}945}{0.4720}\\ &= \text{R}35{,}563{,}672.84 - 36{,}618{,}527.54\\ &= -\text{R}1{,}054{,}854.70\end{aligned}$$

Chapter 2

2.1 Simple interest

(a)
$$\begin{aligned}I &= Prt\\ &= 2{,}000 \times 0.0675 \times 3/12\\ &= \$33.75\end{aligned}$$

(b)
$$\begin{aligned}I &= Prt\\ &= 4{,}750{,}000 \times 0.0825 \times 12/21\\ &= \text{P}223{,}928.57\end{aligned}$$

2.2 Future value

$$FV = P + I$$
$$= 2{,}000 + 33.75$$
$$= \$2{,}033.75$$

Alternatively:

$$FV = P(1 + rt)$$
$$= 2{,}000\,(1 + (0.0675 \times 3/12))$$
$$= 2{,}000\,(1.016875)$$
$$= \$2{,}033.75$$

2.3 Compound interest

$$FV = P(1 + i)^n$$
$$= 100{,}000\,(1 + 8.25/200)^{5 \times 2}$$
$$= 100{,}000\,(1.04125)^{10}$$
$$= \$149{,}813.22$$

2.4 Varying results

$$\left(1 + \frac{r_2}{2}\right)^2 = \left(1 + \frac{r_{12}}{12}\right)^{12}$$

$$\left(1 + \frac{9.8}{200}\right)^2 = \left(1 + \frac{r_{12}}{12}\right)^{12}$$

$$1.100401 = \left(1 + \frac{r_{12}}{12}\right)^{12}$$

$$\therefore\ 1 + \frac{r_{12}}{12} = (1.100401)^{1/12} = 1.008005$$

$$\therefore\ \frac{r_{12}}{12} = 0.008005$$

$$\therefore\ r_{12} = 0.008005 \times 12 = 0.096057$$

$$= 9.61\%\ \text{pa}$$

2.5 Forward interest rate

$$r_{6/9} = \frac{FV_9 - FV_6}{FV_6} \times \frac{12}{(9\text{-}6)}$$

$$= \left(\frac{FV_9}{FV_6} - 1\right) \times \frac{12}{3}$$

$$= \left[\frac{(1 + 0.07 \times 9/12)}{(1 + 0.075 \times 6/12)} - 1\right] \times 4$$

$$= \left[\frac{1.0525}{1.0375} - 1\right] \times 4$$

$$= 0.0578$$

$$= 5.78\%\ \text{pa}$$

2.6 Present value

$$PV = \frac{FV}{(1 + i)^n}$$

$$= \frac{10{,}000{,}000}{\left(1 + \frac{7.25}{400}\right)^{3 \times 4}}$$

$$= \frac{10{,}000{,}000}{(1.018125)^{12}}$$

$$= \frac{10{,}000{,}000}{1.240547}$$

$$= \$8{,}060{,}960.26$$

2.7 Effective yield on zero coupon bond

$$
\begin{aligned}
i &= \left(\frac{FV}{PV}\right)^{1/n} - 1 \\
&= \left(\frac{1{,}000{,}000}{500{,}000}\right)^{1/5} - 1 \\
&= 1.148698 - 1 \\
&= 0.148698 \\
&= 14.87\% \text{ pa}
\end{aligned}
$$

Chapter 3

3.1 Cash flow representation: forward interest rate

$		1 month
+ 2,000,000		

$		6 months
	− 2,075,000	FV = 2,000,000 (1 + 0.09 × 5/12)

3.2 Cash flow representation: forward exchange rate transaction

$		3 months	DM	
+2,000,000		1.4420		−2,884,000

3.3 Net exchange position sheet

Transaction	DG	NEP	¥	NEP
2	− 7,000,000	− 7,000,000		
3			+ 500,000,000	+ 500,000,000
4			− 200,000,000	+ 300,000,000
5	+ 4,000,000	− 3,000,000		

Dealer is short DG3,000,000 and long ¥ 300,000,000.

Chapter 4

4.1 Gapping: normal yield curve: expect upward swift of yield curve

(a) To benefit from an expected upward shift

- borrow for 3 months at 5.50% (before rates rise)
- lend for 1 month at 5.00% (expecting to rollover at a higher rate).

(b) To close the gap after 1 month

- lend for 2 months at 6.25%

(c)

$		spot
+ 1,000,000.00		5.5%
	− 1,000,000.00	5.0%
1,000,000.00	1,000,000.00	

$		1 month
+ 1,012,500.00		FV= 1,000,000 (1+0.05 × 3/12)
	− 1,012,500.00	
1,012,500.00	1,012,500.00	

$		3 months
	− 1,013,750.00	FV_3= 1,000,000 (1+0.055 × 3/12)
+ 1,023,046.88		FV_2= 1,012,500 (1+0.0625 × 2/12)
	9,296.88	Profit
1,023,046.88	1,023,046.88	

4.2 Gapping: inverse yield: expect downward shift of yield curve

(a) break-even rate $= r_{1/3} = \left[\dfrac{FV_3}{FV_1} - 1\right] \times \dfrac{12}{2}$

$$= \left[\frac{10{,}000{,}000\ (1 + 0.07 \times 3/12)}{10{,}000{,}000\ (1 + 0.08 \times 1/12)} - 1\right] \times 6$$

$$= \left(\frac{10{,}175{,}000}{10{,}066{,}666.67} - 1\right) \times 6$$

$$= 0.0646$$

$$= 6.46\%\ \text{pa}$$

(b)

$		spot
+ 10,000,000		8.0%
	– 10,000,000	7.0%
10,000,000	10,000,000	

$		1 month
	– 10,175,000	
+ 10,175,000		
10,175,000	10,175,000	

$		3 months
+ 10,066,666.67		
	– 10,293,708.34	$FV_2 = 10{,}175{,}000(1+0.07 \times 2/12)$
227,041.67		Loss
10,293,708.34	10,293,708.34	

The corporation would lose $227,041.67 because the 2 month rate in 1 month's time at which it will expect to borrow (7.0% pa) is higher than the break-even rate (6.46% pa).

4.3 Gapping: normal yield curve: expect rotation of yield curve

(a)

C		spot
+1,000,000		5.0%
	− 1,000,000	5.5%
1,000,000	1,000,000	

C		3 months
	− 1,012,500	$FV_3 = 1{,}000{,}000\,(1+0.05 \times 3/12)$
+1,012,500		4.5%
1,012,500	1,012,500	

C		6 months
+ 1,027,500.00		$FV_6 = 1{,}000{,}000\,(1+0.055 \times 6/12)$
	− 1,023,890.63	$FV_3 = 1{,}012{,}500\,(1+0.045 \times 3/12)$
	3,609.37	Profit
1,027,500.00	1,027,500.00	

(b)

C		spot
+ 1,000,000		5.0%
	− 1,000,000	6.5%
1,000,000	1,000,000	

C		3 months
	− 1,012,500	$FV_3 = 1{,}000{,}000\,(1+0.05 \times 3/12)$
+ 1,012,500		
1,012,500	1,012,500	

C		12 months
+ 1,065,000.00		$FV_{12} = 1{,}000{,}000\,(1+0.065 \times 12/12)$
	1,061,859.38	$FV_9 = 1{,}012{,}500\,(1+0.065 \times 9/12)$
	3,140.62	Profit
1,065,000.00	1,065,000.00	

Profit under strategy (a) = C 3,609.37 (received after 6 months)
Profit under strategy (b) = C 3,140.62 (received after 12 months)
Strategy (a) is more profitable.

Note: The future value of C 3,609.37 after a further 6 months must be greater than C 3,609.37 and so is greater than C 3,140.62. To draw an exact comparison, calculate the future value using the expected $r_{3/9}$.

$$r_{3/9} = \left(\frac{FV_9}{FV_3} - 1\right) \times \frac{12}{6} = \left[\frac{(1 + 0.065 \times 9/12)}{(1 + 0.045 \times 3/12)} - 1\right] \times 2$$

$$= \left(\frac{1.04875}{1.01125} - 1\right) \times 2$$

$$= 0.07417$$

$$= 7.42\%$$

$$FV\ (C\ 3{,}609.37) = 3{,}609.37\left(1 + 0.0742 \times \frac{6}{12}\right)$$

$$= C\ 3{,}610.41$$

4.4 Gapping: calculation for exact number of days

(a) The company has opened a *negative* gap by borrowing for a shorter period than it has lent.

(b) The company would want the 3 month rate on 1 October to be below the break-even rate.

$$r_{1\,Oct/3\,Jan} = \left(\frac{FV_{3\,Jan}}{FV_{1Oct}} - 1\right) \times \frac{360}{186-92}$$

$$= \left(\frac{(1 + 0.0675 \times 186/360)}{(1 + 0.0675 \times 92/360)} - 1\right) \times \frac{360}{94}$$

$$= 0.6353$$

$$= 6.35\%\ \text{pa}$$

(c)

$		1 July
+ 10,000,000		6.75%
	– 10,000,000	6.75%
10,000,000	– 10,000,000	

$		1 October
	– 10,172,500	$FV_{1\,Oct} = 10{,}000{,}000\,(1 + 0.0675 \times 92/360)$
+ 10,172,500		6.75%
10,172,500	10,172,500	

$		3 January
+ 10,348,750.00		$FV_{3\,Jan} = 10{,}000{,}000\,(1 + 0.0675 \times 186/360)$
	– 10,351,790.31	$FV_{3\,Jan} = 10{,}172{,}500\,(1 + 0.0675 \times 94/360)$
3,040.31		Loss
10,351,790.31	10,348,750.31	

$$\begin{aligned} \text{Loss} &= 10{,}351{,}790.31 - 10{,}348{,}750.00 \\ &= \$3{,}040.31 \end{aligned}$$

Chapter 5

5.1 Bid offer rates

(a) The quoting bank will buy dollars by selling pounds at its offer rate of 1.6025.

(b) The customer will sell pounds at the bank's bid rate of 1.6020.

(c) The customer will sell dollars by buying pounds at the bank's offer rate of 1.6025.

5.2 Bid offer rates

Bank A is the calling bank.

DM is the terms currency.

Bank A will sell deutschemarks by buying dollars at the Bank B's offer rate of 1.5650.

5.3 Bid offer rates and spreads

(a) 1,000,000 × 1.4945 = P1,494,500

(b) 1,000,000 × 1.4935 = P1,493,500

(c) P1,494,500 – 1,493,500 = P1,000

(d) $\dfrac{1{,}000{,}000}{1.4935} = \text{C}669{,}568.13$

(e) $\dfrac{1{,}000{,}000}{1.4945} = \text{C}669{,}120.11$

(f) C669,568.13 – 669,120.11 = C448.02

5.4 Bid offer rates

(a) A customer can borrow dollars at the bank's offer rate of 8.50%.

(b) A customer can invest dollars as the bank's bid rate of 8.25%.

5.5 Bid offer rates and spreads

(a) 1,000,000 × 0.0475 × 7/21 = F15,833.33

(b) 1,000,000 × 0.0450 × 7/21 = F15,000.00

(c) F 833.33

5.6 Brokers

The broker price will be the highest bid and the lowest offer:
105.63 105.65.

5.7 Jobbing

The bank has purchased F10,000,000 at its bid rate of 1.12130.

To square its position, the bank needs to sell F10,000,000.

To make 5 points profit, the bank needs to sell francs at 1.2135.

The bank should quote A: 1.2125 **1.2135.**

Its offer rate 1.2135 is attractive because it is below the market rate of 1.2140.

Its bid rate 1.2125 is not attractive because it is below the market rate of 1.2130.

So the bank is likely to sell francs at 1.2135 to square its position for 5 points profit.

5.8 Arbitrage

To arbitrage:

(1) sell NZ$10,000,000 to Bank B at 0.6826 = US$6,826,000

(2) buy NZ$10,000,000 from Bank A at 0.6825 = US$6,825,000

Arbitrage profit = US $1,000

5.9 Cross rates

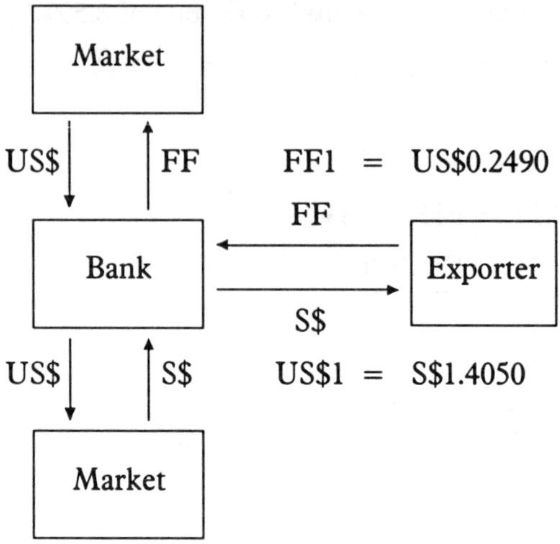

S$? = FF1
FF1 = US$0.2490
US$1 = S$1.4050

$$\therefore \text{FF1} = \frac{\text{S\$ } 1 \times 0.2490 \times 1.4050}{1 \times 1} = \text{S\$0.3498}$$

5.10 Cross rates

<u>Bid rate</u>

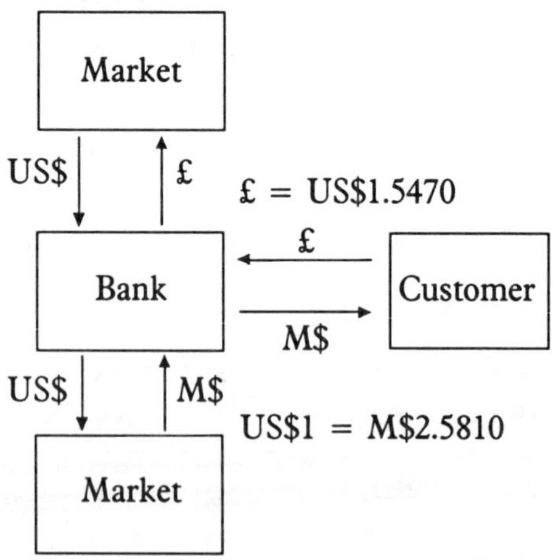

M$? = £1
£1 = US$1.5470
US$1 = M$2.5810

$$\therefore £1 = \frac{\text{M\$1} \times 1.5470 \times 2.5810}{1 \times 1}$$

= M$3.9928

<u>Offer rate</u>

M$? = £1
£1 = US$1.5490
US$1 = M$2.5830
∴ £1 = M$1 × 1.5490 × 2.5830
= M$4.0011

Chapter 6

6.1 Forward exchange rate and forward margin

(a)

$$
\begin{aligned}
f &= s\,\frac{(1 + r_T t)}{(1 + r_C t)} \\
&= 1.5000\,\frac{(1 + 0.03 \times 3/12)}{(1 + 0.06 \times 3/12)} \\
&= 1.5000\,\frac{(1.0075)}{(1.015)} \\
&= 1.4889
\end{aligned}
$$

(b)

$$
\begin{aligned}
\text{Forward margin} &= \text{forward rate} - \text{spot rate} \\
&= 1.4889 - 1.5000 \\
&= -0.0011
\end{aligned}
$$

6.2 Forward exchange rate and forward margin

$$
\begin{aligned}
f &= 70.00\,\frac{(1 + 0.035 \times 7/12)}{(1 + 0.065 \times 7/12)} \\
&= 68.82 \\
\text{forward margin} &= 68.82 - 70.00 \\
&= -1.18
\end{aligned}
$$

6.3 Forward bid rate

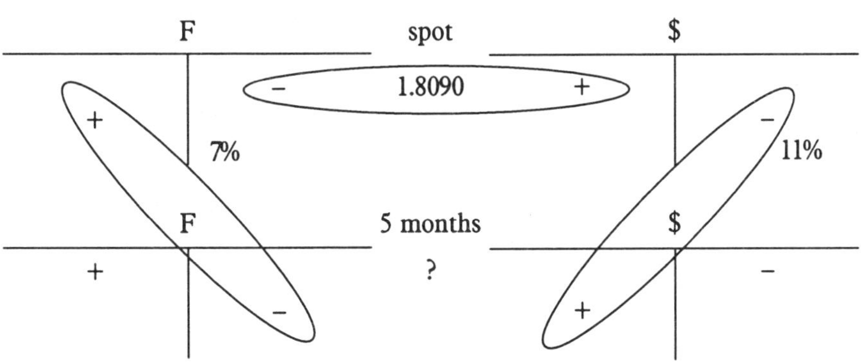

$$
\begin{aligned}
f &= 1.8090\,\frac{(1 + 0.11 \times 5/12)}{(1 + 0.07 \times 5/12)} \\
&= 1.8383
\end{aligned}
$$

6.4 Forward offer rate

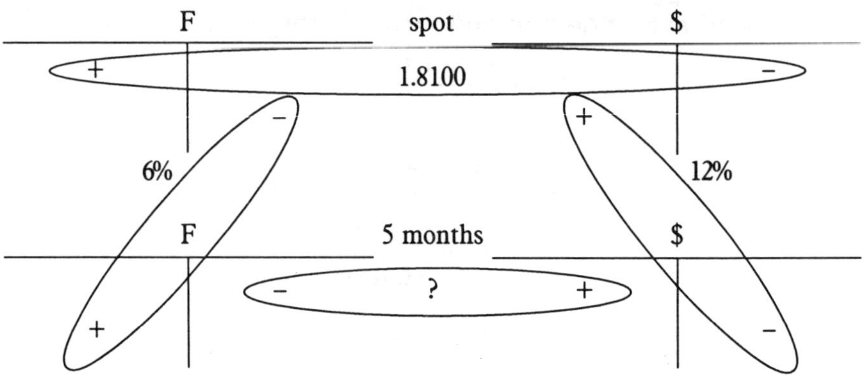

$$f = 1.8100 \frac{(1 + 0.12 \times 5/12)}{(1 + 0.06 \times 5/12)}$$

$$= 1.8541$$

break-even offer rate	1.8541
2 points profit	+ 0.0002
	1.8543

6.5 Long term foreign exchange

<u>Bid rate:</u>

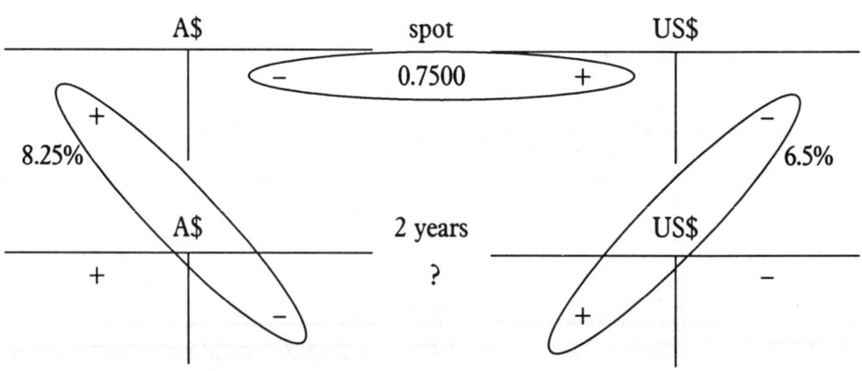

$$f = 0.7500 \frac{(1 + 0.065/2)^{2 \times 2}}{(1 + 0.0825/2)^{2 \times 2}}$$

$$= 0.7251$$

Offer rate:

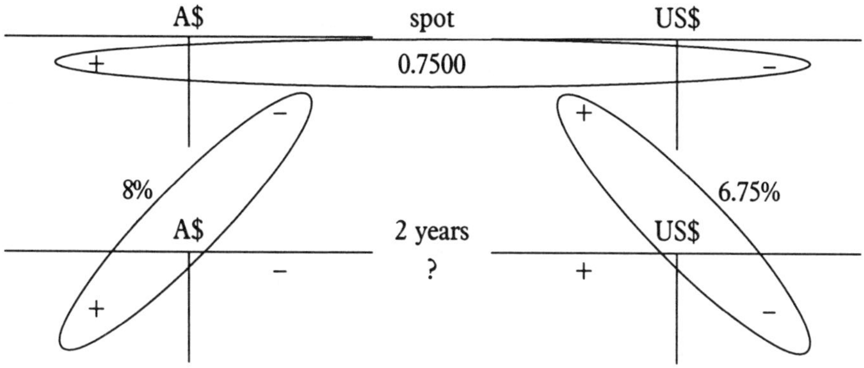

$$f = 0.7500 \frac{(1 + 0.0675/2)^{2 \times 2}}{(1 + 0.08/2)^{2 \times 2}}$$

$$= 0.7321$$

6.6 Short dates

Bid rate:

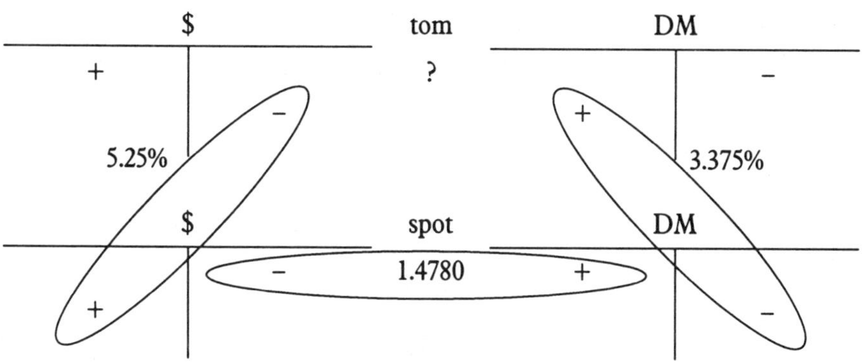

$$t = 1.4780 \frac{(1 + 0.0525 \times 1/360)}{(1 + 0.03375 \times 1/360)}$$

$$= 1.47822$$

Offer rate:

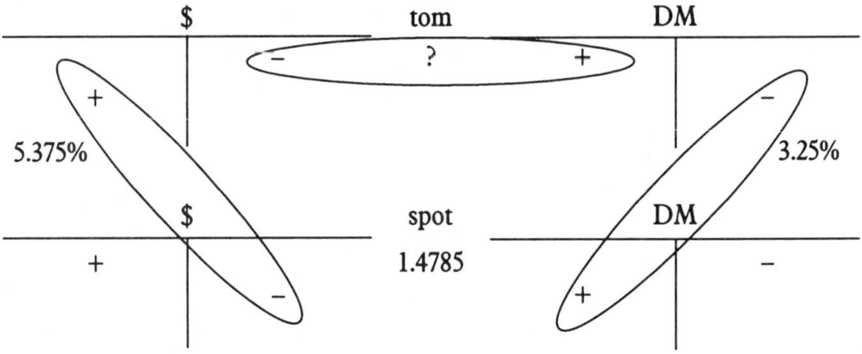

$$t = 1.4785 \frac{(1 + 0.05375 \times 1/360)}{(1 + 0.0325 \times 1/360)}$$

$$= 1.47859$$

Chapter 7

7.1 Hedging export receivables

(a) $$f = 0.6500 \frac{(1 + 0.0575 \times 62/360)}{(1 + 0.0975 \times 62/365)}$$

$$= 0.6457$$

(b) If the exporter remains unhedged, the expected NZ dollar proceeds will be:

$$\frac{4{,}560{,}000}{0.6350} = \text{NZ\$}7{,}181{,}102.36$$

If the exporter hedges, the certain NZ dollar proceeds will be:

$$\frac{4{,}560{,}000}{0.6457} = \text{NZ\$}7{,}062{,}103.14$$

If the expectation turns out to be correct, the exporter will be better off remaining unhedged. However, the spot rate at maturity might not be 0.6350 as expected, so the exporter may elect to hedge to eliminate the risk.

(c) The break-even rate = forward rate

= 0.6457

7.2 Hedged and unhedged foreign currency borrower

(a)

Drawdown $= \$8{,}000{,}000 \times 1.4650$

$= \text{DM}11{,}720{,}000$

DM repayment amount $= \text{DM}11{,}720{,}000\,(1 + 0.045 \times 274/360)$

$= \text{DM}12{,}121{,}410$

Dollar equivalent $= \dfrac{12{,}121{,}410}{1.4540}$

$= \$8{,}336{,}595.60$

Effective borrowing cost $= \dfrac{8{,}336{,}595.60 - 8{,}000{,}000}{8{,}000{,}000} \times \dfrac{360}{274}$

$= 0.0553$

$= 5.53\%$

(b) $f = 1.4650\,\dfrac{(1 + 0.045 \times 274/360)}{(1 + 0.095 \times 274/360)}$

$= 1.4130$

(c) Borrowing deutschemarks unhedged will turn out to be cheaper if the spot rate at maturity is 1.4540.

7.3 Hedged and unhedged foreign currency investment

(a)

Yen	Pounds
$s = 100$	$s = 1.5000$
$f = 90$	$f = 1.4750$
$r_T = 0.02$	$r_T = ?$
$r_C = ?$	$r_C = 0.09$
$t = 6/12$	$t = 6/12$
$90 = 100\,\dfrac{(1 + 0.02 \times 6/12)}{(1 + r_C \times 6/12)}$	$1.4750 = 1.5000\,\dfrac{(1 + r_T \times 6/12)}{(1 + 0.09 \times 6/12)}$
$\therefore\ r_C = 24.4\%$ pa	$\therefore\ r_T = 5.52\%$ pa

(b) The yen investment (which incidentally had the lowest nominal yield) would have provided the highest effective return on the investment.

7.4 Break-even rate on unhedged investment

$$\text{break-even rate} = s\frac{(1 + r_T t)}{(1 + r_C t)}$$

$$s = 106.50 \text{ (investor needs to sell dollars to buy yen)}$$

$$r_T = 0.02$$

$$t = 6/12$$

$$\therefore\ b = 106.50\frac{(1 + 0.02 \times 6/12)}{(1 + 0.06 \times 6/12)}$$

$$= 104.43$$

(b) At maturity, the investor needs to sell yen to buy dollars at 103.40.

$$103.40 = 106.50\frac{(1 + 0.02 \times 6/12)}{(1 + r_C \times 6/12)}$$

$$\therefore\ r_C = 0.08056$$

$$= 8.06\%\text{ pa}$$

Chapter 8

8.1 Pure and engineered swaps

(a) 1.2735 – 0.0030	=	1.2705
(b) 1.2740 – 0.0025	=	1.2715
(c) Customer buys dollars short at		1.2740
and sells dollars forward at		1.2705
Cost of engineered swap		0.0035
(d) Cost of pure swap	=	0.0030

8.2 Calculating swap rate

Bid

$$f = 1.4860\frac{(1 + 0.04/3)}{(1 + 0.08/3)}$$

$$= 1.4667$$

Swap rate = f – s
= 1.4667 – 1.4860
= – 0.0193

Offer

$$f = 1.4860\frac{(1 + 0.05/3)}{(1 + 0.07/3)}$$

$$= 1.4763$$

Swap rate = f – s
= 1.4763 – 1.4860
= – 0.0097

8.3 Simulated foreign currency loan

$$s = 1.4100$$
$$f = 1.3570$$
$$r_C = 0.06$$
$$t = 1$$
$$r_T = ?$$

$$1.3570 = 1.4100 \frac{(1 + r_T)}{(1.06)}$$

$$\therefore r_T = 0.0202$$
$$= 2.02\% \text{ pa}$$

8.4 Simulated foreign currency investment

Swapping deutschemarks into dollars involves:

buying dollars spot at 1.5060
and selling dollars forward at 1.4940

and investing dollars at 5.5%

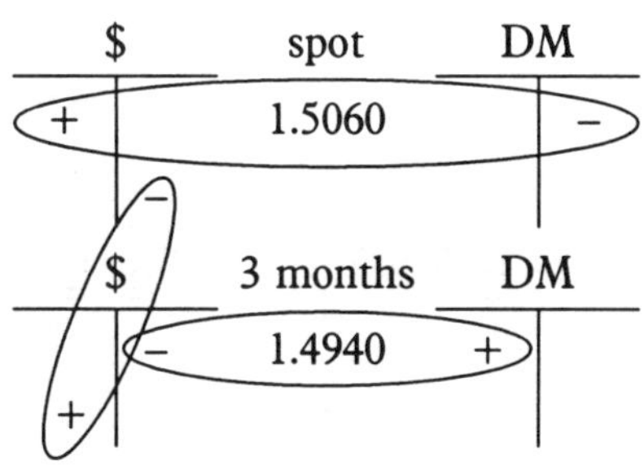

$$\text{If } y = \text{effective yield}$$

$$1.5060 \frac{(1 + y \times 3/12)}{(1 + 0.055 \times 3/12)} = 1.4940$$

$$\therefore y = 0.0227$$
$$= 2.27\% \text{ pa}$$

Investing directly in deutschemarks at 2.4% would provide a higher yield.

8.5 Short dates

(a) Value tom bid rate = 1.4780 + 0.00011 = 1.47811

(b) Value today offer rate = 1.4785 + 0.00042 + 0.00014 = 1.47906

(c) Swap rate 16 July over 8 July = 0.0008 + 0.00011= 0.00091

For example, if the swap was based off a spot of 1.4780, the customer would:

buy dollars value 16 July at 1.4780 – 0.0008	=	1.4772
and sell dollars value 8 July at 1.4780 + 0.00011	=	1.47811
benefit of swap	=	0.00091

Chapter 9

9.1 Parallel shift in a positive swaps curve

(a) To take advantage of an expected fall in swap rates:

buy dollars 1 month at	1554	i.e.	4 points cost
sell dollars 3 months at	1562	i.e.	12 points benefit
benefit of opening gap:	8		8

(b) One month later ...

$		spot	λ	
1,000,000		1554		1,554,000,000
	– 1,000,000	**1600**	**+1,600,000,000**	
		9.5%		**– 46,000,000**
1,000,000	1,000,000		1,600,000,000	1,600,000,000

$		2 months	λ	
	1,000,000	1562	1,562,000,000	
+ 1,000,000		**1606**		**1,606,000,000**
		P + I	**+ 46,728,333**	
		Profit		**2,728,333**
1,000,000	1,000,000		1,608,728,333	1,608,728,333

Profit = λ 1,562,000,000 + 46,728,333 – 1,606,000,000
= λ 2,728,333

9.2 Rotation of a negative swaps curve

(a) One month later ...

NZ$		spot	US$	
	1,000,000	0.6877	687,700	
+ 1,000,000		**0.7000**		**– 700,000**
		6.8%	**+ 12,300**	
1,000,000	1,000,000		700,000	700,000

NZ$		5 months	US$	
1,000,000		0.6801		680,100.00
	– 1,000,000	**0.6955**	**+ 695,500.00**	
		P + I		– 12,648.50
		Profit		**2,751.50**
1,000,000	1,000,000		695,500.00	695,500.00

Profit = 695,500 – 680,100 – 12,648.50 = US$ 2,751.50

(b) One month later ...

NZ$		spot	US$	
	1,000,000	0.6877	687,700	
+ 1,000,000		**0.6800**		**– 680,000**
		6.8%		**– 7,700**
1,000,000	1,000,000		687,700	687,700

NZ$		5 months	US$	
1,000,000		0.6801		680,100.00
	– 1,000,000	**0.6756**	+ 675,600.00	
		P + I	+ 7,918.17	
		Profit		3,218.17
1,000,000	1,000,000		683,518.17	683,518.17

Profit = 675,600 + 7,918.17 – 680,100 = US$ 3,218.17

Note: The lower spot rate adds to the profit from the gap because it results in a positive cash flow rather than a negative cash flow at the 1 month date.

Chapter 10

10.1 Pricing a put using a binomial model

Drift = forward – spot
= 108.92 – 110.00
= – ¥1.08 over 3 months
= – ¥0.36 per month

Up-factor = + ¥2.00 – 0.36
= + ¥1.64 per month

Down-factor = – ¥2.00 – 0.36
= – ¥2.36 per month

This generates the following binomial tree:

			x_i	Intrinsic Value	Probability	Expected Value
			114.92	0.00	1/8	0.00
		113.28				
	111.64		110.92	1.08	3/8	0.405
110.00		109.28				
	107.64		106.92	5.08	3/8	1.905
		105.28				
			102.92	9.08	1/8	1.135
					1	3.445

$$\text{Premium} = \frac{3.445}{(1 + 0.01 \times 3/12)} = ¥3.44$$

On face value $10,000,000,

Yen premium = 10,000,000 × 3.44 = ¥34,300,000

$$= \frac{\$34,400,000}{110.00}$$

= $312,727.27

10.2 Volatility

x_i	$(x_i - \bar{x})$	$(x_i - \bar{x})^2$	p	$p(x_i - \bar{x})^2$
114.92	6.00	36	1/8	4.5
110.92	2.00	4	3/8	1.5
106.92	− 2.00	4	3/8	1.5
102.92	− 6.00	36	1/8	4.5
			1	12.0

$$\sigma_t = \sqrt{\sum p(x_i - \bar{x})^2} = \sqrt{12.0} = 3.4641$$

$$\text{Expressed as a percentage of the forward rate} = \frac{3.4641}{108.92} = 3.18\%$$

$$\text{Annualised } \sigma_A = \frac{\sigma_t}{\sqrt{3/12}} = \frac{3.18\%}{0.5} = 6.36\% \text{ pa}$$

10.3 Pricing put using the Black-Scholes formula

$$s = 110.00$$

$$k = 112.00$$

$$t = 3/12 = 0.25$$

$$\sigma = 6.36\% \text{ pa} = 0.0636$$

$$r_T = 0.01$$

$$r_C = 0.05$$

$$d_1 = \frac{\ln (110/112) + [0.01 - 0.05 + 1/2\,(0.0636)] \times 0.25}{0.0636\sqrt{0.25}}$$

$$= \frac{-0.018019 - 0.009494}{0.0318}$$

$$= -0.865185$$

$$\therefore N(d_1) = 0.1934686$$

$$d_2 = d_1 - \sigma\sqrt{t}$$

$$= -0.865185 - 0.0318$$

$$= -0.89698$$

$$\therefore N(d_2) = 0.1848634$$

$$C = \frac{f\,N(d_1) - kN(d_2)}{(1 + r_T t)}$$

$$= \frac{(108.92 \times 0.1934686) - (112.00 \times 0.1848634)}{(1 + 0.01 \times 3/12)}$$

$$= ¥0.37$$

$$p = C - \frac{s}{(1 + r_C t)} + \frac{k}{(1 + r_T t)}$$

$$= 0.37 - \frac{110.00}{(1 + 0.05 + 3/12)} + \frac{112.00}{(1 + 0.01 \times 3/12)}$$

$$= 0.37 - 108.64 + 111.72$$

$$= ¥3.45$$

It is noteworthy that the crude binomial model used in Practice Problem 10.1 produced an answer which is remarkably close to that calculated using the adapted Black-Scholes formula.

10.4 Put-Call arbitrage

Strike – forward = 1.5200 – 1.4800	= 0.0400
Put premium – call premium = 0.0450 – 0.0100	= 0.0350
Difference	= 0.0050

Buy put and sell call = synthetic sold forward	
DM proceeds of \$10,000,000 sold forward at 1.5200	= DM15,200,000
Net premium payable = 10,000,000 × 0.0350 = DM350,000	
∴ FV (net premium) = 350,000 (1 + 0.03)	= DM 360,500
∴ Net DM proceeds of synthetic forward sale	= DM14,839,500
DM cost of forward purchase of \$10,000,000 at 1.4800	= DM14,800,000
Profit	= DM 39,500

Chapter 11

11.1 Exporter

(a) Call premium paid =

1,000,000 × 1.5/100 = DM 15,000 = \$15,000/1.5100 = \$9,933.77

Put premium received =

600,000 × 1.5/100 = DM 9,000 = \$9,000/1.5100 = \$5,960.26

Net premium payable = \$3,973.51

FV (net premium) = 3,973.51 (1+0.05 × 3/12) = \$4,023.17

(b) Dollar proceeds of selling DM1,000,000 spot

(i) at 1.4500 $= \frac{1,000,000}{1.4500} = \$689,655.17$

(ii) at 1.4900 $= \frac{1,000,000}{1.4900} = \$671,140.94$

(iii) at 1.5500 $= \frac{1,000,000}{1.5500} = \$645,161.29$

(c) Break-even occurs where:

proceeds with participating collar = proceeds if unhedged

$$\frac{1,000,000}{1.5000} - 4,023.17 = \frac{1,000,000}{b}$$

$$666,666.67 - 4,023.17 = \frac{1,000,000}{b}$$

$$\therefore \quad b = \frac{1,000,000}{662,643.50} = 1.5091$$

11.2 Foreign currency borrower

(a) Premium dollar put $= \dfrac{25{,}395{,}300}{1.2500} \times \dfrac{3.0}{100} = \$609{,}487.20$

Premium dollar call $= \dfrac{12{,}697{,}650}{1.2500} \times \dfrac{2.4}{100} = \$243{,}794.88$

Net premium payable $= \$365{,}834.63$

FV (net premium) $= 365{,}692.32\left(1 + \dfrac{0.05}{2}\right) = \$374{,}834.63$

(b) Dollar cost with participating option,

(i) at 1.2000, dollar put is exercised and dollar call lapses

$$\text{Cost} = \frac{25{,}395{,}300}{1.2300} + 374{,}834.63 = \$21{,}021{,}420.00$$

(ii) at 1.2400, dollar put lapses and dollar call is exercised

$$\text{Cost} = \frac{12{,}697{,}650}{1.2300} + \frac{12{,}697{,}650}{1.2400} + 374{,}834.63 = \$20{,}938{,}167.63$$

(iii) at 1.3000, dollar put lapses and dollar call is exercised

$$\text{Cost} = \frac{12{,}697{,}650}{1.2300} + \frac{12{,}697{,}650}{1.3000} + 374{,}834.63 = \$20{,}465{,}550.39$$

(c) Effective borrowing cost $= \dfrac{\$\text{cost} - 20{,}000{,}000}{20{,}000{,}000} \times 200$

(i) at 1.2000, $\dfrac{21{,}021{,}420.00 - 20{,}000{,}000}{20{,}000{,}000} \times 200 = 10.21\%$ pa

(ii) at 1.2400, $\dfrac{20{,}938{,}167.63 - 20{,}000{,}000}{20{,}000{,}000} \times 200 = 9.38\%$ pa

(iii) at 1.3000, $\dfrac{20{,}465{,}550.39 - 20{,}000{,}000}{20{,}000{,}000} \times 200 = 4.66\%$ pa

(d) Dollar cost if borrow in dollars $= 20{,}000{,}000 \times (1 + 0.05 \times 6/12)$

$= \$20{,}500{,}000.00$

$$\text{Dollar cost if borrow in SF} = \frac{12{,}697{,}650}{1.2300} + \frac{12{,}697{,}650}{x} + 374{,}834.63$$

Break-even occurs where:

$$\frac{12{,}697{,}650}{1.2300} + \frac{12{,}697{,}650}{x} + 374{,}834.63 = 20{,}500{,}000.00$$

$$10{,}323{,}292.68 + \frac{12{,}697{,}650}{x} + 374{,}834.63 = 20{,}500{,}000.00$$

$$\therefore \frac{12{,}697{,}650}{x} = 20{,}500{,}000.00 - 10{,}323{,}292.68 - 374{,}834.63$$

$$= 9{,}801{,}872.69$$

$$\therefore \quad x = \frac{12{,}697{,}650.00}{9{,}801{,}872.69}$$

$$= 1.2954$$

11.3 Foreign currency investor

$$\text{Dollar call premium} = \frac{1{,}111{,}152{,}778}{110.00} \times \frac{3.25}{100} = \$328{,}295.14$$

$$\text{Dollar put premium} = \frac{777{,}806{,}945}{110.00} \times \frac{2.00}{100} = \$141{,}419.44$$

Net premium payable $= \$186{,}875.70$

$$\text{FV (net premium)} = 186{,}875.70 \times (1 + 0.05 \times \frac{365}{360})$$

$$= \$196{,}349.26$$

(a) (i) at 100.00, call lapses and put is exercised

$$\text{dollar proceeds} = \frac{777{,}806{,}945}{109.00} + \frac{333{,}345{,}833}{100.00} - 196{,}349.26$$

$$= \$10{,}272{,}952.60$$

(ii) at 110.00, indifferent between exercising and lapsing the call, put lapses

$$\text{dollar proceeds} = \frac{1{,}111{,}152{,}778}{110.00} - 196{,}349.26$$

$$= \$9{,}905{,}039.63$$

$$\text{effective yield} = \frac{9{,}905{,}039.63 - 10{,}000{,}000}{10{,}000{,}000} \times \frac{365}{360}$$

$$= -0.95\% \text{ pa}$$

(iii) at 120.00, exercise call, put lapses

$$\text{dollar proceeds} = \frac{1{,}111{,}152{,}778}{110.00} - 196{,}349.26$$

$$= \$9{,}905{,}039.63$$

$$\text{effective yield} = -0.95\% \text{ pa (again)}$$

(b) If spot rate at maturity is ¥114.00, effective yield = – 0.95% pa (again)

(i) If unhedged,

$$\text{dollar proceeds} = \frac{1{,}111{,}152{,}778}{114.00}$$

$$= \$9{,}746{,}954.19$$

$$\text{effective yield} = \frac{9{,}746{,}954.19 - 10{,}000{,}000}{10{,}000{,}000}$$

$$= -2.53\% \text{ pa}$$

(ii) If invested in dollars,

$$\text{dollar proceeds} = 10{,}000{,}000\,(1 + 0.05 \times 365/360)$$

$$= \$10{,}506{,}944.44$$

$$\text{effective yield} = \frac{10{,}506{,}944.44 - 10{,}000{,}000}{10{,}000{,}000}$$

$$= +5.07\% \text{ pa}$$

(iii) If hedged with a bought dollar call (k = ¥110.00)

$$\text{dollar proceeds} = \frac{1{,}111{,}152{,}778}{110.00} - 344{,}937.88$$

$$= \$9{,}756{,}451.01$$

$$\text{effective yield} = \frac{9{,}756{,}451.01 - 10{,}000{,}000}{10{,}000{,}000}$$

$$= -2.4\%$$

The best outcome would have been to be invested in dollars.

Chapter 12

12.1 At expiry digital call using reverse binomial method

Drift = 0.7520 – 0.7500
= + 0.0020 over 4 months
= + 0.0005 per month

Up-factor = + 0.0150 + 0.0005 = + 0.0155

Down-factor = – 0.0150 + 0.0005 = – 0.0145

Binomial tree				x_i	Value
				0.8120	100,000
			0.7965		
		0.7810		0.7820	100,000
	0.7655		0.7665		
0.7500		0.7510		0.7520	0
	0.7355		0.7365		
		0.7210		0.7220	0
			0.7065		
				0.6920	0

Reverse binomial tree				Value	x_i
				100,000	0.8120
			100,000		
		75,000		100,000	0.7820
	50,000		50,000		
31,250		25,000		0	0.7520
	12,500		0		
		0		0	0.7220
			0		
				0	0.6920

$$\text{Premium} = \frac{31{,}250}{(1 + 0.06 \times 4/12)} = \text{US\$}30{,}637.25 = \frac{30{,}637.25}{0.7500} = \text{A\$}40{,}849.67$$

12.2 Power option

Outcome (x_i)	Payout on Standard 105 Call	Payout on $(x - k)^2$	p	Expected Payout
118	13	169	1/64	2.64
112	7	49	6/64	4.59
106	1	1	15/64	0.23
100	0	0		0
94	0	0		0
88	0	0		0
82	0	0		0
				7.46

$$\text{Premium} = \frac{7.46}{(1 + 0.01 \times 6/12)} = ¥7.42 \text{ per dollar face value}$$

If face value of the power option is \$10,000,000, premium= ¥7,420,000
= \$74,200.00

Chapter 14

14.1 Value at risk

(a) FV cashflows: \$10,000,000 × 4.8308
= FF48,308,000

A 100 point increase would make the spot rate,

5.0000 + 0.0100
= 5.0100

FV Cashflows	Rate	Present Value	Dollar Equivalent
\$ + 10,000,000	5.5%	+ 8,984,524	+ 8,984,524
FF – 48,308,000	3.7%	– 44,922,255	– 8,966,518 (at 5.0100)
			+ 18,006

Factor sensitivity = +\$18,006 per 100 point increase in the spot rate.

(b) $\sigma = 12\%$ pa $= \text{FF } 5.0000 \times 0.12 = \text{FF } 0.6000$ per year

$= \text{FF } 0.6000 \times \sqrt{2} = \text{FF } 0.8485$ over 2 years

$\therefore 1.65\sigma = 1.65 \times 0.8485 = \text{FF } 1.4000$

A 1.65 standard deviation rise in the spot rate would be:

$$5.0000 + 1.4000 = \text{FF } 6.4000$$

FV Cashflows	Rate	Present Value	Dollar Equivalent
\$ +10,000,000	5.5%	+ 8,984,524	+ 8,984,524
FF – 48,308,000	3.7%	– 44,922,255	– 7,019,102 (at 6.4000)
			1,965,422

Value at Risk = \$1,965,422

14.2 Credit risk

(a)

spot	1.6455
swap rate	– 0.0095
forward	1.6360

$$\text{FV (MTM)} = 10{,}000{,}000 - \frac{15{,}170{,}000}{1.6360}$$

$$= 10{,}000{,}000 - 9{,}272{,}616.14$$

$$= 727{,}383.86$$

$$\therefore \text{MTM} = \frac{727{,}383.86}{(1 + 0.05 \times 3/12)} = \$718{,}403.82$$

(b) Potential exposure = Face value × CRF

= 10,000,000 × 0.07

= \$700,000

(c) Presettlement risk = MTM + Potential exposure

= 718,403.82 + 700,000.00

= 1,418,403.82

(d)

PSR limit	1,500,000.00
Exposure	1,418,403.82
Available	81,596.18

Maximum 3 month deal size = $81{,}596.18 \times \frac{100}{7.0}$

= \$1,165,659.86

Appendix
Cumulative Normal Distribution

Cumulative Normal Distribution

N(d) = probability of being below d standard deviations from the mean

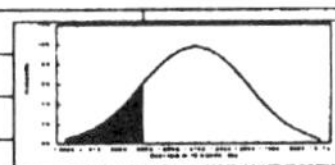

d	N(d)	d	N(d)	d	N(d)	d	N(d)
-1.00	0.1587	-0.50	0.3085	0.00	0.5000	0.50	0.6915
-0.99	0.1611	-0.49	0.3121	0.01	0.5040	0.51	0.6950
-0.98	0.1635	-0.48	0.3156	0.02	0.5080	0.52	0.6985
-0.97	0.1660	-0.47	0.3192	0.03	0.5120	0.53	0.7019
-0.96	0.1685	-0.46	0.3228	0.04	0.5160	0.54	0.7054
-0.95	0.1711	-0.45	0.3264	0.05	0.5199	0.55	0.7088
-0.94	0.1736	-0.44	0.3300	0.06	0.5239	0.56	0.7123
-0.93	0.1762	-0.43	0.3336	0.07	0.5279	0.57	0.7157
-0.92	0.1788	-0.42	0.3372	0.08	0.5319	0.58	0.7190
-0.91	0.1814	-0.41	0.3409	0.09	0.5359	0.59	0.7224
-0.90	0.1841	-0.40	0.3446	0.10	0.5398	0.60	0.7257
-0.89	0.1867	-0.39	0.3483	0.11	0.5438	0.61	0.7291
-0.88	0.1894	-0.38	0.3520	0.12	0.5478	0.62	0.7324
-0.87	0.1922	-0.37	0.3557	0.13	0.5517	0.63	0.7357
-0.86	0.1949	-0.36	0.3594	0.14	0.5557	0.64	0.7389
-0.85	0.1977	-0.35	0.3632	0.15	0.5596	0.65	0.7422
-0.84	0.2005	-0.34	0.3669	0.16	0.5636	0.66	0.7454
-0.83	0.2033	-0.33	0.3707	0.17	0.5675	0.67	0.7486
-0.82	0.2061	-0.32	0.3745	0.18	0.5714	0.68	0.7517
-0.81	0.2090	-0.31	0.3783	0.19	0.5753	0.69	0.7549
-0.80	0.2119	-0.30	0.3821	0.20	0.5793	0.70	0.7580
-0.79	0.2148	-0.29	0.3859	0.21	0.5832	0.71	0.7611
-0.78	0.2177	-0.28	0.3897	0.22	0.5871	0.72	0.7642
-0.77	0.2206	-0.27	0.3936	0.23	0.5910	0.73	0.7673
-0.76	0.2236	-0.26	0.3974	0.24	0.5948	0.74	0.7704
-0.75	0.2266	-0.25	0.4013	0.25	0.5987	0.75	0.7734
-0.74	0.2296	-0.24	0.4052	0.26	0.6026	0.76	0.7764
-0.73	0.2327	-0.23	0.4090	0.27	0.6064	0.77	0.7794
-0.72	0.2358	-0.22	0.4129	0.28	0.6103	0.78	0.7823
-0.71	0.2389	-0.21	0.4168	0.29	0.6141	0.79	0.7852
-0.70	0.2420	-0.20	0.4207	0.30	0.6179	0.80	0.7881
-0.69	0.2451	-0.19	0.4247	0.31	0.6217	0.81	0.7910
-0.68	0.2483	-0.18	0.4286	0.32	0.6255	0.82	0.7939
-0.67	0.2514	-0.17	0.4325	0.33	0.6293	0.83	0.7967
-0.66	0.2546	-0.16	0.4364	0.34	0.6331	0.84	0.7995
-0.65	0.2578	-0.15	0.4404	0.35	0.6368	0.85	0.8023
-0.64	0.2611	-0.14	0.4443	0.36	0.6406	0.86	0.8051
-0.63	0.2643	-0.13	0.4483	0.37	0.6443	0.87	0.8078
-0.62	0.2676	-0.12	0.4522	0.38	0.6480	0.88	0.8106
-0.61	0.2709	-0.11	0.4562	0.39	0.6517	0.89	0.8133
-0.60	0.2743	-0.10	0.4602	0.40	0.6554	0.90	0.8159
-0.59	0.2776	-0.09	0.4641	0.41	0.6591	0.91	0.8186
-0.58	0.2810	-0.08	0.4681	0.42	0.6628	0.92	0.8212
-0.57	0.2843	-0.07	0.4721	0.43	0.6664	0.93	0.8238
-0.56	0.2877	-0.06	0.4761	0.44	0.6700	0.94	0.8264
-0.55	0.2912	-0.05	0.4801	0.45	0.6736	0.95	0.8289
-0.54	0.2946	-0.04	0.4840	0.46	0.6772	0.96	0.8315
-0.53	0.2981	-0.03	0.4880	0.47	0.6808	0.97	0.8340
-0.52	0.3015	-0.02	0.4920	0.48	0.6844	0.98	0.8365
-0.51	0.3050	-0.01	0.4960	0.49	0.6879	0.99	0.8389

Index

CW01618872

Excellent Instructor in an amazing location

Review of Connemara Shooting School

◉◉◉◉◉ *Reviewed 22 October 2019*

Getting back into shooting after an absence of more than 5 years living and working abroad, I have been taking any opportunity to hone my meagre skills. A family trip to Connemara offers the opportunity of meeting Shane Bisgood at the Connemara Shooting School located at Ballynahinch Castle Hotel.

I have to say Shane is by far the best shooting instructor I have had the good fortune to have met. I had two highly enjoyable sessions with him and believe I have gained more from this time than from all of my previous many years of lessons put together. Assessing your issues, Shane will not only explain what you are doing wrong, (or right), but also offers a solution on how to overcome the issue. It seems to work in my case.

I found Shane knowledgeable, informative, patient and effective. I admit I liked him from the get go. A gentleman, he is also a nice guy and a character. I will definitely return to Connemara in the future and look forward to more productive sessions with Shane.

THE COMPLETE Shot

SHANE BISGOOD

© Shane Bisgood 2020 - all rights reserved

First edition
Text, photographs, illustrations copyright © S.R. Bisgood 2020
The moral rights of the author and illustrator have been asserted.
First published in the Republic of Ireland in 2020 by S.R. Bisgood
www.connemarashootingschool.com

All rights reserved

Proof marks, variety of photos
Contact details for associations world wide
International and national competitions for clays

No part of this publication may be reproduced or transmitted by any means, electronic, mechanical, photocopying or otherwise, without the prior permission of the author.

Designed by: Bottlegreendesign | Printed by: Gotoprint

ISBN 978-1-8380193-0-3

Acknowledgements

Over my career I have received so much kindness in comment and in help. I have learned constantly from my clients, the recognition of the right words, in the right order, with the right emphasis, to further ensure their understanding of these methods. Observing their mistakes, they have taught me to make quick diagnosis and then offer them solutions that the client understands and can put into effect. My most sincere thanks to you all.

There are many individuals too who so deserve recognition, all my family from early days to the present, my mother and father, my sisters and brother who tolerated the noise sometimes benefitted from the entertainment value! My extended family, Richard, Kitty, Ems and Jeremy, Gay and Dilly.

Then there are those who have helped directly with this book, Edel Nulty and Jeananne Crowley, both invaluable in their extraordinary abilities to educate a novice.

In recent times I have been fortunate to work with some new friends of mine, Michael Walsh and Dearbhla Casey of the Dubarry company.

My school's location at Ballynahinch Castle, a remarkable gem in the wilds of Connemara, thank you Denis and Catherine.

Veronica Lydon who often rescues and restores me physically, without whom I would hardly be able to move.

And the most important person of all, whom I owe so much gratitude to for her opening doors where I only saw walls, Molly McGuigan, my other half.

Contents

1 Writer's Note

I have written this book with mind to both those who want a full explanation on the reasons why and how, but also in mind of those who would like a quick word of advice.

Therefore you will find subjects covered simply and quickly, early in the book and then returned to later in these chapters to offer the reader a full explanation on the matter at hand.

2 A Word Of Welcome

These following words are usually the first words of instruction given to any of my clients, irrespective of experience, simply to point out to them the most important element of the method used to successfully hit your target.

'Where your gun is pointing in relation to the target, when you decide to pull the trigger, will determine whether you hit or miss your target.' This must always be uppermost in your mind, your determination must be to **'Make the Picture Right'.**

To be successful, you must know exactly where the gun should be pointing in relation to every angle of target, this is called your **'Sight Picture'.** Couple this with **'Follow Through'** and you have the perfect solution.

I know there are other aspects to shooting that should not be ignored and there are methods that make shooting accurately much simpler. That is what this book will give you.

But please remember, the one component of these that can never be automated, that has to be seen to be correct, is the relationship of your barrel to the target, therefore, If you wish to hit your target...
See more on page 62.

Make the Picture Right!
On many occasions I have been lucky enough to be invited to shoot, either on a friend's rough shoot or their driven shoot, or invited to compete with colleagues at clay pigeon shoots. It has become obvious to me that there are a number of individuals who appear content to remain poor shots. If not content, then under the misapprehension

that they are fated to forever be this way. This is most certainly not the case. When I watch guns shooting live birds, the missing of a bird can provoke a number of reactions. Irritation, embarrassment, a laugh, a curse, a scowl or a pensive look. A missed bird at a clay shoot results in much the same reaction. The game shooter goes on to the next drive with a fresh opportunity to excel. The clay shooter will be armed with the same opportunity but may still be discussing, indeed sometimes agonising over the reason for that missed target. There seems to be an interesting disparity here between some game shots and some clay shots, possibly the publication of their score. But this isn't the only factor that drives my curiosity and career.

An illustration of the life I lead can help set the scene. I was invited some years ago to return to Charlottesville, Virginia a wonderful city and historic location to teach some very interesting individuals. On my list of clients that morning was one lady named Patricia. I was in the appointed place at the appointed time and mulling over the information I had been provided on this lady. This is a very important and wealthy individual, do make sure she is treated with 'kid gloves'. Along the track and across the grass travelled a black Range Rover. The car stopped near me, the driver's door swung open and out from the interior stepped a tall slim lady with very shiny, wavy, shortish hair. We walked towards each other and I reached out my hand. It was ignored. I introduced myself saying *"Good morning, my name's Shane Bisgood and I'm your shooting instructor"*. Her reply: *"Good morning, my name's Patricia, I haven't come for a shooting lesson, I want you to check that my guns are clean."* With that she about faced and walked back to the boot of her car, opened the tail gate and undid the leather straps on a very British looking travelling case. Inside were a superb matched pair of best London guns. She turned.

Surprised by her opening gambit, my reply came forth as best I could think up, *"Mrs…….., where I come from, the person who normally checks your guns are clean is your butler, I am a shooting instructor."*

She looked at me for a moment, shut the gun case, then the boot lid, stepped back into the car, shut the door and started the engine. The engine stopped, the door opened and she walked back to me with her hand extended, a very large smile on her face and said, *"Hello Mr. Bisgood, my name's Patricia, I'm here for a shooting lesson."*

What a delightful lady she turned out to be, she was leading a fascinating life and proved to be a very entertaining pupil but admitted that she would frequently test those who were to do her a service and if they stood up to her, she would accept them happily. It is from clients such as her that my life of teaching has been so full of fascination and fun.

Because you are reading this, it is clear to me that you are one of those who do care about the results of your shooting. You would like to add to your abilities. You would prefer to be considered by others as a good shot. So you are going to devote some of your precious time to learning a skill or improving an existing one. What I endeavour to achieve when teaching my clients, is to give them a completely logical and simple set of instructions on how to shoot, be it game birds or clays. What I have written must make sense and must not pose insoluble questions. Having read a section in this book, you may find you have a question unanswered. Make a mental note of it, because the answer will almost certainly be found in a following or subsequent section. I have tried to illustrate this information by using stories or anecdotes, sometimes very much at my own expense. You may revisit this book when things perhaps do not go so well as you would like. With hope that I can always offer some remedy or advice to those who would like to shoot well, I wish you good reading and good shooting.

3 Take It From The Beginning - Right From The Start

These words have been said to me on many occasions as a request, surprisingly by experienced shots and not surprisingly by absolute beginners. It is all too obvious why absolute beginners would utter these words, but what do the more experienced shots want? Why do they wish to be taken from the very beginning when already they have an element of information available, a degree of knowledge, a perception of what to do? There is a possibility that there remains a doubt in their minds that their knowledge is sufficient for them to build confidently upon what exists. Maybe they just want to check their knowledge against another database. Maybe there is a suspicion that no matter how many times you take a lesson, there is always something new to learn. This last is my own philosophy for teaching people. I am constantly learning from my clients, learning new ways to impart information, new ways to effect change in them and realising there must be at least ten different verbal ways to give a single piece of knowledge to a client.

Gun Description

This is purely to introduce the major parts, movable or otherwise, of the shotgun. Yes, there are many more than I have named here. For the time being, all the others are unnecessary to label. Starting at the end of the barrels and working one's way rearwards:

1. Sitting on top of and centred at the end of the barrels is the bead, not a sight but an object to assist one in determining that the gun is in alignment with one's eye. *See photos 12 a,b,c on page 12.*

12a

12b

12c

13a

13b

13c

2. The rib which runs centrally from muzzle to breech above or between the barrels, depending if the gun is configured with barrels over and under (above) or configured with barrels side by side (between). Most O/U guns have a ventilated rib so as to disperse sideways the heat rising from the two stacked barrels and this prevents distortion of your sight image.
   See photos 12 a,b,c on page 12.

3. The top lever, found on the upper surface behind the action, pushed to the right, allows the gun to open at the breech. These are not always to be found on top and to the rear of the action. I've seen several where the lever is situated under the action and wrapping around the trigger guard. Equally well, the gun doesn't always open in the familiar way by hinging between action and chamber. I have seen some that slide apart, dividing between face of the action and your chambers.
   See photos 13 a,b,c on page 13.

4. The chambers where loaded ammunition sits inside the barrels of the gun. *See photo diagram page 153.*

   N.B. Please note advice given on you knowing your chamber lengths and suitable cartridges, page 25.

5. The safety catch, showing 'S' or 'safe', should render the gun inoperable, but being mechanical, potentially renders this service unreliable. Don't depend on your safety catch to be safe. There are variants in the types used. The most familiar are on the gun's Top Tang, to the rear of the Top Lever. This type of safety catch has two positions, with 'S' or 'Safe' showing and if the catch is pushed forward to cover the 'S', enables the trigger to be pulled. It may also incorporate a barrel selector switch in the centre.

This will allow the shooter to choose which barrel fires first when the gun operates with a single trigger. There are also many guns that use the whole safety catch sliding left or right to select the firing order.

The Safety catch can be fitted to the side of the stock near the action. With some single barreled guns such as semi automatics they can be found incorporated in the front and in other makes, the rear of the trigger guard. I saw a gun recently that had its safety catch incorporated in the trigger itself which hardly seemed wise. ***See photos 15 a,b,c,d.***

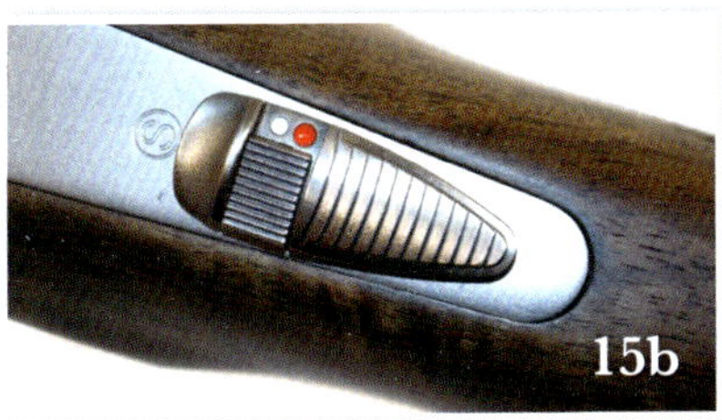

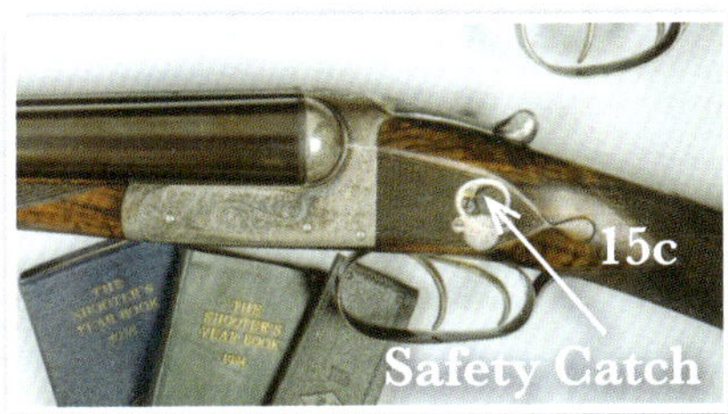

N.B. Most Side by Sides, but not all, will reset to their 'Safe' position when operating the top lever. A high proportion of Over and Under shotguns do not have an auto safety reset and a few gun makers such as Browning, supply a reset push rod which can be fitted by a competent gunsmith. The push rod is attached internally to the cam of the top lever and operates from the action of the top lever rotating when opening the gun.

In my humble opinion, an automatic Safety Catch reset should be uniformly used by all gun makers. There's no question that this is the safest choice and the fear of a lost target due to leaving the Safety catch engaged, is insufficient reason to leave out the auto reset ensuring a greater degree of safety for all.

6. The stock and fore-end, attaches the gun to the shooter. The Grip may be a). 'Swan Neck' or 'Straight Hand', b). Full Pistol or c). Prince of Wales or Semi pistol. *See photos 16 a,b,c,d.*

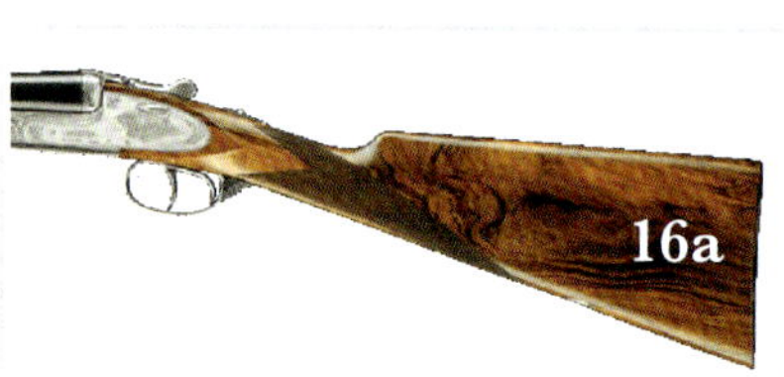
16a

16b

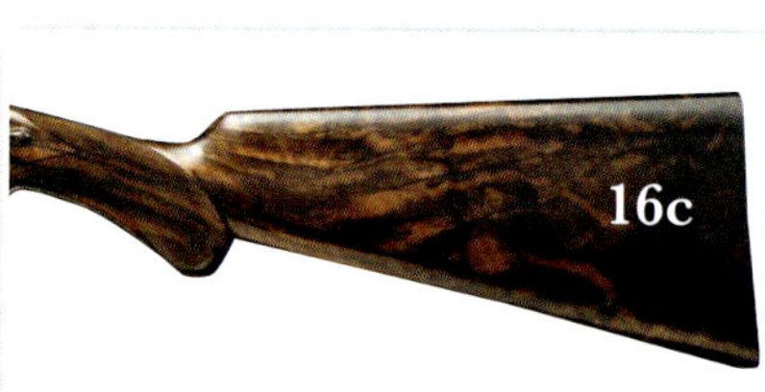
16c

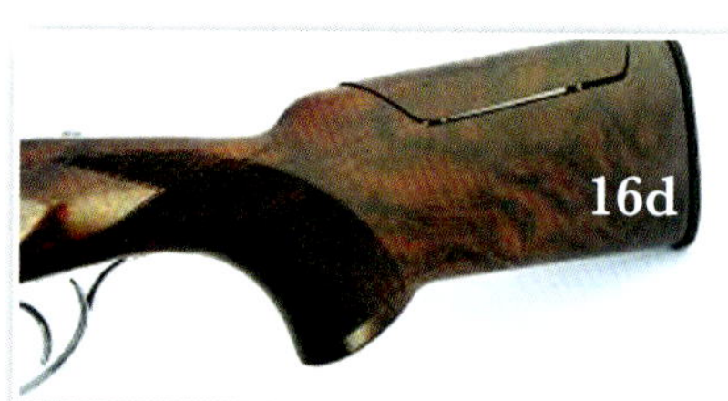
16d

7. The butt, the end of the stock closest to the shooter, which attaches shoulder to gun, composed of centre, heel and toe.

8. The comb, the uppermost part of the stock, which attaches

cheek to gun. This can be fixed or variable in height and centre. *See photo 16d on page 16.*

9. The trigger guard, which frames either one or two triggers, depending on the maker's specification. If two triggers, the front trigger will normally fire the right hand or under barrel, the rear trigger will fire the left or over barrel. *See photos 17a,b,c.*

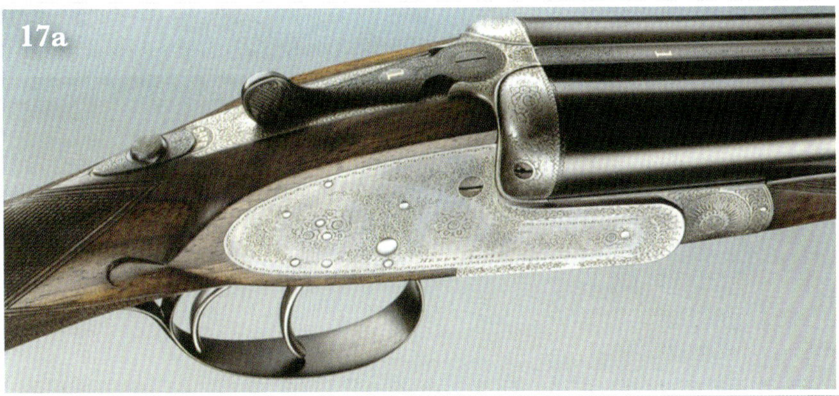

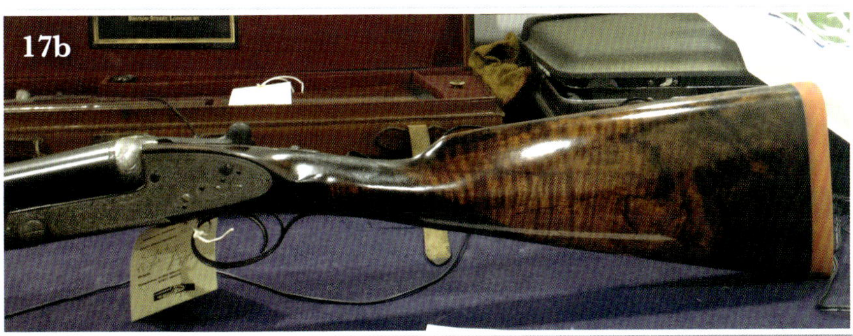

10. The Fore-end which holds barrels and action together, houses other working parts of the gun and may be the part of the gun held by your fore hand. ***See pages 56 and 57.***

11. The muzzle where the shot from the cartridge exits the barrels on its way to the target. The last half an inch being the Choke of your gun. For an understanding of use and variations, see ***Page 159*** on The Choke. ***See photos 18 a,b,c.***

4 The Safety Lecture - A New Angle

So let's take it from the beginning. Whatever I say among these pages will be open to debate, I expect it and welcome it. "You really should have started with…" No matter, I've broad shoulders and I'm happy to debate any issue on this subject which for fifty-five years has been one of my hobbies and for forty two years, my career.

I'm going to start with safety - an issue that all people involved with our sport fortunately agree is of huge importance. The only difference is that I shall take an alternate view to anything I have seen written or heard taught before.

For no matter how long you may shoot, there is one inescapable fact, at some time in your shooting career, you will make a mistake. All you can do is to try and make this mistake as inconsequential as possible. Purely on the law of averages and of diminishing returns, you will make a mistake. Pray that this will not lead to your own or any other person's injury or worse.

Sadly the reality is that we are susceptible to making mistakes. You'll see what I mean.

I teach many people every year. I have spent tens of thousands of hours instructing and yet with someone as familiar with this sport as I am, I have made a mistake. Three decades ago while shooting pigeons on my farm, I was carrying one of the first mobile phones, not dissimilar to a large red brick in your pocket and certainly similar in weight, when from this I received a summons for help from my next door neighbour. There were dogs chasing his sheep and could I come quickly. I slid my shotgun onto the dashboard of my Land

Rover and drove across the farm to our boundary hoping to catch the marauding pack of dogs. Arriving at my neighbour's field, he told me the dogs had run off towards Ballybawn, due south from us. I helped him round up his sheep and deal with two that had been badly injured. Three dead sheep were left in the field. I then drove out onto the lane beyond our farm in the hope that I would spot the dogs. My mission proved a failure and I returned home empty-handed. Taking the gun out of the car I automatically opened the action before walking into my house. I was horrified to find two cartridges still in the gun. In my haste to come to the aid of my neighbour, I had committed the cardinal sin of not unloading my gun when getting into the car. I leave it to you the reader, to conjure up any number of scenarios that may have taken me and my loaded gun and put someone innocent into the path of grave danger. My fortune was that nothing came of my error, but it was only luck that it had not.

As a 'safety rule of thumb', get into the safe routine of always unloading your gun. If in doubt unload, not just break the gun, unload it, no matter how indifferent an obstacle you may have to cross, no matter how familiar the situation. If for one moment there is a doubt in your mind that your gun should be closed and loaded, then break it and unload it.

The first safety element I teach my clients is how to load and close a gun safely. Such a small operation and yet one that is so important to all shooting people everywhere.

Visually check that your barrels are free of any obstruction, whether loading for the first time that day or reloading the gun.

The manner in which you close a shotgun speaks volumes about your own safety practise. Do you notice how people close their guns?

If you do, just what is it that you may notice that will ring alarm bells in your mind? For me it's the gun barrels being lifted to the action rather than the action being lifted to the barrels. What is the difference? Consider where the barrels finish pointing if you lift them to close the gun, they will be pointing on or near waist height. Hardly a safe result. The gun can all too easily be pointing toward another person. Pointing the whole gun at the ground, close your gun by lifting the stock up to the barrels rather than the barrels up to the stock. You will be astonished how many people notice little things such as this.

Loading and closing your gun in the manner above tells those watching you two important facts.

1. That you care about your own safety.
2. You care about the safety of those around you.

I know that when I watch fellow shooters on a gun line, I will all too often judge them on their method of gun closure. Safe or not? I'd rather be with someone who cares for other people's safety than someone who does not. So if you want to be asked back again as a guest or be a welcomed member of a club, adopt these methods, they really pay dividends.

5 Loading The Gun Safely

When driven bird shooting, you make your way to your allotted position or 'peg' that you will shoot from. Each drive has a peg for every gun. Observe where the 'Beaters' may be. These are the ladies and gentlemen who 'work their socks off', fighting through briars, branches and soggy undergrowth, all to find that elusive bird for you to enjoy. Look for where the 'Stops' are positioned in the drive, you'll see them, sometimes along the front of the drive, sometimes down the sides of the flushing point, gently tapping with their sticks to prevent the game escaping on foot. You may also see the 'Flag' men and women on the front of the drive, sometimes there to encourage a bird to fly higher before heading towards the gun line. Sometimes they will be on the wings of the flushing points in order to control the direction of the game. Look behind you for where the 'Pickers' are positioned. The 'Pickers' need special attention as they may well appear only just before the drive starts. Accompanied with their retriever dogs, they may well move their position during the drive to cover an alternative area. Finally check on the whereabouts of your fellow guns. They at least should remain where they started, however, if you are a back gun, you are put there because the shoot captain can really trust you. Don't think you are in a second class position. Remove your gun from its sleeve, ready your cartridges and don't for one moment think there may be a shortage of targets.

When the prearranged signal for the drive to start is given, only then load your gun. Do not shoot the moment you see a bird rise from the flushing cover. Do not shoot along the line of your fellow guns. Do not shoot at a fast dropping or low bird. As soon as you hear the signal to end the drive, unload your gun, replace it in your gun sleeve and make sure there are no live cartridges lying on the ground around your feet.

When clay pigeon shooting, keep your gun in its sleeve or keep your gun broken and empty until you are at the station from where you are about to shoot. Hand your card to the scorer and watch for areas that could be unsafe should your gun at any time be pointing there. When called, enter the station's cage (if they provide one), watch your show birds, (targets that you don't shoot at, but observe for line and speed of flight), only then should you load your gun. Remember you are the person ultimately responsible for what harm you may bring to others. It is you that pulls the trigger.

On completing the card for that stand, unload your gun, check for any live ammunition lying on the ground, collect up spent cartridges and exit the cage. Put your gun back in its sleeve.

When rough shooting, having left public roads, houses and buildings behind, sorted out your gun line, taken note of dogs and plan your directions, then load up. Please understand that there are laws governing the minimum distance there may be between you and a Public Road or Thoroughfare should you choose to discharge your gun. In Ireland that distance is 100 feet from the centre of any public road, track or footpath.

When loading your gun, a glance down both barrels before placing your cartridges in the chambers is essential. I was shooting at a competition on a friend's farm, the station was driven partridge. These are clays that are thrown towards and low over the head of the shooter. I was intent on trying to put up a good score and therefore more concentrated than maybe normal, but I noticed, or maybe I should say, sensed something was amiss after shooting a pair of birds. The sound of the bang wasn't quite right, though the birds had broken and my score was intact. I took two more cartridges and dropped them into the chambers and closed the gun. Something somewhere was ringing an alarm bell. I nearly called for the next pair of birds but stopped, broke the gun and extracted both cartridges. Holding the barrels up to the light, I could see an obstruction down one barrel. My host supplied a gun-cleaning rod and we pushed out the complete plastic hull or tubular section of a cartridge. The hull had separated from the base, normally brass coloured metal, but on this brand, entirely made of plastic. It is open to conjecture what may have occurred should I have fired another cartridge on top of this obstruction, but I would not have retained my fingers should the barrel have blown out.

On another occasion, an old friend and I had gone out rough shooting in some very snowy weather. A foot or so of snow was covering the ground and the dogs were busy searching through undergrowth and quite intent on what scent there was. We, meanwhile, were crossing a barbed wire fence to bring us round the thicket. Quite correctly we unloaded and my friend, then I, crossed the fence. Suddenly from the thicket came a tremendous flapping and out from the branches emerged one cock pheasant and two Labradors hot on his heels. My friend quickly loaded and swung up his gun to fire. There was a loud bang in front of me and the pheasant continued mildly disturbed but totally unharmed. My friend, however, was wondering what on earth he was going to say to his father when he returned home as he had demolished his father's favourite shotgun. While crossing the fence, my friend had brushed the muzzle across the snow and ended up with a little snow in his barrels. When firing the right-hand barrel, the snow was sufficient an obstruction to cause a blow out of the right-hand tube. Normally when the barrel blows, it will often remove the shooter's fingers or thumb, but fortunately for my friend, he was in such a hurry to get off his shot, his front hand was positioned partly under the action, partly on the adjoining part of the fore-end and out of harm's way. More good fortune, depending on your point of view. His father, however, was somewhat distraught at the prospect that his son may have lost his hand.

These are all perfectly true unembellished stories, told so that you will realise that mistakes can be made and accidents do happen, even, as my father would have said, in the best regulated families.

A final word and an important one, before loading your guns, check to see what length chambers your shotgun has. The chambers are the initial part of the barrel, nearest to the action where you place the cartridge. Where the chambers and the barrel proper meet, the excess width of the chamber is reduced by a cone known as the forcing cone. To illustrate what I mean, the average internal diameter of the chamber of a 12 bore shotgun is 810/1000" and the average barrel bore diameter is 735/1000".

Chamber lengths normally measure from:

2”	or	50 mm
2.5”	or	65 mm
2.75”	or	70 mm
3”	or	75 mm

See photo 26 a,b on page 26.

It’s very important that cartridges loaded do not exceed the specified length of the chamber. If this mistake is made, when firing the gun it puts excessive pressures on the structure of the gun, principally on the chopper lumps or equivalent. The ‘Chopper Lumps’ or similar are the parts of the barrel that engage in the action floor or action sides to hold both parts together. Submit them to excess pressure and something has to give way. If this error continues over an extended period of time, the gun’s mechanism or action will become loose. Match your cartridge length to the figure pressed in the steel on the flats of your barrels. This is on the outside section of your barrels

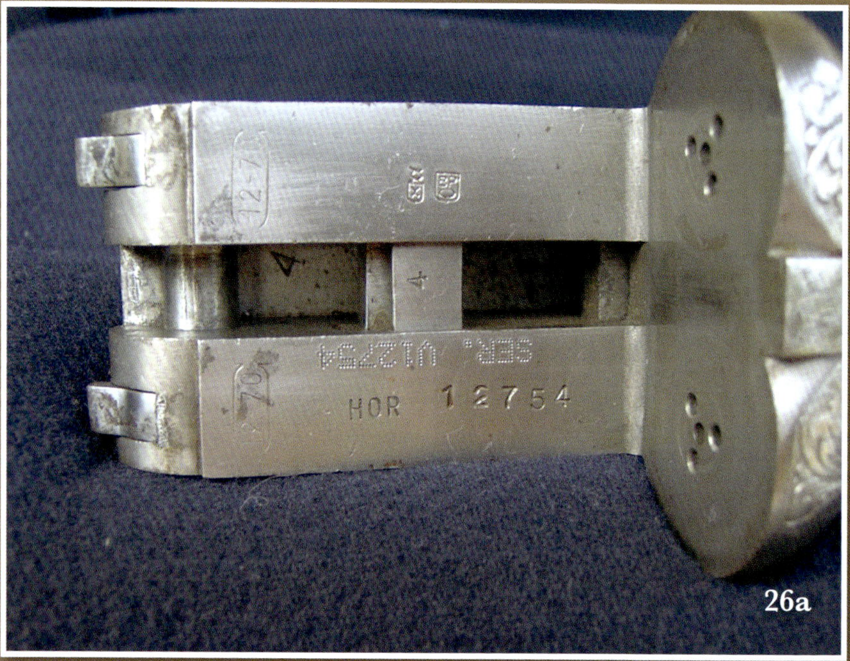

26a

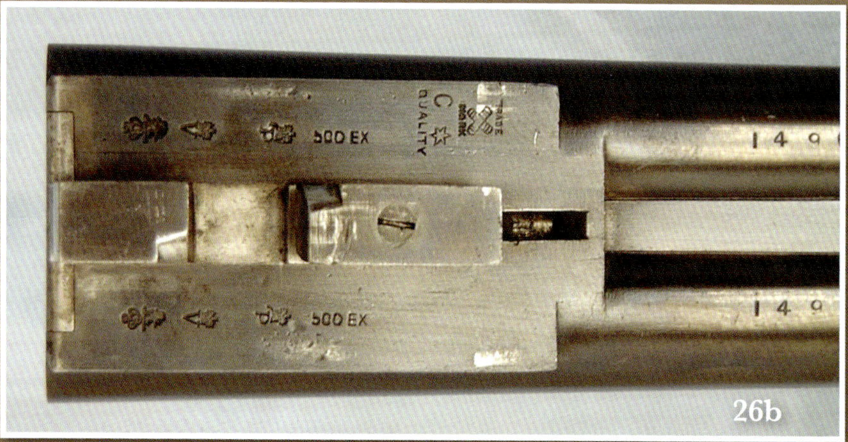

26b

under the chambers that engage with the action floor or engraved on the outside of the barrels near the breach end of the shotgun.
See photos 26 a,b, on page 26.

Together with the chamber lengths, there are a number of other marks which have been stamped on the flats of your barrels. Should you wish to know what these stand for, go to your local gunsmith and ask. It's important information that may be crucial to your safety. For instance, it is of the utmost importance that you should know if your gun is Nitro powder proofed if you are to use modern Nitro cartridges in the gun. It is quite possible that the gun may only have been tested and approved for the use of Black Powder, an older form of propellant producing lower pressures. Indeed it is possible, though unlikely, that the gun may never have been proof-tested. If the gun is not proofed for Nitro powders, you will be subjecting the gun to much higher pressures than the gun is designed to take. If you own a gun that is only proofed for Black powder, ask your gunsmith for his advice. Should you immediately change the barrels? Is it worth the expense of doing so? Is it worth sending the gun to a proofing house with a risk of the barrels being destroyed should they not meet approved standards? If the proofing house find the barrels are out of proof, the gun will be declared unfit for use unless re-sleeved or re-barreled.

Re-barreled means replacing the barrels entirely, so the ribs, top and bottom, the bead, cartridge lifters or ejectors are removed and then everything from muzzle to breach including all elements of chambers, forcing cones and tubes are replaced. Re-sleeved means cutting off the tubes at the end of the forcing cones and affixing two new tubes to the chambers. When this work has been carried out, the barrels are re-submitted to the proof house and tested again. If they pass, the proof house will engrave either re-barreled or re-sleeved on the barrel flats and affix their proof house mark.

However, if the proofing house declares the gun to be fit for use, this will give you a considerable sense of security, rather than a growing element of doubt.

I was invited to a friend's house for lunch the other day. I was led into an old fashioned kitchen with a range and all sorts of curious artefacts. A butter churn on the floor, old pots and pans through the scullery door and the largest copper fish kettle I have ever seen. Beside the range, leaning against the wall, was a very old 12 bore hammer gun. When she saw me looking at it she asked me what I thought of it. Rather a rhetorical question when you are the one invited to lunch. *"Don't you think the engraving is lovely? Aren't the barrels wonderfully shiny."* I picked up the gun, looked at the small amount of very worn engraving on the action, took off the fore-end and then inspected the Damascus barrels. *"Do you really want an honest answer?"* I asked. *"Oh yes, absolutely,"* was the reply. Presuming that this was where I would ruin any chance of being re-invited, I had another long look at the various parts of the gun and then told her that the gun was potentially lethal to any one using it. Her face dropped. Was this some sort of personal affront? She then related to me the previous day's use of the gun, when she and a friend had been out shooting woodcock. *"Nothing had happened then! The gun worked perfectly well."* Looking down those barrels, it was clear to me that someone had mechanically polished them, I would suppose to try and hide the deep pitting throughout both barrels. 'Pitting' is the word to use when there has been severe corrosion caused by burnt powders or rust attacking the metal on the inside of the tubes. There was also a hollow point near the end of the left tube which must have been wafer thin as the hollow inside was not reflected by a bump on the outside of the tube. The fact that someone had done this and then sold the gun on to her was tantamount to a criminal act. Furthermore, there were no proof marks on the barrel flats indicating a weapon built well before 1904 and prior to the laws governing guns sold within the British Isles and excluding Scotland. There was no indication of a tested ability to withstand the pressures of Nitro powder. This weapon was little more than a serious accident about to happen. Picking up some cartridges off the kitchen dresser, I asked if these were similar to the ones she had used yesterday? "Absolutely the same," she said. I explained the problems that she would face when matching a 2.5" chambered barrel and 2.75" cartridge and then explained the differences in black powder compared to modern powder.

The difference is in chemical composition. The much older type of propellant was called 'Black Powder', producing larger quantities of smoke, being very likely to fail in combustion due to humidity or damp and leaving larger quantities of highly corrosive ash within the barrel.

Modern powder, a form of cordite is a chemical composition including major elements such as nitroglycerine, gun cotton and petroleum jelly, producing rods of combustibles then set and flaked as a propellant.

'Caveat emptor' translates to, 'buyer see to it' or 'buyer beware.' In other words the buyer must critically inspect the goods on offer and realise that he or she is the ultimate judge of the item being purchased. Please be careful who you buy a gun from. If you are buying a gun from a private source, ask the seller if you may take it to a reputable gunsmith and get them to check it and approve it. If the seller is a bone fide individual, why would he or she complain if you make this part of the deal?

With a note of relief, we remain friends, thank the heavens, though at one stage it was a close run thing. No one appreciates the messenger with bad news. Should you wish to read more on Damascus barrels, please see definition page 131. ***Photos on page 30.***

Dangers of the game

6 The Master Or Dominant Eye

Just because you are right-handed, it doesn't necessarily follow that you have a right master or dominant eye. Just because you are left-handed, it doesn't… you get the point?

Three different factors will determine one's master or dominant eye. However, before we dip into that, I should explain what is a dominant eye and why it is a factor in successfully shooting a shotgun.

I have never encountered a person that has not got some element of dominance in one eye or the other. Either our right or our left eye will always be the dominant eye. This means that for ultimate control of direction and alignment, for a circumstance that needs precision, the brain uses the pictures coming in from one of our eyes, not both.

N.B. Please note the degree of dominance discussed later.

When shooting with a shotgun, it is advantageous to shoot with both eyes open. Using both eyes gives us judgment of distance, angle and speed, which is an integral part of dealing with a moving target. That judgment is achieved by the use of binocular vision. Shut one eye and your spatial awareness is immediately compromised. If you want to know what I mean, get into your car and try driving down the road with one eye closed (not that I would recommend you should do so on a public road). You won't keep it closed for long!

With both eyes open you also retain peripheral vision with the 'spare' eye. When shooting, if there are multiple targets in the air, possibly coming from other directions than the first you have seen, you may be aware of these before someone with their spare eye closed.

32a

32b

32c

So if you are to shoot with **both** eyes open, you must bring the gun to the eye that is dominant. Bringing the gun up to your non-master eye makes it impossible to correctly direct the gun. Let me further explain:

Let us suppose you have a right master eye. You bring the gun up to this eye keeping the gun on the right cheek. All well so far. Your right master eye is looking straight down the middle of the barrel. Your left eye is now to the left of the centre line and views the gun from the left side only. This side view will not affect the direction of the gun as your master eye has control of the centre line and therefore exactly where the gun points.

Now let's put the cat amongst the pigeons and change the gun to the left cheek and line up supposedly with the left eye. However, because you have a right master eye, the right eye will continue to attempt to direct the weapon, yet the eye is misaligned down the right side of the barrels. The result is that the barrels are 'pulled' to the right so that the end of the barrels align with the master eye and the target. The actual direction of the barrels will now be excessively to the right of the target.

To determine which eye is dominant proceed in the following way. Hold your hands out in front of you at arms length with your palms facing away from you. Now turn your hands so your finger tips face each other. Move one hand slightly in front of the other so they overlap. Not so the fingers interlock, just overlap. Next, drop your thumbs so they create a three sided frame for you to look through. Pick a target, something small and with **both eyes open,** swivel your hands towards each other until your thumbs overlap and you create a very small aperture to look through. Keeping your target visible in the aperture, bring both your hands slowly back to your face all the way to one eye or the other and you can see for yourself which is your master or dominant eye. You have just identified it. *See photos 32 a,b,c on page 32.*

Dominance Left Or Right

You probably remember that I referred to three factors that can affect one's master eye. Normal dominance either left or right is the first. It should be noted that the dominant factor is not simply 100% right and 0% left. In other words, either you have a right master eye or you have a left master eye. Human beings have many attributes which are part 'A' and part 'B'. We deal in percentages of 'A' and 'B'. You can have a domination of 60% right 40% left or I may have a dominance factor 85% left and 15% right. Dominance by degrees. The greater the degree of dominance of one eye over the other, the easier it becomes to shoot with both eyes open. This disparity I believe can change with time and ultimately become more definitive to the benefit of the shooter. If you are someone who finds it difficult to shoot with both eyes open, firstly, get a qualified instructor to determine which is your master eye if you can't. The possible problem that you are having to deal with is a low percentage dominance between one eye and the other (i.e. 55% right to 45% left). Assuming that you are shooting with your master eye, then close your non-dominant eye and shoot this way for several months, practicing on clay pigeons as much as possible. Over time, the master eye may assert itself more definitely and you may eventually be able to open that non-dominant eye and shoot using binocular vision. Determine this by shooting at a straight incoming or outgoing clay. If with your eye closed you hit your target, then open the spare eye and if your shot is then misaligned, you will have to go back to shooting with the spare eye closed. I have taught many persons who have a marginal or small degree of dominance and the option is always to continue with the spare eye closed. Why give up a wonderful sport because someone is advising you that you must shoot with both eyes open?

They don't understand the intricacies of the eyes.

Can dominance change from one eye to the other? Not as a rule but there are two circumstances where I know that the dominant eye has changed.

A teenager, about 14 at the time, was helping his father remove plaster from an interior wall of their house. Being a little over enthusiastic with hammer on chisel, the chisel went through the plaster and struck a lump of stone. From this a chip of granite came off the wall and buried itself in the pupil passage of this lad's right eye. After many complications, the eye was saved but that right eye had been the lad's master eye. It was constantly covered up for many weeks and during that time the lad was determined to continue shooting. With his right eye unavailable, he started shooting left-handed. Eventually the right eye was uncovered but mastership or dominance had switched from right eye to left eye. So the gun stayed put on the left cheek. How do I know this? I was the over enthusiastic lad.

If you are shooting with the gun aligned to your non-dominant eye, you have a decision to make. Do you stay put with this eye (while ensuring that the dominant eye remains closed) or do you change the gun to the dominant side? An important decision. If the decision should be to change to shooting with your dominant eye, find yourself an instructor who really knows how to change people from one cheek to the other to oversee the process. This is not one to tackle on your own. I have changed many shooters over the years and it can be done without difficulty provided the shooter is committed to the change. It actually takes me about 20 minutes to change a person from right to left or vice versa, but it must be done in the correct manner. It also must be their decision, and not one that the instructor persuades or pushes them to take. A clear appraisal of the pros and cons for shooting with or without the master eye should be given to the client and then **they only** should make the decision to change sides… or not.

An old friend of my father, William was his name, spoke to me over a drink at a cocktail party. He was 70 and had shot on Ireland's foremost shoots and travelled to the UK every year shooting right-handed since he was 11. Being a very precise individual, he told me his normal average was one bird shot for every sixteen and a quarter attempted and, for a gentleman who shot on some of the British Isles' most famous shoots, it was a poor return by any gun's standards. I asked him to give me half an hour of his time, which some days later he did. I watched him take three shots right-handed and realised that here was a man with a strong left master eye. Every time he shot, the left eye was wide open together with his right. Each of his three shots had been at a 'medium height driven pheasant' of the clay pigeon variety and straight over his head. Each of those shots missed the target 2.0 metres to the left. His left master eye was busily dominating procedures. So what to do? Here was a man who had been shooting for 59 years but still wanted to improve. I gave him a clear appraisal of the situation and I pointed out that provided he kept his left eye closed every time he had his gun mounted, he could expect reasonable and improved returns from his shooting. Open the left eye at all when shooting and he really couldn't expect to make contact with the target.

"No contest," I hear you say, at his age the decision is *"shut the dominant eye"*. If, that is, you can. He couldn't! Not without the other eye following suit. No matter how William tried, either both eyes would close or both would be open.

Five options are now open to us:

1. Change the gun from right to left cheek… Possible

2. Use a patch over the master eye when shooting…
   Major impediment
3. Use a blotting disc attached to a barrel sleeve…
   Possible but debatable on effect
4. Use a blotting disc on one lens of his glasses… Possible
5. Caste the gun to be an 'across eyed' stock… Very expensive

I asked him if he was right handed?
"Yes" was the reply.
Huge advantage I said.
"Why," asked William?
Hand eye coordination I said. If shooting off your left cheek, which hand controls the direction of the gun?
"The front hand," he said. (He was right-handed.)
If both your hands were in your pockets and I asked you to point at me, which hand would naturally come out of your pocket?
"Probably my right", he replied.
So if the gun was now on your left cheek with your master eye, which hand would be out front in control of the gun?
"My right."
The hand that controls all your sporting activities. Your natural resource for writing and pointing, now in charge of the gun. Better by far than the comparative stranger that is attached to the end of your left arm. Cross domination can have its advantages!

Finally I pointed out to William that as a banker, I was surprised he was prepared to pay for other people to shoot his birds for him!

After a little thought and calling me a cheeky blighter, option number one, to change from right to left, was selected by William. I went through a few words of advice, told him that the first time it would feel very strange, the second time rather odd. What I didn't tell him was that I thought he would make no comment after this. I placed the gun in the correct position on his left shoulder and cheek and then released a clay for him to shoot. He smashed it! After some 5 minutes of shooting, he was confidently breaking clays with his shotgun now on his left cheek. Initially the gun was mounted to his cheek before calling the bird. By the time 15 minutes of shooting was up, my father's friend was starting with his gun semi-mounted or half way to the cheek, after another five minutes he was fully mounting the gun to his cheek and shooting with complete confidence.

As he put it to me:
"The gun's suddenly straight in front of me instead of me seeing down the side of the barrel. I'm now looking straight down the middle of the barrel, the whole operation makes sense in my mind and I'm no longer trying to constantly compensate for a crooked barrel."

His words, not mine. He left me after a few more minutes having paid his bill and exchanged some news about his family. He still shoots as regularly as his time allows and does so off his left cheek. He never mentions the fact but takes great delight in his shooting average which he says meanders between 2.5 and 3.5 to one. Delight for me! I know that when some people read this, they will doubt the time factor of 20 minutes taken to achieve this, they may even doubt that this can be done at all. I can't blame them for that reaction, I myself doubted that this was possible when I first attempted to help a client. I have no doubt now.

I know that the decision to change the side you shoot from, because of one's master eye, should be based on the aspirations and capabilities of the shooter. If you intend shooting clay pigeons non-competitively, then there is little need to concern yourself with the advantages of binocular vision. The target will only have one basic flight path. However, if your intended clay pigeon competition is double-trap, ball trap, skeet, or sporting clays, if you intend shooting any game birds such as snipe, woodcock, duck, grouse, or vermin such as wood pigeon or magpies, consider your options. In other words, if your target is going to be difficult to acquire or your target may suddenly change angle, line, height or speed, you would be better with binocular vision. If you are receiving multiple targets from many angles, if you have both eyes open, your spare eye's peripheral vision will be providing you with some very useful information on targets appearing elsewhere while you are busy shooting the one already selected.

N.B. If you are shooting using your non-master or non-dominant eye, be assured that if your master eye opens during your tracking and shooting at the bird, it will result in a missed shot. Your choice is to change your shooting cheek or be certain your eye remains closed.

A lot of people unnecessarily point out to me that I shoot left-handed. Whether this is still viewed as an oddity or why this should be a subject for comment, I know not. Suffice to say that it is sometimes remarked on. When this comment is made to me, I find it hard to relate to, because all physical direction of the operation is through my right hand. My left hand is there as a minor assistant to the right and there to operate the safety catch, pull the triggers and push the top lever. It's not there to guide and control where my gun points. I still think that the operation is so controlled from the right, how can I call it left-handed? Strange how our minds work. It is true to say that it is my left eye that is governing the relationship of barrel to bird and for that only, it is a left eyed operation for me.

Centre Vision

This is the second of our three factors determining which side we shoot from. In the case of centre vision, I have NEVER met a single person in the last 42 years of professional instructing who have genuine centre vision. This is a natural condition where there is a 50% 50% split between their left and right eyes and therefore no dominant eye. If you find you are in this category, may I be the first to congratulate and sympathise with you. Your rarity value must be phenomenal, but your choice to use binocular vision when shooting is taken away. You have three methods open to you and they are firstly, to keep whichever eye the gun is not mounted to firmly closed. (If you shoot off the right cheek, you must keep your left eye shut and if you shoot off the left cheek, you must keep your right eye shut.) Secondly, to use a blot out patch on your barrels. Thirdly, to use a blot out patch on the lens of your glasses.

NB. A barrel sleeve is available from a good gunsmith and one with a blot out disc attached can still be obtained. Bring your gun with you to test the positioning of the disc is suitable for you before you purchase one. That being said, a much easier way of dealing with the problem is using a patch on your glasses or sunglasses. This is an adhesive disc, a maximum of 2 cm in diameter, which you position yourself on the lens of your glasses serving your 'spare' eye.

Dyslexia

A subject which I have yet to see being addressed in other shooting books. Nonetheless it is a factor with some aspiring shooters. Not all dyslexics will find that this affliction compromises their shooting, but for those who do suffer its indignities, the problem is this. When you test a client for their master eye, you will receive a normal response either left or right. So the lesson begins, all appears well. Ten minutes later you find yourself once more checking the client's master eye for right or left dominance. What tested as right eye or left eye dominance has suddenly changed from one side to the other for no apparent reason. Not only can the instructor see the change, but the client will complain that they are suddenly seeing down the side of the barrels, instead of down the centre of the barrels. So what to do? The use of pink tinted glasses that are sometimes prescribed for those suffering with dyslexia don't seem to make any difference when shooting. If you are one of those who find no effect from these glasses, then the only choice is to close an eye when shooting. The dominance will come back to one eye more emphatically than the other and it is to that eye that you must concentrate your efforts. If you suddenly find yourself seeing the gun from the side, then close an eye temporarily, until the dominance reasserts itself.

The son of some great friends of mine started learning to shoot with me. He was so keen, so determined to do well and become a fine shot. He most certainly inherited his parent's sporting abilities and enthusiasm, he possibly inherited dyslexia as well, but I was not aware of dyslexia being an influencing factor at the time. A natural ability to perform is such a wonderful thing for an instructor to find in a pupil. Geoffrey was one such individual and watching his ability develop was a tremendous return for me. He had arrived with me shooting off his right cheek, but it soon became clear that the eye favoured as his dominant eye was his left. Throwing caution to the winds is not something I'm inclined to do when teaching, and as he was already shooting very well from the right with his left eye closed, I was reluctant to suggest alteration to shooting from the left. Nonetheless, when he tried shooting with binocular vision, it was most apparent that he had a very strong left master eye. If Geoff wished to, it was an ideal time to rebuild his shooting and relocate his gun on his left cheek and therefore aligned with his left eye.

After a lengthy period of discussion with Geoff, most of which was taken up with a question and answer session on his own aspirations and ambitions, he decided that he would take the option of shooting off his left cheek, thereby benefiting from the use of binocular vision. From right to left took the usual 20 minutes and we were underway again. After a further ten minutes of Geoffrey shooting left-handed, to my horror I started seeing his shot consistently being placed to the right of his targets. Had I made a mistake when assessing which his master eye was? All I could do was to check again. Gun down, hands out, back to back, frame made, swivel together the hands with both eyes open… sure enough the dominance went to his right. I had been certain when doing this at the start, that the dominant side was his left. Puzzled, even more concerned, I asked him to change back to shooting right handed, just for a few shots. Within the time in takes to shoot four clay pigeons, the placement of his shots were now wide to the left of his target. His dominance had changed again to the left eye. Gun down, frame made with his hands, eyes both open, aperture created, dominance left and strongly to the left. I could see he was not one of those rare 'centre vision' shooters but what was the cause of this switching? I knew that Geoff had been diagnosed with dyslexia and made notes to that effect. I then spoke to other clients and other instructors, trying to identify a similar case or cases. To my fascination, I found three more records of difficulty in this area, all of them dyslexics. What had I unearthed here and was it something already familiar to experts in the field of dyslexia? My concern in this case, where dyslexia is an interfering factor, is well founded. The dominant eye will change from time to time, creating confusion in the mind of the shooter and potentially denting their self-confidence.

So where did that leave Geoffrey? I'm happy to say that he used his binocular vision shooting from the left cheek with both eyes open, and when the dyslexia effect kicked in and his master eye would change, he would then shoot with his right eye closed for a few shots and then open to see if it had changed back. On almost every occasion it had. Furthermore, he told me that the occasions where it would hop from left to right became fewer and less frequent. I shan't forget him.

7 Gun Speed Or Lack Of It

Preparation for the Novice

Getting the 'feel of the gun' must come next. I'm a great believer in preparing every sensory component that is involved when a client has never shot before. They should be totally familiar with all aspects of the gun firing, so before they point the gun and shoot at a real target, I introduce them to the first of these, the trigger pull. Such an innocent and trifling item, but if you have never pulled a trigger before, it remains a question mark and therefore an uncertainty, even a fear. Handing the gun to the client and positioning their hands, pointing the gun skywards, I then also take hold of the gun, one hand under the Butt, the other beside theirs on the Fore-end. Moving the gun vertically, up and down slowly, I count down from three, two, one, Fire. The client pulls the trigger. As simple as that. If you think this insignificant, watch the face of the new shooter when they pull the trigger. I will ask them to do it again, with the gun still pointing to the heavens, not in the shoulder or to the cheek, this time emphasising to the client to feel the weight or force needed to pull the trigger. This time there will be less suspicion and only slight tension. I will get them to repeat this again until I see the tension leave their face and no flinch at all. Familiarity is important and leads to building confidence. It is the start of learning a skill, and the client will recognise the advantages.

Use Of Leading Hand

At this stage, instead of complicating the issue with an unfamiliar and potentially awkward object such as a gun, I ask the client to put the gun down and instead, hold out their arm and the hand that will hold the front end of the gun, their index and second fingers extended. The arm, hand and fingers represents their gun. The purpose is to show the client the speed of the gun when pointing at a moving target. I often will tell my client the actual speed of the clay pigeon when it leaves the trap and then while pointing at a flying bird myself, get them to watch the speed of my hand. "Did the speed of my hand look fast to you?" Invariably the client will say no.

Why use the arm and not the gun? Your arm and those two fingers of yours are a lot easier to manoeuvre than the weight of the gun. It is all too easy for the client to find it physically demanding if they are not used to holding a gun, or are not that strong. When practising this part of the operation, there is no need to burden the client with the weight of their gun, their leading hand will do the job.

It is often the case that a client when asked to cover the bird, will swing the gun up to the target and when the target disappears behind the barrel, will briefly stop and when the target reappears, they then quickly swing the gun back to the target, each time they cover it, the same slight hesitation and then a rush to cover it again. This is human nature. Concerned where their target might be having seen it disappear, they stop to check its whereabouts and then remember the job they were given.

If you observe a novice shot attempting to point the barrels at their target, when the target appears, you will frequently see them snatch the barrels towards it. Why? A combination of surprise at seeing the target and a wish to get to it quickly in order to save time. Our ability to assess the speed of an object is truly amazing. We can easily determine that the target is flying at considerable speed. Where we tend to err is to assume we must at least match the speed of the target with the speed of the gun. Therefore if the target is flying at 45 mph the gun should be doing the same. In actuality, the gun, when tracking the target, will appear to be moving in slow motion. Extend your arm and front hand towards where you will see your target, two fingers forward, the rest folded away. Those two fingers are representing your barrels. As the bird flies out from the trap, just point at the target and be aware of the speed of your hand during the flight of the bird. You will be amazed at how slowly your hand is moving.

If you understand how slowly the gun needs to move, you are much more likely to take your time and use that time to correctly position the gun in relation to the target before pulling the trigger. If you think there is very little time to shoot, you are much more likely to rush the process and your decision on when to shoot is more likely to be taken before the gun is correctly positioned.

Barrel Speed

The importance of slow gun speed is best illustrated to a client by using my two index fingers. Holding the left finger upright and still, and the other finger horizontal and pointing to the left of my other, I ask my client to imagine that my finger represents the barrel of their gun. I tell them I'm going to move my finger from right to left passing my other finger at a medium speed. I ask them to say 'now' when my moving finger is pointing exactly at the centre of my target finger.

Moving my finger across, the client will attempt to say 'NOW' at the appropriate moment. Almost always the look on their faces tells me that they think their 'NOW' was badly timed. I will ask them are they sure that their 'NOW' was correct, but before they answer, I'll ask them to try again.

This time, moving my hand very slowly from right to left past my target finger, they can see that with slow movement of the indicating finger, it is much easier to be absolutely sure when the finger (their barrel) points where they wish it to be.

Slow hands make shooting easier… keep your gun movement slow.
See photos 47 a,b on page 47.

47a

47b

8 Ear Defence

My next part of the client preparation is to issue headphones or ear 'muffs or defenders' to all present. You may scoff at the necessity for wearing ear defenders, you may find them inconvenient due to you missing the sound of a bird taking off, or put you at a disadvantage when a clay pigeon is due to appear and you can't hear the trap go off, or marvel at how well they block out the incessant words of an instructor! Let me tell you just how damaging the sound of a shotgun firing can be. I was at the till of a local supermarket one morning, prior to spending a few hours writing that afternoon, and the lady at the check out asked me if I had a loyalty card. There was a mixture of piped music and conversation going on to my left (my good side) and my right ear was turned toward the checkout girl. I had no idea what she was saying to me until I turned my left ear towards her and cupped my hand to it. It is true to say that most of this damage was done by a client who pulled their trigger when my head was little more than two inches from the muzzle of his gun. A frightening experience and, I'm relieved to say, a genuine mistake by my client. It has, however, left me almost completely deaf in my right ear. To compound this, I now have Tinnitus in both ears. My long suffering partner has to repeat a lot of what she says and I sympathise with her. I'm told that my remaining hearing is average for a man of my age… whatever that means.

Insofar as equipment for this job is concerned, below I shall give you a list of what is available and how the product performs. That said, it must be on the understanding that my own ear specialist insisted that anything that doesn't cover the bone mass at the back and front of the ear was completely useless. His contention is that any loud sound can be transmitted via bone into the receptor areas within the ear. Damaging sound can be transmitted just as effectively. I leave this argument up to you to decide upon, I follow my specialists advice.

N.B. With the following options the ear canal is blocked and sound cannot travel to the inner ear. However, it is clinically proven that the bone behind the ear can deliver harmful levels of sound into the inner ear. In their opinion and mine, the only safe solution are headphones.

Cotton Wool

Reduces all sounds but I found it tended to work its way loose.

Foam Plugs

Roll them between your fingers until they are very thin and then put in place before they expand. Fairly effective and again all sounds are reduced.

Wax

Moulds to the shape of your ear canal. Most sounds are gone.

Hard Plastic

These ear plugs must fit properly. They need to be specially moulded. Too big and they tend to hurt after a period of use, too small and they leave gaps in the ear canal. Poor choice.

Soft Plastic

These are ear plugs fitted with a pressure equalising valve. Not bad for short periods of wear but I find them starting to ache after a couple of hours. The insert to your ear canal must have two flanges.

Headphones

Check safety standard. Can sometimes get in the way of the gun's stock if they are too bulky. Sounds are reduced safely.

Electronic Plugs

Very expensive, very effective. A similar system to the electronic phones with a sound gate. They are moulded in your ear by a specialist, but I would remind you of the exposed bone around the ear.

The Best Options

Electronic Headphones

Undoubtedly the best, but check safety standard on each make. Buy with rechargeable batteries as you can plug into the cigar lighter in the car whilst travelling to or from your shoot or with disposable batteries. The electronics work using a sound gate which shuts when detecting a noise of 80 decibels or more. They also include two on board microphones so that you can hear really well what is going on around you. Beware of a very wide earphone, it may interfere with your gun mount. A slim profile earphone works without tapping against the stock of your firearm. If you still find this happening, consult with a good shooting instructor and they will show you how best to mount your gun.

And Finally

Parsley

It seemed to work in the 'Asterix' books, but must only be used by genuine Roman Legionnaires and all Gauls.

9 Mounting The Shotgun

The design of a modern side by side or over and under shotgun is an evolution of hundreds of years of gun manufacture. Today's weapon hasn't changed radically since the end of the nineteenth century, and it was designed so that the human body could fit as naturally as possible with it. So when you mount the shotgun consider this question. Would it make sense or is it logical, that someone would have designed a gun where it would necessitate you screwing yourself into any slightly or wholly unnatural shape in order for you to use it? If you find yourself in a uncomfortable position having mounted your gun, there must be something wrong with either your method of gun mount, the gun you are using or both. If you feel you come under this heading, I would strongly suggest you consult an instructor before you do some damage to yourself. Don't fall into bad habits which may have an adverse affect on your performance with the gun and may take a lot of time to rectify in the future.

When you mount your shotgun, your primary thought should be just this: bring the gun to the cheek first. In fact the gun should arrive to both cheek and shoulder but I want you to consider the cheek as your reference point for where the gun needs to be when correctly mounted. By bringing the gun to your cheek first, your head should remain in a totally natural position on top of your shoulders. If you find your head searching for the gun as the gun rises, either by moving forward, down, sideways or a combination of any... **STOP!** ***See photos 52 a,b on page 52.***

Keep your head still and in a natural position when mounting the gun, **bring the gun to your cheek first.** If your gun comes up to your shoulder first, then you will lower your head to the gun, potentially into an uncomfortable and unnatural position, the first

52a

52b

thing your subconscious will do is to return your head to its natural position. This may mean your head lifting before or when you take your shot and can be the cause of several problems, the principal ones being missed birds and possible injuries to your face. The gun mount when executed correctly, leaves the comb of the stock pressed firmly to the underside of the cheekbone with the cheekbone resting on the top surface of the comb, the two both firmly locked together.

There are several problems encountered with someone mounting their gun to the shoulder before the cheek. To begin with, when bringing the gun to the shoulder first, the individual is likely to lower their head to the comb. Remember we are trying to keep the head in an upright and natural position. The next problem is that the individual may only occasionally get their cheekbone all the way to the comb of the stock; more often than not, the head and stock make contact somewhere around the side of their jaw bone. Under these circumstances, their eye is positioned high above the correct sight line and is now inaccurately seeing where the gun is pointing. As a result there is little other than guess work steering the gun. Lastly, when the gun is being brought to the shoulder first, this mistake can often be accompanied by another major error, which is the muzzle of the gun travelling downwards in the opposite direction, therefore pointing anywhere but towards the bird. If your target is going up and your barrels are going in the opposite direction, you are clearly wasting valuable time. While you are bringing the gun to your cheek, your equally important job is to keep the barrels pointing at the target.

Now for the shoulder. The gun having reached the cheek, it also needs to make contact with the shoulder. It just sits on the shoulder, just resting there. **NOT** pulled tight into the shoulder. (For more explanation, see section on 'Recoil'). The butt of the stock should be sitting outside the clavicle and inside the rotator cuff, the heel of the butt in line with the top of the shoulder.

Last but not least, your rear elbow. There's a place for everything and more often than not there's a very good reason behind it. In this case there are three good reasons for its correct position. The position first. Your elbow is held high. If you draw a straight line from point of shoulder to point of shoulder, your upper arm will be a continuation of that straight line, all the way to the point of your elbow. Why this position?

The first reason is that holding your upper arm and elbow at right angles to your body will hold the gun firmly to the side of your cheek. The second reason is best discovered by you lifting your rear elbow to the correct position without your gun and with your other hand feel the area between your rotator cuff and collarbone where the gun should sit, you will feel a vertical slot or pocket. As you lift the elbow, this pocket will become more pronounced. Furthermore, with your elbow raised in that manner, the large muscle that emerges from under one's arm and stretches across to the sternum will afford greater protection to the clavicle. The fourth reason is marginal but I believe it helps. When right handers are swinging a gun to their right, a high elbow tends to keep the gun swinging in a straighter line. A low elbow will sometimes allow the swing to curve downwards, dragging the gun down and away from the correct line of the bird. For those shooting left-handed, this is applicable when swinging your gun to the left.

The Bead

At the muzzle end of the barrels on the upper side will be found the bead. Sometimes made of brass, or other alloy, sometimes of coloured plastic or bakelite and sometimes like the proverbial blue moon, out of gold and even something as exotic as Lapis Lazuli. Irrespective of its composition, the bead is there to indicate whether the gun is in correct alignment with your master eye. When the gun is correctly on your cheek, check that the end of the rib nearest your eye is in alignment with the bead, or that the bead appears to be sitting centred on the rib and therefore centred on top of the action. If this is the case, then the gun will be pointing accurately where you wish it to point. It is also vitally important to realise that if the bead is only very slightly out of line on the rib or action, maybe as little as a tenth of an inch off centre, it will mean that the barrels may be pointing 18" or 0.5 metre to the left or right of a target say 50 feet above you, not straight at it. The higher your target, the greater the mistake. This is equally true on any angle of bird to the shooter.

The bead is not the sight of a shotgun. So if the bead is not the sight, what is? Unlike a rifle or hand gun, which both have a rear sight and a foresight, a shotgun's sights are its barrels. What this means is that when aligning the gun on an incoming or outgoing bird, you use the barrels to cover the target, not cover it with the bead. For a crossing bird, place the target in line with the side of the barrels, not in line with the bead. There are variables on this point and if you are keen to gather more information, it is worth reading the section on 'Fitting the Gun'.

Please note that the 'Top Lever' plays no part in the sighting of your shotgun with the target. A few of my clients have thought that the bead must be aligned with the 'Top Lever', it does not. The misunderstanding comes from rifle or handgun shooting where the firearm has a 'Rear Sight' and 'Foresight".

The Front Hand Position

You now need to control where the gun is pointing and it is with the front hand that most of this movement is managed. Your front hand position is easily determined. Mount the gun to your cheek, extend your front arm fully without holding the gun, then relax the elbow joint. The arm will bend very slightly. Now hold the barrels with that hand. At this point may I suggest that when you take hold of the barrels with your front hand, you extend your index finger along the underside of the barrels, pointing towards the muzzle. It remains as a support but also gives direction to the gun, the barrels being an extension of the index finger. This is not a definitive, some of you may prefer to have the index finger in combination with your other fingers, but it is a method that I have used since I began shooting and find it very successful both for myself and my clients. If you find the gun feels very heavy with your hand in a long grip position, due to a shortage of power in your front arm, shorten your grip until you feel you can cope with the weight of the barrels.

See photos 57 a,b,c,d.

57a

57b

57c

57d

Hand-Eye Coordination

So why such a long grip with the front hand? I'm sure you will agree that the direction and control of the barrels are an all important factor in shooting. The position and control of the muzzle of the gun determines your success. The further down the barrels you extend your front hand, the more control you will have of where the muzzle of the gun will point. The further back towards the action your hand is, the more this hand will become a fulcrum to the lever of your back hand. This is especially so when you are right-handed and shooting off the right cheek and the same for the left-handed shooting off the left cheek. In this case, because your back hand is your natural choice for control, there is a considerable temptation to direct operations from this hand. **Avoid at all costs.** You need to switch over total directional control to the front hand. If you find this difficult to do, before you mount the gun, squeeze the fore-end or the barrels and maintain a strong grip with this hand and I would strongly advise you to lock your wrist. By holding the gun tight with your front hand, your mind will naturally direct operations from here. If however you find, when mounting the gun, that the barrels are always pointing below the target, this can be the result of your back hand dominating the procedure. This mistake will lose you time on your target, because each time you mount the shotgun, you will have to then spend time finding or reacquiring the target. This job should be done before the gun ever reaches the cheek by keeping the whole gun pointing at the target while the gun is coming up to your head. Mounted correctly, when the gun arrives at the cheek and the eye is in a position to see where exactly the gun is pointing, the target should be visible right at the end of your barrel and that is where Hand Eye Coordination is used.

NB If you are shooting a side by side shotgun with a long grip, when you are busy firing at multiple targets such as a pheasant drive, or flush shoot at a clay pigeon event, the barrel will become very hot, frequently too hot to touch and well able to burn your hand or other bare skin. You can alleviate this problem by purchasing a leather barrel sleeve. These are usually made of heavy leather with a sprung steel insert and can be fitted to the gun by sliding them up the outside of the barrels from the muzzle until they reach the fore-end. Be sure that their fit with the barrels is good and tight.

I have on many occasions heard people describe their progeny, or a friend or acquaintance, as having a great eye, a natural eye, a dead eye (USA of course). More often as not, it will be the mother of a young teenager who has been presented to me in order to teach their little Jimmy or Jemima to shoot. The child, mortally embarrassed by his or her parent cringes. "Oh Mum!!" It's OK, I know what they mean, but the Mums (and Dads too), are rarely able to define what they mean by this. Well I shall define what they mean and that will give you an opportunity to 'shoot me down in flames'.

A 'Good Eye' is "the ability to hit a target, moving or still, with foot, bat, racket club etc, and without relating one to the other, make good contact with it."

You don't watch the head of your tennis racket when swinging it towards the ball, you concentrate solely on watching the ball.

We have all heard the phrase 'hand-eye coordination'. I've heard it said that shooting is a hand-eye coordinated sport. Where the coordination is needed is when mounting the gun to your cheek and shoulder. When you are mounting the shotgun, you need to point the whole gun, from muzzle to butt, at your target. A totally efficient shooter requires the successful employment of hand eye coordination when mounting the gun. This is a an extremely useful element to get right, but for those of us who may think we are lacking in coordination, worry not, what we need can for the most part be taught. The result of a successfully coordinated mount is that the gun will be actually pointing at the target when it arrives at your eye.

To do this, hold the gun normally in both hands with your front hand controlling direction. Let the barrels be an extension of your front hand's index finger (which is pointing forward towards the muzzle) and when the target appears, point your index finger, with barrel attached, at what you wish to shoot. Your task is to ensure the **whole gun,** from muzzle to butt, points at the target while the gun is moving to your cheek. With the gun now pointing at your target, all that remains for the shooter to achieve is to correctly lead the target and shoot. The secret to successfully mounting the gun in this fashion, is moving the gun slowly. **Keep your hands and arms slow!** The slower the gun moves, the more easily you will be able to maintain the barrels pointing at the target while the stock is on its way to your cheek. When people initially try this technique, they tend to worry that too much time is taken up with the gun mount. In actuality this method will earn you far more time than you will ever use up by employing it correctly.

The end result of a correct gun mount means that we do not have to waste time re-establishing contact with the target having mounted the gun. As it reaches your eye, you will see the target at the end of the barrel. How more efficient can your gun mount be? Now lead the bird and shoot! I can hear a few voices saying why not point the gun in front of the target while bringing it to your cheek, that is where it ultimately has to go. This is a recognised method but there are pitfalls, especially for a novice. I have seen the barrel over-lead the bird and the shooter either have to stop the gun to wait for the bird, or having over lead it so much, they have actually had to return to the bird. In both these cases, the net result is that the bird overtakes the gun and the shooter then finds themself left behind. More time is lost. It is also worth observing that the hand eye coordinated gun mount, dove tails with 'snap shooting' discussed in a later section (Other Methods, Section 28), but more of this later.

While driven game shooting or clay shooting, people occasionally remark to me that it appears I'm never in a hurry, never rushing the movement of my gun. In reality, there are a few shots where I know I appear to be in a rush, usually caused by spotting a shootable bird going over the line when I'm busily reloading. Save for those occasions however, I do try and keep my movement of the gun to a minimum pace. It simply ensures greater efficiency of mount and that the gun is going to be pointing at my target when it arrives at my cheek. With most of the job complete at this stage, why rush?

Another problem that I see when watching people leading their birds prior to the gun reaching the cheek is as follows. If the target is missed, the reason is frequently a shot missing below the target and very occasionally missing high. This is especially true when the target is at long range. The reason is simple. If you never make visual 'contact' with the target, how can you be certain that your gun is on the correct line when leading the bird? By, metaphorically speaking, touching the target with your barrels before leading the bird, it ensures the gun is on the correct line when you move the gun out in front of the target to achieve the correct lead.

The Rear Hand

I have a section on the front hand, we had better say something of the back hand. It's there principally to assist the front hand, but not to dominate the movement of the gun. It releases safety catches, pulls triggers and opens the action, but it pales into insignificance beside its superior partner. Your grip with the back hand should be light on the gun. The hand should be able to slide on the surface of the stock. To slip the safety catch forward, your hand is obliged to be further forward than your normal grip. For you to maintain contact with the gun and slip off the safety catch, keep your grip light so your hand may return to its natural position.

10 The Sight Picture

'The picture' is the phrase I use to refer to the visual relationship between barrels and target, a split second before you fire the gun. With the gun fully mounted to your cheek, 'the picture' normally features a combination of sky, barrels and the target. It may also include trees, grass, moor or fen, but the important elements are two and sometimes all three of the following. Firstly the barrels, secondly the space between your barrels and the target and thirdly the target itself. These are the important components of your **'picture'.**

If you want to guarantee a hit target, understand this next fact, the 'picture' must be seen to be correct **before** you pull the trigger, not **when** you pull it, nor indeed **after** it is pulled. A matter of just half of a second but a subtle difference and an essential rule to follow. I can tell you what picture to use under any circumstance and can advise you on how to use the pictures and remember them. Read on.

The very first 'correct picture' I introduce my clients to is sky, barrels and **No** target. For a beginner as an introductory shot, I tend to use an incoming clay pigeon, flying at about fifty feet. Incoming means that the clay is flying from a clay pigeon trap set in front of the shooter, firing a clay directly towards them, and some fifty feet over their head. ***See diagrams 63 a,b,c.***

So imagine yourself without a gun, facing towards a hillside covered in gorse bushes, your leading hand pointing towards where you will see the target appear. Out comes the clay pigeon flying towards you. My instruction to you is to point two fingers forward. Raise your hand and arm vertically to catch up with the target. Having caught it, COVER THE TARGET with your fingers and keep it covered until it has a flown over your head. Most people will stop briefly

Straight Overhead Target

63a

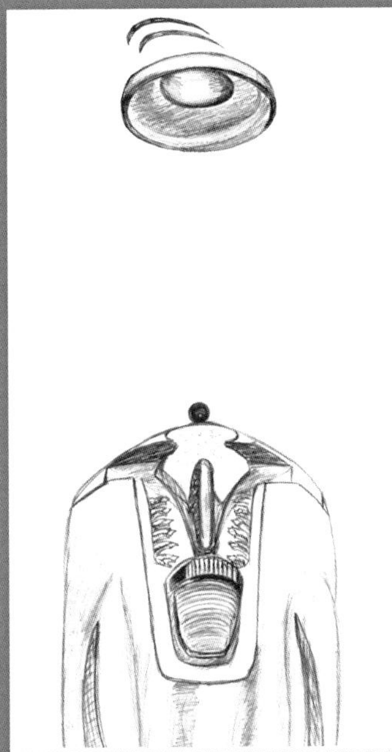

63b

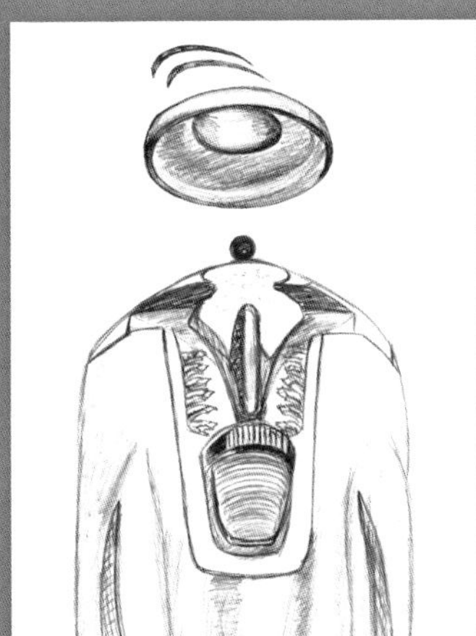

63c

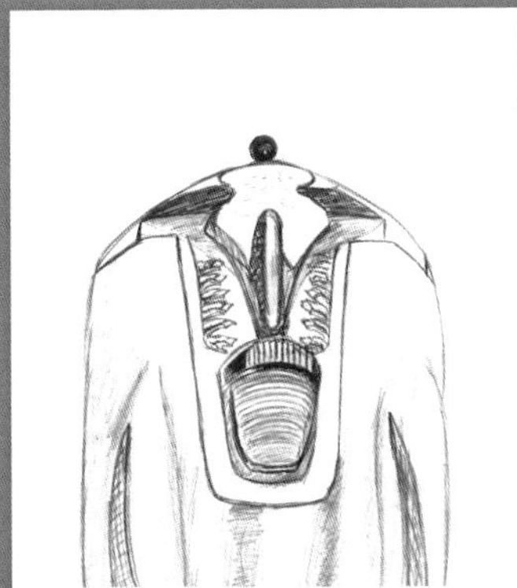

when they cover the bird the first time and then rush to catch up with it again. Worry you not if you stop several times. It is human nature to want to be sure where your target is... well I can tell you where it is, it's just behind your fingers! Remember here, you have a job to do and that is to cover the target. Don't worry about where the target has gone, just cover the target and keep it covered as long as you can. Repeat this until you are confident of covering that target smoothly. Then comes a wonderful moment. With gun in both hands, stock firmly pressed to your cheek, swing your barrels slowly up to the clay pigeon. With you in charge of the gun, your cue to shoot is the very instant your target is fully covered by the barrels. Or to put it another way, the moment the target has completely disappeared behind the barrels, pull the trigger!

Having **'made the picture right'**... SHOOT!

The most normal question to me at this stage is what should the picture be if the target was lower or higher. Answer: It's exactly the same!!

11 The Gap or Lead

What is lead? Lead is the distance that you offset your point of aim from the target, in order to give your projectiles time to cover the distance to the target. To put it in other words, it's the distance in front of the target you point the gun before pulling the trigger.

I hope you were busy reading a previous section called 'The Picture.' In this section I said that I could show you how to discover the pictures for yourself. The technique of leaving the gun on your cheek long after the shot has been taken should be understood and considered for adoption. Instead of targets coming straight over us or targets flying straight up and away from us, we must now give you a picture for crossing birds, those are birds flying at right angles or 90° to you and quartering birds, which are birds flying at a very oblique angle of say 10° toward or away from you. Look at my diagram for further explanation.

I had a fairly accomplished gentleman shooting here one day. He wanted to warm up for the forthcoming season and was shooting a combination of high incoming and high driven targets to his left and right.

The target to his left was causing a problem, so I stopped everything and asked him what criteria he used for successfully shooting the bird. He told me that he worked out the distance and speed of the bird and from that worked out how much lead to give the bird. *"If that is your method,"* I said, *"would you tell me what distance and what speed you think this target is flying at?"* I pushed the button and another similar target appeared. He thought for a moment and then told me that he led the bird by three feet.

"But that's not what I asked you," I said, *"I want to know how far away you*

think the bird is and what speed you think it is flying at."
Again he thought for a moment. *"Well I suppose it must be a fair way from us,"* he replied, *"and flying pretty quick too!"* In reality my client wasn't using the criteria he claimed at all. He couldn't put into words what his method was because I'm sure that he had no cast iron method. Time for some help here.

My question to you my reader is this. How can you be sure what speed and what distance the target may be at? If you feel that you can give an answer, will you always have the time to make this judgement? Will you always be right? There are many occasions when both rough shooting and shooting driven birds, one may only have a split second to mount and shoot the gun. I'm absolutely certain that when I find myself faced with these circumstances, I'm not busily trying to work out distance and speed before firing at my target. If I were to give you a system of lead that works regardless of the distance of the target, wouldn't that make life easier?

The Crossing Bird

For a **crossing target** or a clay that is flying roughly at right angles to us, 'The gap' is purely the visual distance between the target and the side of your barrel when you are pointing the gun in front of the bird. Let us assume that we are shooting at a bird flying across us from our left to our right. To hit the target you need to point the gun to the right of the target when you shoot. The question in everyone's mind is 'how far?' Imagine this: the gun is in your cheek and is now pointing at the bird, you continue to move the barrel to the right and have now overtaken the bird. As you look along your barrel, the target therefore, is to the left of the barrel. As you move the gun out in front of the target, a gap begins to extend between the side of your barrel and the target. Open the gap of daylight until the distance between barrel and bird is 1.5" (Over & Unders) 1.0" (Side by Sides), if you pull the trigger with the barrels thus positioned, the target will break. We have used the visual gap at the barrel as our means of assessing the necessary lead, not the distance the gap represents at the bird.

What you may have noticed about the previous paragraph is that there is no mention of the actual distance between you and the target. I can hear many voices, all giving me estimations of distance to the target, giving me estimated distances of how far in front of the target to point the gun when I pull the trigger. The first voice: *"Shane that bird needs four foot lead."* Another voice chimes in: *"I didn't give it that much I'm sure, maybe three and a half foot."* (You know what they say about those of us hearing voices!) The reason I don't listen is so simple. **It does not matter!** All you need concern yourself with is the size of the visual gap off the side of the barrels. Did someone say *"size matters"*?

Just to be sure you have this indelibly marked on the shooting compartment of your brain, if using a side by side shotgun, the average speed of clay pigeons and game birds will need a gap of 1.0". For Over and Under shotguns and single barrel shotguns, you should use a gap of 1.5". The reason for there being a difference in the gap between the side by side shotgun and any other shotgun is due to two features. The Over and Under has a very narrow sight line when looking along the barrels, as do single barreled guns and semi automatics, pump actions and bull-pup actions. When you look along the barrels of a Side by Side, the fences of the action and configuration of the barrels take up a larger width visually than the Over and Under, though the shot is designed to arrive at the same spot for all. With that additional width of the side by side, the gap can be reduced by a third of what one would use with any of the other barrel configurations. These measurements are what I perceive to be the correct distance. Do take note here that I have found that some clients see these gaps as a little wider than I, and yet others perceive them as a little narrower. Astonishingly some perceive them to be the same as I do! However, the variation tends to be no more than a quarter of an inch, more or less.

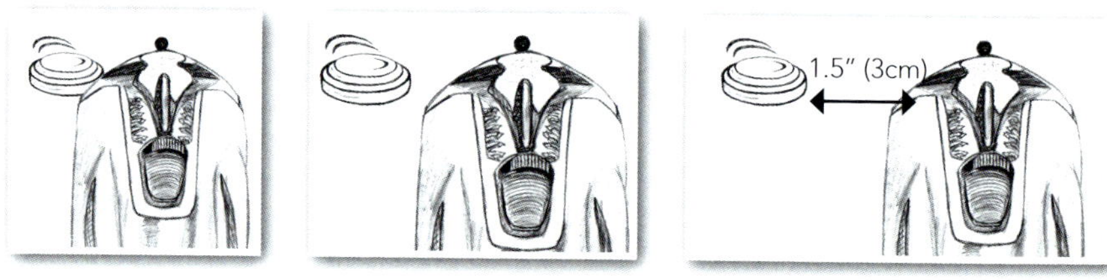

'Crossing Target' left to right.

To better illustrate what we are talking about here, go out of your house or apartment to a garden, a field or a street. Hold up your hand at arm's length and make a gap of 1.5" between thumb and first finger. This will represent the gap between barrel and bird. Select an object roughly 20 yds. away and move your thumb so that it aligns with your eye and the target, your thumb is metaphorically touching the object. Consider now the gap between thumb and index finger. What does that gap represent in actual distance at your target? I suspect you will find that it represents a width at the target of about three feet. Now find yourself something to point at which is fifty yards away. Hold your arm out again, making the same gap between thumb and Index finger of 1.5". Now metaphorically place your thumb on the object you have selected and make an estimation of the distance your gap now represents at the object. The 1.5" gap used on a target at fifty yards distance, represents an actual width or lead at the target of nine feet. ***See photos 69 a,b on page 69.***

Therefore... you don't need to know how far away your target is to estimate lead, your gap of daylight will work at any distance within range of your gun. Whether at 20 yards, 30 yards, 40 yards or 50 yards make the gap 1.5" wide and you will hit that bird. As the target distance becomes further and further away from you, your gap off the side of the barrel represents a greater and greater width and therefore a greater and greater actual lead at the target.

69a

69b

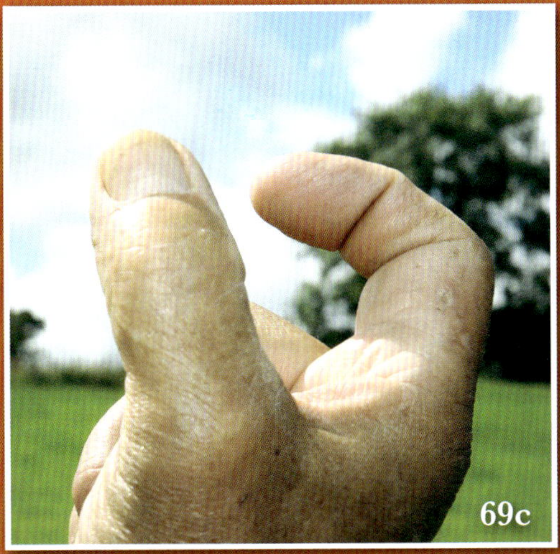
69c

Variables Because Of Speed

Can it really be that simple? There are two variables which can affect the system described above. We can deal with both of these right now. Firstly, the speed of the shot and secondly the speed of the target. Let's take speed of shot, the speed that the small balls of lead from your cartridge, (known as shot), fly while on their way to your target. If you are curious, the cartridge's muzzle velocity is sometimes printed on the top lid of the cartridge box or on the back of the box, but not always. Always use shot with the same or similar velocity, this resolves the first variable of shot speed. I tend to stick to a cartridge with a muzzle velocity somewhere between 1250 and 1350 ft. per second.

Now the speed of target. The gap I have given you is suitable for the average game bird or clay pigeon in flight, providing it is in range, regardless of whether it is at 15 yards or 55 yards. It does not account for a bird that is just leaving the ground or indeed one that is about to land. Their flight speed is massively reduced, a bird descending onto water or a clay pigeon having lost its momentum and coming down, a half inch gap does very well. I've seen many clay pigeons appear to float in a stiff breeze and all I've done is point at them and shoot. Your judgment will have to be the deciding factor of what is the correct picture. The bird breaking will prove your decision.

Not forgetting the other end of the speed spectrum, if there is a force ten gale blowing up the channel and a flight of teal skimming the water towards you with the wind behind them, increase the gap by a quarter of an inch. The same for a driven grouse coming down off the moor with a howling gale trying to overtake it, more lead is needed, try plus a quarter of an inch, if not try plus a half inch giving a lead between an inch and three quarters to two inches. And then of course a clay pigeon called a 'Battue'. They are very thin compared to a standard clay and very fast and definitely need two inches of a gap.

Be observant when shooting, watch to see where you are hitting your targets. If you are consistently hitting the back of the clay pigeon, open your gap by a quarter of an inch. When shooting regular birds, if you find you are missing your birds behind or shooting them in the tail, keep increasing the gap by increments of a quarter of an inch.

Other Pictures

So far we have covered both incoming and outgoing targets, we have also covered crossing birds but there is one more target that needs explanation before you go out and put all of this to good use. It is called the 'Quartering bird'. Neither of the above scenarios will cope with this. The bird isn't quite going straight away from you but it isn't at much of an angle either. Imagine yourself standing on a vast clock face. You are standing at 6 o'clock and facing 12 o'clock. A bird flies past you heading from 5.30 to 11 o'clock . Up goes your gun and you create a gap of an inch and half between barrel and bird. You fire but unfortunately what will happen is that your shot will pass well to the left of the target. Now put down the gun and go back to creating that gap between thumb and forefinger. An inch and a half please with the digits of the left hand. Keep your gap fixed but turn your whole hand so that your digit tips match the same line as the bird has flown. As your hand turns, your gap will appear to get narrower. Just match the line of the bird and use the gap that remains with your gun instead of your fingers. I think you will find the gap appears to be between a third and a half an inch. Use that as your starting point on a quartering bird and adjust by making the gap slightly wider should you not make contact first time. ***See photo 69c on page 69.***

When shooting a Side By Side, then pictures we have spoken of so far have been explained for both. A crossing bird for Over and

Under 1.5" gap, a crossing bird for a Side by Side 1" gap. For the Quartering bird to be shot by the Side By Side, your inch gap when turned to match the line of the target will close completely. Here is the one picture that remains a matter of timing for the shooter, rather than a daylight gap. It really is a matter of getting out to your clay pigeon trap and practicing with your Side by Side on the narrow angled target.

It is worth pointing out that this works in exactly the same manner for a target coming from behind. Let's go back to the clock face we were using. You are standing at 6 o'clock and facing 12 o'clock. A target flies over your head from behind you at 6 o'clock and is heading for 12 o'clock slowly descending. In clay pigeon shooting parlance this target is frequently referred to as 'lighting duck' or 'dropping duck'. Point your gun under the target creating a gap of half an inch between barrel and bird and shoot. Depending on the angle of descent will depend on the width of the necessary gap but start at a half inch and open out the gap in increments of a quarter inch until you break the bird.

Lastly, a clay or game bird gets up and flies away from you and this time relatively flat. Bring that gun of yours up and let the target settle on the bead of your gun. Not covered, just sitting there. If you are a little slow getting your barrels into place then allow a tenth of an inch above the bead. If the target's flight line is rising, then just simply cover the target.

Please note that these pictures depend on the placement of the pattern you are throwing. Please see the section **'Cast and Comb'** which will explain this in more detail.

Why Do We Pull The Trigger?

What makes us intentionally pull the trigger is one of three reasons. Either firstly, the 'picture' (the relationship of barrel and target) is seen to be correct or secondly, we hope that it is correct. Thirdly and the most puzzling of all, we know or suspect that the picture is incorrect but shoot anyway. If you know where you should point the gun, be **determined** to do this, to be perfect each time and ensure you are correct before you shoot. You remain the sole judge on when to shoot, no matter how many times you may have shot this angle of bird, do not assume you will automatically remember where to point the gun, **Make The Picture Right.** Before you call the clay pigeon, before the pheasant drive starts, while you wait in a hide or walk behind your dog, prepare yourself, prepare your mind, think of where you will point the gun.

As you swing the barrels onto and beyond the target, keep asking yourself, what am I seeing? What is the **exact** relationship of barrel and target? Be critical of the 'picture', don't accept a relationship of barrel and target that is almost right, or nearly good enough. So many times I see targets missed by very small degrees. A few inches here, a foot and half there. Do not forget that a positional adjustment of an inch at the barrel, means a considerable change of lead at the bird, and may be the difference between hit or near miss. How long does it take to move the barrel one inch? Surely just a split second. So why not move the barrel just a little more to ensure sufficient lead, or correct line before you shoot? **If in doubt** of what the correct 'picture' should be, as a starting point, always position your gun so that when you fire, you may miss the bird **slightly** in front. Better to have your whole shot pattern up in front of your target and then work your way back to it, shot by shot, than to have your whole pattern starting one millimetre behind.

Consider one more fact here, the less confidence a shooter has in their ability to hit a target, the more they will want to point the gun straight at the target when they pull the trigger, rather than pointing the gun in front of the target.

How To Learn The Correct Picture

If you are fully aware of the relationship of barrel and target just before you pull the trigger, so aware that you could describe it exactly to me after you have taken your shot, you are now remembering and able to use the correct 'picture' for yourself. Your job in hand is to remember the exact relationship of barrel and target the very moment you decide to pull the trigger. Not on the 'B of Bang' or when you see the target break, it's when you actually decide to pull the trigger. If that target breaks or falls you now have the correct 'picture' to use for a similar target and you can store this information in some dusty corridor in your brain!

"Why do you leave the gun on your cheek so long after shooting, Shane?" I've heard that question many times. The simple answer is to help me remember what the picture was when I decided to shoot. I find the longer after the shot I leave the gun stock on my cheek, the easier it is to remember back to the relationship of barrel and target at that crucial moment. It also guarantees follow through.

So then you reload and call for another bird, here it comes, the same as the last, if you make the 'picture' exactly the same again, it will result in the target being hit again. You position the barrels in the same relationship to the target as the last shot and when you see this is matching, you pull the trigger. The bird disintegrates.

However, if you should have missed that first target, keep the gun mounted and you can still use your 'picture' in a positive fashion.

Rather than cursing oneself for any perceived ineptitude, think back to the 'picture' you saw a millisecond before you pulled the trigger. If you can remembered the 'picture', you now have the opportunity to work out for yourself why you missed the target. Was your lead insufficient, was the line of your shot below the target?

If you simply do not know why you missed the target worry you not, you are still able to do something very positive. If you missed the target, and you have remembered the 'picture' you used, at least you know that the 'picture' you used doesn't work, so **change** the 'picture' and try something new, a small increase in the amount of lead, such as adding a quarter of an inch to your gap between barrel and bird. Keep changing the 'picture' until you hit the target. When that target is hit, remember the 'picture' for future reference.

When giving lessons at my shooting school, I have watched many clients who, regardless of missing their target several times, are determined that somehow the picture they first decided to use on a target must be correct and therefore will eventually (and miraculously) hit the target as long as they keep using it. Illogical, but none the less what often happens.

One drawback to being human is a problem with our own decision-making process. When we think we are right, we can be very stubborn or determined that this is indeed the case. Each time the bird is missed, the incorrect 'picture' is confirmed and yet the person continues to shoot the same 'picture'. It's understandable to a degree, as they've originally made a decision to use a specific 'picture' they think should be correct, so when they miss, even though they can see there's a fault, they return to what they originally thought to be correct. It's at this moment that we need to be very determined to **change** the 'picture', deciding specifically what our new picture will be. Before you shoot at the next bird or call for another clay pigeon, ask yourself what am I going to do that is different? Then if you still don't succeed, remember the previous picture and be determined to keep altering it until you make contact with the target.

An interesting observation you can make that relates to the above is when you are out shooting, listen to the frequency of the shots. "Bang, bang", heard as quickly as you would read it, often indicates to me a twice missed bird. The shooter pulling their trigger is not giving themselves time to alter 'the picture' between shots. "Bang, one thousand, bang", heard as quickly as you would read it, indicates to me a shooter who is thinking and trying to change his 'picture' if his first shot has missed. Equally, if there are two birds there to be shot, he has taken his time to make sure of two good kills.

12 Recoil

Next is the recoil of the gun. Everyone seems to have an opinion on this, even when they have never actually seen a shotgun being fired. What we are dealing with here is energy. Energy in the form of compressed gases, created by an explosion inside the chamber of the gun. As the gases expand, they propel the shot through the barrels and towards the target. For those of us who remember our physics classes at school, this will produce an equal and opposite reaction. The 'Equal and Opposite' is a force travelling towards your shoulder, it is energy that you have to learn to absorb so that you will do yourself no damage. The number of times I have heard people say "pull the gun tight into your shoulder" are no longer countable. It leaves me thoroughly dismayed. These words of advice are a technique that has come from big bore rifle shooting and depend on plenty of muscle mass. It is used to maintain a steady platform for the rifle and it has crept into shotgun shooting, but has no right to be there.

It is pertinent here to observe that you hold a shotgun in a different place and manner on your shoulder than to the normal position used when shooting a rifle.

By pulling the gun into the shoulder, what are you doing if you follow this advice? You are compressing the muscular tissue which negates its ability to absorb energy or force. To pull the gun in tight, you have to tension all the muscles in the shoulder and shoulder blade, you will be effectively preventing the whole of the shoulder from moving. Now just bear with me a moment while we talk about a boxer. How does a boxer absorb a punch? He doesn't just stand there holding his head still when he is punched, neither does he move towards the punch. If his opponent connects, he 'rides the punch'. In other words he tries to move in the same direction as the punch, thereby absorbing the energy. If your muscles are relaxed and uncompressed and the shoulder under no tension, when the gun goes off, you too can absorb the energy because the whole shoulder blade can move. If you do not allow yourself the ability to 'ride the punch', it is very likely you will bruise your shoulder.

So when preparing the client, I will load the gun and explain that I am about to pull the trigger, and I request that the client observe what the gun does when the cartridge fires. I point the gun near vertically in a safe direction, hold it firmly between both my hands about a foot from my body. Moving the gun 12" at a reasonable speed, each time from high to low "Three", high to low "Two", high to low "One," high to low "Fire" and pull the trigger. This will show the client the recoil and by allowing the gun to move downwards as they shoot, how they can control and absorb that energy. The operation is repeated, this time with the client holding the gun as well as myself. The client pulls the trigger and I keep control of the gun's recoil. Ultimately one can let the client do this on their own by allowing the gun to move in a controlled manner. An extra bonus will be no damage to their shoulder and the knowledge gained that they are able to control the gun when it fires. All important preparation for the recoil of the gun firing, and preparation for the audio effects too.

When selecting a new or second-hand gun from your local gunsmith, you will find a number of shotguns fitted with rubber recoil pads on the butt. Do I use one on my guns? The answer is no, but having said that, there's nothing wrong with the idea. I'm sure that they reduce recoil to a degree, but should you adopt this 'bolt on extra' may I suggest that you get the pad covered with leather or buy a new one in this fashion. Rubber has an innate ability to grip. As a result, when mounting the gun, the likelihood of your gun dragging on clothing is high, especially when wearing extra clothing in the winter. A leather cover will enable the pad to slide easily across all fabrics and is therefore a much better investment.

Protecting Your Cheek And Shoulder

Not only is the shoulder a recipient of the gun's energy when fired, but the cheek is also in close proximity and can suffer from recoil if not cared for. What we need to discuss is the positioning of the comb of the stock on the cheek. Suffice to say that the underside of the cheek bone 'sits' on the comb of the stock. Providing the cheek remains in firm contact with the stock, during your swing and after the shot, no harm will come to the shooter. However, if the cheek and the stock part company when the gun is fired, the result may be damage or bruising to the cheek. You may observe a small red mark develop on the jaw of a person who has make this mistake a number of times.

These red patches, about an 1" in diameter, usually occur on or just above the jaw line, about midway and it's also to be seen high on the cheek bone, that small bump or 'mouse' will be apparent. To prevent this happening, lock the stock into the underside of your cheekbone before the shot and keep it there until well after the gun has gone off!

Damage is caused for one of three reasons. Firstly, the head lifting off the stock at the moment of shooting. Normally done by the shooter to try and observe whether or not their target has been hit. This happens most frequently when firing at incoming targets. Secondly, sometimes the removal of the head is done prior to firing the gun owing to their fear of recoil. Thirdly, the gun being moved away from the cheek owing to the shooter only using their hands and arms to swing the gun instead of the big muscles in the hips. Whichever the reason, all one needs to do is to keep the stock and the cheek locked together and your follow through is automated. Then consciously, not automatically, dismount the gun.

I have needed to resort to some help with regard to cheek and shoulder in order that I may continue to shoot. Post operative changes have left my shoulder hanging lower than it used to. Removal of muscle across my left shoulder has left the whole clavicle just under the skin and unprotected. An interesting dilemma for a shooting instructor when he has to frequently admit to his clients that he doesn't shoot. What to do?

I have loved riding all my life and was gazing at my saddle thinking how beautifully made it was all those years ago. A thought occurred to me though you may well wonder why this thought has taken 12 years to emerge but I'm grateful it has. The thought was how well padded and how long lasting that saddle has been. Carrying me faithfully for thirty years, ending up one day underneath my horse Hunker Munker in the bottom of a water filled ditch and yet still intact. So if I need something flexible, padded and robust, capable of protecting my bones while lifting the gun to my eye and staying in place on my shoulder with the aid of some straps, then back to my most favourite of saddlers I would go.

So a drive eastwards and some three hours later, Shane is to be seen striding along the pavement in Kilcullen, two shotguns in sleeves over his shoulder and his shooting waistcoat and jacket keeping the winter chills at bay. The locals meanwhile are staring suspiciously at this armed, *'tweeded'* character and on entering Bernie Bros., several startled shoppers are seen to be clearly baffled as shotguns are removed from their sleeves.

One of Bernie Brothers' great saddlers emerged from his workshop, Pascal looking a little relieved since I had put down my guns, reached up to a hook where the breast plate of a martingale was hanging, took it down and positioned it on top of my shoulder with its length tapering down the front of my chest. This piece of harness is normally used to shape and control a horse and direct his energy from his hind quarters. If it could do all that for a horse, what might it do for me? Strongly stitched straps were removed and re-sewn with extraordinary speed, more adjustments made, more debate on position, more movement of straps and finally, *"come back tomorrow, I'll have it for ye."*

And bless him he did. Beautifully padded and covered with soft leather, brass buckles shining and that fresh leather smell, I nervously put it on. We buckled and unbuckled and moved and tightened and suddenly the shotgun was arriving at my eye again. A sight I haven't seen in twelve years and a sight I thought I'd lost forever.

Did it work when actually shooting? Like a dream! Thank you Pascal, thank you Louise and thank you, my old friend, Jim Bernie.

13 Follow Through And Dismount

Having pulled the trigger, there is a fractional time taken by the shot to exit your barrel. It has to leave the cartridge, enter the forcing cone, travel down the tube and pass through the choke. This takes time, not very much I grant you, but unless the gun keeps swinging briefly after the shot, your lead will be lost or your line on the target may be adversely affected.

I so often hear the following words spoken by those lamenting a target missed... their reason for a lost target... *"I stopped the gun." "I didn't follow through"*. Two frequently heard reasons why one's technique can go awry. Firstly, if your head comes away from the stock for any reason, the barrel will stop swinging instantly, has your target instantly stopped flying? If your barrels have stopped while the shot is still travelling down the inside of the tubes, the lead you have given the bird is suddenly lost. This can happen because the shooter wants to enjoy seeing their target break or simply thinks on the 'B' of 'Bang' the job is finished so dismounts their gun.

Secondly, having pulled the trigger, if your dismount of the gun is part of your normal swing through the target, you can automatically start your dismount too close to the moment the gun is fired, possibly before the shot has cleared the muzzle on its way to the target. This will drag the shot below the line of the bird.

What to do? After the shot is taken, if you leave the gun on your cheek, it automates the follow through. Use the cue of the bird breaking or falling as your moment to dismount the gun. Until then, stay with the bird. Make your dismount of the gun a totally separate movement to the swing of the gun. Put this method into use so that it becomes a cast iron habit as it will give you an automatic means to guarantee follow through. That's some claim but, for the experienced shot, I would suggest they already know that this is the answer. All you need to do is to keep the stock and your cheek together after the shot.

Why does this work? Either you will have hit or missed the target; you most certainly will want to know which it is. Your eye will therefore follow the bird, as indeed will your head in order to see the bird break. If your head is attached to the stock, your gun will continue to move.

14 Triggers

Double Triggers: Length Of Stock

It's important to give a word of advice should your gun be fitted with double triggers. There are two problems often encountered with those using double triggered guns, and neither need happen if you know why damage or injury can occur and how to prevent it.

Firstly, a bruised second finger. Our middle or second finger has three sections, the first is nearest the hand. The bruising is most often seen on the inside of the first section of the finger between knuckle and first joint. It is caused by the second finger being either too close or actually pressing against the rear of the trigger guard and when the gun fires, the trigger guard hits that second finger. If your grip with this hand is too tight, it will add to the likelihood of damage. How to solve this?

If you suffer from this problem, consider why your second finger is so close to, or touching the trigger guard. The first possibility is because the index finger has been curled too far around the front trigger. To prevent damage to yourself, just use the centre of the pad of your index finger. You will find it very easy to do, and this will move the rest of your hand, specifically the second finger, rearwards on the stock and away from the trigger guard preventing any impact on gun recoil. It will also benefit you in another way. If your finger is curled too far around the front trigger, it is much more difficult to get this finger off the front trigger and onto the back trigger. Using the tip of the index finger to pull the front trigger, enables this finger to slide across and off the first trigger and naturally engage with the second trigger. The second possibility is that the length of the stock or 'Pull measurement' is too short for you. The solution can be from a number of choices:

- Pad out the shoulder or garment where the butt sits. This can be a problem in hot weather.
- Fit a butt sleeve or boot, best made in leather so it will slide on your clothing but there are cheaper rubber versions.
- Fit a recoil pad to the butt, preferably covered in leather, to suit the length that's desired.
- Ask your gunsmith to fit an extension to the stock in matching walnut. Beware when removing any butt plate or heel piece should there be one. These are metal or bakelite protective parts that may no longer be large enough to cover the new width or height of the butt.

N.B. By extending the length of the stock, you may find your head is in a lower position on the stock and therefore unable to see over the action to the bead. You may be aware of a change in the balance of the gun, occasionally to the benefit of the shooter but check how the gun feels with that addition. If it is a very valuable gun or a treasured piece, discuss the effects on balance with the gunsmith before you act.

As a possibly useful addition to your equipment, you will find in the 'bolt on extras' department of a gunsmith's shop, a small rubber pad that can be attached to the rear of the trigger guard. This is to cater for someone that is bruising their second finger in the manner we have discussed above. My advice to you is to try and cure the problem, as I have outlined, before you go off to buy one of these items. Better to use a preventative measure than to need a cure. The second problem I have seen occurring is the index or second finger getting cut. This is usually caused by a trigger guard or less likely a trigger, which after many years of wear, has ended up with a sharp edge on its side, the problem being exacerbated by too strong a grip with the back hand. If this happens, show the gun to your gunsmith and explain what is happening. He may well file down the offending edge. The alternative is to train yourself to keep your grip very light.

You may wonder, having read this, why anyone would use a double triggered gun. I think the most useful aspect of the double trigger system is the ease to select which barrel you fire first. However, when clay pigeon shooting, this can all be pre-planned before the bird is in the air. When game shooting, you may well need to change your mind at a moment's notice. The double trigger gives you that option faster than a single trigger system with a barrel selector on the safety catch. *See photos 87 a,b.*

It is also true that for many years, some single trigger mechanisms proved to be problematical. This you will be pleased to know, is rarely the case with modern mechanisms, neither single nor double trigger systems prove to be more troublesome than each other.

Single Triggers

There are a few points that you should know about single triggers. Personally I think that they are wonderfully convenient. As the single trigger is normally set to the rear of the trigger guard, it's very unlikely you will damage your second finger as mentioned in the previous section. The speed that one can fire both barrels of the gun can be very fast, though sometimes this is not necessarily a good thing. (See chapter on 'The Picture'.) It's rather like drivers who start by learning to drive a car with an automatic gear box, they would be so much better off if they had learnt to drive a manual box. It may take more coordination to change gear with clutch and gear lever but they will be better provided for in future. Similarly, if you change from double trigger to single trigger, there never seems to be a problem. For those who change from a single trigger gun to double trigger gun, it often results in them placing a panic call to the nearest instructor, but then you know we instructors hate to seem

87a

87b

dispensable.

With a single trigger system, selection of which barrel fires first is normally included in the package. This is controlled by a selector as part of the safety catch mechanism. However, having selected which barrel you wish to fire first, to change your mind mid shot is a much more difficult problem to negotiate. It necessitates putting on the safety catch, sliding the selector into its other position and then slipping the catch off again. Not a very practical proposition when trying to shoot something for supper. In reality, having selected which barrel fires first, I'd stick to it.

Finally, the technique of using a single trigger is best described as pull once, relax your trigger finger immediately, and pull again. There's no need to lift your finger off the trigger, just touch to fire your first shot and relax briefly to fire the gun again. If you find difficulty in pulling the trigger a second time, make sure you are using just the pad of your index finger to pull the trigger and the trigger mechanism is able to reset.

15 A Moment To Savour

For a client who has never shot before, having 'prepared' them (see chapter 6), I will continue my session by getting them to stand correctly. Then I'll place the gun on their cheek and shoulder before the target is released. I will ask them if the bead is aligned correctly, that their 'spare eye' is closed and to call "Pull" when they want to see the target. The client will practise moving their barrels to the target, making the picture right but not shooting as yet. I'll let them use as many targets as is necessary to become confident with this part of the operation. When they are confident they can do this for an incoming clay, and when I can see them covering the target correctly, I'll invite them to shoot at the next clay pigeon. It is important to stress at this point that they are under no obligation to pull the trigger just because a target is in the air.

If the picture isn't right, either make it right or let the clay fly on.

And Then Their First Shot

Feet aligned, weight on the back heel, gun mounted, bead checked for alignment, safety catch off, deep breath, the first bird is called. ***See photos 91 a,b,c,d and 92 a,b,c,d.***

The gun is rising, bird just above the centre of the barrels, they're catching up with the target and it finally disappears... Bang! The target breaks, sometimes shatters, sometimes disappears into a small cloud of black dust. The client looks at me with 'did I hit it?' written all over their face and then the huge grin when I nod and smile. Opening the gun, the cartridge extracted and held smoking under their nose. Smell that! It's surprising how many people at that moment fall in love with the smell of burnt powder.

As they become familiar with the weapon and as they find success by hitting their targets with the gun starting in their cheek, they will then progress to mounting the gun themselves. Once confidence is attained, then we use the 2" mount. Gun pointing to where the target will appear, stock held two inches away from shoulder and cheek. With each stage, the gun will start further and further from their cheek and shoulder, the client mounting the gun each time. When the gun is reloaded, they will bring the gun back to the underside of the cheekbone, feel the comb of the stock correctly positioned there, and then move the whole gun away an inch or two. When ready, they will move the gun back to the cheek and as they do so, I will release another target. From this method, we move on to the gun starting two inches away from cheek and shoulder, but now the target is released before the gun is moved back to the cheek. Ultimately the gun will start fully dismounted in the correct 'present' position. This position is a personal choice but my suggestion to you is to centre the

And then their first shot

91a

91b

91c

91d

92a

92b

92c

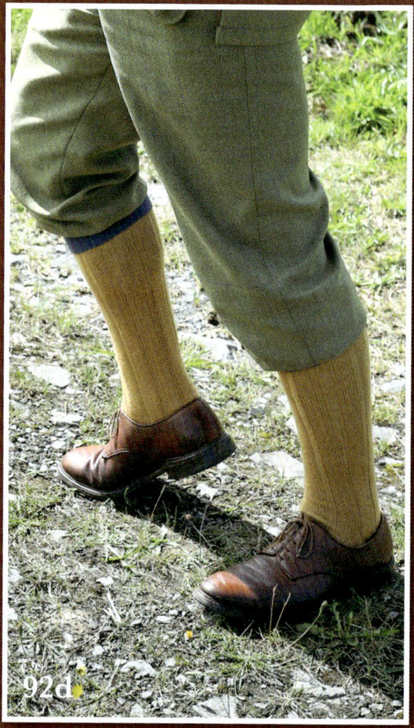

92d

gun on the sternum, barrel pointing toward where you expect to see the next target, providing of course, it is safe to do so. The reason for having the gun centred with the stock on your sternum, is that the gun, when rising, moves in a straight line up the face of your clothing and into its correct position on your cheek. If you watch the gun rising from the sternum, you will see that the stock has to move very slightly backwards as it follows the line of the chest. This is one reason why it will seldom snag on your clothing. See section on 'recoil' for further advice.

For game shooting, if you are walking up birds, it is generally accepted for the gun to be held in one or both hands, barrels pointing at the ground, or barrels pointing to the sky. The classic carrying position is for the gun to be held in the crook of your arm; however, if there is a strong possibility of a bird showing, you may be well advised to adopt a different position for the gun, both hands in control, barrel pointing towards where you think the birds will appear, yet again, providing it is safe to do so. If you find there are people on the ground where the birds are showing, you must be sure to keep the gun pointing skywards. When shooting driven birds or waiting for flighting birds to come over your hide, again the accepted position is pointing your barrels at the sky or pointing them at the ground. I've never been that keen on watching a set of barrels resting on top of the shoulder, but the length of the barrels resting against the front of the shoulder is fine. When you see a target that you judge is likely to come within range of your peg, providing it is safe to do so, point the whole gun at the bird when it's almost in range. Bring the butt up to your sternum and keep the gun pointing at your target until it's definitely yours to shoot at, then fully mount the gun.

Clay pigeon shooting demands different starting points for the gun. The 'correct position' is a variable because, due to the rules of different clay pigeon disciplines, you may be allowed to start with the gun already mounted, or you may be obliged to start with the gun stock on your hip, or you may find that your starting position is yours to choose. There are also variables from country to country, continent to continent.

16 Moving Gun And Body

Movement Of The Upper Body

The gun is mounted, the target is in the air and we have to move the gun and ourselves. Let me first give you a golden rule. As soon as the gun reaches your cheek, your upper body including pelvis, back, arms, hands, shoulders and head, should be one single unit moved by the big muscles of your body, and from your hips. Your upper body should be a single unit, not too tense as we know the effects of tension and we are trying to eliminate it.

So why use the hips? Two principle reasons. The first is accuracy of swing. Having mounted the gun to your cheek and the target, if you try to continue the swing of the gun with your hands and arms, you will find the gun will not follow a straight course. There will be unwanted lateral or vertical movement. In other words, the gun will appear to wobble. Let us assume you are swinging on an incoming bird. The gun rises near vertically but you see it wander slightly left or right of your intended course. That is due to arm/hand interference. Equally, if your target is flying across you, your gun may be moving left to right but it will also be wandering over and under the line of the bird. No matter how strong you may be, trying to control and execute a perfect swing takes greater muscle control than can be provided by the arms. Using your pelvis and to a lesser degree your back and legs, these muscle groups will provide you with an absolutely reliable movement of the gun in all directions.

Secondly, if you are swinging the gun with your arms and not your body's big muscles, you are very likely to move the gun in relation to your master eye. I have seen guns creeping up past the cheekbone until they actually obliterate my view of the client's eye. It becomes increasingly difficult for the shooter to know exactly where the gun is pointing. Equally problematic, it's putting the cheek in danger of being hurt. Remember, if the cheek isn't correctly engaged with the gun and the two not locked together, the gun is more than able to slap you on the cheek when fired. Imagine a gun mounted on the right cheek, following a target flying from left to right. Using the arms to swing the gun is likely to swing the gun away from the cheek and therefore the eye. Rotate (left/right) or elevate (up/down) the gun by principally using your hips and waist, keeping those hands, arms, shoulders and head as a single unit, your gun will remain steady on the cheek and the alignment with the bead and barrels constant with the master eye.

Movement Of The Lower Body

When I first started teaching shooting 37 years ago, I noted, with a degree of dismay, that some of the methods taught by one of the UK's premier shooting schools, didn't allow the shooter full range of movement. Their philosophy was to teach the client to shoot with their weight over the front foot and always the front foot, regardless of the direction the target may be flying. When making enquiries, I was told that they were determined to be different to Robert Churchill's shooting methods. Whether they still adopt this practise I am unsure, but I was astonished that they should adopt this attitude at the expense of their clients. Surely what we should be looking for is a method that will gives maximum balance and maximise each chance we get to shoot safely and successfully.

I once described this part of teaching shooting as dancing classes. It's not far from them as it is your balance, rhythm and the movement of your feet that we are concerned with here. I'm going to give you a rule of thumb, and then explain to you how this is achieved. **All you have to ascertain is where your target is flying to in relation to yourself.**

NB These rules apply whether you shoot left or right-handed.

- If the bird is flying to your left, the weight should be in the left heel.
- If the bird is flying to your right, the weight should be in the right heel.
- If the bird is flying to your front, the weight should be in the front heel.
- If the bird is flying to your rear, the weight should be in the rear heel.

Being an observant individual you will have noticed some common elements to this rule. Firstly, it depends totally on where the bird is flying in relation to yourself. Secondly, the weight is always in the heel, not in the middle of the foot or in the toe. Thirdly, it is never apportioned evenly between both feet. So imagine a target flying towards you. The bird's direction is to your rear. Therefore the weight needs to be in the back or rear heel. To achieve this do the following. ***See photos 98 a,b,c,d.***

Keep your feet no more than six inches apart. Why? The closer your feet are together, the better the all round balance can be maintained. If you stand with your feet two or three feet apart, you may be well braced 'for and aft', but you will compromise your lateral balance. I stand with my feet no more than three or four inches between my heels. If I'm on very uneven or steep ground, I may be obliged to have my feet a little further apart. When shooting walked up game birds, there is rarely time to prepare your feet so best to step up onto the front foot or stay on the back no matter what the space between.

98a

98b

98c

98d

The alignment of your feet should be as follows:
For the right-handed, stand with your feet at the two o'clock position. (Left foot pointing at 12 o'clock, right foot pointing at two o'clock).
For the left-handed, stand with your feet at the ten o'clock position. (Right foot pointing at 12 o'clock, left foot pointing at ten o'clock).

The Hips

It's a curious thing but if you ask a man to move a gun with his hips, he will look at you with a very quizzical expression. And yet the most stable, powerful way of moving your gun comes from both hips or pelvis. The problem is that most men have little idea where their hips are. Ask them to bend at their hips and they will bend from the waist. The best way of demonstrating the correct way to move is for you the reader to stand sideways on to a full length mirror. Position your feet in the two o'clock stance, front foot pointing at midnight, back foot pointing at two o'clock. You are about to shoot a bird coming from in front of you. For a right handed shot, put your right hand on your hip bone and push your hips side ways. Hold the other arm straight out to the left (towards that imaginary bird) and move like a teapot. Allow the pouring spout to rise by pushing with your right hand on your hip bone and equally illustrative return your arm to level by moving your pelvis to your right. Move yourself in that fashion and you have something akin to that teapot pouring.

You ladies know precisely where your hips are, you need no direction from me, but you may have to demonstrate to your gentlemen. I know a wonderful lady, her profession is that of a therapeutic masseuse and she patiently eases the aches and pains of days spent standing in wind and rain, sometimes freezing cold and getting others to achieve their goals. Veronica is her name, she said I could use it and I'd highly recommend her. We were discussing movement and inevitably how one moves a shotgun. I explained about the pelvis, or if you wish, your hips, using them to move the gun. I explained the difficulty of getting men to move from their hips and asked her why she thought ladies could do this with complete ease? Her answer, which is so true: "Get a man to hold a growing baby, he'll soon find his hips!"

For an incoming bird, position your feet as discussed, push your hip sideways towards the direction the bird will fly to. It's that stance that would always earn censure from a strict parent, "Stand up straight Shane!" If done correctly, your rear leg will remain straight and your front leg will bend at the knee. If you wanted to lift your front foot, it should be able to come off the ground without you readjusting anything. Now from the waist straighten the upper body leaving your hips where they were positioned. It will feel that your weight is entirely in the rear heel. As the gun rises to your cheek, your weight should only be in the rear heel. There is no reason to move your weight onto the front foot, keep your weight in the back heel. Finally, if the gun needs to swing all the way to vertical and beyond, then the front heel should be allowed to rise and only the ball of the front foot stay in touch with the ground. Don't lift the whole front foot, just allow the heel to rise and you will find you will be able to swing the gun much further to vertical and beyond than when leaving this heel on the ground. Try it, you'll see what I mean. With the front heel on the ground, your gun will be hard to swing to vertical above your head. With that front heel up, your gun will travel easily to vertical and some degrees beyond, giving you more opportunity and time to shoot your target.

For a bird rising in front and flying away, shift the pelvis forward or if you like, shift your weight onto the front foot with the rear heel rising. This will also allow greater freedom of movement, similar to lifting the heel on that incoming bird.

For a bird crossing the shooter, what follows should afford the greatest degree of improved range of movement on your target but it only works best if your feet remain within a few inches of each other.

Target Flying Left To Right

For a right-handed shot, put all your weight in the right heel. Swing the gun onto your bird and as you do so, allow the left heel to rise. If not rise then let the left heel disengage from the ground and the foot to slightly roll over. Once you have perfected the technique of allowing your spare heel to rise, for sake of experiment, leave the heel in touch with the ground and see how far you can swing the gun to your right. You will notice your ability to turn and the distance you can turn, dramatically reduced. By slightly lifting the spare heel, I suggest you will find an additional 90° degrees of movement to your right. A massive additional opportunity to shoot your target.

For a left-handed shot, weight in the right heel. Swing on your bird keeping all your weight in the right heel, and as you do so, let the left heel rise. This will give you an additional 90° degrees of movement to your right. More opportunity to get to an elusive quarry.

Target Flying Right To Left

For a left-handed shot, weight in the left heel. Swing on your bird keeping all your weight in the left heel, and as you do so, allow your right heel to rise. If not lift then let the right foot roll over. The same result will be achieved. Once you have perfected the technique of lifting the spare heel, for sake of experiment, leave the heel in touch with the ground and see how far you can swing the gun to your left.

You will notice your ability to turn dramatically reduced. By lifting the spare heel, I suggest you will find an additional 90° degrees of movement to your left. Again a massive additional opportunity to shoot your target.

For a right-handed shot, weight in the left heel. Swing on your bird keeping all your weight in the left heel, and as you do so, lift the right heel. This will give you an additional 90° degrees of movement to your left. More opportunity to get to an elusive quarry.

Where Should I Be Facing?

If you are game shooting, always face towards where you expect your targets to appear. With clay pigeon shooting, the issue is much less distinct. It will depend entirely on your proximity to the trap and the angle that the bird is flying in relation to you. I can't wait to use a diagram, but I promised myself I would try and do this without one. So I tried and eventually realised that there are so many scenarios, that this book was in danger of becoming several volumes!

Let's take that crossing bird alone. The **closer** your shooting station is to the launcher and the flight of the bird, the **further** from the trap and the initial flight of the target you should face. The **further** you are from the launcher the **closer** toward the trap you should face. Let's use the clock face again. The trap is at 12.00 throwing its target to the right. If I am 50 yds. from it, I would start facing towards 12.00. With the trap 20 yds. from me I would start facing at 02.00. With the trap 5 yds. from me I'd be facing at 03.00. Providing you use the previous section's system on weight displacement, you will find you will be balanced to shoot these targets and capable of easy movement. You should set yourself up so that you can move at your most efficient when the bird is moving at its fastest. On that basis, if I can afford to, I would stand facing where I will first see the bird, because I may need to be able to move quickly and efficiently.

I can understand the theory of the school that believes you should set yourself up to face where you think you will hit the target, and then wind yourself back to where you will first see the bird. I've tried it many times with an open mind but I feel off balance or artificially tense and held in place while I'm waiting for the bird to appear. I think this has to be a matter of preference. Under these circumstances, I prefer to face as near as possible to the origin of the bird. ***See series of drawings 'Crossing Target' on page 106.***

Still dealing with the crossing bird, when you move closer in towards the trap, twenty yards or less, you will have to start facing further down the delivery line of the bird. If you try and face the trap, the bird will be past you before you can react and then you are playing catch up to the target. So experiment and find where you feel at your most relaxed, where you are most able to move, the place where you can cover the greatest amount of the ground the target is about to fly over. Read on.

Barrels Starting Position

Do not underestimate the importance of this section. Within lies the means to maximise your opportunity of shooting all targets. All too often I suggest to a client that they might consider exactly where they are going to point their gun before calling for a bird. All too often they are busy thinking of all sorts of other things and forget to get this aspect of their shooting technique set up correctly. In the case of clay shooting, there is every reason to do so, as it is you who calls for the bird. In game shooting, the opportunity will not always present itself, but this is by no means a reason to disregard your set up procedure.

In case you have missed these words elsewhere, to dispel any doubts in your mind as to where the rear of the gun should be when finding your starting position, your stock should be ready to bring to the cheek. Remember to bring the butt to the centre of your chest, on or near the sternum. This may vary for the clay pigeon competitor, depending on the discipline and rules that govern it.

Game Shooting

For Game shooting purposes, in a previous section we covered the subject of your starting position and your facing position when shooting a straight forward incoming bird. My advice under those circumstances was to set up the gun, pointing where you anticipate seeing the target, providing it is safe to do so. However, now that we are progressing onto more difficult targets, this starting position for the barrels becomes a variable. It depends on how much time you have to shoot the target. The closer you stand to the point where you will see the target appear, the less time you have to swing on the target, therefore the further down the flight line your barrels need to be pointing. Obviously this is impossible to predict for a game bird, but let us assume you are standing in a forestry ride and the birds are flying over the ride. You have what appears to be a split second to mount the gun and shoot the bird. Starting your barrels on or below the tree line in front of you, is not giving yourself much opportunity to get to the bird. Starting your barrels a third of the way across the window of sky above the ride will help.

Clay Shooting

For the Clay Pigeon shooter we can afford and need to adopt a more scientific approach. A clay pigeon can frequently achieve speeds of 80 or 90 m.p.h. when leaving the trap. Because of this initial speed of the target, you are putting yourself at a great disadvantage if you do not take the opportunity to work out where best to start the barrels of your gun before calling for your bird. ***See diagrams 105 a,b, diagram 106a.***

105a

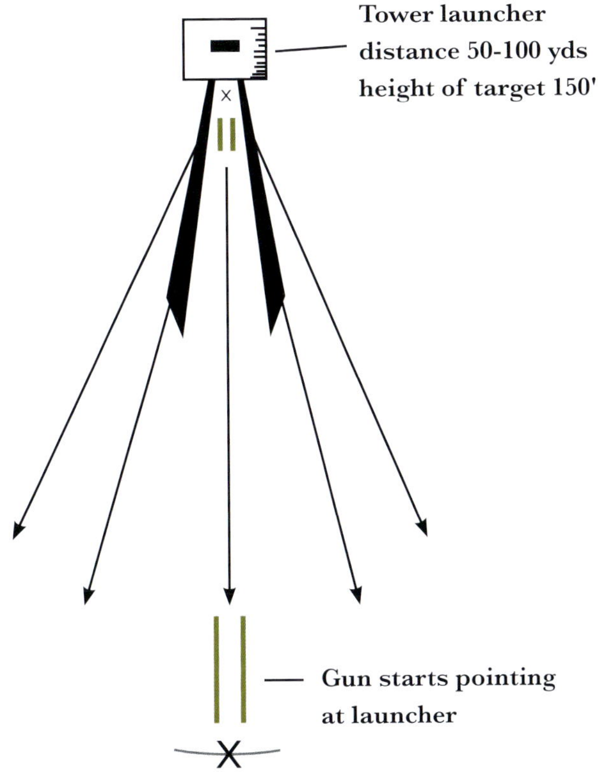

105b

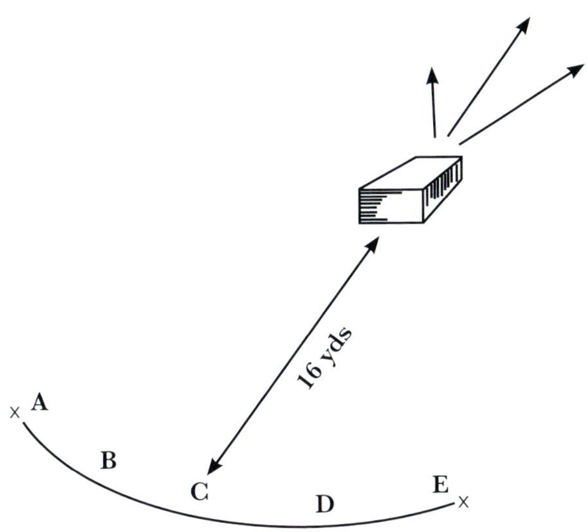

Angle of targets can be variable

106a

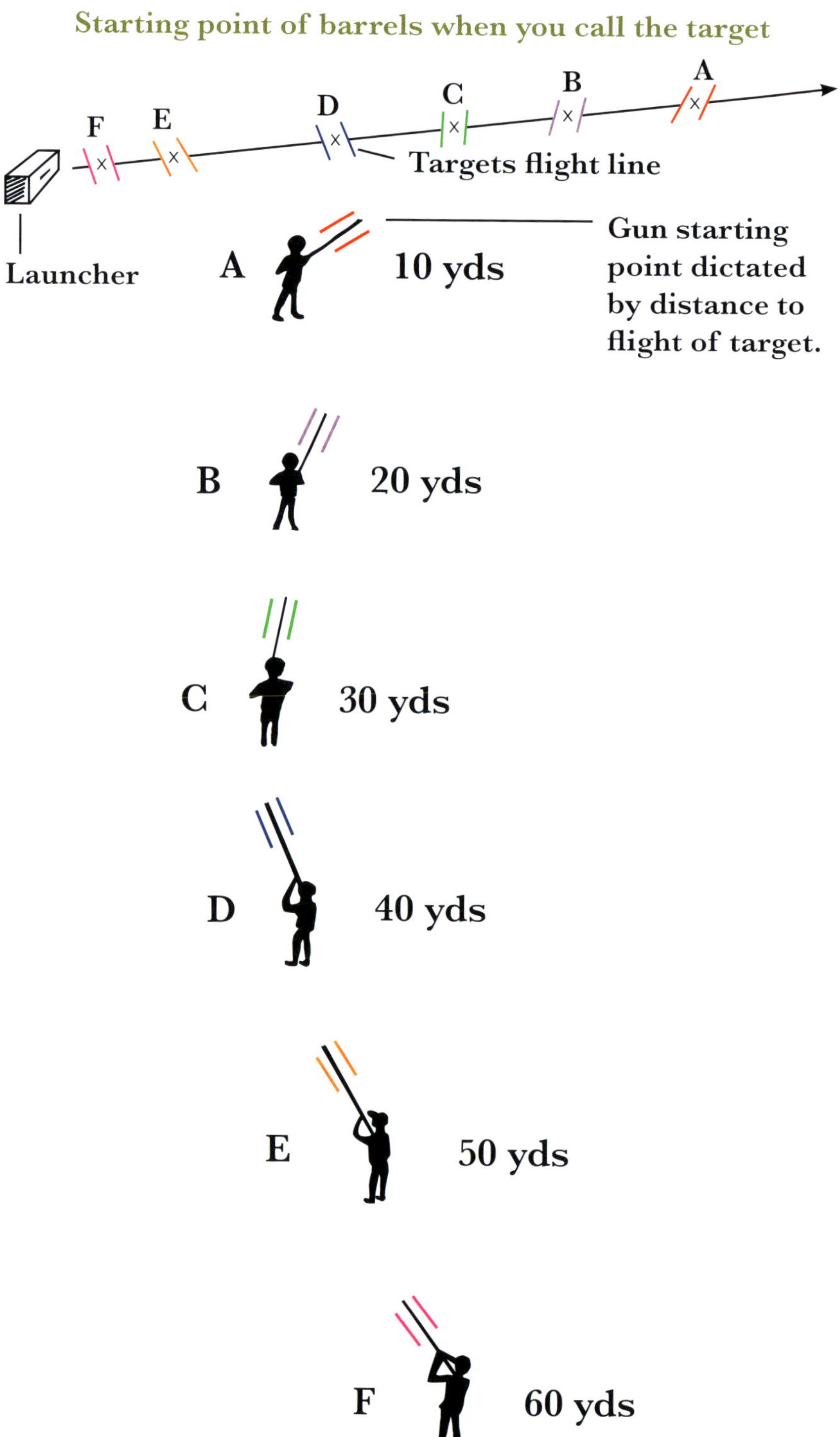
Starting point of barrels when you call the target
F
E
D
C
B
A
Targets flight line
Launcher
A
10 yds
Gun starting point dictated by distance to flight of target.
B
20 yds
C
30 yds
D
40 yds
E
50 yds
F
60 yds

First of all we need to put the gun down and get our fingers out again. Wait until someone is shooting the stand, or if no one else is around, you will have to use your show bird to assess your starting position. Pick a piece of undergrowth or bush or branch or whatever is on the delivery line of the target as a marker. This is to enable you to remember where you started your forehand pointing. With your leading hand's two fingers pointing at your marker, look back to the trap. Watch the bird come out from the trap and move your fingers to cover the bird. If you find the bird out accelerates your fingers, while you are moving them to the bird, and you have to catch up with the clay, your starting point for the barrels is too close to the trap. Move your hand further down the delivery line of the bird and pick a different marker. Point at your marker and look back to the trap. When the next bird appears, again bring your hand to point at the target. If you find yourself behind the bird playing catch up, you know what to do. If however, you find you are waiting for the bird to get to your fingers, then you are starting your 'gun' pointing too far down the delivery line of the bird, too far away from the trap. Move your fingers back a bit, pick another marker, a tree, a fence post, whatever you can remember easily, point your fingers there and call or watch the next bird. If you can move smoothly to the bird without snatching, without being left behind or without having to wait for the bird to get to you, you have just found the correct starting point for your barrels. Pick up your gun and walk onto the station with increased confidence.

17 Parameters, Or A Lack Of Them

FAQ This seems to be the 'buzz phrase' on web sites these days and is pertinent to my profession. Frequently asked question number one: Where during the flight of the target should I be shooting at the target? There are easier places and obviously harder places to shoot at the bird during its flight. I'm quite content to point out to my client where those are on any given bird, but I must emphasise that this should not be your prime reason for pulling the trigger.

Here at the shooting school, providing it is safe to do so, one can shoot at the target anywhere along its flight line. Why give yourself constraints as to when you pull the trigger, it may lead to you shooting and missing. I'll explain. If you set out to shoot the bird at a particular place during its flight, whether the picture is correct or not, you are likely to pull the trigger when the bird arrives at that point. Your primary motivation must always be to make the Picture right. So check that it is safe, then take your time, and use this time to your advantage and only shoot when the relationship of barrel and bird is correct. Perfect your technique and your target will be available to shoot earlier and earlier, should you need to, not should you want to.

There is another type of parameter that shooters give themselves and it is born entirely from human nature. Let us assume that we are shooting at a crossing bird from right to left. If the shooter succeeds in shooting one or two birds late in their flight, inevitably there is a temptation to treat this as a 'comfort zone' or an area of greater confidence to shoot this target. The next target appears and the shooter points their gun at the bird and leaves it pointing there until the bird has reached the area where they have broken those birds previously. Then they lead the bird and shoot. The later you shoot at the bird, the less opportunity you have to correct a mistake and try again. Use the time available as I have said, but do not ride the bird with the barrels. In other words once the barrels have got to the bird, don't stay on the bird, get on with the job, lead it and shoot it.

18 Range - On The Flat And In The Heavens

We ought to discuss the effective range of your shotgun to your targets. To start with we'll assume that we are using a conventional cartridge, normally used for game birds or clays. A cartridge with a shot load between 19 and 32 grams. The generally accepted view is that a target on the flat has a maximum range of about seventy yards. Shooting at clay pigeons at this distance, one needs a very tight choke to hold the pattern together. It is also true that very few people shoot at a target, clay or game over 50m away.

Exceptions will abound. I remember standing in a half filled grain trailer, soft rain was falling and this had stopped our harvest. The machinery had retired to the yard for the day and I was looking for a meal. (There really is nothing to beat marinaded pigeon breast, sliced very thin and pan-fried.) Armed with a shotgun in my semi-elevated hide, I watched as pigeons were flighting onto the crop of barley, beyond the hedge on my neighbour's farm. One of them must realise the exceptional menu on offer over here. And yet I waited. Baffled, and a little bored, I thought I'd head home for a bite to eat and some jobs at my desk. My Labrador, Finn, delighted at the prospect of lunch, charged for the gate out of the field. I remember turning round to have a last look across the field and there, flying across the straw rides at the far side of the field, was one lost pigeon. I brought up my gun and fired, thinking as I did so that it was really only a salute. The bird must be out of range. To my astonishment it fell. So convinced that it should have been too far, I paced the distance to where I estimated the bird was hit, not to where it fell... 84 yards. When plucked I couldn't find a single piece of lead shot in the unfortunate pigeon, so my accusation and eventually my conclusion had to be that the bird hadn't been shot at all, but had in fact taken pity on my grumbling tummy and died of fright. Still and all, as they say in Ireland, Finny got his lunch and I got my marinaded delight. But not since that day have I dropped one at that distance.

We covered the subject of a target on the flat or semi-elevated. The other category we have to look at is the bird in the heavens. Miles up above, the classic tall bird. In the mountains above our farm, miles from anywhere there is a deep quarry valley. Scoured out by the retreat of the glaciers, over the course of time it has grown oak woods up its sides and used to show some of the highest pheasant in the British Isles. There on the face of the valley side, above the timber line, was an Ordnance Survey marker which was well over 300 feet above the valley floor. Far below, beside the river, stood our gun line. Some of the pheasants would appear from holes in the tree line but some would take off from above the tree line, far up by the concrete O/S marker. Watched by Neil Robinson, his superb team of beaters, plus a few wild, rather high mountain goats, there they would catch the breeze coming at them across the valley and with hardly a flap from their wings, they would lift off from the heather and hang glide across the valley, miles out of range. The lower birds would either try for the far side of the valley or dive towards the guns. Inevitably there was competition between the guns to see who, if anybody, could hit the very highest of these birds. I never saw one shot. ***See photo 112a on page 112.***

So how high can you shoot? I have heard people say 70 yards, I don't agree. With a standard game cartridge, 52 yards is normally as far as you can make contact when shooting straight up. Gravity plays too great a part in projectiles fired straight up for you to expect more. If you want to shoot at targets higher than this, you will have to buy a specialist cartridge with shot loads up to 38 grams but do take care of your cheek and shoulder. Any more than this and you may look to a 3" chambered gun or delight in the eccentricities of the punt gun weighing anywhere from 25 to 100 pounds. Including your picnic, carrying punts around a driven shoot can be a considerable burden. A donkey and cart maybe?

112a

19 Concentration And Determination

I have yet to meet anyone who has been involved with this sport for some time, who will not agree that this is principally a mind game. The physical side to shooting is anything but complex. It is the mental side to our sport that determines the good from the marginal, the brilliant from the accomplished.

Here are a couple of thoughts for you to ponder on, which I then want to discuss. Firstly, the more birds you shoot, the more likely you are to miss. If you think this is due to the law of diminishing returns or just sheer probability, you will to a degree be correct. However, I would contend that it is principally due to a loss of concentration as a result of success. Secondly, our inability to sustain concentration, especially when under pressure, leads to an eventual loss of concentration.

Success Leads To Complacency

Let's take the first scenario. You are shooting a succession of incoming clay pigeons with a view to practising your technique. The first four birds shatter without a problem. The fifth is missed. Why? I believe it is due to success. While we are unsure of a result, we concentrate much harder than when we see success. When the birds start to break or to fall, we are inclined to relax mentally. "It's no problem, it's easy, I know how to do this," are all thoughts that vaguely pop into my mind when shooting. I know the most treacherous part of my body can be my brain. Just when you see success, suddenly it feels as if you are running on empty. There is no picture, no method, no deliberate steerage of barrel to the correct proximity with the target. Your determination is no longer a factor and suddenly you find yourself as a spectator to what you are doing, literally watching yourself going through the motions.

As I have said to clients so many times:

Be the dictator to what must happen,
not…
The spectator to what is happening.

When enjoying success, we begin to assume that we can do these things on automatic pilot. If I think what I am doing is easy, I will relax physically. The tension I felt prior to trying to succeed will disappear, the mind will automatically think it too can relax. And when it relaxes, you have lost your concentration, your determination. You are running on empty.

So what should we do? The best thing of all is to understand and recognise this frailty. The next is to try constantly for perfection, both in technique and result. Consider yourself as a demonstrator. You have an audience who wish to be shown just how this should be done. Each shot should be more perfect than the previous. Not just because the target was hit, but because the technique, both mental and physical, was faultless. On rare occasions I will pick up a gun when teaching, to actually shoot at a target. Normally I prefer to teach verbally rather than demonstrating but if I feel that the client will benefit more from watching a demonstration, out comes the gun. When demonstrating a shot to a client, there is no other occasion where I find shooting as simple a process to succeed at. I am at my most motivated, most concentrated and most determined, executing each step as perfectly as I know how.

Concentration Lapse

Our second scenario is the more difficult to control. Here we are competing against our own emotions and aspirations. I have the most enormous admiration for Olympic competitors. They have fought through endless qualifying rounds at home and abroad. The prize they seek is the ultimate in their sport. The competition is the best and they have to sustain their concentration over a period of days, not just minutes. Having competed in a very minor fashion, I have experienced both the dismay and misery of losing and the elation and thrill of winning. We must suffer moments of doubt, moments where victory is in sight if you can just hit those last two birds. The pressure is vast. Don't underestimate the extraordinary difficulty of sustaining your concentration to this level. Having reached these dizzying heights, should concentration suddenly be lost, what should we do?

Think method only… keep your concentration and be even more determined to have a perfect 'Picture'. All you need to remember and use are those pictures from similar targets you have hit before and be determined to keep reusing them exactly, not nearly right, not almost right, not virtually right. Be perfect, seek perfection.

Both in game shooting and clay pigeon shooting, there are major distractions. I used to find it marginally easier to keep my concentration when clay pigeon shooting as it normally extended over a shorter period of time. With game shooting, you may be standing in a hide for several hours, waiting for something to happen. With driven bird shooting, difficult or not, I dread the well meaning individual who is spectating during the driven shoot. They meander slowly towards you, *"Do you mind if I watch?"* And then they hang on your shoulder, talking incessantly, demanding some sort of reply, whether the subject be relevant or irrelevant. They feel obliged to comment on your shooting. *"Oh baaaad luck!"* or *"Good shot, gooood shot!"* Leave… me… be… PLEASE!

There is another potential concentration destroyer in game shooting. It is the target itself. You practise away on clays and get your shooting into order prior to the season, but come the moment there is a live bird in the air above you, or a bird bursting from cover and heading for the far ditch, it is amazing how many people will shoot without thought of 'picture'. What becomes clear is the more live targets an individual has the opportunity to shoot during a season, the better their cartridge to birds shot ratio. If you are likely to only get two or three shots on your day's shooting, there is an anxiety to hit a bird, any bird, that can overrule good gun control. All too often this is driven by a wish to justify the exorbitant cost of the game shooting. If you are experiencing difficulty under these circumstances, think target picture, not bird. Forget the feathers and the beak, the noise and excitement, and think as dispassionately as you can… target.

For clay shooting, there are other influences that may compromise your powers of concentration. I remember shooting in a competition in the eighties. It was our country's yearly grand final of this sport, and I had shot a first round score matched by two others. I was faced with the prospect of a shoot-off between three of us. We were asked who wished to go first. As the other two said nothing, I volunteered. My reasoning being that I would be the one to set the standard and this would put added pressure on them to match or better whatever I scored. As fortune had it, I shot my way through most of the card without dropping a bird. There were just two birds left to shoot. I loaded the gun and brought it up to my starting position and my hands began to shake. My mind had switched to overload, nothing seemed to be prepared for what was about to happen. My hands were shaking so badly that I didn't dare call a bird. I unloaded the gun and put it on the ground. Took three deep breaths, shook my arms until they seemed to relax and wondered if I could be penalised for wasting time? Both of my fellow competitors watched me do this and one of them, an old friend of mine called David, asked me what was going on. *"I can't stop shaking"*, I said out of the side of my mouth. Having picked up the gun I held two cartridges ready to drop them into the chambers, both fell on the ground. He kindly collected the cartridges offering to load the gun and carefully placed one cartridge at a time into each open chamber. A deep breath, another and eventually I recovered enough of my equilibrium to shoot the remaining pair. A 'Possible', (all birds hit). Maximum pressure on the other two shooters, no room for them to make a mistake. The ideal result.

That physical reaction is the result of both pressure and adrenalin, the latter coursing through your body when everything seems to be wound up like a clock's main spring. What I haven't delved into yet was my mental state. Even if I hadn't been shaking, my head was in a spin. I knew that if I called the birds at that moment, my focus was gone and I would almost certainly miss them, my mind was running on empty. I was observing myself shoot, rather than controlling how and when I would shoot. I had to regain my concentration. Re-think what I was about to do, re-plan what I had to get right. How?

Visualisation

In the case of the competition described above, I knew where the next pair of birds were going. I imagined them coming out of the trap and one flying high over me and the next flying high to my left. I then imagined the correct placement of my barrels in relation to each of the targets in order to hit them. I was now prepared for what I had to achieve and nothing would be a surprise and my modus operandi was planned. By doing this, I re-established the process or method of breaking the birds and most importantly, re-established my focus. The rest, as they say, is history and I was on a high for a long time afterwards.

We all prepare ourselves physically for what we are about to do, some in a more detailed fashion than others. What we so often forget to address is preparation of the mind. Think through the process of all necessary physical movement and then prepare your mind for the decisions it will face. In the case of shooting, what 'picture' do we need to break the targets and then most importantly, which target are we going to shoot first. Having selected your first target, watch it break before shooting the second, that moment of watching a shattering clay will provide you with the necessary follow-through.

20 Plan Your Shooting

For clay pigeon shooters always consider your gun's starting position. (This is discussed in depth in the section: 'Barrels Starting Position'). In the case of shooting double targets, make a decision as to which target you are going to shoot first. Have a look at the birds in flight, consider which bird you have more time to shoot. Consider the possibility of taking a natural progression through the targets. In other words, shooting the rear bird first and then the front bird. Consider shooting either the left or right-hand bird first, depending on whether you shoot left-handed or right-handed. For the left-handed shot, shooting the left-hand bird first makes an easier progression and vice versa. If either of the birds is likely to necessitate an awkward shot, try and get this one dealt with before the other. Finally, having planned your strategy, unless something extraordinary occurs, don't change your mind. However, if your strategy proves to be wrong, don't be afraid to take time to re-think your procedure.

For game shooters, don't for one minute think that this is only applicable to clay pigeon shooting. It is just as important an exercise for you to prepare the mind and plan what you will do in the event of a bird appearing. When going out rough shooting, when standing at your peg on a gun line, swing the gun at an imaginary target, following a line you believe the bird is likely to take. Think about the 'picture' you need to drop the bird and then practise a different angle and a different picture. You will be better prepared, more likely to make contact with your target, more focussed and therefore more likely to succeed.

21 Learning Time And Motion

Learning to shoot can be accomplished over a fairly small amount of time. The average time taken by most individuals, who have never handled a gun before, to become safe and competent shots is 5 x 1 hour lessons. The mistake that can often be made is to let too much time elapse between lessons. An ideal scenario is to try and have a lesson at least once every two weeks. Much information and method that has been covered with the client need not be covered again. Less frequent than this and I find that too much time during the next lesson is spent going over old ground and progress is much slower. However, given a frequent attendance, progress is remarkably quick. After five or so hours spent at the shooting school, I would be confident that the client would not disgrace themselves at a driven shoot, rough shoot or clay pigeon shoot. A dear friend and client, Nicola, started shooting with me early in 2002. Other members of her family were indulging in shooting lessons too. To begin with she was the 'ugly duckling' of her clan. A patch was placed on a lens of her sunglasses, she had minimal domination right, difficulty with closing a delinquent left eye. Last Christmas 2002, the swan emerged. She shot at one of our foremost tall bird pheasant shoots in the Wicklow mountains as guest of its gun captain Prof. Harry H. I was phoned by three different individuals who had seen her shoot that day and had been impressed at her sportsmanship and ability with her gun. You too can achieve these levels if you dedicate yourself to learning the art of shotgun shooting.

A word of comment to those of you who wish to learn this skill. A high percentage of gentlemen who wish to learn to shoot, initially find it more difficult than most ladies. I suspect this is due to a preconceived notion that they have some inherent ability to successfully use guns because they are male. Everyone likes to take control of their destiny, everyone wants to dictate what happens when they have a gun in their hands. There is a moment, early on in everyone's shooting career, where the client will themselves determine how to handle the gun and what method they will use. It may be completely at odds with the advice given, will bear no resemblance to method used when they have actually broken their targets but they will not follow the advice of the shooting instructor. They want to do it their way, they want to take control. I can't blame them.

But it is still going against all they have used to find initial success. The scenario goes like this. I give a full explanation on the 'How and Why' of shooting a shotgun. They then take their first shot. More often than not they will hit that first bird. They will use the information exactly as you have instructed. Then it is only a question of time before they will want to see the target break. To be told it has broken is really wonderful but they want to see that moment for themselves. I'm encouraged that this is part of their persona as it proves an independence of spirit, an individualism that shows strength of mind and character. Nonetheless, it is my job to bring them back to the process that works, to get them to abandon their own theories or wishes until they match those of the instructor. Once that is done, we are truly under way with learning how to shoot.

It is from this point that personal experience must be built by the individual as well as instructed by the expert. Go back to your shooting instructor occasionally. Have him or her look at your style, your effectiveness. If you find yourself shooting on an occasional basis or on a seasonal basis, pay a visit to your shooting school before your season starts. Get the creases ironed out of your technique, get back into consistently dropping your targets and then on the first day of the season or at your next clay pigeon competition, you can shoot with increased confidence and efficiency.

22 A Fitting Gun

Off the peg or bespoke; brand new or previously owned; Single Barrel or Double Barrel; Box Lock, Side Lock, Round Action or Hammer; Side by Side or Over and Under; Fixed choke or Multi-choke; Pump Action, Semi-Automatic, Bull Pup or Rotary; Top lever, Side lever, or Under lever; 12 bore, 16 bore, 20 bore, 28 bore, 4.10 bore. You know you could make up some wonderful choices and believe you me there are more variations than you read above.

The reality, as usual, is the more personalised, the more decorated, the more highly crafted, the more beautiful, the more it is going to cost. Currently a new shotgun can range in price from £400 to £110,000 and that's before any precious stones are added or a large quantity of gold inlay. Those prices are going to be out of date as soon as this book is published, so I really put those figures in to entertain future generations who will be amazed just how cheap shotguns were all those years ago. However, when viewing the best made guns in auction catalogue or gun maker's premises, I'm staggered that anyone would question the cost of such an exquisite piece of craftsmanship. What's more, I would love one. It's every bit as good an investment as buying a beautiful property or painting and to use these guns is a delight. Enough of my ambitions and desires, let's get back to you.

I had better take my own advice and start at the beginning, with the 'bore' of the shotgun.

12 Bore: Most widely used for both game shooting and clay pigeon shooting. Perceived to be the adult male's most suitable weapon. It combines both weight of shot and weight of gun to the best advantage for someone strong enough to use one. The implication given here, is that it weighs a great deal. In fact it does not, the average game gun will weigh around 6.5 lbs. But can be found as light as 5.5 lbs. and as heavy as 8.5 lbs. It does produce a degree of recoil that you need to learn how to absorb. Due to this, many ladies and young shots prefer to shoot with 16 bore, 20 bore, 28 bore or 4.10 bore. However, I know of some ladies who will shoot with nothing other than a twelve. I shall illustrate.

The Triathlon is a clay pigeon shooting, fly casting and horse or hunter trial event over rustic fences and through obstacles such as closed gates and anything devious the organisers could think up. Myself plus a very dear friend called Gay, asked another compatriot of ours to make up a team for one of these regional events. Several and a half hours after departure, we arrived at a fine old country estate in the south east of Ireland. Our compatriot Gerald, went off to enter us in the competition, while we unpacked rods, reels, guns, cartridges and one mother (known as Beryl, our head supporter). To our consternation, my team mate's 20 bore shotgun was nowhere to be found. I went off at speed, mission-bound to find a replacement for her to use. No luck, not one on the field. "There's nothing for it, you'll have to sit this one out." This suggestion of mine caused more consternation but Gay wasn't that easily put off. "I'll use your gun," she said. "It's a 12 bore, heavier and with more recoil than you're used to," I replied. I can't repeat what she said to that! Off we went to shoot. I usually went first so we could decide which was the best way to approach any problem there may be. I shot through the card and missed one. I asked the scorer had anyone shot all the birds. "No," was the reply. "So far the best score is yours." Basking, all be it briefly, in the glory of the moment, I watched as Gerald went forward to shoot. Gerald is one of those wonderful countrymen who have shot pigeon and snipe before he was baptised. He also missed one bird. It couldn't be better, we'd share first prize in the shooting and we'd put up a great team score for the overall prize. So finally up stepped our female member Gay with my 12 bore. I dropped in a couple of cartridges while she nervously thumbed the safety catch. "Is it off?" she asked. "Where's the first bird coming from?" Too late to reply, the first bird, a single, came rocketing out of the undergrowth, the gun fired and the clay disappeared in a cloud of black powder. Another cartridge was loaded, another bird this time high overhead. The bird was powdered again. More singles, more powder. Then the same with the doubles. "Don't forget the doubles are slower and take the back bird first," I stage whispered. Two gun shots, two little clouds of black dust disappeared across the fields to settle on a distant cottage's washing line. So it continued with every one of the birds smashed. The the final pair, an 'on report' double, where a single bird is thrown and when the first shot is heard, a second is thrown by another trap. More black powder was left hanging in the air, more white smoke appeared as the cartridges ejected from the gun. Nothing had been missed. She turned, handed me the gun and with a broad grin said "Now I know why you always want me to use a 20 bore!"

16 bore: Once a widely used size of shotgun, convenient in weight if carrying the gun across deep snipe laden bogs in the west of Ireland and over heather covered mountains in the Wilds of Scotland. A small difference in the weight of shot between this and a twelve bore, a small difference in the weight of the gun, in both cases a little lighter. However, if you think this may be the perfect compromise between 12 and 20 bores, check with your gunsmith for availability of ammunition. For us in Ireland, there is a minimal choice of cartridge for this gun. What is available tends to be very expensive as the turnover is so slow.

20 bore: This is a gun that is widely used by many ladies of all ages, and by many young people who are learning to shoot. It is also the favoured piece for many quail shooting people in America. It is an ideal weapon, light and quick to mount. Some think too light, and therefore too quick. I think that's a problem with their technique, not a deficiency with the gun. This is a shotgun that will always be an asset. From one's early teens, you and then your family will benefit from this gun, and when the shoulders get stiff and the back doesn't bend as it used to, you will be reaching for it again. I have started many youngsters on a 20 bore. Two of these boys appeared at my shooting school on a regular basis. I think in those days, their mothers thought of my shooting school as a crèche for small delinquent males. Two impish faces titled Nick and Douglas would emerge from the back of a family car and run riot until the responsible parent had found the nerve to return. By this time I had usually subdued the two of them, by fair means or foul, normally foul. Do I still have to put up with them? Yes. Have they changed? Not the slightest! How old are they now? 40 plus!

28 bore: This is the next size down in the shotgun range. Very light indeed for an adult, very little recoil. A reduced weight of shot load. Again, a very suitable gun to learn on. If you choose this gun, check on the availability of a broad selection of ammunition should this be the only gun you buy. If you haven't a broad choice of shot load and shot size, you may find there are some targets that you should not attempt to shoot. This size of gun is being used by a select number of driven game shooters in an attempt to make their task more challenging. All very well if they genuinely can shoot. That said, I do use one for my less confident clients when they first begin, such as a group of ladies yesterday who were here for a Hen's Shooting Party. Some shot twenty bore, some 28 bore, all left with broad grins on their faces and no bruises on their strapless shoulders later that evening.

4.10 bore: The smallest of the regularly used shotguns. By necessity, it throws an extremely small pattern due to a small shot load. Used by many young boys and girls as their first shotgun, it usually ends up on a gun rack as a curiosity, occasionally lent to a neighbour or friend for their children to learn with. In theory every bit as lethal as the 12 bore, with a much smaller shot load, it necessitates a much greater degree of accuracy at distance due to a very narrow spread of pattern. However, using a three inch cartridge your shot speed should remain the same, therefore your quantity of lead on the target is of reasonable volume.

Single Barrel Or Double Barrel

There are still some single barrel shotguns made and of course one can always find a secondhand one to be bought for very little cost. I remember having one, given to me by a client who didn't want it, never used it and saw no purpose in owning it. Neither did I. I tried selling it and eventually gave it to a friend. Fifteen years later at a wedding, he reminded me of it. "You know Shane, I never fired a shot through that gun. I kept it licensed and in good order for years, but I never even dirtied the barrel." "What on earth did you keep it for?" I asked. "I had ambitions to be a publican and thought it would look good on the wall, but I ended up trying out an angle grinder on it. Then I used the pieces in a sculpture!" he said. Nice to think that it eventually ended up being useful.

I'm sure there are people out there who will be hopping mad at the suggestion that a single barrel, single shot shotgun is a pointless investment. I'm not suggesting it, I'm saying it. It's the cheapest entry level to shotgun shooting but please show some good sense and save your money until you can afford to buy two barrels or a multi-shot shotgun. ***See photos 127 a,b on page 127.***

OK, having made at least one enemy out there, let's see who else I can offend! Next had better be double barrel shotguns.

127a

127b

Side By Side

An elegant shape, generally lighter than an Over and Under. A short or medium length barrel, 5.5 lb. to 6.5 lb. well balanced 12 bore S/B/S is a very useful weapon when rough shooting or driven game shooting. Being lighter than the majority of O/U's, carrying this type gun across country for many hours of walked up shooting can be an advantage. These are durable weapons, simple in design and for the most part reliable. I know that many shooting people contend that no O/U can be as well balanced as a Best London S/B/S. I would agree that one can find beautifully balanced S/B/S shotguns, considerably easier than beautifully balanced O/U shotguns but then I very rarely have the privilege of handling best London Over and Under shotguns. I should travel there and see them more often and hope they may give me one!

Over And Under

Generally more substantial in appearance than the S/B/S and in my opinion, lacking the aesthetic appeal of the S/B/S. I think the O/U's greatest advantage over an S/B/S is its undoubtedly easier sight picture along the barrel, due to a narrow action and barrel configuration. Persist when selecting a new gun, it may be more difficult to find the perfectly balanced O/U but they are out there. Rather than chasing a multi-choke gun, you might consider purchasing an O/U with fixed chokes as they balance better due to lighter barrels. For an all round shotgun, an O/U with multi chokes gives you a huge choice of uses. I have 12 and 20 bore S/B/S, 12 and 20 bore O/U all of which vie for my affection; each has its place. All said and done, my favourite O/U is a Winchester O/U boxlock with fixed chokes, which for 40 years I've enjoyed and used with success. I've never felt the need for a tighter choke on this gun and as it was my late wife's wedding present to me, I dearly love it. ***See photos 130 a,b on page 130.***

Hammer Gun

For those of you who think there is little point mentioning something that is long passed from the gunsmith's window, think again. They are still being made in at least one factory in Italy and I may yet receive a severe lecture from more manufacturers of hammer guns. What do I think about them? Again I'd love to use one for a while before I approved or condemned the idea. If you should be tempted to buy one to use it for shooting and not decoration, please ensure the gun is still in proof. They look wonderful in their own nostalgic

130a

130b

fashion. However, the impracticality of having to pull back the hammers on the old guns leaves me uninterested. On the modern hammer guns, this is done mechanically for you; certainly on the Italian model I saw recently being used on a driven pheasant shoot, the hammers were cocked automatically. When activating the top lever the barrels dropped away from the action and when closing the gun, the hammers self cocked. A safety catch was provided and I can't really see any reason why you shouldn't buy them if that is your wish. For me they looked overly cumbersome and ornate and performed heavily.

Damascus Barrels

Prior to the early 20th century, all shotgun barrels were forged by heating narrow strips of iron and steel and shaping them around a mandrel. This process was referred to as 'Laminating' or 'Damascus'. These types of barrels earned a reputation for weakness and were never meant to be used with modern smokeless powder, or any kind of moderately powerful explosive. Because of the resemblance to Damascus steel, higher-end barrels were made by Belgian and British gun makers. These barrels are proof marked and meant to be used with light pressure loads. Current gun manufacturers make slide assemblies and small parts such as triggers and safeties from powdered Swedish steel resulting in a swirling two-toned effect; these parts are often referred to as 'Stainless Damascus.'

Semi-Automatic

A single barrelled shotgun with tubular magazine. The gun having been discharged automatically reloads a cartridge from the magazine. Where you are when reading this, will dictate on the laws governing the use of these guns. Normally the sporting variations of this shotgun are able to hold five cartridges but restrictions have been imposed in some countries where the maximum number of rounds is limited to three. It is vital that this gun be kept very clean and all foreign bodies removed from the action lest dirt should jam the mechanism when reloading.

Other than this minor 'achilles heel', the mechanical performance of these guns would seem to be reliable. However, although I like the sight picture due to the single barrel, there is a shift in the balance of the gun as the magazine empties. This is considerably more pronounced when using a full complement of five shots in the tubular magazine. With three shots in the magazine, the difference is harder to detect. A characteristic of this weapon, which I do see as a drawback, is the single barrel. This gives only one choice of shot pattern every time you swing onto a target.

These guns can be bought with multi-choke options, so you are not completely stymied but once your choke is chosen, that's it. One final comment must be made. I know it will leave some of you writing furious letters to your favourite newspaper but sadly it is a fact that there are many shooting people, usually from the game shooting department, who view these guns with a great deal of suspicion. I have to say that it is understandable to a degree. The problem lies in the action. With an O/U or S/B/S, when the gun is open it is very obvious to everyone who cares to look that the gun is broken and potentially safe. With a semi-auto, unless you are on the side of the action that has the ejection port visible to you, it is impossible to know if the gun is empty and safe or the action is closed and loaded. Sometimes it is impossible to see at all due to the way the gun is being carried and people naturally are suspicious, if not very nervous of these guns.

Regardless of this, for the person using one, handling is ok and recoil is minimal and many shooters love them. Manufacturers sometimes fit such luxuries as muzzle brakes or ported muzzles to divert expanding gases at right angles to the barrel thereby reducing recoil and in some cases their contention being that it prevents or reduces muzzle rise or muzzle flip affecting your shot pattern. It is worth noting that I for one do not subscribe to the possibility of muzzle flip affecting a shotgun's barrel before the shot has left the barrel. The reactive forces from a fired bullet or cartridge exiting the muzzle act directly down the centre line of the barrel and the shotguns grip is so close to that centre line that rise or flip is impossible and any movement of the barrel has to occur after the projectile has left the barrel. It is after firing and after the exit of your shot that the user will see the barrel has risen, hence the only weapon that this may cause difficulty for the user is the multi shot semi-auto. I note that some shotgun manufacturers continue to use muzzle flip as a great marketing tool for adding weight to the front end of their 'trap shooting' guns and effecting more sales.

For those of you who, like me, have bought these guns, be aware that you can order a new gun with a loading/ejection port on either the right hand side of the action or on the left. The simple reason for this is to prevent the user from having spent cartridges flying out of the chamber near to his or her face. For a left cheek shooter you will need a port on the left of the action and vice versa.

Should there be any out there who would like to know more, the user loads separate cartridges into the gun, one via the ejector port in the

134a

134b

134c

side of the action and the action closed mechanically, usually by a button being pushed. For other ammunition, this is loaded through a sprung floor plate in the underside of the action. The trigger when pulled fires a single round and must be pulled again to fire a subsequent round.

As an additional piece of information for you, there are semi-autos that can hold up to ten rounds in a tubular magazine, up to ten rounds in the 'bullpup' magazine, and up to twelve rounds in a rotary magazine. Quite an armoury but don't indulge in one of these as I suspect you won't be welcomed with open arms if visiting many police stations and I suspect that most European game shoots would despair if they saw such a weapon.
See photos 134 a,b,c on page 134.

Pump Action

All the worries of those who dislike semi-autos tend to hold the same fear. More suspicion, more problems. In fact by the nature of the gun it is easier to see if the action is open and therefore safer. The slide that is used to crank another round into the chamber is a major giveaway as the gun can only be fired when the slide is all the way forward at the end of the tubular magazine. It still doesn't help if your fellow shooters are unfamiliar with this type of action. Perceptions are difficult to change. The actual operation of the gun is interesting but difficult to master. When one is trying to maintain total control of the gun with the front hand, you have to use it to reload. It really is hard to keep the gun steady on a target while activating the slide.

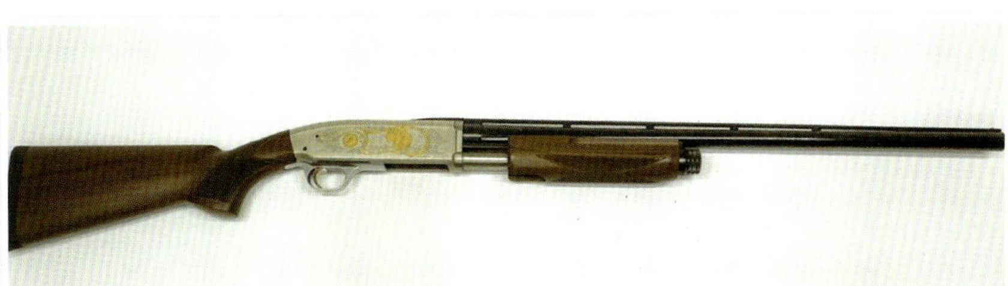

23 Action Types

Box Lock

This refers to the mechanism which is housed in the body of the action and is part of the means used to fire the cartridge. Access is normally through the underside of the action but if you want to service the gun, best leave this to an experienced gunsmith. Box lock mechanisms have a superb track record of reliability. I have yet to encounter a serious problem with one, either my own or my clients'. They tend to be priced below that of their partner the side lock. Solid, dependable, a good investment.

Side Lock

Again this refers to the firing mechanism of the gun. With a side lock, the locks are no longer housed in the under side of the action but on either side of and behind the action. Hence their name. A side lock shotgun appears to have a much larger action than the box lock shotgun. Its benefit to the owner is the ease by which one can remove and therefore service both locks. Many side locks can be removed by undoing a single screw. From an aesthetic point of view, due to the extended plates the locks are mounted on, it gives a great opportunity for the engraver to show his art to its best advantage. If you can afford a good one, buy and enjoy. Caveat emptor the side lock that is miraculously cheap. Shiny and new it may look in the catalogues, it very quickly will become tarnished and worn.

Side Lock

Round Action

This is neither box lock nor side lock, though from an external view there is a vague similarity to the shape of a box lock action. Both locks are mounted on the trigger plate and the ejector mechanism is built into the body of the action. They have, until recently, been an action peculiar to gun makers in Scotland. A famous product of great quality, made in Glasgow by David McKay Brown and in Edinburgh by Dixons. There is at least one copy on the market made by another manufacturer but the McKay Browns and Dixons are the classics of the marque. There is nothing to criticise, no aspersions to cast, they are truly on par with the side lock action. I've organised two matching pairs to be built for clients and they have proved to be a great investment... and I'd love one.

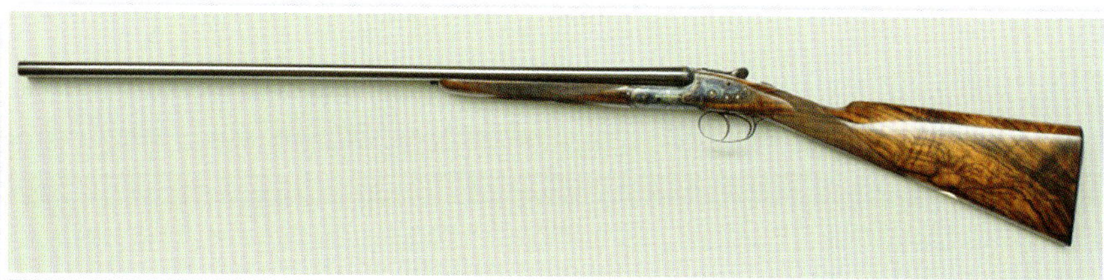

Droplocks

A superb firearm that initially appears to be a standard boxlock but as with the Westley Richards made version, the action floor plate is hinged and when lowered the two locks can easily be removed from the action. This addition makes them as easily serviceable and as legitimate an investment as the side lock.

'Sister act'

24 New Versus Used

Still more decisions to be made. Let's discuss the new versus second-hand gun. One of the most attractive prospects for investing in a shotgun is a gun's ability to hold its value. Indeed, some will increase in value and I'm not just talking about very expensive guns. The gun my father bought me new for £36 is currently worth €450. Do not be put off by a gun being second-hand. Providing the dealer or gunsmith guarantees the gun's in good condition, there are many good deals to be had on second-hand guns. Beware however, if you are not buying from a licensed dealer. With no official blessing on your potential purchase, it is vital that you get the gun checked to ensure it is in proof. This means that the barrels are capable of withstanding the considerable pressure of gas, created when the cartridge fires. We do not have a proof house in Ireland so guns would need to go abroad to be tested. A good established gunsmith should have a barrel gauge and from that be able to establish if the barrel thickness is worryingly thin. However, there are some other pointers that can be considered when making a purchase of a second hand gun before you need start looking for Bore Gauges and Micrometers.

1. Check the stock and Fore-end for any hairline cracks, especially around the grip. Check any areas of the stock and Fore-end where they adjoin with metal parts. If they are very dark in colour and near to places where screws etc. are holding parts together beware. Excess oil over time softens wood. Check all components feel good and tight.

2. Check the amount of wear on the checkering (this is the diamond shaped pattern carved into the wood by the stock maker), both on the Fore-end and on the stock's grip. This gives a good indication of the amount of use the gun has had. Note

that too little wear may indicate the checkering has been redone to aid in the sale.

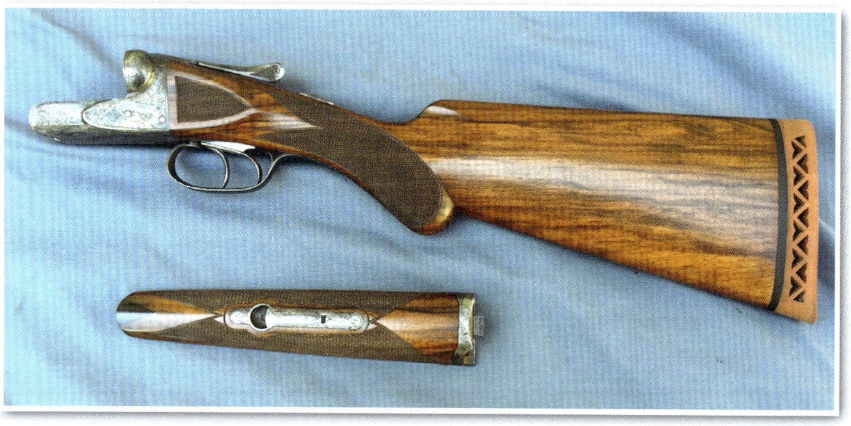

3. Remove the Fore-end and use your finger tips to check for indentations in the barrels. Slide your fingers up and down the barrels and trust your sense of touch rather than your eyesight for this job.

4. Check screw heads in the action and Fore-end for worn slot heads caused by excessive or careless use.

5. Check the inside of the barrels for any pitting in the steel tubes. If you suspect the metal to have been polished to remove signs of pitting then you must ensure that the gun has been proof tested and is currently 'in proof.'

6. Close the gun and holding it in one hand at the back hand grip, shake it to and fro to see if the action is tight. Any vibration or noise needs careful identifying of the source. A very loose fit between action and barrel will result in lost compression within the chambers and therefore shot speed will diminish.

7. Load the gun with snap caps and check the safety catch is

working and the triggers cannot be pulled with the safety catch on. A 'Snap Cap' is a simulated cartridge that is used to 'Dry Fire' a shotgun and maintains resistance for the firing pins when they strike. Failure to provide a resistance for them may result in a broken firing pin.

8. Slip the safety catch off and pull each trigger having loaded the gun with those snap caps. Break the gun and check the ejectors or push rods are functioning (providing it isn't a non-ejector type). It is not uncommon to find one ejector throwing out the spent round and the other ejector only partially pushing the spent round out of the chamber. There are a number of reasons why this may occur, some that are cheap to repair, some which decidedly are not. Many are caused by a lack of simple maintenance, cleaning and oiling of those moving parts. Should you be checking a single trigger mechanism, pull the trigger twice. If the gun will not fire on a second pull of the trigger, give the butt a sharp tap with the flat of your hand and then pull the trigger again. The reason for the non firing will be to do with an inertia system that hasn't been activated by the recoil of the gun firing the first barrel.

9. Check the flats of your barrels to find the proof marks. Ensure the gun is marked 'Nitro Proofed'. Also check if the word 'sleeved' appears stamped on the flats. This will mean that the barrels have been replaced from the forcing cones to the muzzle. This should reduce the value of the gun, but does not mean the gun is unsafe, on the other hand it may affect the balance of the gun. ***See photos 144 a,b,c on page 144.***

10. Check if the action was originally colour hardened and if so, how much colour hardening is still present on the outside of the action and top and bottom tangs. 'Case colour hardening'

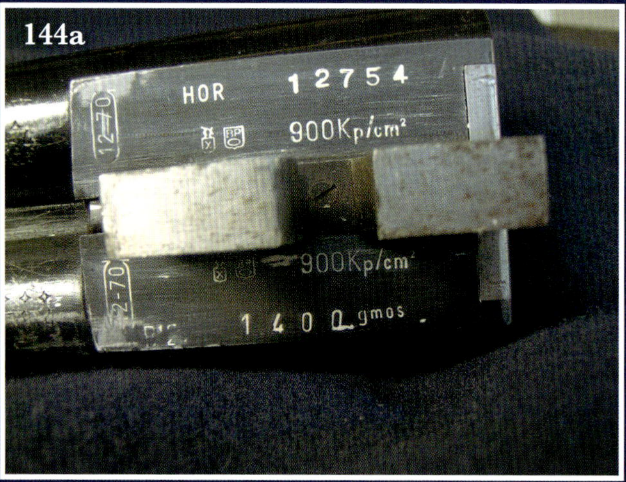

144a

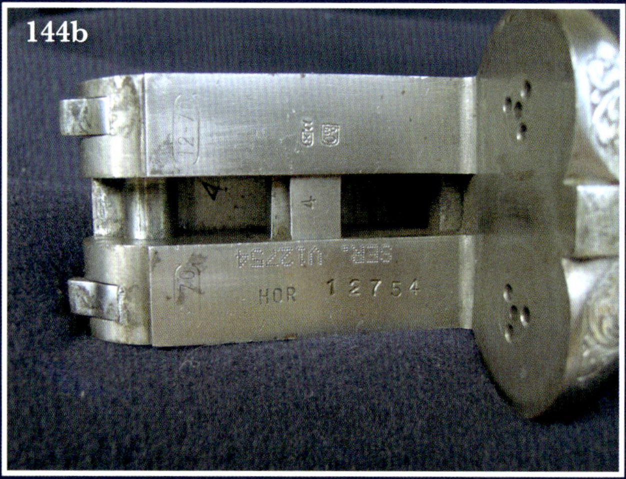

144b

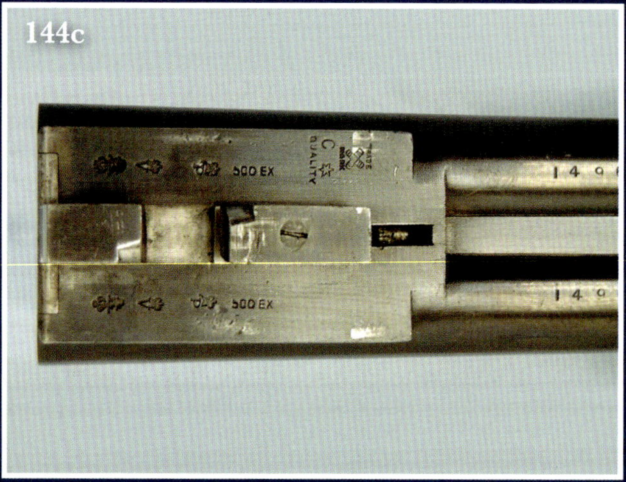

144c

is a process used to chemically harden the outer surface of the steel while leaving the main bulk of the metal softer and therefore more easily machined. The colour hardening is done after the part has been made. Blueing or blacking of the gun are processes that are designed to eliminate the sun reflecting from those metal surfaces. It also gives some small protection to those surfaces from rust. Check both to assess the amount of wear and tear the gun has had.

11. Check the balance of the gun. A correctly balanced gun will feel as if it wants to lift itself. How can that be when we are dealing with an inanimate object? Hold the gun in both hands as you would normally, and bring the gun to your cheek. As you mount the gun, it will 'move' or lift with a greater or lesser degree of ease. You'll feel this best in the tricep which is on the opposite side of your arm to your bicep in the upper arm, the arm that holds the barrels. The amount of force required to raise the gun will be anything from very little, to a major strain. If you are raising and lowering the gun two hundred times in a day's shooting, it will make a huge difference to your efficiency if the gun is well balanced.

12. Do you like the engraving on the action?

13. Is there a stock oval, found on the underside of the stock, and is it already engraved?

14. Is the furniture well figured? (Does the woodwork have an attractive grain?)

15. Is the gun being sold with a travelling case; if so, is it the original case?

16. The final consideration is: does the gun fit? If not, seek the advice of a qualified shooting instructor if you intend shortening or lengthening the stock. Equally seek their advice if the stock needs casting to fit. Be aware that old stocks are more at risk of breaking when you attempt to bend them to suit the person using the gun. Be also advised that the stocks on over and under shotguns may prove difficult to bend and keep bent. This is due to a steel bolt that runs through the grip of the stock and into the back of the action to hold action and stock together.

25 The Bespoke Gun

The bespoke gun is our final category. A gun, tailor-made to your requirements offers virtually no limit to what can be designed and built. There are many manufacturers the world over who will take an order for a gun to be built specifically as a one-off. I regret to tell you that there are some factories who cannot turn out what they promise. I would strongly suggest that you do some research before you place an order. Safe territory may be found in London, Birmingham and Scotland, but there are a few wonderful manufacturers, some of them very small private businesses, who will make guns to order on the European continent. Be prepared to wait for your order as most of the great gun makers have long waiting lists. Even for the most expensive of guns, a waiting list of four years is considered normal.

The whole process of ordering a gun is completed without hurry, without pressure. Time is devoted to you. Choosing the stock blank is the part I like most. A 'blank' is the raw or unfinished stock, made of walnut. Ask to see a selection of finished guns so that you can make an informed choice when selecting yours. If you see a finished stock that you particularly like, ask your gunsmith to find you a choice of blanks that will be of similar type. The joy of owning a really beautifully figured stock is best described by referring you to a lovely piece of furniture you may own or see, where the grain in the wood swirls like large incoming waves rolling onto a beach or reminds you of a summer's sky with high cirrus or mackerel clouds. The grain, figuring or marbling in the wood will be enhanced by the stock maker and as always there are a number of choices. English, French or Turkish Walnut (this latter option seemingly the most popular currently), Circassian Walnut, Birdseye Maple to name but three, there are Black Cherry, Screwbean Mesquite, Bubinga Rosewood and Bastogne and there are many more, research will show you why they aren't all included in this book. There is a decision to be made with regard to the type of rear hand grip you would like for the stock. Whether it should be straight hand or swan neck, a gently curved Prince of Wales or steeply curved full pistol grip. I have to admit a preference here. The Side By Side shotgun looks its very best with a straight hand stock, the Over and Under with a Prince of Wales grip, which is sometimes referred to as a semi-pistol grip, or 25% pistol grip.

The maker will of course build to your specification so should you require a stock designed with a 'Full Pistol Grip', I suspect there may be a few raised eyebrows but nonetheless, think long and hard before you order this design. Elegance in your shotgun is difficult to maintain when built with this as a design feature. I also find a full pistol grip is incompatible with the way I hold a gun and prevents my back hand from staying light on the gun and therefore enabling my hand to slide rearwards as I mount the gun. A personal thing but I know how my own technique works and it isn't as efficient with the full pistol grip.

I have a wonderful B2 Browning, built I'm told in 1933. It was sold to me by a dear friend Pat O'Brien when he decided to retire from his most passionate of hobbies, Pat has been my gunsmith for forty or more years. Such an elegant looking gun, the Fore-end is very slim, the rear hand grip of the stock is 'swan necked' and equally slim, the action blacked with little engraving and this gun is magical and featherweight in my hands. A Best London gun that truly 'moves' would not be better than this Browning... Thank you old friend!

Back to your own gun; the engraving on the action and other parts of the gun is a matter of your choice. You will be offered engraving patterns that the manufacturer will carry out for you. You can specify what you would like to see on the gun, even to the extent of having portraits engraved on the action. Computer aided engraving can perform some extraordinary feats nowadays. I have always hankered after an action with an old cantankerous Cape Buffalo staring back at me. If the manufacturer cannot produce the engraving you would like, ask for advice on getting an independent engraver to work with you on your own design ideas. Look through auction catalogues, gun makers' brochures, books on guns and artistic exhibitions. You will find a huge quantity of information out there and discover that the greatest difficulty is making a final choice.

You will of course be invited to visit a shooting ground that serves the manufacturer, where your measurements will be taken amidst copious cups of coffee, three course picnics and champagne... or should be! This won't be a one off visit either. You'll be back when the gun is nearing completion. Remember the experience, it can be very special, and take your time making your choices; this gun should last many generations of your existing or future family.

There is finally a choice of how many?

I was in a delightful coastal town of Watch Hill, Rhode Island, again with my friend David Lloyd and he brought me to meet a highly entertaining gentleman whom I shall refer to as Peter. Little did I know that I was to be shown one of the truly famous collections of English shotguns. The Graves Collection was made up of 5 or 6 guns of ascending calibers, 12 bore, 16 bore, 20 bore etc, all side locks, all with exhibition grade furniture in a beautiful walnut gun cabinet. Leather lined with drawers below, a piece of art and antiquity all in one. Not only those but another gun was produced for inspection, one of my most favourite of Best London guns by Boss and Co.

A 12 bore side lock that Peter told me wasn't working correctly and would I have a look? I settled in his kitchen, armed with a cut glass tumbler plus contents and opened the gun case. Inside was not only one of the most beautiful of English guns but in the smaller compartments of his gun case, were a complete array of little paper packets, tied with twine and every one carefully labelled. Spare parts for every eventuality. In another compartment a full set of 'Turn Screws'. I removed both locks and marvelled at the precision of the interior, something the owner may never see and yet finished as carefully as the exterior. I found the problem without too much difficulty and took a number of components apart so as to replace a broken piece, I spread them out on white writing paper. The relevant packet with spare part was found, opened and at that moment into the kitchen came Peter. He looked at me, looked at the gun, looked at all those parts, went slightly pale, made as if to say something, decided against and quietly walked out. I can't say I blame him.

A collection of guns like Peter's, exhibited in your home, may enhance your life, or you may consider another possibility? How about a matched pair or even a matched triple. Two or three guns of the same calibre, each numbered consecutively with a number 1, 2, and 3 engraved in gold, usually on the rib at the action end of the barrels. Large leather travelling cases to hold all the guns or single cases for a more modest shooting day?

The idea of having multiple guns is for the game shooter who is intent on shooting big bags or large numbers of birds. Usually this will be driven bird shooting, the birds flying over the gun line in such quantity that the user needs a loader or maybe even two loaders to keep him armed and shooting continuously. Unusual in this day and age but not impossible to find.

26 A Gun To Fit

Before I started this project, I searched my bookshelves at home and took out every book I possess on the subject of shooting. My idea was to try and find a way to order my thoughts when planting them in these pages. While looking through those dusty tomes, I discovered what I think is an extraordinary assumption made by many of these authors. The assumption being that the normal way to shoot is right-handed and if you are about to start, you will be adopting a right handed hold when mounting the shotgun. When commenting or advising on how the stock of your shotgun should be shaped for you, most books make comment on 'cast off', make comment on 'pull', 'drop at comb', 'drop at heel', some even acknowledge 'pitch'. Nearly all give direction on how to shoot, some detailed, some not. Little or no provision is made for the person, with a left eye dominance, that should shoot off their left cheek or, if you wish, left-handed. Don't be put off by this, shooting instructors know the value of shooting with the master/dominant eye and even authors of shooting books are becoming more enlightened. Find out which is your master eye!

The Pull

Why is it important to have your gun fitted? Firstly, let's deal with stock length or what is called your 'pull' measurement. When you bring the gun to your cheek, a stock that is too long is likely to get caught in clothing when you mount the gun. When the stock arrives at the cheek, it may leave your head too far from the action and your master eye may be positioned too low to see the bead. Your front hand may have too short a grip on the barrels; if this is the case, there will be too much weight forward of your point of control. Your rear hand may have trouble reaching the triggers and the safety catch, all of the above leading to a bad body position leaning backwards at the waist in order to counterbalance the weight of the gun.

Several points from the reverse of the above list can cause as many difficulties if the gun stock is too short. Your head can be too close to the action, your master eye too high above the line of the barrels for you to accurately align the bead. Your back hand wrist may be overly bent and your trigger finger difficult to move from front trigger to rear trigger. This will lead to you feeling very cramped when you have the gun mounted.

If any of the above describes how you feel when you have the gun mounted, seek advice from a shooting instructor.
See 153a labeled diagram of the shotgun.

Cast And Comb

When considering the cast of the stock, the pitch and height of the heel and comb, these too may have a major impact on your accuracy with the gun. When looking along the barrels to the bead, your eye must be exactly centred on the action otherwise your shot may be placed to the left or right of the target. The height of the comb will dictate the height of your shot at the target. It will also produce more or less lead on two targets, incoming and outgoing. It is important that you discuss with your gunsmith the various targets that you normally shoot as he will have to ascertain what height of comb would best suit your type and style of shooting. What we are talking about here is a preference on shot placement. At your gunsmith's or shooting instructor's shooting ground, they may have an aid called a pattern plate. This is a large 8' x 4' vertical board with a centred horizontal and centred vertical line drawn on it. Point the barrels below the horizontal line, your bead on the vertical line and move the gun slowly up the vertical line, allowing the bead to pass through the intersection and when the barrels reach the horizontal line and centre on it, pull the trigger. When you fire the gun, a proportion of your shot pattern should be over the line and a proportion under, with 50% to the left and 50% to the right.

153a

Double Barrelled Sidelock

Swan Necked Or Straight Hand Stock, Well Figured

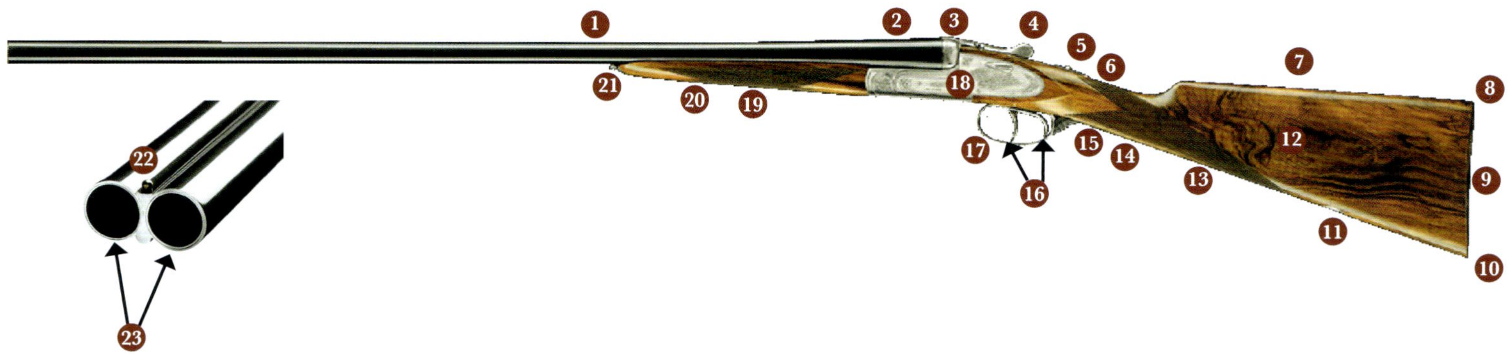

1. Barrels
2. Chambers
3. Fences
4. Top Lever
5. Safety Catch
6. Top Tang
7. Comb
8. Heel
9. Butt
10. Toe
11. Stock Oval
12. Stock
13. Checkering
14. Grip
15. Bottom Tang
16. Triggers Front and Back
17. Trigger Guard
18. Sidelock Action
19. Forend
20. Checkering
21. Forend Release
22. Bead
23. Muzzle and Chokes

154a

Cast And Comb

Starting Point

The Pattern Plate: Usually a timber board with a cross painted on it.

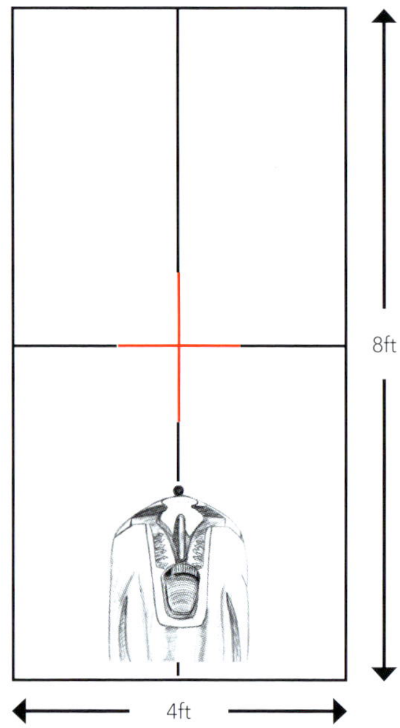

Firing Point

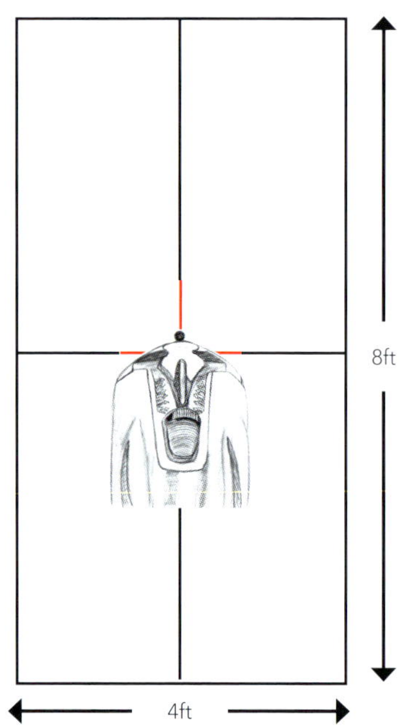

See 154a diagram on Cast and Comb page 154.

Depending on what types of target you intend shooting at, you may think that the obvious answer is to have 50% above the line and 50% below. I myself much favour this approach as it gives me a very true placement of shot. This is known as a 'Half and Half' cast for the gun. However, it may be your choice to have a slightly higher percentage of your shot pattern over the line than a 50% split either side. Let us say 60% above to 40% below? Some guns who shoot only driven birds will ask for as much as 70% above to 30% below. Thus giving them a little additional built in lead on an incoming and outgoing bird. However, when on a crossing bird, aim must always be below the target (which allows constant vision of that target) as you pull through to establish lead. I can see the attraction for this but I still prefer a true placement of my shot as I shoot at every variety and angle of target. If you were shooting at a descending bird flighting into a lake or at a wide variety of 'Sporting Birds' including 'dropping duck' on a clay pigeon ground, 'half and half' cast stocks are vital or you will genuinely confuse yourselves.

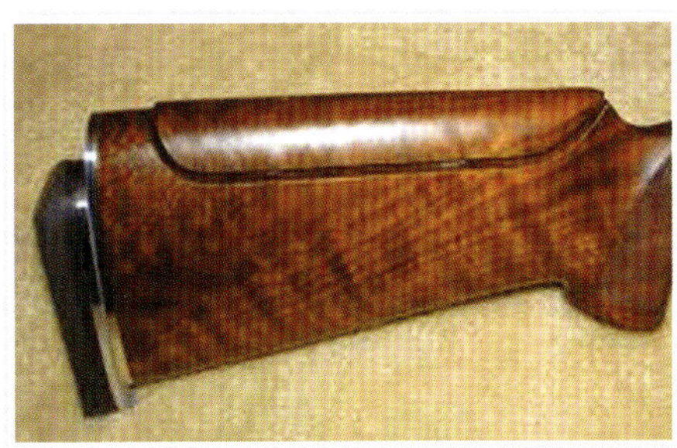

The DTL, Olympic Trench or ABT clay shooter will usually ask for an elevated view of their target enabling a constant view of the target when shooting and again building in a little lead. Indeed there are some guns out there that have what are called 'Ramp Ribs' which leave the shooter's head very considerably elevated from the normal game gun. I think this is more due to the gun's position frequently mounted low on the shoulder and more on the arm and armpit. It will necessitate elevating the rib to prevent the head having to be lowered to see the gun's true aim.

There is also the option of a Monte Carlo stock. This is where the comb of the stock is adjustable in elevation at either the front, the back or both ends, plus the added bonus of the comb being able to move slightly left or right of the stock's centre line.

Consider also your shoulder and its shape relative to the shape of the butt. Some of us have more steeply sloping shoulders than others and it is important that the person shooting enjoys a full length contact with the butt, especially when the gun fires. We require an equal distribution of energy from the stock, via the butt, to our shoulder, so as to minimise the effect by providing the maximum surface area to absorb that energy.

The Try Gun

The easiest approach to fitting a shotgun is to seek the advice of a shooting instructor. Talk it through with your instructor and he will advise the best cast and measurements for your needs. This will be carried out with a 'Try Gun', a weapon where the stock can be adjusted to a multitude of different positions. The overall length, the length to the heel of the butt and length to the toe of the butt, the height of the comb, the height of the heel or bump, the pitch of the butt and the cast of the stock. By adjusting and then firing at a pattern plate, it is possible to see immediately where you are placing your shot. This cannot be done in the gunsmith's shop, it needs to be done at a shooting range. What is also important to bear in mind is that the shooting instructor will ensure that the gun is correctly mounted before measurements are taken. I have observed gunsmiths taking measurements from clients when the gun is mounted incorrectly, ultimately this may be to the disadvantage of that client. The truth is that a gunsmith is not there to instruct, he is there to build a gun to suit the idiosyncrasies of the client. Frequently the customer being measured for a new gun is a novice at shooting. If you are one of those, perfect a correct gun mount with your shooting instructor before you have a gun built to your specifications or a gun adjusted to your measurements.

Consideration is given to a variety of physical measurements and idiosyncrasies:

- The cheek to shoot from
- The shape of head and jaw
- The positioning of eyes
- The length of arms
- The width of shoulders
- The length of neck
- The shape of shoulder and butt
- The way to handle and mount the gun
- Clothing normally worn when shooting

A thought for you on this subject before we move on. When teaching a client, should I need to demonstrate a technique to them, the only gun immediately available is the client's gun. So I demonstrate with theirs. If, heaven forbid, I have to shoot at a target, the issue of 'a gun to fit' becomes a lot more problematical. As you may have gathered by now, I shoot off my left cheek having a left master eye, coupled with a cross dominance due to my being naturally right-handed. What fun! All of you who think this must make shooting very difficult for me, I appreciate your concern! It actually makes it easier. I digress, back to the ill fitting gun. To use a client's gun efficiently, will for me depend on how much 'cast on or off' there is in the stock. Especially if it is 'cast off' for a right-handed shot. Cramming my head onto the stock, I can normally manage to use most guns. I can do so because I know how to. I'm prepared for the eventualities of this but I have occasionally suffered bruising as a result. Should you have encountered these problems, please understand that there is no need to endure pain or discomfort when shooting. Go and talk to a qualified shooting instructor.

The Choke

Your choice of specification is not yet finished. Next comes the choice of what chokes you will have in the gun. What is choke? In simplest terms, it is the internal measurement of the last half an inch of your barrel at the muzzle. This is decided upon by the gun manufacture but, should you be ordering a new gun, you can specify what choke you wish for each barrel. This is described as fixed choke, but if on inspection you find your chokes are very tight and would like to have at least one more open pattern, any gun may have its chokes opened or reamed out by a good barrel borer.

The choke governs the size of your shot pattern. Consider what makes up the shot pattern. Your cartridge is filled with lead balls known as shot. As those balls fly away from the gun, so they spread out. Whatever the distance of the target, our ideal situation is to have the largest shot pattern available to give us the best chance of hitting the target . Let me give you an example, our target is at 20 yds. With a more open choke measurement known as 'improved cylinder', the shot will have spread out to give a coverage at the target of 26". By contrast the spread from a 'full' choked barrel at the same distance would be 16". A shot from a barrel choked Improved Cylinder used on a target at 40 yds. will give a pattern of 51". From the Full Choke barrel, a pattern size of 40". When using an open choke, what we must be certain of is that there won't be any spaces between each shot in the pattern sufficiently large that our target can fly through. With a double barrelled shotgun, you can have a different choke measurement in each barrel, thereby giving you an option of two alternative sizes of shot pattern, one for closer targets and the other for more distant targets. The normal arrangement for a side by side is the right hand barrel is more open than the left, for an over and under, the under barrel is more open that the over barrel.

Distance in Yards	Improved Cylinder Pattern Width	Full Choke Pattern Width
15	20"	12"
20	26"	16"
25	32"	21"
30	38"	26"
35	44"	32"
40	51"	40"
45	60"	48"

The alternative to fixed chokes are multi-chokes or poly-chokes, or interchangeable chokes. Call them what you will, these give the shooter as many options of variable choke as they have in the gun case. It is a fairly modern innovation so you would be unlikely find old best London, Birmingham or Scottish guns fitted with these. The choke tube is screwed into the muzzle end of the barrel. It is up to you which you select, a choice should be made on the basis of what type of target and what range you may be shooting at it.

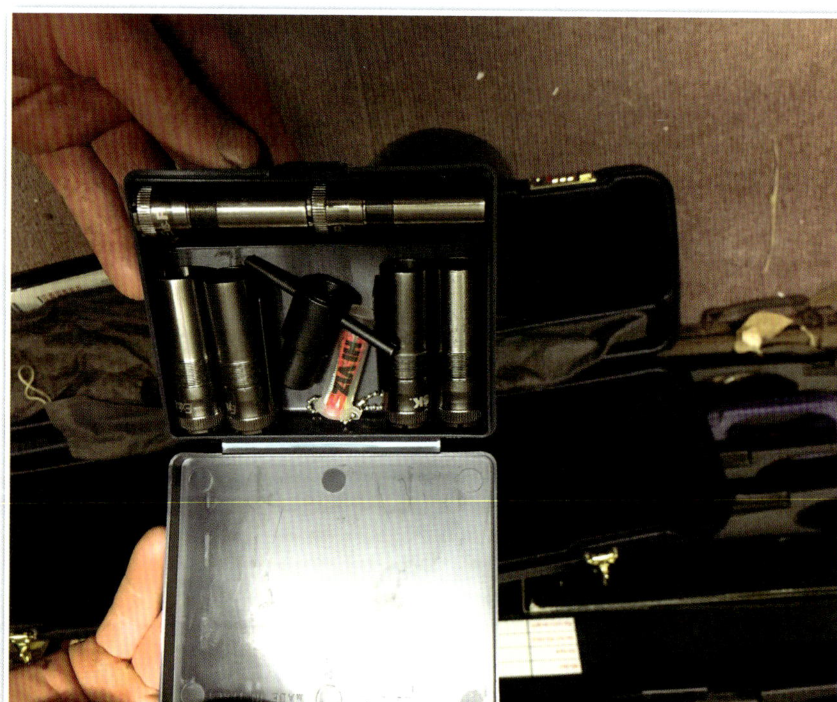

I do believe that a perfect compromise for fixed chokes are improved cylinder in one barrel and half choke in the other. I prefer to have fixed chokes, as interchangeable chokes sometimes leave the gun balanced nose heavy and I greatly value a gun that is correctly balanced. On a more optimistic note, there are specialist choke manufacturers in many countries who can and do fit interchangeable chokes and still maintain the integrity of balance in the gun. I have yet to come across a normal gun manufacturer who manages to achieve this but that said, please note I say 'yet'. I haven't tried every gun on planet earth and there may be some to be found out there.

A word of warning on the seemingly perfectly balanced shotgun. There are a number of shotguns on the market where parts are being made from alloys in an attempt to reduce the overall weight of the firearm. I purchased one of these in recent times because I felt the gun was very nicely balanced and perfect for a lady or youngster to learn to shoot with. It was also extremely cheap. I have since had that gun repaired twice due to parts breaking. Both ejector push rods, one firing pin and a problem yet to be determined in the action design and the Fore-end design that is causing these breakages.

⚠ ***Buyer beware!***

27 Gun Maintenance And Equipment

Good care of a shotgun not only means that the weapon should function properly, but it will pay dividends should you want to sell your gun at some time in the future.

The tools for the job are as follows :
1 set of turn screws
2 Paradox gun cleaning rods
(full length, covered in a fleece like fabric)
1 set of conventional cleaning rods *(for barrel)*
1 phosphor bronze brush
1 mop
Bore solvent
Gun oil
Boiled linseed oil
Toothbrush
Pipe cleaners
1 set of snap caps
1 box of patches
1 brass patch holder
I soft brass bristled brush for suede shoes.
No.0000 gauge wire wool

A quick clean entails cleaning the inside of the barrels with cleaning rods and using the brass brush to scrub the ejector push rods and the muzzles of the gun, plus any other internal surfaces that may be showing signs of burnt powder deposit or rust and then apply oil. For a correct cleaning procedure read on.

Initially, use one of the Paradox rods to clean out the burnt propellant left in the barrels. Insert the rod from the chamber and push through the entire length of the barrel. Draw the rod back and repeat once more. Then use the other paradox rod to polish. When necessary, the rods can be cleaned in washing up liquid and warm water. If you have no paradox cleaning rod, use an old fashioned piece of cloth, about 4" x 2" called a 'Patch' on the brass patch holder attached to the end of a gun cleaning rod and push this in similar fashion through the barrels. Next spray bore solvent down the barrels and leave for ten minutes. Attach the phosphor bronze brush to the cleaning rod and scrub out the barrels paying particular attention to the first six inches of the barrel beyond the chambers and the last three inches of the barrel before the muzzle. These are the areas most likely to suffer from nitro deposits or leading. Nitro deposit is caused when the powder ignites and it will leave a staining on the tube just beyond the forcing cones. Leading is from the passage of lead shot through the barrel. It appears as translucent white streaks and can be quite stubborn to remove. Clean the chopper lumps and the wells in the bottom of the action where they engage. These always build up a layer of debris. Next are the ejectors. Pay particular attention to the wells in the chamber where the ejectors recess. On a side by side shotgun there is a keep screw which can be removed should you need to dismount the ejector push rods, a job worth doing if you have been shooting in wet weather. Use the pipe cleaners to remove any damp or dirt from the tunnel where they are fitted. Use bore solvent to clean the powder deposits on the outside of the muzzle. Use the toothbrush to clean either side of the rib and when dry, lightly oil the whole barrel, best done with an oily rag and some oil on your brush to get into the recesses of the rib. As a final job on the barrels, spray some oil into the barrels and run your oily mop through.

Clean all other working parts of the gun, paying particular attention to the internal works of the action. There are many nooks and crannies which tend to build up dirt if they are not regularly cleaned. Where the moving parts of the gun meet, these are the areas where dirt can inflict the greatest damage if left unattended. If there is a film or layer of dirt when parts close against each other, this creates an unnecessary and un-catered for stress and strain on those parts, something will eventually have to give. Keep all working parts lightly oiled, there's no need to pump large quantities of oil into the gun. In fact over oiling can be nearly as detrimental as not oiling the gun at all. Only use recommended oils on steel parts of the gun and avoid using large quantities of oil that may possibly soak into any part of the furniture of the gun, either stock or fore-end, where screws are seeking a firm grip between steel and timber. **Gun oil will slowly soften the wood.**

When caring for your gun at the end of a day's shooting, clean off the dirt or damp from the furniture and let the gun dry in a normal manner. Don't place it on or near a heat source. When the furniture is dry, use a small amount of boiled linseed oil and rub into the wood with the heel of your hand. Pour a small amount of oil, enough to cover an old penny, onto the surface of the stock. Using circular motions, rub the oil into the wood with enough pressure that the wood slowly starts to warm. You can also use a beeswax-based polish or a silicon-impregnated cloth, but, in my experience, the use of boiled linseed builds a lovely patina on the stock of the gun, enhancing the figuring or grain in the walnut and protects it well. Use a toothbrush to clean the checkering on both the Fore-end and the stock. Be sure to clean any residue of boiled linseed off the metal parts of the gun. It will dry as a yellow scum and isn't that easy to get off.

A cleaning solution

28 A Day's Shoot

Equipment For The Shoot

1 shotgun license

1 travelling case

1 gun slip or sleeve *(ideally without zips, just leather straps and buckles)*

1 ammunition magazine *(optional, heavy, expensive, but good to have)*

1 barrel sleeve *(Side by Sides only)*

1 cartridge bag

1 cartridge belt

1 game bag

1 cartridge extractor

1 pair of ear defenders

1 pair of shooting glasses with interchangeable coloured lenses *(Clay Pigeon Shooters)*

Proof of current insurance

A good range of cartridges kept in stock for all eventualities

Plus attendant cleaning kit outlined above

Proof of Right To Shoot at that location

Beyond these, you can indulge in all sorts of shooting paraphernalia. There are many types of decoys, bird calls, fox calls, camouflage nets, shooting sticks, gun racks and what have you.

What To Wear

Clothing plays an important part in the life of a shooting enthusiast. From either a practical standpoint or from a wish to look well dressed, the following suggestions may well help. Clothing has changed from the original tweeds, through the ubiquitous oiled cotton from England and 'loden' from Austria, to a massive range still including these but now boasting the use of high tech fabrics. Mind you, it doesn't stop there. If you are intent on wildfowling or flighting birds in woodland or on open ground, there is now the age of the photo-print camouflage. The Americans have developed camouflage clothing which if matched for the right environment, renders you completely invisible. You can also purchase camouflaged shotguns to match your different types of clothing. There are cotton waist-coats with suede or leather facings, irritably often only on the right hand side. What do these designers think, that we all shoot right-handed? Headgear and footwear really haven't changed that much. Maybe the inclusion of some more wonder fabric has helped with both. I've worn the same tweed flat cap for thirty years and it still doesn't leak. The baseball cap hasn't found its way onto my head yet, anyway, for an Irishman in an Irish climate, they leak like sieves. *See photo 167a on page 167.*

For rough shooting practicality is your only concern. Just make sure that you can move inside your clothes, especially when they are wet. For those covering really tough country, I use a heavy duty canvas gaiter that grips the walking boot, ties underneath and covers all the way to the knee. Should you be lying up waiting for incoming birds such as wood pigeon or duck, the number of varieties of 'Real Tree' camouflage will undoubtedly provide a suitable garment for your shooting ground under any circumstance.

The clay pigeon shooter frequently wears a shooting 'vest' or waistcoat, deep pockets are helpful and some form of padding on the shoulders can prolong the use of the garment and the use of the shoulder. A deep brimmed tweed cap or baseball hat is ideal as shade for sunshine, and isn't so bad at coping with the odd drop of rain. I'd complement this with a light magazine for your ammunition, a shooting stick and sunglasses plus a good picnic of course.

For driven shooting, be it as a guest or as a syndicate member, there is an expectation that you will be turned out correctly. What

167a

is correct? Plus twos or plus fours, waist-coat, jacket and top coat. Long socks, garters if you must, shirt, tie and good leather shoes. It's an image that recurs constantly across the British Isles on any shooting day. It shows an element of respect for your sport and your fellow beings. There are some shooting people who are content to make do with jumpers, open shirts, even normal long trousers. I don't make comment and I don't question their motives, I just like to dress correctly. For those of you who are like-minded, you may need a little advice on what is suitable and what is available. The best source for that is a good tailor or country wear specialist. A well made shooting suit will last ten to fifteen years and with age, and a few pulled threads, comes a certain provenance. So what choices do you have?

Tweed can be a personal badge. Many of the great estates use their own particular tweed to set themselves apart, their keepers dress in this as a uniform. The colours can be as diverse as the imagination of the weaver and nothing seems to be too eccentric. After a choice of tweed, a choice of trouser Plus Four, Plus Two, or breek. Most 'off-the-peg' versions are appallingly badly made. I suppose the less material they put into the legs, the greater their profit margin. I can't think of any other reason why they would get something so completely wrong. Apparently we all have stick-like legs, so for an ex rugby playing horse rider like myself, you haven't got a choice, go to the tailor. Plus twos or plus fours, for those of you who have wondered what these may be, are an old and much loved design of shooting trouser. They end below the knee and are fixed or cinched under the knee with a strap. When outside on possibly uneven terrain, you need a certain amount of spare material so that the knee can bend and prevent the trouser riding up the leg. Plus Two is an overlap of two extra inches of material overlapping the knee and Plus Four is four extra inches of overlap. The more severe the terrain, the more the knee may have to bend. Make your choice of which, depending on where you think you will shoot. Furthermore, that overlap of material acts as a drip tray in wet and windy weather. Breeks or breeches seem to be built to stop below the knee with no spare material. I always thought that this design was called knickerbockers, but what would I know? ***See 170a on page 170.***

Head gear should be kept to a tweed cap or battered felt hat. Please don't be tempted by a fore and aft or deerstalker. Footwear used to be a long laced leather boot. There are much better pieces of kit available nowadays. Leather lined, zip sided boots seem to lead the field over conventional wellies. I like the neoprene lined boot for warmth, or the half boot with leather-laced upper which the Americans have devised. Buy on the internet and ensure that you get the type with an inner felt boot for temperatures down to minus 15° not the ones for minus 35°, unless you are heading for the arctic or need to have your feet slowly cooked. L.L. Bean are excellent manufacturers and give a life time guarantee.

Coats, those original tweeds and Loden, are now boasting the use of high tech fabrics such as Gortex and Flexothane. What is on the outside may well be old fashioned but these new lining or coating products help keep us dry, warm and stylish. The best of all worlds. For the skiers amongst us, those Merino underclothes you may wear in the Alps give superb warmth and allow me to spend hours outside teaching when externally, wind howls, rain lashes and, very occasionally, a snowflake is seen.

Other equipment must include your gun sleeve and cartridge bag and if necessary your magazine. Leave your favourite cartridge belt at home for your days of rough shooting and possibly include a shooting stick if your back is complaining. Bring your barrel sleeve if you are using a side by side or if not a sleeve then at least one leather glove, a side by side can heat up considerably during a busy drive

170a

and your fingers and hand will appreciate some protection. I find a leather barrel sleeve also makes a side by side shotgun much easier to hold with your fore hand. and don't forget your ear defenders. You might include some good quality sunglasses as well, that low winter sun can hide birds with ease. Some cash would be useful as you will be expected to tip the keeper. A little research with the gun captain will provide you with an answer as to the normal amount. It is also fair to say that some shoots tip the keeper depending on numbers and quality of birds shown. Finally, put your certificate of insurance into the car in case you are asked for proof of coverage. Insurance is necessary for protection of yourself and others should there be an accident and is required by some shoots and I'm told some clay pigeon shooting grounds. The easiest way to obtain this is through one of the related associations with shooting.

A Game Shoot

When meeting at the shoot, take note that the people actually shooting, now have the collective title of 'Guns'. Numbers will be drawn for your pegs, and a card with your peg number or position for each drive issued. This may also include the names of the guns for that day, which I admit is very useful, especially if you are a newcomer to the shoot. Check if the shoot uses its own transport or whether you are expected to follow in your own vehicle. If the latter is the case, you may consider offering space to others or travelling in another car as the fewer vehicles there are, the less likely people are to get lost and delay the drives. An introduction to the day's sport will be given by your host or the shoot captain. An emphasis on safe shooting, instructions on signals for a drive to start and to finish, instructions on birds and ground game which may or may not be shot, a little 'any other business' and now you are underway.

On arriving at the first drive, unload your equipment from your car or other and ensure your gun is in its sleeve. Move quietly onto your peg. At this moment, the job of the gamekeeper is to hold his birds in the drive that is made up of the flushing points and cover, held there until the guns are in position. The task is not easy and will not be helped by a number of guns walking towards the drive noisily exchanging their latest jokes. As soon as you are on your peg, take your gun out of its sleeve and prepare your cartridges and be ready to load. Look to your sides and behind you to see where other people are standing. There may be guns on pegs behind the front line of guns. These are known as back guns and are generally placed where action is thought to be hottest, or placed there because the width of the drive is difficult to achieve for a full complement of guns in one single line. Pay particular attention to where the pickers up are stationed with their dogs, as they frequently will arrive only moments before the drive begins. The tension builds.

A bird breaks from the covert and flies high over the gun line, don't shoot! Wait until the signal for the drive to begin has been given. Only when the horn or agreed signal has been given such as two shots are fired somewhere down the line, whatever the starting signal may be, you may now load and close your gun. Your 'shooting zone' is in front of you and round to either side, but not down the line of guns. Under certain circumstances, shooting behind the line is permitted too. Constantly be aware of beaters and stops that may be positioned or moving in front of you. These are part of the keeper's team that assist him in finding and presenting the game for you to enjoy. They are working on your behalf and appreciation for their efforts doesn't include a load of No. 6 shot flying at or near them. The pickers, who are those wonderful folk accompanied by their dogs behind the line, tend to feel the same way, though they can be remarkably patient! Your fellow guns have the option to shoot back, so best not aim at them either. Shoot only your bird, unless a bird has obviously been missed by your neighbour.

So the drive gets under way and you drop some birds. Remember how many you see fall, don't count what you think you may have hit. If there is a bird you have hit hard, try and remember where you saw it fly to. Take delight in what you do well and try to shoot as efficiently as you can. Look to shoot each bird in the cleanest possible manner, aim to hit each bird in the head and take note where your shot is actually hitting the bird. If you see the bird stagger in the air but fly on, if the bird has a leg down, increase your lead and take note of the line of your shot. The ideal scenario is for the bird to be dead in the air, long before it hits the ground.

And then the horn blows. Unload, put your gun back in its sleeve and find the picker up who is working behind your peg. An accurate count of birds shot is most useful for the picker up. They will compare this figure to what they have seen and should waste no time searching for imaginary birds. You may have been asked to tidy up the spent cartridges around your peg. If that is the case, then make a small pile of them but don't remove them unless directed. The empty hulls are a useful indication to the keeper where the weight of his birds have flown during the drive. It's not an accurate representation of numbers, but it is a useful aid when planning his strategy for the future.

The number of drives held during most driven shoot days are frequently five. This is not a rule and depending on your location, will depend on the day's fare. For instance, I was invited to shoot by a syndicate of Irish guns on one of the most superb driven shoots just outside Edinburgh on the Perth road. At lunch, Wilson, the owner and manager of the Thirlestane Castle shoot, informed us that the afternoon's drive would start on the dot of ten past two and would run all afternoon. It was called 'The Face' and truly was one of the most spectacular drives I have ever seen. We shot and then we walked on a few yards, we shot and moved a few more, the idea being to keep pace with the beaters on the hill to our right. Prior to lunch there had been three drives, a total for the day of four. On most Pheasant shoots we have option 1, the guns stop for a quick break between drive two and three, a hot drink, a bullshot and then on to the next drive. Then shoot your third drive and in for lunch. You may, option 2, 'shoot through', which means shooting all five of your drives and then going back for a late lunch. This is often wisely adopted when the forecast is for deteriorating weather. What may well happen during a day's driven shooting, as the number of birds shot reaches that which has been planned or contracted, the subsequent drives may be cancelled. If it is a 'Sold Day', where teams of guns contract to shoot on just a daily basis, the shoot manager may offer you a further drive provided 'overage' is paid. This means you will have to pay for any additional birds shot, over and above the original price which had been contracted, should the team of guns choose to continue.

As payment is all part and parcel, even to a guest, your final commitment to the days business is to tip the keeper. Ask your host or gun captain what is recommended. If you have been supplied with a loader or stuffer for the day, you should expect to tip them as well. In other words, bring plenty of cash even if you are there as someone's guest. Try not to over tip as this causes problems between the guns and equally well, try not to undertip as you may never see another bird flying over your peg!

Do's and Don'ts A story for you, set in the southern counties of Ireland. The phone ringing in my kitchen one evening brought a welcome but curious invitation. "Hi Shane, would you be busy this Saturday? We have a gap in the gun line and we'd love it if you'd join us." The travel details followed and at the appointed hour I arrived at a very beautiful property, set in old deciduous parkland and among the guests standing there, a number of old friends. My

host took me to one side and asked if I would perform a favour for him and the rest of the syndicate. Having heard the problem and possible solution I agreed to do my best.
We loaded ourselves in a rather ancient farm vehicle and bounced off down the track to the first drive. Onto my peg with gun removed from its sleeve I looked over to my left and received a smile and a wave. Looking over to my right I received a brief nod. My host appeared and quietly explained to me that any bird going towards the gun to my right must be shot before he could do so. "Any bird do you understand? We're fed up with him shooting everybody else's birds."

Now I knew that this individual was considered to be a rather fine shot, the possibility of receiving a load of No. 6 shot in anger and accurately placed at me was interesting. However, the drive started and in short time a bird came between us, I shot it. Another heading directly towards him, I shot that one too. A pair of birds, one towards him and one beyond him... I shot those as well. Finally with a very theatrical gesture, he put down his gun, marched over to me and said "Point taken! May I now shoot a bird?" We remain on good terms and I believe the message was taken to heart.

So what constitutes 'your bird'?
- A bird flying towards you that will clearly go over your head.
- A bird flying between you and the next gun to your right or left.
- A bird missed by the gun to your right or left.

What is not your bird to shoot.
- Anything outside the parameters set above.
- A marginal bird for you, that will make a much higher bird for back guns or for guns further along the front line.
- A bird that necessitates you turning round to shoot it behind the line.
- A low bird within the parameters set above.

Low Bird

This is an issue that will always be hotly debated, as so many factors contribute to a sporting bird, no matter who you speak to. We have all shot at a bird sometime in our life, and it has exploded into a cloud of feathers. Hopefully there are very few of us who are proud of that moment. Depending on what quarry you are shooting, you may find that you only have low fast birds to shoot at. Grouse and partridge frequently cross the gun line skimming over hedge or heather and make very challenging targets. When driven pheasant shooting, you may use a sense of achievement as a yard stick for what you shoot at and what you do not. In other words, only shooting at a bird if you feel it will be a memorable shot if it drops. The problem with this tactic is that you need to guarantee a large percentage of your birds to be 'tall' ones or difficult shots and therefore memorable. If that is the case, consider yourself to be superbly situated. Equally memorable in my opinion, is a really long shot to left or right if you are stationed at the end of the gun line. The economic reality is that the owner/manager of the shoot needs to see a percentage of his birds shot, so that he can justify the expense of this pastime. If he is charging per bird shot, then he will be even more keen to see birds in the bag and a contract made. I have spent a great deal of time managing or advising pheasant shoots and I understand the need for putting birds in the game cart, regardless of the satisfaction taken by the guns. A combination of tall birds and medium birds are really the ideal compromise. So far all I've offered you are variables. What you need is a yard-stick that you can use for most, if not all, occasions.

The yard-stick I would suggest for driven pheasant shooting is for a minimum height of bird at nothing less than 45 ft. Even this is low and I would personally leave the bird for another day. That said, pheasants flitting over a forestry ride can be every bit as difficult as the best highland bird. However, once out in open ground, I find it hard to feel a sense of achievement from hitting a marginal bird. When the bird reaches sixty feet, things start to be a little more interesting and when the birds get to a hundred feet, now things are getting more challenging and when higher still, let's say up to 160 ft. what a delight!

29 A Suitable Cartridge

The shot load table below will give you the number of balls of lead shot in differing cartridge loads, measured in grams for a 12 bore shotgun. A smaller calibre of shotgun offers less weight of shot per cartridge, necessitating a careful consideration for the choke you use at longer distance and therefore resulting in a slightly smaller shot pattern so there are no gaps in your pattern. The speed of the shot should remain the same. It is also under debate as to the performance of shot in plastic wadded cartridges as opposed to the use of fibre wadding. I cannot detect any change in my success rate when using plastic or fibre wads and prefer not to see the countryside littered with plastic wads that will remain there for many years and threaten the health of all grazing and browsing animals.

Table 179a

Shot Size	Shot Load (grams)			
No	32	30	28	24
BB	79	74	70	-
3	113	106	100	-
4	191	181	170	149
5	248	234	220	193
6	304	287	270	236
7	383	361	340	298
8	506	478	450	394
9	-	616	580	508

The table *179a on page 179* gives you an idea just what is travelling toward a target each time you pull the trigger. What I should point out is that the more balls of shot in a cartridge, the smaller the shot must be and of course vice versa. Hence the higher the number of 'shot size' the smaller and more vulnerable your target should be.

A basic guide of suitable cartridges for a choice of quarry species.

Shot Size	Quarry Species
BB	Geese, hare, large vermin
1	Geese, hare, large vermin
3	Wildfowl
4	Wildfowl
5	High pheasant, wood pigeon, corvids
6	Pheasant, grouse
7	Pheasant, grouse, partridge, woodcock, clay pigeons
8	Quail, snipe, clay pigeons
9	Snipe, clay pigeons

N.B. Shot size 7.5 is a continental version of the Imperial 7.

Personal preference will no doubt play a part in what you select for your gun. However, you may bear in mind that too small a shot size may leave your quarry wounded, with all that that implies, too large and you may destroy a good meal.

A word here on shot patterns, when your gun is travelling through and on out in front of the target, when you fire you are throwing a pattern that is tear drop shaped so has a main circular body but also a longer or shorter tail. I believe the tail length has something to do with ignition speed and wadding types but I cannot be definitive. It does also appear that some cartridges have longer tails than others. On that basis it should make a target very difficult to miss in front!

And a word here on shot. Up until now I've referred to lead as being the choice in composition of Shot. Governments are looking at alternatives. Steel, Tungsten and Bismuth are three that have been tested and can be found on the market. Performance of these seems to be very varied and they haven't as yet received a seal of approval. Both expensive and lighter than lead, they offer a more acceptable metal regarding the environment.

Pat Murphy, gun room manager of Holland and Holland, recently wrote: *"All our new guns are designed to be compatible with standard steel shot, but, as far as older English guns are concerned, we advise caution. We have modified a number of older guns to use steel at the request of customers. This would include lengthening the forcing cones – to ease the pressures and passage of the wad and shot into the main bore – and a reduction in choke constriction to a maximum of half. We do not routinely carry out these modifications, however. Nor do we sell steel shot cartridges because of their limited range and lethality. Our preference for classic guns is bismuth and suitable tungsten."* This is a view shared by many other knowledgeable members of the gun trade. It is also significant that no steel loads are available for 2 1/2" chambered guns – the chamber length of the vast majority of older English guns.

The cartridge manufacturer Gamebore made this comment: *"We have been in the lead-free business for over 25 years and have tried and tested a number of different metals with nowhere near the striking energy and characteristics that Tungsten Matrix offers."*

Tungsten Matrix is costly, but there seems little doubt with regard to it's performance or its suitability for classic guns when suitably wadded. Tungsten matrix loses less residual kinetic energy than lead (because it deforms less) and packs a considerable terminal punch. In addition to being quite dense, lead is relatively soft. This softness allows lead to travel through the barrel of a shotgun at great speed without damaging the gun's bore. Where it is still acceptable for use in hunting, clay target shooting and other activities, lead shot remains the best choice simply because it outperforms steel shot by leaps and bounds and it is far less expensive than shot made of other nontoxic materials. Lead shot can also be used in older guns that were not built to handle steel.

For those of you who may be curious as to the designated load size of a cartridge. The system evolved from the following when the internal capacity of the shotgun barrel could accommodate one single round ball of lead:

Shotgun Calibre	Weight of Single Ball of Shot
1 Bore	1 lb
4 Bore	1/4 lb
8 Bore	1/8 lb
12 Bore	1/12 lb
16 Bore	1/16 lb
20 Bore	1/20 lb
28 Bore	1/28 lb

30 Techniques Of Teaching And Learning

"You must have the patience of a saint" or "Don't you ever feel like strangling them?" Words from clients about themselves or others who are being taught.

Patience should not be the one characteristic the shooting instructor depends on, but it is certainly a huge asset. I have been teaching for what seems like most of my life and probably is. The only occasion I feel I really need patience, is when a client is late for their lesson. When I am teaching, the reward, the first motive that feeds me, is from a competition between myself and the client. This competition is a secretive one, the client won't be aware of it going on, but the competition is to see how long it takes for the client to assimilate whatever it is I'm teaching them. You may say it is a presumptive point of view, but I genuinely know that a degree of success for the client is just a matter of time. As long as the client has an open mind and is prepared to adjust their technique, I know that they will learn and succeed with whatever I'm teaching them. If I'm told by a client that I'm a good or great instructor, it makes sense to me to explain to them the following. "I may give them the right advice, but after that it is up to the client to trust me sufficiently to put that advice into effect and to use that information. The client should be complimented too!"

There is another fascination that keeps my interest in teaching stimulated and this is discovery. A new method, a new phrase, a new understanding of the human psyche. It may be an adjustment in emphasis on what I am saying that makes a concept easier to grasp. It may be an addition to information being given, a re-ordering of information given, an inclusion of something that previously I had taken for granted. For example, the system of preparation I put a novice through before they actually fire the gun. This has been discussed earlier in this book, but has elements that are fairly new even to me. I had for years demonstrated the effects of recoil and how it should be managed. What had not occurred to me was to open the process one step earlier. Open with the trigger pull. No cartridge, just a snap cap, and take the client one step at a time. I was so familiar and comfortable with the concept of pulling a trigger, that I assumed this would be the same for everyone. All sensory aspects of shooting must be catered for, not just the obvious ones. The lesson here is to keep an open and enquiring mind to every aspect of what you teach and to do the same for every reaction of your client.

There is a friend of mine called Donald who lives nearby who came for a lesson many, many years ago. I have watched him shoot on frequent occasions and his ability is considerable. When he came here, he used a technique which is a widely recognised method of shooting a shotgun. It just didn't match with the method that I taught my clients in those days. My determination that he should shoot in the manner I suggested left him none the wiser. And why should it? I bumped into him somewhere recently, and during our conversation, the topic turned to shooting. "You know I never could come back for another lesson with you. Your system isn't anything like mine." Why had I been so definitive about my method? Possibly because of my own absolute belief in the method that I taught. Nevertheless, I had lost a potentially long term customer for no good reason, other than I wanted him to do things my way. I was perfectly aware of the method he was using, I knew it worked well for him. So what is my point? Don't deconstruct someone's method of shooting, if it is already working well or even reasonably well for them. If your client already shoots, first and foremost observe the client. Give them time to relax and shoot naturally in whatever style or method they know. Then take your time improving their methods. Modify if absolutely necessary, polish those methods certainly. To deconstruct completely is both time consuming for the client and potentially damaging to their self-confidence. If your knowledge of their method is insufficient for you to be able to contribute to their abilities, then you shouldn't be teaching until you have a full understanding of all methods used to shoot a shotgun. Without that knowledge, how can you debate with any potential or actual client, the practicalities and reasons for the method you normally teach? Tough words but nonetheless the real truth.

For many years I have travelled to the U.S.A. teaching clients there. I came across all sorts of shooting grounds and on them, all sorts of instructors. Some became good friends and others anxious competitors. What astonished me most about their system of accreditation as a bona fidé shooting instructor was that any paying individual could attend a four day course run by a major shooting association in the States. At its end, the course was completed by a graduation ceremony where the participants were certified as shooting instructors. They were given a badge to sew onto their 'shooting vests' and a baseball cap with a similar display. One of these bedecked individuals came to me for a shooting lesson. When I saw these badges, I was intrigued to know what the students were taught. He told me one of the tests they had to pass was to be able to shoot both left and right-handed. They were taught the rudiments of safety and the rudiments of ballistics. He did tell me with a degree of pride, that classes lasted for three hours in the morning… with a half hour coffee break. Then in the afternoon a further two hours of instruction. I observed the gentleman shooting and asked him why he had come for a lesson. "Because I want to learn more," he replied. My compliments to Bob when he reads this, because he realised he still had so much to learn and because of that, he will one day make a first class instructor.

I fear that our profession is sometimes devalued by some of those who teach without the experience, knowledge and skills, necessary to be a competent instructor. As a parent, would you accept a school teacher for your children whose sole education has been a course lasting four days or, for that matter, no course at all? Your success with a gun demonstrates an understanding of how to use one, but does this mean you have a full understanding of those methods and, more importantly, do you have the ability to pass on this knowledge to another person? Can you quickly assess the deficiencies in someone's technique and know how to address the situation? Teaching is a complex and noble profession that cannot be purchased by a quick visit to a discount store.

Everyone can learn, can find means to improve and if with the right person giving the right advice, there comes a time when the more curious collection of individuals will find themselves kindred spirits. Our little country has had its moments of difficulty in recent times. During the eighties, my parents lived in a lovely old property south of Dublin. They would give some wonderful dinner parties to their friends and on occasion those friends would bring some interesting 'bed fellows.'

The British Ambassador or the British Military Attaché would arrive at the front door with another car close on its heels. When the occupants of the first had found their way in through the front door, I would emerge and usher the occupants of the second car to the rear of the main house and out through our farm yard where I had established my first shooting school. The members of our Diplomatic Protection Squad, all crack shots, would then enjoy a half hour or so of instruction at clay pigeon shooting, before we made our way back to the main house for some light refreshment. I must admit I grew to like them all very much and they proved as adept with shotgun as I expect they were with their office hardware.

A Carrot To The Sub-Conscious

Direct words of advice or constructive criticism are the most obvious means to teach a client. There is one other method that I often employ when teaching. It is a back door method to effect change when the client cannot achieve it themselves. Let me explain by telling you another story.

I was teaching in Charlottesville, Virginia as the guest of two great American sportsmen, Jack and Bill. Between them they had organised a series of lessons at Jack's private shooting grounds. All was going well and our bookings were full to bursting. On the afternoon of the third day, a lawyer had come for a lesson. A very likeable individual, he introduced himself by saying he could no longer shoot in any way, shape or form, though he'd been pretty hot stuff once upon a time. I brought him down to the range and asked him to swing onto a couple of birds but refrain from shooting. His gun mount was good, his overall control was good, his lead was good. Having done this, I loaded his gun and called for a bird. An incoming bird flew towards us and over our heads, he fired. The gun suddenly veered away from the target and his shot was about seven feet to the left and three or so feet in front of it. He looked pleased which left me a little perplexed. I loaded his gun again and called for another bird. Again the bird was missed by a large margin. He was still grinning so I asked him why he thought he was missing. "You mean I really missed them?" I thought he may have a problem with seeing the birds disappear behind his barrel so I moved him to an alternate stand where he could shoot at a crossing bird. As before, his shot was well wide of the mark. There is a clue to diagnosing the problem my client had. No doubt other instructors will recognise it immediately. When he pulled the trigger, he would metaphorically pull it with both hands. You could see the whole gun move into his shoulder and more often than not, away from the track of the bird. It is a classic symptom of someone who is closing both eyes just before they pull the trigger.

The reason I have outlined this incident is to illustrate that there are more ways to solve a problem than may at first be obvious. Was my client closing his eyes because he wanted to? I think you will have to agree that the answer is clearly no. Then why were his eyes closing and what part of his brain was closing them? The likely reason for them closing was as a result of too much sound or recoil, or a combination of both, which had occurred at sometime during his shooting career. He was wearing ear defenders so I had to presume that this was damage from some time ago. So what to do? To tell him to keep his eyes open would be pointless because he wasn't closing them on purpose. This was not a conscious act by him, it was an order from his sub-conscious. What I had to do was to find a stronger motive for him to keep his eyes open than the motive employed to shut them. I asked him to put down his gun and then I released another bird, pointing out to him the sunlight shining on the front edge of the clay pigeon. Watch the sunlight I told him. No matter where the gun may be pointing, watch the sunlight and see what happens to the bird. I took his gun and called another bird. When I shot the clay pigeon, I turned and asked him where it had been hit. *"In the middle I guess"*. With the next target I asked him to be really sure where the bird was hit as I was going to experiment on this one. Again I shot the bird and asked him what he had seen.

"The bird smashed into smithereens," he said. I replied: *"It's fun to see them break isn't it?"*

I gave him back his gun and again told him to concentrate on the sunlight reflecting from the front edge of the target. I told him to keep watching the bird so that he could tell me where it broke. I released the bird and he shot. The shot was behind but only just.
"Open your lead a little more but watch the sunlight and tell me how the bird

breaks." I released the bird again, out it came, the front edge glinting in the sunshine. This time the bird shattered. I said quietly in his ear, *"It's good to see them break."*

"Hell yes," he replied. The gun was reloaded. I said: *"Same again, watch that sunlight."* I released the bird and low and behold when he shot, the bird shattered. *"It's good to see them break,"* I said it again, quietly, close to his ear. He just grinned!

The job was done, the stronger motive had taken hold. He shot for another ten minutes and broke all his targets. That big grin was still on his face when he left. I have no doubt that he will continue to enjoy watching the remains of his broken clays for a long time to come.

31 Other Methods Of Shooting A Shotgun

As an instructor, it would be remiss of me not to make comment on all methods of shooting a shotgun. I have called them by their most commonly used names, but you may well know them as something else. I've listed them in no particular order.

- Churchill or Known Lead *(The system advocated in this book)*
- Snap Shooting or Reaction Shooting
  (An ideal partner to the Churchill or Known Lead method)
- Sustained lead
- Insertion
- Pull through

I would like to give an explanation of all shotgun shooting methods, but along with the Churchill Method, the only other method I'm going to explain here is Snap Shooting. This system or technique dovetails exactly with the system already outlined in this book. An explanation of the other methods may satisfy your curiosity, but it may also lead to confusion. My primary aim when taking on this project has been to ensure that I would succeed in eliminating any confusion. My one concern for all the people who come to my shooting school is to ensure that there are no elements of what I teach, which they do not understand or elements that appear illogical in concept or delivery. If one tries to adopt some or even one feature of another system, it may lead to chaos and confusion. So I'm sorry if that leaves you feeling uninformed but I have chosen the system I teach with good reason. I believe that it is the easiest to learn, the most efficient to use and moreover, I can pick critical holes in those other systems.

Snap Shooting

This is the method that should be used when there is very little time available to shoot your target. The initial component parts of this technique are exactly the same as I have taught you already. The gun starts in the same position, centred on the sternum, and is mounted to your cheek. While mounting the gun, ensure that the **whole** gun is constantly and accurately pointing at the target. Where we depart from the previous system is what happens next.

To perform this technique correctly, it is now dependent on perfect timing and good gun control. The barrels are still pointing at the target, the stock about to reach your cheek. The moment the stock hits your cheek, it is crucial to pull the trigger on that instant. Not half a second afterwards but the moment you feel it touch. Keep the gun on the target, the stock on your cheek and follow through will automate itself as before. That was pretty straight forward, I hear you say. Well, think again. It takes practice, lots of practice and completely correct control of the gun. The only time I use this method myself is when I have been practising it a great deal. Any deviation from the method I have outlined, and the target will be lost. If the timing is off by half a second, you will have missed. This is why I only teach the method as the very final act in educating a client.

I should also explain why I am reluctant to teach this method as the sole system to use when shooting. This method is dependent on first class timing and execution. You are committed to the moment. In other words, you are obliged to pull the trigger the split second the gun reaches your cheek and your eye. You have no opportunity to fine-tune the positioning of the gun and the target. You may think that there is a momentary opportunity to check where the gun is pointing but even thinking this will lose you the bird. The gun having touched your cheek, must be fired. Because there is no recourse for correction, there is little point in using a method such as this to shoot a target if there is plenty of time available. If there is time then use that time to be sure your sight picture is correct.

The Snap Shooting system is specifically designed for the bird that gives one a split second chance and then is gone. Picture yourself standing in a forestry ride. A thirty yard gap between the trees. Suddenly a woodcock appears and as you mount the gun you realise the bird is about to disappear again over the trees behind you. Point the whole gun at the target and as the stock touches your cheek, bang! For the clay shooter, imagine yourself at station 8 on a skeet field or in a piece of woodland with a running rabbit dodging between trees and bushes. The snap shot is exactly what it says it is, but unless you truly need it, stick to a system where you have the opportunity to fine-tune the gun's position before pulling the trigger.

32 Shooting Syndicates, Gun Clubs And Clay Clubs

The process of becoming a gun owner and participator in this sport is simple but can take a little while. Go to a good instructor. He or she will teach you the basic elements of shooting successfully. Then enquire as to where to buy a shotgun. Choose wisely, beware of some guns that are purpose built for just one form of target shooting such as trap shooting guns. You need to understand what they are built for and how they will affect your performance when used on targets that they weren't designed to shoot. If in doubt, always ask. Having made your choice, take all particulars of your chosen gun, maker's name, model, calibre, number, current owner and then go to your local Gardai Barracks or Police Station. Having discussed the purchase with your Firearms Officer, return to your instructor and ask if they can certify you for Safety. If so, attend the Safety Course and fill out your gun license application form. Put your Safety Certificate, plus photo, plus form together and hand it in to your Gardai.

One of the services that I have always provided has been to find a place for my clients to shoot. If, as a newcomer to the sport of shooting, you picked up this book and started reading, you will eventually wonder what to do next. Shooting schools are usually listed in the advertising sections of good shooting magazines or at shooting grounds. Word of mouth will supply you with recommendations for the best of these. Most gunsmiths and gun dealers either have their own shooting grounds, or have an arrangement with one. Furthermore, if you are looking for a place on a shooting syndicate or a membership of a gun club, vacancies will occasionally find their way into the advertising columns of the shooting press. However, the better the syndicate or gun club, the more difficult it may be to obtain a place. Talk to your instructor or the local gunsmith and explain what you want to do and what budget you have. Strike up a conversation that will supply you with some local information. The gunsmiths, gun dealers and other professionals in this business, are the people most likely to have their fingers on the pulse of what is happening in their neighbourhood. Other than this, personal recommendation and personal contacts will elicit good information and the means to obtaining the right introductions.

For clay pigeon clubs, a perfect source of information will again be the local gunsmith and gun dealer. However, if you need an alternative source of information, you can contact your national Clay Pigeon Shooting Association. They should have any affiliated club listed. In Ireland, where Clay Pigeon shooting is a very popular form of recreation, there is no problem in joining clay pigeon clubs and new members are very welcome. Needless to say, the internet will provide you with all the contact information you could possibly need. Search first using 'Irish Clay Pigeon Shooting Association' or if reading this book elsewhere around the world substitute 'Irish' for your own country.

For all forms of shooting, you should ensure you are properly insured. The new associations, such as Countryside Ireland and the Countryside Alliance, provide a broking service for good shooting insurance. Proof of insurance is asked by most game shooting syndicates and gun clubs. I suspect the same is true for most clay pigeon clubs. In Ireland the N.A.R.G.C. offer a comprehensive cover and I believe the Irish Farmers Association is offering insurance coverage for this purpose.

I thought it would be pertinent to give a detailed description of quarry species available in Ireland, but a good friend and neighbour Christopher, very gloomily declared Ireland is a country now low on quarry species. "When I was a boy and teenager," he said, "these bogs were full of snipe and the foreshore and waterways were teeming with wildfowl. We would be out shooting, my brother and I, every day of the holidays. I wouldn't let anyone shoot at a snipe on my land now." I think he may have a point as I have walked this area all winter and seen one snipe in the fifteen years I have made the west of Ireland my home. However, rather than there being a dearth of some species, there may have been a redistribution of these species into areas of feeding where they used not to be found. What would be interesting to know is why? Certainly our rainfall has increased, the areas that used to support snipe are desperately wet. Maybe we have destroyed something in one area and provided an easier obtained or alternate food source elsewhere? This is why we need to support our shooting and conservation associations and find the answers to these conundrums.

For those of you who are fresh to the fare and while the quarry species are still in abundance, here for you is a guide to those most commonly found and one or two which are not.

Walked Up Or Rough Shooting

I think before we enter into this section, it is important that for those of you who intend shooting game or vermin, you should first look at each species and consider the numbers that still are available for that species to preserve and promote their existence. They must not become part of the list titled 'Endangered'. It is recognised by many non shooting organisations that the persons who have done most to preserve our Game Species in the British Isles are the shooting people themselves. May that long continue.

Grouse. Larger in size to a partridge with red \ brown plumage, pale 'hirsute' legs and red wattles over the eyes. To be found on mountain and moor land but few and far between in Ireland. Once again, if you are not actively involved with their conservation, you really shouldn't be out hunting them. That said, they are a highly prized quarry and provide a superb target when driven over a gun line.

Mallard. The largest of our hunted wildfowl species. Substantial in size, the male is clearly recognised from its deep green plumage on the head. The bird is no different from the variety seen on most ponds in city parks. With a good offshore breeze, a brace of mallard flying up the channel towards one can challenge most sporting individuals. Often to be found on stubble fields in the winter with a particular affinity for barley.

Partridge. Smaller than a pheasant with a short tail, the grey partridge can still be found occasionally in the Irish midlands I'm told. They are so rare as a wild bird, its seems wrong to pursue them unless you were actively contributing to their conservation. A very family oriented bird, rises in coveys to fly fast and low over thickets and hedgerows. Its cousin the Red Leg is more successful as an import from overseas.

Pheasant. Only the male of the species may be shot if you are hunting for wild birds. They can be found anywhere from the edge of moorland right down to the swampy areas of marsh grass and molinia grass next to the coast. A big bird, not indigenous to Ireland and as a result I have misgivings when they are shot and are not being replaced with hand reared birds.

Quail. The rarest of our game species. No larger than a starling with brown plumage and buff coloured stripes on its back, it has a distinctive black and white face and throat pattern. Living in close family groups it will be found in cereal crops and will flush suddenly and return to the ground as soon as possible. Look after them and protect them.

Snipe and Jack Snipe. Normally found in flat marshy wetlands or red bog. Now I'm told, also to be found on stubble fields in the winter. Small and fast with a characteristic single peep and then three jinks when taking off, they are a challenging target and my very favourite when it comes to kitchen fare. Skin them, pin their legs, put streaky bacon on top and rest on a doorstep of white batch loaf. Cook in oven until the bacon is crispy.

Teal. A pint sized duck by comparison but very fast when flying in to feeding grounds on a morning flight. On ponds or lakes when roused, they have a rocket ship approach to flight with a near vertical take off. They are to be found on water as they are normally surface feeders.

White Fronted Geese are often to be found on the Slobs in Wexford, sadly no longer in the company of a great gentleman in that region called Bill Fiske who ran the North Slob. Bill achieved many memorable things on his estate, one of these as an extraordinarily successful conservationist and shooting man. His wetland and agricultural management worked superbly and brought thousands of these huge birds back to this area.

Widgeon. The last of the common wildfowl species. Slightly larger than a teal with the drake sporting very striking colours. Often to be found grazing on waterside grassland and stubble fields. Just as challenging as his cousin and delicious to eat.

Woodcock. Similar in design to the snipe but much larger, they are darker coloured with brown woodland camouflage. Normally found on the edges of woodland or in openings among the trees, they are deceptively fast with a small body powered by big wings and will dodge left, right, up and down if they spot you first. When arctic winter winds blow in Scandinavia, these remarkable birds take to the air and migrate to warmer locations in the British Isles. Skirting the north of Ireland they travel down our west coast and through three entry points in Sligo and Connemara. They arrive here and then spread out across the country and into the United Kingdom. Not only are there migratory birds but there are residential birds in Ireland. What makes them stay we don't know but they breed and rear their young in our deciduous woodlands. If I come back as a game bird, this would be my choice. Why? Because they are superbly agile in the air, they protect themselves on the ground by only having scent glands under the wing roots and make one of the most difficult birds to successfully bag.

Wood Pigeon. Found during daytime in deciduous woodland where feed is plentiful and a view of the surrounding terrain easily obtained. When roosting they prefer a snugger home and tend to head for the thick conifer woods. They can be found in spring feeding on pasture where the diet is young clover, in early summer young brassicas are particularly popular and toward the end of the summer, most frequently found on ripe cereal crops or harvested fields of stubble. Truly an acrobat in the air, for sheer variety, one of the greatest challenges as a target. To add one more accolade, they are a culinary delight too.

Driven Shooting

Pheasant. A non indigenous species, bred specifically for shooting, this is the ubiquitous pheasant. There are a number of hybrid types on our driven shoots, sporting some interesting names such as Scandinavian, Extra Large, Michigan Blue Back, Ring neck, Black neck, Melanistic, Scotch, French Black, Golden, Reeves and so on. What the shoot owners are looking for is a bird with great flying abilities, good holding abilities (doesn't stray to the next estate) and is impervious to disease. Needless to say, we occasionally come close to making the perfect hybrid and more often than not we don't. Nonetheless, the pheasant when flying high above a gun line makes a first class target and performs well on the dinner table too.

Partridge are also being used to vary the type of target to be seen at the driven bird shoots. Most common of these in the Red Legged partridge, sometimes referred to as a 'Frenchman' as these birds were originally imported from France to augment the stocks of Grey Partridge. The Grey Partridge was the original species of partridge in Ireland and the U.K. and there are still some to be found here but they are much more common in the U.K. The reason for the success of the Red Leg has been its ability to use similar cover to that provided for the pheasants and since the mid eighteenth century, the Red Leg has proved itself to be a major asset to any shoot.

Mallard. The second largest of our hunted wild fowl, there are some shoots in Ireland where Mallard are used as a driven bird. This can be due to the land's suitability for this type of quarry species or because the shoot owners would like to extend the number of 'sold days' shooting available on their property. This is due to the duck shooting season opening in September, considerably earlier than the pheasant season which gets under way in November. From a commercial point of view, the longer overall season will obviously benefit the business if you have both pheasant and duck available to your clients. However, there are very few examples of really good driven duck shoots so should you wish to partake, choose carefully.

Quail. I heard recently of an Irish shoot that were releasing hand reared quail with an idea of doing part walked up and part driven days. At time of writing I have no more information available.

Grouse. During the early 20th Century there were large numbers of driven grouse available to be shot in Ireland on our mountain land

and high hills, this is rarely the case in Ireland currently and shooting this quarry really shouldn't be encouraged here until a much greater number of birds successfully populate those heather clad moors. Should you wish to participate in one of the most exciting forms of driven bird shooting, you will have to board an aircraft and journey to the Yorkshire moors or further north to the Scottish highlands. It is expensive, it is unbelievably exciting and it is by no means easy, but you haven't lived until you've shot driven grouse, they are the royalty of driven birds.

Finally, on this subject, one can find some oddities and curiosities, usually in small numbers, of birds such as **Guinea Fowl and American Bronze Turkeys.** I released a few of the **Wild Turkeys** on a shoot I managed some years ago and implored the guns to leave them be. All I can tell you is that when these vast birds appeared over the gun line at somewhere around 150 feet, it was too much temptation and everyone seemed to let fly at them. Best described as the B52 of driven birds, they really are a lot of fun. Guinea Fowl on the other hand are extremely reluctant to make their way into the heavens and can usually be found up a very thin tree with a very thin beater in close attendance, wringing the tree's neck or the bird's neck. Another great friend who ran the shoot at Birr Castle invited me there to observe. We stood and watched the first drive as a number of pheasant flew forth from the woods near the old castle and performed in a reasonable manner. "Wait until you see what happens next," said James. After a pause of several minutes a despairing voice announced from up in some high branches, "I can't shift the beggars milord! Dey're hanging on here for grim det!" "Or maybe that should be an easy life," replied James.

Across The World A Few More

There are plenty more species to pursue across the world, including trying your hand at **Francolin** or **Sand grouse** in Africa where you too can be on the menu! You can hire a train to take you and your friends on a bird shooting safari travelling through the Kalahari Desert, parts of Botswana or across to the Skeleton coast in Namibia and down into South Africa. **Quail** on the eastern sea-board states of America, hunted from horse back or horse drawn carriage, or down in Texas where you have to dodge the oil and gas wells and hang on tight to a 6 litre bucking Ford Bronco and where you need 50 acres of land just to feed one steer. Don't get lost. Driven **Partridge** in Spain reeks of tanned leather and is both superbly elegant and generously managed. **Ruffed grouse** in Montana, a bit like a cross between a grouse and a hen pheasant with a bad hair day and which I would contend are the most difficult of all game species to shoot. **White winged dove** in the Virginia corn belt and on the gulf coast of Mexico, where the secretarios (the guys who gather the birds you have shot) gamble on how many birds you will shoot, and how many of them will die from the kiss of a coral snake. The problem is the Coral snake doesn't like to move and sleeps for a large part of its life. Wake it by trespassing in its territory and it will be slow to react. If it is still awake when another human or animal invades its territory, it wont be so slow and that will be a fatal bite. It's all out there waiting for you all to thoroughly enjoy, I have.

33 Quarry Species Clay

This time we'll begin at my own beginning. The first clay pigeon trap I ever saw is where I began my shooting career. It was an enormous mechanical beast, certainly designed by Victorian England, and built, like all things Victorian, to last and last. It threw a 'Down The Line' bird which was operated with a tall two-handled noisily clanking, badly squeaking lever. Together with this was built a skeet field with high and low house plus eight stations. Every other week, Brighton's 'E' Division of Police would come to my old school, led by their Commander Tiplady. Myself and a friend would busily load the traps and push the button to release the skeet targets and hopefully avoid being asked to crank the DTL handle. One day we were challenged to a school versus police shoot, Father Edward Cruise (our man in charge) accepted the challenge and much to our delight, we beat them! From that occasion the odd Policeman would turn to me seeking advice and from that moment sprang the notion of a career.

I met another extraordinary human when teaching in Tampa, Florida and make no apology for telling you of him.

I'd received a phone call from a deep American voice, Norman was his name, asking me if I would be available to teach at his shooting grounds. A date was agreed and having flown to Tampa and taken a cab to some woodland on the outskirts of Tampa, I arrived in front of a long low club house. Driver paid, I was about to make for the front door when it creaked open and one of the taller, tougher gentlemen I've met, emerged armed with a large cigar and an unmistakable grin. I know his face... I'm sure I know his face... With his hand outstretched he said one word, "Norman". I replied "Shane" and then the penny dropped. General Norman

Schwarzkopf. Another exceptional human, capable of commanding the entire armed coalition forces for 'Desert Storm' and delivering the rescue of Kuwait and the winning of the first Iraqi War. My attention you might describe as riveted.

He was a fascinating man, full of life, full of fun. A perfectionist when shooting and he had come up with some very novel design ideas for his shooting grounds. One such idea was a large tower with staircase rising 20 feet to a wide railed platform. Immediately below and crossing from left to right was a single bird, shot with the gun pointing almost below one's feet and followed by a going away bird emerging below one's feet and disappearing like a rabbit.

I have a love of military history and an inevitable interest in weaponry and our hours were spent discussing the merits of the M1A1 Abrams Tank and the British Challenger as opponents of the poor old Russian T55 and T72 that faced them in Iraq. He reminded me several times during that first week, that I must tell him to shut up if he started telling me more stories... I apparently was permitted to offload some of mine. To tell him to shut up would be like shutting one of the best books you have ever read when reading those pages. I'm very sorry to hear that he is no longer with us.

Now to get back to the better known of the Clay Pigeon competitive targets.

Down The Line, D.T.L. Or Trap. This is a going away target, rising very slightly and giving a random angled target across a 90° range. Groups of five people shoot this from five adjacent stands and after two shots move No.1 goes to No.2, No.2 to No.3 and so on, while No.5 goes back to No.1. To complete the round you shoot on every stand making a total of 25 shots. To make matters a little more difficult, the five shooting positions are set back 16 yds from the clay launcher.

Double Trap. Similar in style with a pair of targets to shoot at. Very fast work, a round is again 25 birds.

Trap Field

Ball Trap. Similar in style to D.T.L., a going away target but ball trap varies the spread of the targets and also varies the height of the targets. 25 bird round.

Olympic Trench. Again we have a going away target, the birds are launched at ground level, the angles vary but this time we have a choice of 15 traps where the bird can be launched from, and to make that more difficult, there can be a time delay of up to 3 seconds from calling the bird to its appearance.

Olympic Trench

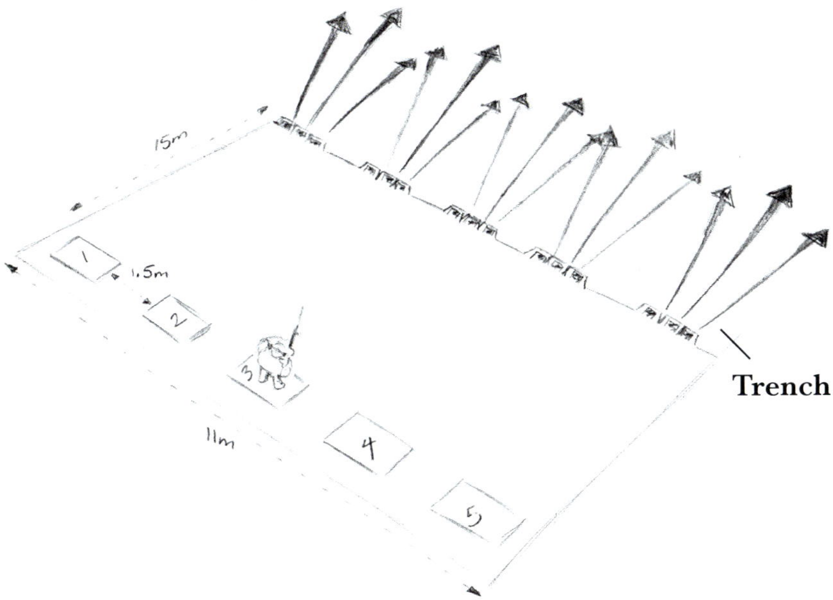

Skeet. A purpose built course with two facing houses, one high delivery, one low delivery, a low and a high with a semi circle of shooting positions from one house to the other. There are two versions of this discipline, the first known as English Skeet, the second known as I.S.U. Skeet. The variables between the two cover the speed of target, the position of gun prior to calling the bird and the sequence the birds are released in and positions from where they are shot.

Skeet Field

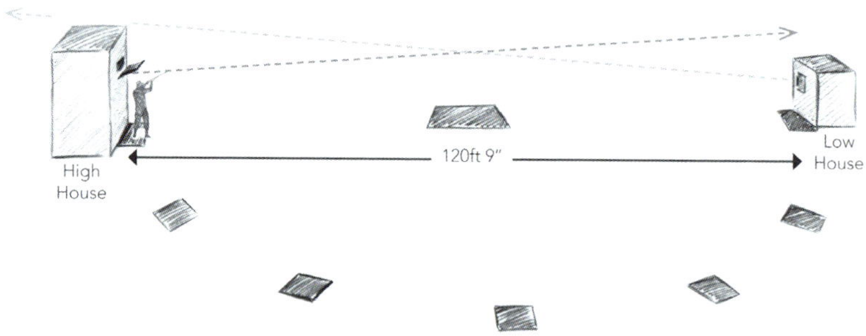

Compact Sporting

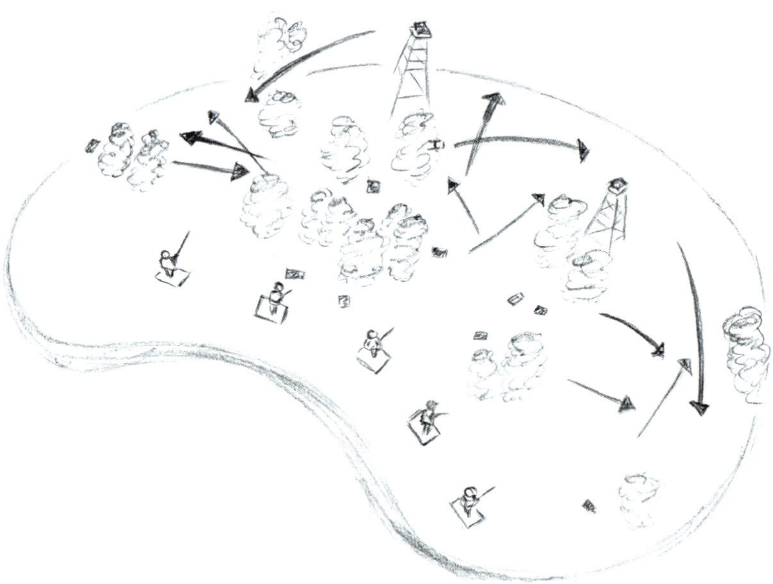

Skeet remains one of my favourites though there have been moments. I was teaching near Matamoros on the Mexican Gulf, a desert-like skeet field. Eight o'clock in the morning and my host Federico wanted to shoot some skeet. We had arrived at station 7, all going well and suddenly I felt this clawing or biting on the toe of my boot. We both looked and watched as a small rattlesnake made its final attempts to get out from under my boot before it was squashed to death. I stepped back thinking 10% conservation and 90% preservation... of the snake of course.

Sporting. This is a simulation of game birds, ground game and wildfowl, usually made up of ten different locations on the shooting ground giving a multiple target round. There are all sorts of targets at all sorts of angles, curves and heights, the only limit to what you may see, is governed by the imagination and ingenuity of the course designer and often the maker of the 'launcher' or 'trap'.

Five Stand or Compact Sporting. A similar idea to D.T.L. but instead of the going away targets seen there, these are targets coming from all angles and various heights and of similar style to the Sporting layout. Again the imagination of the designer is the only limit. Similar to the arrangement at Ballynahinch Castle in Connemara, the current location of my shooting school, the targets are launched in combination from a multitude of traps set up in close and distant proximity to the shooter.

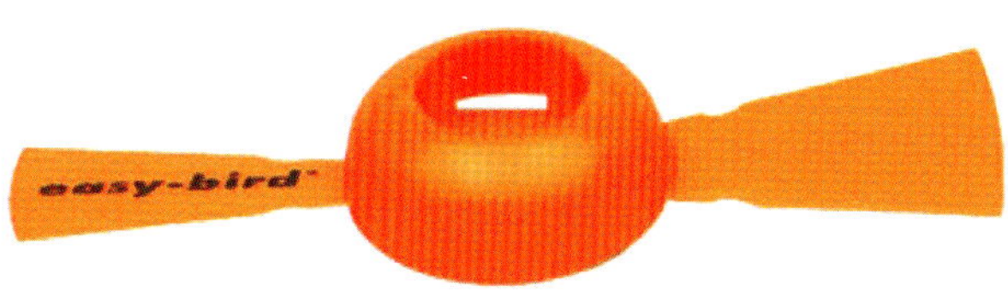

Z.Z. Trap. A system developed in America which may be available currently. What one may consider to be the ultimate in attempting to mimic a game bird. These are a plastic target with metal wings clipped on. When released from the launcher, they fly in almost any direction and change direction during their flight. When the target is hit, the wings suitably drop off! A remarkable idea and brilliantly engineered but as yet there seem to be none of these machines on our own Irish shooting grounds, considerable expense would account for this I suspect.

As with Game shooting, there are always new ideas that appear and sometimes disappear. For a while the talk of the shooting world was for a system called Star Shot. I suppose it was a valiant attempt to get television interested in Clay Pigeon shooting. A celebrity contest was held and televised, shooting at night, a 'going away' target flying across what looked like the scoring sectors from the upper half of a darts board. The bird appeared at the centre and flew towards the outer rim of the target area. The faster the competitor could shoot it, the higher he or she would score. Sadly for those of us who are Clay Pigeon shooting enthusiasts, the almighty clay pigeon doesn't appeal to the television world and while professional golfers and tennis players store away their millions, the great clay shots live an altogether humbler existence. How one can make our sport televisual has perplexed many more imaginative people than I, maybe one day an idea will emerge that eclipses Star Shot.

However, the 2012 excitement of the Olympic Games had me on the edge of my armchair as I watched Peter Wilson bring home his gold medal for the Double Trap but it's a rare occasion that the breaking of clay pigeons amounts to fascination save for the person pulling the trigger. After 52 years of shooting them, I still love seeing a little cloud of dust in the sky.

34 Shooting And The Law

As in most facets of life, the legislators have seen fit to regulate most aspects of shooting. The Wildlife Act and many appendices to it govern what you may and may not do with gun and game in Ireland. No matter which country you live in, talk to your local police and obtain a copy of the rules. How far from the centre point of any public road, path or area must you be before you can legally discharge a weapon? Do you know the answer? Has the law regarding this been changed in the last five years? If you don't know the answer to this question without doing some research or rapid reading, you are potentially a law breaker. If a serious accident should occur while you are breaking the law, your insurance cover is invalid. Your insurance company **will not meet** the terms of that insurance.

Police Contact

There are a number of legalities which, irrespective of where you live, you will have to address as soon as you determine to take up this sport. Firstly, you will have to make contact with your local police station.

In Ireland, if you don't already know your station sergeant, go along to your local barracks and introduce yourself to him or her. They are all part of the community and the Garda Siochana put the importance of human relationships fully alongside the exalted process of the law. Express your wish to buy a shotgun, explain what type of shooting you intend to take part in and where you will be doing it. If you are a clay pigeon shooter, you will be asked for proof of membership of a club, if your interest lies in game shooting then proof of agricultural lands owned by you, or proof of permission for shooting over agricultural lands from the owner. You will be told of the necessity to attend a 'Safety Course' with an approved instructor and they will advise you on how to contact your local Safety Officer, such as myself. The course I give lasts approximately one and a half hours. This is not a shooting lesson, it covers the safe provision of ammunition, the safe usage of the firearm, the transport, maintenance, safe storage and legalities of shotgun ownership. Having attended this, you should be certified by the Safety Officer and when applying for your shotgun license, the certification will accompany your application. The Garda Siochana will request you show them secure storage for the gun and to that effect, you should install an approved gun safe in your place of residence. Note that the safe must be bolted in four places into solid wall fixings, preferably to wall and floor. May I suggest here that the investment and use of a very small heater, 4"x3"x2", powered by a 220v domestic socket, will alleviate threat of damp to your firearm. Your next move is to buy the shotgun. Take your time here, shop around as far as you can and seek independent approval for your choice if you aren't certain you are making the right choice. Once purchased, the gun remains with the dealer or current licensed owner until you receive your license. The details of the gun, its maker's name, number, and description are given to the Garda and you will have to wait until your application is approved. As a first time applicant, this can be a fairly long wait, but all being well, you will receive a licence in about 12 weeks. Once you have been issued with your license, you may collect the gun.

In the UK, having decided to acquire a shotgun, it is necessary to visit your local police station. Explain to them your intention. They will ask you to fill out an application form. You will need a character reference from two specified individuals, photographs of yourself and a medical report from your doctor. Next will come a phone call from the police, in order to arrange an appointment to meet you in your own home. This usually takes about 45 minutes and is both an interview of yourself and an explanation by the police to you of your responsibilities, once you are granted a shotgun certificate. I would suggest you research this by reading the excellent advice offered by the following website:

http://www.shootinguk.co.uk/shooting/start-shooting/how-to-get-shotgun-certificate-licence-32358

The interview subject matter covers topics such as :

- How long have you been shooting for, are you a first time applicant?
- What sort of shooting have you done?
- What are your future intentions?
- Where do you intend keeping the gun?
- Discuss character references
- Have you attended or are you attending a shooting school?
- Are you a member of any shooting club?

Finally you will be phoned back to be told if your certificate has been granted. Once you are in possession of your certificate, you may then go shopping for a gun or collect your gun from its current holder.

If you think the above mentioned rules and regulations governing the possession of a shotgun are restrictive or draconian, try applying for a licence in Austria or Germany. I'm told that you have to go through an instructional process for two years. Your education in the use of the gun is only one facet of their tuition. You must have a complete knowledge of the mechanical workings of your gun, a complete knowledge of the ballistics of your gun. You must have a complete understanding of the ecology, biology and means of conservation of all quarry species and their habitat. You must demonstrate both safe use and efficient use of the weapon. They believe this is a perfectly justifiable means to an end. They say that it restricts numbers shooting and aids conservation. They also say that the failure rate, when sitting the examination on all aspects listed above, is very high and if you fail, you start the course from the beginning again.

European Union: Travelling the E.U. you are required to have a EURO License. This will be provided for no charge if you go to your local Garda Barracks, together with any Irish Gun license for your firearms that you wish to travel with. However, gun laws and shooting are very strictly observed in some European countries and our own Parliament may adopt those rules for all of us. In every way I would be in absolute favour of this being the case. We have a duty to act responsibly, both to each other and to the wildlife around us. If we can demonstrate our integrity as shooting people, we would make a much more difficult target for those people who are opposed to our sport. Equally we would become an even greater asset to our own wildlife conservation.

In the USA the very first question you must answer is which State do you live in or intend to visit? Laws vary enormously from State to State but research via any of the major search engines will provide the necessary information and advice.

35 Shooting Or Related Associations

I am going to concentrate on what associations exist in Ireland as they should all have a plug or I will never hear the end of it! I will give you a suggestion for a couple in the UK and the USA after that you will be doing your own research. As I have mentioned previously, there are Clay Pigeon Shooting Associations in many countries around the globe. The Irish CPSA, the American CPSA and the original CPSA (UK) are all highly proficient organisations.

For game shooting enthusiasts, there are a number of associations available for membership. Firstly though, I should point out to you the work that 'FACE Ireland' does in the EU. 'FACE' is a pan-European organisation that monitors all aspects of field sports and conservation. It is our sole representative within the law making process and is funded by subscription from associated bodies.

One of these is the newly renamed Countryside Ireland. Formerly known as the Field and Country Sports Society, it is a body that has representation from most field and country sports organisations. It is run by a council of elected representatives from their individual sports and is a highly respected and extremely active association. Historically they have championed the cause of field sports in Ireland, have funded scientific research into a wide selection of projects, and monitor any threats to the sporting interests of their members. They also organise support for like minded individuals or associations such as the Countryside Alliance in the UK. If making a choice of organisations to join, I have to say that Countryside Ireland, as the umbrella body, would be very high on my list.

On the same list is the NARGC. This stands for the National

Association of Regional Game Councils. I spoke at length to the Secretary of the NARGC who kindly gave me a definitive description of the association's role. "It is the national representative organisation for game bird shooting in the Republic of Ireland. Its objectives are to promote the sport of game hunting by :

A. Representing and protecting the interests, objectives and traditional rights of residential shooting men and women.
B. Promoting conservation of wildlife and habitat.

I.G.P.A. or the Irish Game Protection Association. After a period of dormancy, this association was reborn to cope with the very real threat to game management from Brussels. Managed game shooting was banned in Holland and Belgium and very nearly banned in Germany. The fear that Brussels might continue to wield its rather arbitrary and ill advised axe galvanised a number of individuals. A meeting was called of Ireland's shoot owners and managers and this meeting was addressed by the President of the Game Conservancy, Hugh Van Cutsem. Since that date the association has contributed enormously to the success of the driven shooting industry in Ireland. Together with this, they have raised tens of thousands of pounds to go towards research into game conservation and have benefited from the scientific data that is produced yearly by the Game Conservancy.

The Game Conservancy established its headquarters in Fording bridge, Hampshire. Originally founded by Maj. H.G. Eley of the Eley Bros. cartridge manufacturers, his intention was to put back as much research for game conservation at the muzzle end of the gun, as his family firm had done from the chamber end. Fordingbridge is the home and headquarters for one of the United Kingdom's foremost associations and has a formidable membership. As previously stated, their remit is both as a scientific research establishment as well as a training institute in related careers. Courses are held in a variety of pursuits such as Game Keeping and Shoot Management. They also offer an advisory service for game shoots with a view to building from scratch or improving existing facilities.

The Countryside Alliance has of course been on the front page of most newspapers in the British Isles, and would rightly claim to have the largest following of any association for country sports. Recently fighting for people's right to determine their own sports and activities, though remarkably successful, I believe their fight is far from won. We shall see a great deal more of their political power and parliamentary lobbying before this decade is out.

Ducks Unlimited is an American organisation who have a similar remit to the English Game Conservancy. Originally formed to ensure the conservation of wetlands for the benefit of North America's waterfowl and wildlife, they have a vast membership which ensures a formidable lobby within government and a most effective network of scientific knowledge.

B.A.S.C. or British Association for Shooting and Conservation. Both the B.A.S.C. and its northern counterparts are associations that identify themselves as the national representative body for country shooting. The B.A.S.C. has five strategic objectives:

- A strong and unified voice for shooting
- All party backing for shooting
- Balanced comment in the media
- Continued opportunity to go shooting
- High standards

36 A Final Thought

I have spent forty-two years or so, putting together a simple system that I hope will be considered by my peers to be a definitive version of how to learn to shoot. Indeed my system may be thought the best option should the reader wish to become an instructor. Providing the reader realises that they must know ten differing ways to explain every nuance of the system to their clients, a lot of my own techniques are here for them to read and use should they wish. Repeating what I say verbatim will work for some clients but may not work in every case. It is up to the instructor to provide verbal information that the client can relate to, it's not up to the client to relate to the instructor.

So where does all this leave me? Could I ever match Robert Churchill the shooting instructor and commentator and longest published author I have read on this subject? It's what I aspire to but some will ask how I could pair myself in such exalted company? Some will ask, why just Churchill? Having studied his words I know he spent a great deal of time thinking through what he would say, it's obvious from his phraseology. I started mentally preparing myself to write this book years ago, it is only now that I feel ordered enough to put these words down on paper. Having spent so much of my life teaching, I realise Churchill and I differ is some respects, both dealing with the eyes, the method of physical movement and management of our thought processes. I know now that this is where we have to concentrate our efforts. A familiar stumbling block is the fact that we shoot because we enjoy shooting. We compete because we enjoy it. It is, you might say, our weekly R & R. When indulging in rest and recreation, the idea is to switch off and let the world go past without undue worry or effort. The problem is that we don't function at our best if we adopt this mode. To be good at this sport, we should really be at the office. The best shots I have seen are undoubtedly wholly intent upon what they are doing. Some can switch from easy bonhomie with their friends, to maximum concentration while a game drive is on or the clays are presented at the next station. Then miraculously it's back to fun and congeniality again. Some find this very difficult to do, but in this scenario lies our means to success. Identify how you best sustain your concentration under all circumstances and employ those means as your shooting bible.

I have had a life full of fascinating people. Take for instance my great American friends David and Susan Lloyd. When teaching in Rhode Island, I was asked to stay at their wonderful home by the ocean and use their house as a base. *"Get the train to New London"*, David had instructed, *"I'll collect you from the station"*. I disembarked at the appropriate stop and stood on the platform watching reunions between parents and children, business men and women, sons and lovers. And finally the station was empty. Save for me and a bucket of anxiety. Was this the only New London station? Was this New London at all? Was this the date agreed? Was this the correct time? I felt a light tap on my shoulder followed by a large pair of arms wrapping around me, a broad grin and then, *"Hi Shane, bring your bag and follow me"*. With that we walked across the railway lines and through a small gate that I hadn't noticed up to that moment. This led immediately to a long spiralling flight of stairs down to a dock by the river. Moored alongside the dock, David's boat, the 'Rolls Royce' of fishing or fast working boats. V8 petrol engine, two computer screens at the wheel giving satellite and navigational information, radar and sonar, more akin to an offshore power boat. *"Do you wanna catch a sea bass on a fly rod?"* David smiled as if he knew my answer. Why do people ask such unnecessary questions? *"Lead on McDuff!"* I stared out over the stern as the boat headed down river, past the General Dynamics yard with its attendant nuclear submarines, black like gargantuan water beetles, sinister behemoths leaning against their quays, innocent waves twinkling with sunlight, foam streaming from our stern and a curious thought occurred to me. I wonder if people realise how much I enjoy teaching, how lucky I am to have chosen this road? If they have, there will be a large queue at the careers counter looking for the words.

'Shooting Instructor'

37 Appendix

Glossary of shooting words and terms

Across eyed = Stock cast enabling shooting from one side using opposite eye
Action = Part of the gun that houses the locks and the barrels engage with
Balltrap = A format for a going away clay target (ABT)
Battue = Very fast clay pigeon with narrow profile
Bird = Clay pigeon or game species
Bead = Used to align eye with barrel, round sometimes brass at end of rib
Beat keeper = Principal person on one part of game shoot rearing birds etc.
Beater = One of the keeper's team at a game shoot to find & flush game
Beavertail and Semi Beavertail = Specific design of Fore-end
Blacking = Protective coating on parts of gun against rust and other corrosion
Blueing = Protective coating on parts of gun against rust and other corrosion
Bore = Internal diameter of barrels
Boxlock = Particular type of design for shotgun's action
Brace = Two birds of the same species
Browning = Protective coating on parts of gun against rust and other corrosion
Bullpup = Gun with the magazine and action housed in the stock
Butt = End of the stock
Cage = Protective frame at the shooting stations on a shooting ground
Cast = Bending the stock to suit peculiarities of shooter
Chamber = Initial part of barrels housing cartridge
Checkering = Diamond shaped carving in furniture to aid shooter's grip

Choke = Final internal part of barrel before muzzle dictating pattern size
Clay = Clay pigeon or target
Colour hardening = Chemical/Heat Colouration giving decorative and protective finish to the outer surface of the action
Comb = Top edge of stock
Crimp = Closing and opening point of a cartridge
Crosser = Clay pigeon whose flight is near to right angles to the shooter
Down the line = A format for a going away clay target
Dropping duck = A clay that descends having passed over shooter's head
Ejector = Mechanical rod to throw out spent cartridge
English style = Specific design of stock grip and Fore-end
Engraving = Decorative carving in the exterior metal parts of the gun
Fences = Back of action upper side
Figuring = Darker coloured grain in stock and Fore-end
Firing Pin = Small pin, housed in the action that strikes percussion cap
Five stand = Compact sporting layout for clay pigeon shooting
Flag man = One of the keeper's team working at a game shoot
Flush = Multiple birds rising into the air
Flush shoot = Multiple target release for team of guns
Forcing cone = Compressing section of barrels between chamber and tube
Fore-end = Third part of gun that engages with action and barrels
Furniture = All timber parts of the gun
Game = Birds and animals with a specified shooting season
Gauge = Internal diameter of barrels
Gun = Shotgun or person using one
Head Keeper = Principal person on game shoot rearing birds etc.
Heel = Upper end of Butt
Hull = Tube section of cartridge

Keeper = Single handed person managing birds on a game shoot
Lighting duck = Clay pigeon whose flight is near to right angles to the shooter
Load = Amount of shot inside one cartridge
Loader = Person who assists gun on game shoot
Lock = Part of a shotgun's mechanism that fires the cartridge
Lump = Part of barrel that engages with the action
Matched pair = Two matching guns made with consecutive numbers
Midi = Medium size clay pigeon
Mini = Small size clay pigeon
Monte Carlo = Specific design of stock making gun shoot a little higher
Muzzle = Opening at the end of the barrels where shot exits
Neck = Narrowest part of stock where rear hand holds gun
Olympic Trench = A format for a going away clay target
Pair = Two clay pigeons launched simultaneously
Peg = Drive position for a gun on a game shoot
Percussion Cap = Small container holding shock sensitive explosive
Picker = Person plus dog who finds and collects shot game
Picture = Relationship of barrels and bird at moment of firing
Pistol grip = Specific design for grip for shotgun stock
Pitch = Angle of the butt relative to the shape of the shoulder
Possible = All targets hit, not one missed!
Powder = Propellant in the cartridge
Prince of Wales = Specific design for grip of shotgun's stock
Rabbit = A running clay pigeon used to simulate the animal
Receiver = Part of fire arm that houses operating parts
Rib = Upper centre viewing part of barrels housing bead at the end
Roach bellied = Specific design of stock
Rotary = Round drum magazine fitted with action to rear
Round action = Particular type of design for a shotgun's action
Safety catch = Small switch used to protect gun from accidental

discharge
Schnabel = Specific design of shape to the Fore-end
Sear = Part of the lock mechanism that holds back the hammer or striker
Selector = Switch to select firing order of barrels
Semi-auto = Self loading single barrelled shotgun
Semi-pistol = Specific design for grip of shotgun's stock
Shooting = Discharge of the shotgun
Shot = Projectiles housed in the cartridge
Sidelock = Particular type of design for a shotgun's action
Skeet = A format for a multi angled clay pigeon competition (EUR)
Skeet = A title used to describe all clay pigeon shooting (USA)
Sleeve = Carrying case for a shotgun fully assembled
Smoked = Hitting the clay pigeon with the centre of the pattern
Springing teal = Very steep rising clay pigeon
Stop = One of the Keeper's team working at a game shoot
Tang = Upper and lower ends to action extending into stock
Toe = Lower end of Butt
Top Lever = Lever to open chamber of shotgun
Trap = Clay pigeon launcher or thrower
Trench = A format for a going away clay target
Trigger = Firing device
Trigger guard = Protective screen to trigger
Tulip = Specific design of shape to the Fore-end
Under keeper = Junior aid to head keeper
Vermin = Pest species with an unspecified shooting season
Wad = Fibre or plastic material between propellant and shot within cartridge
ZZ Trap = A clay pigeon that can change its direction of flight several times

Those Smiling Faces

4x4
SALES

PROTECH

1146

Testimonials

Bite the Bullet

I have been to Ireland more than 100 times, lived there for a couple years in college and it's my favourite place to visit because of the great scenery and even greater people! Shane and his shooting school is no exception.

From the minute you meet Shane he is properly dressed for the part and will take your learning experience very seriously, so you should too. He will lead you in a classic Jeep (with his friendly lab Molly!) to a beautiful remote lake-front location among the hills of Connemara. He will trust you with taking his lessons to heart and will even let you use his personal collection of shotguns for the shooting lesson and they are BEAUTIFUL and lightweight - a combination of black and wood with intricate designs on the trim (he even lets you keep the shells from your shot as a fun, memorable souvenir! I added mine into a scrapbook from our trip). Before the lesson, my biggest concern was the kickback of the shotgun bruising me or hurting because I heard horror stories from friends over the years who shoot rifles and shotguns. Not only did Shane give me the bravery and confidence to hold the gun against my FACE, I left the lesson that day completely UNSCATHED - not a single bruise or mark anywhere! I didn't feel that there was any kickback at all really, because Shane KNOWS what he's talking about and I trusted him and followed his instructions exactly as he said. My fears are abated and I will definitely be back for another afternoon of shooting with Shane in the near future! We were only disappointed it was one day, next time we want to spend a whole week with him at least!

THANK YOU SHANE for the most memorable and didactic experience we've ever had, it definitely surpassed our expectations! We could tell right away that you were serious about your craft and very knowledgeable, and we felt so lucky to have had a private lesson with you and it was no surprise to us that you trained the Irish shooting team! It was the highlight of our trip and the very first story we shared with our family when we arrived home, telling them all about our day in Connemara with the Olympic shooting coach! It's fair to say that everyone was very jealous and we will certainly be bringing more of our family back to you for more formal shooting lessons.

You are obviously a master shooter, but I think you're also a master of teaching – specifically your method of always keeping clear eye contact, checking for understanding, educating us about what the common mistakes or misconceptions are (like keeping both eyes open), and giving us confidence to try (like pointing out our dominant eye/hand coordination or reminding me when I was getting fooled by my own head). We can't rave enough about you and how wonderful of a teacher you are, definitely the best we've seen. You were right to follow your passions and pursue a career in shooting as you are definitely very skilled but more than that it led you to teaching others, which is I what I believe you were really meant to do as you have such a talent for teaching.

We are so happy to have met you and Molly, and we are very grateful for the time and knowledge you shared with us. Outside of the lesson, it was also very nice to just get to know you. We really enjoyed hearing all of your stories about your family background, your skills and hobbies whether it be with horses or shooting, and the interesting people you've met (especially the famous ones!). My favourite was the story about how you still use your family tailor to dress the part and ended up starting a trend in the town where people were starting to dress up more and wanted to look more polished. We had so much fun and it's definitely one of our fondest Ireland memories. Until next time, take care of yourself and never retire! Thanks again!

Notes

Notes

CW01619305

MOMENTS

stories

Wayne Dean-Richards

OUTSIDELEFT books

First published in the UK in 2025 by OUTSIDELEFT Books.

Paperback ISBN 978-1-0684021-1-1

copyright © Wayne Dean-Richards, 2025

Versions of some of these stories first appeared in the following publications, for which I'd like to thank the editors:

Feeders, The Lawn Mower, The Sandman - *Flash: Anthology;*
Maybe Monday – *Culture Matters;*
The Beach Boys in Winter – *Flash Fiction North;* Apprenticeship – *Lumpen;*
Supermarket Shoot, The Quinton Meat Van – *Outsideleft;*
Messages – *Red Fez;*
A Nice Guy – *Earthly Rewards: Anthology;*
New Blood – *Funny Bone: Red Nose Day Anthology;* Not What – *Bunbury Magazine;*
One Day – *Armley Press;*
You'll Never Know – *Writing the Black Country;*
Only Once – *Runcible Spoon;*
Skid Marks – *Ink Pantry;*
The Squatter Above Bossiney Cove – *Brittle Star.*

Thanks to my family.

Cover image by Amrit Kaur

Wayne Dean-Richards image
by Garry Corbett

'There are some things one remembers though they may never have happened. '
Anna - Hard Times - Pinter.

'A little autobiography and a lot of imagination are best.'
Raymond Carver.

FEEDERS

Some of these guys think because they feed you, they own you but it's not so.

Take this one guy who got pissed off when I wouldn't eat only this special super high calorie cake he'd had made and had specially delivered. He offered to pay extra if I'd eat only this cake for a month or so. Now don't get me wrong, I'm an eater and I like cake, cake's one of my all-time favourite foods.

But cake only?

Nope. It's not going to happen. No way.

Only when I said that he told me I was a just fat woman who sat practically naked on a supersize bed all day and got paid to let men watch her eat and I should remember that and not get uppity.

When attitude didn't work, he sent me a dozen messages, maybe more. Is still sending them for all I know. It doesn't matter because I blocked him. Knew what he wanted was for me to get so big I couldn't move anymore and thought I was so dumb I didn't know that.

Thankfully my feeders aren't all like that.

Ken, for example, who's calling me now, is a nice guy. Sure, he likes to see me eat. And he especially likes to see me eat cake. All my feeders like to see me eat cake is the truth of the matter. But not cake only until I get so big I can't move anymore, can't do anything for myself, no.

"Hi, Valerie," Ken says when I put him onscreen.

"Hi, Ken," I say.

MAYBE MONDAY

Managers are mystics. Must be because they're always telling the people who work for them about their fucking vision. Their fucking vision for the company, that is. Their fucking vision for the company always a trigger for what they call revised practices. A catchy little phrase meaning whatever your job was before you've now got to do a shedload more of it. Only what you're now doing a shedload more of isn't called what it used to be called prior to their fucking vision for the company, no. Now it's called something else. Something a lot fancier. Though the truth is it doesn't pay any better. It's just a lot more of the same old, same old. That's more, more, fucking more.

With so much more to do it's no wonder I feel fucking battered at the end of every workday. Hollowed out. A ghost of myself. Except on a Friday night when I hit Broad Street.

ALL DRINKS ½ PRICE B411 say the signs outside the clubs.

But that's not what draws me in. A half-priced drink or two isn't what stops me feeling fucking battered. No way, no how. No, movement is what does it. Movement what counts. I'm talking head, body, hands, feet. I'm talking dipping, swirling, turning. I'm talking, fast, slow, on the beat, off it. I'm talking being inside every move and at the same time watching myself from the outside. None of which has anything to do with half-price drinks.

Some tunes are old favourites. Some are brand new. To me it makes no never mind. Simply, the tunes come at me, and I move. I move and the dark moves with me. Holds me in its arms. Is a mirror reflection of me.

Only it's not only me, no. It's all of us. All of us move to the music. All of us are pierced by it. All of us are impaled by its foreverness, yes. Though I always go alone, I'm packed in with the rest. A seething mass. Love what I feel for every one of us because of this shared thing we're doing in the strobe-lit dark. Which, till they kill the tunes and turf us out, helps me escape the management visionaries and their more, more, fucking more. Gets them out of my head and from under my skin. Fucking saves me, yes. At least for a little while.

Saves me for a little while and makes me sad at the same time, I should say.

Makes me sad because by saving me for a little while it lets me carry on with the more, more, fucking more.

Makes me sad because I can't help thinking that if at work enough of us moved together like we're moving now, maybe managers couldn't keep battering us with their fucking vision for the company. Why, I think, as I move to the music, I ought to try talking to the people I work with again. Why, I think, maybe Monday, I will.

AM I?

Stuart Adamson's black shirt was sticking to him and BIG COUNTRY was reflected off his shy, sweaty face.

Was he shy?

Did I read that somewhere?

Or was it just an impression I got from watching him perform?

I think the latter, though that night he didn't seem shy. Certainly not when he was singing Chance. My all-time favourite Big Country song - track three on The Crossing - Chance alone so great it was worth queuing to get in for.

Which I'd had to do. Queued for so long my first job when I got in was to find a toilet. When I found one was surprised how much it stank: vomit exploded all over the second urinal from the left if memory serves.

Doubly relieved to have emptied my bladder and escaped the stink of that second urinal I made a beeline for the front. Knew from balconies you often got a better view, but the atmosphere wasn't the same. Remember really feeling the heat as I pushed through the crowd. My hair long in those days. A denim jacket, skinny black jeans and a black tee-shirt what I was wearing.

Did Jools Holland introduce them that night?

Or Paula Yates?

Or maybe it was Muriel Gray?

I can't remember. But let's face it the 17th of February 1984 is a lifetime ago so it's to be expected.

Besides which it doesn't matter who introduced them. Could have been Leslie Ash for all I cared.

The important thing was I made it right to the very front. Where my chest was pressed up hard against the stage. I made it right to the very front so although I was too hot, I was excited. Big Country being my favourite band. A band who I'd already seen three or four times. Maybe more. Though I can't watch any of those early gigs again because they weren't filmed.

This one was.

And at this one Stuart Adamson was sweating buckets by the time he urged us all to sing.

At which point the whole audience sang hard before the guitars and drums came in harder still and he took over again, singing, "Oh, Lord, where did the feeling go...Oh, Lord, I never felt so low," under Tyne Tees Television's studio lights.

*

Forty years on I watch it all the time, The Tube perfect for YouTube, that there've been 3.3 million views what it says on the bottom left of my screen.

To which I now add one more.

Then another.

Sit hunched forwards. Alert to the band's every move. Listening intently to their every note. When the camera cuts away from the band to the audience hit pause and lean in close. Not with long hair, wearing a denim jacket and skinny black jeans anymore but sweating as I study the faces of those in the front row. Am I beside the ginger-haired guy Adamson directed the mic towards when he first urged the audience to sing?

I am.

I must be.

"Oh, no, where did the feeling go?"

I remember being there.

I remember the stench of vomit and sweat.

I remember the heat and the glare of the studio lights.

"Oh, no, I never felt so low."

But despite countless viewings I've never yet set eyes on myself.

Not beside the ginger-haired guy or anybody else at the front.

Nor have I ever seen myself in any of the rows immediately back from the front.

Never.

Am I even there? I wonder.

I am, I must be, I tell myself.

But am I?

Am I?

THE BEACH BOYS IN WINTER

"Joan Peterson."

When Miss Gladstone raised her icy blue eyes the attention of the class shifted to eight-year-old Joan.

"Don't keep me waiting," Miss Gladstone hissed.

Trembling like a cornered animal, Joan stood, gathered up her exercise book and stepped back from her desk.

"Bring your pencil, too," Miss Gladstone instructed.

Why?

No answer forthcoming Joan picked it up anyway. Seeing Miss Gladstone glaring at her felt something thicken at the back of her throat. Fear it was that took her by the shoulders and propelled her past orderly rows of desks. Her raging heartbeat a counterpoint to the click of her new school shoes. In exchange for their silence would have borne the hurt of their newness for a week, a month, the rest of her life. Barring that wished the waxed wooden floor would open like a mouth and swallow her whole.

It didn't.

Instead, Miss Gladstone waited for Joan to turn to the page she'd been working on and after a cursory glance at it said, "Show me your pencil."

Nonplussed, Joan nonetheless complied.

"There's nothing wrong with your pencil," Miss Gladstone said.

A second later the thwack of the ruler froze the class –

This was George Road Primary School, 1969. Church-like windows in all the classrooms. Desks with inkwells from another age. Joan's stomach clenching with the realisation that if she told her mom what'd happened, her mom would say she deserved the punishment.

"You need to do better, don't you?" Miss Gladstone said.

Blinking back tears Joan said, "Yes, Miss Gladstone."

*

Her dad said she looked ridiculous in her platform shoes and high-waisted trousers. Looked stern when he said it, then laughed. Was often that way, which confused Joan even though she was fourteen by then and half a head taller than her mom, his words replaying in her head as she walked to the Christmas disco - the first she'd ever attended.

It was held in the school hall and policed by teachers who gossiped to each other rather than peer through the darkness at clumps of gyrating teenagers.

Wearing a denim waistcoat and Oxford bags, Kevin Marshall was there.

From a distance Joan had loved him for a year and wished more than anything that he'd ask her to slow dance to Mud's Lonely This Christmas.

He didn't, but that weekend she bought the single from Sounds Easy in Bearwood and installed in the front room knelt before the record player as if it were an altar.

She played it endlessly but didn't ever play it loud, his hunt for a misplaced fiver what drew her dad into the front room on the second Friday in March.

Only once his search was underway did he even notice her. Had been to The Two Brewers after work but wasn't drunk when he kicked the record player, and the needle leapt. Landed hard. Dug jaggedly through the vinyl.

"Don't play Christmas songs when it's not Christmas," he snapped.

Afterwards he tried to make a joke of it and bought her a replacement copy. When he handed it to her winked and said, "We're keeping Sounds Easy in business," to which Joan smiled though she never played the replacement.

*

They married in mid-May, a week before her twenty-fifth birthday.

Glenn was slim, with thick, dark hair. He had a crooked front tooth about which Joan was glad: would've felt intimidated by a man with perfect teeth.

He was the youngest of four and his sisters Olivia and Trinity visited them every Saturday. Not on speaking terms with Olivia or Trinity his sister Rebecca visited them every Sunday. All Glenn's sisters brought their kids along but not their husbands.

Lucy wasn't yet a year old and whenever Joan held her Rebecca said, "Your turn next."

Convinced Rebecca was right Joan stopped taking the pill and she and Glenn prepped the back bedroom for the sound of tiny feet.

Ready for a new-born, the back bedroom sat accusingly empty for two long years.

Another two years on, when she stepped out of Aldi into a cutting wind and spotted him with his new wife Joan saw Glenn's dark hair had thinned and his body was no longer slim.

Was she glad?

Yes, she was.

Then, no, no, she wasn't.

*

Thirty-nine, now, Joan had worked at Superdrug for a decade.

"Doesn't mean you're a shoo-in for branch manager," her colleague warned her. "Beccy's bubbly."

Donning a wounded look Joan said, "Are you saying I'm not?"

Seeing his distress Joan said, "I'm pulling your leg."

When he'd polished off his tuna baguette she said, "Anyway, they don't want bubbly."

Aston smiled. His smile widening when Joan said, "They don't really want a woman at all. Which is why I'll be wearing trousers for the interview."

It was as well she was - hefty snowflakes spiralling between the shops on Bearwood High Street and clinging to the windscreen despite the dogged thwack of the wipers.

Slowing, Joan saw that Tesco Express and Blunts were gone.

When had that happened?

She had no idea. Knew only that she'd never imagined she could be a branch manager.

Until now.

Miss Gladstone, her dad, Glenn, wouldn't they all be surprised if she got the job?

They would, Joan was convinced of it.

But she didn't turn off Bearwood High Street and slow to find a parking space. Instead, found herself reaching forwards with her left hand, picking up a CD and pushing it in.

Snow fell as The Beach Boys sang and Joan pressed the accelerator.

THE RUNNER

I started running to help stop smoking. At first could manage only a hundred yards. After which, in the grip of the dry heaves, I'd have to stop and put my hands on my knees.

*

But things got better and soon I was running every day. Liked that, before sunrise, only dog walkers, people on earlies, and a few other runners were up and about.

*

A year later I discovered Park Runs.

Some of the other park runners introduced themselves and asked me my name.

Alex, I told Paul.

Shaun, I told Andy.

Told Errol my name was Thomas, but he could call me Tommo.

*

When Errol said I'd suit longer distances I stopped doing park runs, started getting up at 3AM and running until 6AM - leaving just enough time for a shower and breakfast before hopping on the bus to get to work before my shift started.

*

A year into this routine my supervisor stared at the bones in my face and raised his eyebrows.

It decided me.

Up at midnight, I gulped water and set off.

At first the route was crushingly familiar.

But after eight hours it wasn't anymore. Alright, maybe on occasion I'd glimpsed some of the houses, shops, and factories I was now running past from the top deck of a bus, but after twelve hours that was no longer the case as, sweat dripping, I drove with my legs, pumped with my arms, kept running...

NOTES

Last night I dreamed my granddad was using his clasp knife to eat an apple. My granddad someone who always sliced, never bit right in. Told myself it was how I'd eat apples from now on. Remembering he'd been young when he died despite the care that he took eating apples what gave rise to my sudden panic. When I jolted awake saw the bed was a mess. The pillows as if they'd been mauled by a bear.

Truth is the whole place was a mess. With drawers not properly shut and things that'd slipped from my pockets left where they fell. This how it'd been since Carly left.

I intended to clean up. Hadn't yet but told myself not to worry about it. After all this was how ordinary people lived and was the real reason Carly left - not because I'd rather die than listen to anyone but myself.

Slowly, I sat up. The effort left me breathless. Made my head spin. Why, even more slowly, I lay back down. Tried to bring the ceiling into focus. When I couldn't, turned onto my side and saw the first of the notes - a yellow post it stuck to the nightstand. Had to concentrate to make my fingers close around it. Peel it off. Bring it close enough so that I could read it. The scrawled handwriting familiar:

Trust no one.

I called my doctor friend Alex and asked him if he'd done anything to put me on. Listened as he told me he didn't know what I was talking about then hung up, drank two glasses of water and thought about my ex some more.

Could Carly have written the note on the yellow post it?

It occurred to me to call her up, laugh and say, "Hey, you got me." Went so far as to reach for the phone, then stopped. Breathless again. My head spinning so much I was no longer sure I'd rung Alex.

*

The second note was stuck to the fridge.

It said:

A clasp knife won't help.

Once, she turned the bathroom into a steam room and sat there for half a day. When I finally persuaded her to open the door was crying and muttering that I didn't listen. Not to her, not to anyone, not ever. The memory of which decided me: Carly wouldn't have written either of those notes, much less the others.

*

I found post it notes everywhere. Liked that they were never in the same place twice. Knew if I didn't pay attention, I'd miss them. Why I allowed no distractions. Not the ringing of the phone, not the banging of the front door. Convinced myself I had rung my doctor friend Alex after all. Him sounding nonplussed part of his game: Alex who was writing all these notes, for sure.

*

Though not the note posted through the letterbox this morning.

For starters that note wasn't on a yellow post it.

The Alex who wrote that note said:

I just picked up your voicemails.

I didn't remember leaving any voicemails.

The Alex who wrote that note said:

Are you alright?

I was.

The Alex who wrote that note said:

Your bedroom's above the central heating boiler.

So what?

The Alex who wrote that note said:

You don't have a CO2 alarm.

Big deal.

Whoever that Alex was included a list of symptoms, which I didn't read.

Instead, I placed this non-yellow non-post it note back on the doormat and, sure that somewhere sometime soon there'd be a new note that was on a yellow post it, told myself I just needed to be patient and lay back down.

PERHAPS

What prompts her to ask - in perfect English - why I've travelled to Taiwan I don't know.

But without even turning around I do know she looks like one of those beautiful women you see on billboards.

And travelling's certainly what I've been doing. Twenty hours on a Boeing 707 followed by a train journey from Taipei to Tamsui District and now the return to Taipei. Standing room only both ways. Just by chance that she and I are only inches apart. The two of us holding tightly to the overhead handrail and swaying with the irresistible motion of the speeding train. All this travelling almost certainly why, still without turning to look at her, I decide to abandon my mother's good advice never to talk to strangers. Clear my throat and say, "I've travelled here because I'm a McQueen hunter," the two of us rocked like puppets by the movement of the train say, "I flew out here then travelled to Tamsui District because part of McQueen's movie The Sand Pebbles was shot there back in 1966."

Is she surprised or sad to hear this?

Of course, if I really wanted to know I could turn to see the expression on her beautiful face.

Instead, I stare out the windows at jagged mountains zipping by - there-then-gone-there-then-gone-there-then-gone.

"The Sand Pebbles was McQueen's only ever Oscar nomination," I say and immediately wonder why.

Do I expect her be impressed by me knowing that The Sand Pebbles was McQueen's only nomination?

I only know I find myself wondering how she'd react if I told her how much time I'd spent travelling to McQueen sites over the years – places where he filmed, raced, lived.

Or if I told her how much I'd spent on the racing gloves he wore driving a BMC Mini in the British Touring Car Championship at Brands Hatch in the early Sixties.

Or if I told her how many times I've watched: The Magnificent Seven, The Great Escape and, my favourite McQueen movie, Bullitt.

Pushing these thoughts away I say, "They used nine hundred locals from the Tamsui District as extras," tighten my grip on the handrail when the carriage sways more violently and say, "They threw lighted torches at the San Pablo - the American ship that was at that time the most expensive movie set ever built."

My eyes fixed on the distant mountains I say, "I found out one of the extras was still alive, so I came out here to talk to him about his memories of The Sand Pebbles. Of being an extra. Of throwing a lighted torch."

The darkening sky intensifying the clack of the wheels I speak louder when I say, "But I didn't get to see him because he died two days before I reached Tamsui District."

The carriage rocks, I sway, the mountains stare down.

Their stare is what finally forces me to turn to the beautiful woman listening to me tell why I've come to Taiwan - only to see there is no beautiful woman.

Where is she?

Frowning, I turn this way and that, desperately searching the carriage for a glimpse of her.

But all I see is that the carriage is almost empty. Vacant seats to my left and right: no need for anyone to stand.

I tell myself she must have slipped away, mutter, "That must be it," and with my heart racing search one carriage after another until I reach the end of the train and can go no further.

*

My search has been slow. My search has been methodical. But there's still no trace of her.

None.

Why the mountains laugh cruelly at me.

Despite which I don't turn to look at them. Resist the urge and force myself to breathe slowly as - with my reflection thrown back by the darkness beyond the windows - I plan a return trip to San Francisco. Tell myself there, perhaps, I'll hire a car and like McQueen as Frank Bullitt drive west from Bernal Heights, through Columbus and Chestnut, along Filbert Street and Guadalupe Canyon Parkway.

BLUE, BLUE SKY

My friend Marie picks up on the eighteenth ring and I say, "Me and Darren have been married twenty-five years, which's a fucking life sentence in anybody's book am I right or am I right?"

Marie doesn't answer but I push right on, say, "Anyway, yesterday I ask him, I say: Darren, what's the most memorable day of your life? Why I ask him that I don't fucking know but it is what I ask him, and he thinks for a second or two then says the most memorable day of his life was when he was a just kid and he went to this place called Sandy Beach, on Anglesey. He'd been there many times before, he said. Only, despite its name, all those other times he went it wasn't ever sandy. Was always covered in shale. Then this one time, the time he was talking about, all the shale was gone, and Sandy Beach was all sandy. There were acres of golden sand and a blue, blue sky, he said. And he had the beach all to himself that day. And he swam in a warm sea then lay on the sand. And that day, my Darren said, of warm sea, golden sand and a blue, blue sky was the most memorable day of his life…

“Twenty-five years we’ve been fucking married and that’s what he says to me. Can you believe it, Marie? I mean can you believe the fucking nerve of that man!”

APPRENTICESHIP

His back to the prison officer our tutor counts out pencils, hands us sheets of paper and says, "Write about what you know."

How I come to write about what started me on the road to this place:

I was thirteen and some beef between me and another kid needed to be settled. If we'd tried to settle it in the schoolyard a teacher would've broken it up. Why we waited till school was done.

The kid outweighed me but was scared. Why he grabbed me and tried to hold on. Why I butted him, and it was over.

Only it wasn't. His older brother showed up. Was a head taller but wasn't thinking cold.

I was and timed it right, from then on was the go-to guy for such things, just kids' stuff at first but, later, much more than that...

SUPERMARKET SHOOT

I pick the Mauser C96 up off the passenger seat and check it's fully loaded. For its era its range and penetration exceptional though the performance of modern pistols is vastly superior, my choice not without risk, then.

Tucking the Mauser into my waistband and zipping up my leather jacket I get out of the car and eye the car park. See it's almost full already which surely increases my chances of a high score.

*

A familiar song washing over me I step into the cooled supermarket air. Am convinced the fruit & veg and tinned food aisles are key to my success. Know frozen goods will be busy too though the freezers might provide cover. Why I intend to start in fruit & veg then move directly to tinned goods. Skipping clothes, stationary and the deli.

The clock ticking I see three mothers with pre-school children and half a dozen elderly couples.

Unzipping my jacket with my left hand I draw out the Mauser with my right. Dropping to one knee aim at the furthest of the mothers and squeeze off my first shot. Shoot the second mother before the first hits the recently mopped floor. Mothers high tariff, children worth nothing. Why, next, I sight on the third mother and squeeze off another round. Miss because she bends at that precise moment to gather her child up into her arms and run.

The miss is a disappointment, but I don't let it faze me. Empty the Mauser into the elderly couples before striding around to tinned goods. Don't run because I know if I run, I'll breathe harder, which'll make it difficult to keep my hand steady, my aim true.

By now everybody knows what's going on.

But that's alright because I've anticipated this and planned for it though luck still plays a part, I admit.

Today luck is on my side since as one the customers in the tinned food aisle charge towards the exit enabling me to fire at a wall of bodies.

Re-loading, I continue to fire rapidly as I stride towards the crumbling wall.

Am re-loading again when the klaxon sounds.

*

Wiping sweat from my brow I let the Mauser hang loosely at my side as the show's theme plays over the supermarket's sound system - think it sounds different somehow but push the thought aside when Rex Cranston appears with his famous grin fixed in place.

Wearing a blue suit and matching tie, his perfect teeth reflecting the lights behind the cameras, Cranston says, “Congratulations Nick Cahill of Oldbury that was spectacular.”

I say, “Thank you.”

Cranston claps his hands together and says, “Now, the question that’s lit up the network is: what kind of weapon is that you’re carrying?”

I say, “It’s a Mauser C96,” and on impulse hand it over.

Swivelling, Cranston points the Mauser directly at camera #1 and says, “Pow!”

Then, laughing, he hands it back and to camera #2 says, “After that spectacular display with a Mauser C96 will Nick Cahill’s points beat current Supermarket Shoot winner Gemma Cantrell? Find out right after the break.”

When the lights on top of their cameras turn from green to red, the camera operators stand down and Cranston says, “The antique pistol was a nice touch, Nick. After the break, you get to talk about it, OK?”

I nod.

"Roll out your spiel about the gun, I'll announce you as our new winner and when we go off air I'll introduce you to Ellie Moore, who agents for the show."

I nod again.

"You're a man of few words, I like that," Cranston says as behind him the camera operators turn back to face us.

When the red lights turn green to camera Cranston says, "A killing machine, Nick Cahill of Oldbury is going to tell us all about his Mauser C96..."

*

I've seen previous winners make the mistake of looking sullen – Eddie Cooperman's tally yet to be equalled but where is he now? – so after smiling broadly I open my mouth ready to talk about the Mauser -

At which point as if of its own accord I feel my mouth snap shut and I spin around towards sounds of urgent whispers, low sobbing and fast approaching sirens.

What is this?

What's going on?

Intending to direct these questions to Cranston I turn to face him -

I'd have sworn on my life that just a moment ago he was standing right in front of me in his blue suit and matching tie.

But now there's no sign of him.

Or of the camera crew.

How can that be?

I decide it must be a joke they're all playing on me. Why I say, "Guys, please don't do this to me. Come on, now, I'm a big, big fan of the show, have been for years..." and wait.

SHATTERBANGED

He'd bomb up the Wolverhampton Road in a white Triumph Herald, from rolling out of bed to clocking in in twenty minutes flat, always muttered, "Needs must," as he strode into the clinging dark, Barlow's synonymous with the dark: as if the steel mill and the darkness were welded together.

Was it that the only light was from the furnaces and the roller-doors?

It irritated him that he couldn't remember but George let it go. Consoled himself with the fact that he remembered the furnaces well enough - soot-blackened things that showered him with sparks and screamed like banshees every time they spewed out a steel billet.

None of which deterred him: apparently impervious to sparks and banshee screams, in his steel toe-capped boots, leather chaps and work gloves George expertly reaching out to guide the billets with his flat tongs. The veins in his arms thick as rope. According to the old hands young George the top dog at Barlow's when it came to cogging down. The man nearest the furnace. The man in most danger if a billet shifted from true. Tales of those who'd been maimed known to all who grafted there. How George knew a billet had kinked and taken off Ronnie Barrett's right arm a day before the Christmas shutdown. And almost a year to the day later a two-inch shard had put out Ronnie's younger brother Gordon's right eye.

"Bloody unlucky them Barrett boys," George oftentimes said when he piled into the Waggon & Horses with the rest of the lads on afternoons. After a couple of pints was given to yelling at the furnaces to, "Get a move on!" Sweat running in his eyes and his tongue whipping back and forth over his bottom lip like Ronnie Barrett's broom - Ronnie relegated to brush-man after his accident and Ronnie the fastest one-armed sweeper any of them had ever seen.

George's work life being full of sweat, sparks and ear-splitting clanks was why he always told his wife and sons, "I'm shatterbanged," when he got home. The word one he'd invented to convey that he felt shattered and banged out. That and something else. Though exactly what else George couldn't put his finger on till much later - indignation in his voice when he added, "Barlow's is a hell hole not fit for man or beast."

Despite which when they made him redundant, demolished the mill and built a bus station where it'd been George came apart for a while. Using the thumbnail of his right hand to dig at the thinning calluses on his left palm told his wife and sons they'd have to pull up sticks and move to South Africa, "Where a steel man still amounts to something." Might well have done so if his brother-in-law hadn't landed him a job at British Leyland.

*

Rife with the potent stink of thinners Number #2 Paint killed George's sense of smell within weeks and still he was glad of the job - happy to avoid the stigma of being on the dole and pleased with the worker's discount he got on a brand-new brown Austin Allegro.

Not that even in a brand-new Allegro he was able to roll out of bed and clock in in twenty minutes flat anymore - Longbridge being a lot further than Oldbury town centre.

Despite which it was less demanding than being at Barlow's - working in a paint shop he got togging up time for starters.

"Means they pay me ten minutes extra at the start of every shift to put on overalls," George told his wife and sons.

"Sounds cushy," the youngest said.

"Steady on," George countered, "I have to wrap masking tape round the wrists and ankles of my overalls, then put on special gloves."

It was true, though once he was togged up he didn't have to dash like the rest the moment the track started, then spend eight hours rooted to the same spot as the body shells of Allegros moved relentlessly through the spray bays then the ovens then out the other side to the engine shop: was a slip man, whose job it was to relieve other workers for fifteen-minute spells throughout the day.

"Bog breaks," George explained, his utterance drawing a simultaneous smile from his wife and sons.

"It is cushy, then," his youngest son said. The youngest the one who made George laugh the most. Laugh what he did in response to this. Laughed then insisted that after each shift he was still shatterbanged because being a slip man he no longer had just one job he did throughout each shift, rather, for fifteen-minute stretches, he had to be able to do the job of anyone in Number #2 Paint. Do it and get it right, that was. Getting it right the key thing: "Can't have punters turning their noses up at that Allegro because George Richards worked on it," he said. Needed his wife and sons to understand that life at British Leyland - driving over to Longbridge; bagging a space on the car park; jogging over the Bristol Road to Number #2 Paint; muttering, "Needs must"; clocking in; togging up; making a fist of the job of anyone in need of a bog break; at the end of his shift returning his overalls to his locker; clocking out; running back to his car because it was first back first away; then driving home in heavy traffic - was still hard graft. This need in him why when his oldest son said, "No wonder you're shatterbanged," George smiled. His oldest son it was who enabled him to understand the something else there was to shatterbanged: his word embodying his relish of the exhaustion he felt at the end of every shift and the reason why he was in such a state when British Leyland shut down.

*

For weeks afterwards he walked around saying, "People still drive cars, don't they?" to anyone who'd listen - knew only that he had to get another job so was massively relieved to bag an interview at Ash & Lacey's.

"Little firm on the Oldbury Trading Estate who board up empty houses to stop people smashing windows or breaking in," he told his wife - both sons having grown up and left by then, "Only they don't use wooden boards, they use aluminium panels."

To demonstrate that he could handle one of those panels was why after his interview he followed Ash or Lacey - though he'd introduced himself at the start of the interview George had forgotten which the shaven-headed fella wearing a white shirt and red tie had identified himself as – outside to where two ladders waited before a second storey window.

Ash or Lacey offered him a pair of work gloves.

George passed. Considered telling Ash or Lacey he had previous working with metal but decided actions spoke louder than words and elected not to, fiddling first with his donkey jacket then with the waistband of his jeans.

"Kid 'll help," Ash or Lacey said and pointed at the lad in tracksuit bottoms stood by the ladder on the left, the lad wearing trainers instead of work boots, George saw, and a tee-shirt not a donkey jacket even though it was early April and still cold - the sky steel grey.

"It's a two-man job," Ash or Lacey said.

Two men my arse, George thought. Waved the kid off but bent more carefully than he used to. Positioning his feet carefully. Making sure his knees were aligned, and his lower back was flat the way the strongmen he'd seen on telly at Christmas lifted. The difference being that they were enormous, tall and solid, their arms the thickness of young beech trees. Whereas George was short and skinny.

Tentatively, he gripped the panel. First with his right, then with his left hand. Was surprised how heavy it felt but kept the surprise from his face when he pushed his tongue dartingly across his bottom lip the way Ronnie Barrett used to push a broom, then held his breath and straightened up.

Its size was what really put the boot in. The panel five feet wide and three and a half feet high. Big enough for it to be awkward as he took three steps forwards and placed his booted foot on the bottom rung of the ladder on the right. Big enough to be so awkward the breath he'd held bolted out of him and a warrior rhythm began pulsing in his throat.

Pressing his lips together so Ash or Lacey and the lad wearing tracksuit bottoms could see he meant business George began to climb the ladder.

One rung...

Breathing hard.

Two rungs...

Breathing harder.

Three rungs...

The trick of it was to drag the panel up over the stiles, he found.

But almost immediately the muscles in his forearms burned with acid - the muscles in his lower back and thighs, too.

After his demo, he was confident he'd be well and truly shatterbanged but that was alright with him.

No.

That wasn't so.

Remembering what his oldest son had said George realised it was way, way better than alright, and smiled.

Four rungs...

The cold April air burned his throat and the warrior rhythm in his throat became more urgent, but that didn't stop him smiling.

Five rungs...

Now he was older the skin on his forearms was loose, the tattooed names of his wife and sons faded - yet still his veins were close to the surface and as thick as rope, so still his forearms were work-hardened and strong, weren't they?

Six rungs...

Seven…

Eight…

Nowadays there was grey in his hair, and it was thinning in places, but he could still graft with the best of them and if any were needed here was proof of it, George decided.

Nine rungs…

First his right leg.

Drag the panel a couple of inches higher.

Then his left leg.

Ten rungs…

First the right boot, clunk.

Then the left boot, clunk.

On like that.

Slowly.

Steadily.

His smile widening as he worked harder until, sweat running into his eyes like in his Barlow's days and the muscles in his forearms, lower back and thighs fibrillating, George missed his footing -

Slipped -

Plummeted to the ground –

*

"What's he's saying?" Ash or Lacey snapped - whatever the word was uttered through bloodied lips by a bitten tongue.

To which the kid in tracksuit bottoms responded by shrugging, then shaking his head.

MESSAGES

I walk from one end of the long, thin house to the other but it's not enough, so I pick up the phone, check for messages, listen, hang up when there are none.

*

I'm familiar with the cliché about there being hundreds of TV channels but nothing on of interest and still I grip the remote and put it to the test, when I'm done go back to the phone, check for messages, listen, hang up when there are none.

*

I play The Streets Never Went to Church on repeat, singing along until my voice cracks and starts to fade.

What must the neighbours think?

Will there be a message telling me what they think?

There isn't and there are still no other messages, so I hang up.

*

Unable to sleep I creep from bed and move through the dark.

I go to the phone, of course, wait to be connected to messages and listen.

Finally, there is a message and though the voice I hear is my own, I tell myself, "That's OK, that's OK."

A NICE GUY

I felt like shit warmed up. Three nights on the piss was why. Discovered if you drank enough of it your sweat stank like Breaker.

"What the fuck are you playing at, Ronnie?" Alison had snapped.

In the middle of the night this was. I'd been palming Breaker-stinking-sweat from my face and slipped - fallen backwards downstairs and puked. If the noise hadn't woken her, I might have drowned in my own fucking vomit. Couldn't answer her question then because I didn't know what the fuck I was playing at and still couldn't answer it when it came back at me as I was steering a shopping trolley towards the booze aisle.

Never mind, I told myself. Told myself everything would be alright so long as I didn't buy Breaker. Told myself Carling or Bud would be OK.

I liked Carling better than Bud, but Carling reminded me of my old man and thinking about my old man distracted me. That was when our trollies collided.

It was me who wasn't looking where I was going but he was the one who said, "Sorry," and smiled.

His smile spelled out in no uncertain terms that he hadn't ever drunk Breaker till his sweat stank of it and wasn't somebody whose wife had found him covered in vomit and asked him what the fuck he was playing at, so I stomped off.

But when my Carling was being scanned, I saw him again. At the checkout next to me. So close I heard his checkout wasn't just chatting to be polite. No, a proper conversation was what they were having and once it was finished, I watched him leave the supermarket ahead of me, steering his trolley in a straight line.

I hurried after him.

Before I caught up the front wheel of my shopping trolley caught the edge of one of the speed bumps outside the supermarket and I fell to my knees.

Carling, beans, and bread spilled out and was still that way when the nice guy rushed over. Righted my shopping trolley then scooped up the bread, the beans, my Carling. Smiled and said, "There you are." Was reaching out to help me up when I hit him.

Sharp as a new razor Alison's question came back at me.

I screamed by way of answer. Wiped tears from my eyes as my throat closed off and people ran towards us.

THE QUINTON MEAT VAN

The boy says, “It’s really dark here.”

I say, “That’s true.”

We’re at the bottom of the Kings Highway. Good houses in what used to be a good area.

“Kids break the streetlights,” I say beneath a broken streetlight.

It’s not late but it’s already dark, as if somebody painted the sky with tar.

“See?”

Through the tarry darkness we see the cover’s smashed, the bulb gone.

“Why do they do it?” the boy says.

They’d have stood where we are now, and the streetlight will have painted them orange. One would’ve had an air rifle, the other an air pistol. They should’ve been home in bed, but they weren’t. The one with the pistol will have aimed at the streetlight and fired. The casing will have cracked but not shattered, so the one with the rifle will have taken aim and fired. This time the casing will have shattered, the bulb behind it, too, the broken parts raining down.

I think about telling the boy this. Instead, I give his hand a squeeze and say, "The important thing, is if you see the Quinton Meat Van, run as fast as you can."

We walk up the Kings Highway on frosted pavement, to our right a row of semis stretching to the top of the hill - all with their curtains closed.

When the boy says, "What's the Quinton Meat Van?" I tell him what my childhood friend told me, that it's a white box-van with windows you can't see into.

The boy says, "Does it deliver meat?"

We're walking quickly. I say, "It doesn't deliver, it collects," and feel the boy's hand wriggle from his wanting to know more.

I say, "It takes people who don't run away when they see it."

We're halfway up the Kings Highway. Still no sign of anyone and the boy listening attentively, desperate to know more.

I say, "Inside there are meat hooks on a rail attached to the roof."

My childhood friend told me if you didn't run, they hung you like a carcass - the hook ripping through your flesh, digging into your bones. You screamed but no one heard you. Then the cutting started.

At the top of the Kings Highway, we turn left. Well-maintained semis on one side and on the other the backs of a row of shops with space for deliveries, overflowing steel bins, and a white box-van with windows you can't see into.

The boy says, "Look."

I say, "I'm looking," and let go of his hand because not to do so would be to give him no choice.

Seeing the fear on my face when he told of the cutting and screaming, my best friend had laughed and said I was a fucking stupid cunt for not knowing none of it was true, the white-hot disappointment I felt at that moment with me to this fucking day - buried deep, a fire that just keeps burning.

We're three feet from the van and the boy doesn't run so I lift him as if he's a sack of spuds, throw him into the back of the van and climb in after him.

The boy scrambles away. Cowers in the far corner.

I watch his eyes adjust to the darkness and fix on the waiting hooks.

Intent on protecting him from white-hot disappointment, I take off my coat and reach for an apron.

His voice little, the boy says, "Dad…"

Moving towards him I whisper, “I’m sorry…”

UBER CUNT

If anybody asked me why I bought a Fiesta when my Mongoose Villain 1 Mountain Bike finally dropped to bits, I'd look them straight in the eye and say, "Don't be fucking stupid."

I mean if I'd had a choice, I'd have gone for

A Porsche 911.

Or a BMW M4.

Or a Mazda MX-5.

Course I fucking would.

But it'd already taken me two years to save enough for a fucking clapped-out Fiesta.

Clapped out?

Yeah, no doubt about that. Why the cunt who sold it to me was struggling not to laugh in my fucking face as he filled in the V5. Something which could've gone badly wrong for him if I hadn't got other fish to fry.

Lucky for him I did.

Which's how comes I ended up working my bollocks off on a clapped-out grey Fiesta for another two years.

Not just trying to bring it back to some kind of life, mind you.

No.

Working to improve the fucking thing's performance so it'd catch any Uber cunt in the country who wasn't driving -

A Porsche 911.

Or a BMW M4.

Or a Mazda MX-5.

An Uber cunt driving a Toyota it was who finally put me to the test by stopping where he shouldn't to drop off a fare, then without signalling pulling right out in front of me.

It's what I'd been waiting for, so I went after him like a fucking shot. Sounding the horn and flashing my lights.

He got the message loud and clear. Would've had to be deaf and blind not to but thought once he jammed his clog down in that nearly new Prius of his he'd leave me for fucking dead.

Only it wasn't like that. No fucking way Jose.

I mean he hammered it good and proper. No doubt about it. But even when the cunt raced through a red light and bombed round a series of tight corners so fast he was practically on two wheels I stuck to him like glue.

The Uber cunt would've been thinking: How the fuck can a clapped-out Fiesta keep up with me?

Only he wasn't fucking thinking.

Was fucking shitting himself is what he was doing.

Which's how comes he charged away from the city when he'd have been better off staying in it. The odds in favour of something impeding me far greater in the city than out of it that's for sure.

It was his mistake and my lucky day. Luck plus all my hard work on a clapped-out Fiesta paying off, that is - credit where it's fucking due, I say.

Anyway, the Uber cunt in question bombed out of the city and pulled a sharp right onto this housing estate.

At least he fucking tried to.

Only instead he lost control and skidded across the road and mounted the pavement and was still going so fucking fast he smacked into a waist high wall.

I slammed my brakes on, and the Fiesta stopped dead.

Beautiful.

I got out and ran over. Yanked open his door and started in on him. Pounding the cunt. Blood everywhere in no time. Gave it to him till my fists were mashed up and it felt like my lungs were on fire.

At which point I was about to fuck off before some nosey prick with a phone showed up and started filming, when even though he had a mouthful of blood the cheeky cunt asked me why I was doing this to him when he was just an Uber driver.

"I know you're just an Uber driver," I said. "That's the fucking point. See, you stopping where you shouldn't to drop off your fare, then without signalling pulling right out in front of me is just the sort of stunt you and Uber cunts just like you pull all the fucking time, and I've had my belly full of it."

Despite all the blood I saw confusion on his face, and it set me thinking.

I realised the Uber cunt hadn't stopped where he shouldn't to drop off his fare.

No.

Nor without signalling had he pulled right out in front of me.

Nope.

But it doesn't matter, I told myself.

Not a fucking bit, I told myself.

Why I gave the Uber cunt another couple of digs for good measure then told him to take that look off his face and got out of there right fucking sharpish.

AGAIN

Been listening to The Growlers singing Mama Said on repeat play since I finished work - upwards of eleven hours and counting.

How long will I have to keep counting?

How long will I need to keep listening to the same track?

No idea. None. Gripping the wheel - the leather worn away in places - all I know for sure is I'm not there, yet. Need to keep hearing that chorus again and again and again as I drive. Going nowhere in a blue Corsa up to its eyeballs in rust. Work traffic long gone and the dark packed tight around me. Winter coming in hard.

What the song's supposed to be about, I don't know. Can't say. And it doesn't matter. Not to me, anyway.

To me the chorus is the whole thing. That's what gets me. Gets me and holds me. Talks to me. Is why I keep listening to it. Can't seem to stop, though to tell the truth I haven't tried. Not really. The chorus - Mama said there'll be days like this/ There'll be days like this, mama said – what does it for me.

Did she, though?

Dark-haired and rake-thin, did my mom, ever really tell me that or something dressed up very much like it?

Maybe she did.

Maybe she didn't.

Doesn't matter. Either way there are days like this - days when it feels like there's a forest fire raging in my head.

Does that mean The Growlers are fire fighters?

Who knows?

I don't.

I'd say probably not, though the only thing I can say for sure is that right now I've got to keep driving. Got to keep pushing through the dark along roads I know and roads I don't while listening to that chorus - Mama said - again - there'll be days like this - and again – There'll be days like this, mama said - and again…

NEW BLOOD

Eyes wild, face a mass of tics, when he sat at one of the outside tables I made myself extra busy with the orders inside. Hoped he'd sit there just long enough to get himself together then wander off.

When he didn't, I turned to the new blood and said, "He's not buying so you have to go tell him to move on."

I always worried I didn't sound like a real manager, but the new blood started for the door. Only hesitated when the wild-eyed man outside started banging his head against the table.

"Because it's your first day," I said in answer to his unspoken question and seeming to accept that the new blood swallowed hard and stepped outside.

THIS IS NOT ME

'We look at the world once, in childhood. / The rest is memory.' Nostos – Louise Gluck

This is not me -

Whilst in her cot beside my bed my little sister slept soundly my mother lifted me effortlessly with her factory-strong arms.

Impossibly young, blue eyed and blonde she carried me through to her bedroom and placed me on a double bed – sheets, not a duvet.

We were somewhere high up, it was morning, and my mother was laughing or crying.

Averting her face, she sat beside me, the sheets crumpling like waves around her.

Was it my birthday and she'd carried me in here to unwrap presents?

If that was the case, those presents are all long forgotten and gone.

Never mind. What I remember is her speaking quietly to me. Explaining things that, though I listened carefully, I couldn't begin to understand. After which, both of us knowing he'd never come, we waited and waited for my old man.

But it's alright, really it is, because this is not me.

*

This is not me -

It seemed as if I'd waited my whole life for this moment. The uneven pitch so green it hurt my eyes. A wintry sun watching over two teams of 6-year-olds when, nearly as wide as he was tall, Mr Jameson blew a whistle, and we kicked off.

It was all frantic, furious, and desperate until, somehow, the ball arrived at my feet, and I was onside, 6 yards from goal.

If I scored, my life went one way. If I missed, it went another.

Was I aware of this at the time?

Of course, I was.

Of course, I wasn't.

Since the number 6 was sewn onto the back of my shirt, afterwards I stupidly wondered if that third 6 meant I was the devil's own child.

Aged 6 I shot and missed. The ball sailing a yard over the crossbar.

But it's alright, really it is, because this is not me.

*

This is not me -

There were ten of us in the competition and we sat on chairs placed at the front of the school hall with our hands neatly in our laps and the audience before us.

It'd been seven years since I skied the ball, and this was something completely different and exactly the same.

I think I knew that. Think I felt it squeezing at my breathing as, the first to go, I stood and walked to the lectern.

My heart flailing, I placed down my speech, the sheets deathly white against the angled oak.

Miss Dubar had said she believed in me.

I hoped my mother believed in me, too. No longer impossibly young and the blue of her eyes terribly faded, she sat next to my English teacher on the front row.

Where was my little sister, Jenny?

Why wasn't she watching, too?

I couldn't think of that then so, with my eyes riveted to my speech, opened my mouth –

Only to find my voice gone. Extinguished as if it had never lived in me.

The silence clenched around me, and everybody watched as, burning with shame, I returned to my seat and sat squirming. Squirmed even as the next competitor moved to the lectern and began – her fluency an indictment of me.

But it's alright, really it is, because this is not me.

*

This is not me -

A friend of hers was coming to the house, my mother said.

It'd happened before. Different friends each time I thought but didn't know, didn't ever meet any of the friends who came to visit her.

I was to take Jenny to the park as usual.

Ten years old, I nodded to show I understood.

My mother always gave us ice cream money when one of her friends came, and we'd get ourselves 99s and sit on a bench to eat them, then play on the swings, going higher and higher, the two of us laughing harder and harder.

That day it was winter, the lake at the centre of the park iced over - way too cold for 99s.

It wasn't too cold for Cokes though, so I bought us Cokes and we stood by the bench to drink them, the bench coated with frost even though it was past midday.

Since 99s cost more than Coke I was able to buy three cans with the money my mother gave us. Two for me because I was four years older, and one for Jenny.

She didn't complain. It was me who was complaining not long after I'd guzzled them both down. Told Jenny to keep well away from the ice-covered lake while I hurried over to the bushes.

I never saw my little sister again.

But it's alright, really it is, because this is not me.

*

This is not me -

My eyes fixed on the scribbled trees at the bottom of the overgrown garden I calculate it's been 207 hours and counting since Marta left me, everything she owned furiously flung into a faded cream suitcase.

Except that's not right. She didn't take everything she owned. Only everything she wanted. Left both the towelling dressing gown I bought for her last birthday and various explanations as to why she couldn't stand to be with me anymore:

It was my fault, me being how I was, she said.

It was her fault, her being how she was, she said.

The two of us ever coming together was a mistake, we were just too young, she said.

O-r-, maybe it was the stillbirth, she said.

O-r-, I repeated.

At which point Marta screamed and threw the TV control at me. Threw it as hard as she could but seemed shocked when it cut my cheek nearly to the bone. Blood dripping onto my shirt and the petal-shaped settee. A jagged smudge of scar tissue on my right cheek 207 hours later.

There's no one else, Marta had said before she closed the front door.

And I'd believed her until I saw her getting into his Audi on the Asda car park three days after I'd rescued her dressing gown from the bin and stuffed it into the washing machine.

Alright, the Audi didn't belong to the boyfriend she'd lived with before we were together, whose photograph Marta kept in her box of precious things, but he was the spitting image of him so what else was I to think?

There's no one else, Marta had said.

But was that just a lie?

Maybe it was.

O-r-, maybe I'm the devil's own child after all.

Maybe, baby. Like the Buddy Holly song. Which, maybe, baby, one day soon I'll learn all the words to and sing.

In the meantime, I can't help thinking that all the things that keep endlessly repeating in my head are the reason why things have happened as they have.

But it's all alright.

Really it is.

Because this is not me.

This.

Is.

Not.

Me.

NOT WHAT

Cheeky kids are the bane of my life, and this kid is the cheekiest of the lot, comes in two or three times a week, never buys a fish, just a portion of chips with extra salt and vinegar, always some batters.

Sometimes cans go missing from the cooler by the door. I can't prove it, have never seen him do it, but he's my prime suspect.

I serve him because it's how I make a living, though the truth is I'm always relieved to see the back of him.

But tonight, he bounces back two minutes later, and my heart skips a beat. No, more than one.

"Look, mate," he says in that cheeky way of his.

I see he's ripped open the paper I wrapped them in to get at his chips. See the chips in there and something else.

Something moving –

It's a wood louse is what it is, and I could say it's nothing to do with me, but I know where that would lead so I say, "I'll give you more chips, a can of pop and a nice piece of fish - they don't call me the Codfather for nothing."

To this he says, "Mate, it's not what you think...I want the thing battered, that's all."

ONE DAY

One day I decided to focus on the punk band X-Ray Spex. This was some years after Poly Styrene had died. When the band broke through in the late Seventies, I didn't register them or registered them but dismissed them. Told myself it didn't matter which it was. What mattered was now and now the punk band X-Ray Spex was a focal point for me.

I acquired their music on vinyl, on tapes, on CDs. I acquired DVDs, books, articles, and posters. I acquired, really, anything to do with X-Ray Spex that I could get my hands on.

One or two of the pieces I acquired were rarities and quite valuable, though that wasn't what drove me. Certainly, those rarities meant no more to me than my other X-Ray Spex acquisitions. Simply, I wanted anything to do with X-Ray Spex, and immersed myself in acquiring it, everything else secondary.

It's a fad, I told herself.

It's a fad, I insisted four years later to stop it.

*

For two days following this decision I avoided any sort of focus on X-Ray Spex. Didn't look at what I'd already acquired and didn't search for more acquisitions.

On the night of that second no X-Ray Spex Day, I was jolted awake at 2AM.

"What're you doing!?"

The darkness seemed to pulse around me. I was sure it was Poly Styrene's voice, and she sounded angry, which was understandable because I'd abandoned X-Ray Spex. At least, that is, I'd tried to.

*

When the same thing happened on five subsequent nights it was clear to me that if I was ever again to sleep without being jolted awake, I'd have to re-focus on X-Ray Spex.

What did it all mean?

I didn't know. But on that sixth night I told myself that from tomorrow, once again, anything to do with X-Ray Spex, I had to have.

Where would it end?

I didn't know that either. But not knowing what it meant or where it would end, I nonetheless closed my eyes. As ever, I didn't feel calm. But I definitely felt calmer now that I'd made up my mind to resume my focus. Maybe, I thought...

THE REVIEWER

Remembering the times his mother had sent him to take a sandwich to his dad my old man said, “It was like a torture chamber.” Went on to speak of cavernous darkness and flying sparks, the cry of disgorged steel and choking heat, said, “I’d have told them everything,” and winked at me.

Working in a steel mill wasn’t for him, though whenever my old man spoke of his life as an English teacher, he hunched his slender shoulders.

*

I never asked him why, but lately listen carefully when - often in supermarkets, drawn to me by the physical resemblance - those he taught approach, smiling, and tell me what a great teacher he was, how he made reading seem essential.

*

He did.

Yet when my old man handed me his copy of Running on Empty a month after my mother’s death my contempt was apparent.

Even so I took it from him and read it in a single sitting. The story about a young man whose parents are killed in a car crash. Never mind that I'd lost one parent not two and to cancer not a car crash felt as if I were the un-named young man. His thoughts my thoughts. His experiences my experiences. How it was that Running helped me through that dark time.

*

That might've been an end to it but wasn't.

Reading JK Jennings crystallised in me a desire to become a writer myself. Cold Outside the novel Castle Books published a year after I completed my Masters. Its critical and commercial failure a kick in the teeth and why when I saw it sitting in a tattered cardboard box in the corner of a remaindered bookshop depression took me by the throat and squeezed hard.

Feeling as if I were choking, I re-read Running as an act of spite. Hoped I'd find it less powerful now I was older.

Whereas the opposite was true with things I'd missed first time around rising from the pages to embrace and console me. Its power to heal why I read it again when my marriage ended, then again when my old man died.

*

My old man...

I realised I hadn't ever thanked him for directing me to Running and wasn't there when he died - his next-door neighbour who found him sprawled face down next to the hydrangeas in the front garden.

After his funeral I drank myself unconscious, which didn't help, though a third reading of Running did.

It also decided me on another course of action - but I'm getting ahead of myself.

*

When Cold Outside bombed the need to make a living loomed so large I considered becoming an English teacher myself, sat in his conservatory beside a dead-looking cactus that he refused to discard asked my old man what he felt about that.

His fingers steepled in thought he said, "I always thought that piece you wrote on Running was very good."

I'd written it whilst Jennings was working on a much-anticipated second novel and was something which, though I wasn't sure it deserved to be called a "piece" much less that it was "very good," when I went back to my flat that night, I dug out.

After re-drafting it I even had the gall to submit it and got lucky.

Always one to tell the truth as she saw it irrespective of the pain it caused Rosie McConnell said although what I'd sent her was "well enough written" she never would've used it if on the day she received it if aged just fifty-one Jennings hadn't dropped dead of a heart attack minutes after stepping offstage at a literary event.

*

Rosie's use of my timely "piece" led to me becoming a reviewer for Bookworm and was why it seemed fitting not long after my old man's death and my subsequent re-reading of Running to speak to her about doing a new piece on Jennings - after mentioning the lasting appeal of Running planned to write of Savage Day, about which nothing had been heard for over a decade.

Throat infections the bane of her life and the smell of menthol always on her breath, Rosie winked and told me she'd heard Jennings' son had taken to gambling.

*

When I rang him Jennings' son said he wasn't prepared to talk about his father, this the line he'd always taken, had hung up on journalists, slammed the front door in the faces of academics, live on air once famously told a team from the BBC to "fuck off." But now a man with losses to account for he went on to say he'd let me spend "an hour or so" in his father's study for £200.

How I came to be seated before a battered teak desk on which sat two Moleskin notebooks, a box file, and an Olivetti Lettera 22.

As if Jennings were with me and any sudden movement would disturb him, I slowed my breathing. Remembered how a few months before his death he'd donated his hand-corrected draft of Running to the British Library. Something I intended to visit in the hope that it'd add to the first part of my new piece, though for now -

Here Jennings had sat. Here he'd written. I itched to open the dust-covered box file and delve into his final manuscript, but my old man had taught me to be patient and methodical. Traits that had allowed me to forge a career of sorts as a reviewer and why, imagining Jennings rising from his chair to take something from a shelf, dip into and draw inspiration from, I first turned to his bookcase.

Selecting Kafka's Complete Stories, I recalled an interview in which he'd spoken about Metamorphosis bringing him to tears.

I was the same with Running and hoped my mention of it would impel more to read it, though the bulk of my new piece would emerge from Jennings' notebooks and the box file containing his final manuscript - Savage Day.

I hoped to be lucky again. Needed to be in fact.

Since I'm apparently in the mood for admissions let me proffer another. Namely, that from the moment I secured access to Jennings' study I'd entertained a scenario whereby through my new piece I helped facilitate posthumous publication of Savage Day.

Reverentially, I replaced Jennings' copy of Kafka - jumped when my phone rang.

"How's it going?" Rosie rasped.

Looking out through a window at oak trees assailed by winter winds I said, "I feel as if I've travelled a long road."

"Nothing so poetic if you please," Rosie growled. Always demanded concrete in what she published, though Jennings' Moleskins resolutely lacked it. Contained nothing pertaining to plot, theme, or character. Instead, again and again in handwriting that looked as if it'd been carved onto the page simply said he wanted to write something: 'WAY BETTER THAN RUNNING.' Something that was: 'A RUSH TO READ.'

*

I'd sold my old man's house not long after his funeral but an hour after paying Jennings's son his £200, as storm clouds gathered, found myself parked across the road from it in a purple Skoda with a scuffed nearside wing.

The house had new windows and the hydrangeas my old man had tended religiously had been replaced by a block-paved drive. Recognising that such changes were inevitable didn't cull the sadness I felt at seeing them or recalling how the dust-coated box file in Jennings' study had contained only sheet after sheet of blank paper.

When my phone rang, fracturing that image, I saw it was Rosie - her calls more frequent now than they ever were when we were married - but for once I didn't pick up.

Instead, my head spinning, I stared out the window as the sky tore open and rain started to pour.

THE LAWN MOWER

I push that lawn mower and the sun shines.

My customers like that I still use a hand mower. Feel they're getting something extra.

"They like to see you sweat is what it is," my daughter told me this one time.

I said, "That's alright with me, I like to sweat."

She works in a city, calls me on a Sunday.

"You ever feel like you've achieved something, mowing all those lawns?" she asked me another time.

"Yeah, I think I do," I said.

After which there was a silence.

THE SANDMAN

He lies between Boots and Poundstretcher, sculpting and shaping, with sand carefully crafting a life-size dog playing with a beach ball.

Does it hurt to work lying down like that on the cold, hard pavement?

Surely it must?

But it's worse than that because the wind is up. Drying the sand and trying to steal the dog's right front paw –

Trying but failing for the man's hands move quickly, quickly, quickly.

"Go, sandman," I whisper, putting two coins onto his blanket, one for his craft, one for his endeavour.

YOU'LL NEVER KNOW

The old man's rage is inconspicuous behind glasses thick as the bottom of a bottle: no money for the Asda across the road much less thinned lenses.

First one of the younger guys says it, then the other, like an echo, "Fucking old cunt!"

The younger guys decide that the smile the old man returns is a taunt and they're right to, behind them the sound of the M5 a relentless whine or a cry for help, it's hard to say which.

As usual the old man is parked some way from the entrance to Aldi. Where empty wrappers congeal, weeds sprout through cracks in tarmac and stray dogs stop to shit.

"What're you smiling at?" one of the younger guys says, spittle gathered at the corners of his mouth.

"You'll never know," the old man says, striding towards them with years' worth of ready in hand.

READY

It's bitterly cold in the underpass, where the two of us are sitting hunched under the blood red S in SLAM, but I can't put it off any longer - it's time to talk to the youngest. Time to make sure he's ready. The lad nine-years-old now and a lot like the oldest was at that age if memory serves. Long skinny legs and narrow shoulders. Built for speed.

Good job he is. Speed's what you need. Can't have too much speed. "Speed, speed, speed," I've been saying to him practically since he took his first steps. Speed what I used to have till, working together, a deliverer and a have busted my legs, my days as a hunter over from that day on.

Funny how things work out. I mean if my legs hadn't been busted and my hunting days ended it would've probably been worse later - that's how it usually works.

In which case it would've been down to the oldest to teach the youngest instead of me.

How comes I decide to mention the oldest right at the start. No messing about. Say, "Your brother was a great hunter, he got us grub for three years before it happened, which is good going the amount of catching goes on, you understand?"

The youngest says nothing. Stares at me with no expression on his face.

I spread my fingers. then ball them into fists as the cold nips at us and our guts growl with hunger.

"Anybody can slip and fall. What happened was just bad luck," I say. Cup my hands and blow into them to see if it'll help me stop shivering, when it doesn't, say, "Makes no difference how good you are. Such things can happen to anybody. Do happen to anybody."

Sometimes you get caught and the deliverer and any haves will bust your legs. Sometimes they'll do a lot worse. It's why you mustn't get caught and I've said as much so many times before the youngest nods to show he knows without me having to say it again.

Does he really know though?

I can't be sure. Which is why I say, "You got to keep your focus sharp."

"Yeah, yeah, yeah," he says, and I stare hard at him.

He doesn't flinch.

"Good," I say.

Say it twice.

The youngest's hair is dark like his mother's. Why when I look at him it's hard for me not to think of her and keep telling him how much I miss her. How much I wish I could've -

Thankfully, this time at least I manage to avoid saying anything.

But it's as if the youngest has read my mind. Something he's always been able to do and why he says, "If we'd had cash for medical..." Then glances down at my withered legs and says, "If we had some now -" Would say more if I didn't reach out and grab his skinny shoulders hard enough to leave marks.

"We don't take cash, you hear me?"

I don't let go of him till he nods, once, twice, three times.

Then I say, "You go to medicals with cash what's the first thing they ask you?"

The youngest lowers his gaze.

I say, "They ask you where you got cash. Can tell by looking at you it's not yours and never could be. Take it off you and trace it. Find you took it and -"

I slap my right fist into my left palm. Hard. Making him jump.

*

“I kept my focus sharp,” he tells me when he gets back from his first hunt.

With his dark hair flopping down over one of his eyes he says, “Did everything just the way you told me.”

Now, it’s my turn to nod - after which I wait for him to go on:

“Picked a tired deliverer like you said. Knew he was tired from the way he was riding.” He snake-wiggles his right hand to show me and I grin. “Waited till he stopped outside the house he was delivering to and got off. Was so tired he didn’t turn. Didn’t see me coming.” He holds his arms out straight in front of himself and flattens his hands to show me how he charged. “Caught him high up. Sweet as a nut like you said it’d be.” He unzips the carrier, which is sitting waiting on the floor between us, and says, “Man hit the deck, and I moved in, quick, quick, quick.”

With the carrier unzipped the smell of the food rolls over us.

“Didn’t go for cash,” he says. “Knew if I tried to spend it, they’d ask me where I got it - can trace it in no time.”

“That’s right,” I nod.

It was late. Chances are the deliverer would’ve had some cash on him, which makes it doubly tempting I know. Know how you think, at that moment, of the all the things you could do with even just a bit of cash and need to shut those thoughts out.

"You did good," I say.

"I pulled the carrier off him before he knew what'd hit him and ran as fast as I could."

"Speed, speed, speed," I say.

The youngest grins. "I was gone before he could call help or get back on his bike and come after me."

The food's still warm - the two of us close enough to it to feel the heat rising from the carrier.

The youngest nods, then lowers his gaze to the pizza in there, meaning he wants me to have first dibs.

I do, my mouth watering, after which he digs in, and we go at it, the two of us eating fiercely, this our first grub in days, the cold packed tight around us but our bellies being filled at least for tonight.

MULTI-STOREY

1

Roland hated getting up early but needed to train before work. Training an escape, a comfort, and a promise unfulfilled.

Quietly, so he wouldn't wake Kelly, he eased out of bed when the central heating came on. Moving with urgency pulled on a sweat suit and trainers then paused to study Kelly's face in sleep. Her words at him again –

Stepping into the hallway he raised then lowered his shoulders. The tightness easing only slightly. Things said and things unspoken making him feel as if he was being held underwater. Imagining Louis in sleep what gave him the strength to go through to the kitchen.

He made tea, swallowing B complex, C and E vitamins as he gulped it.

The sports bag by the table contained his uniform and his training belt. Roland added two protein drinks then let himself be drawn to the window.

The flat overlooked the council estate where he'd grown up. Standing on tiptoe, he saw the house where he used to live and the alleyway into which the bigger kid had chased him.

Breathless and terrified, eight-year-old Roland had stopped, able to run no more.

The bigger kid had driven his fist deep into Roland's gut.

Roland's house was just yards away but even if he'd had the breath to call for help none would've come for his mom was at work and his dad was by then already long gone.

Ripe tears filled his eyes and when the kid released him, Roland had sunk to his knees, his head bowed as if in readiness for execution.

Framed by the kitchen window, the pain of the boy imposed upon the face of the man, he wanted to offer comfort and hope to his younger self. The need to do so why he couldn't leave the flat though Kelly had demanded that they buy a house.

"Louis needs a garden," she'd said, her eyes narrowing.

"I need time to think," Roland had said. Couldn't remember her ever being so resolute. So distant.

She'd stood, touched the birthmark on her throat with a fingertip and with the flat of her hand beat the creases from a skirt that wasn't the pale green one she'd gone to work in that morning.

That had been two days ago.

Now, as he'd done thirty years ago in the piss-stained alley Roland struggled for breath. His struggle continuing even after he dragged himself away from the window.

*

All available space was filled with equipment though Roland moved dexterously amongst it, at least for now the anxiety that'd been trying to throttle the life out of him anaesthetised.

Ninety minutes slid by like summer sun.

After which he stood before a mirror.

As an amateur Middleweight he'd won twenty-seven of thirty-two fights. Lack of power accounted for his losses - the desire to be stronger and to be a Heavyweight, where the real money and fame lay in boxing, what had driven him to start lifting weights.

He planned to return to the ring once he'd sufficiently increased his size and strength. Liked to imagine commentators raving about him. Shocked that he could emerge from nowhere and challenge for the World Heavyweight title.

It'd been twenty years since he stepped into a ring. Roland now stood six feet three inches tall and weighed eighteen stone nine pounds, stripped, yet felt insubstantial and weak, wasn't the man he wanted to be, wasn't the man his dad would've had him be.

Disappointed by what the mirror had to offer, he headed stoop-shouldered for the EXIT.

*

Roland used his pass to get onto the multi-storey car park. Drove into his allocated space and eased out of the beaten Escort.

Oblivious to the stink of exhaust fumes and engine coolant, the proximity of steel mesh and girders, he headed for the Security Room.

The door should've been locked but wasn't. And Reece should've been patrolling or monitoring the CCTV screen above the door but wasn't. Rather, he was asleep. His feet up on the tin desk. His scarred hands cupping his crotch as if it was a small bird. The Security Room reeking of whiskey and failure.

"I'm a five-star casualty," Reece often said, "and I haven't had a fuck in three years," - was a man who described his life in numbers.

Roland picked up the empty bottle and pushed it into Reece's bag.

In there, he glimpsed a cheese and chutney sandwich that looked like roadkill.

Then looking up, he saw on CCTV that the car park was filling quickly - Christmas Eve always the same: always bringing with it both too many cars and too many memories.

*

Roland had been six when his dad left and his mom ducked into the kitchenette and turned the radio so loud that everything vibrated, emerging not long after with plates full of fried eggs, fish fingers, and baked beans.

He hadn't been hungry but after watching her eat as if she was starving, Roland had done the same, cleared his plate bar the enamel though it was all he could do to keep the food down.

He'd been twelve when he saw his dad again.

He and his Uncle Eddie had stayed in a French-colonial-style hotel in Port Maria, the hotel a dump though from their room there was a view of sun-drenched palm trees and the glittering sea.

Every day they'd eaten freshly caught fish then lay in the sun and laughed at how cold it'd be back in Birmingham. Roland repetitively looking over his shoulder and wondering when his dad would show up as they ate.

During their eighth night in Port Maria Roland was halfway to the bathroom when he heard Eddie's voice and froze. The door separating their rooms had muffled his words but not his tone and when Eddie slammed down the phone Roland had scurried back to bed.

He'd managed to close his eyes a moment before Eddie peered in, though his heart punched angrily at his chest had inhaled slowly and deeply until Eddie withdrew - at which point he'd gripped his knees to his chest, the pain in his bladder acute.

The next morning Eddie had chain-smoked, and Roland had sat in a daze until a resonant voice from behind yanked him into full wakefulness.

Shaven-headed and bull-necked, Alex Mitchell had stood with his arms by his sides and his gut pushing at the silk of his open-necked yellow shirt.

"You look prosperous," Eddie had said, blowing out a tube of smoke.

"You can call me fat and I won't tan your hide, little brother."

"If there's any hide tanning to be done, I'll do it," Eddie had said, and the brothers had simultaneously grinned - Roland noticing the gap in his dad's front teeth before recoiling from the weight of his gaze.

"You've grown," Alex had said.

Frustratingly, though he'd waited eight days for him to arrive, Roland hadn't been sure what to say and had shot pleading glances at Eddie, who'd lowered his eyes and busied himself lighting another cigarette.

"Doing well at school?" Alex had asked and Roland would have told of the daylong drudgery of lessons and his ineptitude for learning but in pausing to gather himself had missed his moment.

"Does your mom say you should work hard?"

Roland had nodded.

"She knows what's best," Alex had said. The sadness in his voice making Roland's heart feel bruised, though when he'd looked up his dad was grinning again. "You want to go for a swim?"

Roland had nodded and, the silence between them awkward, they'd followed their shadows down to the beach.

All skin and bone and self-conscious about it next to his dad, Roland had dived into the foaming blue, swam a dozen strokes then flipped onto his back.

When Alex had swum out to tread water beside him, Roland had longed to ask why he'd left them and if he ever missed him, but those words evaded him, and he'd managed only to ask his age.

"Not too old to give you a race for your money," Alex had laughed.

For half the race they'd been so close they might have been shackled together.

Then a clear leader had emerged, his loss what Roland remembered first when, a month after they flew home, his dad had been found stabbed though the heart outside a nightclub - two column inches all his death merited.

*

It was as cold in the Security Room as the day Roland received news of his dad's death.

Pushing away his memories, he turned to watch a black taxicab progress to Level Three and decided a walk would help.

*

On Level Three it was light enough to make out the yin and yang symbol that he'd drawn onto the chest of his Hi-Vis jacket. The symbol something Roland had come to by way of Bruce Lee. Enter The Dragon a film he'd watched twice the previous night to try and stop thinking about what was wrong with Kelly, though today there was still no balance, symbolic or otherwise: the traffic sounding like a dentist's drill, though that didn't account for the tingling in the pit of his stomach.

Roland loved Spider Man, the superhero's spider sense something he liked to think he possessed, his most notable experience of it when he'd been thirteen...

*

It was autumn and his pockets bulging with conkers Roland had known he had to get home and slog through schoolwork or face his mom's anger.

As darkness closed around him, he'd entered Warley Woods from Barclay Road. Had gone no more than three yards when he stopped. Behind him were terraced houses and the road. Ahead of him were trees erupting from the darkness and myriad, small sounds. Nothing was unusual yet, his spider sense tingling, he'd retreated and taken the long way home.

Decided he'd let fear get the better of him until he saw a newspaper the following night.

Roland had read that a twelve-year-old boy had been sexually assaulted the previous night and had retraced his steps to find an area not twenty yards from where he'd entered the woods cordoned off.

*

Close enough to see that the cab was badly parked, Roland gathered himself, the tingle in his gut intensifying, gasped when a hand gripped his shoulder –

But it was only Reece. His cheeks haggard. His breath 20% proof.

"I've got to tell you something..."

Assailed by the memory of a mushroom-shaped birthmark Reece longed to confess, perform penitence, receive absolution, but instead spoke of the fish and chip shop he planned to buy. Didn't know much about business, he said, but knew people would always need to eat.

"It's a great idea, I hope it works out," Roland said before helping him over to the nearest concrete pillar.

When Roland saw vomit by the driver's side door, he decided the taxi driver had puked and gone to get something to settle his stomach, though he still felt edgy.

"I'm a shit," Reece said, was moving away from the concrete pillar when Roland reached him.

"Don't be hard on yourself," Roland said, and set about helping Reece back down to the ground floor, Reece muttering but Roland not listening, desperate to read Spider Man comics or sit through Enter The Dragon three or four times in succession.

When he sat Reece down and checked the CCTV screen, Roland saw the car park was so full he needed to cone off one of the entrances as a matter of urgency but was suddenly distracted.

"Hit me!" Reece demanded.

Used to his drunken outbursts, Roland eased his friend backwards, the chair creaking alarmingly.

*

Roland was thinking that if he trained harder than ever before he might yet become the man he was sure his dad had wanted him to be as he coned off one of the entrances, from the corner of his eye saw the girl with dark hair look up then break into a run - this the moment at which he followed the girl's gaze and saw the woman atop the perimeter fence.

His whole life he'd wanted to do something that'd bring him acclaim. But instead of reacting immediately, he paused. Imagined reaching out as the woman leapt and catching her with just the tips of his fingers. Like Spider

Man. Or Bruce Lee. Believed that if he was a hero he wouldn't need to be the World Heavyweight Boxing Champion. Would be snapped up anyway. To do just what he wasn't sure. But from whatever it was money would flow and with his newfound riches he'd buy the house Kelly wanted but would keep their flat...

2

Thomas sat in his cab on Stephenson Street, 7.59AM on Christmas Eve, the sky Bakelite, three from the front felt he couldn't wait any longer, didn't know how he'd managed to make it back to the city much less how he'd escaped Carl's house.

His scalp itched. Preferring pain to the itch, he scratched hard. His gnawed fingernails drawing blood. When he was done, drove. Wanted to escape the city but couldn't concentrate. Twice scraped the gutter and once almost clipped a growling bus.

Desperate to get off the road, he pulled onto the multi-storey car park on Brunel Street - checking the rear-view mirror as he pierced the shuddering grey.

Thomas parked, opened the door and spewed.

Thinking about the jacket he'd left at Carl's being examined for traces of blood, he stepped over his vomit.

In one pocket he found a tape recorder no bigger than his palm, though he'd have sworn it wasn't his, pressed PLAY.

After two minutes of white noise Thomas shoved the tape recorder back into his pocket and turned sharply towards the slam of a car door.

But it wasn't the police. Here to arrest him for Carl's murder. And when his heart steadied, he moved to peer through steel mesh at The Mailbox - home of the BBC in Birmingham.

All his life Thomas had wanted to be a famous actor. As if that would salve his wounds and fill his hollows.

But he wasn't a famous actor and with The Mailbox underlining his sense of failure he returned to his cab. Took out his phone and dialled the only number he knew by heart.

"Sam," he said immediately she picked up the phone. Told her that he needed to tell her what he'd done.

*

The run up to Christmas had been hectic. The city like a boil about to burst.

"It's a good time to make money," Howard had told him - the owner of A Number One Taxis a dab of a man who practically wore his weight in gold.

Ever in need of money, Thomas had pulled twenty-hour shifts back-to-back. His hands practically glued to the steering wheel.

It'd been like that for weeks when, on the evening of the 23rd, Carl had climbed into his cab.

"Thomas? Is that you? Fancy going for a drink so we can catch up?"

The Rococo Lounge had been crowded and hot. Though he felt out of place, Thomas had tried to mask it. Certain that buying the first drink constituted a victory of sorts, he'd been halfway to the bar when a woman splashed wine onto his shirtfront.

Nobody, he'd noticed, had spilled wine onto Carl.

They'd drunk greedily and on Thomas the effect had been immediate after a long day of running on empty.

Shouting to be heard above the noise of other conversations and pounding music, Carl had told how he was happy but there was a price to pay, patted his paunch and laughed.

Then his laughter had become something else.

"I need to get home," he'd said.

It had been after midnight when Thomas parked and tipped his head back to study the stars, like chips of ice laid out on asphalt.

“We’re here,” he’d said. That when he was tired or angry he sounded like his old man irritating to him.

Seeing the state Carl was in, Thomas had looped his right arm under Carl’s left, hoisted him out of the cab, and, like contestants in a three-legged race, they’d set off up the drive.

“Have you got your key?” he’d said, the cold air stinging his throat.

Carl had pressed it fumblingly into the lock but couldn’t get the door open.

“Let me try,” Thomas had said. Had opened the door, helped Carl into the hall and switched on the light.

“I need to pay you,” Carl had said and in reaching for his wallet had coughed, spraying Thomas with phlegm.

Afterwards, in a voice plaintive as a child’s, Thomas had said Carl’s name - but leaning close to the figure on the floor had seen that there was no chance of him answering, ever.

3

It was the first Christmas Eve Sam had had off in six years and the night before she and Pete had drunk white wine.

Pete was two years younger than her. That he liked a well-ordered life was why Helen had left him. Had claimed his virginity on his twentieth birthday and moved in with him not long after. Had moved out when Richard came along. Richard somebody who played football for a few minutes most Sunday mornings and dressed in the latest fashions. When Helen told him about Richard Pete had asked how she could leave him when he loved her. "No offence," Helen had said, "but you're really bloody boring." But then Pete had got lucky because Sam turned out to be looking for a man who was kind, thoughtful and reliable. Him, then, not Thomas, who'd just rung to tell her he'd killed an old acquaintance and needed her to meet him.

Pete parked opposite the multi-storey on Brunel Street. That he was parked illegally made him uneasy. Unease something he'd associated with Thomas from the first time he set eyes on him.

*

Looking grubby and drawn Thomas had watched the two of them from his taxicab.

"Is that him?" Thomas had called through the open cab window.

"Take no notice," Sam had said, Thomas following the two of them like a scene from a film.

"You're not really fucking him, are you?" Thomas had called.

Pete had stopped dead. He'd never been in a fight but was ready to fight now.

Promptly intervening, Sam had said, "I'll meet you back at the car."

To Thomas, she'd snapped, "Who I'm fucking is my business. All you need to know is me and you finished a long time ago."

*

The second time Pete set eyes on him had been even worse.

Thomas had turned up at the house looking as if his central nervous system was wired to the mains. When he'd grinned, Pete saw his bottom teeth were cracked - as if he was in danger of falling into those cracks had held tight to the front door.

"I want to tell you about Sam," Thomas had said.

When his rant had finished, Thomas had thrust out his hand to shake but Pete hadn't taken it.

"Only trying to help," Thomas had said, as he walked away his dark clothes becoming part of the darkness, a stain atop a stain.

*

Sam wasn't afraid of Thomas though the sight of him emerging from shadow startled her.

"I left the denim jacket you bought me," he said, then dipped his head like a boy before a beating.

The piss-stink of the stairwell wasn't conducive to clear thinking, but Sam was sure she'd never bought him a denim jacket - then and now Thomas wore his dead dad's clothes, but wanting to get this over as quickly as possible she said, "Where did you leave it?"

"At Carl's house."

"Carl?" Sam drew her shoulders up against the cold. Wished she were anywhere but here.

"The man I killed..." Thomas clenched his jaw so hard Sam heard the crunch of teeth.

"Take me there," she said, then sent a message telling Pete to follow.

*

"Are you still cutting yourself?" she asked when they stopped.

Thomas fiddled with his narrow, blue silk tie.

"Roll up your sleeves," Sam instructed, and Thomas obeyed, showing criss-crossed lines along both forearms but no new cuts.

It made sense since for months she'd received no messages written in blood.

Thomas turned in his seat. His eyes sunken. His cheeks whiskery.

Sam felt sorry for him and angry at him, both, and at the same time.

"Which house?" Sam demanded.

His tongue repeatedly dabbing at the same point on his lower lip, Thomas pointed at the ex-council semi twenty yards to their left – number 22.

When Sam reached the front door of number 22 Thomas's description of events came back at her.

Her heart beating quickly, she raised the brass knocker and let it fall - the sound like a gunshot.

"I'm sure I killed him," Thomas said. Sounded ready to cry.

"Don't," Sam warned. Would've said more if the door hadn't opened, letting her see that he had shoulder length dark hair, wore loose fitting jeans and a blood-stained Mickey Mouse tee-shirt.

4

He should've been at college but had overslept.

Deciding that going in late on the last day was pointless, pointless one of his all-time favourite words, Adam had taken a bus into the city.

Coffee seemed like a good idea, so he'd ducked into the first place he saw.

In the queue, Adam had thought about Natalie - with whom he twice weekly shared assaults on Keats and who had once grazed the back of his hand with her fingertips, accidentally or purposefully, he wasn't sure - at which point the woman behind him had inadvertently shoved a tuna and mayonnaise baguette into the base of his spine.

When he'd turned, Adam had caught sight of his dad at a table by the window. His dad lapping up every word the blonde woman opposite him said. The woman's fingertips close to the back of his dad's hand.

Seeing his nosebleed, the baguette-wielding-woman had reached for a handkerchief, but Adam had hurried out of there before she could hand it to him and, more importantly, before his dad set eyes on him.

Details of his journey home were hazy.

Once there, Adam knew he'd gone to his room and drawn the curtains though it was still light outside.

The next thing he remembered was hearing the front door.

His thoughts disjointed he'd shambled downstairs. Needed to clean his teeth, take a shower, get his thoughts in order, but when the woman asked about his dad had felt his chest tighten.

5

Sam turned to Thomas.

"You're sure this is the right house?"

Thomas nodded, his gaze skipping away from her glare.

Sam hated crossword puzzles. Even the most obvious clues eluded her, and a concerted effort yielded nothing but a low-level headache, this how she felt when she turned her attention back to the young man who'd opened the door.

"Your dad's not home, then?" she said. Felt as if a dislocated shoulder had just clicked back into place.

Adam had been sure he was alone in the house but now, gripped by the all too familiar sense of doubt, needed to make sure his dad wasn't bleeding in some corner, his mother staring down at him vengefully.

*

Passing the Christmas tree, Adam wondered if his dad was really having an affair with the woman sitting opposite him in the coffee shop. For the moment decided he believed somebody grazing the back of your hand didn't necessarily mean anything and as if to affirm it shook his head as he passed through the empty kitchen, the empty bathroom, the empty lounge, and, finally, his parents' empty bedroom.

*

When he returned to the front door, narrowing her eyes Sam said, "Carl isn't your dad's name, is it?"

"No."

"I've made a mistake," she said, "and if I've worried you, I'm sorry."

*

Adam shut the front door, then went and sat cross-legged on the floor of the living room and watched the lights on the Christmas tree flick on and off.

*

At the end of the drive, Sam stopped - snowflakes gathering on her eyelashes.

"What pisses me off most is that I went along with this." She shook her head. "I should've known better." Remembering something else, she rushed at him. "Are you recording this?"

"What?"

"Stop pretending - you're a taxi-driver, not a fucking actor!"

Yet instinctively Thomas turned to see if anyone was watching him play out this scene.

"Give it here," Sam demanded.

"I don't understand," Thomas said.

There were silvery hairs in his eyebrows and the bones in his wrists stood out.

After listening to twenty seconds of static hiss Sam said, "You used to record our conversations on this," and pushed the tape recorder at him as if it were filthy, diseased.

Thomas said, "I beat Carl to death and left the denim jacket you bought me there."

Sam said, "There are no marks on your hands, besides which I didn't ever buy you a denim jacket."

Thomas followed her.

Only when Sam stood beside where Pete was parked, waiting, did she turn. "Don't call me again," she said.

Thomas said, "I'm making a film, I'm the star."

Sam got into the car beside Pete.

"I love you," Thomas said. Used the edge of his hand to wipe snow from his face and said, "I hate you." Touched his tie for reassurance and whispered, "Dad said..." Opened his mouth to say something else and found he couldn't think of a single thing.

6

Natalie was listening to Boulevard of Broken Dreams on her CD player.

To get her attention Marie widened her eyes, pointed at it and said, "What do you think of this?"

*

Marie caught up with her on the down escalator.

"If you won't even look at things for yourself, we might as well get your dad's Christmas box."

Her shoulders hunched Natalie headed for the EXIT.

*

Turning her back on the icy wind blowing along Corporation Street, she lit a cigarette.

Marie hated that Natalie smoked but bit her lower lip to avoid saying so. "What shall we get for him?"

"Are you serious?"

"We need coffee," Marie said, rubbing her hands together in a way that suggested she was frantic rather than cold.

Natalie followed her mother into Macdonald's, to distract herself chewed her cuticles.

"I think it's important for a woman to look after her hands," Marie said and immediately wished she hadn't.

"Don't change the subject."

Marie had the same look on her face as when her marriage had come apart like a pair of cheap shoes -

*

Natalie had sat with her legs draped over the arm of a chair and the telly on, she and Ben in the other room.

Mocked by a nearby family photo Marie had said, "What's her name?"

"What difference does it make?"

Marie had carefully lain the family photo face down on the table and glared at Ben.

"Gemma," he'd said.

"Gemma?"

*

Following the divorce Marie had started a new diet every week and every night had vacuumed the downstairs rooms after she supposed Natalie was asleep.

For Natalie there had been two years of fortnightly Sunday visits from her dad during which time she'd grown taller, hacked off her ponytail with a pair of blunt scissors and unbeknownst to either of them had her left nipple pierced.

*

Natalie gulped more coffee, though it didn't dislodge the taste of too many cigarettes.

"You said my dad was a 'shit'." Natalie pressed her palm against her ragged fringe. "But you want to buy him a Christmas box?"

"Christmas is a time of forgiveness," Marie said.

"What, so you forgive him for fucking his secretary?"

Marie followed Natalie outside.

"I think it's nice to get him something, that's all," she insisted, wind chopping through her words.

"'Nice'?" Natalie sneered, imagining the city razed to the ground like familiar war footage.

*

They went to Boots, where shiny surfaces gave Marie the confidence to say that Natalie was too thin.

"I weigh eight stone," Natalie insisted.

They both knew it was a lie but when Natalie tensed her shoulders, Marie backed down.

“We’ll get your dad some after-shave,” Marie said and strode to an aisle guarded by photos of impossibly handsome men.

When Natalie entered the aisle and saw her mom talking to a man in shoes so shiny they might’ve been coated with shellac she pushed her way outside and plugged her earphones in.

*

Minutes later she dipped into another branch of Boots - this one smaller than the one she’d escaped though just as crowded.

From a head-high shelf she plucked a tube of moisturiser. She pushed it into her pocket, wanted to be caught but when no one grabbed her made her way to the toilets on Stephenson Street.

*

Her head bent over the bowl Natalie pushed two fingers to the back of her throat with practiced ease but managed only a series of dry heaves.

Afterwards, in the smeared mirror above the sink she inspected her face and decided she was fat and ugly despite that Herbie had asked her to go out for a drink with him three times in as many weeks -

*

The first time was in a tiny basement club. Wearing a Boomtown Rats tee-shirt Herbie played lead guitar in Stream of Consciousness and fought the singer for wanting to change their name to Cosmic Fuck Up - a flurry of inexpertly thrown punches leaving them both bloodied, after which they'd played a set that made The Ramones seem like time-wasters.

He'd held a bottle of Coke in each hand when he asked her if she'd go for a drink with him.

"Why?" Natalie had said.

Bemused by her question Herbie had taken a swig of Coke and said, "I'll get back to you."

*

He'd got back to her Friday the following week in the college library, sat beside her and said, "What're you reading?"

Natalie had looked surprised to find the book in her hands.

"Keats," she'd managed.

Nodding, Herbie had run his fingers over the spines of the nearest books.

"I've been thinking about your question," he'd said.

She'd waited for him to continue.

"Because I like you," he'd said and had stood, his body unfolding like a deckchair, and walked away.

*

The third time was on the train back from college.

Weighed down by books Natalie had been staring out the window when he'd plonked down on the seat opposite and asked her if she was still reading Keats.

"Down to three poems a day after therapy."

She'd grinned.

Herbie hadn't.

Instead, he'd beat a rhythm on the edge of his seat with his fingertips and asked more questions, each intended as an opener, each deflected by a straight yes or no from Natalie.

*

As a rule, Natalie was cautious, but in the Stephenson Street toilets she was distracted by thoughts of Herbie - how it was that the woman got so close.

"I used to be pretty," the woman said.

Told Natalie she'd left school, pregnant, at fifteen; her son, Robbie, had weighed nine pounds three ounces; his dad hadn't wanted to know; she and Robbie had lived with her mom till her mom died; after which she'd moved in various men; Craig, a builder, had fixed the house up a treat but when she found out he'd screwed her best friend she'd ousted him; there were a dozen others; then she'd met Gregg, who she liked more than the rest until she'd caught him in Robbie's room; she'd tried to kill him with a bread knife and at that point police and social services had climbed aboard her life; Gregg got to be a guest of Her Majesty though not before he'd painted a damming picture of her as an unfit mother; when they took Robbie away she'd snapped like a frozen twig; that was when she'd found a new best friend; she told her new best friend everything and her new best friend never tired of listening; her new best friend always came hand-wrapped in tin foil.

"I need money," the woman said, her broken nose darting forwards like a boxer's jabs.

Flinching, Natalie looked for a space into which she could bolt. Saw there wasn't one so smiled and told the woman she was skint.

"Liar," the woman hissed, then knocked Natalie to the floor with her fists and rummaged through her pockets.

Finding no money the woman took the tube of moisturiser Natalie had stolen and her CD player and hurried away.

*

Minutes later, Natalie got up, splashed cold water onto her face and stepped outside.

The sky seemed intent on crushing all human life and Natalie wished it would. Snow flurries swirled round taxis and six feet away a man slammed his fist repeatedly against a phone box.

Wounded afresh when she saw her Green Day CD in pieces on the floor, Natalie fed a finger into her mouth and expertly chewed off what remained of one of her cuticles.

Everything was pointless, she decided. Was desperate to escape the city centre but, penniless, believed her only option was to go back to the car and wait for her mom to return.

With her hands driven into the pockets of her jeans, Natalie strode with her eyes fixed on the skyline.

It was how she came to see the spindly figure perched on the fence at the top of the multi-storey, as she ran thought about Adam, Stream of Consciousness' singer and Herbie's best friend, the back of whose hand she'd recently grazed with her fingertips in a lesson on Keats - had no idea what he was thinking as he stared fixedly out of the classroom window but all at once wanted to know.

*

When, gasping, she reached the woman on the perimeter fence of the multi-storey car park Natalie said, "My mom and dad split up." Gulped in air and said, "I've been taking things out on her ever since, but I wouldn't want her to do this."

*

Marie watched from the door onto the roof of the multi-storey car park. When Natalie had ducked out of Boots had panicked, knew it was impossible to find anyone in city-fed Christmas crowds, but had searched anyway.

Returning to the multi-storey had been her last option and Marie was almost there when she'd seen Natalie up ahead of her and began to run.

The distance between them had been closing when Natalie had begun to sprint.

Now, as Natalie spoke to her, and the spindly woman climbed down from the perimeter fence moved closer.

*

Natalie turned when Marie was just ten feet away. "This is my mom," she said, put one arm around the spindly woman's shoulder and raised the other to draw her mother to her.

7

What'd happened, Reece was desperate to explain when he caught up with Roland as he approached a taxicab on Level Three, was an accident.

Roland had gone to get something for his son's birthday and Reece had been happy to cover for him. But Roland had been gone only a few minutes when he'd started to shake. Had wanted a drink, but that wasn't why he was shaking - all at once couldn't stop thinking about the time he'd seen his ex-wife.

She'd driven onto the multi-storey in a nearly new Mercedes, recognised him but looked right through him.

If they'd snapped at each other or pretended to be grown up and made jokes about their time together, Reece would've been able to carry on.

As it was, when she spun dismissively away, he'd stood by the entrance barrier with sweat glistening on his ruined face.

Reece had been shaking so much when Roland's wife arrived, he hadn't recognised her till she rolled down the window and called his name.

After which he'd launched himself at her car as a drowning man launches himself at a life raft, words gushing from him.

8

Kelly was thirty years old. She stood five feet four inches tall, had piercing green eyes and a tiny scar below her bottom lip, worked as a classroom assistant and was midway through an Open University degree in Maths.

It meant that study time was gold dust but that day after dropping Louis off she hadn't gone straight home and begun work, looking up from her books only when Roland got in from his second workout of the day and it was time to eat. Rather, pained by an emptiness that was nothing to do with food had suddenly decided she needed to see Roland, needed to be close to him.

Reece had told her Roland had gone to buy something for Louis' birthday, was in such a state she was sorely tempted to leave immediately.

But that wasn't what happened.

Reece had babbled until the night shift arrived and started sniggering at him at which point she'd said, "Get in," intended to let him talk only for a few minutes - how grateful he was to have a listener what compelled her to offer him a lift home.

"You're a lifesaver," he'd said, his relief vivid as an open wound, his smile boyish despite the ruined face.

Before, Reece's emotions had always been too much for her. His ability to deliver narratives without pause an annoyance. Tales of record players flung from upstairs windows and being known by name at A & E unfunny as far as Kelly was concerned. But now it felt different, and his stories had soothed her as she drove out of the city.

Which was why, diverted from thoughts of her own emptiness, she'd accepted his offer of tea.

Reece's house, reached by ascending ten fractured steps, was small and, Kelly had seen as soon as he opened the front door, untidy - the debris of his life strewn across furniture and floors.

"I know the place is a mess," Reece had said, pointing to an array of bleaches and detergents in brightly coloured plastic bottles, as proud of them as if they were awards, "but it isn't dirty."

When he'd made them tea, he in his crumpled uniform and she in her immaculate pale green skirt, he'd said, "I wish I could hug you."

Kelly had laughed, then looked surprised - as if she hadn't heard her own laughter in a long time. Heard herself say, "You can," and felt like a little girl rolling down a grassy hill, though afterwards, easing from his bed, had trembled with regret.

Reece had slept whilst Kelly dressed, soundlessly, deciding to throw the clothes she was wearing away once she got home.

During her descent, one of the stairs had groaned, and she'd frozen like a thief in the night.

Breathing shallowly through parted lips, she'd listened.

But Reece hadn't stirred and above the rush of her own blood she'd heard only the tick of an unfamiliar clock.

Her progress illuminated by light leaking from the kitchen she'd felt as if she was on a journey through an uncharted land.

Gripping her keys, she'd hurried through the chilled darkness and down the cracked steps to her car.

Opening the door, she'd turned to look up at the bedroom window and seen Reece. Had shaken her head as if in response to a question and got in.

She'd turned the ignition key hurriedly and sped away.

At the bottom of City Road, Kelly had pulled over. Patches of ice had glittered, traffic was heavy, and outside the grocery shop opposite blue tissue paper curled from boxes of oranges. She'd gripped the steering wheel so hard her wedding ring cut into her finger. The face staring from the rear-view mirror looked unfamiliar to her. To shed as much of her old life as possible now an imperative she'd determined to call at an Estate Agent's before she went home, but before pulling away from the kerb brutally used the edge of her palm to scrape make-up from her eyes.

9

Gripping his friend's broad shoulder for support Reece was desperate to explain that none of what had happened was something he or Kelly had anticipated much less planned.

But as Roland moved away from the taxicab and helped him down to the Security Room, instead he blathered on about buying a fish and chip shop...

*

"I slept with your wife," Reece finally screamed. His words warheads. Their impact deadly -

Though they missed their target because by then Roland had left the Security Room.

Reece dreaded telling Roland but knew he must. Saw it as the next step for him and Kelly. She'd help him give up booze and together they'd buy a fish and chip shop and begin a new life.

For several seconds the scene in his head was as clear as the image on the CCTV monitor.

Then it surrendered to it and the CCTV image drew him unsteadily to his feet.

The woman on the perimeter fence looked ready to jump and though the alcohol racing madly through his bloodstream made him feel numb and befuddled Reece determined to reach her in time to stop her.

*

He climbed two flights of steps. Paused to spew then launched himself up two more flights. He'd been a drunk all his adult life. Was just eighteen when he'd smashed his four upper front teeth, tooth, gum, and blood exploded all over his face. Over the years had gone through a dozen sets of false teeth, though miraculously none of his bottom teeth had been damaged.

Until now.

On Level Five he caught his foot and pitched forwards. Reached for the handrail but wasn't strong enough to stop the force of his downward motion. The sound of his lower incisors snapping like a booted foot breaking virgin snow.

"Vuck it," Reece gurgled. Cupped his lower face with his right hand and got moving again, though more slowly than before - why the dark-haired girl beat him to the roof.

Just seconds later Roland, too, hurried past him.

When, one behind the other, the two men stepped out into the howling winds they saw three women over by the perimeter fence. Hugging each other. Smiling and crying at the same time. At which point with blood dripping from his chin, Reece turned to his friend.

"I'm a vucking shit," he began.

10

On Christmas Eve Maureen went through her house tidying and cleaning, making sure there were no nasty smells or stains.

*

When Ken left her, Maureen had burned every photo of him, her features transformed into a mask of anguish that in the rapid, tumbling, years that followed became her face.

She'd told herself her life would've been different if Keith's life hadn't been ruined and Ken hadn't left her, like two shots to the heart at close range.

Alright, she'd still have got old. But more gracefully if not for a life without husband and son. Her loneliness something Maureen had at first fought against, placing an ad in the paper: Mature woman seeks male companion.

*

To meet Ian Maureen wore a new dress and shoes and had sat torturing herself with what ifs.

Ian had worn a dark suit with a shirt but no tie. Like her, he'd been nervous.

"I haven't done this before," he'd said and as if to prove it spilled beer, the splotches on her dress expanding. "I'll pay for it to be cleaned," he'd said, squirming with embarrassment.

"It doesn't matter," Maureen had said.

What did matter though was his need to detail how he'd lost his wife of twenty-six years. Picking through steak and salad had told how the disease first crippled then killed her. Spooning chocolate ice cream told how he'd found clumps of hair all over the house and knelt with dustpan and brush to remove them from carpets and furniture. Sipping beer told how the sunburst clock on the chimneybreast measured the comings and goings of nurses and doctors, the arrival and departure of new oxygen tanks.

Maureen wished she could offer him comfort but knew she couldn't and was glad that she'd pre-ordered a taxi.

*

She'd never seen Ian again, though she went on other dates, all of which left her feeling angry about the divide between the life she was living and the life she wanted, all of which always left her feeling lonelier after the touch of another's hand, the sound of another's voice.

*

Only with Barry had she connected.

Barry was short, with a squarish head and a goatee. Always wore denim shirts with the sleeves rolled up. Was a wardrobe-fitter, comfortable in houses.

Like Ian, his wife had died of cancer. But he'd mentioned it only once, briefly, making it clear it wasn't something he wanted to dwell on. Liked to hear her talk about her dreams, what she liked to eat, what she watched on telly.

They'd held hands, taken turns staying at each other's places, spent hours preparing meals with the radio on, sometimes pausing to sing along with songs they both liked.

They'd planned to get somewhere small and neat that wasn't haunted by memories, but Maureen got cold feet, and Barry told her they'd move in together or stop seeing each other and because she couldn't overcome the nagging fear that what'd happened before would happen again, she'd opted for the latter.

*

Her Miss Lonely-hearts memories made Maureen hungry and that'd come as a surprise, for hunger had never been a part of her plan, but here it was, suited and booted, familiar in its demands.

She ate at the kitchen table, staring out of the window at an iron sky.

When she'd finished, she washed up carefully and put everything away, then examined the kitchen with objective eyes and, judging that everything was as it should be, left after double-checking that she'd locked the front door.

*

Mareen put her handbag on the Fiesta's passenger seat. It contained a photo of Keith taken a day or so before he was destroyed. Showed a handsome young man in school blazer and a crisp shirt, his whole life before him.

She remembered him combing his hair the day the photo was taken. Checking it in the mirror then combing it again, determined to get it just right.

Reaching into her bag she touched the photo before she set off.

*

She parked and walked to Barclay Road, stopping opposite the entrance to Warley Woods and pressing the heel of her hand against her temple - trying to squeeze out a familiar pain, failing to squeeze out a familiar pain.

The trees had a tight hold on what remained of the night. The grass was speckled with dew. Here and there stones glistened like jewels.

When Maureen returned to her car it was necessary to hold the photo tightly in her trembling hands.

*

She drove into the city and turned onto Brunel Street.

It'd have been better if she'd chosen a quieter time, but what she was doing wasn't about choice, was something she'd fought for years, was something she felt unable to fight any longer.

Driving onto the multi-storey was like diving into the sea but she hadn't flinched.

She drove to the roof, parked and turned off the engine.

In the ensuing quiet she remembered a summer holiday, just her, Ken, and Keith...

*

For five days it had rained non-stop, forcing them to stay indoors playing card games, doing jigsaw puzzles, eating sweets.

Then, on the sixth day, the sun had burst through, the roads had dried, and the air seemed to transmit sound more clearly: cows munching in a nearby field, gulls trading insults, the bark of a farmyard dog.

They'd driven to a beach where Keith paddled in the sea, dug in the sand, poked through rock pools.

After which they'd eaten ice creams - their hands overrun by sticky vanilla streams.

*

Happy days become bittersweet memories were what had taken Maureen to the edge of the roof.

Handbag held tight against her body she turned. Seeing no one, she stepped over the knee-high steel barrier to reach the chain-link perimeter fence.

Panting, she grasped the fence and climbed, nearby buildings, the railway station, even the curve of the surrounding roads seeming familiar, yet somehow different.

Maureen had rehearsed this moment many times and, in her mind, there had never been any hesitation - she jumped, and her body was taken to City Hospital, fitting for she'd been born there.

Police, meanwhile, would be despatched, would let themselves in and see how everything was ready for them.

She expected her suicide would make the local news. Saw the headline, CHRISTMAS DEATH LEAP, followed by a single column of text, the word 'tragedy' used once, had intended to climb to the top of the perimeter fence and jump –

But found her hands become claws.

*

Ken had always been strong, but he'd broken as if he were a China figurine. Losing his wallet and keys had become a habit and his walk had slowed. Finally, one Saturday in autumn when the garden was full of leaves that he lacked the energy to clear he'd told her he couldn't go on.

Keith had been fourteen by then, as tall as his father, saw a psychiatrist once a week.

"I just can't," Ken had said.

"Please," Maureen had said.

But it'd been no use.

*

Ken leaving was part of the reason Maureen was on the fence.

What'd happened to Keith the rest of it...

*

Keith was bright, good at sport, and so considerate that on his way home from football that night he cut through Warley Woods so he wouldn't be late home, wouldn't worry her.

There, he was attacked, beaten, raped.

*

Receiving the news, she'd screamed till her throat was raw.

A taste that lingered, though much of what happened next was lost, Maureen a book with its pages torn out and thrown away.

*

She'd been driven to a police station and in a starkly lit room that reeked of bleach had talked to Keith.

That is, she'd talked to what was left of her son.

*

Like the king's men in the nursery rhyme, everybody had struggled to put Keith back together again.

There were meetings with schoolteachers, counsellors, and friends - only they weren't his friends anymore.

"They used to be Keith's friends," he'd said - having taken to naming himself in conversations.

"They're still your friends," Maureen had insisted.

"Humpty D-Dumpty shakes his head," Keith had said, dutifully shaking his head before explaining that they were the old Keith's friends, and he wasn't the old Keith anymore.

She'd tried to persuade him that this wasn't true, though normality or the façade of it became harder to maintain when, aged thirteen, fifteen, seventeen, and nineteen, Keith attempted suicide - tried, each time, to hang himself.

The attempts were not in the same month or on the same day, but once every two years he tried to hang himself and would've been successful if not for the tremor he'd acquired along with his stammer and habit of naming himself: she had to tie his shoelaces for him, so tying a noose was something he couldn't manage and hanging himself using a "proper noose" was something Keith was insistent on.

Four times he'd tried to hang himself and each time the nooses he'd fashioned had unravelled.

Maureen had been told that Keith needed help.

He'd smoked as they discussed it, Keith always smoking, his thin hair giving prominence to a prematurely lined forehead.

"It's b-best if I go away for a b-bit,' he'd said, his gaze on her then the edge of the coffee table then the daddy longlegs throwing itself repeatedly against the windowpane.

Worn out, broken, she'd eventually given in.

"You'll c-come to see me w-won't you?"

"Of course," she'd said, blinking away tears.

*

She'd visited him every Monday, Wednesday, and at the weekends, always taking sweets for him and always talking about the weather and what she'd do if she won the Lottery.

Weeks had gone by, during which Keith had showed little improvement, though she'd smiled when he told her how a change in medication had reduced his tremors.

For his twenty-first she'd bought him a gold-plated lighter.

A month later Keith had stolen three ties from the wardrobe of the man in the room next to his, knotted them together to form a hangman's noose and in a toilet cubicle next to the Day Room had hanged himself.

*

"I wouldn't want my mom to do it," the dark-haired girl said and seeing the look on her face Maureen climbed down and stood with her arms by her sides.

"My husband left me, my son hanged himself," she said and as Natalie moved close and put her arm around her realised it was the first time she'd said those words aloud.

ONLY ONCE

The look on his face told her he thought a Drama specialist wasn't up to the challenge of covering Maths at the Ace Academy but pretending she hadn't noticed she said, "Lydia Bee."

"Tom Webb."

Squeezing his eyes shut for a second then forcing them open again he asked her if she'd like a Mini Mars Bar - an open multi-pack on his cluttered desk.

Lydia shook her head and followed him up two flights of steps - the smell of disinfectant stronger the higher they got, the walls scarred by savage gouges and painted over obscenities.

"Don't let them take your lanyard whatever you do," Tom Webb said when they reached the classroom.

*

It bore the ravages of war, though currently 10X5 sat silent and still, the Head Teacher scowling at them from the front - didn't re-direct his glare from the hostile faces before him even when Tom Webb cleared his throat and announced, “Ms Bee’s here.”

She felt the weight of thirty pairs of eyes on her.

Daring 10X5 to speak or move the Head Teacher pushed out his chin.

His challenge declined he strode from the classroom.

Immediately, movement erupted in the ranks. Students giggled. One stage-whispered, “Supply!”

Tom Webb scowled. “Did somebody comment?”

Through the classroom windows Lydia glimpsed a football field bordered by winter-naked trees.

“Their work ’s on the desk,” Tom Webb said. Looked in need of a Mini Mars Bar himself when he added, “I’ll be back at the end of the lesson.”

*

He hadn’t been gone thirty seconds when 10X5 started in on her, their clamour to inflict suffering manifest as a feral stench that, strong as it was, the disinfectant failed to mask.

It was a stench she was familiar with. Steeled against it, Lydia peered down at the work that had been set as a paper dart sailed from the back of the room and someone called, “Are you a bumble, Ms Bee?” which prompted laughter and a chorus of buzzing.

Experience told 10X5 she'd either shout at or try to reason with them.

Lydia knew if she did either, their cruelty would gather momentum. Why instead she shook herself like a dog emerging from a lake, then cupped her face with her hands.

As she knew it would, the laughter and the buzzing stopped.

Now she had their attention she leaned forwards and sobbed uncontrollably.

Long seconds passed.

A lad near the front whispered, "Are you alright, Miss?"

Lydia held the subsequent silence as if it were a silky thread before lowering her hands to let them see her tears and saying, "My sister, she was...was murdered."

*

When Tom Webb opened the classroom door, he saw that as one 10X5 were hunched over their exercise books, working quietly.

*

On the way back to Reception he said, "Lydia? This is a challenging school. And 10X5? I don't think I've ever... What I'm trying to say is... Would you like to do more supply work here at Ace Academy?"

Lydia said, “I’m flattered, Tom, really I am, but my methods work -”

SKID MARKS

All the time thinking, thinking, thinking, he paced back-and-forth-back-and-forth-back-and-forth, was determined to find who was doing it – who, who, who? - the same thing every fucking day: the first skid mark always saying, Fuck, the second always saying, you, the third always saying, Fitton.

*

His old man had warned him he should get used to people trying to get at him because they were jealous of what he'd accomplished - his old man it was who'd set him on the path to success in the first place, sending him to a lesser-known public school and hammering home that the odds were massively against his playing football ever paying off, whereas the right accent would pretty much guarantee him a top job.

Fitton had a voice that would cut glass, though he steadfastly believed his sheer relentlessness was what had endowed him with the wherewithal to become a CEO: when PQC Logistics appointed him wasted no time in making his relentlessness clear – axing a hundred jobs during month one surely some kind of record.

Early mornings he'd prowled, sometimes slowing to stare out of windows when blue inched up from the horizon but only genuinely moved by the fear on the faces of those who arrived to find him already there, thought of his early starts as an act of will rather than a by-product of insomnia as he strode through empty offices shutting desk drawers that hadn't been properly shut and straightening items of stationary left skewed on desks whilst deciding who should stay and who should go.

*

The final week of his third month in post was when he saw what had been left for him in the second cubicle from the left in the toilets on the first floor – nothing accidental or unconsidered about it, he was sure.

That the cleaners were to blame was his first thought, insulting him as an act of revenge: lowered rates of pay and a raised commitment to productivity things he'd forced their contractor to sign up to.

Deciding if he discovered skid marks at the end of one of their shifts, they were all for the chop, Monday through to Friday he arrived between midnight and 3.45AM…

But there were never skid marks left during those hours, meaning the cleaners were in the clear and why, alone in his office, Fitton gulped Gaviscon as if it was going out of style and re-configured his approach.

A fortnight of surreptitious checks narrowed the time frame at which the message was deposited to between 3.45AM and 9.15AM. It doesn't matter whether it's one, two or three skid marks, he told himself at this point, the message was still unequivocally the same - Fuck you Fitton - believed the fact that the message was never in the same toilet two days running was indisputable proof that whomever it was, was intent on taunting him, teasing him, humiliating him, and promptly put the night-time security man in the frame, Harold Lever someone who smiled agreeably at all and sundry.

Fitton didn't trust any man who smiled, with a clear view of the lobby each night sat across from PQC Logistics in his Mercedes E Class Saloon and watched Lever make his rounds on the hour: always waited till the security man's shift was almost over before he strode in.

Seeing all the porcelain was spic and span Fitton chewed his bottom lip till he drew blood, whilst doing so latched onto the idea that the day-time security woman was the culprit so, following her hourly patrols, relentlessly checked and re-checked the toilets on all floors.

Nothing.

Meaning that like Harold Lever, Sheila Parkes was off the hook. Meaning it wasn't a contract cleaner or contracted site security, meaning it had to be one of PQC Logistics' own staff who was each day leaving him a message in shit.

Claiming it was part of an efficiency drive, ever more desperate to find who was responsible Fitton ordered state of the art CCTV cameras installed everywhere - including the entrance to the toilets on all floors. Would've had a camera placed in each cubicle too if he hadn't anticipated the reaction of PQC Logistics' board of directors to such a directive.

Throughout the installation Fitton lost weight and cultivated dark smudges beneath his eyes, shook when he signed the release confirming completion, then spun to face the monitors occupying an entire wall of his top floor office.

With the necessary means for discovery in place process became everything.

Having first patrolled to make sure all the toilets in the building were spotless he'd study the monitors scrupulously and make a dash every time he saw a worker exit a toilet -

It sounded straightforward but wasn't since sometimes workers on different floors simultaneously left their workstations and headed for the toilets on their floor - PQC Logistics eight storeys high.

Fitton needed to be as quick as he'd been as a boy with a football at his feet, to facilitate this took to wearing lightweight Nikes rather than hand-made leather shoes.

No one mentioned his suited sprints, no one dared, though the fear of his staff no longer comforted him.

Discomforted, Fitton estimated that it'd already been several weeks since the installation of CCTV and still skid marks appeared like clockwork: Fuck you Fitton…Fuck you Fitton…Fuck you Fitton…

Well, fuck you right back, I won't give up, he assured himself relentlessly. Wouldn't give up, couldn't give up, wouldn't, couldn't, wouldn't, why after gulping more Gaviscon, all the time thinking, thinking, thinking, he resumed pacing back-and-forth- back-and-forth-back-and-forth…

SPARROW

It happened not long after Steve had been made redundant and couldn't stop saying the word - was studying himself saying it in the hallway mirror when Rachel stuck her head round the door and asked him what he was doing.

"Nothing," he said and pushed his fingers through his hair as if shaping it was what he'd stood there to do - just that and nothing else.

*

"HiQ are pretty good," Steve told his son Shaun an hour or so later. "Their prices are fair, but it's still way cheaper to do it yourself."

Shaun nodded as Steve used the jack to raise the front nearside of the car - a ten-year-old Ford, its paintwork faded, its sills badly rusted.

Steve said, "The trouble with a trolley-jack is they can slip."

To which Shaun nodded again. His job to stop the jack from slipping by standing with his foot wedged up against it - this and to watch carefully so he'd know how the job was done in case in the future he, too, couldn't afford even reasonably priced HiQ, in case in the future he, too, was made redundant, redundant, redundant.

Following his own advice as he spoke, Steve said, "Always grease the nuts when you take them off so next time it's easier to remove them."

"Right," Shaun said, but wasn't paying attention because Beccy Ellis walked by at that moment.

In the same year as him, word had it Beccy had just chucked Harry Adams, her boyfriend of nine months, why Shaun stepped away from the trolley-jack, ready to speak, though what he intended to say to her he had no idea.

Steve leapt backwards when the jack slipped, and still the edge of the plummeting brake disk caught his thumb and sliced it.

"You were supposed to stop it slipping," he snapped, shaking his head as blood dripped, Beccy Ellis gone, just the two of them standing in Muir Close, a dozen semis under an iron-clad sky, Shaun holding his arms out from his sides as if he'd like to fly away to someplace where was no such thing as rusted sills or redundancy.

*

They were getting ready for bed when Steve told Rachel what had happened, paused when he was done telling and said, "I shouldn't have snapped at him."

*

Overdubbed by the word redundant his conversation with Rachel burrowed its way into dreams from which, at 3.11AM, Steve was wrenched by a sound from outside.

Rachel stirred, but didn't wake, and Steve would've drifted back off if he hadn't heard another noise - when he did, eased out of bed, stepped over to the back window and peered out.

At first, he couldn't see anything.

But when his eyes adjusted, he saw Shaun was knelt close to the back of the house with his head bowed, as if in prayer.

*

Only when he stepped out into the chilled night did Steve switch on the torch - the yellow cone of light highlighting the concern on his son's face.

"It's a sparrow," Shaun said, raised it into the cone of light and said, "It hit the back window."

Initially, he'd been convinced it was dead.

Now, torchlight allowed him to see the rapid rise and fall of the sparrow's tiny chest.

"It's just stunned," Steve said - was able to tell by the sound of his own voice that he was smiling.

Nestled in Shaun's hands, the sparrow's beak described a series of tiny arcs.

"What shall we do?"

Directed by torchlight, after Shaun placed it gently on the bird table and retreated, father and son stood side by side and watched as the sparrow gathered itself, then darted up into the thinning darkness.

COUNTING

I'd been driving for hours. Was determined to break the back of the journey so had had only one cup of tea that morning to avoid needing to stop in a hurry.

The day had started cold.

Then it'd got so warm I'd had to drive with the window all the way down. Was conscious of the noise of the motorway beating away at me for the first couple of hours, after which I became oblivious to it.

*

One cup of tea only is the way to do it if you want to get some miles under your belt, but sooner or later the need to take a pee starts to weigh heavily - both on your bladder and your mind.

I was over halfway there by then. My choice would've been to reach the two-thirds mark. Or, better still, to have got three-quarters of the way there before having to stop.

But it wasn't to be. Why when I saw the sign saying there were services a mile ahead, I moved over onto the inside lane, then signalled and left the motorway.

*

The services were buzzing - how comes the only space I could find to park was by the grassy area with tables and benches for those wanting to eat or drink outside.

Still, parking way back there was alright with me because it gave me a chance to stretch my legs and ease the kinks from my lower back.

*

I entered the services building through the automated IN door and immediately looked up to locate the sign for toilets, glad to see that familiar outline-image of a male and a female because the pain in my bladder suddenly felt a lot more acute from having walked aways.

I followed the directions dictated by the sign:

Straight ahead.

Then left.

Only when I got there, there were no toilets where the sign had said there would be. Just a WH Smith's next to a gambling arcade - the sound of a slot machine paying out even though there was nobody in there seeming to vibrate my bladder, ramping up my discomfort and turning it into something sharper and more penetrating.

People passing by all around me, I stood there a minute: looking and then looking again.

There were no toilets where the sign had said there were.

Definitely.

So, were they on the opposite – right - side, was that it?

I turned to look.

Nope - on the right side there was just a Waitrose with people plucking sandwiches and drinks from the shelves as if they were going out of style, then heading for the self-service check outs.

No sign of any toilets.

Convincing myself that I must've made a mistake I re-traced my steps to the entrance. Walked slowly because the more penetrating pain that'd come on outside the gambling arcade hadn't climbed down any. If anything, it'd gone up several notches. Was no longer a polite request. Was, all at once, an urgent demand. My bladder insisting: You need to pee, you need to pee, you need to pee.

*

Back at the entrance, with people passing all around me - some coming into the building and some leaving it - I looked up at the sign to the toilets and sure enough saw, somehow, first time around I'd got it wrong.

How had that happened?

Never mind, I told myself. Saw that according to the sign the toilets weren't situated:

Straight ahead.

Then left.

Saw that according to the sign they were situated:

Right.

Then left.

After double-checking that this was the case, I set off again. This time around took a right, taking carefully measured steps, my mind fixed on holding my pee in, was certain I would've been able to drive further if I'd kept on driving but now that I'd stopped to pee, badly needed to pee - that something there was no escape from.

When I could walk no further right, as had been directed by the sign, I turned left. Passed a Spud-U-Like and kept walking left till I couldn't go any further.

But there were no toilets there either.

Just a shop selling neckties in a mind-boggling array of colours, some that were slim, some that were wide, hundreds on display.

So where are the toilets?

Where...

...are...

...the...

...fucking...

...toilets?

It was tempting to scream it out loud, but I didn't. Closed my eyes, then opened them again and again looked over at where the sign had said the toilets were.

Where the sign had said there were toilets there was only a shop selling neckties.

I frowned.

Who bought a necktie at a motorway services station - McDonald's, WH Smiths, a gambling arcade, Waitrose, Spud-U-Like, I had no problem with, but a shop selling only neckties?

Never mind, I told myself. Forget it. Told myself it wasn't important, now. Told myself the important thing right now was for me to quickly locate a toilet and pee.

To do that I needed to go back to the entrance and look at the directions for the third time - good old Holy Trinity stuff: Father, Son, Holy Ghost.

Right, I told myself.

Right.

*

This time around I walked way, way slower. The pain in my bladder a stabbing blade. My face flushed. My necktie-free shirt sticking to me. Reached the entrance to the services, looked up and saw sure enough, somehow, I'd managed to get it wrong both times previously. Saw that the toilets weren't:

Straight ahead.

Then left.

Nor were they:

Right.

Then left.

They were the only remaining option:

Left.

Simple, I told myself, and set off, walking super slowly, concentrating hard.

The services had got way busier since I first arrived. It felt like I was swimming through a sea of people, many of whom gave me strange looks, probably because of the tension etched onto my face.

I walked left.

I kept walking left until I couldn't walk left anymore, then stopped.

I was bursting. The pain in my bladder made my eyes ache. Made my heartbeat faster.

Directly ahead of me was a Costa. To the left of Costa was a KFC. To the right of Costa was an M&S.

There were no toilets.

Definitely.

There were no toilets and by now sweat ran, stingingly, into my eyes and my jaw muscles clenched of their own accord.

I'd followed the directions indicated by the sign by the entrance three times, but apparently the signage kept changing, so what should I do?

Surely there was a manager of some sort, someone with responsibility for the whole of this motorway services - so I should find the manager and report what had happened and insist that something be done about it.

Yes.

I should.

Absolutely.

But right now, that wasn't an option.

No.

"Excuse me, could you direct me to the toilets," I said.

I'd tried to sound relaxed and friendly but the woman I'd spoken to had turned sharply away, tugging hard at the hand of her little boy and lengthening her stride.

The next time I directed my question at a man, but it was the same story.

I asked a dozen passersby, maybe more. Men, women, young, old, and every time it was the same - no one slowed, no one answered, all of them hurried on.

The pain in my bladder by now excruciating, I shifted my weight from one foot to the other as if I was dancing to an almost forgotten tune.

Could I make it outside and all the way across the car park to the picnic area and find some cover there?

I was pretty sure not. The pain was too sharp. Too deep. Wasn't letting up. Was why as a seemingly endless stream of people passed me by all I could think to do was keep very, very still and begin counting.

My lips and tongue moved slowly, cautiously as they formed the numbers:

"1...

2...

3..."

WHAT?

Alex had already heard most of the jokes about being tight-fisted - and with good reason - but hours after my old man's funeral, when the few who'd attended had fucked off and it was just the two of us sitting on poorly upholstered, blood red stools on either side of a battle-scarred circular wooden table in the Bar of The George, his wallet got an airing and then some.

"You want another pint, mate?" he kept asking.

"If you're buying," I kept answering.

I was joking, but Alex apparently didn't get it and kept dashing to the Bar.

"Can't be easy losing your dad," he said after he'd got the fourth round in - the two of us gulping Carling in unison and a midweek Premiership game on the big screen TV above the Bar but the sound down. "I mean I know what you've said about him over the years, but even so..."

"I hardly knew him, really," I said.

"How old were you when he left?"

"Eight or nine," I said. "Still in Miss Townsend's class."

"She was fucking fit," Alex said, then shook his head and said, "Sorry, mate, that's well out of order."

"No need to apologise, mate, Miss Townsend was fucking fit," I said, remembering the tight dresses she wore, then gulping more Carling.

"What I mean is I shouldn't be saying stuff like that on the day of your dad's funeral," Alex said and as if to make amends offered to get us crisps.

"I'm alright, ta."

"You sure?"

"Positive, mate."

I don't think I'd ever noticed how dark it was in The George before. Or paid any attention to the swirly-patterned, orange wallpaper. Or the blood red carpet that looked as if it was left over from the early Eighties. Was thinking we'd have been better off going to The Plough when Alex said, "Was another woman, right?" then shook his head even harder than before and said, "Sorry, mate, that's bang out of order even if what I said before wasn't."

"Nah, you're alright," I said, "but what's brought all this on?"

I waited and we did our Carling duet again and the old fella in the corner - his eyes on the game - lifted one cheek of his arse and farted - just the three of us and Greg, the barman, in there, midweek a low-key night at The George to put it mildly.

"It's your face, mate," Alex said.

"I can't help my ugly mug," I said, and because Alex still didn't crack a smile, I smiled for him.

"See?" he said. "There you go again. I can't believe you're like this on the day you've buried your dad. I mean, yeah, you told me he ran off with another woman, but -"

"Wasn't one woman, mate," I said. "Fuck me, every time I ever saw him, he was with a different woman. Liked to put it about and then some. When I was twelve or thirteen said, 'I've had more crumpet than you've had hot dinners, lad,' and winked at me."

"No disrespect, mate, but your dad was a shit of the first order."

"Should've had that put on his gravestone," I said - wastefully because having seen our glasses were empty Alex had snatched them up and made a beeline for the Bar.

"Cheers," I said when he returned, knew Alex liked to drink but could see tonight he wasn't enjoying it.

The old fella in the corner farted again and I expected Alex to remark on it.

Instead, he licked his lips a couple of times and said, "You're not going to do anything stupid are you, Kenny?"

"Stupid? Like what?"

"Like throwing yourself off a motorway bridge," he said, his eyebrows raised, his shoulders tense.

We'd shared a lot over the years, but this was new and the expression on my face must have showed it.

"I saw this programme on telly," he explained. "Sarah made me watch it," he admitted. "'It's right,' she kept saying every time the adverts came on, 'blokes don't talk about their emotions, they keep everything bottled up, then - pop.'"

"I must've missed that programme," I said, some sarcasm in my voice though, like my jokes earlier, it went over Alex's head.

"It's right, though, it is fucking right, Sarah said-"

"-Alex, mate, I know Sarah's got more than her share of GCSEs and all that, but why would you think I'm bottling things up when I've been smiling all night."

"You smiling so much is what I'm worried about," Alex said, the hand holding his pint drained of blood, I saw.

Wolves put one in and the old fella in the corner fist pumped until V.A.R. overruled it, at which point he shook his head in disgust, the three long grey hairs left on top of his head bouncing up and down.

"It's all a show," Alex insisted. "I mean yeah, you look perky enough, but you're keeping your emotions bottled up. You buried your dad today and you're in pieces. I'd be. Anybody would. I mean, it's natural. I mean alright, your dad was a cunt, but he was your cunt when all's said and done, so you're depressed as fuck and hiding it. All that smiling? It's just a façade, mate."

"A façade? No, mate, it's not, I haven't got a façade in me," I said, took another gulp of Carling and put him straight: "What it is, see: I went to view his body last night, and the funeral directors took me into this room where his open coffin was on a big oak table."

About to mount a protest, Alex said, "Kenny, man," but I held up my palm.

"Let me finish," I said as Alex brought his pint to his lips, then lowered it without taking a drink - was clearly at his limit for the night: the whites of his eyes bloodshot and his bloated belly trying to push its way out of his best blue shirt. "My old man was a shit dad who left me and mom when I was only eight or nine years old, but worse than that was how he made me feel my whole fucking life. See, him telling me he was a ladies' man and winking wasn't the worst of it by any means – my old man liked to brag."

Despite himself Alex said, "Brag?"

"Not to put too fine a point on it," I said, "he liked to brag about the size of his dick. Practically every time I ever saw him, he told me he was well hung and then some. Said that was what women saw in him. 'Well, it couldn't very well be my money or my good looks and boyish charm,' he said, and I knew him well enough to know that much was true, so I ended up believing him about the other, too."

When Alex stared at me, I shrugged and said, "I believed my old man had a massive dick and my whole life I felt-"

I noticed the old fella watching the Wolves game was looking my way.

Had the nosey fucker been listening?

I waited for him to turn his attention back to the big screen before leaning close to Alex, lowering my voice and continuing: "- My whole life I felt distinctly inadequate in the trouser department."

Alex tried to swallow.

Couldn't.

I said, "Don't look at me like that - you started all this."

Then I swigged Carling and said, "Anyway, when Greaves and Simpson left me alone, I walked over to my old man - lying there with his hair parted in the wrong place in a cheap suit - leant in close and told him I thought he'd been a fucking shit dad, but I loved him anyway."

Alex rapid-blinked, which made me wonder if he'd got something in his eye. It wouldn't have surprised me because The George was always dusty and tonight it seemed dustier than ever, the place a shithole and no mistake.

"You were spot on," I said. "What you said earlier, I mean. When all was said and done, he was still my old man, so I told him I loved him and I was about to go, but instead stopped. Turned around. Made sure it was just me and him in there, then..." I reached for my pint, took two gulps of Carling and said, "Yep, that's right."

Now, Alex was back to staring at me. "You don't mean you...?"

"Yeah," I said, "I did."

Alex looked down at his pint, then back up at me.

"And it was nothing special," I said. "Nothing to write home about."

I heard a penny drop – as if from a great height and Alex said, "And that made you feel..."

"Better about myself," I said, nodding and smiling at the same time.

"Which's why you haven't looked miserable all night even though we buried your dad today."

"Right," I said.

And let the silence hang between us until, registering a new expression on my face, Alex said, "What?"

"I was just thinking," I said, "if the offer still stands, maybe a bag of crisps wouldn't go amiss after all – see if they soak up some of what we've drunk, eh."

I paused, then, seeing Alex already had his wallet in his hand, said, "Cheese and onion, please."

THE SQUATTER ABOVE BOSSINEY COVE

My current predicament shakes his head officiously and tells me I can't stay in a public call box.

I shake my head back and point out that it's not a public call box anymore because there's no phone in it.

I'd walked to the point where my legs weren't prepared to take me further, not if I asked them nicely, not if I begged them, knew I needed to call someone, just not who, when I saw there was no phone inside the call box decided to stay put, liked looking out at the sky and the sea.

My current predicament tells me I can't stay even if there's no phone.

"I can!"

"You can't!"

"I claim squatter's rights!"

My current predicament performs more officious head shaking and says, "What? That's ridiculous! Who are you?"

OTHER BOOKS BY WAYNE DEAN-RICHARDS

Poems by Two Fat Men

At the Edge

Breakpoints

Cuts

A Box of Porn - Kalman Dean-Richards and Wayne Dean-Richards

Money & Blood

It's A Mad World But Funny

Days of Ordinary Madness

*

thanks to Paul for having faith and all his brilliant work.

Printed in Great Britain
by Amazon

62733489R00097